In Search of Clusters
Second Edition

Gregory F. Pfister

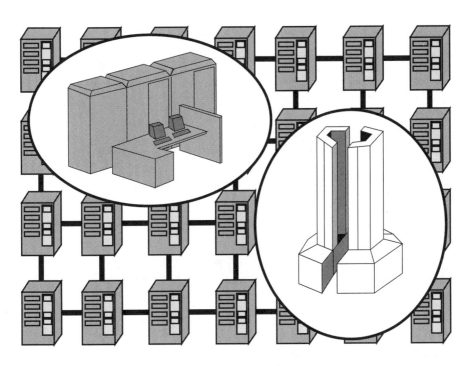

To join a Prentice Hall PTR Internet
mailing list, point to
http://www.prenhall.com/mail_lists.

Prentice Hall PTR
Upper Saddle River, NJ 07458

ISBN 0-13-899709-8

9 780138 997090

90000

 © 1998 Prentice Hall PTR
Prentice-Hall, Inc.
A Simon & Shuster Company
Upper Saddle River, New Jersey 07458

Editorial/production supervision: *Joe Czerwinski*
Acquisitions editor: *Greg Doench*
Manufacturing manager: *Alexis R. Heydt*
Cover design director: *Jerry Votta*
Cover design: *Design Source*

Prentice Hall books are widely used by corporations and government agencies
for training, marketing, and resale.

The publisher offers discounts on this book when ordered in bulk quantities.

For more information contact: Corporate Sales Department, Phone: 800-382-3419;
Fax: 201-236-7141; e-mail:corpsales@prenhall.com.
Or write: Prentice Hall PTR, Corp. Sales Dept., One Lake Street, Upper Saddle River, NJ 07458

Some of the clip art contained herein was obtained from FrameMaker® 5.
Some of the clip art contained herein was obtained from CorelDraw.™
Grim reaper image used on page 438 © Task Force Clip Art.

Printed in the United States of America

10 9 8 7 6 5 4 3 2 1

ISBN 0-13-899709-8

Prentice-Hall International (UK) Limited, *London*
Prentice-Hall of Australia Pty. Limited, *Sydney*
Prentice-Hall Canada Inc., *Toronto*
Prentice-Hall Hispanoamericana, S.A., *Mexico*
Prentice-Hall of India Private Limited, *New Delhi*
Prentice-Hall of Japan, Inc., *Tokyo*
Simon & Shuster Asia Pte. Ltd., *Singapore*
Editora Prentice-Hall do Brasil, Ltda., *Rio de Janeiro*

Trademarks

My esteemed colleagues in IBM Austin Intellectual Property Law have informed me that since IBM expects other people to respect our trademarks, IBM employees must respect theirs, too. That sounds reasonable. But more to the point, their approval is required for external publication of this work, and they won't give it unless all trademarks used are flagged as trademarks when they're first used. They also told me that a section like this, appearing before the text (and in this case, necessarily before the table of contents) satisfies requirements: It's the first use, and it's flagged. So, here's the fine print:

CXT 1000 is a trademark of Ancor Inc. Chorus is a trademark of Chorus Software Systems, Inc. Convex and ConvexNQS are trademarks of Convex Computer Corp. Cray and Y-MP are trademarks of Cray Research, Inc. Data General High Availability is a trademark of Data General, Inc. Alpha AXP, DEC, DECsafe, PDP, Star Coupler, VAX, VAXCluster, VAXen, VMS, microVAX and TruCluster are trademarks of Digital Equipment Corp. Memory Channel, Reflective Memory, and Encore is a trademark of Encore Computers, Inc. Load Balancer is a trademark of Freedman Sharp and Associates Inc. Fusion High Availability is a trademark of Fusion Systems, Inc. Gould and Reflective Memory are trademarks of Gould Computer Systems, Inc. Apollo, Domain, HP, HP Series 700, NCS, Network Computing Services, and Switchover UX are trademarks of the Hewlett-Packard Company. INGRES is a trademark of INGRES Corp. IDS and ISIS are trademarks of ISIS Development Systems, Inc. Informix is a trademark of Informix Software, Inc. iPSC, Paragon, and Intel Scientific Supercomputers are trademarks of Intel, Inc. AIX, CICS, CICS/6000, DATABASE 2, DB2, DB2/6000, ES/9000, ESCON, ESSL, EUI, HACMP/6000, IBM System/370, IBM, JES3, LoadLeveller, MVS/ESA, NETBIOS, NetView, OS/2, POWER/4, Parallel Sysplex, PowerPC, PowerServer, PS/2, RACF, RISC System/6000, RMF, S/370, S/390, SP2, Sysplex Coupling Facility, Sysplex Timer, System/370, System/390, TCF, Transparent Computing Facility, and VTAM are trademarks of International Business Machines Corp. Locus Cluster is a trademark of Locus Computer Corp. FUSION is a trademark of Locus Computer Corp. and International Business Machines Corp. Lotus and Lotus Notes are trademarks of Lotus Development Corp. X Window System is a trademark of Massachusetts Institute of Technology. NCube is a trademark of NCube, Inc. Lifekeeper, NCR, NCR3400, NCR 3600 and Teradata are trademarks of National Cash Register, and therefore probably of AT&T. Novelle, NetWare, and Machine-Independent NetWare are trademarks of Novell Inc. DME, Distributed Management Environment, OSF/1, OSF/1 AD DCE, Distributed Computing Environment, DFS, and Distributed File system are trademarks of the Open Software Foundation, Inc. Oracle, Oracle Parallel Server and Oracle Version 7 are trademarks of Oracle Corp. Express is a trademark of Parasoft Corp. Utopia Load Sharing Facility is a trademark of Platform Computing Corp. Pyramid and Pyramid Reliant are trademarks of Pyramid Computer Corp. Network Linda is a trademark of Scientific Computing Associates Inc. HiAv Symmetry, Sequent, Symmetry 2000/990 are trademarks of Sequent Computer Systems, Inc. SGI is a trade-

Table of Contents

In Search of Clusters ✳

✳   **xi**

List of Figures

List of Tables

Preface to the Second Edition

Well, I had to write a second edition. Too much of what I predicted in the first edition became history.

You know, it feels good to be able to say that.

They even code-named the development project at Microsoft "Wolfpack" after the cover. "Dogpack" or "dogfight" didn't have the right connotations, I guess. Sent me a logo T-shirt, too. I also got some nice e-mail from other developers, but nobody else was that classy.

Before I completely dislocate my shoulder patting myself on the back, I should mention that I missed a couple of rather major things the first time around. I didn't foresee the importance of mass-market high availability. I also didn't foresee how much confusing "NUMA" rhetoric would be used. Neither were left out entirely, mind you, but they certainly didn't get anywhere near the attention they either deserve or require. That's been corrected, in the form of two major added chapters, major revisions to other chapters, and scattered revisions throughout the book.

Another major change is the inclusion of information about cluster hardware and software acceleration, a subject that literally did not exist in sufficient quantity to take notice of when the first edition was written.

Of course the chapter of examples was trash about 40 seconds before the first edition hit the stands. This edition's version probably will be, too. There has to be a better way to do that part; books can't compete with magazines' rates of publication, much less the Internet. I've tried to be more generic in this edition, but you can't ignore the real systems and do that job right.

However, the basic original structure of the book has stood up adequately, for which I'm grateful; this edition would have been far more work were that not true. As a result, readers of the first edition will probably have an odd sense of reverse *deja vu* (*jamais vu*?), like "Hey, I thought I read that before, but it didn't say *that*." Believe me, literally every page of this thing has been changed. Why?

When the first edition was written, it really was true that most people in the computer industry had not heard of clusters, and those that had mostly considered them a lower form of life. Products that really were clusters weren't called that, because there were much cooler things to claim to be: Massively Parallel. Distributed. Hemidemisemicoupled. Whatever.

Now you would have to be deaf to not have heard of clusters. All God's chilluns got a cluster product, or two, or four, and are talking about them—if that's the phrase—with all the power of their collective lungs. The products are mostly (not always) fairly crude, but, hey, you have to start somewhere. At least they recognize the name. I've had to revise things fairly pervasively to take this new milieu into account, and have also removed some of the ranting about how this might actually be a useful thing to do. Not all. Some.

I'd like to think that the publication of the first edition had something to do with this change in the state of affairs. That would be far more satisfying than merely having correctly nailed a few short-term predictions.

Acknowledgments

I of course remain grateful for IBM's rather enlightened policy towards book authors, which still provides both support for writing and motivation to complete the job. The views expressed here are not necessarily those of the IBM Corporation, of course.

I am also again grateful for the support of my family, who once again put up with my lack of attention while immersed in this project, even though the first edition didn't produce all its promised benefits: my children Danielle and Jonathan, and, of course, my wife, Cyndee Stines Pfister—who originally said that was probably her only chance to get her name in a book. Well, lightning strikes twice.[1]

I also again owe a large debt to the many people who have discussed the subjects of this book with me, both within and outside IBM. I feel privileged to say that the cliché remains true: There are far too many to mention all of them individually. However, my manager, IBM Fellow and Vice President Rick Baum, must certainly be thanked for uttering the fateful words, "Don't you think it's time for you to do a second edition?" And then giving me the time to actually do it—possibly more time than he anticipated, and certainly more than I originally estimated, but it did finally get done. Jim Rymarczyk, Dave Elko, and Pete Sargent at least partly repaired my woeful ignorance of Parallel Sysplex. I'm particularly grateful to Dave for the several sessions at which he endured my intemperate questioning. Tom Weaver and Lisa Spainhower provided extremely useful review feedback, as well as much useful discussion over the years. Renato Recio, Tom Chen, Jeff Weiner, and other members of the System Architecture and Performance I/O team are also to be thanked for the times when, hiding behind the clever façade of "we're just dorky I/O guys who don't know nothing about the serious stuff," they filled in large gaps in my understanding of that Rodney Danger-field of computing. Not all the gaps, by any means; but I'm better off than I was before. And Bill ("Rocky") Rockefeller: May he always keep The System off all our backs.

Once again, however, the people who are most to be thanked are the IBM customers I have met over the years, as well as the members of the IBM field force who brought us together. Those customers gave me the opportunity to find out what was really of importance to them, which of course must be of paramount importance to we who serve them. It appears that many of them really do want to understand the kind of information that is in this book—at least when it is properly explained, as I have tried to do. They also unwittingly provided me with numerous opportunities to try out ways of explaining various topics, and to debug the analogies, metaphors, and jokes in response to questions and quizzical looks. As a direct result, getting through many of the chapters that follow will require markedly less caffeine.

Greg Pfister
August, 1997
Austin, Texas
pfister@us.ibm.com

---

1. My wife also insists that I acknowledge our dog, a Bichon Frise named Dallas Bell, also known as Da Stiggy to my wife and daughter (don't ask; I don't know) or as Hosehead to my son (he's a teenage boy...)—Thank her for climbing upstairs to my office to make me walk her while I was working, thereby wake... Harruumph. Never Mind. OK, Hosehead, let's go out.

Preface

Anyone planning to purchase, sell, design, or administer a server or multiuser computer system should buy and read this book.

Key needs of those systems—high performance, an ability to grow, high availability, appropriate cost, and so on—imply the use of parallel processing: multiple computing elements used together as a single entity. Parallel processing, with a bit of distributed processing, is what this book is about; it will give you the background needed to understand where the real issues lie in that realm. However, this doesn't mean that this book discusses "highly" or "massively" parallel computers. Those are flamboyant enough to have already attracted a multitude of variably successful explanations and are really of direct interest only in a vanishingly small fraction of the computer market.

Instead, this book uniquely discusses both the hardware and the software of "lowly" parallel computers, the everyday, practical work gangs of computing: symmetric multiprocessors, so-called "NUMA" systems, and, in particular, *clusters* of computers.

You do not have to be a died-in-the-denim "techie" to enjoy and profit from this book. Its form and content reflect the author's experience in explaining these issues quite literally hundreds of times to people with at best a semitechnical computer background. This has included customers who have better things to do with their time than become computer technophiles; marketing reps, both the technically oriented and the Jag-driving backslappers; and development managers, who too often think they have better things to do with their time than understand the technological basis of their business.

You do need familiarity with the current computing milieu. An ability to (mostly) understand the thick, monthly computer magazines demonstrates a background adequate to get a lot out of this book. In some areas this may even be overkill. If you've understood this preface so far, you're in good shape.

But that this book has been written to be accessible does not mean that it is *Ye Compleate Moron's Guide to a Child's Garden of Stupid Tiny BASIC Tricks*, either. Its content is not technically trivial. Because it approaches both parallel and distributed systems from a nonstandard viewpoint, that of clusters, it offers a fresh perspective that can potentially enrich both. As discussed below in "History," technically sophisticated readers have profited from prior versions that weren't publicly published. Of particular interest have been the analysis of single system image and the characterization of the programming models used in commercial computing.

One result of this unusual perspective is that while many different groups of people will find many items of interest herein, many are also going to find something to be annoyed about.

> ➤ Promoters of distributed systems will be annoyed when the book points out that their already diametrically challenged systems have ignored a significant area, one whose support will of course add even more expense. Also, they may not have realized they were in league with the next category.

> ➤ Vendors and designers of heroically large symmetric multiprocessors will be annoyed when the book warns readers of their necessarily higher costs, and therefore warns them to avoid addiction to their products—a new form of being "locked in," just like the bad old days, but this time "locked in" to an architecture, not necessarily a specific manufacturer.

> ➤ Proponents of so-called "NUMA" systems will be annoyed that this book debunks many of their statements about "maintaining the SMP programming model" and brings out of the closet their never-mentioned high availability issue.

> ➤ Cluster proponents will be annoyed when the book airs the real meaning of the industry-standard benchmarks for clusters.

- ➤ Highly massive parallelizers are already annoyed. "Flamboyant"? "A vanishingly small fraction of the computer market"? For that matter, "highly massive"?

- ➤ All traditional proponents of parallelism will be vexed because, unlike other books talking about parallelism, this one does not try to say that parallel programming can be easy or will be if only enough funding were applied to the problem. Rather, it *demonstrates* that parallel programming is very hard; and therefore mainstream software cannot directly use it, since any increase in the difficulty of writing software simply cannot be absorbed by the industry. There is a way around this conundrum, an already commonly used but formally ignored technique that is often deprecated by parallelizers; that technique forms a major theme of this book.

- ➤ Purchasers of server systems will, I sincerely hope, be happy to be given a straight, comprehensible story for once. It is really for them that this book is being written.

The humor- and irony-impaired will also have a spot of trouble here and there. (That includes one reviewer whose mind is apparently wrapped in sandpaper, to whom my editor thankfully paid no attention.)

Finally, this book will also annoy those uncomfortable unless information is presented using the puritanical parody of "the" scientific method taught to my high-school children: Just the dry facts, ma'am, boring is fine, science is rote memorization of terms (God, I hate that one), and one must not appear to be contaminating oneself with preconceived notions. All that practice serves to do is to hide the actual prejudices of the presenter, be they conscious or unconscious. That situation is far from true here.

The only reason this book exists is that I am convinced that clusters of machines are good for us, the members of the computer industry; clusters will happen whether or not we like the idea; and perhaps we should try to make the inevitable transition less than maximally painful. Its purpose is to convince you, too. Whether or not you end up agreeing with me, this book will explain an awful lot about lowly parallel computer systems—clusters, symmetric multiprocessors, and "NUMA' systems—without the rose-colored classes usually coloring most views of those subjects.

History

This book began back in about 1991, while I was a participating in an internal IBM work group. Formed from members of several development laboratories and Divisions of IBM, the group's charter was to figure out what to do with, or about, the groups of computers just then being called *clusters*.[1]

Clusters had, of course, existed for many years as commercially available products from several computer vendors, although just how common they were none of us really understood at that time. They appeared to have been, if not niche products, at least outside the mainstream of the greater computer milieu. But now they seemed to be popping up all over the place. These new clusters were not formal products from vendors but rather informal bunches of computers assembled by customers. Those worthies were using bunches of computers in a number of ways that were both technically interesting and, we hoped, commercially useful and exploitable. In addition, there were some group members making deep, or at least loud, arguments in favor of clusters as a particularly efficient and attractive product offering.

Interesting stuff. My own interest was less than overwhelming, however. This was not because of the topic, but because of the situation. I was jaded. This was far from the first working group on various parallel architectures in which I'd been involved. I could tell it wouldn't be the last, either, since like most of the others, it was going nowhere fast. A basic problem was that this collection of generally rather high-level, intelligent, and experienced computer architects, software system architects, technical strategists, product designers, researchers, and market analysts didn't know what in Sam Hill they were talking about.

No, that's actually wrong. We did have a problem, but it was nearly the exact opposite of that one. Each individual knew precisely what he or she was talking about. They were (mostly) rather smart folks and were earnestly expressing worthwhile, useful points. But each person's point of view, and often what they meant by seemingly common words, was completely or, even worse, subtly different from most of the others. So the discussion was going in circles and everyone was trying, with decidedly varying intensity and success, to believe that not everyone else was a complete dolt.

Communication was just not happening because we differed at every possible level: feasible market and application areas, appropriate performance measures, the amount and type of software support necessary, whether that support could be "open," what "open" meant in this context, what if anything all of that implied for the hardware, what the "natural" hardware (whatever *that* was) implied for software, where applications and sub-

1. Another group with an almost identical mission, although in far different circumstances, is running as the second edition of this book is nearing publication in mid-1997. *Plus ça change, plus la même chose.* This time I'm not invited. And its difficulties are different.

systems were going to come from, and so on *ad nauseam*. Nobody could even use what seemed simple terms (for example, "single system image") without significant misunderstanding by others.

It was probably fortunate that I was bored. If my mind hadn't been wandering, I probably would have "contributed" more, listened less, and never realized that this meta-problem of communication was lurking below the surface of the obvious morass. Since anything was obviously better than actively participating in yet another accursed work group, I began to work out how some of the various positions were different and what their relationships were.

That lead to my collecting in an organized form various aspects of "clusters," whatever that meant, simply to give us the common vocabulary without which progress was impossible. The outcome was a presentation that was at first short, but incrementally expanded to include possible hardware organization, aspects of software support, a number of examples, and finally a definition of the term "cluster." As I picked up more information or realized something else, I just kept fitting it into the presentation's organization, massaging that organization as necessary to make things flow logically.

The original work group was soon enough disbanded, but this had become a personal project with a life of its own, and it was becoming larger than I realized at the time. I gave parts of the presentation several times, in various circumstances, and the whole thing exactly once. Yes, to Another Work Group. To my amazement, one of the audience observed when I concluded that the complete presentation took approximately 16 hours, spread over two days. That time did include a large amount of lively discussion; otherwise I'd probably still be hoarse.

I concluded that the circumstances leading to my having a captive audience for that long were at least unusual, and certainly unlikely to be repeated. If this material was to be of use to anybody, it had to be in a different form. So I stayed home for two weeks of uninterrupted, intense effort and wrote out in prose a lengthy white paper based on that presentation.

That white paper, an internal document completed in the early fall of 1992, was version 1 of *In Search of Clusters*. I made about 100 copies, informally distributed it to people who I suspected might be interested, and, well, just stopped. There were other things to do.

I later found out that the copying machines had been busy. *In Search of Clusters* had become, informally, what amounted to required reading in the newly formed Power Parallel Systems group in the IBM Kingston laboratory, as well as in the Future Systems group in Austin and several groups in IBM Research. Not that they agreed with all of it or even modelled their projects after its precepts, but it apparently had succeeded in providing a useful set of common terms and concepts in their contexts. Comments and suggestions, both pro and con, of course began arriving.

About a year later, members of the IBM AIX Executive Briefing Center in Austin contacted me. They had been requested to provide the IBM field and marketing forces a paper that would clear up what the differences were between various forms of parallel, distributed, and clustered computing— one of those so-called "market positioning" statements. After spending several months attempting this themselves, they had come across *In Search of Clusters*. It had the information they needed, and they wanted to distribute it. This implied some work to eliminate the company-confidential elements, but at one year old those were history anyway. So, I did that, added a good amount of information I'd collected over the intervening year, did some substantial reediting, and published it electronically by placing softcopy on the internal IBM distribution facility called MKTTOOLS.

That was version 2 of *In Search of Clusters*, an "IBM Internal Use Only" 80-page document completed in September of 1993. About 1500 people obtained copies from MKTTOOLS. The copying machines have also been busy again, since it's not the simplest thing to print a 70 page document in the field in IBM, especially one translated into the common IBM printing format from PostScript® (this process usually creates huge files that print at an incredibly slow rate). I also made it available within IBM development by an easier-to-access electronic means that does not keep track of requests; from inquiries back to me, I know that has seen substantial use. I estimate that at least 2000 copies got into circulation within IBM.

Along with that circulation came a stream of electronic mail and telephone calls from the field with many comments, a fair number of kudos, and could I please make a version that wasn't "internal use only" so they could give it to customers? In addition, word inevitably began to leak out of IBM. I saw several postings to USENET discussion groups on the Internet of the form "I hear there's this paper on clusters or something that somebody in IBM wrote. Anybody know where I can get a copy?" It sounded like time for a completely unclassified version 3.

Well, somehow despite my day job I managed to put that version together. In the six months that had passed since version 2, the entire chapter on "Examples" had been made obsolete by new product announcements, but the basic structure and content had stood up well. Comments from readers indicated that several other chapters needed expansion, so that was done along with some further general tweaking. By this time it had grown to over 140 pages. Problem.

This was too long to be a white paper. I was wondering what to do with it when I accidentally heard of a seminar being run by the Austin IBM "Technical Author Recognition Program," a seminar for anyone who interested in publishing books—at which representatives of publishing companies would be present.

Bingo.

What you are holding is essentially the second edition of version 4 of that original 16-hour presentation. It's been greatly expanded, brought up-to-date, and reshaped by feedback from a large number of internal IBM readers. The book format—translation: more words than I ever thought I'd write in my lifetime—has allowed me to make the treatment of most topics much more self-contained than the original, which more or less assumed that the reader was a competent, practicing computer hardware or software architect. It also allowed me to include several new nonbackground elements, such as the chapter explaining why we need the concept of a cluster.

It's been a long, interesting trip for me. I hope you enjoy the ride, too.

First Edition Acknowledgments

My thoughts about clusters and symmetric multiprocessors, and this book in particular, have benefited tremendously from discussions over many years with a large number of people, both within and outside IBM. There are too many to mention all of them individually, but a few deserve special mention. The elaboration of workload characteristics occurred in discussion with Tilak Agerwala, who set me on the topic of clusters to begin with. (I originally didn't want to do it, since it involved all that ugly "distributed stuff.") Recognition that there were levels of single system image first occurred in discussions with Patrick Goal; a number of "at large" discussions with Patrick also contributed greatly. Jim Cox helped further my understanding of single system image concepts, along with other members of the Yet Another Work Group that met in the fall of '92. Jim also contributed to my understanding of system management issues. None of these fine people is to be blamed, of course, if I mutilate their knowledge in this book.

But the people who are most to be thanked are the IBM customers I met with during the summer of 1991, as part of a kind of technical market survey primarily targeting another set of issues. I began that exercise with a specific notion of what a "cluster" was. The customers I met had myriad other, very different notions. The disparities between the many expressed views are what first sent me in search of clusters.

Greg Pfister
May, 1995
Austin, Texas
pfister@us.ibm.com

Part 1:

What are Clusters, and Why Use Them?

Introduction

There are three ways to do anything faster:

1. Work harder.

2. Work smarter.

3. Get help.

Work harder is familiar to all of us. Ancient Sumerians probably worked extra hours for the last days before a Priest-King's inspection of a Ziggurat. "Crunch time" has been with us forever and applies to artistic-intellectual tasks as well as physical ones: Michaelangelo carried his lunch with him up the scaffolding so he wouldn't have to stop while painting the Sistine Chapel ceiling. We may not like it, but we've all done it and we know it works.

But working harder often isn't enough. It's nearly always better, and often necessary, to find a way to reduce the work needed to accomplish something. That's what *working smarter* is all about. Management consultants found it particularly profitable to hawk this one in the United States during the last decade's preoccupation with Asian competition. Despite that hype, doing anything more efficiently has a positive flavor; everyone likes to get more with less effort. Large examples, such as Henry Ford's automobile assembly line, have become cultural icons.

Finally, if you can't do it fast enough alone, no matter how much you sweat or how much intelligence you apply to the problem, you can always *get help*. This works, too, whether the group formed is a road gang or an army. But this method has a curious ambivalence associated with it. Several people can almost always dig a ditch, build a house, or write a big computer program faster than one. Committees, however, are notorious for wasting time and producing inferior results; "the right way, the wrong way, and the army way" is proverbial; and bureaucrats, who are necessary to coordinate large group efforts, are universally satirized as slow, bumbling, incompetent, and wrong-headed—except, of course, by other bureaucrats. Getting help certainly works, but everyone is well aware that it can go awry.

Despite its taint, however, *getting help* has a significant advantage over the other two techniques, one that may at first seem unrelated to finishing faster: A group can continue to make progress even if some members are lost to illness, waning interest, redeployment, or any of a multitude of other problems. This of course doesn't work if a lost member has unique necessary skills, but it works often enough to make groups much more resilient than individuals. A group may talk itself into doing odd things, and may even finish slower than a single talented individual could, but with the right kind of interpersonal glue it will operate more reliably than a loner. Both causes and companies routinely outlive their founders.

And so it is with computers:

	In a computer:
1. Work harder	processor speed
2. Work smarter	algorithms
3. Get help	parallel processing

1.1   Working Harder

Simply making the basic guts of a computer run faster, as often but imperfectly measured by its clock speed, works very well indeed to increase performance. The beast simply *works harder* on everything, all the time. It has the electronic equivalent of a faster metabolism.

The advances that have been made in this area, and can reliably be predicted to continue, are nothing short of astonishing. Intel, for example, increased the speed of its X86 architecture microprocessors 450 times between the introduction of that architecture in 1978 and mid-1994 [Hal94]. This is an astonishing 47 percent annual cumulative growth rate (CGR) over 16 years. Vendors of RISC architecture workstations have done even better over a shorter haul. Virtually every member of that club—Hewlett-Packard, MIPS, IBM, and Sun in particular—has succeeded or beaten their prediction that they will double their system performance every 18 months. That corresponds to a 60 percent CGR. Never in recorded history has any human-created process increased its speed at a sustained rate like this.

Not all of this speed increase arises solely from clock speed, the purest manifestation of *working harder*; very significant aspects of the other two techniques are involved in a major way both inside the microprocessors themselves and outside of them. When these are more fully taken into account, the growth rates mentioned above are blown away. Overall computer performance on commercial processing has been rising since 1992 at the incomprehensibly fast rate of 154 percent per year, compounded (CGR). That means performance doubles *every nine months*. For every child born in the middle 1990s, the speed of computers at its birth was more than twice that when it was conceived.

The data behind these statements is presented and discussed in Chapter 3. For now, just note that the last shoe has not dropped, nor has the fat lady sung. The advances resulting in ever faster computers will continue, and economic empires will rise and fall as a direct result. There's more in store than anybody realizes, because no one is mentally equipped to truly comprehend the exponential growth that's involved here. If we were, we wouldn't be annoyed that a personal computer or workstation purchased five years ago is now virtually worthless.

This book would never have been written if the speed increases described above were not occurring. The topics treated here are ultimately consequences—possibly not even the most important, but certainly interesting and useful—of this continued rapid growth of microprocessor and computer performance. But how that growth is coming about, and why, will not be discussed here. The saga of the circuits must be found elsewhere.

1.2   Working Smarter

"Using a better algorithm" is a direct translation into mathematico-computer jargon of the phrase *working smarter*. The increases in speed made possible by better algorithms dwarf even the feats of semiconductor integrated circuit technology.

For example, no one would ever look up a name in a phone book by turning to the first page and checking the first name listed, then the second name, and so on up to the name that's wanted. Phone books would be useless without a better search method (algorithm) than that. A start-at-the-first search takes time related to the number of names: in a list of 200 names, you look at 100 names on average before finding the desired one; 1,000 looks for a list of 2,000 names; 100,000 looks for 200,000 names, and so on. The usual alphabetical search, in contrast, takes time related to the number of *digits* in the number of names: 3 looks for 100, and only 6 looks 100,000 names. (In the jargon: It's proportional to the logarithm of the amount of data.) The difference between 6 and 100,000, or 8 and 10 million, and so on, is gargantuan. Using the right algorithm can mean the difference between possible and practical, now; and impossible, ever, on any computer.

Choosing or discovering appropriate algorithms is therefore supremely important. We should be extremely careful that using any of the other techniques does not require us to use an inferior algorithm. But other than that caution, and the citing of a specific violation or two later, this book is not about that topic, either.

1.3   Getting Help

That leaves *getting help*, known for computers as parallel processing or, as it is sometimes called, concurrent computing (among the alliterati).

Some forms of parallel processing are covert. They reside hidden inside the microprocessor, manifesting themselves only as increased processor performance on a single programmed stream of instructions. Covert parallelism is a significant constituent of the increased processor performance mentioned above. It is advertised with terms like "superpipelined," "superscalar," "multiscalar," and so on. This book is also not about covert parallelism; instead, it lumps this form of parallel processing in with processor performance.

If parallel processing is not covert, it is overt. Software—really, the programmers of the software—must at some level explicitly form multiple streams of instructions to "manually" (as it were) exploit overt parallelism. When the unqualified term "parallel processing" is used in this book, it means overtly parallel processing.

Like *getting help*, its social counterpart, (overtly) parallel processing has, or, after discarding the hype, should have, an aura of ambivalence about it. There's an old joke in the field that parallelism is the wave of the future—and always will be.[1] There is a tendency to feel that way because the history

---

1. The first time I ever heard it was in approximately 1982, from Creve Maples, who was then at the Lawrence Berkeley Laboratory of the University of California. I believe he attributed it to someone else, but who that was I do not remember.

of the area has not been the smooth upward climb experienced by the two other techniques mentioned above.

Parallelism was explicitly considered and rejected by Von Neumann during the birth design of the modern computer in the 1940s [BGvN62]. There were of course excellent reasons for this rejection, but nevertheless it was not precisely the best possible start. The basic computer architecture he and his team devised, known as the Von Neumann architecture, has dominated computing ever since. It contains an intrinsic, internal performance limitation called the "Von Neumann bottleneck" that all forms of overt parallelism, and some forms of covert parallelism, attempt to overcome. More will be said about that later.

Nevertheless, a number of fairly early parallel designs were attempted. Parallel processing to do a fair range of things faster—not just specific, one-off applications—probably emerged into its first great visibility in the late 1960s with the ILLIAC IV project at the University of Illinois [BBK+68]. This was not just parallel processing in the sense of getting a couple of friends to help paint the house. It was highly, or massively, parallel processing: recruiting an army of computational elements to do battle with far more massive calculations than were feasible on conventional computers. Nowadays, if your army is merely tens strong, you're certainly not in that club; better make it hundreds or thousands.

ILLIAC IV suffered a number of problems, not all related to parallelism by any means; it also tried to advance circuit and software technologies significantly. It faded into obscurity, finally being extinguished in the early 70s. The field remained an active, collegial area of research at many major laboratories and universities, with results reflected in a number of interesting projects and products that will not be described in this brief overview. It was just less highly publicized and, at least in massive form, it was not terribly successful in the marketplace.

Thanks to that continuing effort, the field was well prepared when a very different sort of demand arose for parallel processing of the highly, massively, build-an-army persuasion. Such processing was one of the significant elements of the Japanese Fifth Generation Project, begun in the mid-80s. Again the justification was to provide vastly more computation than was feasible with conventional computers. Countervailing projects in the U.S. and Europe were begun, including several efforts of the massively parallel persuasion.

Even though the Fifth Generation's goals didn't appear to require numerical processing (as far as anybody could tell), the more traditional scientific and engineering parallelizers seized the moment. Among other events, an official, U.S. Government-approved list was made of problems of intense economic or scientific interest, significant problems that were so large they just had to have massive parallelism for their solution: the Grand Challenge problems [Exe87]. This list was and continues to be used to justify government promotional programs.

The Fifth Generation also faded and was extinguished—again, by no means entirely, or even mainly, due to problems with parallelism. Most of the countervailing projects followed suit, although some have survived and most left a legacy of interesting computer designs and pathways to government support.

Through all of this, the hype and the front-page newspaper articles ebbed and flowed, as is inevitable surrounding projects to build the biggest, fastest, most colossal of anything, including computers.

Starting in the late 70s and early 80s, the parallelizers had noticed, along with everybody else, that microprocessors had superb performance for their price compared with larger computers. They just weren't very fast individually. Well. Talk about a tailor-made situation. All You Have To Do Is Just gang up a huge whacking lot of them, and you get massive amounts of computer power for relatively little money. Almost all the Fifth-Generation-Era projects were microprocessor-based.

The problem was, always was, and still is, that All You Also Have To Do is program the dang things to work together. Why that's a daunting task is a question to which we will return in far more detail. In the meantime, just consider the effort needed to coordinate large numbers of people to do anything, and the mistakes and frustrations typical of dealing with the bureaucracy necessary for control of large organizations. Programming costs money, much more than hardware, and is furthermore in a chronic state of crisis; so if all parallelism gets you is cheaper hardware, it's no bargain. These didn't make it commercially, either.

Then in the early 1990s the continuing rise of microprocessor performance made itself felt. The business end of an exponential growth curve is really just rising as usual, but it feels like it's "kicking in," and kick in this one did. Rather suddenly, large but practical-sized agglomerations of microprocessors didn't just equal big machine performance or provide it more cheaply. They clearly became the way to exceed even the biggest and super-est computers' speeds by large and ever-increasing amounts.

This was potentially a horse of a shockingly different color. Byzantine programming or no, there appeared to be an adequate number of people willing to do quite a lot for significantly faster computers than anybody else has. They ranged across a very broad area.

- ➢ Scientists wanted to verify or disprove things they couldn't before, and just incidentally get the work done faster so they could publish first, establish precedence, get tenure, and receive the other rewards of scientific excellence.

- ➢ Engineers wanted to simulate more of a car, airplane, drug, or whatnot in ever greater detail so they could remove their mistakes before embedding them in expensive prototypes, trials, or even more expensive production, thus avoiding really ugly economic, and sometimes moral, issues.

- ➢ Retailers wanted to examine every one of roughly a gazillion sales records so they can tailor, for you alone, every individual one of you, a whole series of offers so good you just can't refuse them.

- ➢ Airlines wanted to make sure a "full" short-hop flight really had room for that one more person who was using it to get to a high-profit transcontinental connection.

- ➢ Financiers wanted to make an obscene amount of money because their probabilistic analysis of future projections of multilevel tranches of mortgaged-backed securities was 0.1% faster than their competitors'.

- ➢ And, as far as I could tell, nearly everybody on earth wanted to warehouse a huge number of movies for immediate, interactive download to your home, making a high profit at this because absolutely everybody else hates having to return rented video tapes.

That's how things stood in about 1993-1994. Massively parallel computing seemed on the road to commercial success. Established companies like NCR, IBM, and Fujitsu joined in. Startups were in less danger of folding. Intel's Scientific Supercomputer Division (sell lots of chips at once!)[2] was rumored to be making money. Traditional vendors of supercomputers and superminis like Cray and Convex, following the trend or in self-defense, began marketing massively parallel machines based on the newly-potent microprocessors.

Commercial processing seemed to open up, too, with "MPP" offerings from such powerhouses of that area as Oracle, Sybase, Informix, and IBM. Massively parallel processing was the wave of the future again, and this time it actually seemed to be making money. There was an aura of satisfaction in the air, and not a little relief.

---

2. Don't laugh. That's how Digital Equipment Corp. began selling computers. Their first computer, the PDP-1, was a way to sell lots of logic gates—the original "equipment" of Digital Equipment—at once.

Of course, the publicity machine stayed in full gear—although at a tad lower volume, since fewer folks had to be convinced that real profits are possible. It's always easy to hype the biggest, fastest, most powerful. Unusual programming was still required, but hey, get used to it, it's the wave of the future.

There was, and is, a wholly justifiable fascination with huge computer systems. Cathedrals, pyramids, and other Grand Challenges are legitimate objects of awe and rightfully the province of efforts correctly described as "massive." To quest for the biggest and the fastest, to push back the boundaries of the possible—this is to be involved in a grand cause. It feels wonderful, especially when after all those years one finally seems to be winning. Trust me, I've been there [Pfi86, PN85, PBG+85]. The lure of large numbers is powerful.

But this book is not about *that*, either.

1.4   The Road to Lowly Parallel Processing____

In the hullabaloo of the highly massive and the excitement of finally making it, one key point was forgotten, and another issue raised its head. The result was that directions changed, companies collapsed and were absorbed—including the venerable Cray Research, ending the supercomputer era—and the market for massively parallel systems was described in early 1997 as "small and erratic."[IDC97]

Other things also occurred to produce this result. For example, post-Cold War military downsizing really took hold, drying up some markets and eliminating economic props from some of the more speculative efforts. In addition, some markets, like the one for home video on demand, turned out to be mythical. However, the key points were just two.

First: *The microprocessors kept on getting faster. A lot faster.*

Recall the earlier statement that commercial computer performance has been rising at 164 percent per year, compounded—doubling in 9 months. If the basic system speed doubles in 9 months, that means the number of units you need to couple in parallel is halved every 9 months to get the same result.

This puts "massive" systems on a crash diet. They shrink from massive through merely portly to practically svelte at a rapid rate. In just four years, for example, the size needed for a given task is divided by approximately eight. 128-unit parallelism evaporates down to 16-unit parallelism, shrinking from "massive" to merely a comprehensible grouping.

This can be seen in one of the original premier commercial areas of massive parallelism: mining mountains of worldwide sales data to find new competitive information. For example, are people who buy golf clubs also likely to buy something else soon? If they are, targeted advertising material can be stuffed in the box with the clubs. Polo shirts, maybe? Airline tickets? Possibly... The point is that you don't know what you'll find until you've scanned at least Gigabytes of data. This kind of thing is now routinely done on systems much smaller than was originally envisioned. While there are still cases where massive efforts are required, they are restricted to markets that are, indeed, "small and erratic."

Second: *System availability became a mass-market issue.*

There have always been situations in which people are justifiably willing to pay large amounts of money for computers that don't stop working. Just to pick a few examples, consider what would happen if spacecraft guidance systems were to go haywire, medical life support systems were to fail, or stock trading were to suddenly stop. The social, personal, or financial disasters that would result are quite large enough to justify the special prices such special computer systems traditionally commanded. This was, and remains, a lucrative, if relatively narrow, market.

On the other hand, there is a vast legion of people who started using computers because inexpensive ones did useful things. Recently they have begun to realize—and computer vendors have of course been helping the realization process along—that they really are dependent on the dang fool gadgets. A whole firm full of lawyers can't bill hours if their word processor's file server isn't working; a corral of salespeople can't take orders if they can't enter them into the billing system; and Internet servers can't take "hits" from their worldwide audience, justifying their advertising revenue and, perhaps, soon doing real business, when they're down.

So, a very large collection of people now realize that they're strongly impacted by failures of inexpensive computers. These people are decidedly unwilling to pay the ultra-premium prices commanded by traditional high reliability. They're only in the game because the price is right, and won't play if it's too high.

What to do? Well, if they're so cheap, buy two! Then if one fails, you switch to the other.

The many issues involved in making this work we'll discuss later; for now, consider a point unrelated to moving work from one computer to another: The computers aren't really all *that* cheap, and furthermore they're not all *that* unreliable; most of the time, they work fine. Buying another that just sits there getting dusty nearly all the time is at least annoying, particularly to whoever keeps an eye on finances.

So, OK, instead buy two smaller ones and use both at the same time. If either fails, move all the work to one until you fix the one that died. Now you're covered against failure, and it doesn't cost much at all. Good deal.

Ahem.

Both computers are being used at the same time.

That means you just started doing parallel processing across those computers.

It might be rather plebeian compared to heavy-duty database mashing, grandmaster-level chess championships, or simulating whole milliseconds of a nuclear explosion, but it's parallel processing all the same.

However, this time it's being done with a motivation very different from that of traditional parallelism. This parallel processing isn't there to do something so big it can't be done in one computer. It's there to make high reliability cheap. "Massive" numbers of computers aren't involved, even though the people designing the systems may, for reasons discussed later in this chapter, be somewhat confused about this point. Confusion or not, it's certainly true that a potentially massive market is definitely involved.

The use of parallelism in extending high availability to the many, together with the continuing explosion in processing power that was the first point discussed above, together make small parallel systems, mere *clusters* of computers, an extremely important topic.

Clusters are now used in many more places than one would expect, and in fact the notion is not new at all. What is new is their power, and the broad-based need for their intrinsic availability. These will inexorably increase, so that while there will always be a need for highly parallel systems, systems at the other end of the scale—for want of a better term, *lowly parallel systems*—are, and will be, far more widely used by vastly more people.

That, finally, is what this book is about.

Not the armies, the conquering hordes, the multitudes recruited for the grand exploits of whole civilizations, national economies, or massive individualized mail-order campaigns, imbued with some kind of wizardly super- or ultra- or massive quality. This is about construction crews, tightly knit teams, small departments. Groups big enough to handle the majority of jobs today, and even more tomorrow since they're composed of ever-growing giants, coupled to make them immortal.

There would, however, be no point to this book if this were all happening smoothly, if there were not difficulties or issues to be resolved. There are. While many will be discussed, two stand out in particular.

First, there already is a highly visible, entrenched lowly parallel computer organization: the symmetric multiprocessor (SMP). The SMP has been around since at least the early 70s. It is the workhorse lowly parallel computer architecture of both commercial processing and much engineering and scientific processing, the *de facto* industry-standard lowly parallel system. SMPs have some significant advantages over clusters, but they have disadvantages, too. Are they competitors, or synergistic?

In addition, an extension of the SMP organization has recently been the subject of a rather significant quantity of deeply purple prose in press releases: The so-called "NUMA" system (Non-Uniform Memory Access system). This blurs the picture even more, since it claims to extend the familiar SMP organization into territory previously held only by massively parallel systems.

Not that clusters aren't the subject of propaganda and day-long coming out parties themselves. There are hearts and minds to win, and with them many dollars, so the entire spectrum of server vendors maintains an incessant drumbeat of press releases, announcements, and related events.

Whose claims are true? Anyone's? This is a primary question this book seeks to discuss. Clusters are not a perfect parallel computer organization. There probably is no perfect parallel computer organization. At the same time, there are characteristics of clusters that SMP and NUMA systems cannot have that will cause clusters to survive. What exactly is the relationship between SMP, NUMA, the old massive parallelism, and clusters? The comparison is crucial. It appears later in this book, arguably its climax, after an awful lot of preparation.

Another question can readily be asked, however: Why is everybody shouting so loudly? Money is directly at stake, lots of it, and that alone certainly accounts for much of the volume. But in this case something else is afoot. There's an element of the SMP/NUMA/cluster issue that's particularly nasty.

How you program these lowly parallel architectures is different. It is so different that it builds a significant barrier to anyone who would like to move between them. In the jargon: their programming models are different.

If one explicitly exploits SMP architecture in an application, it's essentially impossible to use that same program to efficiently exploit clusters. The program can't exploit "NUMA" systems well, either, although their proponents claim otherwise, speaking a half truth that confuses the issue greatly. The situation is, furthermore, nearly symmetric: If an application explicitly exploits cluster architecture, SMP use is merely strongly degraded, at present rather significantly, and the main features of SMPs are not exploited. NUMA is in a similar position.

Open systems standards do not bridge the gap. There are, or will be, standards—one set for SMPs, another for NUMA, and yet another for clusters. So the bad old days before open systems, when programming locked you into a vendor's architecture, are still around.

The result is a major issue of critical mass: If programs are written for one architecture, they aren't there for another; hardware purveyors look at what's written, shrug, and build what runs the programs; with more hardware available, more programs get created; and a cycle begins that's either virtuous or vicious depending on which side you are on.

That's the reason for the vociferous nature of the debate: Companies will live or die by the programming model they choose, should they choose only one; most hedge their bets and support several. The whole issue of programming models, including how and why they are in fact different and the nature of the barriers between them, forms one of the more important chapters of this book.

Beyond even the question of competing computer organizations, however, there's a completely separate, second problem. It is a distinctly odd one. Despite the fact that clusters, like SMPs, have been around for decades, they're invisible. In a very real sense, they don't exist.

1.5   A Neglected Paradigm

Is there really such a thing as a *cluster* of computers?

To the users and administrators of the hundreds of thousands of clusters in production use, that must seem a remarkably stupid question. Of course there are clusters. You can purchase them ready-made from many sources— Tandem, Digital, Hewlett-Packard, IBM, Compaq, Sun, Pyramid, Sequent, Amdahl, Novell, and many others (a more extensive list, but still incomplete, is in Chapter 2, "Examples"); or you can roll your own using nearly anybody's computers and widely deployed distributed and parallel computing facilities—distributed file systems, network operating systems, parallel programming packages, and the like. There's practically a press release a day on the subject, and it's even become the subject of puns: "Digital Mustering UNIX Clustering" (Network World); "Put Some Luster on Your Cluster" (Datamation). The cluster bluster is reaching a deafening level.

So how can the question above possibly be a serious one?

Consider:

On the one hand, material on clusters enjoys a respectable if not particularly large presence in the technical literature, in the form of papers, books, and chapters in books. It also has begun to form an ever-increasing thread in popular computer magazines. These sources typically describe individual cluster implementations: how they are built, how they are programmed, what they are used for. The books usually amount to reference manuals for specific cluster products. Individual cluster incarnations are described in conferences on parallel and distributed systems and are occasional case studies in textbooks.

On the other hand, while the field is beginning to open up, there is still near silence about characteristics shared by clusters in general. There are no textbooks or textbook chapters that are not case studies; there are no conferences other than product user groups (although workshops are becoming common). There are no standards, benchmarks, openly defined programming tool kits, and other desiderata specifically for clusters, although individual vendors have announced their own versions. Which of those mutually incompatible support structures is better? By what standards can they be judged? For example, hardware vendors regularly trumpet how much bandwidth they have between computers in a cluster, implicitly saying that more is obviously better. Is it, really? Or is most bandwidth useless without reduced communication overhead? The industry has begun to struggle with questions like these, but the answers have not yet crystallized.

In short, the topic of clusters is still not a coherent discipline. Its current state mirrors that of the state of geography in the Middle Ages as described by Daniel J. Boorstein, a time when there wasn't even any common synonym for the word "geography":

> Lacking the dignity of a proper discipline, [it] was an orphan in the world of learning. The subject became a rag-bag filled with odds and ends of knowledge and pseudo-knowledge, of Biblical dogmas, travelers' tales, philosophers' speculations, and mythical imaginings. [Boo83, p. 100]

It surely is overstatement to apply this to clusters, of course. There are no religiously held dogmas, are there?[3] We don't draw our product-positioning maps of clusters with Eden, the unreachably magnificent, at the top, labelled "East" (…with the massively parallel systems)—do we? The sales force is

---

3. For those who are not involved in this field at all: This is rather heavy-handed sarcasm. There are more religiously held-to dogmata in parallel and distributed processing than there are fleas on the Pope's dog.

certainly imaginative, but can we credit them with truly mythic capabilities? Depends on their budget, I guess.

But clusters aren't being used because of metaphysical speculation. The eminently practical reasons why cluster use is growing were discussed earlier. What wasn't mentioned was that the trend to broad market use of clusters is actually following a path long trod by makers of mainframe and midrange computers, who have been grouping machines for decades. The general motives for this were the usual reasons advanced for all types of parallel and distributed computing: Clusters provide users with enhanced performance, capacity, availability and price/performance; in addition, these qualities are extensible—they increase, within sensible limits, as the size of the cluster grows.

There is nothing new about such motivations. They comprise a standard litany that is always trotted out and recited as the list of reasons for parallel and distributed systems of all stripes. But although clusters' general motivations match traditional paradigms' motivations, other reasons for clusters, as well as clusters' characteristics, do not. It is a thesis of this book that clustered systems are not very well described by the most popular standard paradigms of computer systems. As a result, they are not well-served by existing tools, their ability to fulfill their promises is curtailed, and they will continue to be underutilized until their differences are recognized, supported, and exploited. To some degree that difference is now starting to be recognized, but understanding of it is far from widespread. For example, I recently reviewed a new graduate-level textbook, not due for publication until 1998, that hopelessly confused clusters with distributed systems and "NUMA" systems.

This is slippery ground. Paradigmatic distinctions in the realms of distributed and parallel systems are notoriously difficult to make and are usefully ignored in not a few contexts. For example, some recent textbooks (e.g., *Modern Operating Systems* by Tannenbaum [Tan92]) explicitly label all multiple processor systems of any type "distributed," on the grounds that coupling techniques form a continuum, as indeed they do. On the other hand, practitioners of the parallel art have been heard to refer to all multiple-computing-element systems as parallel, which of course in a sense they are. It is all one, big field that invisibly grades from one style of computing to another, so this reductionist logic is impossible to refute on its own terms.

However, there is also, to pursue an analogy, a continuum between the Great Salt Flats of Utah and the Swiss Alps, and one could refer to all topography as hills of different magnitudes. No one does, because distinctions such as flatlands, hills, mountains, and rolling plains are useful and necessary. If they weren't, we would cross Kansas using the cog railways of the

Alps—or use secure remote procedure calls to communicate inside a symmetric multiprocessor. We obviously don't do either.

One class of foothills has been commonly accepted as a useful subparadigm of distributed processing: the client-server paradigm. The unique needs of client-server systems are addressed by a number of tools and techniques, notably the remote procedure call, threads, distributed naming techniques, security services, global time services, and so forth.

Clusters are similarly a subparadigm of the parallel/distributed realm. But their unique needs are not generally understood; they are confused with traditional "massively" parallel systems on the one hand, and traditional distributed systems (also rather massive) on the other.

This is a neglected paradigm. More: The very concept of a cluster, as a unique type of thing of itself, has been missing. It cannot be replaced by any number of product brochures and press releases. Some degree of intellectual cohesion is necessary, a quality notoriously absent from those media.

This lack of an intellectual framework for clusters is not without costs that range well beyond the frustrations of some eccentric and atypically stubborn workers. Broadly used performance benchmarks, lacking the concept of a cluster, give information most people misunderstand and misuse when the benchmarks are used to compare clusters to other types of systems. Research and development efforts are misdirected, wasting effort and losing the recognition and market presence that should rightfully be their reward. There are issues in computer science which remain confused when they might be clarified by considering clusters. Products are maladapted to the greater market they could serve because developers, lacking an appropriate framework, concentrate their efforts on the wrong things.

A later chapter will explicitly address each of these items to show just how much we need the concept of a cluster.

1.6   What is to Come

So exactly what is a cluster, anyway? Well, I'm not going to tell you. Not right now, anyway. There is a reason for this reticence.

Since it's not commonplace to consider clusters a separate sub-paradigm, the first task must be to give examples, focusing on aspects common to the cluster genre. Then the technology trends that lead to clusters and lend them ever-increasing importance will be discussed. The intent is to build up the characteristics that a definition should try to capture, hopefully creating a focus on the thing rather than on its definition. After that background, a surprisingly simple-looking definition will be offered, and the nontrivial distinctions that follow from it will be highlighted.

The bulk of the discussion then begins. Starting with hardware for clusters, SMPs, and NUMA systems, we will continue into software and finally converge to systems—for all overtly parallel issues, be they cluster, SMP, NUMA, massively parallel, or distributed, are system issues: neither hardware nor software alone, but their alliance.

The hardware discussion will cover the myriad possible forms of clusters and what's needed to build a good one of any of several varieties; how they differ from other computer organizations, such as the SMP and NUMA systems mentioned earlier; what an SMP is, really, and what a NUMA system is (really); and, in some detail, the amazing things one has to do to build a shared-memory machine that can run programs which exploit industry-standard SMPs—and not just wind up with a "shared-memory" computer, which in general is *not* the same thing as an SMP.

Then it's off to software: what these systems can be used for and how easily, the ways they are programmed, a demonstration of the difficulties parallelism adds to programming, the great continuing debates in the area, how differing "computational models" can trap you into an architecture, and how commercial, not just technical, parallelism works; and finally, the subject of "single system image" (whatever that means).

The convergence to systems then discusses high availability, a topic which can have (and has had) very thick tomes devoted to it alone, and certainly produced a thick chapter here; then the system discussion interrelates what has come before in a grand SMP-NUMA-cluster comparison. Finally, examples of where we are going wrong without this concept—clusters—will be addressed in detail, and some conclusions drawn about what we should be doing to better exploit the paradigm.

This is a far longer trip, with many more subplots, than I anticipated when I began this project. I hope you can stick around for the ride. It's really not all that bumpy. Most of the issues involved are really common sense when looked at from the right angle, as I've tried to make clear throughout.

In that spirit, I've started the next chapter with an example from an area that many should find interesting:

Beer.

Examples

2.1 Beer & Subpoenas _____

Figure 1, on the next page, illustrates a very straightforward, highly useful cluster that is used in every brewery of one of the world's largest producers of that beverage. There are three computers, used in parallel in a very straightforward way: One monitors the production facilities, one controls distribution, and one is used for administration.

What makes this a cluster, rather than three separate systems, is their linkage in a group that keeps going when there's a failure. If the production monitoring system goes down, its tasks are picked up by the administrative system and administration gets pushed into the background. After all, the beer must be brewed. If the distribution controlling system goes down, its tasks are picked up by the administrative system and administration gets pushed into the background. The beer must be shipped. If the administration system goes down, nobody much cares. (Well, actually, they do care very much when it comes time for payroll.)

Notice that there are no hifalutin' fancy parallel operations going on. They aren't needed. Since each job fits nicely in a computer, the parallelism involved is dirt simple. This style of parallelism is called partitioning the

Figure 1   Running a Brewery

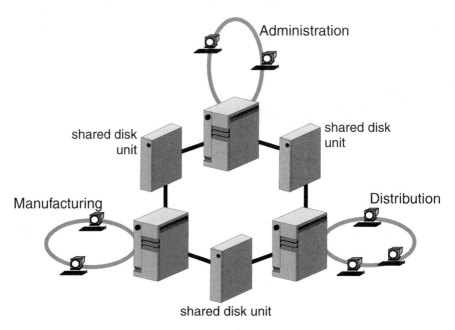

workload, for the simple reason that you put "part" in one place and "part" in another.

However, such simplicity is not shared by the functions that detect failure and move the work when necessary. The issues involved there are also not traditional parallel processing issues, but that doesn't mean they're anywhere near trivial. We'll get into them in Chapter 12. For the moment, just note that they are what makes this collection of otherwise completely separate computers look like a single unit, a cluster.

This style of cluster is not uncommon in manufacturing operations such as this. A similar two-computer cluster is used at the factories of a leading cosmetics manufacturer. There, one machine monitors production and the other is used for administration.

So, neither beer nor mascara would be produced without clusters, a situation that leaves me feeling rather frustrated. I know there's got to be a redneck joke in there somewhere, but I can't find it. Someone suggested it probably has to do with disrupting the breeding cycle.

That's the beer. Now we need some subpeonuts. (Sorry, that's very bad, but I couldn't resist.) There's a medium-sized law firm in downtown Austin, Texas, which, like law firms everywhere, runs on word processing. It's what's known as a mission-critical application for them: If it isn't running, it is extremely difficult for them to rack up hours billable to their clients. Since all standard forms and templates must be available to everybody, the word processing relies heavily on their file server.

To ensure that this is always available, they use an even simpler arrangement than the brewery, as shown in Figure 2.

Figure 2   Mission-Critical Word Processing

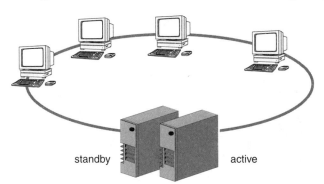

standby   active

There are two file servers, but only one actively serves files at any time. The other just sits there, but it's not completely idle. It copies onto its disks any changes made to the files on the active unit, thus maintaining a complete, up-to-date second copy. Should the active one should drop dead, the standby immediately picks up the load, masquerading as the active one as far as the clients (the computers, that is) are concerned.

The manager of this system isn't concerned about the idle capacity. It's simple, it's completely reliable, and it keeps him from getting beeped at 3:00 AM by irate junior partners. (The senior partners are asleep.) Besides, he considers himself a skinflint. He's quite proud of having shopped around and assembled this two-computer cluster out of the cheapest possible units he could find, any of which was completely adequate to serve the load his users put on it.

Once again, what's being done is eminently simple, except for the part that "fails over" the system; and that was written back at a vendor's shop, by a collection of experts.

2.2   Serving the Web

After being sued, the next least popular corporate activity is, or soon will be, annoying thousands of customers simultaneously by having your Internet

Web server crash—or merely have too little capacity after you were lucky enough to have your web site declared "cool." This is a brand new opportunity to turn an asset into a handicap, as if there weren't enough of those already. Unfortunately, those customers won't stay annoyed long. The browser "stop" button is awfully convenient, and competitors are just a mouse click away.

Several companies are avoiding this opportunity by using an arrangement like that shown in Figure 3.

Figure 3   Serving the Web

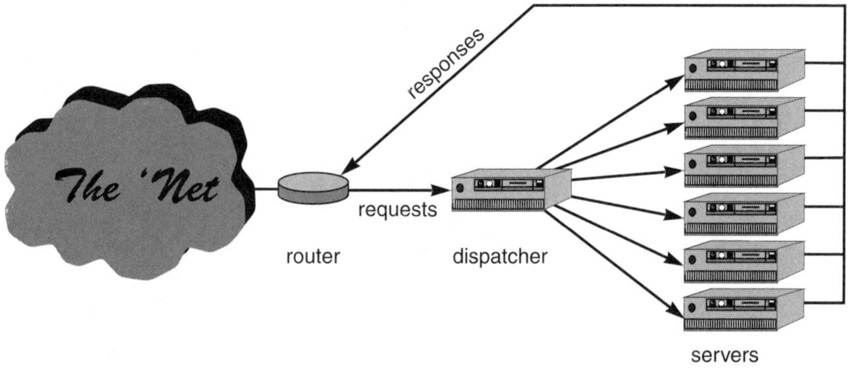

Figure 3 is illustrates what goes on in a highly schematic, simplified form; the reality is somewhat more complex, as is typical of networking.

The basic idea is that just one computer, the dispatcher, advertises its presence on the Internet. It's receives *all* the requests directed at http://whatever.com. But it doesn't service them. Instead, it forwards the requests to a bank of servers that do the actual work, balancing the load among them by getting feedback from each indicating how busy is it. The responses are sent back to the Internet by each of the servers; since responses are much larger than requests, and formatting data to look "cool" is much more complicated than just passing on requests, a single dispatcher can handle the load for at least tens of servers. The users don't know there are multiple servers doing this, and don't care; they just see the one web site, and are happy about the response time they experience.

Each of the servers can handle all requests by sharing access to a file system holding the actual web site data (not shown) and by holding local copies of the information that has to be transmitted. In more complicated cases, a second rank of servers is used to access a database holding the "real" data. The first rank's function is to pull apart the request to find out what's needed in the database, send database requests, get the real data, format it so it looks cool, and transmit it back to the user.

How the system survives loss of a server is fairly obvious from the figure; the dispatcher monitors who's up and who's down, and doesn't send anything to systems that are down. However, the figure makes it look like the router and the dispatcher are single points of failure: lose either, and the whole complex is off the air. That's part of the simplification of the figure. Two or more of both the router and the dispatcher are employed, with the incoming load split among them. How the load is balanced is further discussed in Chapter 4. In addition, the two LANs implicitly shown in the figure—one from the dispatcher to the servers, and one from the servers back to the router—can actually be one.

Arrangements like this were used by IBM for the web coverage of the Atlanta Olympics[1] and the Deep Blue-Kasparov chess match, and will be used at the Nagano Olympics; they're also used at many large, well-known web sites. At Atlanta, a 53-node system responded to as many as 16 million hits a day. IBM's Net.dispatcher product was used there. Several other companies also provide this function, including Cisco, RND Networks, and HydraWEB Technologies. Tandem's WebCharger operates similarly, extending Microsoft's Internet Information Server to a load-balancing cluster of the kind described here.

2.3 The Farm

Sorry, not that kind of farm. Except for a holdout in the flatter eastern reaches of the county, nobody has farmed the region where this cluster lies since pre-Revolutionary times. Back then there was no choice. Settlers arriving at New York piled up in Westchester along the eastern bank of the Hudson River, since crossing the river meant dealing with decidedly uncooperative natives. Once those had been "pacified," the settlers took off to the west and never returned. The trees they cleared have been growing back ever since. I don't blame them for not sticking around, since how they actually managed to farm that area I don't understand. When I lived a bit to the north of there, I once tried to clear the rocks out of a plot for a vegetable garden. After several hours of work I had a large pile of rocks, the level of the ground had dropped about an inch, and I was staring down at just as many rocks as when I started. I gave up. The early settlers obviously didn't have that option or found better locations; when the leaves are off the trees, the stone fences that separated their plots are still obvious, crawling up and over the hills like great, grey, demented snakes.

---

1. This was the part that did *not* take the "opportunity" to annoy lots of press people.

This, however, was a MFLOPS and MIPS farm: a cluster of 22 high-performance workstations officially called the "Watson Research Central Compute Cluster," but known to everyone as "the Farm" at IBM's research center. It actually doesn't exist in the form shown any more; it was one of the early examples of clustering.

Insofar as possible, the Farm is run as if it were a single machine. For example, a user doesn't log onto any specific machine, but rather onto the Farm as a whole. This is done, as illustrated in Figure 4, through a terminal server on a master workstation. The server automatically selects the least loaded of the workstations that function as compute servers. Any user's job must be able to run on any compute server, so the same programs and data are available on all. That's achieved by using an everyday distributed file system: All user files are mounted from file servers in a standard-by-convention position in every compute node's file hierarchy, while each compute server's own disks hold only system software, swap space, and a small amount of temporary (UNIX /tmp) space.

As implied above, the Farm's workstations are partially specialized in function: One is a gateway, the master machine mentioned above, connecting the campus LAN system to the local farm LAN(d); two are file servers with about 15 Gbytes of disk space each; and the remaining 19 are compute servers with large amounts of memory (512 Mbytes or more). While the file servers are rack-mounted machines, to conveniently provide large disk storage capacity, the master and the compute servers are deskside, floor-standing machines. Seeing those 20 in compact rows leaves little doubt about why this type of arrangement is universally known as a workstation farm—

Figure 4   Use of the Watson Farm

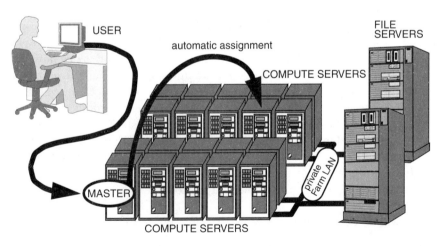

In Search of Clusters ✳

except in Texas. There it's a workstation ranch. Such terms were undoubtedly suggested by a precedent: Back when disk drives were the size of washing machines, large floor-covering arrays of them became known as "disk farms."

What new software was written for the Farm, and that was deliberately minimal, was written to facilitate its use as a single computing resource. This software was the terminal server mentioned above, a central accounting system that provides daily usage summaries across all machines, and a high-level scheduling mechanism called *Share*, which helps distribute compute time based on prior allocations. *Share* does its job by using standard UNIX facilities such as renice, which alters running jobs' priorities. Everything else is assembled out of distributed and open systems technology that is standard, commonly available, and quite broadly deployed. Graphical output is delivered straight to users' workstation displays, using again standard X Windows facilities. Thanks to the Farm, those users can get by with far smaller personal systems than would otherwise be feasible.

Very little software development yielded a bountiful crop of eminently usable MFLOPS.

2.4 Fermilab

Speaking of farms, Illinois has really good dirt. You learn to appreciate stuff like that when you live in places like Eastern New York and Central Texas. (A major difference between those two is that the Central Texas rock—singular—hasn't been broken up.)

In addition to having good dirt, Illinois is also really flat. This makes the building in Batavia, southwest of Chicago, dominate the horizon for miles around with its curved thrust tens of stories tall: Fermi National Accelerator Laboratory. This is the home of the Tevatron particle accelerator, and also of a standard Fermilab joke: The bison living in the restored prairie area within the accelerator ring are *not* cattle mutated by synchrotron radiation.

Good dirt and a big, flat area means megafarms. While amusingly coincidental, this obviously has absolutely nothing to do with the fact that Fermi-Lab ran another pioneering cluster, one of the largest workstation clusters of its time: about 400 Silicon Graphics and IBM workstations.

Unlike the Watson Farm, the workstations here are all small desktop units, mounted in racks that stretch wall-like across rooms. All were chosen by virtue of their having the best cost/performance on the primary FermiLab application, the analysis of subminiature particle events recorded by huge underground detectors of exceedingly tiny things. Analyzing any one of those events, and a whole lot of them have been recorded, has nothing to do with analyzing any of the others; so there's no reason why many analyses can't be done at the same time. That's parallel processing, and that's what the FermiLab cluster is used for.

Analyzing each individual event doesn't require a lot of memory or storage, so no individual machine in the cluster has to be big—but it does have to be computationally fast. Therefore, they use many small but powerful workstations; each has large raw floating-point performance without paying for large addenda to bigger machines: space for more memory, robust input/output subsystems, and so on.

FermiLab researchers are interested in physics, not the computer science of making large numbers of machines cooperate. If writing parallel software is as difficult as has been implied, something had to have been done to make such a collective simpler to use. It was. The FermiLab solution is to do something very similar in spirit to the techniques long used to domesticate parallelism in commercial systems: Users simply don't write parallel programs at all. Instead, the system provides the parallelism. How this works is illustrated in Figure 5.

Figure 5 Fermilab CPS Operation

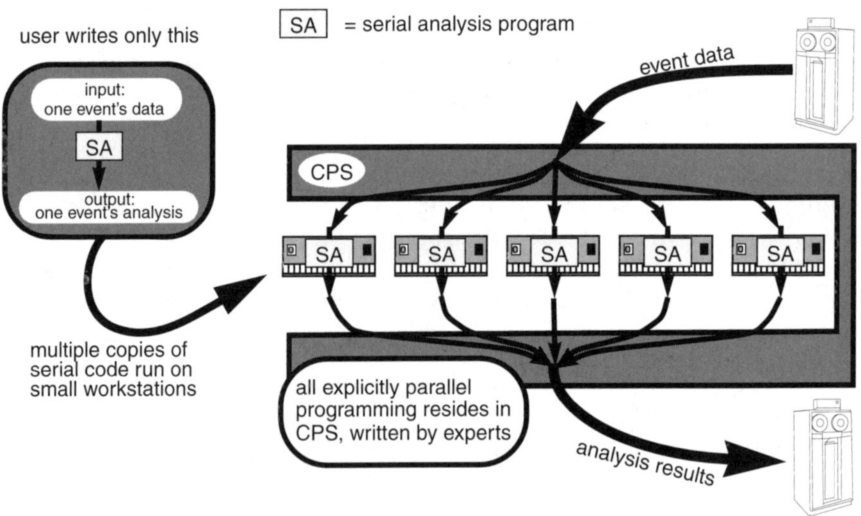

The physicist-user writes an ordinary serial program that analyzes a single accelerator event. That program gets the data for one event, munches on it in complex ways having to do with the physics involved, and delivers output describing what happened in the event. This analysis procedure is then given into the care of a Fermilab-developed subsystem called Cooperative Processes Software (CPS), which causes the procedure to run many times, simultaneously, on multiple machines. CPS reads accelerator events data from input tapes and feeds that data to those multiple instances of the user's analysis procedure, one event's data for each instance. As each individual event analysis finishes, CPS collects the results and writes them to storage, to be perused by the user.

CPS is a parallel program. It was written and is maintained by a coterie skilled in parallel programming, not necessarily physics. That one supervisory parallel program, however, allows many physicists to get the benefits of parallelism without the pain: Many serial programmers are reaping the benefits of a select few parallel programmers.

This is a common pattern that was also implicit in our initial simpler examples. (Remember that complicated high availability code?) Subsystems like transaction monitors and database systems fill the same role in business and commercial use of clusters and other forms of parallelism: An application programmer writes a (comparatively) simple serial program, a program containing no parallelism; the subsystem runs it many times simultaneously, in parallel, and has the job of keeping the many instances from interfering with each other. Perhaps less obviously, operating systems and batch monitors also provide this service for stand-alone programs that don't visibly run under the care of a parallelizing subsystem; the system provides the parallelism.

This **serial program, parallel (sub-) system (SPPS)** technique is by far the most common way for nearly all computing to use *any* of the forms of overt parallelism: cluster, symmetric multiprocessor, highly parallel, you name it. By hiding the complexities of parallelism from the run-of-the-mill user, SPPS effectively turns overt parallelism into a higher-level form of covert parallelism. In this form, it is even commonly done on a single processor to overlap I/O and processing; there the technique has long been known as multiprogramming. The individual programs don't go faster. But they wait less for the resources they need, since those resources have been multiplied (parallelism) or their use has been overlapped (single processor). The Watson Farm described above effectively uses parallelism that way. Up to now, a term for what is here called SPPS parallelism has been missing.

FermiLab to the contrary, SPPS parallelism is a rather uncommon way to get individual technical programs to run faster. Most technical problems aren't as obviously composed of many independent tasks, and single common structures usable by many are not common. As a result, aside from multiprogramming whole programs, it is more common to find users applying parallelism within their programs. A number of tools and techniques have been developed to make that easier; these will be discussed later.

FermiLab has developed some software which, while very representative of a general technique of exploiting parallelism, is in the technical computing realm uniquely suited to the atomistic nature of their problem. Of course, it's not just Fermilab's problem; it is *the* data processing problem of high-energy physics, common to all particle accelerator laboratories—CERN in Europe, SLAC (Stanford Linear Accelerator) in California, and so on. There is definitely motivation for some unique development that harnesses as much computing power per dollar as possible, because the colliders have created their own kind of information overload. There are quite literally warehouses full of tapes holding collider-generated event data that have never been processed, simply because the required computing capacity isn't available. There's just got to be a Nobel Prize hidden in there *somewhere...*

2.5 Other Compute Clusters

In one respect, the two compute clusters mentioned above are quite atypical of clusters being used today. They were some of the earliest practitioners of the art of assembling clusters from high-performance workstations and therefore had to roll their own software support almost completely. Today, cluster assemblers have a much easier time of it; they can pick and choose among a good range of commercial offerings that provide the necessary functions of cluster-wide batch queueing, interactive login, and parallelization. Earlier editions of this book attempted to list a large sample of those facilities now available, but the field has grown and is growing and changing so fast that this is now impractical. Faster-moving sources like magazines and, of course, the Internet are far better sources.

Despite that proliferation, an area that is still less than perfect is system administration. Keeping a flock of dedicated workstations in line is nowhere near as bad as doing the same to a huge crowd of individuals' personal machines. The latter is like trying to sweep up ants, while cluster management is more like herding sheep. An administrator can enforce far greater uniformity within a cluster, because the machines don't have individual owners who are free to mess around with their machines or demand to be different. This uniformity means that there's a much higher likelihood that the same command, performed on each machine, will yield the same result; that simplifies the problem immensely.

Nevertheless, you still need a sheepdog or two. Trading the administration of a single, large machine for the administration of eight, ten, or more requires forethought and work. In assembled clusters, this task is usually accomplished for compute clusters by a combination of standard distributed-system facilities, judiciously chosen "mount points" for shared file data, and a local collection of Shell Scripts from Hell that actually use those tools to do what's required.

The many product offerings that now exist in the compute cluster area, and there are a fair and growing number, would not have been developed in the absence of customer demand, and demand there certainly is.

While the exact number, or even a good estimate, isn't known, it can safely be stated that there are at least thousands of assembled clusters out there, primarily in technical settings: universities, industrial research laboratories, government laboratories, and so forth. For example, Florida State University's Supercomputing Research Institute (SCRI) has a large heterogeneous cluster containing workstations, massively parallel machines, and a conventional supercomputer. Philips Research Laboratories in The Netherlands has a cluster based on Hewlett-Packard hardware for computer-aided design support; in this case, most users have only X-Stations (UNIX graphics terminals); all the "real" work is done on a cluster of machines that provide login, computing, and file services [vDR94]. Among many others, Cornell has a cluster, as does Lawrence Livermore National Laboratory. Eugene Brooks of that laboratory has been quoted as saying "One computer center after the other is lining up to put a cluster of microprocessors on the floor. Their budgets are shrinking and these systems are much more cost-effective [than traditional supercomputers]." [Mar94]

While system vendors can be facilitators in this category, they are for the most part not the ones doing the work. Users and administrators are creating clusters, using software and hardware that is generally available. However, there's obviously a product opportunity here, too, so several vendors have begun marketing clusters-in-a-box that make what are really assembled clusters more compact and tolerable—"preassembled" clusters, in other words. Those are by no means the only cluster system products, but have characteristics that merit some discussion.

In a number of cases, the products provided are rather straightforward. Versions of the companies' mainline products are simply sold in groups, usually with little if any modification. For example, the HP 9000 Model MPS10 and the DEC TruCluster consist of those companies' high-end servers, repackaged to allow them to be conveniently placed in a rack or similar enclosure, connected by standard communication offerings such as Ethernet, FDDI, or Fibre Channel Standard, and packaged with third-party software offerings pre-ported to the platform; the spectrum of those software offerings will be described later. HP's preassembled compute cluster is typical; it's shown in Figure 6. For IBM, small versions of its RISC System/6000

Scalable Parallel systems fill this role and offer IBM-supplied software that makes system administration simpler. In some cases (DEC, IBM, and others) special fast inter-cluster communication hardware is also available.

Figure 6   HP 9000 Model MPS10 Computational Cluster

© Copyright 1994 Hewlett-Packard Company

Preassembled clusters have a quality that can make it advantageous to buy and sell even a one-machine cluster rather than the corresponding workstation. This is true even though the singleton workstation is likely to be a bit less expensive; after all, the workstation price does not include the cost of the larger rack or the less-common (and therefore more expensive), single-machine packaging used in the cluster.

The advantage arises because the whole cluster is typically labelled with a single serial number. This sounds trivial. However, it makes the purchase of additional machines an upgrade, not a new purchase. Upgrades of existing systems typically do not require the bureaucratic approvals needed for new machine purchases, approvals that would be required if another stand-alone workstation were purchased. In addition, software license arrangements are typically resolved at the outset for the entire cluster, making that aspect of adding a new machine easier, too—and often less expensive.

For example, the IBM RS/6000 SP system is the least expensive way to purchase that company's server products in even modest quantity. It you're purchasing more than four or five of them, buying them already racked and stacked in a "Scalable Parallel" enclosure has a lower total bill than buying them separately. This is true even though the individual hardware boxes are, in fact, slightly more expensive. Why? You get a deal on the software: Rather than separate licenses for each machine, you purchase a single scaled license for the operating system, compilers, and other standard software. Other vendors have similar pricing arrangements.

2.6   Full System Clusters _____

Bolted-together copies of a vendor's standard systems are not the only form in which clusters are offered for sale. While such clusters are offered by virtually every vendor of server products, hardware or software systems, three offerings are different. They stand out in that clustering is built into the system at a deep level, and its support is pervasive, encompassing most system services: administration, files, databases, workload management, and so on. Those three current kings of clusters, in a class by themselves, are DEC's OpenVMS Cluster, IBM's System/390 Parallel Sysplex, and Tandem's Himalaya series. Each is described below, along with some offerings that at the time this book is written are not available, but are either possibilities or announced directions.

2.6.1   DEC OpenVMS Cluster

Digital Equipment Corporation's OpenVMS Cluster [Dig93] was introduced in 1984 as the VAXCluster [KLS86, KLSM87, Sha91]. A name change was appropriately made when this clustering technology was extended to heterogeneous mixtures of VAX and AXP systems; today virtually any AXP or VAX system can be part of an OpenVMS Cluster—large, small, uniprocessor, symmetric multiprocessor, workstation, whatever. Furthermore, clustering is an integral part of the OpenVMS operating system. It is, in effect, not possible to purchase OpenVMS without cluster support; it isn't used until you attach a second computer, but it's always there.

OpenVMS Clusters, in contrast to assembled clusters, are very often connected by sharing input/output devices: Multiple computers are attached to the same disk or tape devices and the computers can read or write all the devices. Obviously something has to keep them from stepping all over each other's handiwork, and that's the OpenVMS Cluster software—which does much more, as will be discussed below. The hardware aspect of this sharing was originally supported by Digital's Star Coupler and CI Interconnect; later lower-cost connection called Digital Storage Systems Interconnect (DSSI) was introduced, and more recently a SCSI hub allows non-proprietary storage attachment. OpenVMS Clusters can also be connected without shared storage, using standard LANs like Ethernet or FDDI. Using the latter, nodes can be placed up to 40 km (5 miles) apart for disaster tolerance. An extremely low-overhead interconnect called Memory Channel can also be used, particularly for synchronization and message traffic; Memory Channel is discussed in detail in Chapter 5, "A Cluster Bestiary."

Multiple types of interconnect can be mixed in the same cluster. This is illustrated in Figure 7: Several workstations, AXP systems, and VAX systems combine with terminals over an Ethernet; the APX and VAX systems share access to a collection of common disks attached via CI and Star Coupler.

Figure 7 Digital OpenVMS Cluster

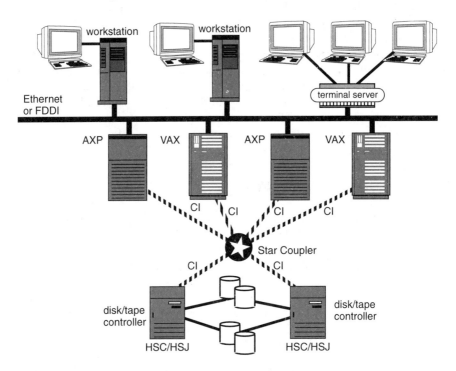

And the whole conglomeration is made to look very much like one computer.

What this means is: When you log on, you get put somewhere in the cluster. Unless you explicitly ask, you may never find out where, nor, in most cases, will you care. Those three terminals on the top right side of the figure, seemingly hanging in midair, aren't attached to any specific machine—they're attached to the cluster-as-a-whole; the "terminal server" shown is typically a small computer that serves only as an attachment point and communication

In Search of Clusters ✳

concentrator. When you submit a batch job, it gets done somewhere—again, don't know where and don't care because the same environment is available for all jobs: I/O devices have cluster-wide single names, and their use is the same from everywhere; the file system is likewise universally available, through shared disk if that's used; and to the outside, the cluster as a whole has a single "alias" to DECnet. Administration is similarly made uniform: all operations on user information, security, software installation, and so forth, are performed as if the cluster were a single, albeit extended, machine. Monitoring facilities allow all jobs running across the cluster to be seen, as well as the load on individual machines. In effect, the image of a single system is created across the cluster.

The OpenVMS Cluster must be regarded as a highly successful product on several grounds.

First and most basic, they've sold a lot of them. According to Digital, there are over 25,000 installations worldwide [Dig93 page 1-3]. This number must be interpreted in light of the fact that many cluster installations arise because a customer has outgrown the biggest machine a vendor makes. So, in all likelihood, many of those 25,000 represent multiple copies of Digital's largest machines. (Digital says that by 1997 they had sold more than 50,000 clusters, but that number includes cluster products other than OpenVMS Cluster.)

Second, this market success spawned important technical advances in the form of several cluster-supporting database systems—systems that provide the image of a single database across multiple machines and pass that image down to ordinary serial programs via the SPPS (Serial Program, Parallel Subsystem) technique mentioned in the discussion of Fermilab's cluster. In addition to Digital's own Rdb, Oracle originally developed the Oracle Parallel Server for what were then VAXClusters, and Ingres (now Computer Associates) similarly developed parallel support there. This heritage is reflected in the structure of those systems: They require disk systems shared by computers, as is provided by CI and Star Coupler in OpenVMS Clusters (and in other ways on other vendors' clusters). More recently designed database systems—Sybase's MPP, IBM's DB2/6000 Parallel Edition, Informix' XPS—eschew shared disk, targeting conventional intermachine communication such as LAN instead. Which is better—"shared disk" or "shared nothing"—is a hotly debated topic that will be discussed in Chapter 10.

Third and finally, coupling this database technology with the robust performance of Digital's Alpha AXP processor-based symmetric multiprocessors has allowed OpenVMS Clusters to demonstrate rather considerable aggregate commercial performance. In May of 1994, Digital announced that a four-node OpenVMS Cluster composed of DEC 7000-650 AXP machines, each of those a five-way symmetric multiprocessor, all running DEC's Rdb cluster-parallel relational database, achieved a new world record in the standardized TPC-A performance benchmark: 3,692 tpsA, at a system cost of $4,873 per tpsA. This was stated to have exceeded all other relational database systems' performance by a factor of at least three. That benchmark has since been retired, so OpenVMS Clusters hold the permanent record. Later, the transaction-processing benchmark record was held by a four-node cluster of Digital's AXP 8400 SMP systems running Digital's UNIX clustering product, TruCluster; that has achieved 30,390 tpmC at $305/tpm on the TPC-C benchmark, eclipsing the prior record by about 150%. (That prior record was also held by a cluster; see below.)

By the way, the current record as this book goes to press (it changed two days ago) is held by a two-node cluster of Sun Microsystems' servers running the Oracle Parallel Server database system, producing over 50,000 tpmC at a little over $100/tpm.

Notice how the number of nodes keeps getting smaller.

2.6.2   Tandem Himalaya

Tandem is well known for selling fault-tolerant, online transaction processing (OLTP) systems. What is perhaps less well known is that all their systems have always been clusters. That it's less known is partially explained by their preference for referring to smaller configurations as "loosely coupled multiprocessors." Nevertheless, except for recent Intel-microprocessor-based products, all their machines down to the smallest are composed of multiple uniprocessors that happen to be packaged in a single box, just like a preassembled cluster. Tandem calls the individual separate machines "cells," or "processing cells." The structure of a current high-end Tandem system, the Himalaya [Tana] is shown in Figure 8. Tandem uses clustering for both increased performance and for high availability, which it refers to as "software fault tolerance."

As it must, this fault tolerance begins with detecting the faults; if you don't know something's wrong, you can neither fix nor tolerate it. Fault detection in a cell is provided by, among other things, duplexing processors: two processors are run in lock-step, and if their outputs disagree, a fault has been found. That alone is neither clustering nor any other form of parallelism; no benefit other than fault detection accrues from the second processor. (Fault detection is, of course, not a trivial function to provide.) Once a fault is detected, it is "tolerated" by switching the affected operations to another cell—failing over to another machine in the cluster that is running a synchronized backup copy of the failed function. These topics will be discussed in far more detail in Chapter 12, "High Availability."

Figure 8   Tandem Himalaya K-Series System Architecture

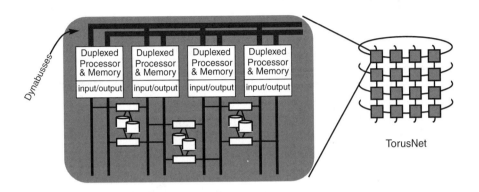

TorusNet

Failover is assisted by providing internode disk multi-tailing; as shown in Figure 8, two machines can access each disk. However, this connectivity is not used the way it is in the DEC OpenVMS Clusters. In VMSclusters (and in systems running the databases that were originally developed for VMSclusters), multiple machines simultaneously read and write disks to obtain and update shared data.

This is not done in Tandem systems, which instead use the "shared-nothing" approach: Only one machine "owns" and is allowed to use each disk at any time; if a non-owner needs to do something to data on a disk it doesn't own, a request is sent to the owner, who then performs the requested operation. The multiple access that's provided is for increased system availability only: If the owner dies, and so is definitely not using the disk any more, another machine can take over as the owner. Multiple access is also used for the same fault-tolerating purposes in OpenVMS Clusters and the commonly provided availability clusters discussed in a later section.

Increased performance on OLTP and database applications is achieved by parallel operation of the clustered cells [EGKS90]. This proceeds in multiple levels [Tanb]: Four "cells" are connected by a Dynabus [HC85]; four of them are connected by TorusNet 40Mbyte/second horizontal connections to form a 16-cell (machine) "node." Vertical connections are then made with four Mbyte/second connections, forming up to a 14-node (225 cell) "domain." Domains can themselves be connected to achieve systems with more than 4000 cells.

Tandem's latest series of high-end products, the Himalaya S-series, follow the same general architecture as the K-series described above, but do not use the TorusNet. Instead, it and all I/O connections are handled through ServerNet, a type of architecture that Tandem has dubbed a System Area Network (SAN). SANs in general and ServerNet specifically are discussed in detail in Chapter 5.

Tandem's NonStop Kernel, as well as their database system, makes such collections of units again appear to be a single unit for administrative and programming purposes.

Tandem is in the benchmark race like everyone else. From 1994 to 1997 they held the world record on the TPC-C standard benchmark—by what they stated was a factor of almost ten over the closest competition: 20,928 tpmC at $1,532 per tpmC. When this record finally fell in 1997, it was to another cluster—Digital's, as mentioned above.

A comment about this is in order: The system used to reach that mark was a 7-"node" system, where each "node" contained its full complement of 16 "cells" (machines). This is a total of 112 processors; but it was benchmarked as a 7-element cluster, treating the groups of 16 as if they were single machines—"loosely coupled multiprocessors," in Tandem's terminology. As will be explained in Chapter 14, "Why We Need the Concept of Cluster," this is quite significant.

Finally, Tandem put some publicity-garnering spice into the game. So sure were they that others will not be able to surpass them soon that they publicly made a wager: Should any company beat their record within a year, they'll donate $20,928 to the charity of the winner's choice. Nobody collected.

2.6.3   IBM S/390 Parallel Sysplex

The concept may boggle the mind of those attuned to microcomputers, personal computers, and workstations,[2] but massive, room-spanning clusters of old-style water-cooled mainframes have been used for a very long time. IBM's Job Entry System (JES) has eased the task of distributing work to a user-constructed cluster of mainframes since the mid-1970s; enhancements over time produced JES2 and JES3 [IBMb].[3]

---

2. Thereby showing their age. Back in 1972, I stood *inside* the CPU of the TX-2 computer at Lincoln Labs. The accumulator was a three-foot wide, one-foot high unit on the right with many, many lights. I guess I'm showing my age, too.

3. Virtually every press release from DEC mentioning clusters says "DEC, who invented clusters..." IBM didn't invent them, either. Customers invented clusters, as soon as they couldn't fit all their work on one computer, or needed a backup. The date of the first is unknown, but I'd be surprised if it wasn't in the 1960s, or even late 1950s.

In the early 1990s, the emphasis changed. While everyone else was prematurely predicting the death of the mainframe, internal IBM development was predicting the death of bipolar transistor technology. CMOS technology would surpass bipolar in speed, and furthermore was cheaper to manufacture and far less expensive to own.

Problem: It hadn't happened yet. The fastest CMOS didn't match bipolar speeds, and wouldn't for a while, yet customers required as much horsepower as could be thrown at their problems. (It hadn't quite happened by mid-1997, either, but it will.) Furthermore, there wasn't enough money to pursue both CMOS and bipolar in the interim. Aside from system development, they required different, conflicting, fabrication facilities; semiconductor fabs are *really* expensive.

The solution chosen was to shut down bipolar and put all the eggs into the cluster basket, focusing on using clusters of CMOS systems to provide the aggregate power needed, with the not inconsiderable added advantage of high availability. The result emerged over time, but was complete in full outline with the introduction of the S/390 Parallel Sysplex (for **sys**tem com**plex**) in 1994. [IBMd, NMCB97]

I recounted that history because it motivates a very significant design requirement for Parallel Sysplex that in turn makes a point common to all clusters.

Parallel Sysplex had to be acceptable to generally conservative customers as a replacement upgrade for large SMP mainframes running heavy commercial workloads, such as transaction processing with thousands of users and large I/O-intensive batch jobs massaging Gigabytes of data. Furthermore, those workloads had been extensively tuned over the years by generations of programmers who were not shy about taking advantage of the ease of data sharing among and within applications that is natural on a single computer with multiple processors (an SMP). Moreover, it had be an upgrade for such systems using processors that individually were *slower* than the processors in the systems upgraded. In Chapter 8, "Workloads," we'll see how nearly all workloads that can be handled well by an SMP can also be handled by a cluster, but that chapter by itself is theory. Parallel Sysplex proves it in practice, on large, difficult workloads. Anyone wondering whether clusters are up to handling the worst workloads in existence can point to Parallel Sysplex as an existence proof.

To accomplish this, Parallel Sysplex adds additional special functions to a collection of machines, and relies on the data sharing facilities already in place on S/390 systems. As illustrated in Figure 9, the added function is the Sysplex Timer, and the Coupling Facility.

Figure 9   IBM Parallel Sysplex

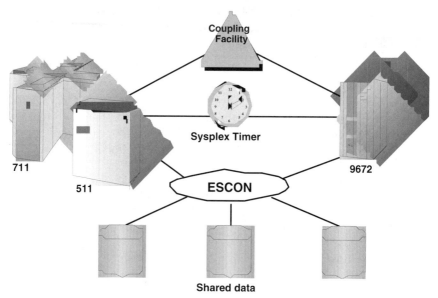

The timer provides a uniform time base for keeping track of committed transactions. The Coupling Facility will be described in more detail in Chapter 5, "A Cluster Bestiary," and Chapter 10, "Commercial Programming Models." It provides low-overhead, high-speed intersystem communication (100 MB per second), synchronization, cluster-wide data caching, cluster-wide work queues, and a number of higher-level functions such as consolidation of transaction logs across the entire cluster.

The data sharing approach previously described for DEC's OpenVMS Cluster is used here, also. Among other issues, the idea was that customers should not have to change the layout of data on their disks when installing a Sysplex. The multiple machines get access to shared data through ESCON Directors: I/O switches that simultaneously provide access to disks and other input/output devices from multiple sources. (ESCON, "Enterprise System Connection," is the normal 20-Mbyte/second I/O connection to S/390s.) ESCON Directors serve much the same function as Digital's Star Coupler, but at significantly higher performance because they are switches that allow multiple simultaneous data transfers.

However, the hardware and low-level support code, while necessary, was the small part. To drop in, replacing a single large machine, means that *all* the major software subsystems had to be modified to run in parallel across the computers of the cluster. That of course includes the parts that commonly have support for multicomputer operation, like databases and transaction monitors, thereby transparently supporting customer applications using them via the SPPS paradigm. It also includes the less-common pieces: performance monitoring, security, access methods (mainframe-ese for "file systems," approximately), communication, and cluster-wide workload management that can dynamically shift both interactive and batch loads across cluster nodes in response to changing conditions, customer priorities, failures, the time of day, and probably the phase of the moon. Here's a list of acronyms for some of the subsystems involved to tell mainframe-literate readers what's involved: DB2, IMS DB, CICS, VSAM, RACF, VTAM, JES2. All of these exploit the Coupling Facility and data sharing facilities either directly or indirectly.

Replacing a single existing large system also means that system administration cannot be handled by the mainframe equivalent of Shell Scripts from Hell. In Parallel Sysplex, the specialized tools developed for this task have each been extended to provide a single point of control—one console from which their target area can be managed and administered for the entire cluster. For example, the ESCON Manager monitors and manages cluster-wide I/O configuration and status; RMF provides cluster-wide performance monitoring and capacity planning; CICSplex System Manager monitors and controls CICS (transaction monitor) resources across the Sysplex. There are many others [IBMd]. These facilities are good enough that in many cases customers install them just to make their systems more manageable, without using any of the deeper Parallel Sysplex technology.

The result of all this work is that a Parallel Sysplex looks and acts like one single giant computer. This is not only true from the point of view of administrators and users, although that alone is impressive. It's also true from the point of view of applications—even if those applications are continually in each others' shorts sharing data extensively.

As this is written, Parallel Sysplex is considered a qualified success in the marketplace, with the qualification gradually getting better over time. Mainframe customers are a conservative, cautious breed, and many were perfectly happy running back-level system software that wouldn't support Parallel Sysplex. If it ain't broke... That was a larger problem in many cases than the introduction of cluster technology after the base support was at the right level.

Also, there are obvious difficulties handling the one application class that neither clusters nor any other overt parallel technology cannot significantly speed up without changing the application: Single, purely serial, large jobs, usually batch, which must be completed with a specific time window (like, you want your paycheck on time, right?). This problem is being alleviated as the microprocessors get faster; CMOS really is catching up.

Despite these difficulties, by June 1997 there were 1,500 installations at 850 customer sites, which is not a bad record for multimillion dollar installations. Perhaps more telling is the fact that by the same time, Parallel Sysplex was responsible for 50% of IBM's S/390 gross revenue, and the number was rising.

2.6.4   Future Candidates

There are many other vendors who now have clusters that are not as full-function as the three described above, or are purely software efforts that use standard or semi-standard hardware. Those are covered in later sections of this chapter. Two, however, have indicated that they are moving towards what I would class as full-system clusters, but as this book is written have not yet become available.

Sun Microsystems is the first. Sun has announced a road map for its Full Moon Cluster[4], which will be gradually phased in through 1999. At that time it will have graduated to the ranks of a full system cluster, since it will have high availability, a cluster file system, global (cluster-wide) networking, load balancing across nodes, global device access, and administration as if it is a single machine. Sun's current clusters use Fibre Channel Standard for disk connectivity, and a version of the Scalable Coherent Interface (SCI) links (discussed in Chapter 7) for internode communication; Full Moon will do likewise.

Silicon Graphics is the second, and is arriving at a full system cluster from a very different direction. SGI has stated that they are developing Cellular IRIX, their version of UNIX, to allow multiple "cells" within their "NUMA" Origin 2000 systems. At present, Cellular IRIX has only one cell—the whole system; this doesn't count. They may not agree with me that the result, once they have multiple cells, is a cluster with a low-overhead proprietary interconnect; this is discussed in Chapter 7, "NUMA and Friends."

2.7   Cluster Software Products _____

Proprietary systems have a potential advantage in supporting a new programming model, which clusters are in many cases. Since the hardware and all the system software is under the control of a single vendor, they can move both together to the new plateau. This advantage may be only theoret-

---

4. This name was specifically chosen because full moons make wolfpacks howl.

ical, since other aspects of their system structure may pose distinct, unique problems, but that it can work is illustrated by the cases of DEC's OpenVMS Cluster and IBM's Parallel Sysplex. (Tandem never had to change.)

However, that advantage can be drowned out by inter-vendor cooperation, standards, and the sheer aggregate mass of "everybody else," which can amount to far more development resources than any single proprietary vendor can amass.

That is illustrated by the enormous proliferation of cluster products that are purely software and run on multiple hardware vendors' platforms.

A number of the software products for clustering are briefly described below by category. Many are treated in considerably more detail in later chapters. The tables provided should be considered only a sampler, since new products and entrants are arriving regularly.

2.7.1   Batch and Login

Several products for batch submission to clusters exist, from the venerable JES systems mentioned above, which works on IBM and compatible mainframes, through more recent systems based on modern distributed processing software. Many also support interactive login in the manner described for the Watson Farm.

Examples of the more recent systems include DQS, the Distributed Queueing System developed at Florida State University SCRI (not a commercial product, but widely available "freeware"); NQS/Exec from The Cummings Group; and the IBM LoadLeveller. The latter was announced with IBM's Scalable Parallel systems, but runs on any collection of IBM, HP, and Sun workstations that communicate using the *de facto* industry standard IP (Internet Protocol). The same is true of the other packages. A number of other systems provide similar functions; several are listed in Table 1.

These systems provide job submission to a cluster, perform at least rudimentary load balancing, and allow users to query the status of jobs. The degree to which they hide the multiple-machine nature of the cluster varies widely. Some (for example, IBM LoadLeveller) also provide checkpoint/restart facilities for more reliable operation; others (for example, The Cummings Group's NCADMIN) provide cluster-wide administration and accounting services. At this time, only one provides multistep job submission or conditional job step execution: Utopia Load Sharing Facility from Platform Computing. At this time, none can be really considered a complete, full-function commercial batch system with conditional job steps, step monitoring, priority queues, resource enqueueing, and so on. This may change, and in any

Table 1   Some Cluster Batch and Login Systems

Who	What	Description
Freedman Sharp & Associates Inc.	Load Balancer	batch queueing, interactive login
IBM	Loadleveller	batch job submission; runs on heterogeneous collections of machines
	Job Scheduler for AIX	batch job submission with multiple queues and other features; runs only on IBM's AIX
Platform Computing Corp.	Utopia Load Sharing Facility	batch queueing with multiple job steps, interactive login, development
The Cummings Group	NCADMIN, NCLOGIN, NQS/Exec	accounting, managing, reporting, and such; load-balanced interactive login; batch job submission

case the systems now available are certainly adequate for some commercial and most technical use.

Batch systems, of course, have the major advantage of being SPPS: They allow clusters to be effectively used without altering applications in any way. Normal (serial, not parallel) jobs can be submitted to a cluster and run without further ado. Some batch systems (e.g., IBM LoadLeveller) have facilities for running parallel jobs too, but it's not required in order to make effective use of the cluster. These issues are discussed in more detail in Chapter 8.

2.7.2   Database Systems

As Table 2 indicates, every major vendor of database software either now has, or has in development or plan, a version of their database that operates across multiple computers—in other words, across the machines of a cluster. In doing this, these systems effectively merge the machines into a single database entity for application and database administration purposes. Oracle's Parallel Server is the most mature; it has been delivered for many years [Llo92, LC94]. The others—IBM's DB2/6000 Parallel Edition [Fec94], Sybase's MPP [Ber94], Informix-Online's XPS [Chr94]—are all available, shipping products. The different techniques used by all of these, and they all do differ very significantly, are discussed in Chapter 10.

Table 2   Some Cluster/Distributed/Parallel Database Products

Who	What	Description
IBM	DB2 Parallel Edition	Relational Database; OLTP, Query for open system clusters and parallel machines
	IMS DB for Sysplex	Hierarchical database manager for IBM Sysplex
	DB2 and VSAM	Relational DB and storage management, statement of direction for Sysplex support
INFORMIX-Online	XPS	Relational Database; OLTP, Query for open system clusters
Oracle Corp.	Oracle Parallel Server, Oracle Parallel Everything; Oracle V7 on NCube	Relational Database; OLTP, Query; many installations on clusters and highly parallel systems
Sybase	MPP	Relational Database; OLTP, Query
Tandem	NonStop SQL/MX	Relational Database for Windows NT; OLTP, Query.

Like the batch systems mentioned above, such database systems are also SPPS, and hence are application transparent: No change to the application is required. This enormous advantage, and other aspects of the whole issue of exploiting parallelism, will also be dissected in detail in Chapter 8.

2.7.3   *Parallel Programming Facilities*

There are also packages available that enable applications to be programmed to run in parallel, that is, to run faster because they've been reorganized to execute simultaneously on multiple nodes in a cluster. Examples, listed in Table 3, include Parasoft's Express [Kol91], Scientific Computing Corp.'s Linda [CG89], Applied Parallel Research's FORGE 90, and two popular "freeware" packages: P4 from Argonne National Laboratory [BL92, LO87] and the very popular, highly portable package from Oak Ridge National Laboratory and the University of Tennessee, PVM (Parallel Virtual Machines) [GS93, BDG+91].

A standard program interface for message-passing parallelism has also been developed, called the MPI (Message Passing Interface) standard [Wal93,

Table 3   Some Cluster Parallel Programming Facilities

Who	What	Description
Argonne National Laboratory	P4	portable parallel C and FORTRAN programming; free package
Myrias Computer Technologies Corp.	PAMS Parallel Productivity Tools	virtual shared memory - based parallel programming tools for message-passing (cluster) systems
Oak Ridge National Laboratory.	Parallel Virtual Machines (PVM)	portable, heterogeneous parallel C and FORTRAN programming; very popular free package
Parasoft Corp.	Express	parallel C and FORTRAN enablement; message-passing, collective operations
Rice University	Tredmarks	virtual shared memory-based parallel programming system for message-passing (cluster) systems
Scientific Computing Associates, Inc.	Network Linda	parallel C & FORTRAN enablement; a relational-database-like shared memory is emulated
The MPI Forum	MPI	widely-supported, highly detailed specification of a standard C and Fortran interface for message-passing parallel programming

Mes94, SOH⁺96]. MPI has been defined by an international *ad hoc* group called the Message Passing Interface Forum that is very well supported by many industrial members, universities, and research laboratories. Many other systems for parallelism, particularly message-passing parallelism, have been developed; for example, there's also PARMACS [Hem91], CHIMP [Edi91], EUI [FBH⁺92], and so on.

Many of these facilities began life as university or research laboratory projects in providing programming support for massively parallel systems; Express, Linda, and P4 are examples of this. They were then were ported to collections of workstations connected by LAN, simply as an expedient way to allow multiuser program debugging that didn't use up expensive and/or limited time on a massively parallel machine. The workstation/LAN version proved to be a valuable tool in its own right, to say nothing of a profitable product. PVM was different: Its avowed original purpose was to support parallelism across heterogeneous clusters of machines.

The installation rate of these systems is at least as large as the rate of installing assembled or preassembled clusters in noncommercial accounts. Virtually everybody with one of those clusters at least thinks they want to explicitly exploit its parallel capabilities, too. As has already been emphasized, explicit parallel programming is not for the faint of heart (or the credulous). Circumstances in which it is feasible and warranted are discussed in Chapter 8.

2.7.4   Operating Systems

The products previously described are tools or subsystems that run under the native operating systems of the clustered machines. There is still a copy of the operating system per machine; the facilities described are independent of that. They also, particularly in the case of the database systems, provide their own whole-cluster administration tools for maintaining themselves.

There are also, in contrast, at least the beginnings of extensions to operating systems themselves that start to make multiple machines look unified in general, not just for one specific purpose. This potentially equals the "single-system" capabilities of the proprietary full-function clusters, but most are special purpose, not generally available, or not yet shipped. Those software operating system products are listed in Table 4.

While there is an exception, these, for the most part, provide the internal requirements for cross-machine operation. In the jargon, they implement unified name spaces: The name for something is guaranteed to be the same, and unique, across all the machines connected. For example, files are globally named, processes (running programs) likewise, normal forms of communication inside an operating system work between machines with no application code change, new processes are created on different machines in accordance with load balancing, and so on. These are necessary technical underpinnings for SPPS execution of general programs on a cluster, not just programs submitted to a special cluster-wide batch system.

Locus Computing's Transparent Network Computing (TNC) does this for the UNIX personality of a microkernel [Thi91, PW85], and has been included in the Open Software Foundation's OSF/1 AD TNC product used by the now defunct Intel Scientific Supercomputers' massively parallel offering [WLH93]. A prior non-microkernel version of Locus' technology was used in an IBM product, Transparent Computing Facility (TCF), which made a single system out of S/370 mainframes and PS/2s all running UNIX [WP89]. Convex uses similar Locus-derived OSF/1-based support to emulate Hewlett-Packard's HP/UX across their highly parallel machine.

Table 4   Some Cluster-Supporting Operating Systems

Who	What	Description
Chorus Systemes	Chorus/MiX Operating System	microkernel-based system, Unix SVR5 personality; transparency among machines
Locus	Transparent Network Computing (TNC)	UNIX process, device, etc., transparency between machines
Novell	"Wolf Mountain" (code name)	cluster-unified operating system, communication, object directory store, and other subsystems
QNX Software Corporation	QNX	microkernel-based system for real time and control operations spanning multiple machines
Santa Cruz Operations	name not known	extension of SCO kernel to provide transparent cross-machine device, process, etc., access across machines. Based on Locus TNC, ported to SCO UNIX by Tandem

Chorus Systemes' Chorus/Mix is another microkernel-based approach to distributing UNIX [A+92], which has been available as an alternate operating system for several years.

Santa Cruz Operations has indicated that they will be including in their UNIX kernel the Locus TNC capabilities; these were ported to that version of UNIX by Tandem, for a product initially aimed at the telecommunications industry. The Tandem version has been demonstrated on a cluster of Compaq servers connected by Tandem's ServerNet as will be described in Chapter 5.

In addition, QNX markets a microkernel-based system of the same name, particularly targeted at embedded and control applications, that provides a large degree of single system image across multiple machines [Hil93].

Novell has announced a system called Wolf Mountain (funny how Wolves keep showing up) with the characteristics listed, and demonstrated it on 12-node cluster of Intel-based systems.

While these systems provide a way to run applications across multiple machines, they seldom, if ever, adequately tackle the larger, more amorphous, and highly practical problem of similarly modifying the parts of operating systems not talked about in operating system textbooks: system management and administration facilities. This and related areas are further discussed in Chapter 11.

2.8   Basic (Availability) Clusters _____

Hey, so far we've missed a few. See Table 5. Almost every major manufacturer of server systems, and several independent software vendors, have some facility for coupling at least two machines in a cluster. The hardware vendors' offerings are usually tied to a hardware product or product line; the software vendors listed most usually run on Microsoft Windows NT on Intel-based platforms.

Note that Table 5 is a mixture of products with quite varied characteristics, as will be discussed below. Also note that it is absolutely guaranteed to be incomplete; not only can I not claim to have a list of all of them anywhere, the announcement rate is fierce.

Table 5   Some Basic (Availability) Cluster Products

Vendor	Products	Hardware Assist
Amdahl	EnVista FS/R Cluster, running Windows NT "Wolfpack"	Fibre Channel
Compaq	Recovery Server Option Kit	
	strategy, but no product announced yet; to run Microsoft "Wolfpack"	Tandem ServerNet, Fibre Channel
Data General	DG/UX Cluster	
	AViiON NT Cluster	
DEC	TruCluster Availability Server	Memory Channel, Gigaswitch
	TruCluster Production Server	
	Digital Clusters for Windows NT	

Table 5   Some Basic (Availability) Cluster Products

Vendor	Products	Hardware Assist
Fujitsu	High Availability Manager	
	DS/90 7000 Cluster	
HP	HP High Availability Enterprise Clusters, MC/ServiceGuard,	Fibre Channel
	NetServer System Cluster; runs "Wolfpack"	
Isis Distributed Systems	Isis Availability Manager	
IBM	AS/400 Opticonnect/400	Opticonnect/400 interconnect
	HACMP/6000 (High Availability Cluster Multi-processor)	Serial Storage Architecture (SSA) disk connect
	PC Server Cluster; runs 'Wolfpack" or Vinca	
	RS/6000 Scalable Parallel Systems	High-Performance Switch, Virtual Shared Disk
Microsoft	Windows NT Enterprise Server Cluster Services ("Wolfpack")	likely support for Tandem ServerNet
NCR	NCR Lifekeeper FRS (Fault Resilient System)	
	WorldMark series	BYENET
Novell	Software Fault Tolerance III	
Octopus Technologies	Octopus Server 2.0; add-on for Microsoft Windows NT	
Pyramid/ Siemens-Nixdorf	RM1000	MESH interconnect
	RM600E Cluster	

Table 5 Some Basic (Availability) Cluster Products

Vendor	Products	Hardware Assist
Siemens Nixdorf	BS2000/OSD HIPLEX	
	PRIMERGY high availability clustering	
Sequent	Symmetry 5000 ptx/ CLUSTERS	
Sun	Ultra Enterprise Cluster PDB Server,	Cluster Channel inter-node, Fibre Channel Standard disk attach
	Ultra Enterprise Cluster HA Server	
Silicon Graphics	IRIS Failsafe	
Stratus	RADIO Cluster	
Tandem	CS150; runs "Wolfpack" and Tandem NonStop database and transaction monitor	ServerNet communication
Unisys	UClusters	
VERITAS Software Corp.	VERITAS FirstWatch; add-on for Microsoft Windows NT	
Vinca Corp.	Standby Server for NT; add-on for Microsoft Windows NT	

The entries in Table 5 weren't listed in the prior discussion, even though many are primarily software, because they don't fall into any of the categories I happened to choose: They aren't databases, batch, or login facilities; and they certainly aren't full operating systems. Instead, they are add-ons that provide valuable cluster services on top of an existing operating system. Usually great pains are taken to not disturb that operating system base; extensions are kept to a minimum, and, preferably, only system-architected extension mechanisms are used.

Most notably and usually, these products provide high availability; this is usually their original *raison d'être*. They can't be classified as "only" high-availability systems, however, important though that may be. For example, most also provide extensions to ease cluster administration, which is certainly desirable.

In addition, nearly all include some means of overt performance scaling on a single job. Particularly for commercial purposes, this often includes an arrangement with one or more cluster-enabled databases or transaction managers to support, prepackage, or otherwise associate themselves with the product. When one of the associated cluster-enabled database is Oracle Parallel Server, which is almost always the case, they also include as a separate product some form of cross-cluster lock manager, something required by Oracle's shared-data (or shared-disk) organization; this is discussed in Chapter 10. Several, like IBM's RS/6000 Scalable Parallel systems and NCR's 3400 and 3600, regard themselves as massively parallel systems, capable of supporting hundreds of nodes. Some specialize in highly-parallel database functions like data mining, on-line analytical processing, and the like.

Particularly in the massively parallel cases, aggregate performance support may include optimized support for communication, either with or without special hardware support; this is usually made accessible by standard or popular means, such as TCP/IP (always), MPI, or PVM (mentioned earlier, in section 2.7.3). In some cases, the database systems have been modified to use these optimized facilities.

The high availability characteristics that virtually all provide are implemented by what is called failover. This and the techniques associated with it will be discussed in detail in Chapter 12. The basic idea is that the machines listen to "heartbeat" signals from each other, and when one stops the other takes over its work. (That makes it sound simple. It's not.)

The number of vendors with products in this area is large; their individual capabilities are varied; and announcements of new features, functions and capabilities appear regularly. Go to any major hardware or software vendor's Internet web site, and search for "cluster"; in nearly all cases you will find more information than you can handle.

Therefore specific point-by-point feature comparisons are clearly inappropriate here. Such comparisons are now a regular feature of computer industry trade press at this point, and will be more up-to-date than even the list of products that appears here.

However, Microsoft's offering is clearly important because of their market position. It is described in some detail as a case study in Chapter 12.

Where these systems generically have a weakness, it tends to be in system administration and workload management. Not a whole lot of additional administration is required for a simple duplicate system used as a backup. However, as these systems are used for higher performance in addition to availability, the number of machines in the cluster rises and the multi-machine administration required becomes a deterrent to sales. It is hardly surprising that commercial customers, buying multiple machines for enhanced availability, are unwilling to entrust their corporate jewels to Shell Scripts from Hell.

2.9   Not the End

An amazing thing about clustering is how widespread it is. There's just so much of it going on, and it's been going on for so very long. There are so many products, so much new product development right now, and such significant market presence. The author was, frankly, overwhelmed by the product variety and forced to retreat to generic descriptions in the previous section. Cluster products are being announced faster than they can be catalogued and documented by any one person.

An obvious question to ask at this point is: Why?

What has turned this field, in just the last few years, from a steady but low-key stream of announcements into a bandwagon that has attracted virtually everyone, complete with inevitable camp followers and mountebanks, in the entire computer industry?

That's the topic of the next chapter.

Why Clusters?

The prior chapter makes it clear that clusters have achieved pride of place in many users' server lineups and, therefore, in many vendors' product lines. There are a number of reasons why people should go through the bother and expense of creating clusters—and certainly it is a bother and an expense; many "simple matters of programming" are involved, and the technical issues involved are certainly not simple. There are both general reasons and specific reasons for going to that trouble.

The general reasons arise because clusters are a form of parallel or distributed system. As such, they inherit many of the reasons for which their more well-studied brethren are pursued. These general reasons are by now neither particularly new nor even exciting, but they are not to be brushed aside; they also apply to clusters and form a broad general motivation for their development.

But why, specifically, clusters? The general reasons can't explain that. Are there specific factors that exist now favoring clusters as opposed, for example, to ever larger symmetric multiprocessors or so-called NUMA systems? There are. Those are the specific reasons, the reasons why clusters are actively being promoted and expanding their sweep, rather than dying out in the face of significant competition.

Most of both the general and the specific reasons have actually already been mentioned in the introduction and the examples. This is where we pull them together and examine them as a whole.

3.1   The Standard Litany _____

Every time anybody tries to sell a parallel or distributed system, or obtain funding for the development of a new one (which amounts to the same thing: selling), a fundamental collection of standard reasons is always recited. This litany hasn't changed one whit for 30 years. Slotnick probably used it when he asked for the money to build ILLIAC IV. Dewy-eyed neophytes declare themselves by chanting it with ingenuous enthusiasm. Here it is.

- ➤ **Performance:** No matter what form or measure of performance one is seeking—throughput, response time, turnaround time or whatever—it is straightforward to claim that one can get even more of it by using a bunch of machines at the same time. In some cases there is a proviso that a wee bit of new programming is involved for anything to work. Those cases are best avoided.

- ➤ **Availability:** Having a computer shrivel up into an expensive doorstop can be a whole lot less traumatic if it's not unique, but rather one of a herd. The herd should be able to accommodate spares, which can potentially be used to keep the work going; or if one chooses to configure sparelessly, the work that was done by the dear departed sibling can, potentially, be redistributed among the others.

- ➤ **Price/Performance:** Clusters and other forms of computer aggregation are typically collections of machines that individually have very good, if not industry pace-setting, performance for their price. The promise is that the aggregate retains the price/performance of its individual members. While this, like the other reasons, can be true, it always makes me think of committees...

- ➤ **Incremental Growth:** To the degree that one really does attain greater performance and availability with a group of computers, one should be able enhance both by merely adding more machines. Rolling an old, smaller computer out and rolling a new, bigger one in should not be necessary. This collaterally avoids the attendant trauma of justifying a whole new computer, to say nothing of getting everything to work again on the new one. Good show.

- ➤ **Scaling:** The marketing community, ever alert for new synonyms for "good," seized on "scalable" as an important buzzword for open commercial systems. As a result, its definition has devolved to the point where it means little. It actually has (or did have) something to do with how big a computer system can usably get. Since there's no limit outside a buyer's pocketbook to how many machines can be stacked side by side, parallel and distributed systems in general and clusters in particular are good... er, I mean offer great scalability. This will be discussed at far greater length later, since despite the marketing hype it's a crucial element in the differentiation between clusters and symmetric multiprocessors.

The above is the Classic Standard Litany. There is an addition to it that was spawned with the wide deployment of personal workstations and computers. Adding it to the above results in the Enhanced Standard Litany.

> **Scavenging:** Every Information Services (I/S) manager on earth possessing two neurons to knock together lusts after all those "unused cycles" spread across most organizations' personal computers and workstations. As the saying goes: Computers may grow ever cheaper, but unused cycles are *free*. Putting those spare cycles to productive use appears to be just another application of clusters, since the collection of all those personal machines is "just" a large, rather diffuse cluster. For reasons to be discussed later, however, rounding up spare personal cycles into a usable herd complicates cluster support very significantly. It's rather like trying to herd cats.

The rather jaded rendition above to the contrary (well, partially), the standard litany is real. The benefits promised are without question highly desirable and are actually being accomplished—gradually—by aggregate computing in general and clusters in particular. This was demonstrated by the examples in the last chapter.

The important points are that the litany is certainly neither (a) new, nor (b) accomplished by merely waving a parallel-hardware magic wand. Hardware provides potential, and potential alone; fulfillment lies in the software. Painstakingly incremental development of the requisite software has proven to be required, has been going on for years, and will continue. Software is not riding the same kind of exponential growth curve that hardware has, so there is no business end of an advancing curve to appear to kick in and make the most recent advances look spectacular.

In addition, the litany explains why parallelism or distributed computing in general has always been desirable. It does not explain why clusters, specifically, should become a popular form of parallel or distributed computing. One must still answer the question "Why *now?*"

3.2 Why *Now*?

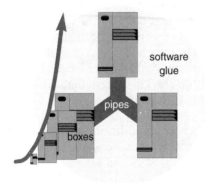

Figure 10 Fat Boxes, Fat Pipes, Thick Glue

There are three technical trends, and an enormously increased market requirement for one of the standard litany items, that explain why clusters' popularity is now increasing and will continue to increase. The trends are fat boxes, fat pipes, and thick glue; and the requirement is for high availability.

1. Fat Boxes: Very high-performance microprocessors. As mentioned in Chapter 1, microprocessors have kept, and will keep, getting faster. This takes the wind out of the sails of "massively" parallel systems in short order. Furthermore, there are very few "big" machines that aren't aggregations of these potent beasties. Mainframes are made from them. Supercomputers in the classic style are an extremely endangered species, if not extinct for all practical purposes. Just a few years ago the situation was different; hundreds or thousands of microprocessor-based systems had to be ganged up to achieve interesting aggregate performance levels. More recently, this point was a story about relatively exotic technical RISC workstations. No more. Mass-market, inexpensive microprocessors, originally segregated from technical workstations, have crawled up the tail pipe of the workstation market just like workstations crawled up the tail pipe of larger machines. There are no more supercompu*ters,* but there is supercomput*ing,* performed on aggregates of microprocessors.

2. **Fat Pipes: Standard high-speed communication.** Communication technologies have advanced rapidly, allowing common off-the-shelf (COTS), industry-standard parts to achieve levels of performance that previously were possible only with expensive, proprietary techniques. This technology saw a jump in capability starting in the early 90s when fiber optics started phasing into commercial use; the competition, of course, spurred refinement of more traditional technologies. The introduction of such standardized communication facilities as Fibre Channel Standard (FCS), Asynchronous Transmission Mode (ATM), the Scalable Coherent Interconnect (SCI), and switched Gigabit Ethernet are raising intercomputer bandwidth from 10 Mbits/second through hundreds of Mbytes (not bits) /second, and even Gigabytes per second. This is

not limited to inter-system communication. FCS and other I/O mechanisms are now providing standard, high-speed methods by which many systems can share access to many I/O devices, particularly disks.

3. **Thick Glue: Standard tools for distributed computing.** The requirements of distributed computing have produced a collection of software tools that can be adapted to managing clusters of machines. Some, such as the Internet communication protocol suite (called TCP/IP and UDP/IP) are so common as to be ubiquitous *de facto* standards. Higher level facilities built on that base, such as Intranets, the Internet, and the World Wide Web, are similarly becoming ubiquitous. In addition, other tool sets for multisense administration have become common. Together these provide an effective base to tap into for creating cluster software.

Finally, there is the rise of mass-market high availability:

> **High Availability**: Nobody has ever wanted computers to break. But never before has high availability become a significant issue in a mass market computer arena, nor has high availability acquired as stringent a collection of requirements. Clusters are uniquely capable of answering the needs of both sides of that spectrum and, unlike prior hardware-based fault-tolerant approaches, clusters do so in a way that is inexpensive and capitalizes on economies of scale.

An important aspect common to all four cluster promoters is that all, for reasons having nothing whatsoever to do with clustering, will be enhanced over time: There will be faster microprocessors, faster standard communication, and more functional tools for distributed computing, and an increasing need for high availability. This means that if those factors do indeed favor clusters of machines, and there appears to be little question that they do, clustering bids fair to become even more common.

Most aspects of the above four cluster promoters are well-known and will not be expanded on here, with two exceptions: The actual speed with which computing capability is increasing—how fast the boxes are getting fatter—is not well-known; and neither are many of the reasons behind the requirement for high availability. Those will be discussed in later sections.

However, clustering is still not, in fact, the most prevalent kind of computing today. The thousands of installations mentioned in prior chapters are but a drop in the Brobdingnagian bucket of the computer industry. The reasons for that need to be examined also.

3.3 Why *Not* Now?

So if they're so good, why haven't clusters already become the most common mode of computation? Two reasons:

> **Lack of "single system image" software.** Replacing a single large computer with a cluster of, say, 20 smaller ones means that 20 systems have to be managed instead of one. The only reasonable response to that is a feeling of intense nausea. The distributed computing facilities currently available are piece parts; they are toolkits, not solutions providing "turnkey" single system management and administration. A study by International Data Corporation [Int94] which surveyed hundreds of actual midrange UNIX installations in the United States and Europe showed that the largest component of cost, around 50% of the total, is not hardware, software, or maintenance—it is staffing. Since staffing is intimately related to system management and administration, an increase in system management workload is a huge cost disadvantage for assembled and preassembled clusters. This, of course, has been recognized in the industry, leading to such endeavors as "network computers" and attempts to produce "zero-management" systems. Those efforts, aimed at clients, do not help clusters.
>
> The three primary cluster full-system offerings, IBM's Sysplex, Tandem's systems, and Digital's OpenVMS Cluster, are exceptions that probe this rule. But each of them is a unique solution, both tailored to and a product of its unique hardware/software surround; as a result they have not spread beyond their proprietary bounds and are not likely to. It would be absurd to consider dropping the Sysplex code, for example, into the middle of a UNIX system; it depends heavily on the internal structure of OS/390 and its hardware surround, which is totally different from that of UNIX.
>
> This general lack of "single system image" effectively limits the use of open-system-based clusters to technically sophisticated sites with the expertise to construct and maintain the required solutions using the available tools.
>
> **Limited exploitation.** Only relatively few types of subsystems now exploit the ability of clusters to provide both scalable performance and high availability: databases, transaction monitors, and some batch submission and login facilities. These provide an SPPS mode of operation that extends their capabilities to numerous applications, but clearly don't cover anything like the entire spectrum of server applications. Nearly all file systems can exploit high avail-

ability, as can most Internet servers (as explained in Chapter 12, "High Availability"), but with some exceptions for the Internet, they don't scale well. Batch and login systems exploit scaling, but seldom if ever delve into high availability except in a limited way.

This is a direct result of the substantial difficulties that arise in parallel programming, difficulties that are further reflected in the lack of single-system-image software mentioned above. Everyday sequential software is already notorious for being the bottleneck in computing of all kinds; parallel is substantially more complex. A later chapter illustrates this in great detail.

The reasons "why," listed in the prior section, were all hardware. The reasons "why not," listed above, are all software. In other words: **The problem is not hardware. It's software.**

This fact bears more than a little emphasis.

Any number of hardware products and proposals for clustered or parallel systems continually appear, willy-nilly, especially for intermachine communication. I don't know what it is about switches, networks, and strange communication architectures, but they really must be lots of fun for engineers to design and build, since there are so many of them proposed. Their proponents all universally chant the Standard Litany of advantages listed above; some—especially those using optical fibre—have progressed to the Enhanced Standard Litany. *All such claims are intrinsically without merit unless the proposed hardware facilitates solving the real problems, which are all in software.*

In the past, few if any cluster hardware organizations have demonstrated any such ability to simplify software, other than the distinctly neutral advantage of doing standard things faster or more cheaply, without appearing different; the lack of being different supports existing software with minimal fuss.

Fortunately, this lesson appears to be sinking in to at least some segments of the industry. A collection of hardware assemblages that actually begin to help solve some real software problems in clusters have begun appearing, and will be discussed in Chapter 5. They are, however, still rather few in number and a consensus has yet to emerge on what features are really most useful beyond the obvious (low overhead).

This situation—easily proposed and constructed hardware, recalcitrant software—has been true of parallel and distributed systems since their inception. In the colorful phrase of a colleague,[1] two blind men and a lame boy

---

1. Justin Hall, then of the IBM RISC System/6000 Division in Austin, TX.

can assemble the hardware for a cluster. But programming it takes sophistication, experience, and gumption—and the time of people with all three is very expensive.

The rest of this book delves into these issues in greater detail. A word, first, about the exceptions.

The statements above could be taken to apply to any and every parallel or distributed system. That would be incorrect. For one parallel system, software issues have been addressed to a great degree, and in the process it has become an industry-standard organization: the symmetric multiprocessor (SMP). It alone has the single-system-image management required (and by the way, its hardware organization requires this), and for it alone has the necessary parallelization been performed on virtually every major subsystem required for effective general use: databases, file systems, communication subsystems, and so on.

In addition, there's a new kid on the block called a "NUMA" system whose proponents claim that it has all the advantages of the SMP—single-system-image management, and all your old SMP code just runs—and eliminates the disadvantages.

These architectures, therefore, obviously become the benchmark for clustered systems, as well as for any parallel or distributed system, and must be discussed in some detail. Later whole chapters are devoted to explaining the hardware of SMPs and so-called NUMA systems; this is in support of another chapter specifically comparing clusters, SMP, and "NUMA" systems. As we shall see, the NUMA proponents are not completely correct in what they would let you believe.

But first, let's cover the two cluster promoters for which I promised more detail.

3.4   Commercial Node Performance

Microprocessor performance is of course increasing dramatically, and the near future—just before and after the turn of the century—will see developments in this area that will once again shake this industry; it has more fault zones than the entire Pacific rim. This topic been written about repeatedly, and needs no expansion here.

More important to clusters than individual microprocessor performance, though, is the total node performance—a node being a computer in the cluster. That has been undergoing an increase in performance for commercial processing that is so dramatic it is practically bizarre. Furthermore, the true extent of this change is practically unknown.

At least it was unknown to me, until about a year ago when I discovered that a colleague, Joel Tendler, had been keeping a private record of every result ever published by the Transaction Processing Council (TPC). This historical data is not available from the source one would expect, the TPC itself, because is part of the TPC rules that member companies can withdraw submissions at any time, and when this is done the records are no longer part of the TPC publications.

So there was this nice pile of historical data sitting organized in a spreadsheet, and nobody had done anything with it. I immediately started charting it, got some apparently more than interesting results that raised eyebrows enough for others to recheck it, find out that it was wrong in detail, and correct it. The most interesting format found is the one shown in Figure 11.

Figure 11   Historical Best of Breed TPC-C Results

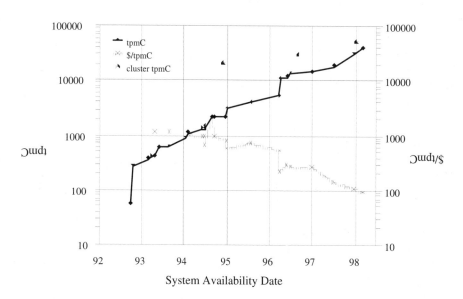

System Availability Date

This graph shows the highest benchmark result, measured in "transactions per minute - C" (tpmC), at any given time since the introduction of the benchmark in mid 1992. That's the line trending up and to the right. It also shows cost per transaction ($/tpmC) of those systems over a five-year period as required by the TPC rules; that's the line trending down to the right, with the two additional points between 1993 and 1994 (not all data was available for costs). The graph extends beyond the publication date of this book because the dates shown are the dates when the systems benchmarked are available for purchase, which is usually in advance—often by as much as six months—of the date the benchmarks are performed and announced.

It's worth emphasizing that these are the highest results achieved. At any given time, the chart shows the record-holder. Many other results have been published, since commercial system vendors also publish results on smaller systems that are in many cases more cost-effective than the largest. As a result, the cost/performance figures on the graph are not always the record lowest costs; by mid-1997, those were even below the value shown. Were all the results to appear on the graph, they would form a massive cloud of points below the upper line shown. In fact, the first point is more indicative of those systems than the best of breed; it gets on the graph only because it happened to be the first result ever for this benchmark, and therefore by default the best (also the worst).

The line deliberately excludes results for clusters. Three of those, for reference, are shown; they are actually the literal record holders, but for reasons discussed in Chapter 14, I don't count them. It is interesting, however, that the size of the clusters involved has been decreasing: The first point represents a seven-node system, the second a four-node system, and the third a two-node system. This is consistent with the proposition that increasing processor and node performance puts large systems on a crash diet.

The result of excluding clusters is that the line shows are results for symmetric multiprocessors (SMPs) that can be used as nodes in clusters.

Note that the scale is logarithmic. The range of values from first to last is very large, going from around 200 to around 20,000. It also looks roughly like a straight line, meaning that a uniform cumulative growth rate may be going on. This look is not deceiving. Regression analysis on the data, excluding the leftmost point since it's clearly an outlier, indicates that best-of-breed performance is increasing with a CAGR of 164%. Furthermore, the tracking to that rate is rather close, with an R^2 (confidence indication) of 92 percent.

A 154% CGR is absolutely astonishing, and certainly not anticipated by anybody I've been in contact with. It means that performance more than *doubles* every year. In fact, it doubles just about *every nine months*.

This is definitely not all due to microprocessor performance. That has been tooling along at "only" a CGR of 60% or so. The high rate of performance increase is basically due to vendors throwing just about everything they have at it, for the eminently rational reason that this is the area of the computer market that makes the most money. Everything has been made bigger, faster, more numerous, and more efficient:

> individual microprocessor speed goes up, of course;

- so does the number of processors used, from one to 16 or more; the highest result is for a 20-processor system;

- that puts pressure on hardware memory and I/O subsystems, which also are enhanced—memory requirements, in particular, tend to outstrip processor speeds, and dramatic improvements were made over time in this area;

- but none of the above does anything useful unless software is altered to use all those processors, so great effort is put into "fixing" that in:

  - operating systems,
  - transaction monitors,
  - databases,
  - compilers, and so on;

- beyond changes to "just" use more processors, all the software listed above is enhanced to use better algorithms, making it more efficient no matter how many processors there are;

- and finally, of course, there is the inevitable tuning to the benchmark itself, attempting to exploit its unique characteristics whether they relate to real use or not. This is a source of error in any benchmark. It is not particularly prevalent in the case of the TPC-C benchmark applied to SMPs. (Clusters are another story.)

Figure 11 charts the combined result of all those efforts, which is indeed impressive.

Will this trend continue? It won't be charted as a direct extension to Figure 11, since the Transaction Processing Council is in the process of defining a replacement for TPC-C that will be less costly to run and more indicative of more recent workloads. So Figure 11 is likely to be close to the entire history of that benchmark.

In any event, as the cliché used in money management goes, past results are no guarantee of future performance. There is, however another guarantee in force here: It's guaranteed that the entire server segment of the computer industry will continue to focus its best hardware and software efforts on this problem, since that is where the largest amount of money is. Whether the combined result lives up to past performance or not, it will undoubtedly be the largest performance increases of any subarea of computing.

And the combined best result is what counts here. As far as clusters are concerned, it doesn't matter where the performance comes from. The whole individual systems—hardware, software, SMPs, whatever—are the piece parts from which clusters are made, and unless clustering does something to mess up the efficiency of the parts (it doesn't), this is a wave that clusters can just ride.

This means that the rationale for "massive" groupings is eroding at a rapid rate. While all the elements of the standard litany are always duly chanted, the real rationale for the massive parallelism has always been performance, performance far larger than what is available in a single system. That means this actually massive single-system performance increase hits those systems at both ends of their market:

> Every time single-system performance doubles, a chunk is ripped out of the lower end of the market for "massive" systems, and the lower end is where the sales volumes are.

> Similarly, every single-system performance doubling halves the number of systems that need to be aggregated, reducing the number of customers who need the high-end design targets and making them less economically viable.

High end customers will still maintain the over-fair share of attention that their large, unified payments inevitably produce; it's just human nature to respond fastest to the biggest threat or reward. However, the number of those customers who need the ministrations of massivity have decreased precipitously, and will continue to decrease as fast as the hardware and software efforts of servers can make it so.

At the same time, this nearly incredible increase in performance does not eliminate the need to use multiple systems at once, in clusters. Somehow application growth always expands to more than fill the available computing containers. Also, for reasons having to do with high availability, it may well be advantageous to aggregate systems that individually are not large and fast enough to perform a desired task individually. That particular discussion appears in a later chapter. Let's now move on to the need for high availability in general.

3.5   The Need for High Availability

The reliability of computers has always been important. That's not saying much, since the reliability of everything is important, right down to pencils. Just ask a kid taking the college boards.

There has always been a moneyed elite extremely concerned with computer reliability, and willing to pay whatever it takes to get it: financial traders, the military, the health industry for patient-serving equipment, and real-time controls for transportation of all kinds—people who, hearing "the computer crashed," immediately respond, "Into what?" This collection has in the past been served by a similarly narrow elite within the computer industry that provided special "fault tolerant" computers to these special customers at special prices.

Now, however, the concern for computer reliability has spread out and down through society, becoming something that concerns everybody, either directly or nearly directly. How can you tell that's happened? Because it's in the part of the newspaper that, unlike the financial section, everybody reads: the funny pages.

No, I don't mean *Dilbert*. The pointy-haired boss has of course said that he wants 24-hour advance notice of all unplanned network outages. Such mention is a good indication that the issue has passed beyond "elite" status, but *Dilbert* doesn't target a general audience; it's not even carried in markets that don't have a high-tech subculture. So it doesn't count as a good gauge of how widely spread the concern for computer reliability is.

Blondie, on the other hand, has been around since the roaring '20s; the title character used to be a flapper. You simply can't stay broadly syndicated in the comic strip business for that long unless you follow the large-scale trends and talk about things that nearly everybody can identify with. On January 3, 1997, millions of readers saw Dagwood pounding on his desk and crying in front of a smoking computer because he hadn't saved the figures for the big presentation. That means millions of ordinary folks understood, and sympathized with the guy.

And that's a robust indication that computer reliability is now a mass market issue.

There are other indicators. One such is how the issue has affected the language we speak. How many ways can you say "That computer doesn't work"? I ran an informal survey on this. The results aren't nearly as robust as the *Blondie* reference, since the people surveyed were in IBM and, as a group, are obviously far more computer-oriented than the general public; they're not a *Blondie* audience, they're a *Dilbert* audience. It was, however, done through a company-internal electronic news group devoted to discussing words, a group frequented by writers, lawyers, and others who enjoy and need to discuss nuances of the English language. So at least the respondents weren't wholly people who design and program the fool things. I asked for words or phrases they had used or heard used to describe broken hardware or software. In a few days, with few (surprisingly few, just three or four) additions from *The On-Line Jargon File* [RS96], I had 104 ways to describe the state of computational brokenness. See Figure 12.

That quite handily exceeds the possibly mythical fifty words the Inuit have for different kinds of snow [Bry90], even taking into account the tendency of

Figure 12 The Dead Computer Sketch

This computer is a basket case. It's all over the floor, and all Borked up (after the unsuccessful nomination proceedings of a certain US Supreme count nominee). It's a back-in-the-box (initial bring up failed). It's gone belly up (the original from which 'casters up' came, q.v.), it has bit the big one and the dust. It's blown away (mostly files), out, and up. Beam me up, Scotty, it's sucking mud again. (Star Trek & Dallas regionalism) It has bombed (chiefly software). It has bought the farm, and is BLR (Beyond Local Repair). It's braindead, broken, and it's BRS time (Big Red Switch; main power switch on earlier IBM mainframes and PCs). It's busted. It is in casters-up mode. It has checked out, and has choked and died. It's gone into a core dump frenzy (Commonwealth Hackish), has coughed and died (from unexpected input), crashed (mostly software), crashed and burned, croaked. It is dead and gone, dead as a dodo, and deep-sixed. This computer is defunct. It has died horribly. It DNFed (Did Not Finish; racing term), and was DOA (medical: Dead on Arrival). It is down. More, it's down the drain. It has expired. It has EXXONed (from the EXXON Valdez oil spill). It not only fell over, it fell over hard. It is FFFF. (The last "F" stands for "Fried." The expansion of the rest is not suitable for a family book.) It has flamed out (jet pilots), has flunked the smoke test (I was present for one of those; power and ground had been switched on a very large circuit board), folded its tent, and is four paws up. It's fried, frotzed, and FUBAR (F*d Up Beyond All Recognition; WWII). It has gone awry, bozo, flatline, haywire, south, swimmies (from kayaking), west (UK equivalent of "gone south"), and to pot. It is gronked. It has had it. It's high sided (motorcycles), and has hit the dirt as well as the wall. This computer is hosed, hung (mostly software), in the bit bucket, and in the ditch. It is history. It's dead, Jim. (Star Trek). It is kaput, has kicked the bucket, and is lit up like a Christmas Tree (bad case of "red lighted," q.v.). It has lost it, locked up, and is an MHSS (Melted Heap of Smoking Slag). It's had a network meltdown (as caused by a Chernobyl packet). It's nonfunctional, off fighting Klingons (Star Trek; software locked up), on the fritz, out of order (oldie but goodie), out of whack, and out to lunch. It is pumping mud (Dallas regionalism). It's PVS (in a Persistent Vegetative State). It has red lighted (from when red lights indicated errors). It is retro-sand. It is rubber side up (from motorcycles, cars), has run aground (from boats, obviously) and sunk. It screamed and died (like coughed & died, but with an error message), screwed up, shuffled off, and is six feet under. It's a case of squirrelcide (one chewed through the power cables and electrocuted itself). It has struck out, and is sucking mud (Dallas regionalism). It's T-zero (failure to power up the very first time), and tanked. It's taking a dirt nap, is toast, and took a Brodie (colloquially correct, but strictly incorrect; Steve Brodie survived his publicity-stunt jump off the Brooklyn Bridge). It took the pipe (???) and is US (also U/S, unserviceable; RAF jargon). It is was headed off at the pass, waxed, wedged, went that-a-way, and went the way of the dinosaur. This computer is whacked. It is wonky (Australian). It is in yo-yo mode.

This is an ex-computer! (Inspired by Monty Python's "Dead Parrot "sketch, as was this form of presentation.)

English to be richer than most languages in vocabulary with slight shades of meaning. Apparently broken computers are more of a factor in our lives than is snow to people who live near the Arctic circle.

We arrived at this state, of course, due to the proliferation of personal computers. Paradoxically, this attempted massive decentralization has lead to a situation where the availability of more centralized systems—servers—is an issue to the mainstream of the population. The reason, of course, is that PCs are more useful to more people when they are connected, able to share or send information. Hence the need for a server, whether it serves files, mail, or other more complex things. Of course, if the server croaks everybody connected to it is affected.

Uncountable numbers of people have bought into word processing, electronic mail, simple databases, on-line appointment calendars, on-line billing, time and inventory control, and any number of other small-scale, relatively straightforward business and personal applications. They're hooked. And when it breaks, they're mad. Or sad. Or both, pounding the desk and crying like Dagwood.

They're also unwilling to pay elite prices. The only reason they got hooked was that the price was right. Well, clusters to the rescue.

Unlike prior solutions, cluster make high availability systems by combining standard, commodity parts that can, unlike the fault-tolerant systems of years gone by, share economies of scale with the more numerous client systems they serve. One analyst has estimated that "adding" cluster-style high availability to a midrange server is now averaging only a 15 percent increment in cost. How it can be that low is discussed in detail in a later chapter; for now, just note that many people will find that very attractive cost for an insurance policy that can keep those now oh-so-necessary computers alive. Clusters are the best known solution to providing low-cost, mass-market high availability.

They are not, however, limited to that area. The midrange has been mentioned, and the high end is there too as an area where high availability is becoming even more important.

Obviously, the larger the number of people depending on a server, the worse the results when it goes braindead. There is an immense laundry list of reasons why more people are becoming more dependent on larger servers than ever before. They do not exclusively apply only to the midrange or high end of the computer market, but in many cases the sizes of the businesses that see these reasons gravitate towards such larger systems.

The list of reasons for this trend—increasing need for high availability—amounts to a list of virtually every major trend in the business use of computing. My eyes glaze over just contemplating it. Some even have really ugly names. Here's a representative sample that is by no means complete:

> **The Internet**: This is clearly the most extreme and unforgiving example. If you're lucky or skilled enough to have a "cool site," an outage of your web server can now disappoint millions of people at once. That's millions of *customers*, all getting mad at the same time.

Furthermore, there's no time to do system maintenance; even Saturday at 2:00 AM is a prime time somewhere in the world. So there's not only no time for unplanned outages, there's also no time for planned outages. To top it all off, your competitors are just a mouse-click away, probably right next to you on the screen produced by that search service. If your system doesn't respond, it's trivially easy for prospective customers to try somebody else.

➢ **Partner Connections**: Actually business-to-business Internet use, this refers to subcontractors or outsourcers obtaining the information they need, or providing you with information. Clearly, if the Internet or file servers involved go down, work by multiple companies is strongly affected.

➢ **Mobile Computing**: It's now nearly routine for sales forces to obtain information needed to quote prices using a modem, or to download presentations on demand. Obviously a server that suddenly goes inert in the midst of this will affect a large fraction of a sales force, to say nothing of prospective clients.

➢ **Telecommuting**: Electronic mail and file servers are a primary way in which workers at home stay in contact with their company. It's the way they obtain work and information, and the way they deliver results. This is now part of the business landscape, and of course the ability of these remote workers to be useful comes to a swift halt if the servers they connect to are on the blink.

➢ **PC Management**: The cost of managing all those personal computers has finally hit home. Every solution to the problem has the effect of making PCs more dependent on more centralized service.

➢ **Recentralization**: More than one company is discovering that finding adequately skilled personnel to manage far-flung systems is at least difficult, if not impossible. Piling up all the servers in one location, where one centralized staff can service them, solves the problem. It also makes outages at that central location even more disastrous.

➢ **Disintermediation**: This really ugly word refers to the fact that human intermediaries between customers and a business are going away. If you call a mail-order house, and its computer is down, the person on the other end can stall until the system's up or even write the order down on paper, for later entry. No such person exists when the service is completely automated, as in kiosks, automated teller machines, or, of course, the Internet. As far as a customer is concerned, *your computer is your business*. This has ramifications far beyond availability, but certainly how reliable a business is can be a very significant factor in using it.

> **Business Competition**: The ante for entering more and more businesses now includes hours of operation far beyond the traditional 9-to-5 regime; in many cases—particularly for providing food and money, for some reason—this tendency has maxxed out to full 24-hour service. That means the servers providing inventory, stock control, accounting information, and everything else have to run around the clock, too; a server outage now becomes close to a business outage.

> **Time Zone Tyranny**: The extension of many businesses to global concerns means that there is never a time of day when their operations cease. Of course, the Internet allows any garage shop to reach this state almost instantly, but the problem is even more severe when physical remote offices need to communicate even though they are geographically remote. The "home office" services must be provided continuously; outages are planet-wide.

It's worth noting how often in the above the notion arose that even planned outages for system maintenance—upgrades, preventive actions—are becoming unacceptable. Clusters are unique in their ability to provide for even that. Even if one were willing to pay for the older style of fault tolerance, it doesn't address the issue.

So, high availability is the wave of the future, and the direction in which all the vectors of the computer industry are pointing. Get with the program or you'll be left behind.

Summary of this chapter: The clusters are coming! The clusters are coming!

OK, so what's a cluster?

Funny you should ask. That's the next chapter.

Definition, Distinctions, and Initial Comparisons

Having given more examples than was perhaps needful, and pointed to the reasons for clusters and some of their problems, a definition of a cluster is obviously in order if not rather grossly overdue.

The definition in itself is not complex and may initially appear rather vague. This is at least in part because it is attempting to avoid being prescriptive. I am not attempting to define what a cluster "ought to be" or how it "ought to be constructed" independent of what others may be (misguidedly) doing.[1] Rather, the definition tries to be descriptive of what many are constructing, informally or formally, as clusters. I have seen too many, too dogmatic definitions of the term "cluster," all contradicting one another, to be a prescriptivist in this area. Furthermore, without some grasp of the breadth of possibilities, it is impossible to make an intelligent choice of what might be pursued.

---

1. I once gave a presentation whose theme was that there are many ways to build a cluster. I was immediately followed by someone who began by saying (approximately) "Greg may be right that there are many ways to build a cluster, but there's only one *right* way. That way is..." Sigh.

While being descriptively inclusive, the definition must distinguish "cluster" from the traditional realms of parallel processing and distributed computing. The definition in fact does that, but why it does so requires more explanation. That is why the rest of this chapter is devoted to distinctions between clusters and other forms of parallel and distributed computing.

4.1 Definition _____

A cluster is a type of parallel or distributed system that:

➤ consists of a collection of interconnected whole computers,

➤ and is used as a single, unified computing resource.

The term "whole computer" in the above definition is meant to indicate the normal combination of elements making up a stand-alone, usable computer: one or more processors (symmetric multiprocessors (SMPs) or "NUMA" systems are acceptable cluster nodes), an adequate amount of memory, input/output facilities, and an operating system.

Well, that seems simple enough. (Earlier versions I used were much more complex.)

But it may not be immediately apparent that this definition does effectively separate clusters from other forms of aggregate computing. Distinctions in this area are notoriously difficult and under some circumstances they are usefully ignored. However, the intention is not to define clusters as something different from parallel or distributed systems, but rather to distinguish them as a *subspecies* or *subparadigm* of distributed (or parallel) computing. The next sections discuss the distinctions more fully.

4.2 Distinction from Parallel Systems _____

There is an analogy I find interesting and surprisingly useful in this context. Here is a dog:

Figure 13 A Dog

She seems a friendly type, though a bit close-mouthed. Figures 14 and 15 below, on the other hand, show a pack of dogs and their competition, a Savage Multiheaded Pooch[2].

Figure 14   A Pack of Dogs

Figure 15   A Savage Multiheaded Pooch

Dog packs and (pardon the abbreviation) SMPs are both more potent than just plain dogs. They can both bring down larger prey than a plain single dog, are more ferocious at guarding things, eat more and eat faster than a single dog, and so on.

These two dog organizations differ in important ways, though, and many of those form a surprisingly good mnemonic for the differences between clusters and (computer) SMPs. Many of the statements below describing those differences prefigure far more detailed discussion that appears later in the book.

───────────────

2. This savage pooch is, by the way, no relation to the well-known Kerberos who guards both the gates of Hades and distributed systems (an interesting equation, that). The Grecian pooch has only three heads.

- **scaling**: The Savage Multiheaded Pooch obviously can take many bites at once. What happens when it then tries to swallow? Obviously, it also needs a proportionally larger throat, stomach, intestines, and so on. Similarly, to scale SMPs you must do more than just add sockets in which to plug processors; the entire rest of the machine must also be beefed up. When you add another dog to a pack, on the other hand, you add a whole dog: head, legs, lungs, memory, I/O system, and so on. If the original dogs individually had balanced capabilities to begin with, adding more doesn't change that. Likewise, clusters.

- **availability**: If the SMP breaks a leg, well, as the down-home Texan phrase goes, that dog can't hunt. It doesn't matter how many heads it has. If a member of the pack is injured, however, the rest can still bring down prey.

- **system management**: You only have to walk a Savage Multiheaded Pooch once. It takes a good deal of training to get the dog pack to behave well enough to make such mundane, but necessary, tasks simple. In general, obedience training is easier with the SMP—at least after the heads learn basic cooperation, something that had better come very early in life (like, it had better be built into the operating system).

- **software licensing**: If you walk into your friendly local government department of animal licensing with a Savage Multiheaded Pooch in tow, well, they'll probably look at you funny. But they will also, in all probability, sell you one dog license. Not the case when you walk in with a cluster of dogs in tow.

This distinction—whole computers vs. replicated computer parts—also serves to separate clusters from other parallel systems. For example:

- SIMD, or instruction broadcast machines such as Masspar systems or early Thinking Machines systems (but not later versions) replicate only an arithmetic and logic unit (ALU), along with registers and some memory. (This type of system is described further in Chapter 9.)

- Massively parallel multicomputers such as the Intel Paragon, Convex Exemplar, Cray T3D and the IBM Scalable Parallel series replicate whole processors and memories, and each has an I/O system. This makes them quite akin to clusters and, in some circumstances, they shade over into clusters with attendant confusion of marketing focus. But usually not all nodes need have complete I/O resources; there is usually less than adequate memory for a stand-alone machine at each node; and until the Intel Paragon, and later the IBM

SP series and the Convex Exemplar, there was no attempt to provide access to complete conventional operating system facilities at each node.

➤ There is similar confusion between clusters and what are called "NUMA" systems. Like MPP systems, they look like they're composed of separate machines, glued together at the memory. However, at least the first generation of those systems has a single copy of the operating system spread across all the nodes; this makes them distinct from clusters. (It also induces one of their high availability issues, since it's a single point of failure. See "Lowly Available Systems: SMP, CC-NUMA" on page 445. Chapter 7 discusses NUMA in detail.)

So, like distributed systems, but unlike most parallel systems, clusters are composed of whole computers. That's not to say that parallel systems cannot be made out of whole computers; they can. When that's done, what you get is a cluster used for parallel programming.

4.3 Distinctions from Distributed Systems ___

The distinctions between clusters and many distributed systems are somewhat more devious. They come in several areas, discussed below.

4.3.1 Internal Anonymity

Nodes of a distributed system necessarily retain their own individual identities. For example, it is quite important to the functioning of a node in a bank's distributed system that a particular node is the one physically located in the office in East Overshoe, Maine. That physical location is an intrinsic part of its function; it's there to serve customers residing in East Overshoe. Equally, it is important that the workstation in my office is physically in my office; that is key to the response time it provides to me. There are other important aspects of individuality; for example, particular distributed nodes may have software licensed to them that are unique to that node.

The elements of a cluster, on the other hand, are usually viewed *from outside the cluster* as anonymous; as much as possible, they are "cogs in the system," facelessly and interchangeably performing a function, much as the processors of an SMP are not individually addressed from outside the machine. Hence the phrase "single, unified computing resource" in the definition. There may be functional differences between a cluster's nodes—one may have a vector unit or communications facilities that others lack; and it is not uncommon to designate one or more nodes as "keepers of the data," specialized with large disks to hold the cluster file system, while the others provide computation (but see below). From the outside, however, one would like to log onto the cluster, not cluster node 4; submit a job to the cluster, not to node 17; and so on.

Some vendors have encapsulated this concept in the notion of a *virtual server* (Microsoft), or consider clusters as exporting *virtual resources* (DEC). The idea is that clients see the same "server" or the same "resource" no matter where it is instantiated on the cluster, independent of load balancing considerations or failure of a node. How this is accomplished is discussed in Chapter 12 (Section 12.10.2 on page 430).

Current distributed system facilities do not support this notion of internal anonymity very well. This will be discussed more completely below.

4.3.2 Peer Relationship

Another distinction between clusters and traditional distributed systems concerns the relationship between the parts. Modern distributed systems use an underlying communication layer that is peer-to-peer: There is no intrinsic hierarchy or other structure, just a "flat" list of communicating entities.

At higher levels of abstraction, however, they are popularly organized into a client-server paradigm—a two-level hierarchy, with clients as the leaves and servers as the root(s). This results in a valuable reduction in system complexity. It also serves as a distinction from clusters, but one that is deliberately not part of the definition used because it is not universal: a peer-to-peer relationship between the cluster elements themselves.

The reason this distinction is not universal stems from the utility of specialization among the cluster nodes, for example the use of file-serving cluster nodes within assembled and preassembled clusters. Being built out of the distributed-systems kit of parts, these often use distributed file systems following the client-server paradigm: A cluster node is designated the file server and equipped with large disks; the other nodes are the clients and have little, if any, disk storage.

This arrangement is adequate for processor-intensive technical computing, which uses relatively little input/output, and this is the use to which many assembled and preassembled clusters are put at present. But the disk bandwidth available within the entire cluster is thereby limited to that of a single node—actually, it's limited to the bandwidth of the communication between the file server and the other nodes; this bandwidth is typically LAN speed, in the low Mbits/second. So, this arrangement is inadequate for I/O-intensive commercial computing.

This inadequacy is recognized by the creators of many commercially oriented clusters and cluster subsystems (IBM Parallel Sysplex, OpenVMS Cluster, Tandem, and various distributed database systems in particular), which instead access data in a peer-to-peer fashion, as illustrated in Figure 16. In a typical distributed, client-server file system the clients access files on the server; they do not access each other's files directly. In commercially oriented clustered systems, on the other hand, the files are typically a mutually shared resource: By hook or by crook, every machine must access most (if not all) of the data in the cluster; if it cannot, the ability to balance the workload within the cluster and hence achieve scalable performance is curtailed.

In practice the need for mutual data access has lead to two organizations, illustrated in Figure 16. On the one hand, there are shared (multi-tailed) disks that all machines can physically access—used for example in the Parallel Sysplex, OpenVMS Cluster, Oracle's Parallel Server database system, and many availability-oriented clusters. On the other hand are "shared-nothing" systems in which requests for disk access and other I/O requests are "shipped" to the appropriate machine—used for example in Tandem Himalaya systems and several database subsystems such as Sybase MPP, Informix XPS, and DB2/6000 Parallel Edition. Either way, the cluster elements are peers; there is no hierarchy among them.

Figure 16   Client-Server Hierarchy vs. Cluster Peer File Systems

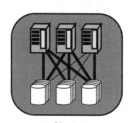

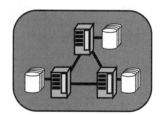

Client-Server One-level Hierarchy	Cluster Peer Access Physically Shared Disk	Cluster Peer Access Shared Access by I/O Shipping

This is one area where clusters are ill-served by distributed system technology. Disk sharing is simply anathema in that regime, for good and sufficient reasons; it's hard to scale up active disk sharing to thousands of nodes, and similarly hard to share disks over physically large distances.[3] The effect of

3. However, disks attached through Fibre Channel Standard (FCS) can be kilometers away. FCS is not usually considered a "distributed" technology, however. Also, long-distance access is important in disaster recovery (see Chapter 12).

I/O shipping could be obtained by having each machine be a file system client of all the other machines and a file system server to all the other machines. But managing such partitioning is an administrative nightmare unless appropriate tools are available. They generally are not.

4.3.3   Clusters within a Client-Server Organization

The above should not be taken to imply that internally peer-to-peer clusters, adequate for commercial workloads, cannot be part of client-server distributed systems. A cluster running a peer-to-peer file system can serve quite well as a scaled-up file server, for example, as illustrated in Figure 17. Here the cluster is (most desirably) viewed as a single "node" of the distributed system; any of the clients can use it as a whole, without necessarily indicating which node they access it through, to get at any of the data on any of the attached disks.

**Figure 17   A Cluster as a Server: Logically One
Distributed Node**

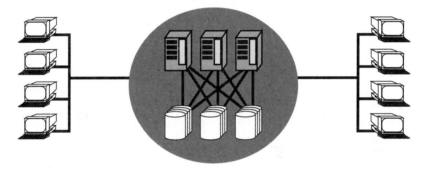

Viewing a cluster of machines as a single node is another area not well served by traditional distributed system technology, although some support exists. There are commonly available naming schemes—both Sun's ONC+ and Tivoli's DCE, for example, provide this—that decouple the physical location of a resource from its designation, allowing a logical name to designate any of several sources of the desired resource. A prospective client queries the name server, which could (for example) respond with the physical location information of any of a cluster's nodes. This approach has two difficulties when clusters are considered, both problems of modularity:

> First, it places the primary load-balancing decision outside the cluster, in the naming facility. The cluster itself is the natural location of such decisions for many reasons. For example, the cluster might be able to dynamically move work from one internal node to another

to better balance the node. But the client, having obtained a name translation, is using a physical node designation and cannot easily change it.

➤ Second, it similarly places decisions about reaction to failure outside the cluster, in the naming facility. This may be an appropriate thing to do for the catastrophic case of whole-cluster failure, but part of the Classic Standard Litany of reasons for clustering is to allow failure of a part without failure of the whole. (In any event, disaster recovery will require more than this, as discussed in Section 12.11.2 on page 436.) How this is done and how it affects clients is more naturally encapsulated within the cluster itself. In some ways this is the ultimate dynamic load-balancing act: all the work must be moved from one node onto others. The difficulties involved are similar to those mentioned for load balancing but, if anything, more severe. (How node-locked program licenses, or license servers, "fail over" in the event of an internal cluster failure is another interesting issue not well addressed by any system the author is aware of.)

➤ It doesn't work all that well. Routers and other network nodes cache the translation of names into IP addresses and re-use the IP addresses over an indefinite period of time. That means that the first association of a "logical" node name with an IP address "sticks," potentially in an entire network region, because it is cached; neither load balancing nor high availability are affected by it. Attempts to fix this by giving a very short period during which a name should be cached are sabotaged by routers which, for their own efficiency, ignore requests for very short hold times.

Another distributed approach has become available as the increasing popularity of clusters prompts network folks to take explicit notice of them. In this case, the load balancing and high availability function in a router that sits in front of the cluster. The router effectively subverts the routing process, forwarding requests from the IP-specified destination node to the real destination—one of the computers in a cluster. This avoids the address caching problem, since the router always presents the same IP address to the network, and can work quite well; see [DKMT96] for more details. However, it does not address the first two problems mentioned above. Some vendors are trying to do so by providing for feedback from the cluster nodes to the router; if that is done, this may be an adequate solution. However, note that it was only achieved when the network facilities explicitly took notice of clusters and supported them directly, rather than trying to squeeze them into the existing distributed paradigm; they do not fit.

Of course, clusters have gotten around many of these issues directly for quite a while. Turing still reigns, so the cluster can get around many of these issues by telling a lie, and moving the network addresses (IP addresses) to another node. This has a number of interesting aspects, as well as pitfalls. See "Failing Over Communications" on page 411.

4.3.4   Clusters and Three-Tiered Applications

Clusters also appear to be arising in a natural way in the evolution of distributed systems. Look again at the part of Figure 16 illustrating a typical distributed client-server file system. That same system organization has been used for client-server database systems: The clients run the application code, which requests and updates data in the database system much as a file system would be accessed (but, of course, with very different access techniques, durability guarantees, etc.).

However, a funny thing is happening as the database applications implemented in this manner become larger and more sophisticated, extending their reach throughout large enterprises. These applications do substantial work. As a result, they have become too big for the clients. The alternative of performing the entire application on the "back-end" database engine is also problematical, since as the enterprise grows it runs out of capacity.

Figure 18   Three-Tiered Distributed Hierarchy, a Cluster

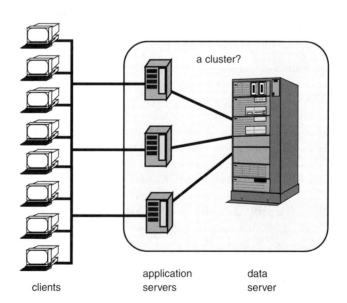

clients   application   data
                   servers   server

In Search of Clusters ✳

A response to this conundrum is an organization with three levels, as shown in Figure 18. This organization is, for example, used by the run-your-whole-business application suites sold by SAP and Baan. On one end, client workstations concentrate on the human interaction, parsing users' inputs and displaying results by using graphics in an appropriate manner. On the other end, the database engine grinds away, making sure everything is consistent and stably stored. In the middle, application servers, a new class, perform the application work itself. The middle tier is a server to the workstations and a client to the back end.

This whole arrangement sure looks like a cluster to me.

4.4   Concerning "Single System Image" _____

A term that may appear conspicuously absent from the cluster definition provided is "single system image." There are two reasons for that.

First, "single system image" turns out to be an interestingly complex subject that is, at least in part due to prior overly simplistic renditions, subject to some controversy. Chapter 11 is devoted to this concept.

Second, and highly related to the complexity of the issue, clusters can be very useful entities even though they lack much of what might be called a "single system image." Database systems that operate against "raw" disk devices, for example, may neither require nor usefully utilize a single cluster-wide file system. At some level a single system image should still be present, of course—a statement that anticipates the discussion to come.

The phrase "utilized as a single, unified computing resource," on the other hand, appears to capture the intent of clusters without raising the complications that the term "single system image" entails.

4.5   Other Comparisons _____

Other distinctions between clusters, distributed computing, and parallel systems are summarized in Table 6.

The distinction drawn here is between traditional "highly parallel" and cluster, rather than the general parallel area and cluster, because the only interesting "lowly parallel" system is the symmetric multiprocessor (SMP). A summary comparison of SMPs and clusters was given earlier (woof!), and a detailed comparison of clusters and SMPs appears later. "NUMA" systems are also ignored, since they are really a variety of SMP (see Chapter 7).

Some of the rows in that table require explanation.

Table 6   Comparison of Cluster, Highly Parallel, and Distributed

Characteristic	Highly Parallel	Cluster	Distributed
number of nodes	thousands	tens or less	thousands
performance metric	turnaround time	throughput and turnaround time	response time
node individualization	none	none	required
internode communication standards	proprietary, nonstandard is OK	varies depending on type; proprietary often used	strict standards adherence required
node size	smaller (< 1 problem)	larger (≥ 1 problem)	larger (≥ 1 problem)
inter-node security	nonexistent	unnecessary if enclosed; required if exposed[a]	required
node OS	homogeneous	varies depending on type; often homogeneous	must be heterogeneous

a. "Enclosed" and "exposed" are defined in the next chapter.

In the "number of nodes" row, the point being made is that neither highly parallel nor distributed systems are particularly interesting if they are not designed to scale to thousands of elements, while the same is not true of clusters. This factor eliminates from the hardware of clusters many constraints that exist in highly parallel or distributed systems. For example, communication by multi-tailed access to disks is a clustering technique that has been used more than once, is in common use now, and looks like it may become more widespread. However, because it does not scale to thousands, is disparaged in the highly parallel and distributed arenas.

"Node individualization" is meant to indicate whether individual nodes are typically personalized and/or different from others. For highly parallel and cluster systems, this is not usually the case—although cluster nodes, and in some cases MPP nodes, must be separately operable (bootable) for diagnostic purposes, if nothing else. For distributed systems, on the other hand, individualization is a necessary characteristic—even if the node hardware and software is homogeneous in the sense of being the same hardware and software models.

In another metric, clusters are closer to distributed than to highly parallel systems: Since highly parallel systems typically spread a single problem across many nodes, each node need not be capable of running an entire job. Nodes of clusters and distributed systems, on the other hand, must be able to run at least one entire job at a time. Clusters must do this because they are often used for execution of serial jobs in a batch execution mode. Distributed nodes must do so because, while parts of a job (like file access) may be performed elsewhere, the bulk of the work of a job is typically performed in a single place. That is the point of the "node size" row.

"Internode security" refers to whether communication between nodes must be made secure for either the proper functioning of the system or for protection against illicit access. Within highly parallel systems, no security firewalls are present any more than they are between a processor and its memory—which is to say, they may be present, but the situation is tightly controlled and has hardware support that allows them to exhibit very low overhead while maintaining system integrity. Distributed computing, on the other hand, deals in communication that is in general exposed to external view, so its communication generally requires protection from malicious or unintentional tampering. Clusters may or may not need internal security measures, depending on the type of cluster ("enclosed" and "exposed," terms that are defined in Chapter 5).

4.6 Reactions

At this point I have hopefully convinced the majority of readers that a cluster is a subtype of aggregate computer system distinct from the traditional parallel and distributed varieties. The intent here was not to be legalistic. As has been noted before, there are clearly senses in which all aggregate computing scenarios are parallel, and equally valid senses in which all aggregate computing scenarios are distributed. But to the extent that there are useful distinctions to be drawn at all in this area, "cluster" is as distinct as any.

If there is still confusion or disagreement, it is my experience that it resides in the minds of active practitioners of the arts of parallel and distributed computing.

Parallel computing specialists have typically responded to the distinctions being drawn by remarking that they can clearly see a difference from distributed computing, but there's no distinction from parallel computing. Conversely, distributed computing mavens readily acknowledge a distinction from parallel processing, but state that there's no distinction from distributed computing.

Part of this is undoubtedly simple territoriality. I've yet to see a definition of distributed computing, for example, that did not implicitly claim all of parallel processing in its bounds—despite the fact that the actual day-to-day concerns and operation of parallel systems use techniques and concepts that are foreign to the distributed world, and vice-versa. Another part of this disagreement is submergence in the Turing tar pit that afflicts all of computer science: Any computer or type of computation can, with (ahem) *sufficient* ingenuity, motivation, effort, and resources, be made to look like any other.

There is a final interesting comment I've received from some of the members of both camps: There may be a distinction between clusters and where their field used to be, but there is no distinction from where it is heading. This sounds quite deep and is possibly very revealing, but I fear I'm really not quite sure what it means, and certainly am not ready to herald the coming of a Grand Unification.

Part 2:

Hardware

A Cluster
Bestiary

A more detailed discussion of the hardware of clusters and of their competitors, SMPs and NUMA systems, is the topic of this and the next two chapters. The chapters following those two deal with software; then the threads of discussion rejoin for system discussions. The divergence begins with this chapter, which purports to describe the ways that clusters can be built.

It may seem odd to treat cluster hardware first; after all, it's been emphasized that the primary issues facing clusters are software. There are several reasons for doing so.

First of all, it's the simpler topic, and so the easier one to get out of the way. Also, the treatment here and in the other allegedly "hardware" chapter consists only in part of hardware issues. Several of the distinctions made are far more relevant to how clusters must be programmed than to the hardware implementation, which can vary quite a bit within the classes to be mentioned. The limitation of clusters to combinations of whole computers also forces a nontraditional view of the topic. The traditional views of types of parallel machines will be covered, both for completeness and to show that many of them have little relevance to this discussion, in one of the software chapters, chapter 9, on programming models. Another, rather plebeian reason for "hardware first" is that it's hard to talk about software without knowing what kinds of contraptions the software is supposed to make into something useful.

A somewhat more interesting reason for treating hardware first is that you have to start somewhere. Clusters, like all of the forms of overt parallelism, is neither a hardware nor a software issue; rather, it is a *system* issue: an issue that involves the interaction of the software and the hardware with each other, each affecting the other in nontrivial ways. Many of the items presented in this book, and the way they are presented, are in fact the result of having gone 'round and 'round in circles from software to hardware to software to hardware… more times than anyone should admit to. This is a primary reason why these issues historically have been so difficult to explain; it's not simple to untangle this knotted mass of threads into a nice, linear presentation. Hardware just happens to be the thread that my mental fingers happen to seize first. I've tried to keep things as linearly readable as possible, but be prepared for a large number of references to the software chapters from the hardware ones, and vice versa; or busting out into code in the midst of greasy hardware details; or discussions of hardware effects while wallowing in software.

So, that's why hardware is the first topic. Before we begin, however, another digression is in order. This one is to explain why this allegedly survey-like, all-encompassing chapter is fairly short.

There are two types of people. Aside, that is, from those who think there are two types of people, and those who do not. Old joke. Anyway, the two types I'm thinking of differ in their mental apparatus.

There are, on the one hand, people who glory in diversity. They love the richness and multiplicity of the many heterogeneous variations of things that are presented to us by the world, be those things people, other living entities, natural objects, or artifacts. Simplicity, including the simplicity created by organization, bores them; there's not enough of it. They tend to be chemists (particularly organic chemists) not physicists, cataloguers rather than taxonomists. They like the unstructured, repetitive documentation that typically accompanies GUIed programs, but they never read it, rather dipping in here and there. In the words of a colleague of mine, they luxuriate in the Dionysian richness of androgynous, chthonic nature. And they have mental machinery that easily, pleasurably, remembers and recalls a multitude of examples of that variation, which fact probably has more than a little to do with why they like all those examples. They are better equipped to know than to deduce.

On the other hand are people who glory in structure. They like having one rule that rings them all, that unifies all the heterogeneity they can see, and like to think that such rules "explain" that variation. Unconstrained diver-

sity bores them; it's just mush. They tend to be physicists (particularly particle physicists) not chemists, taxonomists who relate things to one another
rather than cataloguers who insist on listing them all. They don't understand how anybody can sit down and read the documentation that typically
accompanies GUIed programs (probably nobody does, but these folks try).
Again in the words of that colleague, they typify Apollonian, western males.
And their mental machinery has an absolute *blast* "understanding" specific
cases by spontaneously flashing down a deduction chain, dynamically generating any of a combinatorial explosion of individual cases by intensely
massaging a few logical rules; which fact probably has more than a little to
do with why they like those rules. They are better equipped to deduce than
to know.

I am a structure guy. A physicist-type. A taxonomist. I actually try to read
the documentation of GUIed programs from front to back, linearly (it's usually incredibly boring, unstructured, and repetitious). In mental structure[1] I
am a typical, Apollonian, western male, and unrepentant about it. I deduce
like a madman, and I remember nothing.

And I hate surveys.

Particularly surveys of parallel computers.

I am bored to tears by compilations of seventy-three "interesting" variations
of partially fault-tolerant, multi-path parallel interconnection networks, all
treated in that academically diplomatic style that implies they're all equally
good, to say nothing of worth mentioning. I have an identical reaction to the
eighty-fourth of the limitless possible recombinations of arithmetic and parallel communication gear, none but an infinitesimal number of which could
conceivably be programmed by anyone but a graduate student starving for
a thesis topic. (A significant but thankfully declining number of graduate
Computer Science thesis titles can be best translated as "How I Actually
Managed to do X on the Y Machine My Advisor Thought Up.")

In short, I could never write a typical parallel processing textbook.

So this discussion of possible cluster hardware will not be typical. It instead
consists of a small number of dichotomies, two-way distinctions, that indicate axes along which cluster hardware can vary, with a few examples illustrating the differences highlighted. In one case, two pairs of dichotomies are
coupled, creating what I suppose might be called a quadrichotomy, but it's
still dichotomous at heart. Combine these at will to create variations on the
theme of "cluster." Anything that doesn't fit I've felt free to ignore. This is
followed by discussion of several particularly outstanding, important, and

---

1. But not necessarily politics or sociological attitudes, please.

practical examples of hardware designed to accelerate processing done on clusters.

By the way, structuralists like to say that there are two types of people. Diversity lovers always disagree.

5.1   Exposed vs. Enclosed _____

The first distinction to be made is decidedly nontraditional. It refers to the security characteristics of intracluster communication: As illustrated in Figure 19, intracluster communication can either be **exposed** to outside view, or **enclosed** within the cluster itself.

Figure 19   **Exposed and Enclosed Clusters**

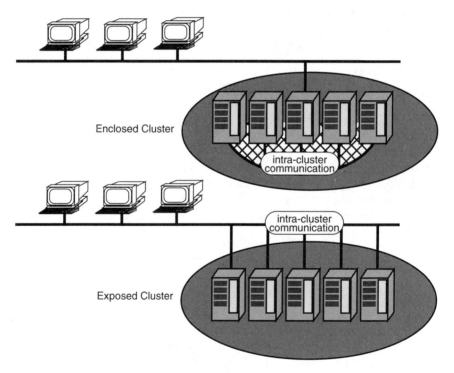

An exposed cluster shares public communication facilities with other computers not part of the cluster. This sharing has several consequences.

> ➤ The cluster nodes necessarily communicate by messages, since public, standardized communication is always message-based.

- Communication has fairly high overhead, since it must use standard protocols designed for robustness in the face of adversity.

- The communication channel itself is not secure, so additional work must be done to ensure the privacy of intracluster communication that carries security-critical data.

- Since public, potentially widespread communication channels are used, this type of cluster more naturally enables "scavenging" of otherwise unused workstation cycles across a campus, enterprise, or, in a military context, battlefield. The latter use has acquired the name "metacomputing" for funding purposes.

- It's really easy to build. In fact, you often don't have to build it at all. All you have to do is pick some workstations on a LAN, say "I dub thee a cluster," and start writing and/or buying software.

An enclosed cluster, on the other hand, has its own private communication facilities. Those facilities could be standard ones; for example, one could use a second Ethernet or token ring residing solely within the cluster. The important thing is that it is private. However, the possibilities are broader than standard communication techniques.

- Communication can be by a number of means: shared disk, shared memory, messages, or anything else.

- Communication has the possibility of having very low overhead because designers' imaginations need not be limited to standard mechanisms. Those mechanisms also don't have to be agreed upon by an international committee, so they can be defined and implemented faster.

- The security of the communications medium is implicit, so data can be transferred between nodes with only the same security provisions used, for example, between sections of an operating system kernel. Which is to say, very low cost security provisions; in many cases, none at all are necessary. (Advocates of capability-based operating systems will disagree with that last statement, and I might join them.)

Figure 19 on page 90, used to illustrate this concept, also implies that the cluster has only one communications path to the outside world. That need not be the case. Other paths were left out only to make the enclosed/exposed distinction graphically self-evident in the figure. (Multiple paths into a cluster are also not well supported by the current wave of distributed programming, though, as was mentioned in Chapter 4).

While the above distinctions are interesting and useful, they are not the major reason for making this distinction. That is: It is markedly easier to implement cluster-enabling software on an enclosed cluster. The reasons are several.

Communication can easily be faster and cheaper, which always helps a lot. Security is not an issue (or at least much less of an issue), which helps tremendously. It can be made at least highly unlikely, if not intrinsically impossible, that the cluster will be accidentally partitioned into two or more separate, individually survivable parts, which then later have to be merged; this is an unbelievably big help. In addition, it is possible to make use of shared storage to hold what would otherwise be replicated distributed data structures. The latter is not a theoretical issue; there are well-known techniques for maintaining such structures correctly (discussed in Chapter 9, but more in Chapter 12) that do not rely on the seeming crutch of actual shared storage media. But it is definitely an issue of implementation difficulty. It is far easier to whack a lock around a block of storage than to debug an asynchronous algorithm that reliably replicates data structure with multiple sources of updates.

Putting this another way: The programming of an enclosed cluster does not have to surmount all the challenges traditionally associated with distributed systems in addition to providing the function desired on the cluster.

Unfortunately, to take advantage of this relative simplicity, the hardware engineers often have to convince the software engineers to do nonstandard implementations. This is an enterprise fraught with difficulty and "full plate" syndromes, since software is usually fully occupied adding function to the "standard" facilities in a race with their competition. This is a reason why fast, *and standardized*, communication is an extremely important piece of the cluster puzzle.

Speaking of fast standards, in the hardware area at least: Facilities like Fibre Channel Standard and ATM require care when applying the enclosed/ exposed distinction. It is possible to implement communication switches that themselves provide security, allowing only certain endpoints to connect to other endpoints. This ability to embed partitioning in a communication switch implies that a single switch could, despite looking to all the world like a widely used common communication facility, host one or more enclosed clusters, each with its own private communication. At the same time, it could be hosting a multitude of randomly communicating nodes that can, along selected paths, communicate with the cluster(s).

The multi-kilometer reach of such technology also dissuades one from assuming that any cluster, exposed or enclosed, is necessarily geographically compact. At least it will unless (I am too pessimistic to say "until") software overhead is low enough that one can detect the fact that the speed of light isn't infinite.

Of course, assembled and preassembled clusters are very often exposed, primarily because the hardware for doing so is usually already sitting right in front of the assemblers, ready to be dubbed. That and the "standards" argument account for the reason why much home-grown open system cluster software is designed to run on exposed clusters, even though that makes it much more of a challenge to write.

5.2 "Glass-House" vs. "Campus-Wide" Cluster

While I was discussing clusters with one of the pioneers in the assembled-cluster area,[2] he mentioned that all his users' individual workstations were part of his cluster.

"Then why," I asked, "do you have a room with a rack full of machines?"

"Because we ran out of desks. If we could use [the machines] as plant stands in the lobby, we'd do that, too."

This points to another distinction between cluster types: Whether, on the one hand, the nodes are fully dedicated to their use as a shared computational resource; or, on the other hand (the case above), the nodes are also used as personal systems that must provide the response time that's characteristic of local, personal, dedicated workstations. In the first case, the cluster nodes will typically be located together in a geographically compact arrangement for ease of management: a "glass-house" arrangement. In the second, they will generally be scattered across a campus. Hence the dichotomy: "glass-house" clusters vs. "campus-wide" clusters.

The attractiveness of campus-wide clusters—also known as NOW systems, for "Network Of Workstations," a catchy term coined by Prof. Dave Patterson of Berkeley[3]—lies in their potential for scavenging unused computing resources from personal workstations, which, like private automobiles, have notoriously low average utilization. This is the additional verse that turns the Classic Standard Litany into the Enhanced Standard Litany of reasons why parallel/distributed computing is good. To repeat the old saw men-

---

2. Dennis Duke of Florida State University's Supercomputing Computation Research Institute.

3. The NOW project also has a roomful of racked-up workstations connected by a fast (Myrianet) switch. I guess they didn't have enough desks, either. I don't think anybody does. For many reasons, server systems distinct from desktop workstations are always necessary. Dave Patterson has a real knack for catchy acronyms; he also coined RISC.

tioned in Chapter 3: While the workstation cycles that form the basis of cluster cost/performance are cheap, unused workstation cycles are *free*.

Two factors distinguish campus-wide clusters from glass-house clusters: Nodes of campus-wide clusters operate in a a less-controlled environment; and they must quickly and totally relinquish use of a node to a user.

The campus-wide environment is less controlled in several ways. It is less reliable in the sense that power cords are accidentally unplugged, machines have coffee spilled on them, are bumped into, have users of decidedly mixed expertise messing around with system configuration files, and so on. It is also obviously a less physically secure environment. In addition, there are likely to be uncontrolled variations in the configuration of the nodes; storage, availability of software, and so on, will vary widely. For example, how does a campus-wide cluster batch system ever find out that a user has installed more memory or disk storage, or upgraded to a new, buggy beta release of a compiler? It cannot—unless control is exerted over users' systems, more control than is often the norm.

Enforcing such control requires a loss of autonomy, perhaps rather substantial, by the individual workstation owner/user. In many cases, the owners will gladly give up that control in exchange for lessening their burden of system management—or for the benefit of using others' machines for their long-running jobs. Other owners regard their workstations as being as personal as their toothbrushes and will be harder to convince. In the end, this is a sociological issue. Commercial enterprises have recently become extremely sensitive to this issue, because maintaining all those toothbrushes turns out to cost a huge amount of money. As a result, more centralized control is becoming popular, especially when coupled with even less expensive computing hardware—nearly a reincarnation of the original Stanford University Network's[4] "diskless" workstations, now called Network Computers. So the necessary control may end up existing for reasons having nothing to do with clustering.

Of course, when this concept is extended to the "metacomputing" environment mentioned earlier, its potential battlefield-wide use adds an enormous load of loss of control. At least the machines in the campus-wide case aren't usually shot at.

The second of the two factors differentiating campus-wide from glass-house clusters is the need to totally relinquish use of a node when a local user wants it. This might appear to be a simple matter of scheduling priorities on

---

4. Bet you didn't know that "Sun" was originally an acronym.

each node: Give the scavenging job such a low priority that it doesn't get in the way.

However, even an idle scavenging job is using up local resources—operating system data structures, buffer space in memory, paging space on disk, and so on. Also, private workstations are often sized to just barely handle an owner's personal needs—and if they're larger than that initially, such an oversight is always temporary; Gresham's Law applies, and the needs grow to the maximum that can be accomplished with the available tools, even if the "need" is a collection of humorous screen savers. Amusing cases aside, the full capabilities of one's workstation really must be available. No user who understands the situation is going to allow some *thing* to come in from who knows where, essentially at random and, for example, use up the paging space needed by the desktop publishing system that must be used to turn out a report in ten minutes. (I'll leave it to your imagination how desirable it is to have a metacomputing system locally used for weapons control suddenly and randomly lose some of its capacity.)

The issue is not how to turn down the scavenger's use of resources. Rather, it is to how make it completely *gone* at the tap of a spacebar, the twitch of a mouse, or in more sophisticated cases, the reaching of some resource threshold.

That this is not so simple is indicated by the several solutions that have been applied where it has been attempted. Here are some examples:

> ➤ The Condor system of the University of Wisconsin takes periodic checkpoints of scavenger jobs; these are sent to a separate controlling site. Then, when a user implicitly requests his machine back, the scavenging job instantly commits suicide and is reborn somewhere else from a prior backup. This is used in IBM's LoadLeveller batch system [IBMc].

> ➤ The Piranha system of Yale, based on the Linda programming paradigm [CG89], sends a scavenging job an "exit" signal on return from which the job is instantly purged. The programmer of the scavenging job must write appropriate code that executes in response to that signal if the scavenging job's work is to be partially or wholly saved.

> ➤ Sprite [O⁺88, DOKT91] and Locus [PW85] (the latter used for the IBM TCF facility [WP89]), do cross-machine job migration when a user wants his/her resources back. This is the best solution from the point of view of the scavenger, since no forward progress is lost and no special code must be written. But it is far more complex. In addition to memory contents, open files, threading, and so on, must

be moved. Also, it relies an significant surrounding infrastructure (a "distributed" operating system) and is possibly slower to relinquish the local machine than either of the other two.

Just like the prior distinction made between exposed and enclosed clusters, the primary reason for distinguishing glass-house from campus-wide clusters is not whether one or the other versions is feasible in the sense of a Turing machine; in principle, anything can be programmed. Rather, the issue is the sizeable number of nontrivial, additional problems that arise when one wants to scavenge computer time in a campus-wide cluster. Such clusters are by no means impractical—they see very significant use—but they are more difficult to program into fully robust, usable life.

A factor not yet mentioned is that campus-wide clusters will assuredly be heterogeneous, composed of nodes using hardware and software from differing vendors. The issues involved in heterogeneous systems have been beaten to death in the distributed computing context; there is no point to rehashing them here. Suffice it to say that this also can certainly be solved, but it nonetheless increases the general overhead and makes life more difficult for the programmer.

Of course, once again the nonstandard/full-plate software syndrome enters the picture. Unlike the enclosed/exposed case, this one is will be resolved only when campus-wide clusters become a buzzword of sufficient pervasiveness that they must somehow be shoved onto the plate, too.

A question: Are campus-wide systems actually clusters? Earlier it was stated that the definition of a cluster implied that internal nodes were anonymous as viewed from the outside. There's a bit of a problem here. Where's the "outside" of a campus-wide cluster? To me, my workstation obviously isn't anonymous. Yours, on the other hand, is just another resource.

Individual office workstations in a campus certainly are not anonymous from the point of view of the owner. But from the point of view of a batch submission system wanting to use a workstation for a job, each workstation is indeed anonymous. It might be said that what is involved here is a "virtual cluster" that can occupy part, but not all, of the machines on which it is hosted. So the workstations involved have a split personality; it's even been called schizophrenic computing [SSCK93]. The difficulties discussed above are caused by the need to switch between those two personalities and the tension between them. If it hasn't happened already, somebody should call such a system "Eve."

Finally, a thought: It is entirely possible that the goals which campus-wide cluster developers are trying to achieve—better resource utilization, provision for running large jobs—can be realized better, and more easily, by using a single roomful of computers as a central, shared, cluster server; and plunking inexpensive Network Computers (NCs) on everybody's desk. After all, the folks who are serious about this already have the roomful of servers.

5.3   Cluster Hardware Structures _____

Describing all the possible hardware structures usable for clusters is difficult and quite possibly silly, because every conceivable technique for gluing computers together has been called a "cluster." When a hardware designer is not even limited by worries about scaling to large numbers—a cluster of four, or even two machines is quite usable—all kinds of strange and wonderful things are both feasible and practical. About the only thing they all have in common is that they are most definitely *not* symmetric multiprocessors, that is, they are not composed of processors with equal, uniform access to main memory and I/O. (This is further discussed in Chapter 6.) Beyond that, well, there must be 60 ways to build a cluster.[5]

There are many ways to attempt to organize this unbridled chaos, and most are probably equally good. Here I will use an organization based on two nearly orthogonal characteristics: the method of attachment to the whole computers involved; and whether the communication medium is or is not some form of shared storage. How these "paired dichotomies" related to each other is shown in Figure 20, which also gives some examples of each type. By no means are the lists anywhere near complete; your personal pet version probably does not appear. Several of the systems mentioned will be discussed in more detail in a later section. Also, hybrid systems that simultaneously use multiple quadrants are definitely feasible, so this categorization is not mutually exclusive (and neither is any other categorization of which I am). The most common hybrids will be discussed below.

These categories, while reasonably inclusive, do not do adequate justice to the special techniques that have been created to speed up cluster operation. Those are discussed later in this chapter.

5.3.1   The Four Categories

Clusters are composed of whole, conventional, traditionally organized computers. Such machines have a limited number of places at which connection to other such computers can be carried out. In fact, there are exactly two such places: at the I/O subsystem and at the memory subsystem.

---

5. Slip the data out the back, Jack / send it on a LAN, Stan / a store to employ, Roy / but not an SMP. / Drop it on a bus, Gus / no need for coherence / share it on DASD / set those hardware jocks **free**. *Pace* Paul Simon. Sorry. I couldn't resist.

Figure 20   Categories of Cluster Hardware

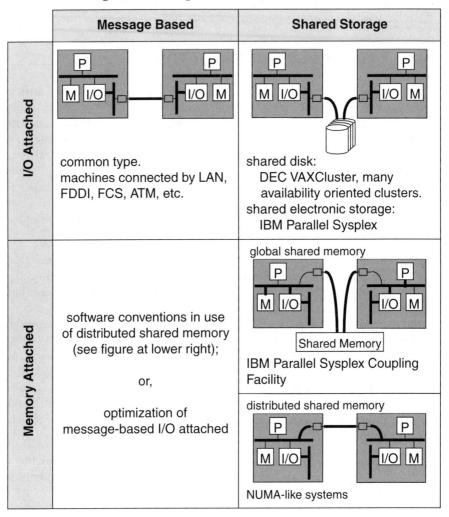

P = Processor
M = Memory
I/O = Input/Output

In the case of I/O attachment, communication is performed by using I/O operations that are usually mediated by an operating system. In the case of memory attachment, processor-native, memory-based load and store operations result, possibly indirectly, in data motion between nodes. Memory-mapped I/O may appear to smear this distinction, but really does not. Memory-mapped I/O loads and stores don't affect the real memory hard-

In Search of Clusters ✳

ware subsystem; they get trundled off to diddle hardware that is nowhere near the usual memory attachment point but rather is on a (usually slow) path to a standard I/O bus. Therefore the hardware attachment points remain distinct. (The software may not, entirely.)

The properties of the communication medium itself are largely independent of where it is attached. That forms the basis of the second distinction: whether the communications medium does or does not contain explicitly used shared storage of some sort.

If there is no explicitly used shared storage, the system is referred to (in this book, at least) as message-based or message-passing. In such a system, communication is completed when data have been received by the target node. A message-based system may contain incidental storage—pipeline registers and the like—used to hold data during its transfer to another node; such storage is not explicitly used in programming the beast. In shared storage systems, by contrast, communication from a node is complete when the data is placed in the shared storage; the location in the storage is explicitly used by the processor as the target of communication.

Unfortunately for those of us who like simple dichotomizing, the shared storage category admits a few subcategories. The shared storage can, for example, be electronic (fast memory), or it can be electro-mechanical (slower, disk). That difference, while very practically significant, does not affect the system structure, only the data rates—possibly by orders of magnitude, so this is not a trivial distinction. However, there is another distinction, this one structural: where the shared storage is located. In particular, is it distinct from each node's own main storage, or is it part of them? This is a structural distinction that is quite significant, which is why the lower-right entry of Figure 20 has been split to accommodate that distinction.

Each of the possible combinations of those two characteristics, attachment point and type of medium, are discussed in the sections that follow.

5.3.2   I/O-Attached Message-Based

I/O-attached message-based systems are the most common and the most fundamental. Clusters connected by common LAN, FDDI, ATM, and FCS fall into this category, as well as clusters connected by proprietary switching systems. They are fundamental in that all the other combinations also include some form of this attachment, at least at the level of a simple inter-node interrupt that can inform another node when data is waiting for it somewhere. They are also the easiest to construct because off-the-shelf hardware can be used.

5.3.3 I/O-Attached Shared Storage

The most common manifestation of I/O-attached shared storage systems is the shared disk system. In this case, a disk controller is able to take commands from two (or more) computers, each of which can read data the other has written onto the disk. The DEC OpenVMS Cluster is a well-known example of such a system, as is the IBM Sysplex, and the SPARCcluster x000 PDB series, and anybody else who wants to run Oracle's Parallel Server systems (which is a very nontrivial collection of commercial UNIX system vendors).

Many of the "basic (availability) clusters" mentioned in Chapter 2 are also of this type, but not all, even though all of them contain cables to disks from multiple machines—multi-tailed disks. The reason some are not of this type is that in several cases, only one machine at a time ever uses a given disk; the multiple tails are there only to allow one machine to take over the disk if the other one buys the farm. Since only one machine ever accesses a disk at once, it obviously is not being shared.

In addition to disk sharing, various forms of semiconductor store can also be shared in this mode. The IBM Sysplex Coupling Facility is an example. The ill-fated IBM POWER/4 RPQ, a very short-lived, limited availability product, was also of this category; it had in addition a special cluster-wide "lock box" providing fast cluster-wide synchronization facilities, like some of the features of the Coupling Facility. (No, the two had absolutely nothing to do with each other.)

Systems sharing I/O-attached storage, like systems sharing any form of storage, require some way to adjudicate ownership of segments of the storage, so they do not step all over each other's data. (How this can happen, and ways to get around it, is discussed in more detail in Chapter 9, "Basic Programming Models and Issues" on page 235.) This arbitration is usually done by some form of software-based coherence control, since one machine may have in its memory a block of data that has been updated but not yet written back to disk; particularly when semiconductor storage is used, however, hardware assists may exist [IBMe], as will be described both later in this chapter and in Chapter 10, "Commercial Programming Models."

5.3.4 Memory-Attached Shared Storage

Memory-attached shared storage systems come in two varieties: those with at least one physically common block of shared storage separate from the storage of the individual nodes; and those in which the storage contained in the individual nodes is shared. Systems connected via the Scalable Coherent Interconnect (described in more detail in Chapter 7) will usually be of the latter type, although it is logically possible to use SCI to access a common storage module. The IBM POWER/4 RPQ (RIP) was an example providing only a common shared storage block, with no accessibility between individual nodes' local memory. The IBM Parallel Sysplex Coupling Facility is arguably a member of this class, too, since the route from the systems to the Coupling Facility may not be I/O (such distinctions are a little blurry in S/390).

Shared storage of this type can also be "logically shared," as is the case with Encore's (Gould's) Reflective Memory facility, which is the basis of DEC's "Memory Channel" facility mentioned in Chapter 2; it will be further discussed later in this chapter, in Section 5.5.3. In this case, writing into the shared reflective storage region results, at some point, in each processor seeing that data—but the actual data storage is replicated at each node. In effect, a store into Reflective Memory is "reflected" into all other nodes.

5.3.5   Memory-Attached Message-Based

The fourth category of cluster hardware, memory-attached message-based systems, contains no current examples of which I am aware. However, software can obviously use memory under conventions that limit it to message-passing; this is common in SMPs and perfectly possible with other memory-based systems, but the hardware base in those cases is nevertheless shared storage.

There is a possible exception to this, since as will be discussed. DEC's advice to programmers is in most cases to use their Memory Channel as a message-passing device. There are extremely good reasons for this, discussed in Section 5.5.3.

5.3.6   Discussion

All of the above communication strategies can and have been used for clusters of machines. Which is best depends on the application area and the available software support.

5.3.6.1   I/O vs. Memory-Attached

I/O-attached message-passing is currently the only way to construct clusters from heterogeneous machines. For only that case have standards been created and deployed that allow meaningful data transmission between machines from different manufacturers running different software systems. In theory, SCI should allow such heterogeneity for memory attachment (why else make it a *de jure* standard?), but the many levels of software protocols required to make such attachment safely usable have not been addressed. One can only imagine the chaos that would result if, for example, a Hewlett-Packard HP/UX operating system and a Sun Solaris operating system could write willy-nilly into each other's memory. Neither would survive the boot process.

Memory attachment in general is harder to accomplish than I/O attachment, for two reasons:

1. The hardware of most machines is designed to accept foreign attachments in its I/O subsystem. This attachment point is generally a well thought-out, architected interface that does not vary too much, at least within a single manufacturer's line. Memory subsystems, on the other hand, generally have more stringent hardware attachment requirements and are usually not "architected," in the sense that they change dramatically from one machine model to another within a single manufacturer's line. Thus, different memory-attachment hardware may be needed for different models of the same machine. This is not a good situation.

2. The software required for the basic functioning of memory-to-memory connection is more difficult to construct. Again, I/O is where attachment is expected, in hardware as well as software, and device drivers for new attachments are routinely written to an explicitly designed interface. The corresponding support required for the bare functioning of memory attachment affects at the very least an operating system's memory management subsystem; unless this is an externalized interface, changing it may require pervasive changes in the operating system.

Once memory attachment is operational, on the other hand, it can potentially provide communication performance that is dramatically better than that of I/O attachment, because unlike I/O, memory subsystems are designed for efficient access directly from user-mode applications. Inter-user protection at the memory access level has extensive, optimized, hardware support built into virtual memory-mapping mechanisms. Inter-user protection at the I/O level, on the other hand, is largely semi-interpretive, most usually enforced by disallowing direct user-mode access. I/O-attached communication (and graphics) is therefore usually in a pitched battle with system software over latency reduction. This potential advantage of memory attachment can of course be dissipated if the necessary communication protocols—always necessary at some level—are not extremely lightweight, if not completely "compiled away."

There is a further conceptual complication with memory attachment for clustering: It gets entwined with issues of "NUMA" and cache coherence, causing no end of confusion among customers, marketeers, and, yes, defi-

　　　　　　　　　　　　　　　　　　In Search of Clusters　✳

nitely system designers. This can only be meaningfully discussed after cache coherence is covered, so further discussion will be put off until Chapter 7, "NUMA and Friends."

5.3.6.2   Shared Storage vs. Message-Based

Which of shared storage or message-based systems is preferable is the subject of a long-running heated battle with techno-religious overtones that is not likely to be settled any time soon, if ever. The dispute is most often over shared electronic memory—we'll cover it in Chapter 9, "Basic Programming Models and Issues"—although shared disks also participate, as will be discussed in Chapter 10, "Commercial Programming Models."

To quickly summarize that argument: Shared storage advocates claim that because their computational model is closer to the traditional uniprocessor model, it is easier to program and furthermore is more efficient, particularly in aspects such as workload management under varying loads, failures, and so on. Message-passing advocates claim their solutions are far more portable and adaptable to larger-scale systems with more nodes, as well as being simpler to debug, and if our minds weren't polluted by conventional programming we'd all understand that fact intuitively. Each disputes the other's claims, and neither position is provable now, if ever; it is more than likely that other issues dominate, like the characteristics of a vendor's base of installed machines, or how well each implementation is executed.

Finally, note that the above has been primarily a hardware discussion. All these things being Turing machines, the appearance that software puts on any hardware can be arbitrary, specifically including the exact opposite of the hardware's innate characteristics. Such cross-dressing is rather more common than one might expect. Here are some examples.

> ➤ Reference has already been made to shared storage systems being made to appear as message-based systems; a particularly important example of that is communication techniques of the Mach microkernel operating system [BRS⁺85, Ras86]. Every entity in that system communicates by messages, no matter what the hardware. To speed the passing of large messages between processes residing on the same machine, a message may be "passed" by remapping the memory of one process into another.

> ➤ In the other direction, the technique of distributed virtual memory has been developed to give the appearance of shared memory between machines connected only by message-based hardware. These, and related issues, are discussed later (Chapter 9).

> ➤ Disks are not immune to software cross-dressing, either. The appearance of shared disk storage can be obtained when there is none,

as was mentioned in Chapter 4, in the discussion of cluster file systems. This technique was originally developed for databases, where it is known as "I/O shipping." More will be said about that in Chapter 10.

5.4   Communication Requirements_____

Something none of the above has yet addressed is how much power any of these interconnection schemes must have to create a usable system. The answer is naturally quite dependent on the use to which the system is put—the workload—and also bears on the perennial shared storage vs. message-passing issue.

The discussion here focuses on the use of clusters for "scaling," that is, for obtaining additional performance by using the clustered computers at the same time. If one uses a cluster solely for high availability, the inter-node communication requirements may be utterly trivial—although this is certainly not true in all cases, as will be discussed in Chapter 12, "High Availability." However, focussing on high availability to the exclusion of scaling sacrifices a good part of what makes clusters an inexpensive way to get high availability, as will also be discussed in Chapter 12.

5.4.1   *Computationally Intensive Workloads*

For long-running, computationally intensive, serial jobs executed in a batch environment, the system-to-system connection between machines may as well be wet string. They don't exchange enough information often enough for the robustness of the interconnect to make a significant difference in the overall performance on their workload. That is why the many systems like the IBM Research Farm or the Philips Research cluster mentioned in Chapter 2, along with a host of other assembled and preassembled computational clusters, make sense in their context. One or a few file servers within the cluster provide adequate access to data, even though the aggregate disk capability of the whole cluster is limited to a conventional LAN's throughput and latency; the demand for data access is simply quite small.

Very unfortunately, the most popular commercial processing benchmarks also fall into this category; they are thus incapable of demonstrating the utility of most intra-cluster communication. This is discussed at length in Chapter 14, "Why We Need the Concept of Cluster."

5.4.2   I/O-Intensive Workloads

Commercial and technical workloads that intensively use input/output facilities are another issue altogether. The discussion here is primarily concerned with the inter-system bandwidth required for shared-nothing systems; shared-disk systems replace most of that bandwidth with I/O bandwidth, and so do not require much inter-system bandwidth (unless they also use shared storage as a cache, like IBM's Parallel Sysplex).

It is straightforward to show that adequate internode communication bandwidth of a cluster for such workloads *should equal the aggregate bandwidth from all other I/O sources that each node has.*

To be crystal clear about this: Suppose a computer can, for the workload of interest, achieve a total, aggregate bandwidth of N Mbytes/second when you add up the contribution of every disk, tape, graphics device, or other I/O thingamabob attached to it. If that computer is to be used in a cluster that performs the same kind of workload—just more of it—the internode cluster communication should provide an *additional* N Mbytes/second between nodes.

Of course, the system will still work if that bandwidth isn't there. It'll just run the workload more slowly than you would expect, unless you have the Great Galactic Genius as your job scheduler, and maybe not even then.

This surprising and seemingly overwhelming bandwidth requirement can be derived by considering two different I/O-intensive workloads: batch processing, and distributed ("parallel") query processing. Latency requirements are a bit harder to get a grip on at the present time.

5.4.2.1   I/O-Intensive Batch

First, consider commercial batch jobs, or, more generally, I/O-intensive batch jobs. Such jobs' execution time is dominated by how fast they can move data in and out of the computer, not by how fast the processor is; that might as well be a lump of putty, except for its role in scheduling I/O (and more than occasionally, its role in sorting the data). As we'll see (Chapter 8), serial batch jobs of any kind are potentially a very usable workload for clusters, one to which cluster designs should cater.

Drop such a job down in a cluster. How likely is it to land on the node where all its data resides? Not very, because optimizing the placement of a job on a node so that both its computational needs and its storage access needs are satisfied is an exceedingly difficult task and in general will be impossible to perform. What can even a perfect scheduler do, for example, if a job needs data that's attached to two different nodes? In general the job will not be on the node where its data resides. Since its execution time depends on how fast it gets its data, it will slow down if it can't get its data equally fast no matter where it is. That means each node must be able to supply that data at the original, stand-alone speed, as well as receive it at that same speed.

Conclusion: For I/O-intensive batch systems, the inter-node bandwidth should at least equal the aggregate I/O bandwidth of each node, or throughput and turnaround time will suffer. The processor overhead required to use this bandwidth cannot get out of hand, either, since no system is used purely for one type of workload or another and the processor requirements of the other jobs will be compromised. The "at least" qualifier is there because in addition to end-use job communication, there undoubtedly must be some communication related to running the cluster itself; how else can the cross-node scheduler work? Telepathy?

5.4.2.2   Query Processing

The second case concerns database query operation.

Anticipating some of the discussion in Chapter 10, a large relational join (for example) may be split up so that is performed partly on each node of a cluster (without any user reprogramming, by the way); each node performs a subset of the operation by working on the subset of the whole table that's directly attached to that node (or, with shared disk, primarily used by that node). The data for that local subset is streamed off disk into memory as fast as its I/O system can pump; the database was specifically written to do this.

While that's happening, the data being read is joined with data from another table—T—and the result sent to another node. Joining finds rows that match and creates new rows that concatenate the matching rows: In other words, whenever a join finds a match, it outputs a row bigger than the rows either table had. Suppose table T happens to be sufficiently small that it all fits in memory. Then the outgoing data, if there are a lot of "hits" in the join, will be *larger* than the original data being read: There can be more data that needs to be sent between nodes than can be read off disk at its maximum rate.

There is actually no theoretical limit to the multiplier that can be applied here. But something on the other end must absorb that stuff, and dump it onto the receiver's disk. (There's always more data than fits in main memory in a database system.) Since the receiver can't get rid of the data any faster than it can write it, the maximum it can receive—so the maximum that it makes sense to send—again turns out to be equal to the maximum aggregate I/O bandwidth of a node.

5.4.2.3   Transaction Processing: Latency and Overhead

Transaction processing, at least as typified by popular benchmarks, does not intensively use intra-cluster bandwidth. It does, however, stress the ability of a system to initiate a large number of I/O operations, each not transferring much data. This assuredly implies requirements on internode latency and overhead.

However, those requirements are hard to pin down. This is partly because of the large differences in software architecture used by different database systems; that variety is discussed in Chapter 10. That difficulty is exacerbated by the fact that popular transaction-processing benchmarks do not stress intra-cluster communication of any kind, as discussed in Chapter 14. For more realistic workloads, however, the normal millisecond-level latencies for standard communication, are surely a drag on this use of clusters. Proprietary systems, such as those of Tandem (Chapter 2), have apparently solved them, and Intel's Virtual Interface Architecture, described later in this chapter, takes direct aim at this problem.

5.4.3   What Can Be Done?

The requirements described above are fierce. They may also be somewhat overstated.

For the I/O-intensive batch case, systems often provide more peak I/O bandwidth than any real program can use because the need to connect many devices may boost aggregate bandwidth beyond usability. Inter-node bandwidth need only add an amount equal to real aggregate programs' use, of course. Furthermore, some experience now being gained in the actual use of clusters indicates that realistic query processing is actually more processor-intensive than I/O or intersystem-bandwidth intensive. This is likely to be a temporary phenomenon, however, caused by the relative immaturity of the software involved.

Even if the full, possibly overstated goals are accepted, however, clusters do not have to be consigned to a compute-intensive ghetto or restricted to proprietary, special-purpose communication hardware and software.

In part this is because shared-disk clusters, accessing all disks equally, today at least come close to meeting the bandwidth requirements, if not completely meeting them in some configurations. They are currently the undisputed leaders of commercial cluster architecture, and meeting this bandwidth requirement is part of the reason. They do have their own difficulties, as will be discussed in Chapter 10, but they are certainly in the right ballpark, if not always in a scoring position, as far as bandwidth is concerned.

For techno-politically-correct "shared nothing" systems, however, something more than conventional communications seems to be warranted. Shared-disk systems can also stand a bit of acceleration if they are designed for particularly rigorous workloads. The most common or interesting techniques are discussed in the next sections, along with one acceleration technique used in a shared-data environment.

5.5 Cluster Acceleration Techniques

A number of techniques have recently arisen for lowering communication overhead, decreasing latency, and increasing the bandwidth between nodes of a cluster. This is an area that is technically in its infancy; the technology hasn't settled down, and as a result the techniques vary widely. I would anticipate that stranger and more wonderful facilities will be developed relatively quickly, since there are a hoard of untapped possibilities. This section discusses several of the more interesting and important versions now available or being discussed.

5.5.1   Tandem's ServerNet System Area Network (SAN)

The System Area Network, or SAN,[6] is an interesting general architectural innovation initially developed by Tandem (before it became part of Compaq) [Hor95]. It can be seen as the result of looking at a common server problem from a nonstandard, cluster-oriented, perspective.

Here's the problem: Everybody would like to use a standard I/O bus to attach devices to servers; that way lies economy in numbers, and ability to reuse devices developed in other areas for other purposes. The best current choice for such a standard is Intel's PCI bus, since it is used in a whopping number of PCs. Unfortunately, PCI has a problem (not the only one) when used as a server I/O bus: too few device slots. The more powerful the version of PCI used, in fact, the fewer slots there are. For example, the widest (128 bits), fastest (66 MHz) version of PCI has two slots. A server only able to plug in two I/O devices is silly.

It's possible to "bridge" multiple PCI busses together to get more slots, connecting one to another in a daisy chain, but this introduces problems. For example, access out on the tail of the chain takes a long time, and a single device can hog the whole chained mess. This is not good for the heavy I/O loads for which servers should be designed. It's better to instead drive multiple independent PCI busses from a source connected to the system bus.

---

6. Unfortunately, some people in the press are now beginning to use the acronym "SAN" to refer to "Storage Area Networks," typified by Fibre Channel Standard. That is not what is being referred to here. Not that it makes any difference, but this use of "SAN" came first.

That works. However, server I/O connectivity requirements are large. For big systems, when you add up the disks, communication adapters, printers, and so on that are to be attached, it's easy to convince yourself that your design should accommodate hundreds of slots, and hence half-hundreds of 2-slot PCI busses. You just can't do that with a single chip connecting on one end to a system bus and the other to PCI busses; saying there are not enough pins is gargantuan understatement. In fact, the pins probably ran out with just two busses. However, this problem can be fixed, as illustrated in Figure 21.

Figure 21   A Server I/O Structure Using Standard Busses

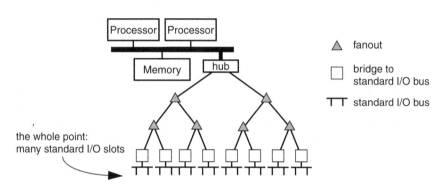

The fix is to insert some additional chips that fan things out, terminating in "bridge" interfaces at the leaves of the tree that actually drive the PCI busses. This has the added benefit, if designed appropriately, of being able to expand that collection by inserting more "fanout" chips. Systems sold by both IBM and HP are along these lines and have this property; probably others do too.

Now step back a bit. What you've got there is a special-purpose, hierarchical I/O network that routes data and commands down to busses, and back from the busses to the processor(s). It's not standard, but who cares; it's wholly internal to the system. For anyone familiar with the techniques used in more general networks, it's just a short step from that organization to a more general network. Relatively little additional logic is required to do general, not just hierarchical, routing; and besides, the chips involved are all pin-limited anyway—they have relatively little silicon real estate, just lots of pins. So the additional logic is "free." (Well, not really; power can still be an issue. But close enough).

What does general routing in a network like this get you? Well, the I/O devices could talk among themselves, transferring data directly to each other without involving a CPU. This is often touted as a significant feature, but its utility is limited for at least two reasons. First, few device adapters are smart enough to do that unaided; for example, you can't just send a disk file to a printer without a disk adapter that can be told to move a sequence of discontiguous disk blocks, and error handling is rather complicated. The second reason is that data format changes are often needed between devices, requiring CPU intervention anyway (consider printing that file on a Post-Script printer).

What you can do that's rather useful is plug multiple hosts into the same SAN. The resulting system (Figure 22) is rather different architecturally from anything else on the planet. There is no I/O directly connected to any of the hosts at all; they are just CPU/memory units with attachments to the SAN. The only I/O devices are out on the SAN, equally accessible by any of the "compute nodes."

Figure 22 A SAN-based Cluster Architecture

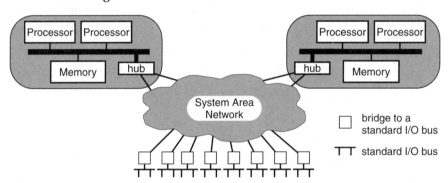

Having all devices available to all the nodes immediately makes it possible for any node to take over any device in the event of a node failure, simplifying workload reallocation on failure. (This is discussed more fully in Chapter 12.)

General accessibility by any node also potentially allows the nodes to actively share all devices in a massive shared-everything-but-memory organization; however, that isn't as straightforward as it might seem. Standard adapters, whose use was the original point of this exercise, don't understand talking to multiple hosts. To which host do they send the response to each command? Sharing on outboard busses beyond the adapter, like SCSI, FC-AL, SSA, FCS, or IBM's channel architecture, is designed into those outboard bus architectures, including tags saying who to send the result back to. It is not designed into many, if any, adapters.

There's a second reason why a SANs generally aren't used as a share-everything-but-the-sausages technique. Tandem originated this scheme, and is the only computer vendor actually selling it in its full form. Tandem is the classic, premier, dyed-in-the-wool, shared-nothing zealot; it's the company technical philosophy (or possibly religion). Forget sharing *anything*. It's the Work of the Devil.

However, having made the network general, another thing happens: The hosts can now send messages to each other *directly through the SAN*, basically the same way they send data to I/O devices.

There is two implications here that make this communication better than the usual LAN or WAN arrangements.

First, notice that there are no I/O adapters involved. Communication goes from the system bus (memory) directly into the SAN, and from there directly to another node's system bus (memory) again. The "hub" that connects to the system bus, and mediates all I/O transfers, is involved; but no additional adapters or busses intervene. That means that the seemingly overwhelming intra-cluster I/O bandwidth requirements discussed in the earlier section can be satisfied without self-contradiction: The inter-node bandwidth can be as large as necessary without making the entire I/O system double its own size (which would be rather hard in any event).

High bandwidth is not useful without low overhead. Fortunately, that is something a SAN design strongly affects, too. Since the network was designed from the ground up to talk to I/O devices, it is intrinsically far more reliable than usual communications.

Normal communication networks are assumed to be nasty. They drop data packets on the floor and don't pick them up, put errors in them, change their order, and do other terrible stuff. There are layers in the communications stack multilayer cake that are there to fix these problems; it's considered part of normal operation to run these, since WANs and LANs are basically sloppy media.

So, what would happen if you used LAN/WAN-style communication when talking to a disk drive, *ad lib* sending data in the wrong order, with some of it occasionally missing or incorrect? Scrambled gorp on the disk? Actually, the result would probably "just" be really bad performance, or no performance at all if things never got sent right—which can happen on a LAN; the software fixes it up (at a cost). While data sent to I/O devices is certainly checked (well, except for some really inexpensive LAN adapters), the basic assumption is that errors are few and far between, and the protocols and code are optimized to the non-error case.

Thus, SAN inter-node communication potentially has lower overhead than normal standard communication. In fact, Tandem's ServerNet SAN implementation is described as performing the lower levels of the usual communications stack "in hardware," meaning among other things that it's the responsibility of the ServerNet hardware to deliver data in order and without errors.

Good for it. This can significantly reduce communication overhead if it is coupled with a special communication stack (for TCP/IP, in particular) that has the hardware-implemented layers optimized out; Tandem has done such an implementation. It would be nice to quantify how much this really buys, but no firm data are available as this is written; a rumored number is a 50 percent reduction in CPU overhead, a statement which may or may not be significant depending on the (unknown) workload under which it was measured.

Several companies had by mid-1996 joined with Tandem to use ServerNet as a cluster communications medium, among them Compaq, Dell, and other vendors of Intel-based systems. The combined Compaq-Tandem announcement of their collaboration, done before those companies merged, declared that they had defined the industry standard cluster. Apparently this was definition by the well-known technique of blatant assertion, since nobody else joined them in saying this. While ServerNet is by no means a bad thing, one would have thought that industry experience with the IBM PC AT design would have inoculated everyone against once again defining a high level standard as hardware.

However, the ServerNet collection of companies are not using ServerNet as shown in Figure 22 on page 110. Instead, they use it as shown in Figure 23, solely as a way of communicating between computers.

Figure 23   Common Use of ServerNet

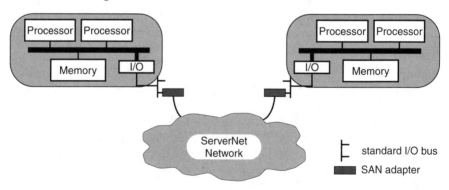

Each node, now a regular old whole computer with its own normal I/O, has an adapter card that connects it to the ServerNet. Tandem does use Server-Net as a true SAN in its Himalaya-series systems, but everybody else takes the architecturally less-innovative route of using this SAN as an efficient intra-cluster LAN. That's not necessarily a bad thing. Nothing that reduces communication overhead in clusters is a bad thing. It does, however, slightly cripple the systems by throwing away the bandwidth headroom of a real SAN architecture directly attached to the system bus, and introduces some overhead and inefficiency due to the need to go through another level of bussing.

That, though, is the most common way it appears that ServerNet will be used.

5.5.2   Intel's Virtual Interface Architecture (VIA)

There is another completely separate effort that also bills itself as a SAN: Intel's proposed Virtual Interface Architecture (VIA). This is also the subject of a consortium; for good and obvious reasons, getting others to agree with you about communications is a rather popular thing to do. People involved with Intel on this one include Microsoft, IBM, Tandem, Compaq, Santa Cruz Operations (SCO), and a host of others (around 20), all participating in refining the initial definition of VIA proposed by Intel.

Wait a minute. Tandem and Compaq? Have they abandoned ServerNet? No. VIA is not a hardware architecture. It is a low-level software interface architecture for communication on an intra-cluster network. Its entire stated purpose is to provide a communication standard that has low overhead. The motivation quite correctly cited is the fact that the use of high bandwidth communication is now hideously throttled by the overhead of normal standard communication protocols. How much of a problem this is will be further described in Chapter 5.

Since VIA is an interface specification, it does not, of itself, immediately reduce overhead. It could even be implemented on top of a high-overhead communications protocol, just adding to the problem; this might actually be desirable for portability and application debugging on systems without other support, and undoubtedly will be done by someone. However, unlike common protocols like TCP/IP and UDP/IP, it is designed to allow a software and hardware implementation that is efficient.

VIA uses three techniques to reduce communication overhead: **zero-copy messages**; **elimination of interrupts**; and **user-mode (virtualized) communication**. Each of these is discussed below.

"Zero-copy messages" refers to the fact that most standard communications facilities effectively require that message data get copied at least once within the sending system before they are actually transmitted. This can occur for several reasons:

> Communication protocols commonly require appending or post-pending header and trailer information on the message data. These additions hold information like the length of the message, information about the recipient, its priority, error-correction codes such as checksums, and so on. Since most communications adapters require that their data be neatly packaged as a single contiguous block of memory, these additions require copying the data so the additions can be made contiguous with it. In some unoptimized implementations, multiple copies are made as the message is passed through different layers of the communications stack. At least one particularly bad case required as many as five copies before the communications adapter was finally invoked. The receiving side can require just as many copies by the time the data is finally placed where the user wants it.

> The data the user wants to send may itself not be a contiguous block in memory to begin with. For example, the data might be a row of an array that is held in column-major order, so the row is actually in many separate locations separated by a regular address stride; or, the message data might be inherently disconnected, consisting of many separate data items—this usually being the case for the arguments of a remote procedure call, where pulling the separate data items into a contiguous structure is called "marshalling."

> Surprisingly, the defined characteristics (semantics) of the message may require copying for greater efficiency. In most message systems, the application is free to alter the data sent immediately after a send() invocation returns; it sends the data present then, not something else. In this case, copying the data to a buffer to await the attention of a slow or very busy communication adapter allows the application to continue doing something useful while communication takes place in the background.

Whatever the reason it is done, copying can be a source of considerable overhead when large amounts of data are transmitted on fast, error-free communications media. VIA allows avoiding copying—"zero copies"—by two means: First, it includes scatter/gather lists in the specification of the data to be transferred or received. These are lists of the addresses and lengths of data to be concatenated into one message for sending, or used on receipt to say where the data goes; this takes care of the first two items in the list above. To take care of the third, VIA does a second thing: it provides for asynchronous send operations that may return to the application before the data has actually been sent. Changes to that data made after the send operation returns will willy-nilly be included, unless the application waits for the send's completion. For VIA's intended use, the operation of high-speed communication hardware, this wait may not be long. Asynchronous sending has been done many times before in other message passing architectures, but involves the overhead of an interrupt to signal completion.

That brings us to the second technique VIA uses to reduce overhead: the elimination of interrupts. While the number of interrupts presented by typical LAN and WAN communications adapters is often quite high, this doesn't have to show to the application and so isn't an intrinsic overhead. What does show is communications of events to the user program, such as "message received" and "message send completed" (for asynchronous send operations). For short coordination messages, which the application has nothing to do but wait for, the overhead of the system fielding the interrupt (thus trashing the cache, discussed in Chapter 6) and passing it down to an application program can be considerable.

Furthermore, there is an 80/20 rule involved here: 80 percent of all messages are short affairs whose purpose is primarily inter-system coordination, not massive data transfer. Measurements and estimates of "short" vary by system and use, but it's not uncommon to find that 80 percent of all messages are 200 bytes or less in length. One study showed 99 percent of messages less than 200 bytes in TCP/IP traffic [KP97], and one study of transaction processing showed *all* messages less than 200 bytes [KAP97].

It does not make sense to go through interrupt processing to receive a 200-byte message sent at a Gigabit or faster, particularly when, as is often the case for coordination, the program has absolutely nothing to do but wait for that message. So VIA allows for efficient polling, meaning a program loop that simply keeps asking "Are we there yet?" like an obnoxious kid in a car. This does use CPU time, but the application can instantly respond as soon as "we're there" with no additional hidden overhead; this tradeoff is right for many fast, small communications events. In addition, VIA provides for using a single polling operation to check for the presence of multiple outstanding messages; this is particularly useful to the coordinator of multiphase group operations such as two-phase commit; these are important in high availability and transaction processing, as is further explained in Chapter 12.

The third item VIA provides for reducing overhead is arguably the most important. It is in any event certainly the most elaborate, and the source of the "virtual" in "Virtual Interface Architecture"[7]: **user-mode communication**, or more specifically **virtualized communication**.

7. Which certainly ranks right up there with ATM as one of the worst names of all time. A "virtual interface" to what?

The problem this addresses concerns the sharing of communication hardware within a node. All communications hardware—adapters and the switching fabric itself—must be shared among not just programs running on different systems but programs running on the same system. Multiple applications coexist on the same node and each, necessarily if they run in parallel across cluster nodes, wishes to communicate to others elsewhere. Even single large subsystems or applications, running in parallel across nodes, usually have separate elements that must communicate with their counterparts elsewhere, independent of any other communication taking place.

In normal LAN and WAN communication, using standard protocols, this sharing is accomplished by software that runs in system mode (also called supervisor state, privileged mode, and so on). That code is up inside the operating system, running in that special mode that allows it to directly access the communications adapter hardware. User-mode (or problem state, and so on) normal applications and subsystems cannot have such direct access precisely because the hardware is shared. No one program "owns" the adapter or knows what another is doing, so no program is allowed to manipulate it directly. Instead, application programs must perform communication by requesting it of the operating system through a system call. This immediately incurs the overhead of switching state. In addition, significant amounts of information must be manipulated inside the system to track who is using which adapter for what and where it is in the course of a communications event.

This is precisely the same thing an operating system does for nearly all hardware resources: The system shares them among multiple, competing processes. It is one of the primary functions of an operating system to share resources like this: disks, printers, processors, memory, and so on.

However, in nearly all computers, the software has some hardware assistance for carrying this out in the case of memory: Virtual memory facilities—segment and page tables, memory translation hardware and the like—enable the system to keep out of the way once it has established the sharing pattern it deems appropriate to the requests received, since software interpretation of every memory access would be an intolerable burden of overhead.

VIA defines something similar for communications. It defines a multitude of "virtual" communications adapters that can be used directly by applications, in user mode, without resorting to software-implemented sharing. If the actual communication hardware doesn't support this, the usual software-interpreted sharing can be done. However, VIA's software interface was designed to allow a direct hardware implementation of this "virtualization" of communication, and a reference implementation was done by Intel before releasing its proposal for comment.

This effectively elevates inter-machine communication to the same status as memory access: Not something done at long intervals using slow devices, but a normal element of program execution that gets the hardware support it needs to be done often, and efficiently. And it's about time, I say.

So VIA makes a strong bid for significantly lowering communication overhead by eliminating copying, interrupts, and the need to run interpretive operating system code to multiplex communications hardware.

But it does not guarantee reliable communication.

The position being taken as this book is written (mid-1997) is that reliable communication should be a vendor option, provided, should a vendor feel like it, as their added value. The data received so very efficiently in user mode cannot be trusted. It may be incorrect, have parts missing, or have sections out of order. This follows the communications "datagram" model, in which the reliability of message transmission is a function of the application, not of the communications subsystem. This is a viable model, of course; it is used in UDP/IP, to which VIA performance is most often compared. However, it also stands in sharp contrast to ServerNet, and, like UDP/IP, implies that the user-mode code must effectively implement those portions of the communications stack that fix up communications problems.

Presumably one could provide different software communications libraries that either provide this function or, if reliable hardware is installed, don't have it. The complexity of doing that in the context of zero-copy communications does seem like a challenge, however.

An advantage of this definition is that it allows relatively simple hardware to implement VIA's virtualization while using ATM as a communication fabric, since ATM, having been designed primarily with voice communication in mind, will when pressed drop packets and deliver things out of order (you'll never hear it). Intel's reference implementation uses ATM.

This unreliability makes one wonder about the use of the term "System Area Network" for VIA. The stated intent is to deal with inter-node communication first, and later with I/O, in a revision of the specification. If that is done, the reliability issue must be addressed as was discussed earlier (page 111), unless I/O adapters all become rather more intelligent than they are now.[8]

---

8. This possibility is not slightly foreshadowed by Intel's otherwise unrelated I₂O effort, which standardizes device interfaces and moves parts of what is now in system device drivers onto microprocessors located in I/O adapters.

Several of the features of VIA already exist in many communications systems. Some vendors have adapters with scatter/gather facilities, which they use with special implementations of standard protocols to eliminate copying; and many communications systems have asynchronous send/receive primitives. However, none that I am aware of offer the possibility of virtualizing communications in hardware. Perhaps most importantly, none has really caught on as a widely-implemented standard used in the normal course of events by the people who bring value to clusters—the subsystem and application developers. The industry position of the participants in VIA may, if it is wholeheartedly adopted with adequate implementations by many system vendors, be enough to bring about this necessary widespread use.

5.5.3   DEC Memory Channel

On the other hand, it's hard to have lower overhead or more virtualized than a single store instruction.

That's the basis of Memory Channel (MC) [Gil96, LBD$^+$96], which DEC obtained from Encore, who obtained it in a merger with Gould (where it was originally named "Reflective Memory"). Once it has been set up, a user-mode store instruction on one node of a cluster causes its data to be written directly into one or several other node's memories. The setup does require operating system intervention, but once that is accomplished, it's all user mode operation; normal memory-mapping hardware provides the protection between user programs that virtualization requires.

DEC's current PCI-based implementation, illustrated in Figure 24, works using two things: the fact that PCI I/O adapters are memory-mapped, meaning that loads and stores can be directly received and operated on by adapters; and additional memory mapping tables contained in each MC adapter.

Using the first fact, the normal memory mapping facilities of the processor are set up so that a section of a transmitting program's (really process') address space points into a section of the addresses that are owned by the MC adapter. Different processes get mapped to different sections, which is part of how virtuality is achieved. On the receiving side, tables in the MC adapter are set up to make that corresponding section point into a region of the receiver's memory; different receiving processes use different sections of memory. The receiver's section of memory must also be flagged by the operating system as not pageable (also known as "wired" or "pinned"); it wouldn't do to have that be on a disk when the write comes through.

Figure 24 DEC Memory Channel

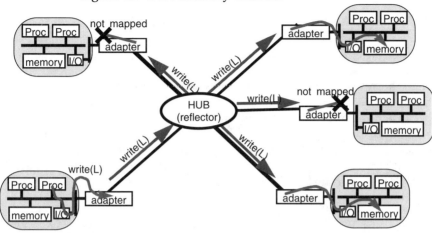

When the transmitter does a store into that mapped section of its address space, the adapter picks it up and sends it off to a hub that indiscriminately broadcasts it to all the nodes, as shown in the figure. If some receiving processor at a node has mapped that section into memory, the store is done to that memory; otherwise, it gets ignored. In the five-node cluster of Figure 24, two of the possible receivers store the data and the other two ignore it.

In most cases, MC is used with exactly one receiver so it provides node-to-node communication. Such one-to-one communication can be used to send messages between nodes by code like this:

```
                    /* Start with flag == FALSE */
/* Processor in Node Able */          /* Processor in Node Baker */
while (...) {*abuf++ = <message source>    while (!FLAG); /* wait */
}                                          /* read message */
flag = TRUE;
```

The processor in Able simply performs a loop of stores until the data has all been sent, and then sets a flag. The processor in node Baker continuously tests that flag, in what's called a spin loop, until Able has set it; then the data has all arrived and can be used.

There is, however, a crucial assumption being made here: The stores by Able get performed over in Baker in exactly the same order they were issued in Able. Were the flag set before some of the data had arrived, Baker could see wrong data. This is by no means guaranteed in all memory or memory-like systems (see Section 6.5 in Chapter 6). In this case, however, the combination of PCI bus operation and MC does guarantee it.

Even though they're in order, however, the transmitter doesn't necessarily know when the stores in the receiver(s) are finished. There could, for example, be contention at the hub with other nodes using the MC, causing an unpredictable delay. In any event, the operation is far from instantaneous: It can take several microseconds for a store to complete. If the transmitter needs to know when data has actually been received—and it often has to, because until received an error could occur, invalidating the transmission and requiring recovery—something else must be done: The transmitter should set his own adapter to take his own messages and send them back to him. It wasn't shown in Figure 24, but the hub reflects everything back to everybody, including the original transmitter; when he gets it, everybody has it.

Obviously, while MC does use normal store operations and appears to be a kind-of-maybe-perhaps-sort-of-like shared memory, it is not particularly intuitive to use it as a shared memory mechanism. DEC's documentation, in fact, warns that "in some cases" it might be better to just build a message-passing library and use that. I would be stronger: With a very few special-case exceptions, no sane and intelligent programmer should try to use this as shared memory. (The situation is very different with another type of system, usually called "NUMA," that is discussed in Chapter 5. NUMA hardware is also very different from MC hardware.)

DEC has implemented popular message-passing program libraries on MC (including PVM and MPI), and those constitute a far more judicious way to use it. Even through those higher-level interfaces, good performance can be attained; it's reported that even for very short messages, 40M bytes/second throughput can be achieved, with five microsecond latencies; longer messages get up to over 60M byes/second for point-to-point traffic, which is a sizeable fraction of the current implementation's hardware peak rate of 100M bytes/second. (Note that this capacity is, however, shared by all the computers connected through MC, since it is a broadcast medium.)

There are, however, some special cases that can be worthwhile. It's reported, for example [GK97], that Oracle's Parallel Server database initially suffered a bottleneck on DEC TruCluster using Memory Channel because it couldn't hand out the globally successive serial numbers (system commit numbers) it needed fast enough; those are used in the database log to keep track of which transaction is which. Special purpose shared-memory-like code, using the MC's multicast capability, was written that fixed this case. I would add that it was probably done by extreme experts, writing very carefully.

5.5.4   The S/390 Parallel Sysplex Coupling Facility

With the exception of the special case just mentioned, the cluster hardware assists so far discussed have focussed on the basics: moving bits from point A to point B with low overhead and/or high reliability. This is obviously necessary. However, it is hardly sufficient to get a fully functioning cluster.

Higher-level functions, built using that communication, must also be performed. Exactly which higher-level functions are needed depends heavily on the general organization of the software run on a system, particularly on whether the "shared data" or the "shared nothing" philosophy is used. For many hardware vendors, a consistent choice of one of these is not possible. Much of the substantive function run on their systems is provided by other companies over which the hardware vendors have no direct control. So, for the most part, cluster hardware vendors have contented themselves with doing basic communications well, and letting other companies build their own unique higher-level functions on top of that. Shared-nothing leaves few openings for support beyond fast, efficient communication, anyway, so explicit hardware support tends to smack of favoritism towards one or a few software vendors (to be avoided) and is difficult to justify since it's not widely applicable to everybody.

There are exceptions to this. They are the whole system vendors, rather than just hardware vendors, who have written a substantial portion of the software that most usually runs on their own hardware—practically the definition of "proprietary" systems. Since they own key software elements, if they're interested in clusters there is the possibility of consistently choosing one philosophy and then providing higher-level support for it. Several have done this. Notable examples are: Tandem, which has always chosen shared-nothing, and has always provided special communications hardware like ServerNet; DEC, particularly wearing its VMScluster hat, which did shared data hardware such as the Star Coupler in the past and whose more recent efforts will be discussed later; and IBM's S/390 products.

In the late 1980s, IBM's S/390 Division decided that for a variety of reasons shared-data clustering was the way to go. The history has been recounted in Chapter 2; the technical rationale is spelled out in [KDY97]. They proceeded to incorporate specific support for that paradigm in both their hardware and system software, calling that the Parallel Sysplex **Coupling Facility** (CF) [NMCB97]. As the necessary dropping of the second shoe, they also incorporated CF exploitation in all the major subsystems under their control—databases, file systems, system management, workload balancing, communication, transaction monitors, etc. [AE$^+$97, BARM97, BDM97, Joh97, JMNT97, Str97] Several important subsystems not written by IBM also exploit the CF; for example, Oracle has a version of their Parallel Server that exploits the CF on S/390s.

So, what is it? Conventional marketing diagrams (like the one I used on page 38 in Chapter 2) show the CF as a mysterious disembodied triangle floating among the nodes of the cluster, giving the impression—at least, it initially gave me the impression—that it's some fancy hardware stunt box that does all kinds of high-level functions in hardware.

Nonsense. It's a plain old S/390, a regular general-purpose computer, as shown in Figure 25. It's just got a code load specialized to perform just the coupling facility functions, and those with great efficiency.

Figure 25 Parallel Sysplex Coupling Facility

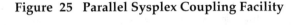

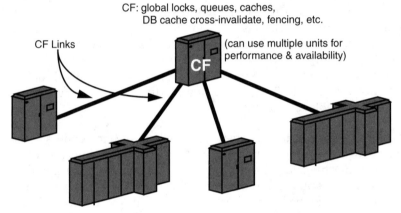

CF: global locks, queues, caches,
DB cache cross-invalidate, fencing, etc.

CF Links

(can use multiple units for performance & availability)

CF

There is, however, a sense in which Figure 25 is also misleading, since a CF is not likely to be a stand-alone physical piece of hardware. It's more likely to be what's called a "logical partition" of one of the S/390 multiprocessors in the complex—either some processors, memory, and I/O separated out and dedicated to that function, or, effectively, a very low-level (below the OS) "time share" of processors and memory that's similarly dedicated. So Figure 25 is effectively a "logical" view: There's a cluster node that's been singled out to do the CF functions for the Sysplex. That functional centralization could result in a serial bottleneck in the parallel operation of the cluster, but does not because it can be expanded as required. The CF can be a multiprocessor (SMP), or even several, effectively forming a cluster-within-the-cluster for additional power and, importantly, high availability; if a CF "node" fails, its duties can effectively be failed over to another.

For the coupling facility to do its jobs, there must be fast and reliable communications to it.

OK, that's one instruction.

Well, if you've got a complex instruction set, why not use it? A single added S/390 instruction transfers data using the **coupling facility links** (CFLs) to the CF (meaning, between nodes) and sets a flag there; that flag is polled by the CF code, avoiding the overhead of an interrupt. The CFL also provide gather/scatter as was described for VIA. It is used to allow zero-copy transfer of large data blocks, possibly discontiguous, directly into CF data structures that store data in fixed-size units to simplify storage allocation.

CFL communication is not user-mode, but that matters less because its use does not require a task switch. The program goes into system state without changing address space, something that is possible in OS/390, Windows NT, VMS, and some other operating systems, but not UNIX; then it checks arguments for validity; executes the instruction; and returns. Communication can be synchronous—done immediately, completed when the instruction finished—or asynchronous, in which case the instruction completes before communication is over. In the latter case, bits are set when communication completes, allowing the program to test for completion without an interrupt. With the current (mid-1997) link speed—100M bytes/sec—the developers decided to use the asynchronous version when more than a page (4K bytes) is transferred in one instruction.

However, there's still a large difference from the cluster accelerators previously described, because communication to the CF isn't just movement of bits. What is transferred is a CF command and the data needed to do that command. The commands perform a wide variety of high level, cluster-wide functions:

➢ node registration, used to identify a node with the CF for other functions; a node registers its existence with the CF when it first joins the cluster.

➢ global queues, used for workload balancing across the cluster by the OS and subsystems; a piece of work can be noted on a queue for any node to perform. They are also used as "mailboxes" for inter-node communication, and can have other functions. Queues can be LIFO (normal queueing), FIFO (push-down stack queueing), sorted by a specified key, sorted LIFO or FIFO within a key synonym, and so on. I've been told that one would be hard-pressed to find a data structure in Knuth Volumes 1 and 3 [Knu97a, Knu97b] that isn't supported.

➢ create, acquire, and release global locks, used to establish ownership of globally-held data (the function of locks is discussed in Chapter 9, and their use in shared data systems discussed in Chapter 10). These are fairly high-function locks, actually implemented as a form of queue.

➤ fast cluster-wide caching of data; this provides a globally-accessible place to put things that are updated (read and written) by several cluster nodes.

➤ "fencing": disconnecting a node both from other nodes and from all I/O. As will be discussed in Chapter 12, this function is required when it is suspected that a node has failed.

➤ functions for cross-invalidation of buffers in different nodes. This seemingly obscure function is used to make the caching of data on each node more efficient in a shared data environment; it is discussed in Chapter 10 (Section 10.5.4 on page 336).

➤ some combinations of the above. For example, a single command can lock a section of a queue (or a whole queue) inside the CF and insert data into it, or atomically swap data: put this data in, and return the data that was there.

All of these are functions that must be done by somebody in a shared-data cluster—and several, like fencing, mailboxes, and others, are useful or required in shared-nothing clusters, too. For example, the seemingly over-the-top sorted queue function is used extensively since it can create, in one fell swoop, a cluster-wide log: Log records are sent to the CF, sorted by a cluster-wide timestamp, and pulled in FIFO order onto one or more a log devices. This is used by many subsystems, including both file and database systems, to ensure transaction semantics. (This is discussed in more detail in Chapter 12, "High Availability.")

Each "communication event" in Parallel Sysplex actually does an entire function of the kind listed above, not just a simple movement of bits from one point to another. In one instruction? Well, the data structures feeding that instruction—function code, pointers to data, etc.—have to be set up, and that will require multiple instructions. But having been set up, a single instruction acquires a system-wide lock, or enqueues data, or sorts and merges a cluster-wide log, or whatever. Note that while it's one instruction in a normal cluster node, it can consume multiple instructions on the CF.

The CF is actually a functional, or architectural, specification. Any implementation that provides that set of functions can be used. Figure 25 on page 122 need not be even a virtual description of Sysplex in the future. Right now it describes the centralized implementation that was done, but nothing prohibits others. For example, the CF functions could be performed in a distributed manner, spread across all the cluster nodes, using something like Memory Channel as the underlying hardware support. Nothing prohibits it, that is, but one heck of a lot of reprogramming. For that reason, I wouldn't expect a change any time soon.

The intention of providing all these functions, not just raw communication, is system-level efficiency. All of the CF functions have an implementation that is fast enough—unlike I/O operations, for example—that there is no reason for the OS to switch to another task while they are being performed. Locks and, in particular, the cross-invalidation functions mentioned above, don't even require communication with the CF in many cases. Instead, the CF broadcasts key data back out to all the nodes, where it is held locally in special bit vectors. It is tested there first, locally, to see if (for example) the data is known valid; explicit communication to the CF is brought into the act only in the "hard" cases that must take more time anyway. This is in sharp contrast to traditional distributed implementations of cross-machine locks, which in nearly all cases begin with inter-node communication that takes long enough to warrant task switching or other multiprogramming while waiting for the communication, not even the function, to complete. Several of the SAN and Memory Channel communication techniques described earlier in this chapter also target efficiency that is at this level, and their actual successful use in this mode will likely be reported at some point.

All of this exists to obtain higher system efficiency. Does it work?

When Parallel Sysplex were first announced, IBM discussed efficiency in a way that must go down in the annals of the industry as the paradigmatic example of shoot-yourself-in-the-foot, self-toxic marketing. Everybody else talks about speed*up* and how much *more* performance than single nodes their clusters produce. IBM proceeded to describe only the *slowdown*—the performance *loss* you get: Coupling two systems with Sysplex was described as having an *overhead* of 20 percent for two systems, 21 percent for three, and so on, the formula being 20%+(1% x (N-2)), where N is the number of nodes.

This happened during the time when Lou Gerstner's dog joke[9] was in full force, so naturally IBM was pilloried by unsympathetic computer industry analysts. Several of those had already been converted to the "NUMA" religion (to be discussed in Chapter 5) and used this as an excuse to say "NUMA good. Clusters bad. Dummy IBM following old-fashioned, inefficient, bad paradigm. Bad IBM. Buy other computers. Sell stock."

IBM probably thought it had to talk about things this way because many customers already had multiple systems, and wanted to know how much it

9. At the height of the "mainframes are dead" IBM-bashing, Lou Gerstner said that if he were to invite the press to his house to see his new dog, and he threw a stick into a lake and the dog walked on water to fetch the stick, then the next day's headline would be "Gerstner Buys Dog That Can't Swim."

would cost them in performance to get the availability and manageability benefits of Parallel Sysplex.

On the other hand, IBM really could publish a chart like the one in Figure 26, which shows the current true situation.

Figure 26 Parallel Sysplex Commercial Speedup

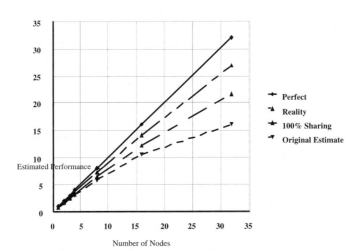

In that figure, the overhead formulas IBM has published [IBM97] are converted into speedup results: How much performance you get compared to a single node's performance, compared with perfection (the top solid line). The original published estimate that sticks in everybody's mind is shown as the bottom line. Since the time that was published, however, there have been improvements to the Coupling Facility Links, the CF code, and exploitation of the CF by subsystems. They have lead to the second line from the bottom: 17% overhead for a two-node system, plus 0.5% for every node added. Even that, however, doesn't reflect reality. The reason lies in the workload.

The industry in general is likely to compare any result with TPC-C, and for reasons discussed in detail in Chapter 14, TPC-C is not a good cluster benchmark. You could get excellent performance scaling on TPC-C even if the cluster nodes were connected using a pack train of camels. The exact composition of the workload IBM uses in these comparisons is unfortunately known only to IBM, and, for reasons best known only to their engineers, is overly pessimistic compared with what is seen in the field. In particular, it assumes that every element of data accessed in the Sysplex is shared across all nodes, so every data access must undergo the overhead of cross-system locking and coherence management. This situation is noted in the graph as "100% Shared." In comparison, TPC-C shares *at most* 15%, and in many cases less than that; this is a serious underestimate of what's seen in the field. What IBM now states that its customers are seeing, however—reality—is about one-half the overhead of the 100% shared case, which is the line immediately below "Perfect" in Figure 26. This corresponds to overhead of only 8.5% in the two-node case, with only 0.0025% added for each additional node.

Do note, however, that these graphs extrapolate beyond the level of experience. No customer has reported that low overhead for a 32-node Sysplex, simply because there are no 32-node Sysplexes installed anywhere. One was on order. Then a new generation of faster processors was announced and, as a result, the number of nodes required to do the job dropped by more than 50%. (See, the microprocessors are still getting faster...)

What about the other guys? Do ServerNet, Memory Channel, VIA, whatever, also fulfill their goal of higher performance? Unfortunately, there's no way to tell. Everybody else relies on the TPC-C benchmark, and that would show good scaling on clusters whose communication consisted of trained mice that ate the data on one node, then ran over and deposited it on the other.

5.5.5 High Function, Low Function

There is no question that IBM's Parallel Sysplex Coupling Facility contains the richest set of cluster functions yet discussed. Does that mean it's necessarily the best? This is profoundly unclear. There is a possible difference in implementation level and a difference in general support philosophy to take into account here.

The difference in level arises because the CF functions are, in other systems, implemented inside the operating system. The most clear example of that is DEC OpenVMS Cluster. Memory Channel (for example) is most closely analogous to just the Coupling Facility Support Facility, a sub-element that runs the CF Links; the other function that IBM puts in the CF is there, but considered part of OpenVMS. On the other hand, Memory Channel doesn't have an opcode for "merge this record into a system-wide log sorted by time," and the CF does; so something more than just the position of a function is involved here. It's a difference in viewpoint.

One school of thought—call it the high-function school—holds that the underlying system should provide rather high-level functions that directly perform operations required by applications or subsystems. These functions can then be heavily optimized, at multiple levels, within the system.

Another school of thought—call it the slick & simple school—holds that the specific features required for a wide variety of programs form a very broad set that can't be predicted in advance. So the best form of support is very efficient low-level functions that don't do much by themselves, but do allow applications and subsystem to build anything whatever they want in an efficient fashion.

The high-functioneers accuse the slick & simples of avoiding the hard decisions and not providing any real function. The slick & simples accuse the high-functioneers of having a simplistic view of what people will want to do, and say that if a program doesn't need exactly the particular high function provided, it can incur much more overhead working around it. They also talk a lot about layering and structure, giving the high-functioneers a chance to talk about the performance loss that results from going through all those layers, to which the slick & simples reply that their well-defined interfaces make it easier to exploit new technology sooner, and so it goes.

Like many other dichotomies, this argument isn't resolvable. It certainly doesn't exist solely, or even primarily, in the cluster context. The classic case is the original UNIX (slick & simple) versus nearly every prior operating system (high function). In another arena: Microsoft Windows and OS/2 Presentation Manager are high-function windowing systems; X-windows, on the other hand, is slick & simple (well, simple, anyway). The same issue often appears within or around arguments of mechanism vs. policy, but it runs deeper than that. Slick & simple is certainly the more popular approach in academia, but that doesn't guarantee correctness, just familiarity by recent graduates.

In the terms of that dichotomy, systems providing basic, fast, low-overhead facilities—like the SAN efforts and DEC's Memory Channel—are operating in a slick & simple context. They quite likely will never want to directly provide the kinds of capabilities that the high function Parallel Sysplex offers. So it is in a real sense not fair to directly compare them with it.

However, these schools aren't mutually exclusive. In particular, within Parallel Sysplex, there is layering: The part that concentrates on moving data and transferring commends between nodes is a separable part, called the Coupling Facility Link Support. Except for its orientation to transmitting commands, it is at least somewhat analogous to the communications elements of others.

Interestingly, there's also a subset of the Parallel Sysplex implementation that's at least slightly slick & simple, namely the part that does locking. This arose because the various subsystems that were to be supported—including DB2, VSAM, CICS, and others—already had their own, highly idiosyncratic, locking facilities that did exactly what those subsystems wanted, but did it only within one node (one SMP). To change the code of all the subsystems to use one new high-level Sysplex-wide lock manager was not feasible. So the

In Search of Clusters ✳

lock facility of the CF is, in effect, a slick-ish & simple-ish "lock manager toolkit" that can be, and was, used to re-implement the lock managers of the various subsystems to make them cross-machine, Sysplex-wide lock sub-systems (as well as providing lock recovery if a node or a CF fails). As a result, the locks native to Parallel Sysplex look—hold your breath for this one—positively *primitive* in comparison to other high-level full-function locking facilities like those in DEC's OpenVMS operating system to support VMScluster. The function is still, of course, gargantuan compared with sub-systems that solely concentrate on communication.

A final comment about cluster hardware in general: This chapter contrasts very strongly with the one following, which deals with symmetric multipro-cessors. In that case, due to the widespread use of SMPs, not only are the requirements far more clear (although not well understood outside a limited technical coterie), but a huge number of incredibly sophisticated techniques for meeting those requirements have been developed and published.

Symmetric Multiprocessors

Symmetric multiprocessors (SMPs), NUMA systems, and clusters are the primary forms of lowly parallel computing. Since they address approximately the same range of parallelism, they can strongly overlap each other in aggregate performance and other characteristics. Yet they differ, grossly in some ways—overall system organization and programming model, for example—and more subtly in others, such as their utilization of memory. Since their overlap often makes them competitors, a comprehensive discussion of the differences is very important. That comparison appears several chapters later, because it must be a system discussion incorporating both hardware and software issues.

It's obviously impossible to understand such a comparison without understanding the relevant characteristics of SMPs. Hence this chapter, which is not about clusters at all. It is a discussion of the characteristics of the other lowly parallel system, the SMP. The next chapter takes on NUMA, and necessarily follows this one, since the technical basis of NUMA systems is to be found in SMPs.

Unlike the salient characteristics of clusters, which are at present primarily external to a whole computer (or are software), the crucial characteristics of SMPs are deep in the heart of the hardware. What an SMP looks like to software—its *architecture*—is very important, as will be discussed. But the things that have to be done create that appearance, to implement that architecture—the *machine design*—are where the meaty comparison issues lie. So this chapter gets rather deeper into computer hardware innards than most other parts of this book.

It's not going to be that hairy, however, and there's a reason beyond cluster comparison for paying close attention to this chapter: Inoculation against processor architecture hype. You'll notice that, like much of this book, this chapter is about performance. But it doesn't say much about processors, only about memory systems. In fact, the performance of a computer is now very heavily dependent on memory system performance rather than on processor performance. If the processor is fast enough to push the memory to its limit—and most of them are, as will be explained below—its architecture may not matter very much. What will always matter, however, is how fast and clever the memory subsystem is—a part of the computer that is woefully unsung in the current atmosphere of RISC/CISC/VLIW wars.

6.1 What is an SMP? _____

A symmetric multiprocessor, an SMP, is a computer variation that, well, has multiple processors that are symmetric.

Figure 27   Simplified Diagram of a Symmetric Multiprocessor (SMP)

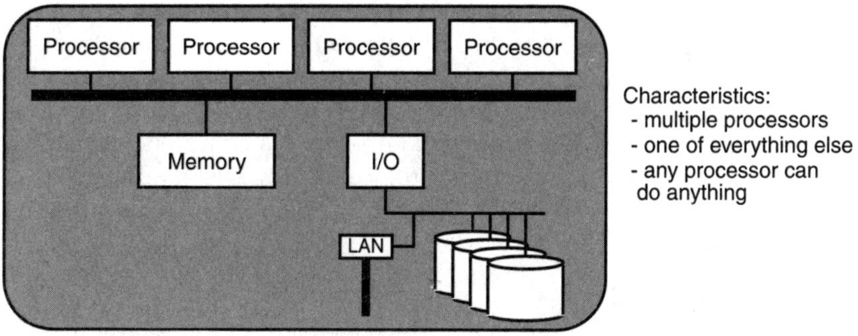

Characteristics:
- multiple processors
- one of everything else
- any processor can do anything

Being a bit more informative (also, see Figure 27):

>   **It has multiple processors.** And *only* multiple processors. It does not have multiple I/O systems, it does not have multiple memories, it does not have multiple anything else, either, like cabinetry. Actually, any of the above can be physically packaged as multiple units, but that is not visible to any program that runs on the machine: ap-

plication, subsystem, operating system, or whatever. Figure 28 shows an example of a multiprocessor that is not an SMP because it has multiple separate memory systems.

Figure 28 Two Multiprocessors that are Not SMPs

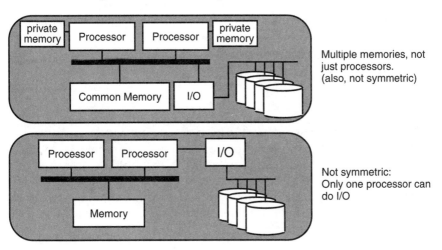

Multiple memories, not just processors. (also, not symmetric)

Not symmetric: Only one processor can do I/O

The fact that there are multiple processors, however, definitely *is* visible to programs running on the machine, although that fact can be hidden from some software by other software. A prime example of a program that hides multiple processors is the operating system. The OS must be exquisitely, intensively aware down to its bones that there are multiple processors, but by default hides that fact from applications. If an application wants to be multiprocessor aware, it can perform operations that find out there are multiple processors and exploit that fact; but by default applications think they're running on a uniprocessor. This is true of every commercially available SMP operating system. It doesn't mean you can't use the multiple processors, just that by default no single program does. Multiple programs, running simultaneously, may. Many database systems are MP-hiders, too. They find out from the OS that there are multiple processors but hide that from their applications. This hiding of the parallel nature of the hardware is key to the SPPS paradigm, which allows plain Jane serial programs to make effective use of SMPs.

➤ **Those processors are symmetric.** What this means is that each of the processors has exactly the same abilities. Therefore, any processor can do anything: They all have equal access to every location in memory, they can all equally well control every I/O device, leap to any interrupt at a single bound, and so on. In effect, the rest of the machine looks the same from the point of view of each processor; hence the term "symmetric." There are multiple-processor systems where this is not true. In a common variant, also shown in Figure 28, all the processors can access all of memory, but only one has the ability to do I/O. Not too surprisingly, these are called *asymmetric* multiprocessors, or, historically, attached processors (referring to the processor that can't do I/O). Such systems can have slightly simpler hardware than SMPs but are less efficient at doing I/O (big surprise) and slightly more difficult to support with system software.

Deviations from these two characteristics are often related, because the most popular way to incorporate multiple memories or I/O systems into a computer is to associate them (tightly) with each of the multiple processors. The top example in Figure 28 illustrates this. There are three memories, which violates the first requirement. However, what primarily makes two of the memories separate is that only one processor can access each—in other words, a violation of symmetry.

SMPs are occasionally referred to as "tightly coupled multiprocessors,"[1] as distinct from "loosely coupled systems," the latter being more or less the systems referred to in the book as clusters. These names open the door to variations on the adjectives—firmly coupled, very loosely coupled, and so on. I have avoided this terminology because it implies that the types of system described are architecturally similar, differing in only one dimension: the mysterious "coupling." In fact, SMPs and clusters differ tremendously along many dimensions, including most of the important issues that concern how they're programmed. Therefore, terms not implying similarity are better. (The "firmly," etc., variations also differ tremendously, a fact hidden by the terms.) Also, the term "tightly coupled" completely misses the necessary emphasis on symmetry that is a crucial element of SMPs; the asymmetric processors mentioned above were, in fact, tightly coupled.

The definition of an SMP is more than just a sterile academic description of one of the legion of possible parallel machines. This definition has teeth because it is what software expects an SMP to be. In the jargon: It is the *programming model* to which software has been written.[2]

---

1. "Tightly Coupled Multiprocessors," as defined by IBM, are SMPs but have additional characteristics. Some of those additions are discussed in Chapter 12.
2. There will be later chapters devoted to programming models. Also, there are elements of the SMP programming model not mentioned here, such as sequential consistency, that are covered later in this chapter.

If a machine does not adhere to this programming model, the difference can in some cases be wallpapered over by system software. For example, suppose only one processor can do I/O. The operating system can run jobs anywhere until they request input or output, at which point they're effectively stopped and rescheduled onto the I/O-enabled processor. This is not as trivial as that sentence makes it sound, but is certainly feasible and has been done. It allows applications and possibly subsystems, like databases, to run on a machine supporting only a non-SMP programming model, with at least some performance degradation.

But in this age of portable system software—UNIX, Microsoft Windows NT, Novell Machine-Independent NetWare, Linux, and others—you must count the cost of altering that standard system, since it has been written assuming the SMP programming model. That will more than likely be far more expensive than just giving in and doing a true SMP, especially when you consider keeping that modified OS up-to-date with every new software release. (The fact that somebody other than hardware development usually pays the bill causes a lot of fights, however.)

That's it. Except for one little thing. Just how many is this "multiple"? How big can an SMP get? *Do SMPs scale?*

There are very possibly few, if any, limits on how many processors sharing memory in some manner can be coupled together. Having to preserve the complete SMP programming model, including total symmetry of memory access, presents graver problems. It is certainly possible that very big SMPs can nevertheless be built, but the cost of maintaining that programming model will increase ever more rapidly as the maximum system size increases.

The question of SMP scaling will be taken up again when SMPs and clusters are compared in Chapter 13, after a great deal more preparation. For one thing, it's necessary to say exactly what "scale" really means. This chapter provides the background needed to understand how SMPs work and therefore to appreciate why there might be difficulties building really big SMPs out of ever more powerful processors.

That background begins, of necessity, with a discussion of computer memories and caches.

6.2   What is a Cache, and Why Is It Necessary?

Memory access and cache memories (or just *caches*) are at the core of many of the issues with SMPs. This section describes caches and relevant aspects of how they work, starting with the question of why they're used in the first place.

Despite the fact that this whole discussion will appear to go into incredibly gruesome detail, it comes nowhere near doing full justice to the richness and complexity of this topic. Caches have been around for a very long time; their first use was on the IBM Stretch 7090 project in the early 1960s. Since then, many extremely intelligent people and a veritable army of lesser lights have spent their entire careers inventing and simulating variations on the theme of caches—simulating, because no completely satisfactory, closed-form mathematical analysis has been devised, although everything from simple linear equations to fractals has been tried. The result of all this frenetic, high-quality effort is an immense store of hard-won information about myriad cache mutations and rococo embellishments. This chapter does not even try to cover them all.

Rather, it focuses only on the key structural elements of caches relevant to SMP design. That alone is a lot; this became—not by design, by any means—one of the longest chapters in this book. I've added a section that at least hints at some of the complexity not covered, both to salve my technical conscience and to avoid being pilloried by the experts, but that section need not be read to understand the overall picture. Far greater detail is available in existing textbooks on computer architecture [HP90, Man93].

6.2.1   The Processor-Memory Speed Problem

Figure 29 shows the basic problem that caches were invented to solve: There is a huge mismatch in speed between memories and processors. I really do

Figure 29   Processor Memory Speed: What's Wrong with this Picture?

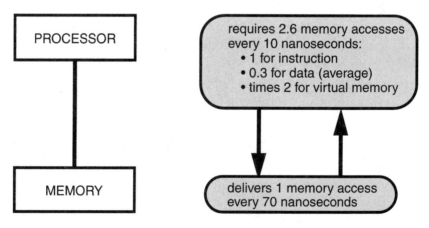

In Search of Clusters ✳

mean huge. Current, typical memories are at least 20 times too slow for current typical processors. Why this happens is described below.

Main memory is commonly built out of inexpensive, large, dense memory chips called Dynamic Random Access Memory or DRAM chips. When such chips are asked for the data stored within them, they take (at present) 50–100 nanoseconds before disgorging the information requested. In the jargon: their access time is 50–100 nanoseconds To keep the discussion simple, let's say such chips take 70 nanoseconds. While that's how fast the memory chips themselves operate, it actually takes much longer to access a large bank of memory chips, correct (or at least detect) errors that might be there, and pass the result to a processor. Thus, 70 nanoseconds is really a gross underestimate, but the problem is quite bad enough for the current discussion if we pretend that the whole memory system runs at chip speeds. So let's do so.

Processors, on the other hand, currently run with a clock speed anywhere from 50 MHz to several hundred MHz. This means that their internal cycle time (1/clock speed) is somewhere between 50 nanoseconds and around 2 nanoseconds Again, to keep things simple, let's take 10 nanoseconds as a typical cycle time, corresponding to a 100 MHz clock.

A modern, superscalar RISC processor works quite hard, and often succeeds, at executing *several* instructions in *one* of those cycles [Joh91]. Some CISC machines whose developers have deep pockets work hard at this, too, and one of the previously highly-hyped phenomena in town is "very large instruction word" (VLIW) machines that may attempt to do tens of instructions, or more, every cycle. But you certainly don't always get several instructions executed simultaneously. How many do get done depends heavily on the processor, compiler, other hardware factors, and very heavily on the particular program being executed. As a result, on a good RISC you can get anywhere from three or more cycles/instruction to 0.2 cycles/instruction (five instructions/cycle). Again, rather than deal with ranges, let's pick a simple number: one instruction per cycle.

So, what we've got here is a processor able to execute one instruction every 10 nanoseconds and a memory that can respond to a request every 70 nanoseconds This is starting to sound bad. Now: Every instruction (10 nanoseconds) requires at least one, and usually more than one, memory reference (70 nanoseconds). This is rather obviously a major problem. Why are all those references to memory required?

Well, you first have to fetch the instruction itself. That's one reference to memory right there. In addition, the instruction might tell the processor to reference memory—for example, a load instruction saying to copy a memory location into a processor register or a store doing the opposite (for a RISC machine, those are practically the only such instructions). Not all instructions will require a memory reference, but enough do require one that the effect is definitely noticeable. Typically, somewhere around 25-30 percent of all instructions are loads or stores referencing memory [HP90, Joh91]. That means up to 30% of all instructions require an additional memory reference. Adding the reference to the instruction itself, gives us 1.3 memory references (on average) per instruction. Wish we were done, but we're not.

In addition to the above, we have to account for the fact that with modern "general-purpose" computers and operating systems, all but a tiny fraction of memory references are *virtual*—meaning that the memory address given by the instruction (or the program counter, for instructions) isn't really the address in the memory. I'm not going to explain all about virtual memory here. It's a standard technique allowing programs to be written as if there were much more memory than really present; it also keeps programs from stepping on other programs' data, to say nothing of stepping on the other programs themselves. See a textbook on operating systems, such as [Tan92], for more details.

For our discussion, what's relevant is that the virtual address (the one in the instruction or the program counter) has to be checked against a table of bounds for validity and then "relocated"—have a number added to it—to get the real address in memory. Those bounds and the numbers added are kept (where else?) in memory. So every time the processor references memory, it really does so twice: once to get the virtual-memory checking and relocation information, and then again to do the reference that the programmer asked for in the first place. Actually, more than one reference is necessary to get that bound and offset information, but for illustration here we'll just use one; that's bad enough.

Having to get the virtual memory information means that our original 1.3 (on average) memory references per instruction is doubled. The processor somehow has to do $1.3 \times 2 = 2.6$ memory accesses for each instruction. Each one of those memory accesses takes at least 7 times as long as we'd like the whole instruction to take. Since $7 \times 2.6 = 18.2$, we are trying to fit nearly 20 lbs. into a 1 lb. bag.

There is absolutely no point to having such fast processors if they are hobbled by this slow memory. It's like superglueing an eyebolt to a tortoise's shell and chaining a hare to it. What can be done to fix this problem?

6.2.2 Why Faster Main Memory Alone Doesn't Work

Something that obviously suggests itself is using faster memory chips. There are such chips. They're called Static Random Access Memory chips, alias Static RAMs or SRAMs. They operate at the same speed as processors because they're made out of the same kind of circuitry as the processors, rather than the different, smaller ("denser") and slower circuitry used in DRAMs (Dynamic RAMs). This solution has been used in the past on expensive supercomputers. Seymour Cray, the famous supercomputer architect and designer, is alleged to have said "You can't fake what you haven't got" (actually referring to caches), when equipping his original machines that way.

But SRAM chips are far more expensive individually than DRAMs, and you need more of them because each chip holds fewer bits (they're "less dense"). For example, in 1994 I purchased 4 Mbytes of DRAM memory for a PC, packaged on a card, ready to plug in.[3] Those 4 Mbytes cost me $132. At the same time, 256 KBytes of SRAM cache cost $76. This was from the same source, for the same machine, under the same price structure, and like the DRAMs, the SRAMs were packaged ready to plug in. So SRAM in that form costs $76 × 4 = $304/Mbyte, while DRAM costs $132/4 = $33/Mbyte. This is nearly a factor of 10 difference. At those prices, if I had bought 4 Mbytes of SRAM rather than DRAM it would have cost me $1216—which is more than the entire computer cost me including 8 Mbytes of DRAM memory. SRAM main memory is not a solution for people lacking very deep pockets and long arms.

All microelectronics are, however, continually getting faster and cheaper. Will DRAMs catch up with processors? Will SRAMs get so inexpensive they can be used? DRAMs are getting faster, and variations on the DRAM theme are appearing which are even faster. For example, there's Rambus [Ram] and synchronous DRAM (SDRAM) that's available at slightly higher cost than normal DRAM from many manufacturers, and EDO (Extended Data Out) has caught on in PC circles. This will help and may in fact help quite a bit. But speed relative to the processor is what counts, and the trend is for processors to speed up even faster than DRAM memory does. (This is elaborated on in the next chapter.) SRAMs are also getting less expensive, but not fast enough. The problem isn't going away and is more likely to get worse than to get better.

Even if the problem were going away, who wants to wait? The problem exists now. Also, don't forget that processors need more than one memory access per cycle, so completely solving the problem means the memory must somehow be faster than the processor. Forget that. If the memory were made out of some kind of new, faster stuff, everybody would instantly turn around and make the processors out of the same stuff, bringing us back to square one.

---

3. By now, the prices quoted for memory will seem large; but the ratios should stay about the same.

In part this is a vicious (or possibly virtuous) circle: Because caches work so well, as described below, designers are more motivated to improve density (bits per chip) and therefore cost ($ per bit) than to improve speed. This makes caches even more crucial, therefore more universally used, further decreasing the motivation for really fast memory, and so on.

6.2.3   Locality of Reference and Caches

There is a relatively inexpensive way to fix the memory-processor speed problem that works quite well and, as a result, is used by just about everybody, from PCs to mainframes: cache memory. To understand why it works, we must begin by looking not at hardware but at the behavior of most programs.

Programs don't access memory here and there, willy-nilly, in a random fashion that scatters across the entire memory. Instead, they repeatedly read and write a relatively small collection of memory locations over and over again; then they move to a new collection of memory locations and access them over and over; then they move again, and so on. That this is a reasonable assertion can be seen by considering a simple program loop. The instructions in the loop are used over and over until the loop finishes. The same is true for at least part of the data used in the loop: temporary memory locations that hold partial results are reused each time the loop is executed. This behavior of programs is called *locality of reference*. Not all programs have good locality of reference—some really do access memory in a nonrepetitive fashion—but the vast majority have quite a bit of this quality.[4]

It is this program behavior that suggests a solution to the memory speed problem.

Suppose you kept just a small amount of the data from memory, specifically the most recently used part, in a small amount of that fast, expensive memory (SRAM). Snuggle that fast memory up close to the processor, inserting it between the processor and its memory, as shown in Figure 30. Now, whenever the processor requests a memory reference you don't go directly to memory; instead you first quickly check the small, fast memory. If it's there, you return the answer right away—at speed comparable to the processor's speed. If it's not, you trundle off to memory as usual to get the data. But when the main memory (finally) gives you that data, you do two things: Give it to the processor as ordered, and tuck it into that small, fast memory.

---

4. What's described here is more specifically known as "temporal locality," since it operates over time. There is also "spatial locality," which asserts that when a program references one memory location it's pretty likely to reference nearby memory locations too. Spatial locality comes into play later.

That way, subsequent references will find it in the fast memory. Locality of reference means you'll find it in the fast memory quite often and will seldom have to go to the slow main memory. As a result, on average you get much faster memory access. And note: The program doesn't have to change one bit to make use of this; it's fully automatic.

Figure 30   A Cache Memory Between Processor and Main Memory

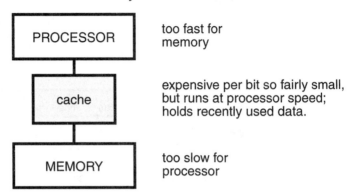

That small, fast memory, holding recently used information, is what is called a **cache memory**. Caches work better than we have any right to expect. How well they work is expressed by what's called the **cache hit rate**. This is the fraction of the time the desired data are found in the cache, normally expressed as a percentage: 100% is perfect: everything's found in cache; 50% means half the time you find what you want in cache; etc. The inverse (0% is perfect) is symmetrically called the **cache miss rate**. The exact numbers achieved for hit rates vary and depend very strongly on the size and other qualities of the cache memory, as well as on the specific program being run. But computer hardware engineers and others concerned with performance get decidedly bent out of shape and instantly start trying to fix things if cache hit rates fall much below 90%. So, at least 90% of the time, your machine acts like it has that expensive fast memory, while you've only paid a very small fraction of the cost. This is one heck of a deal, otherwise known as a wonderfully good engineering tradeoff.

But we noticed that each instruction requires more than one memory reference. As discussed above, you can't go faster than the SRAMs; if you could, you'd build the processor using whatever it was that was faster, and so the memory wouldn't be faster any more. The solution is to use more than one cache and get data out of all of them simultaneously. Result: modern processor-memory subsystems are positively dripping with caches of various types.

For example, Figure 31 shows a system with three caches: One holds instructions, one holds data, and one holds the virtual memory translation information. (The latter is usually called a "translation lookaside buffer" for obscure and primarily historical reasons; it's still a cache). Using all three caches simultaneously, the processor can get an instruction, data and the virtual memory translation information it needs, all at the same time and all in a single one of its own cycles. (Yes, something special must be done with the translation lookaside buffer if two translations—instruction address and data address—are to be done in a single cycle.) (And doing more than one instruction at a time can get even trickier.)

Figure 31   A Processor Festooned with Many Caches

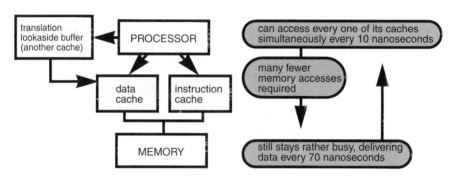

Here's a specific example of the difference a cache can make: The IBM RISC System/6000 model 530 is an aggressively superscalar (five instructions/cycle peak) cached machine. In doing dense linear algebra, it's been demonstrated that the machine can do about 44 MFLOPS when its peak performance[5] is 50 MFLOPS—if it is explicitly programmed to take advantage of the cache [AGZ94]. By such explicit programming, I mean doing two things: First, organize the program so that you reuse data in the cache as much as possible (this will be discussed in "Chunking and Blocking" on page 271 in Chapter 9). Second, include carefully positioned, seemingly useless load instructions whose results you do not immediately use. Their only purpose is to cause data to be moved into the cache ahead of time, so the data are there when they actually are needed. These loads don't slow things down because the RISC System/6000 (in common with other manufacturers' designs) simply keeps doing other instructions until it comes to one requiring the data loaded. Eliminating just the seemingly useless instructions that

---

5. Jack Dongarra of the University of Tennessee, Oak Ridge National Laboratories, and LINPACK benchmark fame, has defined "peak" as the performance the manufacturer guarantees you cannot exceed.

In Search of Clusters ✳

prefetch data, but keeping the reorganization, causes performance to drop from about 44 MFLOPS to around 36 MFLOPS—a 22% loss of performance. Eliminating both optimizations can cause performance to become Very Bad, since completely loading a full cache line (defined later—a hunk of data) from memory to cache can take 18 cycles on that machine, and its memory system is rather aggressive compared to others.

6.2.4   Level 2 Caches

As I hinted a while back, and showed in the example above, I've dramatically understated the slowness of main memory. By the time you send a request to memory, do the access, and send the (multiword) cache line back, it really isn't 7 times slower than typical processors. More typically, memory is 10, 20, or even more times slower. This means a processor is really out to lunch when it has to get data from memory rather than cache—implying a very large cache is appropriate, since the larger the cache, the less often you "miss."

But very large, very fast caches have very large price tags. Another alternative is often used to keep the cost down, called the **level 2 cache** [BW89]. This is, as its name suggests, a second cache inserted between the other caches (now called **level 1 caches**) and memory, as illustrated in Figure 32. The level 2 cache is intermediate in speed between level 1 and memory. For example, it might respond in 5 to 7 instruction cycle times, rather than 10, 20, or more. In addition, there aren't several of them to provide multiple simul-

Figure 32   A Processor with a Level-2 Cache

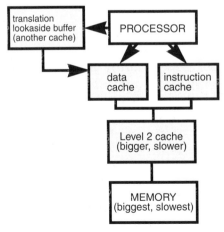

Characteristics		
Element	Typical Size	Typical Speed (nanoseconds)
Processor	(not applicable)	10 ns
Level 1 Caches	10s–100s of KB	10 ns
Level 2 Cache	100s of KB to MBs	40–60 ns
Main Memory	MBs to GBs	100s of ns

taneous accesses. The tradeoff is that it can be larger, which helps immensely in running anything other than tiny programs on tiny data. Commercial processing (database systems, for example) and operating systems aren't small programs and don't operate on small amounts of data, so they can benefit significantly from a large level 2 cache. "Large" in this case is typically somewhere from half a Mbyte to 8 Mbytes, depending on the system's target price and application domain. In contrast, when level 2 caches are used, the level 1 caches are typically in the 8 to 32 KByte range. Some manufacturers have opted for extensive large level 1 caches instead (Hewlett-Packard in particular), but that is the exception rather than the rule.

6.2.5   Cache Lines

Another aspect of caches that will become important in our discussion of SMPs is how much data they get from memory at a time. They certainly don't get only what the CPU asked for, which could be as little as one byte; among other problems, that would require them to manage variable-sized pieces of data, which is hard.

Instead, they grab a fixed- and convenient-sized hunk of data surrounding the address requested. "Convenient" means a power of two and can range from 4 bytes to 64, 128, or even 256 bytes for an aggressive level 2 cache (which typically takes bigger bites than a level 1 cache). **Cache line** is the term for that hunk of data moved between the cache and memory. The term has no mnemonic value I can detect, except for the fact that it is deliberately not the same as "word" or "byte," the units the processor operates on. A cache line is usually at least several consecutive words, all moved in and out of memory and at the same time.

Good-sized cache lines are a good thing for two reasons.

> First, they exploit *spatial locality* of programs. When the processor asks for an instruction, guess which instruction it's most likely to ask for next? Yup, the one right after it in memory. If the cache gets a hunk of memory surrounding the instruction, it's quite likely (but not guaranteed) that when the processor asks next, what it wants will already be there in the cache. Data also exhibits spatial locality, although not to the extent that programs do.

> Second, they allow a designer to get more data faster out of the DRAMs. Many chips can be cycled at once, getting more data in the same time. In addition, most DRAMs have a mode of operation ("page" or "nibble" mode) that takes less time to get data if what's asked for is right next to what you asked for before. So, you can

whip out more data faster if you ask for it in larger chunks, like cache lines.

It's possible to carry this good thing too far, though, which is why I said "good-sized" cache lines above, rather than "big" cache lines. If all the program really wants is one byte and it never refers to any of the other bytes near that one byte, then you've wasted time, and space in the cache, by getting a big hunk of memory rather than a smaller amount. Overall, cache lines at least several words long are a good bet and therefore commonly used.

6.2.6   Now, Let's Simplify Things

All of this complexity of multiple caches with multiple levels and cache lines can be intimidating. Thankfully, it's not necessary to keep it all in mind. In fact, for the remainder of this discussion, we'll ignore the presence of anything but a single data cache, simply labelled "cache," as shown in Figure 33. All the issues we're discussing come up there; nothing is lost.

Figure 33   What to Keep in Mind

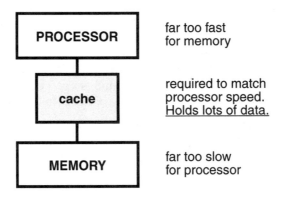

Also, remember that there can be a lot of data in a processor's cache—in many cases, megabytes of it, in fact. And it's kept in hunks, cache lines, bigger than a typical word.

The rest of the discussion above was to prove it and tell you why. Those few things are all you really need to keep in mind.

6.2.7   The Cache as a Messy Desk

Well, almost.

There's an aspect of how caches operate that is crucial to SMPs and has been glossed over so far. It concerns how they function, rather than their size and speed.

Cache memories effectively "know" when the processor starts using some data, since new data isn't in the cache. But caches have no way of knowing when the processor is finished using a given piece of data.[6]

As a result, caches operate using what might be called the "messy desk" principle. Here's the analogy suggesting that name:

Suppose you walk into an office and start to work on some project. You dig the files out of a desk drawer or cabinet, put them on your desk, and work. Then you start something else. No, don't put the old stuff away; restrain your tidiness even if you completely finished the previous job. Just get out the new things you need, find an empty spot on your desk, and work there. Do the next task in another empty spot, and so on. Eventually, of course, your desk will be a mess with no more room left on it. That's when you clear some space off by putting some of the items on your desk back in the files— but only clear enough space to do the next thing you need. Gradually, the next task's stuff replaces older stuff on the desk.

Notice that the desk never, ever gets clean. In fact, except for the initial period when you first start using it, the desk is always completely filled with "old stuff" of various ages. Sometimes this saves you time, since a new task may refer to things you already have out on the desk. In fact, you're maximizing the chance of that by never cleaning things up. (I personally find this a delightful rationalization for the usual state of my own desk.)

Cache memories work exactly like that messy desk: Nothing is emptied out of them until the space it occupies is required for something else.

How this works for caches is illustrated in Figure 34 and Figure 35, which show the life cycle of a cache line.

As illustrated, the life of a cache line has four phases.

1. **Get the cache line**. Initially, let's assume there's nothing in the cache. The processor kicks things off ① by asking for location 23.

---

6. An oversimplification. Several systems have specific instructions allowing the processor to tell the cache to just wipe some stuff out ("**purge**" it) or write it back to memory and then clear the space. But for the most part they're only used in special circumstances; programs aren't usually written to use those instructions.

Figure 34 The Life Cycle of a Cache Line, Phases 1 and 2

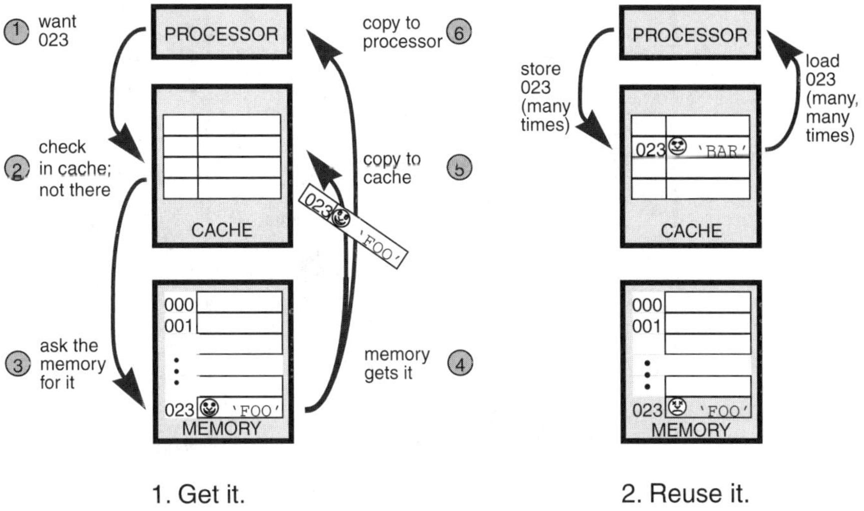

1. Get it.   2. Reuse it.

The cache is checked ② —nope, not there—so we go off to memory, ③ which after a while responds with the contents of location 23. ④ In the illustration, that happens to be the character string 'FOO'. The fact that memory location 23 contains 'FOO' is stored ⑤ in a slot in the cache; simultaneously 'FOO' is given to the processor ⑥, which has been waiting patiently.[7]

2. **Reuse the cache line**. This is the phase that's the whole point of a cache. Assuming the program has reasonable locality of reference, the processor hammers away at location 23 for a while: It writes a new value into it ('BAR'), reads that again, forgets it and reads it a few more times, writes another value ('MUMB'), and so on for quite possibly many, many times. We want it to be many, many times, because each time we find the data in the nice, fast cache rather than that slow, old main memory. No waiting, runs fast, everybody happy.

3. **Ignore the cache line**. (see Figure 35) The program has moved on to other things, so the processor doesn't call on location 23 any more. The cache line for location 23 just sits there in the cache, bored, since nothing tells it to get out. This is the messy desk factor.

---

7. ...to wake up the cat ⑦ who jumps on the modem ⑧ pushing the dip switches ⑨ that put a squawk through the multimedia speakers ⑩ which wakes up the opera singer ⑪ whose scream breaks the monitor... oh, sorry, wrong strip.

Figure 35 Life Cycle of a Cache Line, Phases 3 and 4

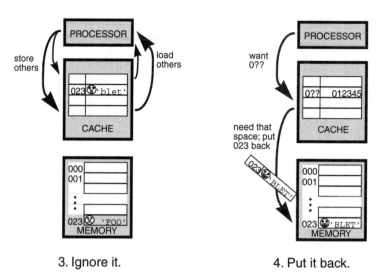

3. Ignore it.   4. Put it back.

4. **Put the cache line back in memory.** At some point, the space that location 23 is using in cache is needed for some new stuff. To clear out that space, location 23 is bumped out of the cache and written back into memory.

That's the life of a cache line.

But, wait a minute. Something odd is going on.

We've been watching the cache. Instead, take a look at the memory in the illustrations. Until the cache line was copied back, location 23 in main memory had the original value in it: 'FOO'. The value in the cache changed to 'BAR', then 'MUMB', and so on, but the memory stayed 'FOO'. So the value in memory is *wrong*. Only when the cache line gets written back does the memory change to the value the processor "thinks" it has—actually, and more importantly, the value the *programmer* thinks it has.

This doesn't matter, of course, because the processor always looks in the cache first, so it always gets the correct memory contents. Right? Right.

Watch this space.

6.2.8   Caches do it at Random

Up to now, I've not said how caches decide which "old stuff" gets put back when you have to make more room on the messy desk. That omission was deliberate, to save a punch line: *Caches do it at random.*

You might think that it would be better to specifically pick the oldest item (really, the least recently used one) and put that away. It would be better, but nowhere near as much better as untrained intuition would indicate. The reason follows from relative sizes.

Even a small cache holds several thousand items (cache lines) from main memory. If you were to close your eyes and randomly pick an item to put away out of several thousand, chances are that you would not pick the exact one you need next, or even one you need pretty soon. Sometimes you'll be unlucky; that's why this method isn't perfect. But most of the time it works rather well—and boy, is it cheap. So it's not optimal, but it is an excellent engineering tradeoff.

An effect of this randomness is that some of the things left on the messy desk can get very old indeed. In fact, you can't predict how long anything will stick around in a cache. It's random! Some things are booted out early and have to be obtained again from memory almost immediately (bad luck). Other things could be loaded into the cache when a machine is first turned on, used exactly once, and then stay there until it's turned off—days, weeks, or months later—just because, at random, they weren't picked to go back into memory.

Those wrong values in memory are corrected only when things are moved out of the cache. That means that values in memory might be quite recent (when bad luck abounded) but they can be wrong for a very long time, too. At random. Since caches can be big (especially level 2 caches), many locations in memory—megabytes—can be randomly wrong. But it doesn't matter, since the processor checks the cache before looking in memory. (Keep watching this space.)

Figure 36 What Else to Keep in Mind

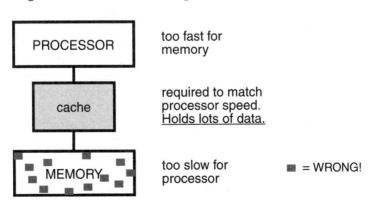

An update to the "What to Keep in Mind" diagram is now appropriate. See Figure 36, which points out that main memory is not only slow, it's measled with incorrect values at random locations.

So much, finally, for caches.

6.2.9   An Aside for the Incurably Precise

The topic of caches is one of the more embellished in computer architecture. To simplify the explanations above, I've made some approximations that stretch the truth a tad, and I've ignored much of the diversity of cache design that exists in contemporary computers.

If you don't care a fig about that, skip to the next section; this one is not necessary to preserve the flow of the discussion. This section may, however, explain a few terms you've heard elsewhere, and fixes some of the inaccuracies for those who already know something of this area. For a far more thorough description, please see a textbook on computer architecture such as [HP90]. Unfortunately, such textbooks all seem to stop short of a good discussion of SMP-related cache issues, which will be our next topic. I suppose there are only so many hours in an undergraduate degree.

First topic: All right, I lied. It's not really random. An algorithm is used, so cache replacement is at best pseudo-random. What happens is that the address of the referenced data is pummeled and mashed to pick a location in the cache memory. If the desired data is there, then you've got it. You find out it's the desired data by storing the full address in an associated memory called "tag memory" along with the data, reading that address out and comparing it with the desired address. If the desired data isn't there (the tag didn't match), whatever is there is put back in memory, and the desired data is fetched from memory and put there.

The picking of the location in the cache's memory is the element that's effectively "random." That location is chosen by shredding the address given by the processor: A scattering of bits from that address is taken; their order is switched around; and they're mixed up with each other by exclusive-ORing some of them together. The process is repeatable: Given an address, it will always pick the same cache location. Nevertheless, no programer can make effective use of that algorithm to predict what's left in the cache, so it might as well be considered truly random. The exact algorithm used—which bits, switched how, exclusive-ORed with what—is seldom if ever published and in any event changes from machine to machine, both between manufacturers and within a manufacturer's product line. Don't get the impression that you can pick any old address bits, do any old thing with them, and get a cache that works well. This is very deliberate, careful shredding whose exact characteristics are established only after a nontrivial amount of work.

Another topic: What's described above is what's called a direct-mapped cache. This is the simplest variety. There are also set-associative caches, which pick a group (set) of 2 (or 4, or...) items at (pseudo-) random as described above. Then within the chosen group, the least recently used one of just the 2 (or 4, ...) is picked and put back in memory. This is a bit more expensive than a direct-mapped cache; figuring out which is least recently used costs circuitry, although not much since it's done over just a few entries. However, it does work better in most circumstances than a direct-mapped cache. For example, going two-way set-associative more or less helps keep data from kicking instructions out of the cache. The general designers' rule of thumb is that a two-way set-associative cache needs half the size of a direct-mapped cache to achieve the same cache miss rate [HP90]; since SRAM is expensive, this is an extremely good thing. Note that the choice for replacement is still mostly (pseudo-) random: There are thousands of sets, versus a small number (2, 4, ...) of things from which the hoariest is picked.

In addition to direct-mapped and set-associative caches, there are also, or at any rate used to be, fully associative caches. These really do figure out the least-recently used of all the data and chuck it out. The expense of figuring that out limits them to very small caches, appropriate in some circumstances but seldom used more generally. Translation lookaside buffers are usually small enough that fully associative techniques are useful and often, but not always, used there.

Yet another topic: The whole running theme that the memory contents can randomly be wrong is a description of a particular cache policy called "write back": The cache remembers that the data has changed and writes it back into memory when that part of the cache is needed for something else. (It never writes back stuff that hasn't changed; why bother?) There's another policy, "write through," that writes data into memory every time the processor writes into the cache. In effect, every store (write) goes "through" the cache to memory. A write-through policy is simpler and therefore cheaper, because you don't have to remember which cache lines are changed—you never have to "write back" anything when making room. This is good. It also keeps main memory correct. This is also good. But it requires more main memory cycles, often many more, which is unbelievably bad in the SMP context we are about to enter. SMPs using it—there are a few in PC-land—are so focused on cost that they don't care at all about performance. (An arguably valid design position, by the way.)

Finally, I've undoubtedly given the impression above that use of a cache always results in faster system performance. That is almost always true and will probably become even more generally true in the future, because processor speeds are increasing faster than DRAM memory speeds. But there are exceptions. If you're running a program with very little locality of reference (it may be incredibly pathological to everybody else, but hey, it's your program), the presence of a cache can slow you down. There's no need to take the time to check whether data's in the cache, for example, because it never is. And the cache will pull a whole cache line out of memory, taking additional time, when your program might use only the first byte out of (for example) 64 bytes; that can *really* hurt. If execution speed is an issue, however, the near-universal deployment of caches makes it wise to look at ways of rewriting that program to increase its locality of reference. You'll probably end up with a more complicated program, but it could end up running 10 or 20 times faster on nearly every computer made.

6.3 Memory Contention

We've almost reached the first main point of this chapter. Plug a second processor with all its caches into a memory, and *voilá!*, we've got a multiple processor system, as shown in Figure 37. And boy, are we in trouble.

Figure 37   A Naive Multiprocessor System with Caches

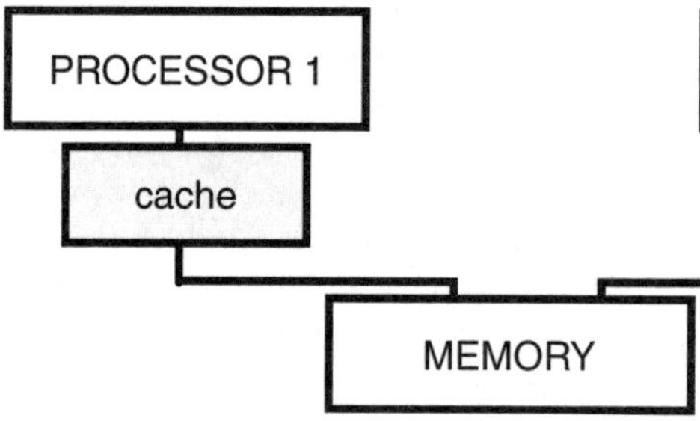

In the first place, even if you could just "plug in" another processor (the memory has to be built to allow that), the whole reason for caches is that a single processor is quite capable of completely overwhelming a memory all by itself, thank you. Remember that a processor's memory appetite is like 20 lbs. trying to fit into a 1 lb. bag, and that was an underestimate. One-twentieth is 5%. If only 5% of the processor's memory accesses "miss" its cache, that memory is *used up*. It is running at full speed and can't produce any more data. Now you know why system designers get bent out of shape when cache hit rates fall below 90%.

Actually, the situation isn't quite as bad as the above description makes it seem, in good part because processors and the programs running on them aren't so boring as to miss cache accesses on a uniform, regular schedule. They smack on the memory a lot, running slowly; then they run full tilt, hitting solidly in the cache with very few misses; then smack the memory some more, and so on. All in all, cache misses have a generally rather jagged behavior profile. (This is why fractals once suggested themselves as a modeling tool.) As a result, one can be smacking away at the memory while the others are buzzing along using cache or at least buzzing a bit between smacks.

Nevertheless, the processors can't run as fast as they could when they were alone. On an irregular but statistically predictable basis, each processor will have to wait because another happens to be using the memory. In other words, the processors now must contend with each other to gain access to a single resource, the memory. That's why this is called "memory contention." It is always mentioned as the conventional canonical reason why SMPs don't scale. (That thinking ignores a great number of interesting things that can be done, as we'll see.)

This particular form of contention is often referred to as the **Von Neumann bottleneck**. It was Von Neumann's original design—and a good one, too—that separated the processor from the memory and put everything, data and instructions, in the "memory organ" of the computer. But if you naively add more processors, you quickly find that the system speed is limited not by the processors but by how fast the memory can produce data: the connection to memory is a bottleneck. As was hinted earlier, with modern (particularly superscalar) processors, it can be a bottleneck for a single processor, too.

6.3.1 Great Big Caches

Without caches, the SMP situation would be hopeless. Well, it would be hopeless with even one processor, so big deal. But with caches, there is the option of making them bigger and bigger until they contain essentially all the data and instructions most programs' locality requires. If the processors very seldom use memory, they aren't likely to run into much contention.

The term "most programs" is particularly application-dependent in this case. There are nontrivial programs that just sit and grind on a fairly small amount of data for a rather long time: Start one of those programs on each processor, and all the processors can buzz along at full speed for quite a while, even with tiny caches.[8] Obviously this doesn't make any of those programs run faster—you get greater throughput rather than faster turnaround time—but at least they don't go slower than they would on a uniprocessor. The system *scales* in performance when running those programs.

Scientific and engineering programs are generally the most likely to have this property of running mostly out of cache. There's no standard term for it, so I'll call it "processor bound" here. (It's not the same as "compute bound," which can have cache misses galore, just no significant I/O.) Not all technical programs are processor bound. Seismic data processing for oil exploration, which literally uses truckloads of tapes[9] as input, is the standard counter-example. Some commercial applications fill this bill, too. For example, I was recently surprised to find that with sufficiently large caches (for example, 4 or more Mbytes per processor—obviously they're L2 caches) many systems that are used to keep track of hotel, car, and other reservations are processor bound, even running under commercial databases. That, however, is the exception rather than the rule for database applications.

Other programs are not processor bound either because they do more input and output operations (we'll get to I/O eventually), or they're parallel and talk among themselves a lot. Or, they may just refer to more data than fits into the processor's cache. That last type may still have decent locality of reference; they've just got a rather large locale. Examples of the latter include operating systems, database subsystems, and communication subsystems. Since such programs are rather widely used, rather large caches appear to be a good idea for SMPs.

This, by the way, is the first indication of why there's a larger cost *per processor* in larger SMPs. If a system is to support more processors, it needs bigger caches to help reduce memory contention. There's a limit, of course; it seldom helps to have much more than 8 Mbytes of cache per processor. But 8 Mbytes is much larger than systems need if they're not designed to scale up. As we've seen, the SRAM memory required makes large caches expensive.

---

8. I know of one program that ran for an entire year at multi-Gigaflop rates and produced as its entire output exactly one single-precision, floating-point number. It was a *very* interesting number. (To be fair, they did do checkpoints, too.)

9. A major oil company actually did the calculation and concluded that, for the distances they were interested in, the highest possible data bandwidth was achieved by 18-wheel semitrailers loaded with tapes. That's as opposed to jumbo jets full of tapes, or all possible electronic transport available to them at the time.

6.3.2   Line Size, Memory Banks, and Pipelining

There are ways to alleviate memory contention that are independent of caches. They rely on understanding a distinction that could be sloughed over up to now (including in our discussions of intermachine communication). The distinction is that between **latency** and **bandwidth**.

Latency is how long something takes. Bandwidth is how much of it you can do in a given time. They're related, but different. Imagine passing buckets of water from person to person in a bucket brigade from a well to a fire. How long it takes any specific bucket to pass down the line from the well to the fire is the latency. How many buckets of water per minute get dumped on the fire is the bandwidth.

The original single processor-memory speed problem is primarily, though certainly not entirely, a latency problem: The memory can't produce a result fast enough. If we've got a cache-memory combination that adequately fixes latency for a single processor, adding more processors is primarily a bandwidth problem. The data can make the trip fast enough; more of it just has to get there simultaneously. How can this be done?

One way to move more data is to increase the cache line size, the amount of data passed to the cache on a miss, and widen the data path over which the data travels—use more wires, so the pipe is wider. This works, but has other ramifications to be mentioned later. It also costs more, since it uses additional pins on the chips, and pins are often more precious than silicon area.

Another technique is to use or increase pipelining in the memory subsystem. Pipelining is exactly like the bucket brigade in the latency/bandwidth example. In this case, you divide each memory operation into successive stages and do each stage simultaneously. For example, one stage might receive requests from the cache, while the next actually runs the DRAMs to retrieve the data for the previous request, another checks for errors on the request before that, and yet another sends the checked data for an even earlier request back to the requesting processor. The only problem here is that the speed is limited by how fast the slow guy in the middle—the DRAMs—can do things. But it definitely helps and only costs a little more in control logic.

Yet another technique is in the category of "blindingly obvious." If you need more water than a well can deliver to a fire, set up another bucket brigade to another well. If you need more data, use more memories. All the processors have to be able to access all those "memories" equally, though, or you've broken the SMP programming model. So, arrange it that there's only one memory as far as the processors are concerned—one collection of addresses—but it's divided into independent units. These are called **banks**, each able to independently and simultaneously read and write data.

This doesn't make any individual memory any faster; the latency stays (about) the same. However, processor 1 can be reading or writing data from bank 1 while processor 2 is doing the same to bank 2. They're not contending with each other as much. That's true at least part of the time, anyway; the rest of the time they want to get at the same bank and so do contend.

Figure 38 A Multiprocessor with Interleaved Memory Banks

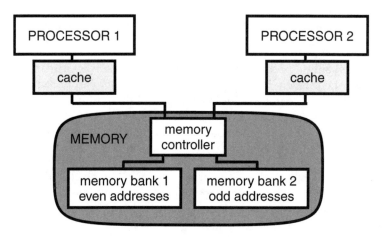

Figure 38 illustrates this. Requests come into a central memory controller from each processor and are directed to one or the other bank depending on the address. Figure 38 also shows the typical solution to a problem banks of memory bring about, namely: Which memory locations do you put in which bank of memory?

You could, for example, put the first N locations in bank one; the second N in bank 2; the third N in bank 3; and so on. That would work, but it starts to bend, if not break the programming model because getting the bandwidth required to scale now means explicitly programming the location of information in memory relative to the banks.

Instead, banks are typically interleaved: odd-numbered locations (really, cache lines) are put in one bank and even-numbered locations in the other. This can clearly be extended to four, eight, or even more banks. With interleaving, there is decent average behavior without explicit programming. It won't be perfect, but you can increase the effective bandwidth of memory quite a bit.

In Search of Clusters ✳

The memory controller shown in the figure is more important than it might appear at first glance. It has to be able to satisfy one processor's memory request while at the same time satisfying the other's, at least whenever they don't go to the same memory bank. See Figure 39. Proc1-Bank1 while Proc2-Bank2 should be possible, but so should the cross-connection: Proc1-Bank2 while Proc2-Bank1. The idea is to allow everything that's possible, but that doesn't mean everything is possible. The controller must delay cases where multiple processors want to get to the same memory, as also shown in Figure 39, while maintaining fairness—never "starving" any processor.

Figure 39 Data Flowing in a Crossbar Memory Controller

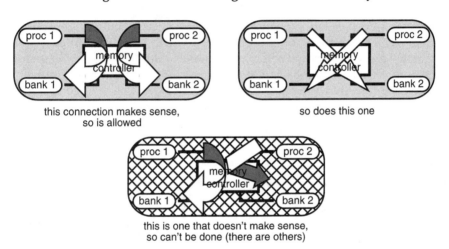

this connection makes sense, so is allowed

so does this one

this is one that doesn't make sense, so can't be done (there are others)

Keeping all the possible paths available at the same time and not allowing the forbidden ones means that this controller must walk, chew gum, pat its head, and rub its stomach all at the same time, or the system will not get the benefits possible from interleaving. This gets more complex the more processors and memory banks there are.

All possible nonconflicting permutations can be simultaneously allowed; it just takes more hardware. The primary data path hardware required, known as a **crossbar switch**, goes up in size as the square of the number of processors: Double the number of processors and memory banks; the switch doesn't just get two times as big, it gets four times as big. This rather quickly gets very expensive. As a matter of fact, going up in cost with the square of the size is the primary reason why crossbar switches are conventionally considered not scalable.

For reasons to be discussed in the next section, the kind of memory controller described above is seldom used in that form in SMP systems. It was presented here to allow considering it separately and more simply. We'll use the concepts later. Rather than having multiple points where processors attach, there is more usually a single input point, shared by the processors (and that sharing involves other complexities). The back end of the controller still talks to multiple banks with a (smaller) crossbar. Now, to get the higher bandwidth, you absolutely must use pipelining; that's the only way to get all the banks going at the same time.

6.4   Cache Coherence _____

Even without considering memory bandwidth, there's another problem. It's far more serious than the memory bandwidth problem, since that is "merely" a performance problem that "merely" inhibits scaling the system up in size. This problem is one of correctness. You can build computers or write programs that go really, really fast if they don't have to get the right answer.

Remember that space I told you to watch? We're there now.

Figure 40   The Cache Coherence Problem

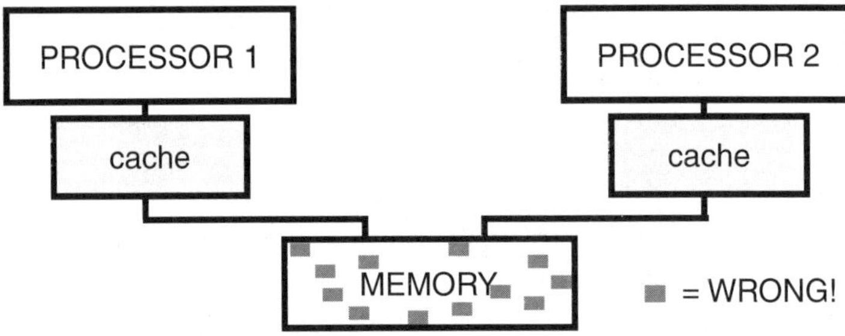

See Figure 40. Thanks to the messy desk effect, the memory has random wrong data in it. What happens when a program running in processor 1 loads data from a memory location that was last written by processor 2? The value in memory might be the correct value, meaning the one most recently stored, because, at random, it just recently was written back out of the cache. Then again, it might not. The system might run for hours or days, getting the right value each time. Then, at random, it gets the wrong value. Whatever the final outcome is, it won't be pleasant. Unrepeatable, randomly occurring errors. Everybody just hates when that happens.

This difficulty is referred to as the memory coherence problem or, much more commonly, the **cache coherence** problem: The system must somehow provide a coherent, uniform view of the memory to all processors, despite the presence of local, private cache storage. If it doesn't, it's not an SMP because it's not symmetric: It doesn't look like it has one memory. That means standard system software will not run on it, so you might as well not build it. (And you certainly shouldn't buy it if you are using it for conventional purposes.)

Cache coherence problems are not an odd occurrence that happens only infrequently. Even if they were, the threat of their occurrence would warrant taking care of them. But loading something that another processor stored happens all the time, although hopefully it is not extremely frequent for reasons that will become clear later. It arises in several common circumstances.

1. **Process migration**. A running program (otherwise known as a *process*) is executing on processor Archie. For any of a number of possible reasons, it stops running there and is moved ("migrates") to processor Buela. All the data it happened to leave in Archie's cache has to be read by Buela. With a big level 2 cache, this could be multiple megabytes.

   - Process migration could occur, for example, because the running program initiated an input or output operation. When that happens, the operating system stops running the program because it will be waiting for the device for some time. Later, when the I/O operation is over and the program is to resume execution, the place where it used to run (Archie) might be busy doing something else while Buela is twiddling her thumbs. Rather than wait for Archie, you'd like to use Buela to continue execution.

2. **Parallel communication**. If a program is actually written to run simultaneously on multiple processors at the same time, it is a parallel program. The parts of parallel programs running simultaneously must invariably communicate with one another. On an SMP, this is done when one processor reads data that another processor has written.

   - At least one such parallel program always exists on every SMP: the operating system. For example, when it begins running a user process on one processor, the operating system had better let every other processor know that process is being executed; it wouldn't do to run it twice. (It would probably end up charging you double.) Heavily used subsystems, such as databases, are also often written to run in parallel on symmetric multiprocessors.

3. **False sharing.** This one is reminiscent of a slapstick routine. Suppose two processors never have anything to do with one another. They never read or write the same memory locations. They can still get in trouble if they simultaneously work on *different* data that happen to be in the *same* cache line.

   - See Figure 41. Two processors load the same cache line. One stores into one part, the other stores into another. One is flushed to memory. When the other flushes, it wipes out the first one's store. This stepping on each others' toes is called **false sharing**. Obviously, the longer the cache line size, the more false sharing you'll have. This is why an earlier comment was made: long cache lines can be too much of a good thing.

Figure 41 Coherence Error Due to False Sharing

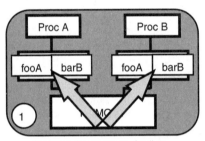

Both get the same cache line.
A needs only fooA, B needs only barB.

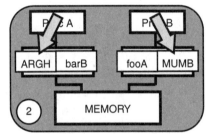

B changes barB to MUMB, and
A changes fooA to ARGH.
Neither touches the other's stuff.

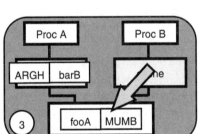

B's copy is written back to memory
(or A could go first; doesn't matter).

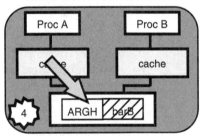

Then A's copy is written back,
clobbering B's data.

So a multiprocessor system does not have to do things that are in any sense exotic to run into the cache coherence problem. It's there all the time. How do we get around it?

In Search of Clusters ✳

6.4.1   *"Fixing" it in Software*

It is possible to build a usable, cached, multiprocessor system with just a little bit of hardware and a sufficient quantity of software. Just add two instructions to the processor: The first immediately forces a cache line out of the cache and back into memory; this is known in the jargon as a cache line flush. The second just empties a cache line in the cache, without writing it to memory; this is a cache line purge.

Now the software can take care of itself. It just flushes things out when it's finished with them, in particular when a process migrates or information has to be passed to another processor. The purge is used in the opposite direction: If a processor is about to start using something that it might have touched before and not flushed, there might be old data left around in its cache; purges get rid of that data. Software also must be careful to avoid false sharing. This isn't hard for nonparallel application programs manipulated by the system; it's rather a bit more tricky for parallel programs like the system itself.

A good thing about this approach is that it allows you to use one of those crossbar memory controllers that was discussed earlier under "memory banks." This lets you have lots and lots of memory bandwidth, so considering only hardware and assuming a captive collection of tame programmers, it could scale well in a raw "break the Von Neumann bottleneck" sense. This is all some application areas need.

But there are a few problems.

> ➤ **The software must be inhumanly careful not to mess up.** Because of the random nature of cache contents, errors in cache management are of the nasty sort: unrepeatable and transient. They'll never be visible in the lab; instead they'll always happen in the field, during your best customer's peak busy period. In general, mere mortals should not be allowed to explicitly program cache management that is required for correctness.

> ➤ **The approach is inefficient.** A process that is to be migrated, for example, may have accessed many megabytes of data. Some of that data might, at random, still be in even a small cache. Which is left around? The only thing to do is execute cache line flushes on all the megabytes to make sure none of the data is still there.[10] Alternatively, there could be an instruction that allows scanning the cache itself, rather than searching it for memory addresses. But caches can

10. Games can be played with the virtual memory system to reduce this inefficiency somewhat. See my proposed book, *Stupid Virtual Memory Tricks*.

themselves contain megabytes, so it's still a long scan. Another alternative: Don't migrate the processes, or at least do so only under extreme circumstances. This avoids the inefficiency mentioned above but runs into another. Because process migration is more painful, you now can't balance the computing load as evenly among the processors. As a result, the system won't scale as well. It obviously would be better to move only the data required, and then only when necessary, but the random nature of caches makes this impossible for software.

> **The approach breaks the SMP programming model** to smithereens. SMP programs expect to see one consistent memory, and requiring use of flush instructions makes the caches into visible private memories, one per processor. This is another one of those things that could be wallpapered over by a deeper level of system software,[11] but the system software will have the two problems mentioned immediately above, along with the cost of being different that has been discussed earlier. In this case the difference is rather major.

The next several sections will describe ways to maintain cache coherence automatically, in hardware alone, which is the standard industry approach.

6.4.2 Central Directory

With only one processor, memory could be incorrect without catastrophe because the processor always checked the cache first. That remains the basic answer to the cache coherence problem: Check the caches first. *All* the caches, on all the processors. If somebody else's cache has what you want, somehow get it from that cache, not from the memory. And better be quick about that checking, because you're adding an additional delay to the amount of time it takes to get data from memory.

How do we know which cache to ask for data, or whether any cache has it at all?

There is a technique for doing this that's extremely fast. It's also quite expensive and gruesomely complex. That technique is to have a single central unit that maintains a centralized collection of tables—a **directory**—keeping track of whose cache has what data. Everybody's cache. Everybody's data. Lots of tables. Rather than ever directly going to memory when data is needed, you instead request the data from that central unit. It "knows" where everything

---

11. *Ibid.*

is and so can get it from the appropriate place, be that the memory or any of the other caches.

A diagram of a system with such an all-seeing, -knowing, and probably singing and dancing, central unit appears below as Figure 42, with a couple of memory banks for a typical situation. At the level of detail of the diagram, it looks deceptively like the relatively simple, multiple-banked memory of Figure 38 on page 156, but there are two major differences from that situation.

Figure 42 A Central Directory Scheme

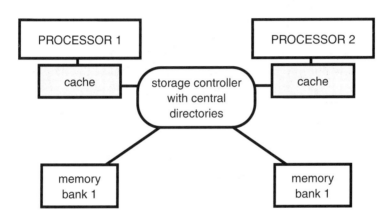

> First, additional data transfer paths are required, because data must be transferred between all the caches directly, as well as between caches and memory. This has more crossbar-ishness than the original (see Figure 39 on page 157). It will be even more expensive.

> Second, unlike the other crossbar, this one is smart. It doesn't just stuff data directly where directed, it looks up referenced addresses in internal tables and figures out where they are. It can know where everything is because everything flows through it: For example, whenever it delivers a line to processor A's cache, it notes in an internal directory that processor A in fact has that line. When it sucks that line out of A and gives it to B, it deletes the entry from its A table and puts it in its B table.

One thing making this method particularly interesting is that it has to do everything at once. All the processors could miss in their caches simultaneously. To avoid increasing memory delay, it has to be able to do all those lookups and transfers at the same time. Doing this requires an increase in cache complexity, too, since the cache has to be able to disgorge a line at the central unit's request while it is waiting, itself, for a line it has requested. This, by the way, just happened to come up at this point; all the other hardware coherence schemes also require it from their caches.

Another important optimization: Much of the information that processors get from memory never gets modified by the processors. Programs, for example, are never changed by the processor (not any more, anyway, and except for special circumstances like compilers and loaders). So, it is quite correct and reasonable for more than one cache to have a copy of some information.

If everybody has recently run the same program (like the operating system scheduler), then bits of that program and its data are probably in everybody's cache. But you never really know that it's just a program, and there is, in addition, non-program data that everybody looks at without changing. So, a processor can turn around and decide to write into a line that everybody has a copy of.

Interesting things must then happen. All the copies in all the other caches have to either get marked "invalid, wrong, not correct, don't use me any more" or they all have to be updated. Which of these two is best is the subject of endless simulation, and in some cases schemes have been proposed that adaptively change from one technique to the other [CF93]. But whichever is used, in the technique being discussed here the central unit coordinates it all, including yet another amusing case:

Two processors might just happen to want to store into the same location at the same time. (Loading and storeing simultaneously is just about as bad.) Somebody's got to go first—having a memory location with two different values is the no-no all this stuff attempts to solve—and it is the central unit that picks the winner and sequences everything.

The rather complicated central directory unit that's been described is known as the **storage control unit** of the big, bad mainframes of yesteryear. It, and not the processors, was undoubtedly the most complex element of those systems. Its size and complexity grows tremendously as the number of processors and memory banks increases. For a small number of processors, it can be so efficient it is frightening. It certainly does not scale. It is no longer used.

6.4.3   Snoopy Bus

Rather than have a central authority that knows everything, another alternative is to have every cache continuously tell every other cache what's going on. This solution, called **cache snooping**, is currently the overwhelming winner of the technical popularity contest for best solution to the cache coherence problem in SMPs. It trades a central active unit for a central broadcast communication channel called a snoopy bus.

The snoopy bus is like a telephone conference call to which every cache and every memory unit is attached. Systems working this way necessarily have all the processors and all the memories on one bus, as shown in Figure 43

Figure 43   SMP with a Snoopy Bus

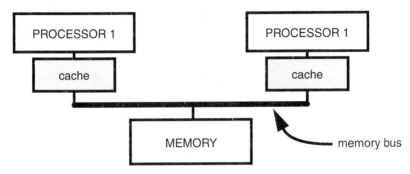

The way snooping works is illustrated in Figure 44.

To understand it, let's go back to the messy desk analogy. This time, however, we have a whole roomful of messy desks, covered with forms, and seated at each one is a clerk. The clerks have green eyeshades, sleeves rolled up, and all exercise regularly; they're scribbling on the forms like madmen. They're the processors.

Across the room is a nasty old codger with creaky bones sitting next to a rusty collection of musty old file cabinets. That's the memory, from which all the forms originally came.

Now, suppose a clerk needs a form—call it form A—that's not on his desk. There's a copy in the file cabinet, but that one might be old; another clerk might have one with more recent data.

So, he shouts out into the room: *"WHO'S GOT A?"*

Everybody immediately starts looking for A.

All the clerks start madly searching their desks for A, and the codger slowly gets up and walks to the cabinet labelled "% through C."

Figure 44 Snooping

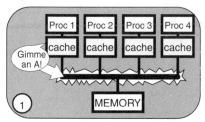

Processor 1 needs location "A"
and broadcasts that on the bus.

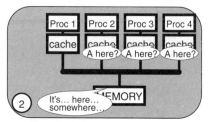

Everybody looks to see whether
they have "A." Caches should be faster.

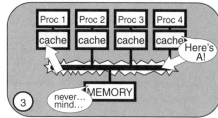

Processor 4's cache had "A," so broadcasts it back
to 1. If no cache had it, the memory would have it.

The codger always finds a copy of A. But he's slow. If there's a more recent one on a speedy clerk's desk, the clerk always beats the codger to the guy who originally asked. So we always get the most recent copy of A.

That's basically the way it works. When a cache wants to read something from memory, it shouts: grabs the snoopy bus and broadcasts to everybody a read request for that particular location. The memory, listening to the bus, hears this request and begins to respond. But all the other caches are listening, too; they're snoopy. They proceed to check their own caches to see if they've got the data being requested.

If one of caches has the data, it essentially pretends it's the memory: It grabs the bus itself, puts the requested data there, and in the process implicitly tells the memory to forget that request. The requestor sees that the data is there and gobbles it up.

It doesn't matter if the contents of memory are wrong because you always get the most recent value direct from a cache. If this is all done correctly and things line up right, you can even get data faster than you would otherwise: you're getting it from (someone else's) fast cache rather than from the slow memory. It's not as fast as your own cache, because the snoopy bus is slower than the processor-cache connection, but it's faster than memory.

That's the basic idea. There are, however, a cornucopia of variations on this theme. They come in two classes: Fixing things up when the cache is not faster than memory; and reducing the number of times a cache has to broadcast something on the snoopy bus.

The first class seems odd given the discussion so far. How can the cache be slower than memory? It's not—when accessed from its associated processor. But when accessed via a secondary path from outside the processor, the cache can be slower, particularly compared to an aggressively pipelined memory system.

One common way to fix this is illustrated in Figure 45. A request is made as usual. The memory, however, always wins and puts its data on the snoopy bus. While that data's being transferred, one of the caches might come along and indicate, through some additional control lines on the bus, that the data being transferred is wrong. This doesn't stop the transmission from memory; that's a fixed operation. After that transmission is over the receiving processor discards the (wrong) data from memory and instead receives data from the other processor's cache, using another bus cycle.

Other techniques for solving this problem exist, including updating the data in memory and then retrieving it from there, perhaps a second time. All have the common property that they result in lower performance when data must be obtained from another processor's cache. The reason is that more than the minimum number of bus cycles must be used. As will be discussed in a later section, this is not a desirable property when the target workload is a commercial database or transaction processing system (see "Commercial Processing: Cross-Interrogation and Shared Caches" on page 171).

The second class of refinements, those aimed at reducing the bus traffic, cover a wide range. For example, suppose a cache already has a line and the processor wishes to modify the data in it—do a store. In the general case, the processor would have to broadcast that write request on the bus. Other caches might have their own copies, which must be purged or rewritten with the new value. But if the writer knows it has the only copy of that line in any cache anywhere, it can just go ahead and write, quietly, without broadcasting anything. This is a valuable optimization because different processors often end up running programs that have nothing to do with each other—they're just separate programs and share no data. Under those circumstances the caches might never, or hardly ever, have to broadcast a request to write.

A cache can know it has the only copy by maintaining a small amount of information about each cache line, referred to as the line's **state**. Suppose, when a line is first loaded, it came from memory; that can be determined in a number of ways, including having the memory transfer the data on the bus

Figure 45   Snooping with Slower Caches

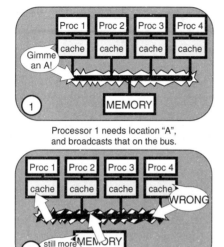
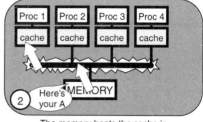
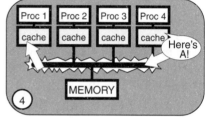

Processor 1 needs location "A", and broadcasts that on the bus.	The memory beats the cache in putting A data on the bus
Processor 4's cache had a new "A" value, so indicates that the data being sent is wrong.	After memory's done, Processor 1 discards the old data and Processor 4 sends the right stuff.

with a marker indicating "from memory." Since it's from memory, it's the only copy in any cache—otherwise you'd have gotten it from some cache. The cache receiving that line from memory thus has exclusive use of the line and records that fact. But the owner keeps snooping the bus; if anybody else issues a read requesting that same line, it dutifully provides it (to speed things up) and changes the line's state to "shared." If the owner of a line wants to write data into the line, it first checks the state: Exclusive? Just do it, quickly and quietly. Shared? Grab the bus, broadcast that you're writing, and don't write until everybody says they've purged it (or done something else to update everywhere).

The particular collection of snoopy bus messages and responses a machine uses to maintain coherence is called its cache protocol. There are lots of cache protocols, using varying amounts of state information per line. A popular one is called the MESI protocol (pronounced "messy"), after the four states of its cache lines: Modified, Exclusive (this is the only copy anywhere), Shared, and Invalid [PP84]. Others are named after machines or institutions: the Berkeley protocol [KEW+85] and the Firefly protocol [TS87] are two examples. Comparative surveys of cache protocols have concluded that the more complicated protocols, with the most states, produce the best performance [AB86]. This isn't terribly surprising. Chalk up another increase in complexity and cost the bigger you make an SMP.

Trading out a central controller for a snoopy bus to solve cache coherence is a good complexity tradeoff, because the central unit, the bus, is passive, and the complexity that remains is focused in relatively simple units replicated in each cache controller.

The obvious weak point is the snoopy bus itself. Every processor's memory requests must traverse the bus, making it a classic Von Neumann bottleneck that inhibits scaling: Rather than being directly inhibited by memory speed, since memory can be readily built in multiple banks and pipelined—just attach multiple memory banks to the bus—the system is limited by the latency and bandwidth of the bus. If you keep the bus the same, you can increase the speed of the processors and caches forever and never go any faster.

A common response to this problem has been to haul out the electrical engineering textbooks, grease up the circuit simulators, and design some really heroic busses. Bandwidth is increased by making the busses wide: hundreds of wires are used (296 in one case [Gal93]). Width is limited only by "data skew": You have to wait until all the wires transfer their data, and the more wires there are, the more speed variation there is. Latency is decreased by making the bus physically short, so the signals take less time to traverse its length; even the speed of light matters, a lot. Many systems, for example, halve the physical length of their buses by using a "midplane" rather than a conventional backplane: The bus lies on a central circuit board, and processor cards plug into both sides of it.

Such buses can achieve peak bandwidths at or well above a gigabyte a second, and in a triumph of electrical engineering have been successfully delivered in production machines, and have proven to scale up adequately. But those dang microprocessors just keep getting faster, so even heroic busses are now falling out of favor.

Another issue with any snoopy bus is that it is of necessity a shared bus. Recall that when a cache wants to read something it first grabs the bus. This "grabbing" alone takes some time. Somehow all the units on the bus must agree about who's going to talk now in the conference call. This bus arbitration, as it's called, can be made fairly fast. But its speed pales in comparison to not having to arbitrate at all—which is the case in uniprocessors and centralized systems. Up to 30% of the bandwidth of a bus can be lost by sharing, not just because of arbitration but also because of queueing delays that accrue because of sharing. (A switched system, since it has only point-to-point links, does not require this arbitration.)

Bus arbitration, bus and switch size, speed, and the packaging implied by those factors are thus a very significant way in which SMP systems increase in cost to support more or faster processors. A snoopy-bus-based SMP that is designed to support many fast processors must have a wide, aggressive, expensive memory connection—even if you only happen to plug one processor into it.

6.4.4 Snoopy Bus and Switch

One possible response to need to the make SMPs out of even faster processors appeared first, to my knowledge, in the IBM RISC System/6000 PowerPC-based SMPs; they're now also used in the Sun Ultra Enterprise 10000.

Those systems use a combination of transfer methods: a snoopy bus or busses for cache coherence, and a crossbar switch to move the data. This organization is illustrated in Figure 46. Processors put memory requests on the bus where they are snooped as usual. In a pure snoopy bus system, the bus is also used to transfer the data from wherever it's found to the requestor. That transfer does not have to be broadcast and takes significantly longer than the request because there are more bits in a cache line than there are in an address. In this bus-and-switch arrangement, processors get off the bus after making the request and await the data through a separate path that does not have to be snooped—the switch.

Figure 46   A Bus-and-Crossbar Switch Combination

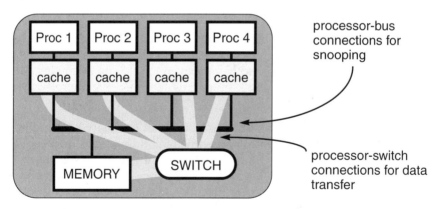

Since the bus is less occupied with each transfer and the switch can perform multiple transfers simultaneously, the result is substantially larger aggregate bandwidth, using rather less heroic electrical engineering in either the bus or the switch. Furthermore, adding more processors increases the data transfer speed because more ports are used on the crossbar switch. The same is not true of the snoopy bus, however; in the case of the Sun system, four separate snoopy busses are used. All processor/cache units watch all four

Figure 47 Operation of a Bus-and-Switch Combination

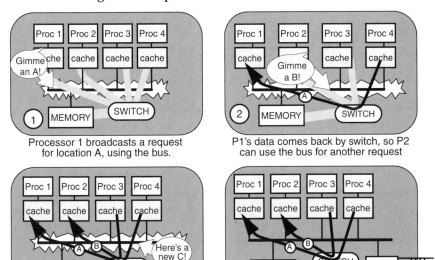

Processor 1 broadcasts a request for location A, using the bus.

P1's data comes back by switch, so P2 can use the bus for another request

While those data are coming back by switch, I/O can make yet another request on the bus

One very busy switch.

simultaneously, and when a cache wants to send out a request it picks the first bus that's unoccupied.

The initiation of multiple transfers with such a system is an interesting operation. As shown in Figure 47 (part 1), a processor requests information as usual. While the data for that transfer is flowing back from another processor's cache on the switch, the bus is free, so another processor can make a request (shown in part 2 of Figure 47). Both of those transfers can be proceeding while yet another is requested, for example, from the I/O subsystem (part 3). So at its peak operation, (part 4), a six-port switch can be doing three transfers simultaneously.

6.4.5   Commercial Processing: Cross-Interrogation and Shared Caches

In the previous sections the discussions of latency and sharing may have left the impression that most uses of SMPs do not do very much actual sharing of data. Nothing could be further from the truth.

There is evidence, as was cited, that there is little interprocessor data sharing in at least some scientific and engineering problems that have been explicitly rewritten to run in parallel. But commercial processing—a much larger market—makes heavy use of database systems and transaction monitors. These, too, have been rewritten to run in parallel on SMPs. They share data. A lot. In fact, they slosh it back and forth between caches like madmen.

Why this occurs and what can be done about it (little, by system vendors) is treated in more detail later in "Commercial Programming Models" on page 311. For now, we'll just note that it happens a lot on commercial workloads. As caches get larger—1 or 2 Mbytes is usually adequate, and 8 is nearly always enough—entire programs and all local data structures are completely cached. This by no means caches all the data, which in databases can be Gigabytes residing in main memory (there can be Terabytes out on disk, of course). But while this irreducible memory traffic does not go away, it becomes a smaller overall factor. Inter-cache traffic can become the dominant use of a snoopy bus, exceeding cache-to-memory traffic and becoming the primary system performance limitation. This is a large enough problem in commercial systems to have its own name: the **cache cross-interrogation** problem.

As a result of heavy cross-interrogation traffic, the performance of SMPs on commercial workloads can actually be improved by doing something that, given the earlier discussions in this chapter, looks monumentally stupid: Have multiple processors *share* a single cache.

Using a shared cache, as illustrated in Figure 48, reduces the *apparent* bandwidth available to each processor, making the Von Neumann bottleneck worse: Access to everything—all programs and all data—is slower than if the cache were not shared, because the processors must now contend for access to a single cache. However, it may increase the *actual* bandwidth.

Figure 48 Sharing Level 2 Caches

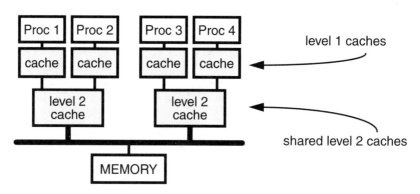

Data that's found in the shared cache is obtained more quickly than getting it from another processor; there's much more bandwidth between a cache and its processor—even when shared—than there is between units on the system bus. Data that's shared and found in a shared cache will therefore be obtained more quickly than if it had to be transferred on the bus. All you need is enough cross-interrogation to overcome the general loss of bandwidth that sharing produces for all other data accesses. There is very often enough shared data to overcome this loss—in commercial workloads.

Whether shared caches make sense depends on the details of a system and the workload: the bus bandwidth, the time required for a cross-interrogation, the penalty incurred by the interrogatee, the amount of shared data, and so on. Whether it's the right solution for any given system is best established by detailed simulation of the system under the chosen workload. In general, it's easier to share caches at level 2 or higher; level 1 caches are simply too busy.

Sharing a level 2 cache, however, reintroduces coherence problems between the level 1 caches, since they no longer directly snoop the bus (or participate in other schemes). Since sharing is seldom among many processors and performance is an issue, a central directory scheme is often effectively embedded in the level 2 cache.

Shared caches might lead to less total expense because of smaller aggregate cache size: A shared cache holds the data of, for example, two processors, and therefore should be larger than a cache for a single processor to get the same hit rate. But because programs and other data are shared, it need not be double the unshared size. The practical limitation of caches to power-of-two sizes can negate that advantage, however. The advantage can also be negated if the shared cache must be faster than an unshared one to avoid excessively degrading the base processor performance. In addition, the complexity of another coherence scheme within a level 2 shared cache will add to the development and design testing bill.

Systems incorporating shared caches can be SMPs. If the other requirements are satisfied (primarily universal access to I/O), the difference in memory access time between processors sharing a cache and processors in another sharing group is measurable, but small enough to be ignored. In point of fact, their whole purpose is to enhance the performance of programs that truly believe in the SMP model: All data is equally accessible, at any time, by any processor.

Cache sharing can also strongly affect the availability of a shared-memory cache-coherent system, as will be discussed in "The Case of the Tightly-Coupled Multiprocessor" on page 449.

6.5 Sequential and Other Consistencies _____

Back in 1979, Leslie Lamport earned the envy of every scholarly person by publishing a two-page, straightforward paper with a catchy title that has been referenced countless times over the years since it was published. The title of the paper, actually published as a short note, is *How to Make a Multiprocessor Computer That Correctly Executes Multiprocess Programs* [Lam79]. It sounds eminently straightforward and is logically clear. But its implications are enough to make your hair curl, turn grey, and fall out. What that paper pointed out is that cache coherence is not the only correctness problem that SMPs face. There is also the issue that paper dubbed **sequential consistency.**

The consistency involved here has to do with the order in which loads and stores are performed. In a single processor, the issues appear simple enough. Consider the following, silly-looking code fragment:

```
y = 0;
x = 1;
y = 2;
if (y < x) then panic();
```

You would never expect y to be less than x in that if statement. That's because the loads of x and y in the if statement occur sequentially after the stores of x and y implied by the assignment statement. (A good compiler might not actually store either x or y in memory, keeping them in registers instead, but let's assume a stupid compiler for these examples; the hardware has to work regardless of compiler intelligence.) This is uniprocessor ordering. Simply put, it means actions on memory take place in the order the program says they do.

But what about the order in which *another* processor sees them? Suppose, on one processor, the following even sillier fragment is executed (obviously created by somebody paid per line of code written):

```
x = 1;
x = 2;
x = 3;
/* etc., up to */
x = 99;
```

You would expect another processor to see these in the order they're programmed, too. So far, so good. Now consider that the other processor could be simultaneously executing a program that reads the values of x, so the following is going on:

Everybody starts with x = 1.

/* In Processor Able */	/* In Processor Baker */
x = 1;	y[0] = x;
x = 2;	y[1] = x;
x = 3;	y[2] = x;
/* etc., up to */	/* etc., up to */
x = 99;	y[99] = x;

The stores of x should occur in the order given. The loads of y[] should occur in the order given. But in what order should they occur *relative to each other?* They clearly can't be relied on to execute in lock step; a cache miss might occur in one and not the other, or a stray alpha particle could cause a short pause for memory error correction in one and not the other. Baker might, for example, execute y[2] = x before or after Able gets around to storing a 2 there. Will y[2] end up containing 0, 1, 2, or 99? Can't say. Could be any. Can anything useful be said about what's stored in array y?

Yes, but only if the multiprocessor involved obeys some rule about the order in which memory actions occur between processors. *This does not happen automatically.* Just because cache coherence has been maintained does not necessarily mean that processors will see the events in other processors in any useful order.

Lamport's sequential consistency is one useful rule, which actually turns out to be the strictest feasible one. To see what that rule is, imagine that the statements above have been written on ordinary playing cards, one to a card. Make two stacks of those cards: One with the stores of x, the other with the loads of y[], each stack in the order shown in the code fragments above. Now shuffle the stacks together into one stack. Any shuffle at all creates a single stack that is a legal ordering of one processor's actions relative to the other's. You can interleave them, one from one stack and another from the other; you can put a bunch of one first, then interleave, then end with a bunch of the other; you can bunch, interleave, bunch, interleave, whatever. You can even put all of one on top of all the other. But—and this is the sticking point—you can *never, never, ever* alter the order of the cards relative to one another *within* either stack.

Processor and SMP designers just hate that rule. Why that's so we'll get to in a bit. First, what does it allow us to say about the contents of that array y? It lets us be sure that Baker never sees x values in decreasing order. Because the x stack can't be reordered, any change to x must be seen by Baker as an increase. The increase might stop for a while, or might never get started, or might be completely over before Baker even starts, but for sure x will never get smaller. So we can say something, anyway: $y[i] \leq y[i+1]$ within the array bounds.

Now, as it happens, a multiprocessor would have to be rather pathological for successive stores into exactly the same variable to get out of order. The problem is much more often encountered when multiple variables are involved. Consider the following, which is the standard example originally used by Lamport. It's far more typical of the convoluted logic typically found in this sort of thing:

Everybody starts with x = y = 0.

/* in Processor Able */	/* in Processor Baker */
x = 1;	y = 1;
if (y==0) print ("Able wins!");	if (x==0) print ("Baker wins!");

If sequential consistency is operational, only one processor will ever think it has won. It might happen that neither wins: they could both assign 1 before either test is done, causing both tests to fail. You surely can't tell which will win. But if there is a winner, it will be alone. Here's the logic behind that.

Assume that Able won. That means:

1. Able must have found y to be 0.

Since that's the case, two other things must be true.

2. Able must already have done x = 1, since that happens before testing y; and

3. Baker cannot already have done y = 1, since y is 0—it was just checked.

Since point 3 is true, we can conclude a third thing.

4. Baker cannot already have tested x, since that test comes after y = 1.

Now combine facts 2 and 4: x is already 1, and Baker hasn't yet looked at it. That means:

5. Baker must sooner or later find that x is not 0, and lose.

When we assumed that Able won, we were forced to conclude that Baker lost. Just turn it around to conclude that Baker winning means Able lost. So only one, at most, can possibly win. *Q.E.D.* and *voilá!*

Operations akin to the above, but even (gak!) more complex, keep multiprocess programs from making a mudpie out of shared data because they provide what's called **mutual exclusion**—they restrict access to one processor at a time. The "more complex" part comes from ensuring that somebody always wins, and nobody keeps losing forever, neither of which desirable characteristics is true above. The use of these operations for mutual exclusion makes them crucially important for the correct operation of SMP software. Numerous ways of doing mutual exclusion have been devised and published over the years, the first (or the first best known) by Dijkstra [Dij65]; an entire book of techniques has been published [Ray86].

But suppose that, somehow, sequential consistency is violated. In particular, suppose Able's load of y manages to complete before the Baker sees the store of x. The logic falls apart because fact 2 isn't necessarily true—from Baker's point of view. (It may still be true from Able's point of view.) Since it's not true, Baker could still look at x before seeing the store, find it 0, and declare victory too. One could readily conclude from this that letting loads get ahead of stores, or any other alteration of order, is definitely a Bad Thing.

But that's exactly what processor designers want to do, and for good reason: performance. Is there ever any other reason for anything in hardware? Oh, yes, cost.[12] Anyway, here's why processor designers hate these rules.

When a processor is told to do a load instruction, it will often have to completely come to a stop and wait for a while. This is true for even the most ambitious uses of covert parallelism to simultaneously do multiple instructions inside a single processor, because the load wouldn't have been requested were there no intention of using the data. Some later instruction is going to test that data, or add it to another, or something. That later instruction simply must wait until the data has arrived; you can't add what you haven't got.[13] This is called in the jargon an **inter-instruction dependency**: the later use depends on the load having completed.

Result: You would really like to get loads done as fast as possible. They hold you up.

A store, on the other hand, has no instructions depending on it at all (except later loads of the same data; we will get back to that). As a result, it doesn't matter when a store "really" happens. Could be immediately, could be sometime next year. We don't much care, because the processor will never have to wait for it to finish.

So, to go as fast as possible, meaning to stop as seldom as possible, loads should get a higher priority than stores. High-performance processor designs do this. They let stores hang around in a **pending store buffer** while

---

12. And a couple of other minor things like manufacturability, reliability, availability of applications, and so on. That was a joke, folks.

13. Well, actually, you can guess what you think you'll get, go ahead and use that, and check your guess later, after the data actually arrived. If you were wrong, throw away everything and start over. It turns out that this can win—programs load the same data values a surprisingly large number of times—but the complexity involved is truly intimidating.

loads are done, even loads that appear after the store in the program. The notion is that at some future point, the program will probably be busy doing something that doesn't need memory access at all; the stores can be slipped in then, where they won't slow anything down. But do the loads right away.

This scheme works well, and it's not the end of this type of optimization. It's typically combined with other techniques that similarly allow entire instructions to execute out of order as long as a program can't tell the difference. Johnson [Joh91] estimates that such techniques can speed up program execution by as much 50%. That's definitely worth the bother; whole careers can be based on performance differences as low as 15%.

Of course, successfully pulling this off requires checking the pending store buffer whenever the processor does a load. You might be re-loading something that's still hanging out, so you must get the correct data from the buffer and not from the cache or from memory.

Iiit's baaaaaaaack!

Remember that space I kept telling you to watch during the discussion of caches? We're there again.

A processor checks its own pending store buffer before going to cache, so it never sees the wrong thing. This time, however, the *cache itself* can be randomly wrong, not just the memory. All the cache coherence on earth can't help, because the cache never gets into the act.

This may seem a bit unfair and inaccurate, because store buffers and their ilk aren't the only places in a multiprocessor system where loads and stores can get out of order. A store could be aimed at one memory bank, and a load, another. If one bank happens to be busy, say, because it's responding to I/O, the actual access to the data can be out of instruction order. Systems with multiple stages of communication between the processor and memory, such as SCI allows, might wind up with a load and a store, or two stores, taking very different paths to different memories; so they may finally happen in who knows what order.

However, all such memory and communication-related reordering can be eliminated by a straightforward expedient: Just make sure the cache never shoves out a memory request before the previous one is finished. In systems with very long memory latencies (such as really occur in so-called NUMA systems, discussed in the next chapter), this can be a significant issue. In a snoopy bus system it will have a much smaller effect, however, since the use of a single bus serializes lots of things anyway. (Unfortunately, I know of no published data that quantifies this issue. It must be out there somewhere. Sorry.)

In contrast, reordering inside the processor cannot be so easily fixed. All that's required is a processor aggressive enough to attempt some modest reordering and your goose has been cooked. That's any current high-performance processor design right down to recent PCs. So, in terms of most current SMP systems, sequential consistency truly is in the same space as cache coherence.

The consistency problem isn't quantitatively as bad as cache coherence, because the amount of data involved is much smaller. Pending store buffers are typically only a few entries long, as opposed to the kilo- or megabyte sizes of caches; the in-transit storage between cache and memory isn't large either, so relatively few memory operations are available for reordering.

Qualitatively, however, it's just as bad. Get some of the crucial operations that enforce mutual exclusion out of order—the others don't matter—and interesting programs like operating systems and databases, which commonly run simultaneously on multiple processors, get into each other's shorts. *Whomp!* Down goes the system. Transient, random errors again. Everybody *still* hates when that happens.

What's to be done? The key lies in two points: First, sequential consistency isn't the only rule that lets you say something meaningful about cross-processor memory interactions. Second, the only place this really matters is when mutual exclusion is involved. Let's talk about the second one first.

Most programmers of parallel programs do not spend their lives taking logic like that described above and spreading it throughout their programs. They'd go insane. More to the point, the programs wouldn't stand an ice cube in hell's chance of working. Instead, they write—or, better, select someone who's both extraordinarily smart and extraordinarily careful (not the most common combination) to write—a small number of primitive operations that can be very strongly relied on to do the right thing.

For example, on an object-oriented basis the smart, careful one might create a "lock" object to be used by all. Send one of them a "lock me!" message, and you are guaranteed to wait until it is absolutely, positively certain that the running program is the *only* one coming out the other side, even and especially if two processors say "lock me!" at precisely the same time. What happens during the wait we will discuss later. Send a lock an "unlock!" message, and someone else is allowed through, but only one other; if multiple programs have said "lock me!" and are all waiting to get in, one and only one makes it. (Which one, we also get to later.)

Now suppose there's a shared object with a hunk of shared data to be updated. Embed a lock in it. Never touch it without a "lock me!" and always "unlock!" as soon as you're done. This alone is complicated enough to keep track of. Instead, it should, if feasible without unacceptable overhead, be embedded in the object protocols of accessing the shared object itself. That way, it's impossible to update the object without passing through the object's lock.

Much of the complexity involved here has little to do with sequential or any other consistency. How do you wait? Continuously reload and retest a word of memory in a tiny **spin loop** until somebody else sets it to 0? Sounds wasteful; the processor could be doing some useful work instead. How about going over to the operating system's scheduler and put the process on a queue, waiting, so the processor can do something else in the meantime? This has lots of overhead and takes a long time; the lock holder might unlock really soon now. Besides, suppose the lock-er is an application program; must every lock involve a system call to allow possible rescheduling? Let's try again, combining those two attempts: Gradually move from a tight spin to increasingly lengthy intervals between checks (for example, **exponential backoff**, which is harder than it sounds), eventually resorting to rescheduling. Maybe. Sounds complicated, and this stuff has to be really, truly, verifiably correct. Where's that careful genius? Also, you have to come out the other end of a wait with some amount of guaranteed fairness; it wouldn't do to have a process wait forever just because others kept butting in front of it. Simple spin locking doesn't deal with that issue adequately except in special circumstances.

The whole point is: This stuff isn't trivial.

With such complexity involved, encapsulation is a must. Any programmer who persists in spreading mutual exclusion logic throughout a program, rather than encapsulating it rigorously, is either certifiably insane, woefully ignorant, or never writes a program more than 20 lines long. In any event he should search for an occupation more suited to his capabilities (or she, hers).

Where I'm going with this is the following: In a sane world (heck of a qualification...) sequential consistency need not be enforced at all times. You just have to guarantee that it's true at certain crucial, encapsulated places in the code. So, at those places, and only at those, apply instructions whose purpose is curb all the covert parallelism going on—to fully serialize the machine. Those instructions wait until all outstanding memory operations are complete: Pending store buffers are empty, caches are updated, memory has acknowledged that all stores are complete. The program will be using special operations in those spots anyway, ones that are more convenient for constructing locks than basic loads and stores. Those instructions can have this "serializing" characteristic built in, or it can be a separate operation.

This is the thesis of other ordering guarantees, such as weak ordering [AH90]; another, release consistency [GLL+90] is similar but allows greater overlap when accessing multiple locked blocks of data in sequence. Either is a relatively simple and efficient solution to the problem of sequential consistency.

You may have noticed that the solution proposed here is quite a bit different from that in the seemingly similar discussion concerning cache consistency. There, I railed against hardware-assisted software implementations. Here, I'm all for very similar solutions. But it's in the same space and can cause the same kinds of ugly problems. What's the difference? Locality.

After a lock is acquired, all access to the shared data is a cache coherence issue. It spreads throughout the code, not just in the locking itself. It can involve uncontrollably large quantities of data, whose movement through a machine is better handled by brute hardware, because the software can't know precisely where it all is (the messy desk factor). In contrast, Locking and mutual exclusion involve a few key storage locations for each instance of a lock. Furthermore, simple access to shared data does not intrinsically involve complex, easily goofed-up logic chopping—once you've established an appropriate locking regime, anyway. Locking and mutual exclusion are logically complicated operations that had better be encapsulated or it won't matter if the machine is sequentially consistent; nothing will work anyway.

Unfortunately, in the not too distant past we were all woefully ignorant. "Heritage" operating and database systems are riddled with programs that assume a simple store can reset a lock. Even purveyors of reasonably modern systems, designed for the open systems market, can get a bit nervous over whether all of their hundreds of programmers were as religiously correct as they should have been about using standard locking primitives at every point where they might be needed. As a result, this issue remains at least somewhat open. Some newer SMPs are sequentially consistent or follow one of the similar sibling protocols. Others have taken the plunge to weak consistency. The latter now seem to be setting the trend.

One final note on this subject. If everything is under tight control, for example, with a big, bad central directory, corners can be cut and additional nontrivial performance enhancements are possible. The reason is that systems don't actually have to *be* sequentially consistent. They just have to *appear* sequentially consistent to *every possible* program. Like covert parallelism within a processor, this is committing the perfect crime: You can get away with murder if no program, or programmer, can detect that fact.

And if you immediately see how to exploit this across a whole system, not just within a single processor, you were born in the wrong century. Grab a yarmulke and a time machine and make for the 12th century; you stand a good chance of becoming a definitive Talmudic scholar. This stuff gives me a splitting headache. Such distinctions were actually exploited in mainframe storage control units, where they distinguished between sequential consistency and **observable order**. They are the kind of thing required to make "heritage" programs run really fast. There is at least one whole textbook devoted to issues like this, and it is far from trivial [Col92]. There had to be some reason those mainframes used to cost a lot, didn't there? Just imagine trying to test such stuff ([Col92] tells you how). And pass the aspirin.

6.6 Input/Output

Input and output. The Rodney Dangerfield of computing. Everybody agrees that it's incredibly important, and it always gets stuck at the back of the chapter. Or the end of the design. There was one very large system project that had a virtually completed architecture and much of the "critical" hardware and software designed, before anybody bothered to tack any I/O at all onto it. This from within IBM, traditional home of massive I/O. (The project wound up a terrific success, by the way.) I/O really does deserve more attention than it usually gets, but that age-old discrimination isn't really going to be rectified here.

The reason it's not is that there's actually not much to say about I/O that is unique to large-scale SMPs, other than: There has to be a lot of it and it, too, must participate in cache coherence and consistency protocols.

There has to be a lot of it just because large SMPs are (intended to be) (or at least advertised as) powerful data processing facilities, and too little I/O means that the system can be limited by that rather than by computational capacity.

"A lot" means many, because disks, tapes, communications adapters, and the like are fairly slow compared with the system speed. A high I/O data rate means the system looks like it's dying the death of a thousand cuts, not hemorrhaging from a torn artery.

"Many" means enough space to plug it all in must be provided, and that requirement aggravates the need for even larger cabinetry. The many "slots" for I/O adapters that are needed necessitate large, long I/O connection buses which require that much more electronics to drive them.

All of this really falls into the category of the (nearly) blindingly obvious. It's necessary, and therefore interesting, but not particularly intriguing except for the usual battles over how much of a machine's cost budget it gets to use.

I/O must also participate in cache coherence protocols, just like any processor attached to the memory. This might appear obvious on the surface. After all, reasonably intelligent I/O devices move data out of memory on their own; if they're not careful, they can pick up wrong values, too, just like a processor, only this time they'll make a nice permanent record of their error on permanent storage. They have to rip the correct data out of processors' caches like any other processor. In the other direction, when the I/O system does its input, it had better act like any other processor doing writes; otherwise it is the processor cache contents that will be wrong.

There is a bit below the surface here, however. Doesn't this reasoning make a cached uniprocessor with its I/O subsystem effectively a two-way SMP? So, even uniprocessors have to do all that hideous cache coherence and sequential consistency gorp? Not necessarily, but it doesn't hurt.

In a uniprocessor it's feasible, just not very pretty, to maintain the required I/O-memory coherence by explicit programming. This uses the cache flush and purge operations mentioned in "'Fixing' It in Software" on page 161. The reason it's feasible is the same reason it was feasible to "fix" sequential consistency with software: The complexity involved can be localized.

This time the locale is the operating system's device drivers or some generic "wrapper" programming surrounding each of them. Before initiating a transfer of data out of the memory, the device driver flushes it all from cache into memory; now memory is correct, so off we go. Transferring data into the system is the contrapositive: Potentially incorrect old data must be purged from the cache before any program is allowed to touch what was put into memory by an input device.

As with any form of software-mediated cache coherence, this operation had better be done very carefully (transient errors again), and it's less than optimally efficient. In addition, it makes device drivers more expensive to develop. But it can be argued that it's not grossly inefficient: You can do a whole lot of cache purges while you're waiting for periods like 20–30 whole milliseconds for a disk's rotational latency. At least it's arguable until you find yourself doing a whole lot of I/O and discover this overhead is eating your processor alive.

Importantly, software-based coherence for I/O does not break the SMP programming model. Well, this is, after all, a uniprocessor; so that's a little hard to do. But portable system software is usually prepared to accept all kinds of weirdness, including things like this, from an I/O subsystem. Such oddities are expected to be encapsulated in the device drivers, which have to be rewritten for every new machine anyway; and so it is encapsulated. Therefore software-mediated I/O coherence is feasible and has been done.

Why not do the same on a large SMP? Well, such systems are often targeted at commercial workloads, so the threat of eating the processors alive with cache flushing and purgeing is even stronger. But there's another reason.

Just which cache did you say the data is in?

If the system is a uniprocessor, you know the answer. It's in the cache. The only cache. But if cache coherence between processors is handled in hardware—and that's been argued for strongly enough already—the correct values to be transferred to a device could be scattered throughout all the caches. You simply don't know where it is. It's not part of the SMP programming model to know this. Data in memory are just in memory, the only memory, period, so the system probably being run has no idea. Purges and flushes of all the processor caches in the whole system is just too much backbreaking overhead to consider.

So, in an SMP, I/O subsystems must participate in the cache coherence protocols used.

Oh, yes, and the entire discussion above was concerned with good old-fashioned slow I/O, like single disks, tapes, traditional communications adapters and the like. It did not discuss the new, really fast communication or really high bandwidth multi-disk RAID subsystems. How that gets attached in is, as far as I'm concerned, a very interesting question. But it had better participate in cache coherence at least as well as a processor.

6.7   Summary

This chapter has been devoted to displaying both the problems that must be solved in building SMPs and the collection of tools available for solving them. The tool set presented here must be considered intrinsically incomplete; there are too many smart people feverishly working on this topic for any published record to be more than a belated snapshot.

The discussion did not encounter any adamantine "brick wall" prohibiting the enlargement of SMP systems beyond some set number of processors. It also showed how the tool set available to an SMP designer today is large, ingenious, and altogether admirable. But unless some genius works a miracle, it does not solve the problem that more and bigger versions of all the support gadgetry—caches, buses, switches, bus-driving transistors, protocols, and so on—are needed as the number of processors increases if the industry standard SMP programming model, the repository of multiple millions of lines of code, is to be maintained. "More and bigger" always means more expensive.

The implications of this will be discussed in Chapter 13, "Symmetric Multiprocessors, "NUMA," and Clusters," where SMPs and clusters are compared. But the background for a meaningful comparison is not yet completed. We must press on, first encountering NUMA systems and then entering a whole other dimension: Software.

7

NUMA and Friends

NUMA stands for Non-Uniform Memory Access. Like SMPs, NUMA systems are a key competitor to clusters; so like the prior chapter on SMPs, this one is necessary if the ultimate comparison to clusters is to be done meaningfully.

However, more is involved here than understanding the competition. There is a nontrivial relationship between NUMA systems and clusters. This can cause, and has caused, intense confusion about the issue. Further, this relationship may ultimately result in systems that bridge between clusters and NUMA systems, with one shading into the other. How and whether that can happen is a significant part of this chapter.

NUMA has been the subject of intensely purple prose in press releases, magazine articles, and interviews with CEOs of NUMA-vending companies; the level quite possibly exceeds even the ultraviolet of cluster bluster. It has been made to seem the ultimate answer to computing, scaling, life, the universe, and everything. NUMA is said to be "scalable to hundreds of processors" but "keeps the SMP programming model" so your code doesn't change, while "avoiding the management complexities of clusters," leaping tall buildings at a single... Oops, sorry, slipped into the wrong fantasy.

On general principles, nothing sounding that good can possibly be true. In this case those general principles are right. Like all good propaganda, these statements do contain just enough truth that sound bites don't suffice to answer them adequately. Yes, it maintains *part* of the SMP programming model. Yes, the hardware can be scaled up to hundreds of nodes, but what about software? Yes, NUMA's current incarnations are easier to manage than *some* clusters, but P.S.: The NUMA systems involved aren't highly available.

The first round of NUMA systems, which were shipped in 1997, are definitely not clusters as defined in this book. Nevertheless, some confused technical press writers, and some analysts who are supposed to know better, blithely talk about "NUMA clusters." What they are, at least as they start out, are SMP systems with a pituitary problem leading to gigantism. Where they will end up is another issue, to be discussed.

The problem here is not that NUMA systems aren't a valuable weapon in the computing arsenal. Rather, the problem is the propaganda. I'm fulminating against NUMA being oversold, not against NUMA itself. As will be discussed in Chapter 13, NUMA systems and clusters are closely related. Furthermore, NUMA systems are important for a reason I've not heard broadcast by NUMA zealots: There are a set of real arguments to the effect that NUMA systems are unfortunately inevitable, and possibly will end up ubiquitous in nearly all sizes of servers. It's probably not been mentioned because "inevitable" and "desirable" are not synonyms. Nevertheless, there are technical trends that argue in this direction, as will be discussed.

Like the SMP chapter, this one necessarily goes into some hardware detail. The reason is the same as that for SMPs: How NUMA must be implemented is the key to its characteristics. What's here is not quite the hip-deep presentation that was made for SMPs, but there is necessarily more technical depth than in most chapters of this book.

Before discussing how NUMA works, however, it's necessary to begin by talking about why the term "NUMA," all by itself, is a source of confusion.

7.1   UMA, NUMA, NORMA, and CC-NUMA

The term NUMA comes from a taxonomy of parallel computers that used to be popular primarily with those who design operating systems. It was originally devised by David Black, then at Carnegie Mellon University and working (surprise!) on operating systems. It is based on one dimension of difference between machines: accessibility of memory.

- ➤ **UMA: Uniform Memory Access.** Every processor has equal access, using normal loads and stores, to all of memory. This is the way memory appears in the standard SMP programming model.[1]

- ➤ **NUMA: Non-Uniform Memory Access.** Every processor has access to all of memory using normal loads and stores. However, there is a noticeably different, often very noticeably different, delay depending on what parts of memory are accessed; hence "non-uniform."

- ➤ **NORMA: NO Remote Memory Access.** Processors cannot access other processors' memories by normal loads and stores, but instead must communicate by other means. For all practical purposes, this is another term for message-passing systems.

This taxonomy was developed prior to the widespread use of, or need for, caches in microprocessor systems. The research hardware system that suggested it, called CM*, had no caches.

That turns out to have been unfortunate, for two reasons:

First, the key technical advance, defining the unique properties of what are now sold as "NUMA," is scalable cache coherence, cache coherence applicable to large numbers, potentially hundreds or thousands, of processors. After getting through the last chapter, you will probably agree that getting past the bottleneck of the usual snoopy bus is quite a trick. All the purple press releases have been about systems that are CC-NUMA, Cache-Coherent NUMA.

The second, and even more important, reason is that cache coherence or its lack makes an enormous difference in the way multiprocessor systems are programmed, their programming models. A non-CC-NUMA system is, at its heart, a cluster. A CC-NUMA system is something else, something so different that the union of the two represented by the term "NUMA" alone is practically meaningless. From here on in, I'll refer to only to CC-NUMA and NC-NUMA (for Non-Coherent NUMA), unless referring to propaganda.

There is, by the way, at least one other name for "NUMA." Silicon Graphics calls its version "Scalable Shared Memory Multiprocessing" or S2MP, which just coincidentally happens to be what Stanford folks call it, as well as the title of a book on the subject written by a Stanford folk.[LD95]

---

1. This UMA is not the same as "Unified Memory Architecture" originally introduced in the Apple II and now becoming popular again. That UMA refers to putting video buffers in the same memory used for normal CPU and I/O operations, rather than in a separate specialized graphics memory.

7.2 How CC-NUMA Works

Both CC- and NC-NUMA systems are formed by coupling whole computer hardware systems, almost always SMPs, at their memory busses. This is shown for the simple case of two NUMA nodes, each a two-processor SMP, in Figure 49.

Figure 49   A CC-NUMA System

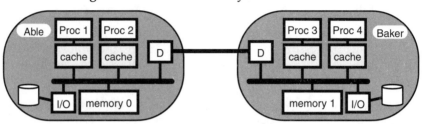

The system of Figure 49 is very much like the type of cluster pictured in the lower-right-hand corner of Figure 20 on page 98, in Chapter 5, "A Cluster Bestiary." Indeed, NC-NUMA systems are such clusters.

The difference between NC-NUMA and CC-NUMA lies within the boxes labelled "D," attached to each node's memory bus. The D boxes act as local surrogates for all the other nodes of the system: They redirect memory requests appropriately across an interconnect to the other nodes. For simplicity Figure 49 shows just a direct connection as the interconnect, but it could be a complex network connecting many switches.

The diagram shows two memories, labelled 0 and 1, in nodes Able and Baker. But that isn't what the processors see. As far as they are concerned, all of the memories in all the nodes are glued together, forming one large (real) address space. This address space starts in location 0 in the memory in node 0 (Able), then location 1 in that node, and so on until all the memory in node 0 is accounted for; then (probably after a gap), it continues at the first location in node 1 (Baker), marches through that node's memory, and continues through all the nodes.

When any processor, anywhere, says "location 798," the exact same location in the exact same node is referenced. In all likelihood the high-order bits of the real address are what is used to pick out the node; how many are used will depend on the system.

The "map" relating addresses to nodes is known to the D box. So, if Baker's Proc 4 calls for location 3, which is in Able's memory, this is what happens (see Figure 50 and Figure 51 for a road map):

1. Proc 4 says "Who's got 3?" on the snoopy bus in Baker. (We'll assume the nodes use snooping for their cache coherence; that's most common.)

2. Baker's D, watching the bus, sees the "3" and realizes that it lies in Able. (Nothing else in that node responds; they know there's no "3" here.)

3. Baker's D sends out a request to Able, which is picked up by its D.

4. Able's D, acting as a surrogate the original Proc 4, re-requests the value of location 3 just as if it were a processor.

5. This time the memory on Able responds, coughing up the value in location 3.

Figure 50 Getting a Remote Value (part 1)

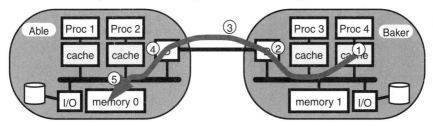

6. Able's D picks that value up from the bus.

7. Then the value is transferred back to the Baker's D,

8. …which places it on Baker's bus, acting as a surrogate for the memory that originally held it.

9. Finally, the value is picked up by Proc 4 and placed it in its cache.

Figure 51 Getting a Remote Value (part 2)

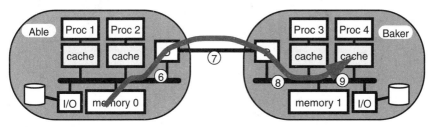

That's all well and good. Proc 4 has the data, and all's right with the world. At least it's all right until Proc 4 alters it. What happens then if Proc 1, back on Able, asks for the contents of location 3? As usual in cached systems, the data in Able's memory 0 is *wrong*. But Proc 1 will just put a 3 out on the bus, and memory 0 will respond. Does Proc 1 then get the wrong data?

If it's a non-coherent NUMA system (NC-NUMA), that's exactly what happens. The "wrong" data—the original value in the memory—is returned. Presumably one "programs around" this, so the "wrong" value is the one that was expected, and so is really "right."

Hmm.

Actually, what's needed is to treat "memory" not as normal memory, which is the point: NC-NUMA and CC-NUMA are different. The DEC Memory Channel discussed back in Chapter 5 (on page 118) was an example of a NC-NUMA system, and DEC's recommendation (with which I heartily agree) was to in most cases not treat it as memory; instead, as quickly as possible write (or find) a message-passing package and use that.

If it's a CC-NUMA system, on the other hand, the idea is that memory is to be used as regular old memory. To make that work, something happened back in step 6 that hasn't been mentioned, and is the key thing separating CC-NUMA from NC-NUMA:

Able's "D" box kept a record of the fact that somebody else has the data for location 3. That record is in a "directory," which is why the box was called "D" (I'll bet you were wondering about that).

This enables Able's D to act as if it were itself a processor, with a cache that happens to hold the missing value of location 3. Of course, it doesn't really have the value; that's held back in node Baker. D does, however, know how to get it; see Figure 52.

Figure 52 Getting Remotely Cached Data

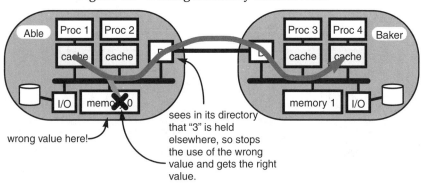

The fact that it has an entry for "3" tells Able's D that it indicate that the memory data is wrong, basically telling Proc 1 to "hold on a minute, the correct data is coming." Then it proceeds to go get the data from Proc 4's cache, using a sequence very much like the one that got the data in the first place: It sends a request to the Baker's D, which in turn acts like a processor on the other side and requests the data on the other bus. Proc 4's cache coughs it up, it gets transferred back to the Able's D and from there into Proc 1's (patiently waiting) cache.

There are other cases to worry about. Suppose there are three (or more) nodes, and look at Figure 53 to more quickly get the idea here. Proc 4 on Baker has gotten some data from Able's memory (location 3 again), as in Figure 50. Now Proc 6, on node Cherise, asks for the value in location 3. Cherise's D intervenes and asks Able's D for it, but it's not there. Able's D, however, knows where it is; it's on Baker. So Able's D ping-pongs the request over to Baker. From there it goes back to Proc 6 on Cherise, either indirectly through Able or, as an optimization, directly. Optimization or not, Able has to update its records to keep track of where the data is.

Figure 53 Remote Access to Remotely Cached Data

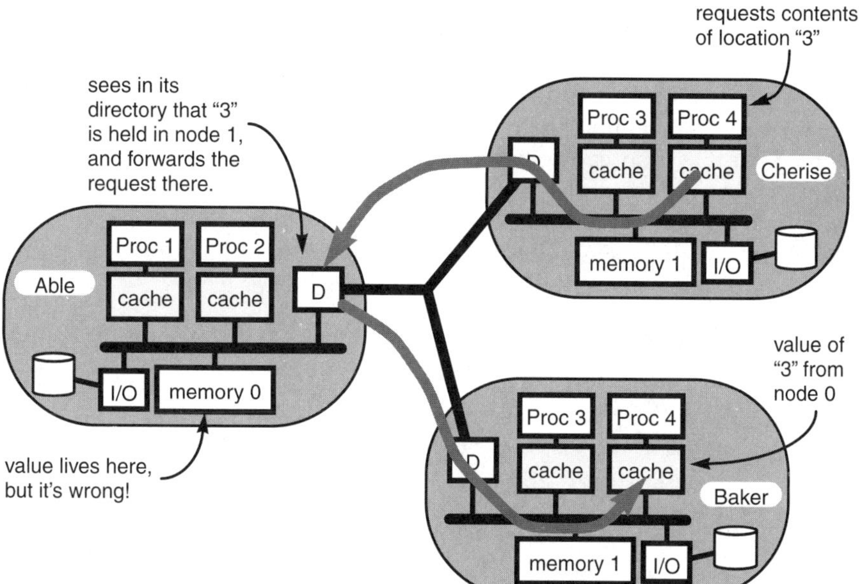

Now, let's have some real fun. (No diagram this time; I'd run out of ink. Use your imagination.) Remember that if a value isn't modified, it can be present in multiple caches simultaneously. This is good; for example, a program (which is also data) can be retrieved from one node by many others and, at least as long as it stays in cache, run simultaneously in many places without bugging the original source. But there's also data that's "almost" read-only. It is set up, and used by many processors, but then later in the game it gets modified—and then used again by many processors, and so on. The "current time" value in a simulator is a good example of this.

So, this value is out in lots of caches, all over the system, and some processor innocently says "I'm going to modify this." Well, good old D has to have kept track of *all* the places that have a copy, and then get all those places to purge their copies, so the modified copy will be the only one in the system. This can be done by a broadcast to everybody holding the value, but that implies the D unit holds some form of entry for every node having a copy. This can cause problems if you want to build one of these things with hundreds or thousands of nodes.

In fact, it results in the major difference between the two different styles of CC-NUMA implementation: the DASH style, named after the Stanford research project that developed it; and the SCI style, which is a scalable standard developed by a committee. A third published style, the FLASH style, can be viewed as an extension of DASH.

For completeness, the next section describes these two in more detail, but those details aren't really necessary for the main line of the discussion. You can probably get along quite well knowing that the DASH directory uses a bit vector, with one bit for each NUMA node, while the SCI directories hold a linked list that is spread across the nodes. So DASH can broadcast, but has limits on how many nodes there can be (the number of bits). SCI cannot broadcast, but must follow the linked list from node to node instead; however, it doesn't impose a meaningful upper bound on the number of nodes. Other techniques will undoubtedly be developed over time.

So, the curious or precise can keep reading linearly; others can skip to "The "N" in CC-NUMA" on page 199.

7.2.1   *Two CC-NUMA Implementation Styles*

Two NUMA implementation styles, as mentioned above, are the Scalable Coherent Interconnect (SCI), which primarily originally targeted massively parallel implementation; and the Stanford DASH projects. SCI will be discussed first, since it has appeared in far more purple prose with less explanation.

7.2.1.1   *Scalable Coherent Interconnect (SCI)*

The Scalable Coherent Interconnect [Gus92] is very often cited as being used in NUMA systems. However, almost no claimed uses of SCI use the entire set of protocols, as will be discussed later. Its original form is more closely associated with massive parallelism than with lowly parallelism. In that form, it is a way to glue uniprocessors together to make large shared memory systems, as opposed to gluing SMPs, as described above. The original form appears as shown in Figure 54. Its most conspicuous element is that it replaces a conventional snoopy bus with a ring (a circular bucket brigade).

Figure 54 Scalable Coherent Interconnect

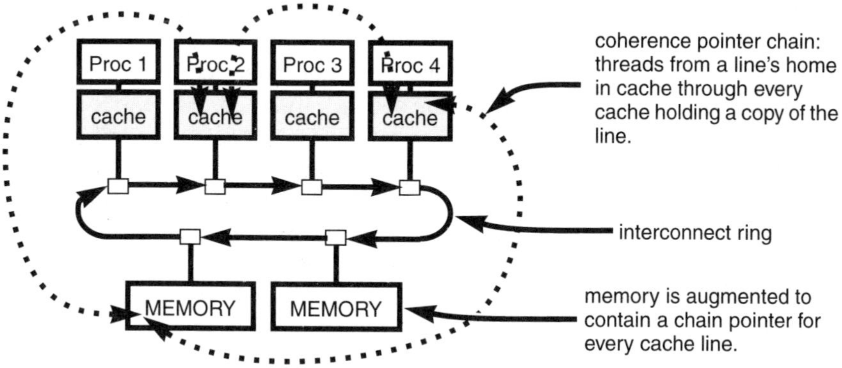

coherence pointer chain: threads from a line's home in cache through every cache holding a copy of the line.

interconnect ring

memory is augmented to contain a chain pointer for every cache line.

This has a number of good effects.

> Ring links are point-to-point, not arbitrated buses, so are electrically easier to run faster. SCI links run at 1 GByte/second, and may go even faster in the future.

> Multiple ring links can be active simultaneously, so the total available bandwidth is higher than that of a single shared bus of the same speed. The ring is still a shared resource subject to contention, so processors do not each have 1 GByte/second available; but the bandwidth available per processor is nevertheless impressive.

> There is no limit to the number of processors and memories one can put on a ring, other than physical distance limits on each individual link. Since that limit is 10 meters, a very large system indeed can be constructed. Of course, if you put a large number of units on a single ring, the memory latency rises to impractical levels and processors become inefficient unless they run with quintessentially perfect cache locality.

> While the connection must look like a ring to SCI-conforming caches and memories, it doesn't actually have to be a simple ring. It could be a ring connecting to a switch of unrestricted topology, for example, or interwoven rings, or other topologies that have fewer

stages between processor and memory than a single ring. This is a necessary part of scaling to very large numbers of processors.

All of this is fine, but snoopy broadcasting is impossible and a central directory is impractical, so another solution to coherence had to be found.

The SCI solution is to use pointer chains (see the dotted arrows in Figure 54) to keep track of the whereabouts of cache lines. If a line is in a cache, the memory has a "pointer" to that cache that it keeps associated with the line. The pointer is a numeric identifier for the processor/cache unit. The chain continues if, as illustrated, the line's in more than one cache. The first cache associates with the line a pointer to the second, the second to the third, and so on, and the last back to the memory (which also has an identifier). The chain is actually bidirectional, meaning that each chain pointer is actually two, one to the next and one to the previous unit on the chain. This makes insertions and deletions easier: When a processor flushes a line from its cache, it (first!) uses the ring to notify both its neighbors to point to each other, thus snipping itself out of the chain. When a processor requests a line for reading, the memory links it into either the head or tail of the chain by (first!) notifying the head or tail unit to link the new one in, then sending the data back with information about who to point to. If the memory doesn't have an up-to-date copy, it tells the requester where to find one—the first cache on the chain. When a processor wants to write into a line others have in cache, messages must proceed around the chain that instruct each cache to purge its entry and snip itself out of the chain. All communication is, of course, done using the ring (don't confuse the ring with the chain!).

You know, this can get a little complicated. Imagine keeping things straight when two processors adjacent in the ring simultaneously decide to purge their copies of the line and snip themselves out. Similar issues are involved when two or more processors simultaneously request the same cache line. These cases certainly can be done correctly, but testing the implementations is guaranteed to be interesting. (Still, not quite as interesting as testing a central directory scheme.)

This can also take a long time. Boppin' 'round a ring alone takes longer than a simple bus broadcast, even though each individual bop may be faster than a bus transaction. In addition, many traversals are required: When a cache requests a line, it doesn't get it back straightaway. Instead, it gets an immediate acknowledgment that the request was received. This is done for reliability; it doesn't do to lose memory requests somewhere out there on multiple 10-meter links. Sometime later, after the memory DRAMs have done their thing and all the chaining is sorted out, the processor gets a message with the information requested; that message gets immediately acknowledged back to its origin, too.

The obviously worst comparison occurs when a cache must convert a widely-shared line from read-only to write. With a snoopy bus, the request is broadcast and every cache does its thing simultaneously. With SCI, it's a serial process: One cache after another must individually purge and detach from the ring. How bad this is depends heavily on the sharing characteristics of the programs running on the machine. If there's seldom any sharing, and then among few caches, the slow behavior of SCI in the worst case simply won't matter. There are too few implementations of SCI, and insufficient published data on the cache-line sharing characteristics of programs, to predict at this point how it will come out. However, at least one unrelated study indicates that on some applications, primarily scientific but including a sort, the degree of sharing is in practice so low that even software-implemented cache coherence is quite competitive with hardware [BMR91]. Some of the competing DASH system results are similarly positive, as mentioned in the next section. The authors of the study weren't looking at commercial workloads, as will be discussed later.

SCI is not limited to connecting individual single processors and creating configurations like those shown in Figure 54 on page 193. It can also be used within the "D" directory units as described at the start of Section 7.2. In that case, the ring (or other topology) runs between the "D" units, as do the chains.

SCI is unique among cache coherence protocols in that it did not arise directly from published research or from product development. Instead, it was developed in committee as an IEEE standard. Standardization can potentially produce a valuable virtuous circle: multiple, compatible implementations compete, thus lowering the price, thus increasing use and raising the volume of sales, thus encouraging more companies to get into the market, increasing competition again, and so on. Formal IEEE *de jure* standardization between different companies at the memory bus level, however, seems a tad bizarre. For SCI to be a generally usable intercompany standard, many other much higher-level standards are required. Not only don't such standards exist, they're rather unlikely. Imagine competing operating systems—Sun's Solaris and Hewlett-Packard's HP/UX, for example; or, even more unlikely, IBM's OS/2 and Microsoft's Windows NT—married, coupled in the guts of their memories, loading and storing into each other's internal data structures, setting each other's locks, and generally mingling at the most intimate possible levels. The mind boggles. Software standards don't even exist that would support message passing by load/store through shared memory.

The explanation is that the SCI standard was driven by the high-energy physics community. This is not to say that large, serious computer vendors didn't consider this effort meaningful and participate quite actively. For example, Hewlett-Packard, Convex and lesser lights were active participants; many others including IBM lurked about the fringes with undisguised interest, and Convex has begun marketing a highly-parallel machine, the Exemplar, containing SCI technology. Sequent's NUMA-Q systems and Data General's NUMALiiNE, also use SCI technology.

However, not all users of SCI technology use the whole standard. Quite to the contrary, as of mid-1997 only one (Data General) does. The standard is defined in layers, so there is an SCI electrical signalling standard, and SCI cable standard, SCI connectors, and so on before one gets to chaining of cache lines. Those lower electrical levels are popular, since the availability of matched high-speed drivers, connectors, and cables eliminates many thorny electrical system design problems and enables faster product introduction. Most of the users of this technology have not, however, implemented the entire standard. There are several possible reasons. Some have considered it overly complex and therefore difficult to debug and slow. Others have considered the internal communication protocols insufficiently reliable, and at least in one ad-tech project I am familiar with replaced it with protocols having more error correction and a more robust signal acknowledgment mechanism.

Standards are good, but the reason for SCI being a formal standard rather than a public research project, the other obvious alternative, comes from high-energy physics. This community would dearly love to be able to buy processor and memory boards from the lowest bidders and sling them together into massively parallel machines that execute their application under their chosen portable runtime system. They have both justification and inclination. High-energy physics, as a social entity, is very conversant with organizing people to move governmental institutions to their own ends; otherwise colliders would never get built. So, an institutional standards route naturally suggests itself. That's the inclination. The justification was described back in Chapter 2, in the FermiLab example: Warehouses full of data, unanalyzed; enough to make a grown man cry.

7.2.1.2   DASH

The second style of CC-NUMA implementation is being taken in a project at Stanford University called DASH: **D**irectory **A**rchitecture for **Sh**ared memory [LLG+92]. DASH is organizationally very close to the "generic" CC-NUMA organization discussed at the start of Section 7.2.

Rather than taking individual processors as its building blocks, DASH used whole, snooping, bus-based SMPs and connected them to form a larger system with an SMP requirement: a single uniform address space. The DASH prototype couples Silicon Graphics POWER Station 4D/340 systems, with four processors each [BJS88]. Confusingly for this context, the DASH team calls these SMPs "clusters." In the discussion here I'll depart from DASH terminology and call them "nodes."

The nodes are connected as shown in Figure 55: Each snoopy bus has an attached directory unit that is connected to all the other directory units. The detail of the connection isn't relevant; anything able to carry messages could be used. The prototype happens to use a two-dimensional mesh. Each directory entry contains information about a cache line that is used outside a node. In particular, it contains a collection of "presence bits," one for each node in the complex; a bit is 1 if the line is present in the corresponding node. There is also a "modified" bit indicating that the value in memory is incorrect.

Figure 55 DASH

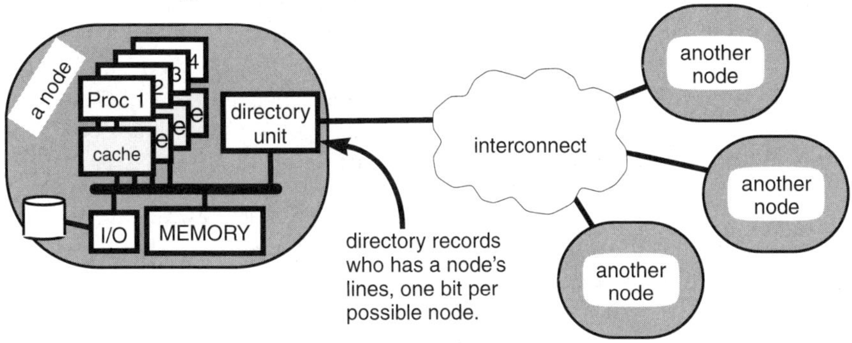

directory records
who has a node's
lines, one bit per
possible node.

The directories are used to do a hierarchical search for cache lines that matches the one implicitly described at the start of Section 7.2. For example, suppose a processor issues a read request for data.

> If the cache line with the data is found in that processor's cache, you're done.

> If it's not, broadcast a normal request on the local snoopy bus. If that finds the line, you're done.

> If that doesn't work, go through the directory unit to the directory of the "home node" of the line, the place where it would be in memory; this location is determined by high-order address bits. If the home node directory says it's unmodified, a copy is shipped to the requestor and noted in the presence bits, and you're done.

> If the line was modified somewhere, the home node's directory requests it from the node that modified it through that remote node's directory unit. It's noted as being in two nodes, and the contents are returned to the requestor. Now you're guaranteed to be done.

If a processor attempts to modify a cache line, the process is similar. But if the quest reaches the home node, the directory unit uses its knowledge of where all the copies are—all the bits that are on in the line's entry—to reel them all in: It multicasts to the nodes holding copies a request to purge that line from their cache(s). Only when they've all finished that process does the home node directory grant the requestor write access and mark the line "modified."

In comparison to SCI, DASH deals with processors in nodal snoopy groups and can multicast, simultaneously sending requesting that everybody with a line copy get rid of it. That's obviously faster. But the process can still take a long time. In the prototype (which of course is just a prototype), a worst-case fill from a dirty (modified) remote node takes 132 processor clock cycles—compared with a best-case 8-cycle fill using the standard SMP snoopy bus within a node, or 1 cycle to access the first-level cache [LLJ$^+$92, LLJ$^+$93]. The time taken if many nodes must be purged is not documented but must be substantially longer. And to think we were getting upset back at the start of this chapter because memory was only 20 times too slow; that factor of 20 corresponds to the 8 cycles mentioned above.

The difference in memory performance between local and remote access means that programming must adapt to this regime or risk low efficiency. This issue will be discussed in general in Section 7.3. Here, we'll just note that published experiments done on DASH support this conclusion. When there is little sharing of data or the sharing is local, individual parallel applications can achieve impressive results; applications with those characteristics achieve 30 to 47 times uniprocessor speed on a 48-processor system. Significant data sharing degrades performance to only a factor of 20, or even a factor of 7, on the same system.

This does not mean, however, that commercial CC-NUMA systems necessarily have such large inter-node memory delays. This topic is discussed in more detail in Section 7.3.

Interestingly, the follow-on project to DASH, called FLASH (**F**lexible **A**rchitecture for **S**hared **M**emory) [KOH$^+$94] builds the system from uniprocessors rather than SMP nodes. FLASH keeps track of which nodes have copies of a line using a supplemental linked list of node numbers—not distributed across nodes, like SCI, but held within each node. If you think this is starting to sound a bit like SCI, you're not alone. Similar goals—in this case, support for thousands of nodes—breed similar conclusions. However, FLASH is more than "just" a NUMA implementation. The "Flexible" of its title comes from its software-based communication protocols that allow it to experiment not just with cache coherence, but with a number of purely message-based organizations also.

In Search of Clusters ✳

7.3 The "N" in CC-NUMA

Starting back on page 189, Figures 50 through 53 implicitly made a point that should be obvious: References to remote memories take longer than references to a node's local memory. That is the "N" in "CC-NUMA": Non-uniform access time. All processors everywhere consistently see a single collection of values in memory, thanks to cache coherence, but some (most) memory locations are harder to get to.[2]

So, how are we to interpret the claim that "NUMA [sic] maintains the SMP programming model"? Will programs developed for SMPs just work? Clearly, any SMP program run entirely within a single SMP node of a CC-NUMA system will run as well as it ever did, and the CC-NUMA system can (potentially) run many of them at once on different nodes. But that's a fairly vacuous statement; you could say the same about a cluster of SMPs.

The real issue is whether SMP-targeted programs will run well when spread across multiple nodes in a CC-NUMA system. They will in all likelihood execute *correctly*, thanks to cache coherence.[3] However, will they run *efficiently* enough to make that matter? A key issue in answering that is: How big is that nonuniformity? Is it a Numa system or a nUMA system?

A useful way to measure this is as a ratio: the access time to remote memory, compared with the access time to local memory. Call that ratio N. Now we're asking "How big is the N in NUMA?"

If N is small—for example, 1.4:1 or lower, a nUMA system—nobody cares. Software can and does treat the system as if it were a normal, UMA, SMP. This has been proven in practice. The IBM S/390 model 3094 was actually a 2-node nUMA system with a 1.4:1 access ratio when more than four processors were installed. IBM never told anybody, and no software cared, specifically including the operating system. (That was a hardware design requirement, in fact.) The difference could nevertheless be detected if you looked hard enough. If you examined a graph of system performance as processors were added, the graph didn't rise quite as much as expected between adding the fourth and the fifth processors. Other than that, there was no visible effect.

---

2. This, and the discussion following, implicitly mentions only latency. Particularly for technical applications, the bandwidth available between nodes can have a strong effect, too, but it ends up being seen as latency: When bandwidth starts to run out, the latency gets enormous.

3. This assumes the program's authors haven't inadvertently, or as part of the design, made various sorts of timings a prerequisite to correctness. This is not particularly good design practice, and is unlikely, but that doesn't mean it hasn't been done.

However, if N is large—for example, 3:1 or larger, a Numa system—then people definitely care; software with performance requirements must be modified. Every software jock I've talked to, when a 3:1 (or larger) ratio was mentioned, immediately started worrying about how to modify his or her code. Well, actually, they started worrying about it when 1.4:1 was mentioned, since they didn't believe it would stay that low. They're probably right.

What happens between the ratios of 1.4:1 and 3:1? Even were my feet held to a fire I wouldn't be able to give a general statement. Even at large ratios it can still depend heavily on the characteristics of the program involved. Some will, in fact, work fine; others will become as slow as molasses. Somewhere between 1.4 and 3, however, there's a threshold that's probably as much programmer-psychological as not and modifications start getting planned.

The first round of CC-NUMA systems, which shipped 1997, have range from 2 or 3:1 (SGI's Origin series [SGI97], an admirably "tight" design) to larger than 7:1 (Sequent [Seq97], Data General [DG97]), although you generally won't find that out directly from their promotional material. That information comes from a mixture of informal sources. It does indicate that they all require software modification to get the performance that might be expected.

There is another way N could be measured, but so far has not to my knowledge. It makes CC-NUMA look less attractive, and is discussed in Section 7.6 on page 205.

7.4   Software Implications

What do these modifications entail? They begin, but certainly do not end, in memory allocation and processor scheduling.

To put the memory allocation issue in an obvious way: When a program asks for a page of memory, you *really* don't want to allocate that page in a node where the program isn't running. However, if your memory allocation code hasn't been modified to be aware of the boundaries between nodes, that is precisely the most likely occurrence, because a location will be chosen "at random" (with UMA, you didn't care). Since there are more nodes where the program isn't than the one where it is, a "bad" remote choice is more likely.

Similarly, when a processor runs out of work, you really don't want to start it up on a job that has all its data in another node. Well, except when…

Clearly, these core issues have numerous ramifications. For example:

In Search of Clusters   ✳

- In the long run, you probably do want to migrate jobs between nodes to balance the load more evenly. That will involve not just scheduling a processor to do a job held elsewhere, but explicitly or on demand moving user memory space, operating system data structures associated with the job, and so on.

- The above indicates that, in general, workload management will have to be significantly modified. This isn't too much of a problem if the workload management programs used are simple, but there are rather complex variants out there. Performance monitoring similarly needs modification.

- What if a program asks for memory, the node it's on has none free, but there are free pages available on another node? Do you start stashing less-frequently used pages in other nodes, as a really fast page store? Like workload management, storage management must be altered, and the more features it has, the more work that will be.

- What about shared data pools that are updated by multiple processors? There's no one place to put them that makes them close to everybody and, since they are updated, maintaining multiple copies is at least rather complicated.[4]

Certainly it's the case that the more a program has been optimized to make use of the uniformity of UMA SMP systems, the more work it will be to similarly optimize it for CC-NUMA.

There's an additional issue: Who does the modifications?

Vendors of CC-NUMA systems can, and generally have, modified their operating systems to do the right thing with memory allocation and scheduling, at least to an initial approximation that's adequate for the first shipment of these systems; improvements can certainly be expected. This, of course, assumes they own the OS; if their chief direction is to run another vendor's OS, such as Microsoft Windows NT, those modifications are at least more difficult.

These OS modifications by the hardware vendor will make many straightforward serial applications and single-node parallel applications work well; and they will probably be done well enough to allow more of them to run on

---

4. This kind of issue is the motivation behind the Parallel Sysplex Coupling Facility ability to hold system-wide data caches, described in Section 5.5.4 on page 121. It can be argued that this makes the data uniformly hard to access by everybody. However, it's a lot faster than keeping it on disk.

a system without debilitating overhead. However, as noted above, the same can be done with non-CC-NUMA systems like clusters.

However, subsystems such as databases, OLTP monitors, batch schedulers, and so on, do their own memory management and scheduling. In particular, there has never been a database system that did not think it could do a better job of memory allocation and processor scheduling than the operating system, since it knows the data and what's being done.

So those all have their own memory allocation and scheduling subsystems, which naturally must be modified, just like the OS was, to run across multiple nodes in CC-NUMA. In many cases, the harder issues must be faced immediately. Databases, once again the example, typically make heavy use of a central pool of shared memory called the database cache, which all processors access and update. Figuring out how to deal with a centrally used, large hunk of data is not easy, as noted above.

The ultimate success of CC-NUMA is heavily dependent on how many important software vendors decide to make this investment—it is, in essence, a programming model issue, as will be discussed in Chapter 9.

Until these modifications are done, and good techniques are found to get around problems like globally shared, updated data, the performance of CC-NUMA systems will be best on workloads that are quite easily partitioned into completely separate units. This includes, for example, running many separate jobs for throughput. Unfortunately, it also includes the most popular commercial benchmarks, an issue discussed further in Chapter 14.

However, it's wise to note something: The raw inter-node bandwidth of most CC-NUMA systems exceeds that of most clusters; and raw CC-NUMA inter-node synchronization has lower overhead and latency than most clusters, since normal SMP locking instructions can be used. So over time, if a significant software effort is applied, even difficult workloads could yield results on CC-NUMA systems that *may be*, if normalized to compare equivalent numbers and types of processors, at least as good as clusters if not better. The reason for the italicized "may be" arises from current CC-NUMA systems' use of a single operating system, discussed below. Various semantics within an OS require more locking across the complex than is done in most cluster implementations. Examples for UNIX are file locks and the signal state of a process. This must result in more serialization than most clusters have to bear, and will degrade efficiency. How much of an effect this will have is hard to tell at this point.

(High availability is another issue, as we'll see in the next section.)

In Search of Clusters ✳

7.5 Other CC-NUMA Implications

There are additional implications of the CC-NUMA organization, both advantages and disadvantages, that aren't directly related to the performance-oriented discussion above: Single system image, and high availability.

7.5.1 Single Operating System

The first wave of CC-NUMA systems, unlike clusters but like SMPs, naturally look like one system to administrators, developers, and users for the most elementary of reasons: There is only one operating system.

That one OS has its data spread across the memories of all the nodes; doing so efficiently is one of the modifications that are necessary to running a CC-NUMA system efficiently. However, no work has to be done to make that data usable everywhere in the system. It's in "the" memory, and plain old load and store instructions, following plain old pointers that can cross node boundaries with impunity, can always get at all the data with no program modifications.

Therefore, NUMA does not suffer from the painful administration issues that are solved for clusters only by arduous programming of a "distributed" single system image, as will be discussed in Chapter 11. This is the one benefit cited in the ultraviolet "NUMA" press releases that is unreservedly true.

However, that benefit has a two flip sides.

The first comes from the fact that a single operating system must maintain the semantics of one operating system. This has serialization implications that can significantly affect the amount of programming effort which must be applied if the system is to continue to provide more performance as additional nodes are added. This issue was mentioned in the previous section.

The second is high availability, which is discussed below.

7.5.2 CC-NUMA and High Availability

Like SMPs, CC-NUMA systems in the form initially shipped provide no inherent high availability. Loss of a *single* processor, anywhere, results in the *entire system* going down.

This is true for both hardware and software reasons, as is discussed in detail in Chapter 12, "High Availability" (particularly the section starting on page 445); but a significant part of the reason is tied to the very fact discussed above: there is a single copy of OS data. That makes it clear that if a single node fails, arbitrary chunks of the OS's data will become unavailable and the system as a whole will swiftly cease operating in a sane manner. (It's also true on single processor failure, as you'll see in Chapter 12.)

To address high availability as well as clusters do, significant architecture beyond the basic CC-NUMA facilities is required. This includes: hardware for turning off or otherwise controlling cache coherence; "fire walls" in the global memory address space to contain "wild writes"; and the ability to hot plug nodes into the NUMA connection fabric.

In addition, even more significant software is required because the system resulting from these modifications is no longer a pure CC-NUMA system. It is, in effect, a cluster, with all the software implications of clusters.

Unlike clusters, however, subsystems and applications sharing memory in a partitioned CC-NUMA system could still span partition boundaries. This is potentially an advantage. However, such shared-memory software sub-systems or applications themselves are very unlikely to exhibit high avail-ability. Only software with the right characteristics can do so (see Chapter 12), and to date none have been so endowed except for cluster or massively parallel implementations. Simple use of memory in the normal way is alone enough to sabotage high availability, as explained in Chapter 12.

Furthermore, there's a significant problem if the target is not just high avail-ability, but also continuous availability: The system stays up not just through unplanned outages (something broke), but also through planned outages (the system is upgraded). This is an increasing part of the "high availability" requirement set, and is discussed in more detail in Chapter 12. For now, notice that if a new version of the operating system is to be put on the system, doing so node-by-node is made very difficult if each node implicitly knows, and uses, addresses and data formats in the other nodes. The insulation of a message-based communications layer makes this process substantially more feasible.

Even though the new-architecture systems that will arise from NUMA with high availability are effectively clusters, they will undoubtedly be called "NUMA" systems. Of course, that's true. But they're not CC-NUMA, which is what "NUMA" usually means, with its associated SMP-like programming model and single copy of the OS. So CC- and NC-NUMA will be confused more heavily than they are now.

Some vendors began actively addressing these issues in 1997, notably SGI. It began developing a version of its UNIX system called "cellular IRIX" that partitions its O2000 system into independent "cells" that can independently survive if one or more fails. This is undoubtedly based on or suggested by the "Hive" operating system of the Stanford FLASH project, which has similar characteristics and similar goals.[CRD[+]95]

Developments like this will without a doubt proceed on many fronts in the foreseeable future, which is why the phrase "CC-NUMA as it was delivered in the first wave" was used regularly in the preceding sections. Any type of server system, if it is sufficiently large, eventually becomes partitionable by customer demand. Mainframes have had this feature (called LPARs, or PR/SM, or other names) for well over a decade. Sun Microsystems recently announced 64-processor UMA SMP (egad!), the UE10000, can be partitioned into logically separate systems.

However, note that the result after the partitioning is not CC-NUMA as it was delivered in the first wave; it is a cluster, with cluster software characteristics.

7.6   Is "NUMA" Inevitable?

Users want ever more server processing power, and infinitely fast uniprocessors cannot exist. Therefore, despite the fact that taming parallelism in any form is a Genuine Royale Paine, we have SMPs, clusters, and other parallel processing systems. In that sense, parallelism was and is inevitable. It is the inevitable result of a technical truth (limited processor speed) meeting a marketing truth: People will pay good money for more computing power.

It is arguable, and certainly has been argued, that CC-NUMA systems are similarly inevitable. This would bring one to the conclusion that, other than (UMA) SMPs with few processors (4, perhaps 8), eventually all shared-memory multiprocessors will be CC-NUMA. The size of the nonuniformity, N, will vary from smallish to very large, but N will not be UMA's 1:1.

There are four arguments that lead to this conclusion:

- ➢ the argument from memory speed,
- ➢ the argument from production volumes,
- ➢ the argument from existing levels of parallelism, and
- ➢ the self-fulfilling argument from mindshare.

The first two parallel similar arguments for clusters, and will be revisited in that context in Chapter 13. All are interwoven, and cascade upon one another; the key technical basis is the first one.

There is a fifth argument, the Overwhelming Memory argument, that is more complex than the others will be discussed after them.

7.6.1   The Four Basic Arguments

The four basic arguments are as follows.

The argument from memory speed: Although both are getting faster, memories are rapidly getting slower relative to processors. In other words, processor speed increases are substantially larger than memory speed increases. Professor David Patterson of Berkeley has pegged the historical rate of divergence at 50% CGR. That is a *lot*. Therefore fewer and fewer processors saturate a memory system over time. CC-NUMA is a way around this reincarnation of the Von Neumann bottleneck that "maintains the SMP programming model" at least in part.

The argument from production volumes: Vendors always sell many more small systems than large systems. CC-NUMA is a solution to the memory speed problem that allows vendors to cost-optimize their small system and then, with a relatively small incremental hardware development expense, satisfy the much smaller market for big ones by making big ones out of the small ones. In addition to development cost issues, these big ones then theoretically keep the cost/performance characteristics of the small ones (we saw this before, in Chapter 3, as part of the classic litany of advantages of parallelism). This is a particularly persuasive argument among vendors who reuse so-called "commodity," "standard" SMPs, such as Intel's Standard High Volume (SHV) board, as several already do. Those vendors need do (and have done) only the development of the inter-node glue. I'd not be particularly surprised, if CC-NUMA does take off, to find that they eventually won't have to develop the inter-node glue chips, either, any more than PC vendors now develop memory and I/O controllers.

The argument from existing levels of parallelism: There are a fair number of large-ish SMP systems out there, sporting 12-16 processors, and there is a significant customer demand for high single system performance. In fact, there are enough of both of these that important third party software vendors have gone to the not inconsiderable expense of modifying their code to actually make effective use of that many processors. Neither the software vendors nor the customers are particularly interested in backing off from this level; it's already in place. So hardware product requirements—which have major marketing and psychological components, as well as technical ones—dictate that a way has to be found, despite the memory speed problem, to keep the number of processors up there. If the software guys swallow it, CC-NUMA offers a way to do that without going bonkers (and broke) trying to get around the ever-slower-memory problem.

The self-fulfilling argument from mindshare: Hey, this is the wave of the future, don't you know? Get with it or be left behind! There is a reason for the deep UV nature of the "NUMA" press releases, and it's a reason all new parallel organizations have in common: Either a new parallel programming model becomes a self-fulfilling prophecy, or it withers and dies. This is a common computer industry phenomenon not limited to parallelism. It's also called the critical mass issue and the virtuous circle or spiral. If enough software is written to exploit CC-NUMA, then its cost and hardware commoditization elements will cause other hardware vendors to pick it up, which will produce more software, and so on. The industry press, seldom understanding the issues but ever happy to pretend anything is revolutionary, and you have to learn about it from them, of course aids and abets this process.

7.6.2   The Overwhelming Memory Argument

There is a fifth argument that leads to the conclusion that the nonuniformity ratio of NUMA systems will, over time, either remain the same as it is now or decrease because the memory access time becomes the dominant factor. If this happens, of course, the argument from memory speed is strengthened significantly. This "overwhelming memory" argument runs like this:

The time to access memory from a processor has several components that are additive: The time to get in or out of the processor (Pin, Pout), the time to traverse the memory interconnect (I), and the time required for the memory chips to actually do their thing (M). For an (UMA) SMP, those add like this:

$$Tuma = Pout + 2 \times I + M + Pin$$

since the memory interconnect must be traversed twice, once going out and once going back. This is literally false, since the time to traverse the interconnect (I) varies depending on whether one is transferring an request and address (one direction), or a cache line (the other direction), and the effective time varies depending on whether the processor can start using the first bytes of a cache line before the rest arrives when doing a read. Those added complexities don't affect the argument however. The point is that the time for a cross-node access in CC-NUMA (or any NUMA) is

$$Tnuma = Pout + 4 \times I + 2 \times N + M + Pin$$

Where two network traversals (N), out and back, have been added; and two more memory interconnect traversals (I) were needed to get the data from the remote node.

The argument is then that all the other terms will become small compared to M, which does not decrease as fast as the others over time.

This is likely true for the terms Pout and Pin, getting into and out of the processor. It can be true for the network and memory interconnect, but only if the entire system becomes physically smaller. While this is less strongly arguable, it also is possible; techniques like mounting a whole CC-NUMA system in a single multichip module could well be used.

However, the entire argument assumes that the majority of data references are to data that actually resides in memory. If references are, instead, to data that resides in the cache of a remote node, then the M term does not get proportionally larger. Cache speeds increase at a rate that's much closer to CPU speeds than main (DRAM) memory.

So, where does most of the data come from? For much technical computing, the purveyors of this argument may well be correct. Many of the cache misses come from insufficient cache capacity; the vectors and matrices being used are just too large to fit in any cache.

On the other hand, for transaction processing in databases, there is good evidence that a large fraction of the memory traffic is between caches; this was the rational reason for using shared level 2 caches in SMPs. (See "Commercial Processing: Cross-Interrogation and Shared Caches" on page 171.) Inter-cache transfers are also more likely for synchronization variables (locks); while not a large component of the traffic, such transfers have a disproportionate effect on system performance since they are serialization points at which at least some system parallelism ceases. Other workloads—multimedia, web page construction, decision support—haven't been well characterized yet, and in any event their code is relatively immature and will tend to mature towards heavier cache utilization. Ever-increasing cache sizes naturally add to the likelihood of cache transfers in general, of course.

So while this argument may be valid for common forms of technical computing, and may be true for now on some new commercial workloads, it doesn't fly for what is probably the most commercially important area.

This and related issues are taken up again in Chapter 13.

7.6.3   So, Is NUMA Inevitable?

None of these arguments alone is worth any more than the usual arguments for non-SMP (UMA) parallelism have been in the past. However, they do reinforce one another, and for all I know may end up carrying the day. They also, as is usual with such arguments, focus on hardware cost, not software cost; and the preceding discussion has hopefully convinced some of you that the software cost and complexity issues aren't exactly trivial.

These arguments do, however, ignore the skeleton in the CC-NUMA closet: lack of high availability. Any system large enough to need this technology is rather likely to require that. And satistfying that is, basically, impossible while maintaining the part of the standard SMP memory access model that

CC-NUMA maintains, as we went through here and will cover in detail in Section 12.11.4 on page 445, "Lowly Available Systems: SMP, CC-NUMA."

7.7   Great Big CC-NUMA

Several of the vendors who were part of the first wave of CC-NUMA offerings took advantage of another obvious advantage of this organization: Stick a reasonably scalable network between the nodes, and you can have a system that can plug in more processors than the largest SMP ever, potentially right up into MPP territory.

This raises a few hardware issues, such as: How do you keep the latency low with many nodes generating lots of traffic? How do you build directories able to "scale up" to MPP territory? Answer to that one: Use something like FLASH, or SCI-like techniques, or just swallow the cost of a whopping big DASH-style bit vector. Those issues, however exciting they may be to the hardware engineers (and people who have smoked too many press releases), aren't really where the issues lie.

They lie in software.

(Do I hear you muttering "as usual"? You should be starting to say that about now.)

To get performance out of those processor slots you need to have all the ducks in a row, from hardware through final application: hardware, operating system, file system, subsystem (like database), application, communications, and anything else that gets involved.

If *any one* of those can't "scale up" to meet the load, you might as well stick chocolate bars into the processor slots. They won't do any worse than processors, and might actually do better. It is absolutely not uncommon to find that a system will *speed up* when processors are *removed*, just because some element of the software is stepping on its own feet too much.

Note that this has absolutely nothing to do with the hardware being CC-NUMA. The effort required to just make the software scale in a shared-memory context, even if it is a lily-white 1:1 ratio UMA SMP, increases dramatically as the number of processors increases. For large numbers of processors—and I'd peg "large" at 24 or more—it may well *exceed* the effort required to take the NUMA-ishness of the hardware into account.

Which is a long-winded way of saying: Just because you have an application that works well on, for example, an 8-way SMP, don't assume it will go any faster just because it's run on a 64-way CC-NUMA (or SMP). It's easy to build scalable hardware; MPP vendors have been doing so for years. Software has always been the problem, and continues to be.

All of this of course is even further applicable if the CC-NUMA model is pushed up into the MPP range—which I personally peg at 100 processors or more (your own mileage may vary). Over time, a collection of techniques has been developed that scale software up to that range. These are the techniques of distributed memory programming originally developed for message-based (NORMA) techniques also used within clusters. They are, for all intents and purposes, the only proven way to use that many processors at once.

So MPP-CC-NUMA can surely be used, if it's programmed sort of like a cluster, explicitly using a distributed memory (but not necessarily message passing) programming model; this may be an advantage, as will be discussed in Chapter 9. It might seem to defeat the whole purpose of CC-NUMA, except that the inter-node communication it provides can be used as a truly fine accelerator of cluster communication. Like the NC-NUMA methods discussed in Chapter 5, it's virtualized, it's got nicely low overhead, and it's got high bandwidth. So CC-NUMA hardware is very nice cluster hardware, indeed, and I expect it may be used as such as high-availability support winds its way into "NUMA" systems.

7.8   Simple COMA

The performance difficulties that can occur with CC-NUMA systems arise from having access to data in a remote node.

In other words, they only happen when the data is in the wrong place.

Pause.

A hand goes up in the back of the room. It's attached to somebody who looks like he's played too much helmet-optional extreme football.

"Yes?"

"So, un, like, hey, dude, ah, why not put the data in the *right* place?"

Indeed. If this is done "manually," by explicit programming, it is the use of an explicit distributed memory programming model. This is discussed in Chapter 9. However, it would be nice to do so automatically, avoiding having to even think about the problem.

One way to approach automatic positioning of the data "in the right place" is to move it using every operating system's favorite unit of data access, the page. Pages can be moved as units between nodes by software, similar to the techniques of demand paging. Some CC-NUMA operating systems do that at least to some extent in the first round of CC-NUMA offerings. However, doing so results in difficulties similar to those of a technique called "Distributed Virtual Memory," which will be described in Chapter 9, notably an increase in the "false sharing" problem to cataclysmic levels caused by effectively using page-sized cache lines.

Simple COMA [SWCL95], also sometimes called s-COMA, is a hardware/ software technique that attempts to alleviate this problem. It had not yet appeared in products by 1997, but may in the future.[5]

s-COMA treats significant portions of main memory as a kind of cache, hence the acronym COMA: Cache-Only Memory Architecture. This acronym actually refers to an earlier architecture, to be described briefly in Chapter 9, that did it all in hardware. The added "s-" or "Simple" refers to hardware: s-COMA uses software to do page allocation, and then uses facilities like those of CC-NUMA to actually move the data a cache line at a time, on demand.

I've found that the easiest way to understand s-COMA is by tracing through its operation after assuming some initialization. It also really helps if you understand how virtual memory works, which I've assiduously avoided describing in this book. If you do not, a basic text on operating systems will help here a lot, such as [Tan92].

Let's assume that a parallel shared-memory program (really a process) has been started on each of the nodes of a system looking a lot like a CC-NUMA system. Somehow, the code is available to every node, and the data has been distributed amongst the nodes. Never mind how it got there; it's there, as illustrated in Figure 56. (Notice that the little connection boxes changed to "M" boxes. They're going to have different stuff inside.)

Also at initialization, the address spaces of the processes are set up so that all of them have addressibility to all the data, just as in a CC-NUMA system. However, the process in node Alice in the figure has only those pages on Alice actually marked "resident" in that processes' memory map: pages 1 and 2. Similarly, the process on node Barb only has pages 3 and 4 marked as "resident." In both Alice and Barb, all remote data is in the memory map, but marked "not resident in memory" even though it is, but elsewhere.

---

5. Actually, as I write the second edition of this book, Simple COMA pretty far out, about as far out as DASH and SCI did in the first edition. Since they spawned a whole dang chapter and significant rewriting, I figured I had better cover myself on this one.

Figure 56   Simple COMA Initial Layout

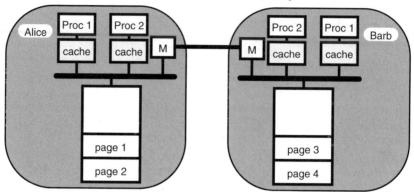

As long as the Alice and Barb processes access only their resident pages, they both just run along as usual; obviously, there's no communication between the nodes then, either.

Now, suppose Alice references location L in page 3. That process immediately gets a page fault. The fault handler then does the following:

> ➤ allocates a page in Alice's memory corresponding to page 3. We'll call it page 3'.

> ➤ puts page 3' into Alice's process' memory space where page 3 used to be.

> ➤ tells Alice's M box that page 3' is in memory, but empty, and associates with it a source address—the location of page 3 in Barb.

> ➤ restarts the process.

When the process restarts, it immediately tries to address location L again. This time it succeeds—L is mapped into page 3' in Alice—but Alice's M box is snooping on the bus. The M box sees that L is in a page it knows, and now acts somewhat like a CC-NUMA D (directory) box. The sequence is as follows:

> ➤ The M box short-circuits getting data out of Alice's own memory, just like a CC-NUMA D box would stop the retrieval of invalid data that was present elsewhere.

> ➤ Then the M box uses the location of page 3, which the fault handler gave it, to create the address in Barb where L really resides.

> ➤ It then sends a request to Barb for the correct L data; this is again just like a CC-NUMA D box.

In Search of Clusters   ✳

> ➤ Receiving the data back from Barb, it makes a note in its own directory that location is now over in Alice, with correct data.

> ➤ Finally, the M box returns the information on Alice's memory system to Alice, again just like a CC-NUMA D box.

Now, Alice has the data in its cache, and proceeds to use it.

So what has all this accomplished that CC-NUMA doesn't do, beyond injecting a great deal of overhead into the process? Taking a software interrupt in the midst of a memory reference is, obviously, a great deal of overhead; and besides, to make room for that page the fault handler might have had to do a disk operation to move some other page out to disk. Whew!

What s-COMA does doesn't become clear until that location L gets pushed out of a cache in Alice. It does *not* go back to Barb. Instead, it goes into the place reserved for it in page 3', right in the local Alice node. The whole process is illustrated in Figure 57.

Figure 57   Simple COMA in Operation: The Point of it All

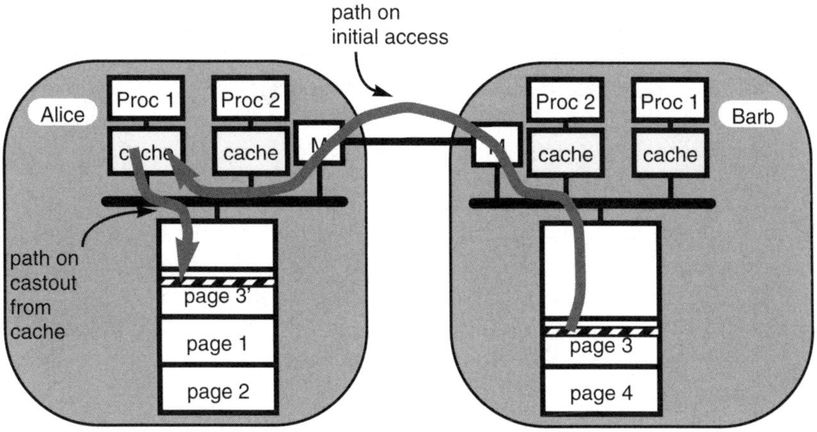

So, when you access a remote page for the first time there's a definite hit in s-COMA. There's no particular hit other than normal CC-NUMA remote access latency for additional lines in that page. But if you access a line another time, after you've finished with it previously, there's much lower overhead: It's now in local memory, and that's where you get it. In fact, if you access a lot of the data in a particular page, that page will gradually migrate over to where it's being used, "pulled" over, a cache line at a time, from its source. s-COMA advocates, therefore, call the memory used to hold previously-remote data "attraction memory," a term taken from COMA, which took it from a project called the Data Diffusion Machine. [WH88]

Furthermore, suppose some other node, call it Carla, also starts messing around in page 3. Carla will create its own copy of that page—page 3"— with its own copies of the cache lines Carla uses. If Carla picks lines that Alice already has, a three-step CC-NUMA shuffle is used to get them from Alice via Barb (see Figure 52 on page 190), but that shuffle has to have an added relocation step, since the lines are in a different physical location in Alice; that's done in Alice's M box, since only Alice knows where they are. (Actually, they might even be paged out…) However, if Carla uses different lines than Alice uses—not an unlikely scenario, given that write access is usually exclusive, controlled by software—they come directly from Barb.

Notice, however, that something really interesting has happened here. There are now three (and there could be many more) copies of page 3 in the system. Some lines of page 3 are copied in Alice, and some different lines in Carla, both of whom have a place allocated for their own versions of page 3. Somebody has to keep track of where this all is, and that somebody is Barb's M box; doing so is no harder than doing so in a CC-NUMA system.

The point is that page 3 is potentially scattered all over the system. Only if somebody wants a copy of that whole page in one place do the pieces of page 3 necessarily come together; when that happens, a page-load of three-step CC-NUMA shuffles—Barb to Alice, then Barb to Carla, then Barb to Alice, and so on—sorts it all out. There is, of course, no particular reason that only three nodes are involved, aside from maintaining our respective sanities while trying to understand the example.

The effect of s-COMA is to reduce the inter-node traffic that's associated with a particular kind of cache misses: capacity misses. These occur because the cache isn't large enough to hold all the data. s-COMA uses main memory as a cache, so the effective capacity is increased enormously. Capacity misses can occur under many circumstances, but one place where they are common is in technical code which, for whatever reason, scans through a lot of memory over and over again. Typically such code then changes the data layout and starts doing multiple scans again. Code with an access pattern like that is an ideal match to s-COMA.

Now, about that initial placement. The reason I sluffed over that initially is that, basically, it's irrelevant. The data is going to be moved to where it is used.

A disadvantage of s-COMA is that it's possible for multiple copies of pages to proliferate, using up valuable main memory space, unless something is done to keep their number reduced. Page replacement is also more complex than usual, since there is a level between disk and main memory to be considered: consolidation on another node that has a frame for a page, but only part of the data.

At the time this is written, It is unclear how suited s-COMA is to commercial applications. I've heard s-COMA advocates say "it's just another level of cache" and therefore should not be a problem. However, unless the database vendors themselves get interested in tuning for it I personally remain sceptical, since database writers barely believe in operating systems, much less virtual memory. They know what's going on, and can handle the job better themselves. They say. Pretty often, they're right. With that attitude, are they going to pick up on Simple COMA?

There has, however, been a study of the use of the original hardware-implemented COMA (the KSR-1) on commercial workloads run under an unmodified version of the Oracle 7 database. [RBG95] For an OLTP workload (the now-obsolete TPC-B benchmark) it showed approximately a 30% increase in speed using 16 processors if capacity misses were eliminated (which is what (s-)COMA designs do). For 32 processors, the increase was slightly higher. Also, a large sort was shown to have one third the capacity misses of an equivalent CC-NUMA system. These results are suggestive, but certainly not yet conclusive, and in any event do not take into account the additional overhead involved in Simple COMA. It's entirely possible that the success of this technique may ultimately hinge on how well the page fault overhead can be minimized.

Part 3:

Software

Workloads

All right, that's the hardware. So what? Hardware alone never did anything for anybody.

How can it be used? What do you have to do to use it? What good is it?

The next several chapters will address those and related issues, under the general and somewhat misleading rubric of "software"—misleading because the real topic is how that software can, must, or need not be aware of the hardware's characteristics. (*Systems* again.)

It seems appropriate to begin by discussing the goal of all this effort, namely, the kinds of work we can reasonably expect to perform on lowly parallel systems. That's the subject of this chapter. Subsequent chapters take up the issue of how that work is accomplished: parallel programming issues, programming models, and the avoidance of parallel programming. Finally, what is possibly the most significant issue for clusters will be discussed: single system image.

8.1 Why Discuss Workloads? _____

Installing a parallel system of any kind, or "scaling up" an existing parallel system with more processors or nodes, is not like installing the next-generation uniprocessor system. When you put in the new uniprocessor system, just about everything simply goes faster (an approximation, but good enough in most cases). Parallelism is nowhere near as uniform in its effects. Not all work will speed up, different types of work may speed up in different ways, and—depending on what exactly you did in adding parallelism—some things might actually slow down.

The reasons for this perverse behavior lie in how the different types of work can exploit parallel hardware or, to put it the other way around, how well the hardware can work on different types of workloads.

So, it is worthwhile to understand the characteristics of those workloads and what kinds of workloads are reasonably targeted by clusters and SMPs. As indicated above, this is where that's done. The entire discussion is summarized in Table 7, which will be explained in subsequent sections. While the table and discussion appear fairly universal, they are both limited to the workloads typical of server systems. A similar categorization of client workloads, tasks for individuals' personal computers, would probably turn out to be different.

Of necessity, this discussion is in terms of "pure types" of workload. Of course, there is no such thing. Nearly all real systems must deal with a mixture of these types.

8.2 Serial: Throughput _____

There is no such thing as running only serial programs on a parallel computer system of any stripe. If you attempt to do so, the beast will at best just sit there and hopefully not destroy itself.

Some people are shocked to hear this. Those who are then react as if they've been tricked when it's explained that at a bare minimum, the operating system must be rewritten to run in parallel. "Oh. I thought you meant *application* programs." There is more than one kind of program in the world, and the degree to which the operating system is effectively parallelized will have a very strong effect on how well any type of program runs under its auspices.

Many, if not most, clusters, however, don't run an operating system that is parallelized across their nodes. Instead, they run multiple copies of operat-

Table 7   Workload Characteristics

Type	Purpose	Classes		Examples and Comments
SERIAL	throughput	no software application changes required	batch	Load Balancer, NQS/Exec, etc.
			interactive	NCLOGIN, etc.
			multijob parallel	boulder-size granularity; would be separate jobs on a uniprocessor
PARALLEL	turnaround time or response time	large software application effort is justified	Grand Challenge	no serial hardware will do it, so there is no choice
			research	parallelism is the wave of the future, and graduate students are inexpensive, intelligent, and motivated.
			heavy use: dedicated and/or widely reused	software cost justified by heavy use of a single important application or subsystem that will run often and/or long. some potentially significant commercial use of clusters examples: seismic migration, data mining
		little software application effort: mainstream parallelism	commercial	automatic exploitation of parallelism via SPPS techniques manually parallelized subsystems: OLTP, DB (SQL)
			technical	parallelized libraries special SPPS frameworks (HEP) automatic parallelization; requires language, programming change for good exploitation of parallelism (High Performance FORTRAN?)

ing systems, one on each node, and glue the assemblage together at a different, higher layer such as a cluster-parallelized batch system.

Given a parallelized operating system and/or batch submission system, serial application programs can of course be run on a parallel system. Many can be run simultaneously, each utilizing just one of the several processing units: one SMP processor or one cluster node. In this case they individually will not go faster than on a serial machine with the same processing facilities. So the appropriate measure of performance is throughput, the aggregate amount of work performed per time period.

This is an example of the SPPS (Serial Program, Parallel (Sub-) System) paradigm first introduced in Chapter 2. An important characteristic of this class is that there are no software changes whatsoever required for any application. Compared with the other general class, in which applications must be explicitly written in parallel, this is an enormous advantage.

Three types of serial workloads can be distinguished: batch, interactive, and what is here referred to as multijob parallel. They are discussed below.

This category is such a straightforward, immediate application of lowly parallelism that it might be asked why it's discussed at all. Its very straightforwardness is precisely the point. There is no magic; there is no heavy-duty high technology; it is perfectly plain and simple. It is also extremely useful.

8.2.1   Batch

For batch processing, there are subsystems available today to handle batch submission of jobs to a cluster of machines. A sizeable list of them was given in Chapter 2, and at least one full-system cluster, IBM Parallel Sysplex, has extensive facilities for this class.

It is clear that virtually any type of cluster or SMP is a natural for this workload. There are two issues to keep in mind, however. Does the system provide adequate I/O to match the job mix? Is the job mix perverse enough to run afoul of load balancing issues? Otherwise, this one is a natural.

As discussed in Chapter 5, the I/O issue is often a limiting factor for assembled and preassembled clusters, since distributed client/server, not true cluster, file systems are all that are readily available outside of full system clusters. For technical workloads this is not a problem, but commercial batch workloads will often be hamstrung if they are limited to aggregate I/O equal only to the throughput of the LAN connecting to a file server. Cluster system products designed to run batch jobs against a file system, such as the Digital OpenVMS Cluster and the IBM Parallel Sysplex, have software and hardware specifically designed to provide a file system across the complex; as a result, they do not have this problem.

Another issue is workload management. Doing an effective job of workload management across several systems when the workload consists of very large, I/O-intensive batch jobs is far from a trivial pursuit. There are clusters that accommodate that, however, particularly including IBM's Parallel Sysplex. Its workload management can, under indirect control by users who "merely" set priorities and schedules, automatically do things like varying the number of batch initiators on each node in response to the applied workload.

8.2.2 *Interactive*

Two categories of possible interactive use are connecting onto some subsystem or application, such as an transaction management system, database system, or Internet server; and directly logging onto the native (for example, UNIX) multiuser operating system as a user. The reason for splitting this case in this way is that the application/subsystem case is covered under parallel applications and will not be discussed here further.

The second class, native login, can very nearly be considered a subset of batch processing after you have added standard distributed processing facilities such as X Windows and **rlogin**. You still run the same, unchanged serial applications; reprogramming is unnecessary. The "very nearly" aspect involves the fact that the workload management involved needs some way to intercept a request to login and divert it to a chosen machine; this is effectively built into the scheduler in the batch case. There are, as were listed in Table 1 on page 42 in Chapter 2, a number of packages available to do this.

This class makes little sense for low-computation, highly interactive applications such as editing, which are more reasonably hosted on a personal machine. However, for interactive use of a heavy number-crunching applications, for example, resource sharing using a cluster is quite a reasonable thing to do. The interaction comes in for "application steering": partial results are displayed as they're generated, and if things are found to be going awry early in the process, the application can be aborted, saving significant personal and computer time. This type of interaction is why an important measure of even these systems is throughput, although that may be perceived by a user as response time.

8.2.3 Multijob Parallel

Another category of basically serial workloads is what is called here Multijob Parallel. This category is explicitly discussed here to separate it from the "true" parallel systems discussed below.

Workloads in this class consist of a number of very large, very loosely coupled steps. In terms of the parallel-processing metric of granularity (discussed in the next chapter), they may be said to have the grain size of Mt. Everest, or the rock (it's just one rock, and it's in my back yard) that underlies central Texas. In general, these steps are so loosely coupled that even on a uniprocessor batch system they would have been submitted as separate jobs. Typically, they interact not at all during their execution; instead, each separate job step places its output in a file somewhere. A final cleanup job, often separately submitted, collects it all together.

Some forms of simulation fit this description, particularly those that check correctness or parameter sensitivity by re-executing the same model many times. Each simulation run is done with different parameters, often pseudo-randomly chosen, and when they're all complete their output files are collected into a single unit for human perusal. Multi-frame computer graphic animation also fits this description quite often: Each frame is a separate, large computation; there are a lot of them; and they don't interact with each other.

Multijob parallel is clearly another shoo-in for clusters (or SMPs), and most of the examples I'm aware of do not run afoul of cluster I/O bottlenecks—on the other hand, the ones I'm aware of are not commercially-oriented, either.

So much for serial or serial-like workloads. On to more conventionally conceived parallelism.

8.3 Parallel

In true parallel processing, a single application or subsystem is spread across multiple processing nodes, and there is communication between the parts during execution. The performance metric most usually applied is turnaround time. In the case of commercial parallel systems, response time (effectively a form of turnaround time), coupled in many cases with throughput, is used instead.

An unpleasant fact of life must be faced with regard to parallel processing: *It is hard to write parallel programs.* Designing, debugging, and performance tuning parallel programs is significantly more complex than the same operations performed on their serial counterparts. This will be demonstrated quite vividly in Chapter 9, "Basic Programming Models and Issues."

This unpleasant fact is particularly vexing when one realizes that software is *always* the problem; software is in a state of chronic crisis; the software application backlog is notorious; and the software community's greatest challenge consists of dealing with the often overwhelming complexity of plain, ordinary, serial programming.

This is not to say that parallel processing does not work. On the contrary, it can be made to work very well indeed and is in regular use throughout the industry in any number of situations.

It does mean that quite significant justification is necessary before one embarks on complicating software even further by introducing parallelism. Therefore this workload characterization splits parallel cases into two subcategories: those where a large effort is justified, and those where it is not. Each is discussed separately below.

8.3.1   Large Effort Justified

There are three primary cases in which the effort required to use parallel processing is justified: Grand Challenges, research, and heavily used applications.

8.3.1.1   Grand Challenge Problems

The official, government-approved definition of the Grand Challenge problems, with examples, appears in Figure 58 [Exe87]. These are well-defined problems whose solutions have major scientific or commercial value, but which require so much brute computation that they cannot be done in a practical period of time on any existing serial hardware, and often not on any existing hardware at all. For purposes of having a number to hang on them, they have recently been referred to as requiring "TeraFLOP" levels of computation: 10^{12}, or a million million, floating-point operations per second (FLOPS). (Yes, it should be "TeraFLOPS," but everybody ignores that persnickety "S".) The Accelerated SuperComputing Initiative (ASCI) (talk about overloading an acronym) is a government program aimed at acquiring a succession of ever-larger computers with peak speeds in this range, primarily motivated by example (3) in Figure 58 as applied to creating a safe, test-free nuclear stockpile.

Since no existing serial hardware will run these problems, if they are to be attacked at all, a parallel approach must be taken. There is simply no other choice.

These problems would be of very significant commercial utility were they solvable on a regular basis. Their other great utility—securing funding for

Figure 58 The Grand Challenge Problems

> "A grand challenge is a fundamental problem in science or engineering, with broad application, whose solution would be enabled by the application of the high-performance computing that could become available in the near future. Examples of grand challenges are: (1) computational fluid dynamics for the design of hypersonic aircraft, efficient automobile bodies, and extremely quiet submarines, for weather forecasting for short and long term effects, efficient recovery of oil, and for many other applications; (2) electronic structure calculations for the design of new materials, such as chemical catalysts, immunological agents, and superconductors; (3) plasma dynamics for fusion energy technology and for safe and efficient military technology; (4) calculations to understand the fundamental condensed matter theory; (5) symbolic computations including speech recognition, computer vision, natural language understanding, automated reasoning, and tools for design, manufacturing, and simulation of complex systems."

highly massive computing—has declined very significantly from its Cold-War highs and may never again achieve its former greatness.

This is not an arena in which clusters or SMPs play. They do not at present achieve the performance levels required.

Wait a few years for processor performance to climb a bit higher.

8.3.1.2   Academic Research

The second case where large effort is justified is one in which the large, high-quality effort required is dirt cheap: academic research in parallel processing. Everybody knows parallel processing is the wave of the future, from the *New York Times* through federal grant-approving agencies. As a result, otherwise impractical parallel hardware can be quite effectively used as thesis-generating machines. Graduate students are generally substantially above average in both intelligence and motivation, and at the same time are notoriously inexpensive. So, normal economic rules are suspended.

8.3.1.3   Heavily Used Programs

The third case is the one of greatest economic importance. Certain applications or subsystems see extremely heavy use. Either systems will be dedicated to executing them, or they will be used on a very large number of systems, or both. Examples include databases, OLTP systems, and Internet servers in the commercial arena; or seismic migration, crash analysis, and general-use subroutine libraries (LAPACK, LINPACK, MASS, and others) in the technical area.

In this case, the additional software effort required for parallelism is economically justified because it produces an economic advantage. For a database vendor, his system produces greater performance on less-expensive hardware than competitors', in a field where price/performance is a very important sales advantage. For an in-house seismic application, an oil company can extract more from its existing fields, for less expense, when the fields are modelled more accurately and in a more timely manner.

The expense of tying up highly skilled application and (sub-) system programmers to parallelize such systems must always be justified. In this case, we are talking about cases where that justification, realistically performed, comes out in favor of parallelizing the application or subsystem—quite often heavily in favor of parallelization. Of the three cases where heavy parallelization effort is justified, this one alone represents a real, substantial, marketable economic opportunity for the use of parallelism in single applications for either SMPs or clusters. One of the more popular portable packages, LAPACK, has been parallelized into SCALAPACK for cluster and MPP use.

8.3.2   *Minimal Effort Justified*

What about the multitude of Suzy Cobol and Freddy Fortran programmers out there? Is parallelism ready for the mainstream? In this case the use of parallelism must at the very least not increase the complexity of the programmer's task. There are definitely uses for true parallelism in some aspects of the commercial computing market, and at least a possibility in the technical market.

8.3.2.1   *Commercial SPPS*

Much commercial computing is done under the aegis of large subsystems, in particular OLTP (On-Line Transaction Processing) and database subsystems. As was noted above, those subsystems are good candidates for manual parallelization because of their heavy use. As a result of that work, applications running under those subsystems take advantage of parallelism with no effort. There are two categories: transactions and large database queries.

Transactions are computations with the property, guaranteed by the surrounding subsystem, that they are either completely done or completely fail; the idea is that your bank balance never gets debited without also crediting whomever the money goes to, which I, at least, consider a very good idea. Chapter 12, "High Availability,", will have a lot more to say about transactions and how their characteristics are achieved.

Transactions are traditionally also considered fairly short, but some can take minutes to perform. Whatever the length, there are always a lot of them to do. A single cellular telephone call, for example, ends up causing tens to hundreds of transactions to be performed by the time you hang up and the billing information is generated. In this case, having lots of transactions is a virtue. The parallelized OLTP system "simply" runs many of them—in unchanged, serial form—simultaneously. No code changes needed. Pure SPPS parallelism. This is referred to as **inter-transaction parallelism**.

The second category, large database queries, requires **intra-application parallelism**, parallelism within a single database operation, to obtain the desired result: decreased turnaround time. The queries are "large" in the sense of requiring the processing of quite a lot of data; the application area typically addressed is decision support.

For example, a product manager might want to know who his best distributors have been, for which product feature codes, over the last six months so that he can make sure they receive appropriate treatment. This is just one question, but the system might have to scan through lots of data to get the answer.

Furthermore, there are lots of such questions that could be asked. Which distributors are fastest in paying? What about similar questions about suppliers? None of these individually is a heavy-use application, reused by many people in the firm. Even though the manager really wants the answer, he or she is alone in wanting that particular; so the justification for heavy parallelization effort doesn't exist.

In this case of parallelism, what saves the day is a standard high-level language for expressing queries: SQL (Structured Query Language). SQL provides a high enough level of expression that the database system can, without explicit action on the part of the application programmer, extract significant parallelism from queries large enough to worry about. The application programmer may eventually have to learn how to express queries for best parallel execution, which is a new discipline but not that much different from learning the idiosyncrasies of any compiler. However, explicit parallel programming is not required.

So, a significant fraction of commercial computing can make use of both SMP and cluster parallelism without running into the complexity of parallel programming. The reader should note that the complexity of the subsystems has not diminished. Making them do inter- and intra-transaction parallelism well is by no means a simple task. Making them do both well simultaneously is at least a challenge.

8.3.2.2 Technical SPPS

How about technical computing? Remember that we are not here discussing large, important technical applications, nor similarly important widely used subroutine libraries, nor the amazing things that graduate students do for peanuts. All those cases have been separated out into the "Large Effort Justified" category.

We are instead talking about the numerical bulk of technical applications. There is abundant data that even in the heyday of vector supercomputers, that bulk was not even tuned to vector processing, even though vectorization had been current in technical computing for decades. How can it possibly be parallelized?

Some is fruitfully tackled by making use of the large-effort subroutine packages mentioned above. This is partially an analog of the commercial case and works if the application spends the vast majority of its time in those subroutine packages. Otherwise it will run afoul of Amdahl's law, discussed later in this chapter.

There is one case of "minimal effort" technical computing that is interestingly unique: event reconstruction in high-energy physics, which, as discussed Chapter 2, can make good use of SPPS parallelism. This is the transaction processing of technical computing.

8.3.2.3 AMO Compilers

The only possible answer for the rest of the technical field is what one customer I spoke to referred to as "An AMO Compiler": You put a serial program in the front end, A Miracle Occurs, and a parallel program emerges from the nether end.

It might sound like this customer was an ill-educated fellow, since there are many automatically parallelizing compilers on the market. Virtually every vendor of SMP hardware, along with well-established third-party vendors, sells them. But their output on the majority of unmodified applications (and *any* modification is prohibited in this category) is at best barely adequate to keep the few processors, say up to four, of a modest SMP busy—and that is the simplest, easiest target of parallelism; any form of cluster, because of higher communication overhead, is more difficult.

The difficulty with automatic parallelization is not the fault of the compilers. Even if the compiler were utterly perfect, able to extract every ounce of parallelism present, the same result would be obtained. The difficulty lies in the programs. They simply do not contain adequate parallelism in the expression of their algorithms.

A parallelizing compiler does not, and cannot, modify the algorithms of the program it is compiling. Users never want their algorithms modified at all. They worked hard to make them produce the desired result, and strange things can happen to boundary cases, numerical precision, and so on if compilers willy-nilly do algorithm modification. So, hands off. You can't replace serial algorithms with parallel ones (and, by the way, it would be more than a little difficult to make such substitutions anyway).

And the algorithms expressed by programmers are likely to contain significant serial elements that block parallelism. The reason this happens is that current languages used for programming, the techniques used to think about and express algorithms, are entirely serial. There is no benefit to a programmer to choose, even out of equally good possibilities, an algorithm that is parallelizeable over one that is not. The language used must change to something that gives Freddy Fortran a good reason, in his own terms, to program in a way that puts possible parallelism into his work.

This is a tall order. There is a possibility: Fortran 90's array constructs allow scientific programmers to express algorithms the way they originally developed the mathematics—in terms of matrices and vectors. Therefore, it passes the Freddy test: It makes his life easier. In the process, it also implicitly expresses some parallelism, although not always the most usable form. Compiling this at least has hope of increased parallelism.

There are other attempts at languages, in particular High-Performance Fortran (HPF) [Ste93], that add to FORTRAN[1] constructs describing how data is distributed for message-based machines such as clusters. This enables compilers to produce correct parallel code for such systems. (Why the primary issue is data distribution will be covered in Chapter 9.) This is a very useful thing to do, and undoubtedly will save much grief in the programming of applications and subroutine packages that pass the "Large Effort Required" test; in the process they will lower the value of "Large" and make the test easier to pass.

Unfortunately, that's not what's being discussed in this section. Such constructs, unfortunately, fail the Freddy test: Unlike array notation, they make expressing *parallelism* easier, but they do not make expressing the *problem* easier; rather, they are an extraneous complication.

So for the bulk of numerical parallel programs, there is some hope. But it will be a long pull, and mainstream technical parallelism will not come easily.

---

1. At least one person has commented that no matter what programming language technical computing uses in the future, it will be called one of two names: FORTRAN, or Fortran.

8.4 Amdahl's Law

A factor that affects parallel workloads and the parallel operating systems and subsystems used for serial workloads is known as Amdahl's Law. Gene Amdahl, who did not believe that parallelism was a correct direction to take at all, ever, expressed it first in a paper published back in 1967 [Amd67].

Basically, what Amdahl noted was that there is always some irreducible part of a job that cannot be split up to run in parallel. For example, after doing a large mathematical calculation, one must print or display the results. Even if the calculation itself can be done in parallel, there are few if any printers that do not take a purely serial string of bytes as input, so that part must be done serially. A simple mathematical formulation of this is that the execution time of any program can be split into two parts: part that can be done in parallel, and part that cannot.

> total execution time = parallel part + serial part

Suppose there are N processors available to do the parallel part. The best that can possibly be done, ignoring all overhead involved in coordinating and synchronizing those processors, is then:

$$\text{total execution time } = \frac{\text{parallel part}}{N} + \text{serial part}$$

which is known as Amdahl's law.

This calculation is straightforward but has interesting implications. Suppose only 5% of a task is irreducibly serial. That sounds fairly good; but Amdahl's law implies that the most you can speed it up, no matter how many processors you use, is a factor of 20.

If the number of processors (N) gets indefinitely large, the parallel part (divided by N) can get indefinitely small. So, say you use a whole lot of processors. You use so many that this part goes so close to zero it can't be measured. Then the total execution time just equals the serial part—and since that was 5% of the total to begin with, you are stuck with at best a factor of 20. Even though you may be using hundreds processors, even thousands of processors, and getting tremendous speedup for them—on the parallel part.

Amdahl's law has obvious implications for parallel workloads, as was noted above, and is particularly applicable to highly massive parallelism. If something useful is to be obtained from using 1,000 processors in parallel, for example, the serial part of the job had better be substantially below 0.1%.

For serial workloads and SPPS parallelism, there is still an effect from Amdahl's law, although it is somewhat less obvious. The serial jobs themselves constitute the "parallel part," since they appear to have nothing to do with any other job on the machine. This appearance can deceive, because the jobs interact in their use of system resources—memory, processors, I/O—mediated by the operating system.

For example, suppose the hardware used is not an SMP but an "attached processor" system in which only one processor can do I/O. Then all I/O done by any job becomes a piece of the serial part. Insufficiently-parallelized operating systems can produce similar restrictions, allowing I/O to be performed by only one job at a time (obviously, such operating systems are not suitable for commercial workloads).

SPPS exploitation of parallelism using parallelized middleware, such as a database system, similarly depends on adequate parallelization of the middleware. In addition, applications can themselves create a "serial part." For example, if every transaction executed in a particular application adds a row to one specific database table, there is little the database system can do; all the transactions, no matter how many processors there are or how many transactions could be done at once, must line up to alter that table. In this case, neither the hardware—SMP or cluster—nor the middleware is to blame. It is the application structure itself.

What Amdahl's law really points out is that parallelism is a game of elimination. For it to work, every last one of the ducks must be lined up:

> ➤ The hardware can be adequately parallel—have low intrinsic serialization in every respect—and it won't do you a bit of good if the operating system isn't.

> ➤ The hardware and the OS can be adequately parallel, and it won't do you a bit of good if the middleware (DB, communications, whatever) isn't.

> ➤ The hardware, the OS, and the middleware can all be adequately parallel, and once again you lose if the application isn't.

> ➤ If the hardware, the OS, the middleware, and the application all have low intrinsic serial content, then you have a good chance.

Of course, the more you are trying to do in parallel, the smaller the serial fraction has to be in all the layers involved.

Amdahl's law is actually an aspect of serialization in general, which will be covered from a different angle in the next chapter.

8.5 The Point of All This

That lowly parallel systems exhibit a broad range of useful, practical applicability is hardly surprising. SMPs have been plowing this turf for a couple of decades, so the utility of lowly parallelism is very well established. In fact, it's so commonplace that it's justifiably considered rather boring by those engaged in research in this area. Lowly parallel systems cover most of the usable possibilities with the exception of the Grand Challenges, academic research, and "no effort justifiable" AMO compilers. The first is not now a commercially viable area, the second doesn't have to be, and the third looks pretty difficult from my vantage point.

What the point of this chapter is, is this: The number of times the phrase "SMPs and clusters" was used, taking them together, when describing whether an area was amenable to parallelism. The broad utility of SMPs is matched just as broadly for clusters. Neither apply to Grand Challenges and research. Both apply to everything else, with one exception: Clusters are worse for "no effort justifiable" AMO technical parallelism. Although there are people who have devoted much effort to that case, in the broader picture I fear it's not going to make that much difference itself. The analysis techniques developed as part of that effort are another story entirely, finding immense, practical use in instruction scheduling for covert parallelism—to pick just one example.

This is not to say that there are not missing ingredients and holes in cluster support. There is the I/O problem for assembled and preassembled clusters; and at present the cluster-enabled SPPS subsystems for batch, OLTP, and the like must usually be separately purchased. SMP support, in contrast, is included in very many systems at no extra charge. And, of course, there's the cluster bugaboo, system administration. But there are no massive technical challenges in applying clusters to a rather broad, immensely practical set of workloads.

So, why have two architectures—three, counting CC-NUMA—that do the same thing? Because, at least potentially and with ever-increasing advantage, clusters can do it better, bigger, and cheaper than heroically large SMPs, and with characteristics like high availability that are unavailable in CC-NUMA. But SMPs are here now in a form many customers find more usable.

However, these *architectures* also do it differently, which is a major theme of the next chapter.

Basic Programming Models and Issues

Back in the introduction, I mentioned that there was a particularly nasty issue involved between SMPs and clusters. That issue is both basic and crucial:

> Programs written to exploit SMP parallelism
> *will not work* on clusters, and programs written to
> exploit message-based cluster parallelism
> *will not work* on SMPs.

CC-NUMA is nearly as bad, although CC-NUMA-oriented programs will work on plain SMPs.

This is not like the bad old days, when everybody wrote programs in assembler language and was locked into a particular manufacturer's instruction set and operating system. *It's very much worse.*

It's not a matter of translating a program, algorithms intact, from one language or system to another; instead, the entire approach to the problem must often be rethought from the requirements on up, including new algorithms. Traditional high-level languages and Open Systems standards do not help.

As a result, application developers, middleware developers, subsystem developers, system developers, and through them, users, can wind up locked in, not directly to one manufacturer's system, but to a system architecture. If another architecture turns out to be dramatically more efficient, you can't use it without incurring significant rewriting costs.

Like all generalizations, this one requires qualification. SMP-parallel programs, if otherwise compatible with respect to operating system, programming language, and so on, will run on clusters—in the trivial sense that they'll run on one cluster node. Since that doesn't use the cluster to exploit the program's parallelism, it's close enough to "not working" to satisfy me. They will also run correctly, if more slowly, on CC-NUMA systems as was discussed in Chapter 7.

Cluster-parallel programs are a little trickier, since—again, if otherwise compatible—you can make them run on SMPs and exploit SMP parallelism. The problem is that they will be significantly less efficient than equivalent programs written specifically to exploit SMP parallelism as well as possible. That matters, since SMPs have a good market position; there are a lot out there, so many native SMP-based programs have already been developed. Cluster-parallel programs on SMPs must compete with those. In most cases, the cluster-based versions' lower efficiency will put them at a very distinct disadvantage. As a result, they might as well not work; you can't use them on SMPs and make money from it.

Cluster-parallel programs can run on CC-NUMA systems, but like their execution on SMPs, they'll be slower. The disadvantage on CC-NUMA is likely to be less than that on SMPs, however.

Unfortunately, the statement about being "locked in" requires no qualification. I guess high-level languages and Open System standards make the rewrite easier than in the days of assembler, but that's it.

The computer-science jargon for these intractable differences between SMPs and clusters is that they have different **programming models**. That topic is what this chapter and the next are all about. In the process of showing what a programming model really is by example, this chapter will also substantiate the oft-repeated prior claims that parallelism adds significantly to the difficulties of programming.

9.1   What is a Programming Model?

A programmer is usually about as aware of using a programming model as a fish is of water. It is the all-pervasive atmosphere, the internalized set of assumptions about how a computer works that imbue every program written for that computer. Almasi and Gottlieb [AG94] make the rather good analogy that a programming model (they call it a "computational model") is the set of rules for a game. Programs and algorithms are then game plans or strategies; they indicate how to achieve particular goals within the game, but clearly they are not themselves the rules.

A bit more technically: A programming model is the architecture of a computer system, both hardware and system software, *above* the level that's hidden by traditional high-level languages—C, FORTRAN, COBOL, and their ilk. It is an application's high-level view of the system on which it is running.

Because there is virtually universal agreement on the serial (nonparallel) programming model that everybody uses—the Von Neumann model—the issue of programming models seldom arises except in parallel systems. Hence, the term "parallel programming model" can be taken as synonymous with "programming model."

A large number of programming models have been invented. They differ in ways that are truly basic; in fact, the differences are radical enough to frustrate attempts to construct a completely satisfactory taxonomy of them or otherwise relate them. Not that taxonomizing hasn't been tried; we'll see a few attempts later. Thankfully, all this wild difference doesn't really matter because only three of them, currently implemented on widely available, production computers, currently have a wide following that includes a significant number of economically important programs and systems:[1]

1. the **uniprocessor model**, otherwise known as the Von Neumann model;

2. the **symmetric multiprocessor model**, also referred to in this book as the shared-memory model (although there are other shared-memory models);

3. the **message-passing model** (used in clusters).

In addition to these, the sheer volume of purple prose and confusion requires addition of a fourth:

4. the **CC-NUMA model**.

The SMP, message-passing, and CC-NUMA models will be described in this chapter; it's assumed that the uniprocessor model is well known, even

---

1. For technical computing, there is arguably one more well-used programming model embodied in vector-processing facilities. While vectors are related to the SIMD model, discussed later, in this book vector processing is not discussed. This is primarily a pragmatic decision; were vectors included, a host of other topics unrelated to the main theme would emerge.

though most programmers aren't consciously aware that they're using it. This will be followed by a section giving a brief overview of some of the other programming models that are possible, but for various reasons are not widely used, are *passé*, or never have been the basis of a practical system.

It is important to note that a programming model is not exclusively, and in some cases not even primarily, a quality of hardware. The hardware may have been designed with a specific programming model in mind, but since when has any hardware system ever been used the way the designers envisioned? (Or any software system, for that matter.) Software-induced computer cross-dressing has been mentioned before; it applies here, too. Turing guaranteed that this is always possible, even with the most conventional hardware and the most *outré* programming model imaginable (or, commonly, vice versa). This scarcely makes this chapter's discussion irrelevant, since whether constructed by hardware, software, or a mixture (the usual case), some programming model must be used. Without rules, there is no game.

The treatment of programming models in the rest of this chapter is both different from and similar to that which can be found in more technical detail in textbooks on advanced and/or parallel computer architecture (for example, [AG94, Hwa93]).

It differs because rather than talking *about* the models, with a few examples, its focus is on *using* them. A simple example program will be constructed and reconstructed in different models to demonstrate the differences. In the process, many of the traditional issues of parallel programming will emerge: speedup, races, deadlocks, repeatability, and so on. These problems will be discussed primarily in the context of shared memory, simply because that's treated first; message-passing is by no means immune to such problems.

By the time we've finished, you may well be of the opinion that parallel programming is like trying to turn the Keystone Kops into a precision drill team. That's not far wrong; processing elements will trip over each other's feet at every possible opportunity.

The similarity between this chapter and most discussions of parallel processing is that it is implicitly about processor-centric technical computing, in that it says nothing whatsoever about input/output. That is why this chapter is called *"Basic* Parallel Programming Models." The chapter following this one, which discusses where and how different programming models are actually used, brings in those additional issues; they are obviously quite important for commercial applications (not that they aren't also important in some technical contexts).

By the way, particularly for the shared-memory model, many of the issues discussed are identical to issues arising in multi*programming*, especially within operating systems. In that context the term "process," for an active program, is appropriately used for the active entities. Since we're concerned with parallelism here, the term "processor" will be consistently used.

When we're good and sick of programming model details, we'll return to the reasons why this stuff is so crucial. Grounding ourselves in the examples will make the general discussion much more meaningful.

9.2 The Sample Problem

The simple sample problem used in this chapter comes from the mathematico-technical domain, because only there can we find a simple case that actually does something useful. The techniques we'll end up using definitely apply to commercial processing.

The specific sample problem is based on a two-dimensional grid of data values, as shown in Figure 59. What we'll do is keep the values along the outer edges constant—those edge values will be the input to the calculation—and attempt to set all the interior values in such a way that each value is the average of all its neighbors. Those interior values are our output. The fixed, outer edge values at the boundary are known, logically enough, as the *boundary values*, or *boundary conditions*.

Figure 59 A 2-D Grid of Values and a 4-Point Stencil

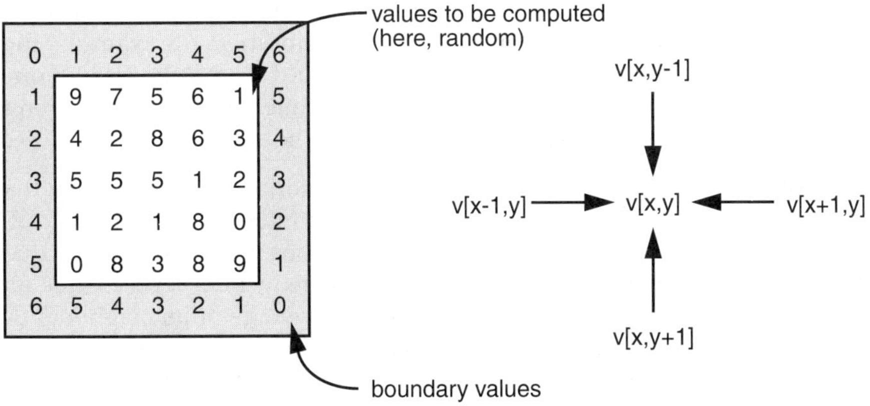

This task might seem like a waste of time, but it actually accomplishes something useful. When the interior values are successfully set to their neighbors'

average, they satisfy a simple approximation to the two-dimensional LaPlace equation *(which you do not have to understand at all)*:

$$\frac{\partial^2 f}{\partial x^2} + \frac{\partial^2 f}{\partial y^2} = 0$$

where x and y represent coordinates in space, and f is the function, the values we're computing.

This equation predicts the shape of things that can bend and stretch when they're pushed or twisted. If you grab a piece of rubber balloon in both hands and twist it, the shape it takes between your hands is predicted by this equation; your hands supply the boundary conditions. Likewise, when an airplane wing, or a steel beam, or anything else is placed under load, its shape is predicted by this type of equation. So, think of LaPlace the next time you land in an airplane or see its wings flex.

Why setting the values to the average of their neighbors ends up satisfying that equation, God only knows. Literally. Nearly all differential equations are "solved" by guessing a solution and then showing ("proving") that the guess was correct. You usually leave some fudge factors in the guess; part of the proof is finding consistent values for the fudge factors (if there aren't any consistent values, you guessed wrong). Somebody—maybe LaPlace—guessed averages, and that turned out to be right.

A couple of other things have to be specified before we start programming.

First: What does "neighbors" mean? We'll take the neighbors of a value to be the ones immediately above, below, left, and right of it. This defines what's called a 4-point stencil, also illustrated in Figure 59: the four points shown contribute to the average. There are other possibilities; for example, the entire box around a value, all eight values, could have been used. Four points is quite enough to illustrate the issues of interest here, which aren't really mathematical; the math is just a carrier for the discussion.

Second: When do we stop? We can't set each interior value to exactly the average of its neighbors, since that would require infinite precision. Instead, we'll be satisfied if it's "close enough." That will be another input, a value called close_enough. We stop when every calculated value—every value on the interior of the grid—is close_enough to the average of its neighbors. A value for close_enough that is, for example, less than 0.01% of the total range of boundary condition values is usually adequately close enough.

That's everything. Let's start. Put on some mental reinforced hip boots, because we're going to beat this problem to death and in the process more or less deliberately step on every cow patty, mantrap, and land mine that parallel processing has to offer.

9.3 Uniprocessor

The way all those intertwined averages are actually computed is so simple it's practically embarrassing.

Want all those values to be nearest-neighbor averages? Go through them all and set them to exactly that: the average of their neighbor's values. Once that's done, ask a question: Did anything change when we did that? If the answer is no—nothing changed significantly, everything was already close_enough—then quit. Obviously, all the values are now close_enough to the average of their neighbors, so we're done. If the answer instead is yes, something did change—some of the values were not already close_enough— just go do it again, *starting with the last set of averages computed*. Each iteration gets a bit closer to the mark, so sooner or later the program gets it right.

Figure 60 shows the business end of some pseudo-code which does exactly that, ignoring the usual details of reading in the boundary values and writing out the output.

Figure 60 Serial Program

```
do forever
    max_change = 0;        /* The largest error we've seen. Initially that's 0. */
    for y = 2 to N-1               /* do all rows, but not outer boundary rows */
        for x = 2 to N-1           /* do all elements in a row, but not boundary*/
            old_value = v[x,y] ;          /* record v[x,y] before changing it */
            /* replace each value with the average of its neighbors */
            v[x,y] = ( v[x-1,y] + v[x+1,y] + v[x,y-1] + v[x, y+1] ) / 4 ;
            /* keep max_change at the largest magnitude change we've seen */
            max_change = max(   max_change,
                                abs( old_value-v[x,y] )   ) ;
        end for x ;                       /* done with that row */
    end for y ;                           /* done with all the rows */
    if max_change < close_enough then leave do forever ; /* are we done? */
end do forever;
```

The nested loops that do the work go from 2 to N-1 over an array of values, v[], that goes from 1 to N in both dimensions. The outer elements—row 1, column 1, row N, and column N—are skipped because they're the constant boundary conditions. They don't get changed.

In order to answer the "did anything change" question at the end of each complete pass through v[]—known as a full iteration—the program must keep track of the biggest change in value that it has seen. That's done using the variables max_error and old_value. max_error holds the largest change made to any element of the value array v[]. Before changing any element of v[], we first tuck the element away in old_value. Then we set max_error to the larger of two things: (a) whatever it currently is; and (b) the magnitude—absolute value, abs()—of the latest change done. That change is the difference between old_value and the newly computed value. After we've done all the points (completed both for loops), we look at max_error; if it's close_enough, we quit.

That's all there is to it.

The technique described above is certainly not the only way to solve LaPlace's equation or ones like it, known as elliptical equations. This is what's known as an iterative technique, using finite differences. It repeatedly "iterates" some operation until the right answer appears or, rather, as close an approximation to the right answer as you like. There are also direct techniques; those don't iterate, they "directly" produce the correct answer. They involve creating banded matrices, inverting them, and other stuff that is, to me, anyway, not as much fun. Direct techniques sound much faster, but that isn't necessarily so in all cases. Iterative techniques are a perfectly valid, viable solution technique, and have the advantage that you can "dial in" the amount of accuracy you want, trading it for execution time as you like. There is a common variation on the iterative method used here, known as successive over-relaxation (SOR), that is far preferable if you're doing this stuff for a living; these and generally more mathematically rigorous parallel techniques for approaching the problem can be found elsewhere, for example, [FJL+88].

Another reason for using iterative techniques is that they're fun to watch. While it's traditional to begin the iteration with everything set to zero, that's boring. Figure 61 shows what happens when the program above is let loose on a collection of 24x24 essentially random points in the range 0 to 745,[2] with only four points tacked down as boundary conditions: the four corners. Initially, as expected, it's a mess. After just one iteration, a lot of the chaos has already dissipated; after four iterations it's already assuming a decent form, but is still pretty bumpy. It takes 61 iterations to get everything close_enough, in this case within 0.1 (out of a 0–740 range, that's around 0.01% accuracy), resulting in what's traditionally called a saddle-shaped curve.

2. Why that odd range of values? Since you can literally start these things out with any values whatsoever, I used my last 576 scores from the Microsoft Windows solitaire applet. Less boring than a random number generator.

Figure 61   Iterating to a Saddle-Shaped Curve

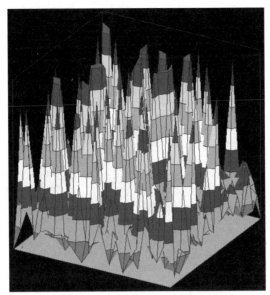

Start: Solitaire Random

After Iteration 1, max_change = 553
A swift reduction in "randomness."

Figure 62 Iterating to a Saddle-Shaped Curve, continued

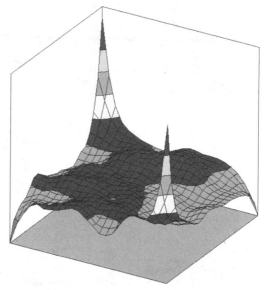

After iteration 4, max_change = 38
Starting to look smooth

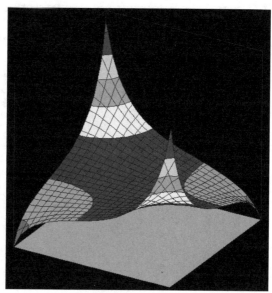

After iteration 64, max_change = 0.1,
which was good_enough.

In Search of Clusters ✳

Figure 63 Iterating to a Turkey Curve

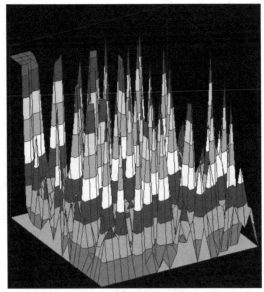

Start: Solitaire Random

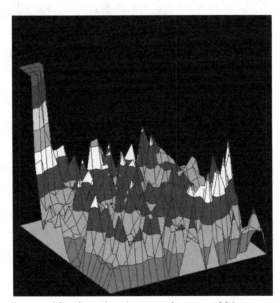

After Iteration 1, max_change = 661
A swift reduction in "randomness."

Figure 64   Iterating to a Turkey Curve, continued

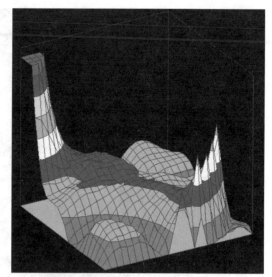

After iteration 4, max_change = 43
The turkey emerges.

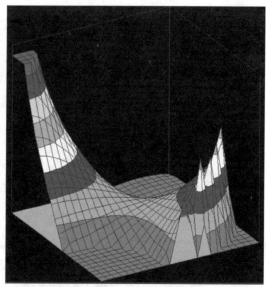

After iteration 46, max_change = 0.1,
which was good_enough.

You can also, by the way, have "boundary" conditions in the middle. Imagine taking a rubber sheet, stretching it between both hands, and bringing it down on top of a coffee cup. The top rim of the cup becomes a set of interior boundary conditions. It's straightforward (though a little tedious) to modify the program above to allow any point to be a fixed boundary position. That's what I did for Figure 63, which I intended to iterate to a Western saddle-shaped curve, complete with pommel. Owing partly to a lack of resolution on the 24x24 grid used and partly to having too high a pommel, I got a turkey curve instead.

9.4   Shared Memory

All right, what parts of this can be done in parallel—which is to say: what parts can be done at the same time? The comparison of max_change with good_enough looks like something that cannot be done in parallel; it needs to intervene between iterations to determine whether to do another iteration. On the other hand, we've got a whole lot of averages to do during each iteration, so that sounds like a good place to start. The shared memory, SMP programming model is the first case we'll tackle.

Because all the data is available to all the processors in the shared memory, we can assume the program is still basically serial and just "turn on" parallelism at the points where it's useful. The parallelism, in other words, is primarily involved in the program's self-control—control parallelism, as distinct from what we'll see with message-passing.

To keep this discussion fairly simple, we'll assume some seemingly straightforward programming language constructs which turn the parallelism on and off.

The first is the forall statement (elsewhere called doall, foreach, pardo, etc.). This is just like a usual iterative for statement, except that it doesn't actually iterate. Instead, it says "just get all these things done, in any order, using as many processors as are available." The number of processors available to the job may be specified or limited in some way, but that's usually outside the domain of forall; rather, it's in job initialization or some other parallelism support.

Simply using forall in a straightforward manner gives the program shown in Figure 65. It looks just like the original serial code, except for that shared, private, and lock stuff. Those additions are a direct consequence of the fact that several processors are going to be executing the code in the middle of the forall loops, all at the same time.

Figure 65 Shared Memory Parallel Solution

```
lock max_change_lock;         /* declare a lock for max_change*/
shared v[], x, y, max_change; /* indicate that v and max_change are shared, */
private default;              /*...and nothing else is. */
/***** The main loop *****/
do forever                    /* The outer main iteration loop is serial */
  max_change = 0;             /* Still serial. */
  forall y = 2 to N-1         /* do all rows at once, in parallel */
    forall x = 2 to N-1       /* do all elements in a row at once, in parallel */

      old_value = v[x,y] ;    /* record v[x,y] before changing it */

      /* replace each value with the average of its neighbors */
      v[x,y] = ( v[x-1,y] + v[x+1,y] + v[x,y-1] + v[x, y+1] ) / 4 ;

      /* keep max_change at the largest magnitude change we've seen */
      acquire ( max_change_lock ) ;  /* wait for access to max_change */
      max_change = max(   max_change,
                          abs( old_value-v[x,y] )   ) ;
      release ( max_change_lock ) ;  /* finished with max_change */

    end forall x ;            /* done with all columns*/
  end forall y ;              /* done with all rows */
  if max_change < close_enough then leave do forever ; /* are we done? */
end do forever;
```

The shared statement indicates which data is actually accessed by all the processors using the same names. The private default statement reinforces the fact that sharing is not the default; only things explicitly shared are used in common, and every processor has its own private copy of everything else. This seems counterintuitive. After all, the hardware makes everything shared; something special has to happen behind the scenes to give each processor its own private copy of something, and even then it's private only by convention—the processors all have to agree to abide by the privatizing rules; nothing's forcing them to stay out of each other's turf. But sharing is tricky, as we shall see. Therefore, it's better programming practice to explicitly label the things that are shared, so there's at least that much of a reminder that they have to be treated specially.

9.4.1   Races and Locks

That special treatment of shared data is typified by the locking statements. For the program to work, the end of each full iteration must find max_change set to the maximum change made to any element of v[]. That means every processor has to test and potentially adjust its value, which is why the max_change adjustment is inside the nested loops.

But all will not be well if each processor simply whacks away at max_change. To see why, consider how a maximum is actually computed:

```
1       load reg_1 with newest change
2       load reg_2 with (old) max_change
3       reg_1 > reg_2?
4       Yes: store reg_1 in max_change
```

Two registers are loaded with the values to be compared, the comparison is done, and a store is performed if the new change is bigger than the old max_change. This is straightforward. But it contains an assumption: It assumes that the copy of max_change in reg_2 is the correct, current value during steps 3 and 4, where the comparison is made and the store is done.

That assumption is trivially true on a uniprocessor; you don't even have to think about it. But if multiple processors are whacking around on max_change at the same time, that assumption may be false. Somebody else could change it during that time it's held in the register.

The program for the kind of thing that can happen is shown in Figure 66, and a graphical illustration is in Figure 67.

Figure 66   A Race Condition

time	processor Able newest change = 100	max_ change	processor Baker newest change = 10
1	load reg_1 with 100	0	
2	load reg_2 with 0	0	load reg_1 with 10
3	100 > 0?	0	load reg_2 with 0
4	Yes: store 100 in max_change	100	10 > 0?
5		10	Yes: store 10 in max_change

Everybody starts with max_change = 0

WRONG!— reg_2's copy of max_change is out of date

Figure 67   A Race Condition, Graphically

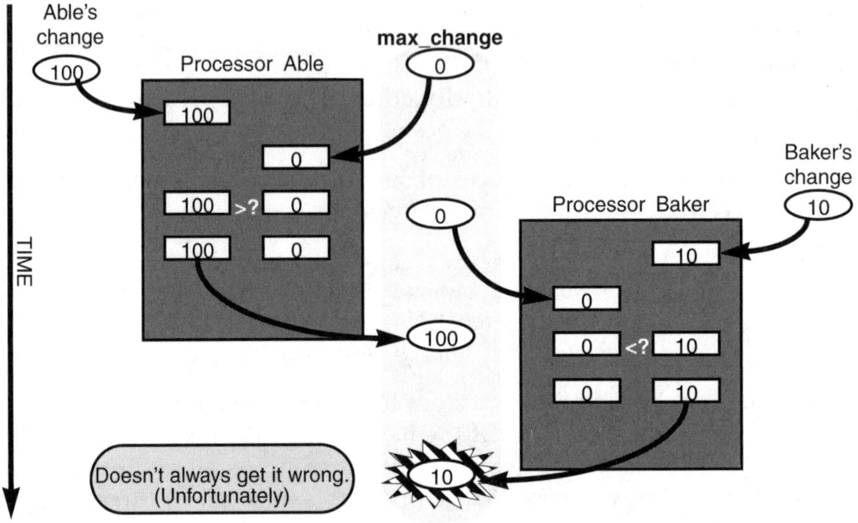

Processor Able initially makes a copy of max_change (time 2 in the code). Processor Baker innocently makes its own copy while Able is munching along (time 3), oblivious to Able's actions. Then, in the middle of Baker's comparison, Able goes and changes max_change. Bzzzzt! max_change does not end up containing the actual maximum change.

However, this is not always going to lead to an incorrect value. If both processors happened upon max_change when it contained 400, both comparisons would have failed and, since neither one did an update, no damage would have been done. On the other hand, if both processors happened upon max_change when it contained 75, Able would have stored its 100; but Baker's comparison would have failed, so it wouldn't have stored anything. Result: max_change ends up at the right value. So, sometimes the right answer will be produced.

That's much worse than failing consistently.

If the fool thing got the wrong answer *every* time, you would: (a) at least be certain something was wrong and not be tempted to attribute it to gremlins; (b) be able to examine it, time and time again, meticulously checking all the possibilities, until the cause was determined. That's not possible if it happens only sporadically.

The kind of difficulty we're discussing is called a **race condition**, because whether the program works depends on the relative timing and speed of the processors involved—in effect, it is a race among them. To keep this horrible stuff from happening, we must only allow one processor at a time to get at max_change. This is mutual exclusion, as was mentioned back in "Sequential and Other Consistencies" on page 174, and it's what the lock does.

A lock, as we're using it, has the effect of turning a block of code into a kind of voting booth: Only one processor can get in it at once; once one's in, another can't enter. Unlike a voting booth, a processor can stay inside it as long as it wants without getting other processors mad (but it may get you annoyed; stay tuned). Once out, somebody else is allowed in. The block of code is more formally known as a **critical section,** I suppose because it's "critical" that nobody else be in there.

The program we've written uses the procedure acquire() to "get" the lock ("acquire possession" of it) and be allowed into the critical section. release() is used to "let go of" the lock, letting the system know that it's out of the critical section. There can be many different locks in a parallel program. Each has associated data needed to implement the locking function itself, which is why acquire() and release() take an argument; in the program, that's the data structure named max_change_lock.

Applying that lock to our race condition of Figure 66 results in the execution shown in Figure 68 (code) and Figure 69 (graphically).

Figure 68   Race Condition Resolved With a Lock

Everybody starts with max_change = 0

time	processor Able newest change = 100	max_ change	processor Baker newest change = 10
1	call acquire(max_change_lock)	0	call acquire(max_change_lock)
2	load reg_1 with 100	0	… waiting inside acquire()…
3	load reg_2 with 0	0	… waiting inside acquire()…
4	100 > 0?	0	… waiting inside acquire()…
5	Yes: store 100 in max_change	100	… waiting inside acquire()…
6	call release(max_change_lock)	100	… waiting inside acquire()…
7		100	load reg_1 with 10
8		100	load reg_2 with 100
9		100	10 > 100?
10		100	No: do nothing
11		100	call release(max_change_lock)

Figure 69   Race Resolved with a Lock, Graphically

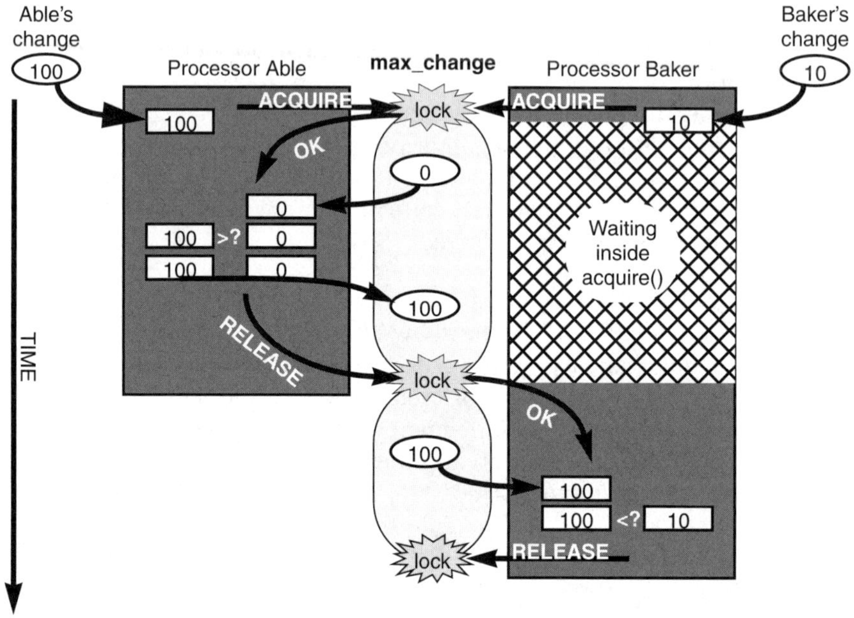

Able's change
100

Processor Able

max_change

Processor Baker

Baker's change
10

ACQUIRE
lock
100

OK
0

0

100 >? 0

100 0

100

ACQUIRE
10

Waiting inside acquire()

RELEASE
lock

100

OK

100

100 <? 10

lock

RELEASE

TIME

The procedure acquire() is written extremely carefully; even if two (or more) processors call it at exactly the same time, only one returns. The other, or others, wait inside acquire() until the lucky one that got through calls release(); then, if anybody's waiting, exactly one more returns from its wait inside acquire(). (If a "lucky one" forgets to call release(), or aborts for some reason, the program is in bad shape; other processors will wait in acquire() forever. Ominous parallelism bug #2769.)

The figures illustrate this process for the case in which Able and Baker both happen to call acquire() simultaneously, and Able won. Baker waits in acquire() until Able calls release(). Now the assumption made by the "maximum" program fragment is correct: Nobody else can change max_change while a processor is in the critical section. It works.

It's also slower. Notice that in Figure 68, the program takes 11 time steps, not counting the time spent in the acquire() and release() procedures, which can be considerable. The original in Figure 66 took only five time steps, with no procedure calls. As usual, you can be really fast if you don't have to be correct; but there's something more going on here.

In Search of Clusters ✳

9.4.2 Serialization

As a result of the lock, which was necessary for correctness, all the processors have to line up to update max_change. That means that when they're updating max_change, they're not working in parallel any more: They've been serialized. This has been spoken of previously in the context of Amdahl's law; why it comes about has not been discussed, nor has there yet been any real indication of its effects. We've now arrived at the point where those issues can be discussed.

Figure 70 illustrates the effect of a serial section like this on a program. Time flows downward in the figure; think of it as taking the program fragments of Figure 68 and Figure 69, eliminating all the detail, coloring the "useful work" white, the update to max_change grey, and the wait crosshatched.

Figure 70 Serialization

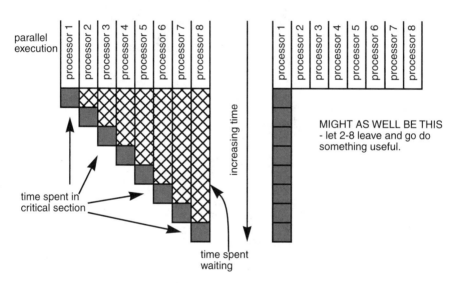

At first, all the processors are doing useful stuff in parallel. Then, they have to update something in common, such as our max_change variable. If the work is perfectly distributed to begin with, they'll reach the critical section at the same time, but only one will get through; as shown in the left side of the figure, that's processor 1. It does its thing, and then another gets in, followed by another, and so on. Now take a look at the right side of Figure 70. You might as well not have all those processors any more—one alone can do the job just as fast.[3] That's serialization.

Our program, however, doesn't execute like that diagram. We've got lots of averages to do, so when each processor finishes with the critical section update of max_change, it goes back and does another average—and then waits for the critical section again.

This is shown in Figure 71. Processor 2, for example, does some work, then waits, then goes through the critical section, then does some more work, waits, and so on. So does every other processor. In this simple case, they will eventually form a pattern. It generally won't be as clean and uniform as that illustrated, because none of the times involved are exactly repeatable; cache misses, memory errors, and so on will affect processing time pseudo- (or truly) randomly.

Figure 71 Re-execution During Serialization

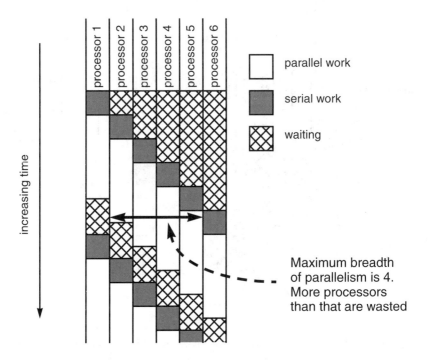

But notice something in Figure 71: Processor 1, the first one through, is finished a *second* time and waiting again before processor 5 has completed its *first* wait. Something is wrong here. If processor 1 gets back in the queue (and there is a queue involved, inside acquire()) while 5 and 6 are still in the queue, why bother having 5 and 6? All they're doing is spending time wait-

3. Actually, it can probably do it faster than many could, because it will have better cache locality. More about this later.

ing. Looking at the diagram more closely, you can notice (check the horizontal arrow) that only four processors are active at any given time. That says the same thing: Don't bother with processors 5 and 6. But there are potentially thousands of averages to do. Only four processors are useful no matter how much work is to be done? Is this an artifact of the diagram?

The specific number of processors, four, is indeed an artifact of the diagram. But limits like this are a general phenomenon. The issue is how much time is spent in serial code, compared with how much time is spent in parallel. Given N processors, once (N × serial time) > parallel time, you don't need any more of them—if they're running in the kind of pattern shown in Figure 71. That's one kind of pattern; there are many other possible patterns, and all have their restrictions. The point: Even if you have a ton of completely separate, different things to do, you can still be limited in the amount of parallelism available, limited by the need to keep the processors from tripping over each other's feet.

How long is our example's serial time compared with the parallel time? Actually, it's pretty bad. The only thing we're doing in parallel is a single averaging operation, and serially we're doing two things. One, updating max_change, has been discussed. As to the other: Where did you think the values of the indices x and y were coming from? That's right. Hidden inside the forall implementation is a lock. The "forall x=..." statement must acquire() a lock for x, then increment x, then release() that lock on every iteration of the inner loop. The outer loop does the same for y.

This doesn't seem that bad. After all, the things we're doing in those critical sections are pretty trivial: taking a maximum, doing a single integer addition. The floating-point operations in the "real" work should, one might think, overwhelm that. Unfortunately, something else is going on in addition to that.

Recall the discussion about sequential consistency back on page 174. Suppose, in order to let the processor run fast most of the time, a technique like weak ordering or release consistency is used. This means that for the program to work at all—for example, for the correct value of max_change to be picked up when it's first loaded—the entire, mile-long, anthracite-loaded freight train of a processor's superscalar, pipelined operation has to come to a shuddering halt on each lock. That's what is needed to let the changed data values percolate through the system.[4] The acquire() and release() proce-

---

4. If it's not using those weaker orderings, it's running more slowly all the time, not just part of the time. Using a slower processor so you can be more parallel is almost never the correct tradeoff.

dures must contain the appropriate, processor-specific instructions causing this to happen.

This means that a processor that could scream right along, completing a floating-point add every cycle, must wait, often as many as 10, 20, or more cycles when a lock must be grabbed. Synchronizing the data across the whole system, and that's what locking requires, is *expensive*.

Net: The program as so far written is in very bad shape serialization-wise. Fortunately, there's a relatively simple way to fix it: Don't try to use so much parallelism. We have lots of rows and lots of columns. Right now we're trying to use them simultaneously and tripping over our own feet in the process. Instead, let's use parallelism only on different rows and do each entire row serially.

That is what is shown in Figure 72, where the inner loop has been changed back into a serial for statement. This necessitated some additional changes: Now a running maximum change is kept in a private, per-processor variable, row_max. When an entire row is completed, row_max is used to update the global maximum, max_changes.

Instead of synchronizing on every point—N^2 times—the program will only update max_changes and get a new parallel index y on each row—N times. That's a factor of N reduction.

As a result, the program will run much faster and, *by deliberately using less parallelism*, be able to use *many more* processors.

As a matter of fact, there is published evidence that this technique achieves the best speedup of any we will consider in this chapter: as much as 3.95 times faster on four processors [EY92]. Sounds pretty good.

Too bad it never gets the same answer twice in a row.

9.4.3   *Consistency and Chaos*

The program we've got so far will produce *a* correct answer; the values of v[] it produces will be good_enough averages of their neighbors. But for any one set of input values, there are any number of sets of v[] values satisfying that criterion. Running our current program twice, under exactly the same conditions, with exactly the same input values, will give two of those correct answers. Different ones. They will most likely differ down in the umpteenth decimal place; the harder you screw down good_enough, the larger "umpteen" will get; you might not even notice it unless your output format shows enough decimal places; but they will differ.

Figure 72   A Better Shared-Memory Parallel Implementation

```
lock max_change_lock;        /* declare a lock for max_change*/
shared v[], x, y, max_change;  /* indicate that v and max_change are shared, */
private default;             /*...and nothing else is. */
/***** The main loop *****/
do forever                   /* The outer main iteration loop is serial */
  max_change = 0;            /* Still serial. */
  forall y = 2 to N-1        /* do all rows at once, in parallel */
    row_max = 0;             /* reset running maximum for this row */
    for x = 2 to N-1         /* do the elements in a row serially */
      old_value = v[x,y] ;   /* record v[x,y] before changing it */
      /* replace each value with the average of its neighbors */
      v[x,y] = ( v[x-1,y] + v[x+1,y] + v[x,y-1] + v[x, y+1] ) / 4 ;
      /* keep row_max at the largest change made on this row */
      row_max = max( row_max,
                     abs( old_value-v[x,y] )   ) ;
    end for x;               /* done with one entire row */
    /* keep max_change at the largest magnitude change we've seen */
    acquire ( max_change_lock ) ;  /* wait for access to max_change */
    max_change = max ( max_change, row_max ) ;
    release ( max_change_lock ) ;  /* finished with max_change */
  end forall y ;             /* done with all rows */
  if max_change < close_enough then leave do forever ; /* are we done? */
end do forever;
```

This kind of behavior can be disturbing. Lots of people expect computers to act like machines, after all, not like other people, and machines are alleged to do the same thing, time after time, except for certain specifically-designated, exceptional circumstances usually involving "random" number generators and Art.

Of course, if you don't know why the system is acting that way you've no guarantee it won't go completely nonmachine and give you a genuinely wrong answer, not just an alternative right one. That would be bad. So, why is this happening?

If something looks, smells, and acts intermittent, variable, and unrepeatable, it's probably a race condition. This is no exception. In fact, it's the mother of all race conditions. We don't have any controls in place that coordinate updating all the many values of the v[] array itself.

As a processor—call it Charlie—lays its stencil down on the array and computes an average for v[x,y] in the inner loop, it picks up values of v[x,y-1] and v[x,y+1]. It also uses v[x-1,y] and v[x+1,y]; those don't matter to us here, because they're in Charlie's own row and therefore under its own control. The y-1 and y+1 cases, on the other hand, are in the rows above and below the one Charlie's working on.

Those are possibly being whacked at by other processors, but, as usual, only possibly: There might be processors working the rows above and below Charlie's, or there might not. If there are, (see Figure 73) they could be consistently behind Charlie as it cranks across the row, or consistently ahead; or they could be neck-and-neck, duking it out for the same cache lines (about which more in a bit); or, since there are two other processors involved, one could be ahead and the other behind, or vice versa, or they could switch in the course of a row, or... you get the idea.

Figure 73 Charlie's Fortunes in the New/Old Value Race

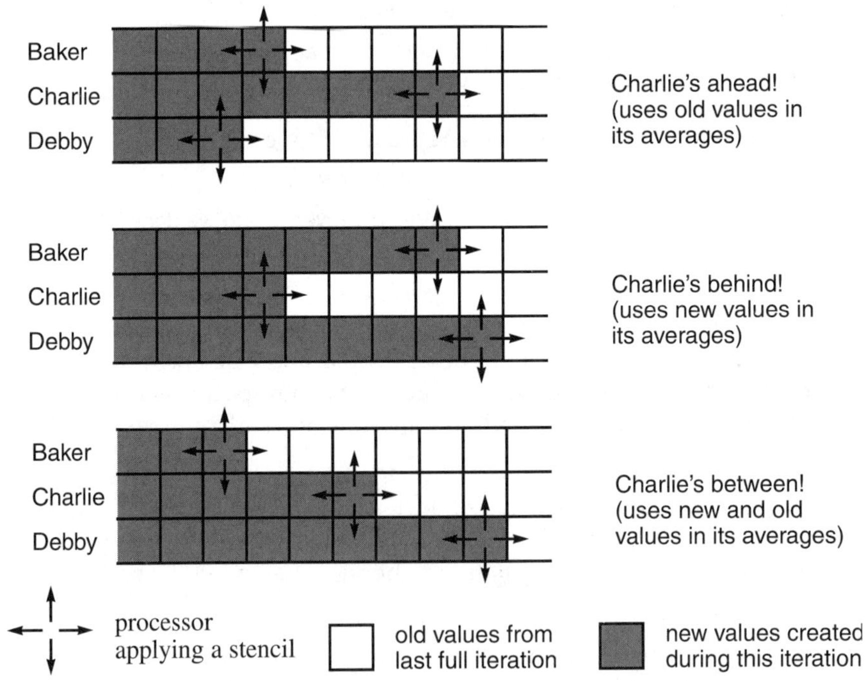

Charlie's ahead!
(uses old values in
its averages)

Charlie's behind!
(uses new values in
its averages)

Charlie's between!
(uses new and old
values in its averages)

processor
applying a stencil

old values from
last full iteration

new values created
during this iteration

Things are pretty chaotic. The reason we get *a* correct answer at all has nothing to do with computer science, but rather with the mathematics of the iterative technique itself. It happens that Charlie never picks up a truly incongruous, random-like value because there are only two possibilities. For each value, either

> ➢ Charlie got there first, in which case Charlie gets the value that was in v[] before this full iteration started—an **old** value; or

> ➢ Charlie got there last, in which case Charlie gets the value that will be in v[] after this full iteration ends—a **new** value.

So all the possibilities for the input values to the averages aren't totally off the wall; they're at least on their way to a final solution.[5] Therefore, the averages computed from those values aren't bizarre either, which makes the next round of values reasonable, and so on. But the randomness of the situation produces different, but still correct, results each time.

It's a bit amazing to me that this method works at all, but work it certainly does. There's even a body of mathematical work behind it, complete with a formal name: chaotic relaxation. That mathematics, and not the "computer science," gives us assurance that it will work. There are many circumstances in which not only does it work, it converges to a solution faster than other methods. It even has been cited in cases of superlinear speedup: N processors produce a result in less than 1/Nth the time it takes one processor.

Before the marketeers start blowing this one to all four winds simultaneously: It doesn't always work. There are mathematical circumstances surrounding its use that have been quite carefully delineated, and I, for one, don't understand them at all.

In any event, most people don't like their computers acting this way. So how do we stop it?

---

5. There is another hidden assumption here. The possibilities listed assume that when a processor writes into the array, it does so all at once; it doesn't write part of a value and then another part. This is called an atomic—indivisible—operation. There are systems in which updating a double-precision floating-point number is *not atomic*. In that case, Charlie could just happen to read a value between the time one part is updated, and the time another part is updated. Result: Sorry, Charlie. You picked up garbage: a half-updated value, half old, and half new. This has happened, in practice. It's yet another nonrepetitive, intermittent horror story.

9.4.4 Many Locks and Deadly Embraces (Deadlocks)

Locking got us out of a race condition before. But we certainly do not want to create an array of locks, one for each element of v[], and lock the y-1 and y+1 elements before computing an average, for three reasons.

> ➤ We just finished removing the acquisition of one lock for every average, the lock on max_change. Adding two doesn't sound terrifically smart. The serialization won't be as bad as the max_change case because at most three processors are ever contending for a value and because many times they aren't even going to go after the lock at the same time. But there is still the intrinsic overhead of system synchronization on every lock operation.

> ➤ How many locks was that again? Just locking the values above and below isn't enough, because you somehow have to keep other processors out of the value being updated. It sounds like you have to lock the whole stencil. The overhead is now in the category of "tremendous."

> ➤ It just plain doesn't work in the first place. Say the program successfully locks everything in sight. Has it locked them before or after they've been updated? Will the average be based on old or on new values? This is the same problem we have without locks.

It sounds like we really don't want to lock each element. How about locking whole rows? There could be a lock for each row, and the code could grab all three row locks needed before doing anything, then do an entire row, then unlock them. This doesn't sound as ridiculous as locking every element; the overhead is back to reasonable amounts. Unfortunately, there are two reasons why this is a bad idea, too.

The first reason has to do with the danger, in general, of acquiring multiple locks. Suppose a processor—Charlie again—successfully gets the locks for its row, row **c**, and the one above. However, Charlie is blocked when it tries to get row **d** below; somebody else—Debby—already got that row. Oh, well, Charlie just has to wait until Debby's done.

Wait a minute. Debby also has to get three locks.

Suppose Debby successfully got row **d**, *and then tried to get row **c** after Charlie already locked it?*

Charlie's stuck waiting on **d**; it won't ever let go of **c**. Debby's stuck waiting on **c**; it won't ever let go of **d**.

If that happens, Charlie and Debbie have effectively locked onto each other, nevermore to separate. Their relationship is illustrated in Figure 74. They'll wait forever. The application locks up, because the iteration they're trying to do never finishes.

Figure 74 Charlie and Debby's Deadly Embrace

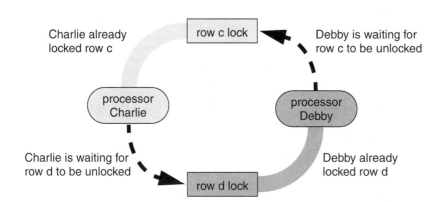

This kind of thing used to be called, rather evocatively, a **deadly embrace.** Nowadays it's more well known as a **deadlock.** The name change was probably done in pursuit of unnecessarily meticulous terminological exactitude,[6] since this situation can happen to more than two processors at once: Charlie's stuck on Debby's stuck on Pat's stuck on Charlie. "Deadly embrace" is "correctly" used when there are only two participants.

Can it happen here? As it turns out, it's possible. It depends on the details of the way program is modified to acquire those row locks. It might avoid the problem by accident, but a slight change in the problem statement could reintroduce them. Here's why.

To get a deadlock (deadly embrace), you need—as shown in Figure 74—a circular pattern: a cycle of references to resources of any kind, not just locks. All that matters is that only one entity can own each resource at a time. They could be tape drives or printers, for example. The circular pattern is the issue: No cycle, no deadlock.

To get the cycle in the example, Charlie had to ask for row **c**, then row **d**, and Debby had to ask for row **d**, *then* row **c**. They had to ask in the opposite order, creating a cycle in their lock requests, to get in trouble. If both had asked in the same order—say, **d** then **c**—there's no problem. Here's why.

6. To say nothing of a lack of imagination.

Since both ask for **d** before **c**, Debby (say) would get it and Charlie would wait there at **d**. So Charlie, waiting at **d**, can't interfere with Debby getting **c**. Debby would get **c**, work, and then release both **c** and **d**. As soon **d** was released, Charlie could get it and **c**, and do its work.

Now, one likely way to have programmed the locks is to have stuck these three lines in front of the loop that does a row:

```
acquire ( row_lock[y-1] ) ;
acquire ( row_lock[y] ) ;
acquire ( row_lock[y+1] ) ;
```

If this is done, all the row locks are always acquired in the "natural" order of their rows and in the same order by everybody. There are no cycles, so there will be no deadlocks. We win. Another likely possibility is to acquire the locks in the opposite order; that would have been just as good. We win again.

However, had it been programmed as

```
acquire( row_lock[y] ) ;
acquire( row_lock[y+1] ) ;
acquire( row_lock[y-1] ) ;
```

then there would be a potential deadlock, because no consistent order is followed in acquiring the locks: the order is up, then down, not consistently down or up. We lose. Several other similarly inconsistent orders exist, too. Which order would you have written? (*Before* you had read this.)

Even if a right order is (perhaps accidentally) chosen, the acquire() statements above will fail if the problem is changed slightly, to a common variation called "periodic boundary conditions." In that variation, there are no constant values on some pair, or both pairs, of sides. Instead, the requirement is that the top and bottom edges (for example) end up at the same values. The solution obtained with periodic boundary conditions is one that's valid for long strips or big areas: Copy after copy of the array can be pasted together at the edges, since opposite edges have the same values.

Computing the correct averages when using periodic boundary conditions is easily accomplished. Just run the averages around the edges of the array, "wrapping" the stencil from top to bottom (for example). This is done by computing the row indices y+1 and y-1 modulo the size of the array (if an index is greater than N, subtract N and continue; could do the column indices, too).

Unfortunately, this introduces a great big cycle into the "natural" way to acquire the locks, since the row indices now cycle around the whole array.

Looking at it another way: The modulo'd value of y+1 can be less than the modulo'd values of y and y-1, so we've lost a consistent order.

It's admittedly extremely unlikely that the whole cycle, all the way around the array, will lock up at once. The longer a cycle is, in general the less likely it is to be encountered. But it still could happen and of course will happen at the worst possible time. It is still possible to acquire the locks in an overall total order, but special attention is needed—and, of course, the need must be anticipated.

As was hinted when the more general term "resources" was used in place of "locks," deadlock avoidance is clearly a far more general problem than this discussion has indicated so far. Operating systems, transaction managers, and database management systems must be alert to the possibility of deadlocks.

Rather than deadlock avoidance or prevention, which has been discussed here, a strategy of deadlock detection is more often used. Occasionally the system fires up a subprogram that checks out all the locks (one lock for each resource), looks at who's waiting on them, and sees if there are any cycles. If there are cycles, one or more of the embracers in a cycle is told to give up: release all the locks it's holding, and start all over again. If this doesn't break all the cycles, another is told to give up, and so on. Once the cycles are broken, continued progress can be made. Obviously, this doesn't work unless the lock holders have specifically been written in a way that lets them give up and start over; in databases and transaction managers, for example, it's the required operation of "aborting a transaction," and the database or transaction manager provides that property for all applications running under it without their having to explicitly deal with it—as long as the applications only access information that's part of the data base; step outside, and anything could happen.

Now we know how to lock the rows in a way that avoids deadly embraces and deadlocks. This solves the first problem with using row locks. However, it was mentioned that there was a second. The second is much simpler and, unfortunately a little harder to deal with:

I've been leading you down a primrose path. Which processors get which rows is still the luck of the draw inside acquire() and can vary from run to run, so this method doesn't solve the problem we are worried about. The answers obtained will be somewhat more consistent from run to run, probably, but the program still isn't guaranteed to get the same right answer twice. Other methods have to be found.

9.4.5   Alternation Schemes

The difficulty we're having with consistency arises because some averages are based on old values present when the iteration started, others are based on new ones computed during the iteration, and there's no real control over which of the average calculations use which values. When the problem's stated that way, it's fairly obvious that some control must be exerted over exactly that aspect: who uses old values and who uses new values. There are several ways to apply such control, all based on knowingly segregating old from new values and alternating between them.

A rather obvious way to segregate the new from the old values is to keep them in separate arrays, as illustrated in Figure 75. Every processor reads values from one array, A, but never writes into it. Instead, the new averages are put in array B. When B is completely filled, assuming another iteration is required, you either copy B into A or, less expensively, exchange some pointers so now everybody reads from B and writes into A.

Figure 75 A/B Alternation (Gauss-Jacobi Iteration)

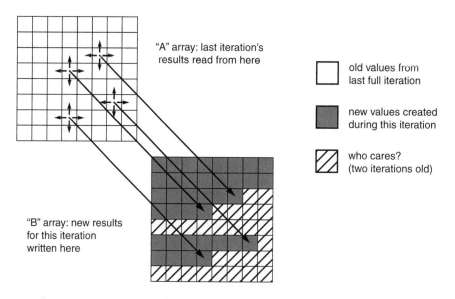

The iterations now proceed through time by flipping from A to B, then B to A, then A to B, and so on. No matter what order the system does the averages, they're all consistently based on old values, because there's nothing *but* old values in the source array. The program will give the same result with the same inputs, time after time. We have achieved complete, total consistency. Congratulations, us.

We have also used up twice as much memory. This is not good on general principles and is likely to get in the way when (not if) the calculation is done on a finer mesh (a bigger array) or extended beyond two dimensions to three.

Well, how about segregating old and new within the same array? That can be done, too.

The simplest way to do this with the program we started from is to divide the rows into two groups: odd-numbered rows and even-numbered rows. We'll call these "red" and "black" rows for a reason that will soon be clear. Now, we split each iteration into two phases. In phase 1, we read the red and write the black rows; in phase 2, we read the black and write the red—or, equivalently, flip what we call red and black.

Figure 76   Red/Black Iteration with Alternating Rows

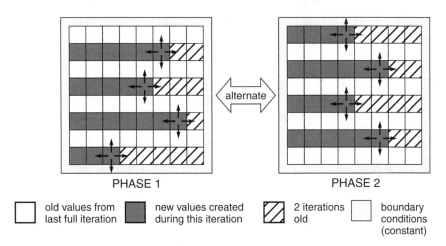

PHASE 1   PHASE 2

☐ old values from last full iteration   ■ new values created during this iteration   ▨ 2 iterations old   ☐ boundary conditions (constant)

This red/black row alternation is illustrated in Figure 76. It also yields consistent results, because all the processors read only red (outside their own rows, anyway), and write only black. That means that during any phase their results never mingle, so the order in which they perform their computations doesn't matter at all.

That's not the only way to segregate within the array, however. We could also apply red/black labels like a checkerboard, alternating within each row, as illustrated in Figure 77. This is obviously where the red/black nomenclature comes from. It, too produces consistent results, for the same reason the row-by-row scheme does. Also, it will usually require fewer iterations than row-by-row because it percolates value changes more uniformly and quickly throughout the array.

Figure 77   Red/Black Checkerboard Alternation

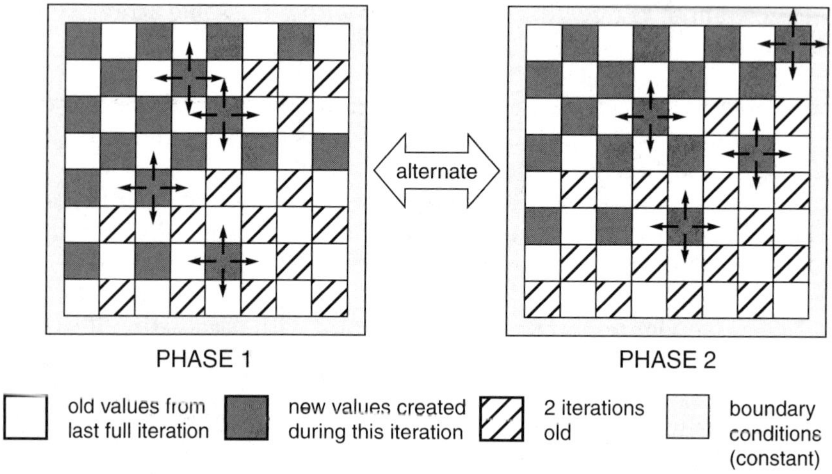

| | PHASE 1 | | | PHASE 2 |

| | old values from last full iteration | | new values created during this iteration | | 2 iterations old | | boundary conditions (constant) |

We now have a parallel program that uses no more storage than the original, except for locks and a few other minor things. It also runs fast and gives the same answer every time when given the same input. Pretty good.

The problem now is that the answer it gives is not the same one the original program gave. Groan.

9.4.6   What Went Wrong?

Once again, we're getting *a* correct answer; the values of v[] are all good_enough. We also get the same answer every time, which is soothing. But the answer produced is not *the* correct answer—the same one produced by the serial program.

In addition, the parallel program often takes more full iterations than did the original to get all the values into the good_enough range. Each of those iterations does go faster, but the fact that more of them are required cuts into the speedup we're getting. This is at least annoying and should be troubling.

Those two facts are linked. What's happened is that we changed the mathematical type of iteration being performed when we segregated the old and new values to achieve consistency.

The original program did *not* use all old values when it computed an average. Ignore the constant boundaries for a moment. As shown in Figure 78, whenever the program computed a new average for a value, the row above was already done; it contained all new values. That meant that the component at the top of the stencil wasn't old, it was new. Similarly, the program had already computed the previous point on the row, so the value on the left of the stencil was also new. The other two components of the average, the bottom and right parts of the stencil, hadn't yet been computed. So, they were still old. The original program used new on top and left, and old on right and bottom.

Figure 78 What the Original Program Really Did

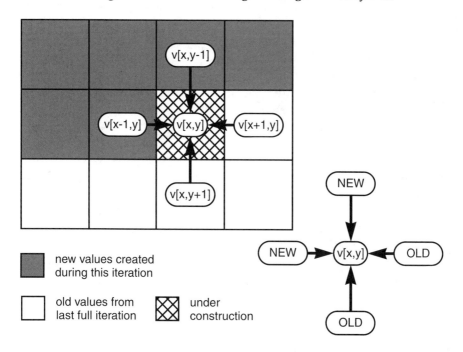

new values created during this iteration

old values from last full iteration

under construction

The red/black schemes, particularly A/B whole-array alternation, use all old values to compute each new average. This is not the same thing the original program did, so it's not surprising we get a different answer.

What may be surprising to those not heavily into the mathematics of iteration is that the different types of iteration used—the original program's and the alternating schemes—have been studied extensively. They even have names. A/B alternation is Gauss-Jacobi iteration, while the original serial program used Gauss-Seidel iteration.

Unfortunately for us, while there are exceptions, the original Gauss-Seidel method is the superior one: It usually converges to a result faster (fewer iterations). There are even cases where Gauss-Seidel does converge to a good_enough result, and Gauss-Jacobi never does. Instead, Gauss-Jacobi ends up with two (or more) sets of values that it just keeps alternating between, never settling down to something good_enough. While unlikely, when it happens this is Very Bad. It is not nice to have programs that never stop. Our changes resulted in using an algorithm that is worse than the original.

This is not parallel processing bug #2769 or any other such high number. It is Classical Parallel Error #1: Parallelizing an inferior algorithm because it is the easier one to parallelize. While there may be a bizarre exception here and there arising from particularly crazed circumstances, it is virtually never the right thing to do. That was emphasized way back in the introduction, where I stated that "working smarter" meant using the best algorithms: "Choosing or discovering appropriate algorithms is therefore supremely important. We should be extremely careful that using any of the other techniques does not require us to use an inferior algorithm." This is where that statement comes home to roost.

While this error is committed regularly, one particularly egregious example stands out in my mind. It involved the publication, in a highly respected, widely read, quasi-popular computer journal, of a long article extolling the virtues of a particular massively parallel machine on the basis of how fast it was able to do a certain type of search. Literally tens of thousands of processors were used, and the authors were obviously quite proud of that fact. A very few months later, another article appeared in a more-or-less competing journal of the same type. It referenced the first article, and showed how exactly the same search could be performed, *much faster*, using a *single* processor instead of thousands—a processor that was exactly the same type and speed as just *one* of those thousands. Exactly the same total amount of memory and exactly the same input/output facilities were also used. A better algorithm was the difference. It was not as easily parallelizeable, but was more than 64,000 times faster.

Spectacular as it is, 64,000 isn't infinity. By switching to Gauss-Jacobi, our program doesn't just run slower. There are cases where it does not converge, meaning that max_change never gets less than good_enough. Therefore it will never exit the outer loop; it will just run forever. In effect, in those cases it runs *infinitely* slower. In all fairness, this doesn't always happen; the circumstances where it arises are not terribly common. Red/black schemes are practical and can be altered to use Gauss-Seidel iteration, too. Nevertheless, we need a way out of our current jam.

9.4.7   The Wavefront (Hyperplane) Method

If we want to get exactly the same result as the original program and keep its good mathematical properties, we obviously can't compute any old average at any time. What can we compute?

The analysis showing which stencil inputs are new and which are old provides a clue. Wherever the pattern shown in the lower right of Figure 78 is found—new on top and right, old on left and bottom—we can compute an average. That will preserve the new/old relationships of the inputs and produce the desired output.

When an iteration first starts, there's exactly one place where that pattern holds: The upper-left point, v[2,2]. (Figure 79, Step 1.) That's because the topmost and leftmost values, v[1,2] and v[2,1], are the boundary conditions; because they're constant, they're always "new" (or old, take your pick). This is exactly what the serial algorithm does first. So, wonderful, we can do one point. Big deal.

Figure 79   Which Points Can Be Done, When?

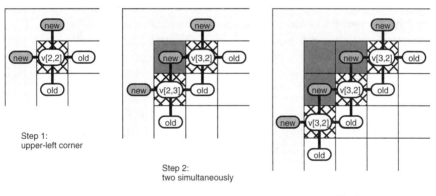

But after that one point is computed, there are *two* places where the new/old template holds (Figure 79, Step 2): v[3,2], the next one the serial algorithm did; *and* v[2,3], the one below the point just computed. That lower point wasn't used by the serial algorithm, but it can be computed immediately because the boundary, in this case v[3,1], is available as a "new" value. So we can do both of those at the same time—in parallel—and still produce the same results that the serial algorithm produced.

Once those two are done, by the same logic we can do three at once; then four, then five, and so on. Now things are looking up. In effect, we can run a diagonal wave of computation through the array, doing everything on the "wavefront" in parallel as shown in Figure 80. This technique was originally described by Lamport [Lam], who described this wavefront as a hyperplane through the space of indices traversed by the loops.

Figure 80 Wavefront of Computation

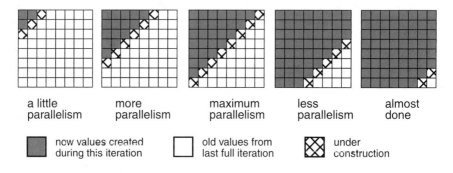

The parallelism available with this method isn't as uniform as in the previous techniques. It starts small, then increases to a maximum across the diagonal of the array, then decreases again. But the array size is likely to be hundreds or thousands square, so, after the first few wave steps and until the last few each wavefront will have more than enough points to keep all the processors busy on any SMP of rational size. (And, hey, it gets the right answer.)

How can we take advantage of this more irregular parallelism? As was the case with the rectilinear approach we pursued up to this point, there are several possible techniques. A few will be discussed below.

9.4.8   Let "forall" do the Work

The first approach is simply to create a serial program that iterates along the diagonals and simply use forall to parallelize it, like this:

```
for max_x = 2 to N-1
    forall x = 2 to max_x
        y = 2 + max_x - x ;
        v[x,y] = ( v[x-1,y] + v[x+1,y] + v[x,y-1] + v[x, y+1] ) / 4 ;
    end /* of forall x */;
end /* of for max_x */;
```

That does the average computation, but what about keeping track of max_change? Locking it in the inner loop is bad because of serialization and, unlike the previous example, there's no second-level inner parallel loop to turn serial to lower the overhead.

Notice: In any execution of the forall loop, each row is visited by a processor exactly once. (So is each column, but we'll use rows.) Suppose we do the following: Make an array of row_max values, one entry for each row, and maintain each entry as the largest change in the corresponding row. Because each row is visited exactly once, the row_max entries don't have to be locked when we update them inside the forall. An additional simple loop, or even a forall, can compute the maximum over that array; if a forall is used, we have exactly the same number of calls to acquire() and release() that the old row_max version did, and for the same reason: We're accumulating the result over rows again.

9.4.9 Chunking and Blocking

There's something wrong with the argument at the end of the last section. Just because there are the same number of calls to acquire() and release() doesn't mean the code is as efficient. Doing something as simple as a single maximum just has to cause serialization problems, and it does. It's obviously going to be much faster to compute a number of maxima serially, locking and combining them fewer times, like this:

```
forall i = 2 to N-1 by 200

    local_max = 0 ;

/* Accumulate 200 of the maxima */
    for j = i to max( i+199, N-1)
        local_max = max( local_max, row_max[j] ;
    end /* of forall x */;

/* Merge local_max with the global maximum */
    acquire ( max_change_lock ) ;  /* wait for access to max_change */
    max_change = max ( max_change, local_max ) ;
    release ( max_change_lock ) ;  /* finished with max_change */

end /* of forall i*/;
```

Now we have 200 times less serialization than we had before and have lost no speed—in fact, the program is probably faster. This is a technique called "chunking": making each parallel iteration do a sizeable chunk of work to overcome the various overheads that must be built into locking and forall, which, if you recall, has to lock at least the index. Worse, it may, depending on the implementation, do system calls to recruit processors.

Speaking of speed, sorry to bring it up, but there's yet another problem this version has. (Won't it ever be right? We're getting close.) It has lots of parallelism, but as we add processors it does not speed up very much. It may even start slowing down. Where that behavior starts depends on the machine being used, but it can happen.

Part of the problem is again serialization. As in the computation of max_change above, there's serialization within the forall statement. A single average is just not doing enough to offset the locking serialization needed to update the index of that loop. All right, we know how to fix that: "chunk" the loop, so each time through the forall we do several elements on the diagonal.

That helps. We're now getting speedup. It's pretty fair when we compare this algorithm running on N processors against itself running on one processor. But try comparing it, not against its own one-processor speed, but against the original serial algorithm running on one processor. This is the only valid measure; beware people who compare against the one-processor version of a parallel algorithm. They are cheating (possibly without knowing it), and here's an example of why that's so: Our latest version, even chunked, is, frankly, in the toilet when you make that comparison. The versions that went across rows were much better (of course, if you don't have to get the right answer...). What's going on now?

Remember caches, cache coherence, and cross-interrogation? This wavefront version has a major problem with locality of reference.

Assume the rows are stored in a way that puts successive row entries next to one another in memory. Then, the versions that went across rows had at least reused cache lines when they loaded the left and right stencil elements and possibly also when they did a store of the new average value. Access to the up and down values, however, likely caused a cache miss because somebody else was storing in those rows. We had some cache reuse, but were doing a fair amount of cache line shuffling and cross-interrogation even there.

In comparison, the diagonal wavefront version is a cache-locality disaster. Will a processor *ever* use two things in a row that are close to each other in memory? Who knows? It's completely up to the luck of the draw of index values inside the forall statement. Chunking helps; successive diagonal elements do reuse some off-diagonal elements. But in general, the more processors we use, the less likely it is that a needed line will be found in the processor's cache. Result: cache lines are being ripped out of processors' caches at a fierce rate. This slows things down terribly, as was emphasized in the earlier chapter about SMPs. It also has a nasty effect on speedup, of course: When the memory system is saturated, it doesn't matter how many processors you use; they don't determine the speed of the computation, the saturated memory system does.

In that earlier chapter, it was also mentioned that programs can be reorganized to get better cache locality. Here's where we do that.

Suppose, instead of each processor computing the average for just a single point, it did so for a rectangular block instead? That still follows the requirements of Gauss-Seidel iteration as expressed in the serial program. As illustrated in Figure 81, when a whole rectangular block is completed, work on the blocks to the right and below can begin. The upper-left corners of each of those blocks is enabled, which is all that's needed for the serial computation in the block; once the first row is completed, the second can begin because the left block acts like a boundary condition; then the third row can be done, and so on.

Figure 81   Blocking and Block Edges

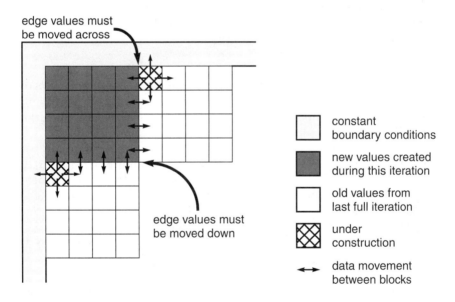

Doing work a block at a time will have a very salutary effect on cache locality. Consider:

When a processor traverses the first row of a block, the up and down elements of the stencil pull parts of two array rows into its cache, and the left and right elements pull in another (or possibly two others). The processor will miss a lot when doing this first row, but the fact that it's working on successive elements helps: several elements are undoubtedly in each cache line, so misses occur only every few repetitions of the inner loop. But when the next row's started, things get really good. Two of the three row sections needed are already in cache; only the bottom row need be brought in. You can even avoid waiting for the cache miss on that third line. If the processor is sufficiently clever (many are), there will be little or no overhead involved if the program references the data before it's needed. Doing so will load the line into the cache before it's needed, overlapping that load with the time the processor is busily computing on its current cache contents. This kind of thing is what was done in the cache prefetching mentioned in "Locality of Reference and Caches" on page 140.

Furthermore, this is the only processor reading or writing those sections of those rows, so it's got the only copy of those cache lines in the system. Remember the commonly implemented cache coherence optimizations that triggers? Before, when a processor wrote the average, it had to broadcast that it was writing, probably causing other processors to purge copies from their caches and wait for a system-wide "all clear" before continuing. But when it's got the only copy, a processor doesn't have to tell anybody anything—it just goes ahead and writes, silently, without bugging or waiting for anybody else.

The net of all this is that the processor can run almost entirely out of its own cache, interacting nearly not at all with other processors, pumping along at very much closer to full speed than was possible before. This is the nirvana of parallel processing—lots of work to do and little communication.

How big a cache is needed to pull this trick? Let's assume 8-byte (64 bit) data values. All we need in the cache are three rows at a time, so in a measly 8Kbytes we can fit a row segment that's 8K / 3 / 8 = approximately 300 elements long. That means with a square block, each processor is doing more than $300^2 = 90,000$ averages per block, with little overhead. You will be hard-pressed to find a system with so little cache memory that 8 Kbytes of data won't fit. If you do find one, don't buy it.

On the other end of the scale, how small you can go is limited by the cache line length. If you don't use at least one full line's worth of data from each row, you are wasting effort and inviting cross-interrogation. Very few systems use a line size larger than 256 bytes, and that size is usually in a level 2 cache. That's 32 of our 8-byte elements, yielding $32^2 = 1024$ averages per block. Is that enough to offset the cache re-loading needed when a new block is started? Quite possibly. It depends on how fast the system is at loading data from main memory into its cache; larger is better, as long as all three lines needed fit in the cache. A larger block also helps offset the synchronization overhead when a new block is started.

With the warning that larger is generally better, there is a very broad range—about 30 to 300 elements, a factor of 10—over which good efficiency can be obtained on most systems.

A square block was used in the above examples, but a square block has no particular advantage for maximizing cache reuse in a single processor. What should the aspect ratio be? Notice, as also shown in Figure 81, that the edge values of each block must be pulled into the processors doing the neighboring blocks. It is desirable to minimize the amount of data moving between caches; the less cross-interrogation the better. Since a square has minimum perimeter for a given area, a square block will minimize the number of array elements cross-referenced between blocks. However, this does not necessarily minimize the amount of data transferred in an SMP, because data are packed into cache lines.

Each individual value pulled into the computation of a block to the right requires a whole cache line. This happens because rows, we've assumed, have their values adjacent in memory. For that same reason, pulling a cache line into the computation of a block below one brings in several values; the exact number depends on how many data elements fit into a cache line.

Result: To minimize the amount of data transferred and the number of cross-cache interrogations, the aspect ratio of the block should be in proportion to the number of elements in a cache line. While this is obviously line-size dependent (as well as problem dependent), for our current problem making the block two or four times as wide as it is high will obtain most of the benefit. For example: four of our 8-byte data items fit into a 32-byte cache line. With a square 8x8 block, 10 cache lines must be transferred: 8 on the right, and 2 below. A 32x4 block, on the other hand, has four cache lines on each side; so a total of 8 lines must be moved instead of 10.

We're now down in the nits. Dealing with a specific line-size dependent aspect ratio reaches the stage where cache-oriented tuning gives an increasingly smaller payoff. There is an exception: You need all the help you can get when using systems where cross-cache interrogation is particularly slow, such as in several of the CC-NUMA systems currently available (but not all).

There is an important point to be noticed about this entire cache-related discussion: It is not optimization for a particular manufacturer's architecture. More could be done if it were; for example, the ideal block aspect ratio could be used, and the block width could be made an even multiple of the cache line size. But even without such detailed tuning, blocking within broad limits will yield very improved performance on any system with a cache. As emphasized earlier, for all practical purposes, that is all systems, period.

9.4.10　Load Balancing and a Global Queue

Our program is now rather good. It can get good real speedup compared to the original uniprocessor program, also (praise be!) gets the same answer every time, and (Hosannas to the highest!) that answer is the same answer produced by the original program.

However, it still doesn't achieve "linear" speedup; it does not run N times faster when using N processors. This is partly inevitable; there is coordination activity in any parallel program that doesn't exist in the serial version, and that coordination overhead inhibits perfectly linear speedup. But even discounting that, we still aren't running quite as fast as seems reasonable.

The reason is illustrated in Figure 82. Suppose we have four processors. While the fourth diagonal is processed (iteration 4 of the for x loop), all four are in use; each is doing a different block down the diagonal. This cannot produce a speedup of exactly four, owing to inevitable variations in processing speed and the time to initiate each processor's work; but it can get very close indeed. No problem there.

Figure 82　Another Source of Parallel Inefficiency

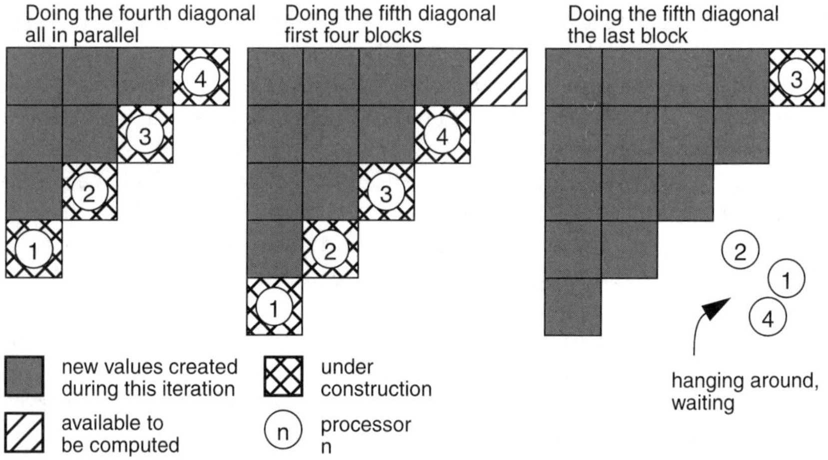

Doing the fourth diagonal all in parallel

Doing the fifth diagonal first four blocks

Doing the fifth diagonal the last block

new values created during this iteration

available to be computed

under construction

(n) processor n

hanging around, waiting

Iteration 5 of that loop, when the next diagonal is processed, is a different story. All four processors chew up the first four blocks, again speeding things up nearly four times. But whoops, there's another block to be done. Whoever finished first—processor 3 in the figure—does that block. The other three can do nothing but mill around the water cooler until processor 3 has finished. The result is a speedup for that diagonal of at most 2.5: The first four blocks are done in the time it takes to do one block (elapsed time = 1), the last block takes the time it takes to do one block (elapsed time = 1), for a total time of 2. In that time we did the work the serial algorithm would have done in 5 time units, one per block. So the speedup is 5/2, or 2.5.

This is a form of the **load-balancing** problem. If the amount of work each processor does is not the same as the amount every other processor does, you can't reach full speedup because part of the time some of the processors are idle; the "load" on each processor is not "balanced." Load-balancing problems are much more common where problems are decomposed into different functions, rather than splitting one function across processors as we are doing here. It is usually nearly impossible to evenly balance the processing requirements of different functions.

Load balancing gets better as the diagonals get longer—in other words, when there are more blocks available to do in parallel. For example, using four processors, a 31-block diagonal would do $4 \times 7 = 28$ of the blocks fully in parallel, in seven stages; and then it will do the last three at once. This is a (maximum) speedup of about 3.9, which is not bad at all. This implies that more blocks are good, so dividing the matrix up into more, smaller blocks is good because you get better load balancing. This characterization is general: with many, small amounts of work to do—or, in the jargon, fine **granularity** of parallelism—you can get good load balancing.

But wait a minute. We just got through finding out that small blocks are bad. They increase serialization overhead and lose cache efficiency. There is a problem here.

In most cases there is no perfect solution to this problem. You just have to find a hunk of work that is big enough to overcome serialization and cache effects, yet small enough not to suffer dramatically from load-balancing problems. Such intermediate sizes quite often exist. When they don't, the problem is simply not efficiently parallelizeable, at least not in the form being investigated; often other formulations will work.

In this specific case, however, there's a way around the problem. It's different enough from our prior approaches that it might be called another formulation.

See Figure 83, which looks more closely at the last stage of doing the fifth diagonal. When the first four blocks of that diagonal are done, there are other blocks that can be computed without violating any of the requirements, since the blocks above and to the left of them are complete. That means there's no intrinsic reason why those three underutilized processors have to just hang around waiting—there are other blocks available to be done. The difficulty is that the blocks to be done are in the next diagonal, and the way we've written the program, nothing on a diagonal can be started until the prior diagonal is completely finished: The forall statement, the source of the parallelism, operates only on one diagonal at a time.

Figure 83 Why are those Processors Waiting?

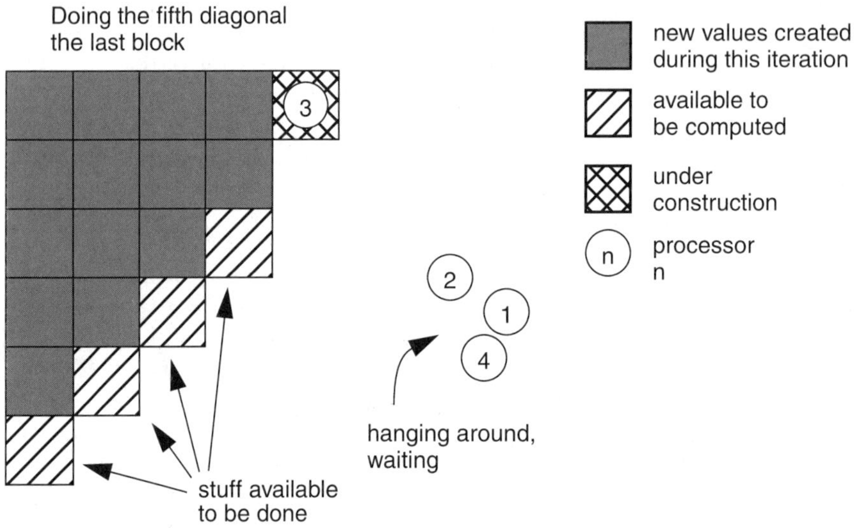

Doing the fifth diagonal
the last block

☐ new values created during this iteration

▨ available to be computed

▩ under construction

(n) processor n

hanging around, waiting

stuff available to be done

There is no straightforward way that I know of to fix this within the bounds of a forall statement. But there is a way to fix it. It involves what is probably the most quintessentially shared-memory approach to parallelism: Keeping in memory a shared, global queue containing items of work to be done. Each of the processors repeatedly goes to the queue, pulls off an item of work to be done, performs it, and goes back to the queue. When the queue is empty, we're finished. What keeps the queue replenished is that putting something on the queue is often part of doing "the work" that's taken off the queue.

What we want to do in our case is put a block on the queue whenever the blocks above and to its left have been done, no matter what diagonal it's on. Figure 84 shows the control needed to perform this.

Much detail has been left out, most notably initializing the block data structures and resetting their left_done and top_done flags before each main iteration. Locks on the block data structures are required because a race in setting the flags might otherwise result in a block being enqueued twice. The queue itself can be an ordinary circular queue, with a lock protecting it. (There exist techniques for enqueueing and dequeueing items from a global queue with little or no serialization; see [AG94]. They are seldom used in practice for a

Figure 84   Processing a Global Queue

```
/* Prime the while loop below by getting an initial block from the queue */
block = get_from_queue() ;

while (block != NULL)              /* quit when queue is empty */

  perform(block) ;                 /* stuff block full of averages */

  /* mark the block to right, and put it on the queue if it's ready */
  acquire ( block.right->block.block_lock ) ;
  block.right->left_done = TRUE;
  if block.right->top_done then put_on_queue ( block.right ) ;
  release ( block.right->block.block_lock ) ;

  /* mark the block below, and put on the queue if it's ready */
  acquire ( block.below->block_lock ) ;
  block.below->top_done = TRUE;
  if block.below->left_done then put_on_queue ( block.below ) ;
  release ( block.below->block_lock ) ;

  /* get the next block to do, if any */
  block = get_from_queue() ;

end /* of while loop */;
```

PROCECURES, ETC.:

get_from_queue() returns a pointer to a block of work currently on the queue, or
      null if the queue is empty.

put_on_queue (block_ptr) puts the block of work that is its argument on the queue.

perform(block_ptr) does an averaging operation on the block that is its argument,
      including updating the global max_change variable.

Each block is a data structure containing:
    indices and spans identifying the section of the array to be averaged.
    left_done and top_done, two booleans that are true if the blocks to the left
      and above this one have been completed.
    right and below, pointers to the blocks to the right and below this one. (Blocks
      at the edges point to a null block that put_on_queue() ignores.)
    block_lock, a lock structure for the block.

---

number of reasons, including innate complexity and the number of times
they require processor serialization.)

9.4.11   Concerning Global Queues

To say that global queues are very widely used is to be guilty of vast understatement. They are the basic mechanism by which work is distributed

among the processors in every SMP operating system: When a job is eligible for execution, it is placed on a queue; some processor eventually pulls it off and executes it. It is also used in the same manner in many database systems, again on chunks of work—usually partial transactions. Other global queues are used to hold jobs that are inactive for some reason—waiting for I/O, waiting for a lock, whatever; when the I/O completes or the lock is acquired, the job is moved to another queue where it will get picked up for continued execution.

The technique is so pervasive that it would not be much of an exaggeration to say that the global queue is *the* SMP programming model. It isn't stretching the point too far to claim that every use of forall in the previous examples was effectively a global queue: A bunch of work in shared memory was identified, and all the processors just had at it from the pile.

Global queues are easily used in SMPs and without a doubt are marvellous for automatically balancing the load among processors. This stands in sharp contrast to message-passing systems, which, as we'll see, have nowhere particularly good to put a global queue, accessible by all.

However, as the number of processors grows, global queues break down in the sense that they are a potential source of inefficiency. This is true in two ways. First and fairly obviously, they can induce serialization delays; if the units of work aren't large enough, the processors can spend much of their time waiting on the global queue's lock, limiting the utility of additional processors, as indicated in Figure 71 on page 254. Second, they can really hurt cache locality. That requires a bit more explanation; it can occur for two more reasons.

In the first place, consider the queue itself: control pointers, data, and lock. It is seldom, if ever, accessed by the same processor twice in a row. As a result, the cache lines holding the queue are real road warriors, forever bouncing among the caches. But the amount of data involved is usually small, and therefore this is not very likely to be a problem—except, again, for systems with unusually large cache cross-interrogation times that effectively bend the SMP model.

The second reason is more likely to cause trouble. When a processor puts a unit of work on a global queue, it has essentially randomized the location where the work will be done next. Any of the processors could pick it up. This is fine if, having picked up a piece of work, a processor settles down and grinds on it for a while. We've been careful to use a large block of computation in our problem; can everybody do that? Hardly. Our example is a straightforward compute-bound process, without significant I/O. Database transactions, for example, often perform tiny squirts of work amid a thicket of I/O requests before they settle down to work, if they ever do. On such work, the randomization among processors done by a global queue eliminates nearly all chance of getting a head of steam up inside a cache; the application data is continually whipped about the caches; this was discussed as a reason why shared caches are often, counterintuitively, a good idea for commercial workloads ("Commercial Processing: Cross-Interrogation and Shared Caches" on page 171). Even in our own problem, if an operating system time-slices one of our nice big blocks, all that cached data will probably get cross-interrogated over to somewhere else.

Such difficulties, together with "straightforward" battles with serialization or Amdahl's law, have traditionally limited SMP systems to modest numbers of processors. At four or six processors (eight stretches it) many of the cache effects mentioned can simply be ignored. Beyond that, programmers must acknowledge that not all memory is created equal—recently used stuff is "more equal" than the rest—and include in their scheduling schemes something called **processor affinity:** making it more likely that an interrupted chunk of work is picked up by the processor that worked on it last. Processor affinity can be obtained by using multiple queues, one per processor, with each processor checking its own queue first before looking elsewhere for work. This works, but makes it more difficult to get the properties that arose easily with a global queue: load balancing, fairness, priority of execution, allocations, and so on. As was the case with the scaling of SMP hardware, there is no intrinsic reason this cannot be done—it's just expensive, and difficult.

9.4.12   Not the End, Again

At this point we have just about beaten this problem into submission for SMPs. That is not to say that there isn't more we could do.

For example, notice that there's still some loss of parallelism at the start and end of each iteration. At those points, there just aren't enough blocks to be processed—ultimately, just the single ones in the corners. This could be attacked, too, by overlapping sequential iterations: Start a new iteration, in the upper left, while the current iteration in the lower right is finishing up. Trying to do that would make it a challenge to keep max_change under control, and we'd have to convince ourselves that an extra fractional iteration is all right to include in the answer or do something else about it, since it will produce a deviation from the serial program's answer. This technique could be extended to N simultaneous iterations, a different one running simultaneously on each diagonal.

But enough already. Let's move on.

9.5 Message-Passing _____

When we started doing our problem using shared memory, we began with the flow of control in the application and asked what was being done often enough to merit parallelizing. The location of the data wasn't an issue; it was just right there, in the shared memory.

Not so with message-passing. In fact, a key element of this model is not that messages are passed; it is the fact that messages *must* be passed because the data isn't in one place. Rather, it's distributed among multiple, separate machines, each with their own private storage. Nonlocal data cannot be accessed without the active participation of another processor. Exactly how it is distributed is the primary issue.

Many years ago, when distributed processing was in its infancy and the Internet (then ARPANET) was just getting off the ground, someone commented to me "Distributed processing, fooey. Tell me where the data is, and I'll tell you where the processing *must be*."[7] That was a very true statement and captures much of what message-based programming is really all about.

Our journey through message-passing will be much more brief than the one through shared memory (both you and I are sighing with relief). For one thing, issues of different kinds of relaxation are already covered; they're obviously the same. More importantly for this book, many of the issues that arose in the shared-memory context are general issues of overt parallelism, and there is no point to covering them a second time.

Some of those parallelism issues have different immediate causes, but they come down to the same thing. Races, for example, can occur when an indeterminate order of message arrival changes the results of the computation; deadlocks typically involve a processor waiting to receive a message that never arrives; serialization is still serialization, although waiting on one processor now becomes really obvious, not a matter of analyzing lock waiting times. Locks, on the other hand, often don't exist as such; they rear their heads again when data is shared on disks (next chapter), for the same access-control reasons that exist for shared memory. And there's no such thing as a global queue; load balancing is explicit, a function of how the data is distributed, except for truly boulder-sized granularity of parallelism. The reason is that it takes much longer to transmit the data required from node to node: tens or hundreds of megabits per second are more typical communication speeds, rather than Gigabytes per second within SMPs.

7. I wish I could remember who, but I can't. I was in graduate school at the time—it was a *long* time ago—so the quote was probably, more accurately, "Distributed processing, *foo*."

One thing that explicitly will not be discussed is the interconnection topology—which machines are directly connected to which, with what message routing. This used to be the favorite topic of the parallel processing genre, an obsession Gordon Bell has called "topomania" [Bel92a]. He hopes we're all over that, and I agree wholeheartedly. It will be assumed that a message can be squirted to any other processor; if the interconnect system can't do that, it's time to buy another. (Or, time to put an appropriate software wrapper around that interconnect, a wrapper that makes it look functionally adequate.) For relatively few machines in clusters, connected by standard interconnection mechanisms, universal connectivity is in any event the correct assumption.

One final item, concerning notation: Since each computing entity in a message-passing system is more than a processor (it at least has memory and something to send messages, too), it's rather silly to call it a "processor." We'll call it a "node," which is more or less standard terminology.

9.5.1   Jacobi/Seidel/Chaotic "Mixed" Relaxation

Possibly the most straightforward data distribution that can be used is illustrated in Figure 85. We've simply taken the array, split it into equal-size rectangular blocks, and put a block in each processor.

Figure 85   Message-Passing, Mixed Iteration Strategy

				Each node
Node 1	Node 2	Node 3	Node 4	1. Exchanges edge values with its neighbors:
Node 5	Node 6	Node 7	Node 8	
Node 9	Node 10	Node 11	Node 12	2. Averages its portion of the array, using exchanged values as boundaries.
Node 13	Node 14	Node 15	Node 16	3. Helps compute global max_change; if it's good_enough, everyone quits.

The overall plan of execution is then:

1. Every node exchanges "edge values" with its four neighbors: above, below, left, and right; these are the values at the periphery of the array blocks owned by each.

2. Using the received edge values as if they were boundary conditions, each node does a normal serial (Gauss-Seidel) averaging calculation on its own data.

3. If everybody's max_change is good_enough, quit; otherwise, do it all again.

This leads to a style of iteration that mixes Gauss-Jacobi with Gauss-Seidel and, because it's a mixture, comes under the "chaotic" rubric. Recall: Jacobi bases new averages entirely on old values, Seidel uses a very specific mixture, and chaotic is, well, chaotic. The iteration style has elements of Seidel because each machine uses Seidel internally, but it treats the data from neighboring machines as if it were constant, that is, uses the old values. That's like Jacobi. This mixture is certainly no worse than the chaos we started out with in the shared-memory case; unlike that case, it is in fact already eminently usable.

Step 2 is obviously straightforward; it's the same thing the serial program did and won't be discussed further. While discussing the other steps, we'll refer to each node's block of the array as if it were the entire array v[], with NxN elements.

To exchange edge values, we must get some identifier for the nodes to the right, left, and so on, of the one we're on. Many message-based programming packages provide this directly, as part of a facility laying out nodes in any-dimensional Cartesian grids (examples: [Hem91, Kol91, Mes94, Wal93]). So, for that identification that we'll just use an opaque procedure. The actual sending we'll do as four data-shifting operations: to the right, left, up, and down. The start of the code, shifting values left, might look something like this:

```
get_neighbors( &left, &right, &above, &below ) ; /* Set node ids*/

send( right, v[N-1,*] ) ;    /* Send rightmost column computed here */

receive ( v[1,*] ) ;         /* Receive left's rightmost column into my boundary */
```

Time to worry about deadlocks (deadly embraces) again.

The reason we worry is that we haven't yet specified exactly how send(to_who, message) works. In particular, when is it finished? Does it simply pick up the message, ship it out in the direction of right, and, having consigned the bits to the howling ether, wash its hands, say "all done," and return? Or does it wait until it gets some word from Mr. right, saying the message was successfully receive()d on the other side? The former is called **nonblocking** message-passing, the latter **blocking**. Many message-passing systems offer both.

Blocking communication is easier to use because if something goes wrong, it either gets fixed then, invisibly, inside the send(), or you find out right there and can tell which procedure call caused the problem. Nonblocking can be faster, but if there's an error in transmission, you'll find out about it in some other piece of code, long after the send() has finished. The error needn't be something having to do with hardware, by the way; it could be an application-induced deadlock (deadly embrace).

Suppose the send(right,...) above is blocking. Then, everybody is inside send(), waiting for the receive() that will complete the blocking send(). But since everybody's in send(), nobody can reach a receive() and the application waits forever. We could deal with this by using nonblocking communication, but there are two ways around it that stay synchronous.

> Checkerboard it. Label even/odd nodes red and black. All the reds send while the blacks receive, then all the blacks send while the reds receive, like this:

```
get_neighbors( &left, &right, &above, &below ) ; /*Set node ids */

if I_am_odd() then {
    send( right, v[N-1,*] ) ; /* Send to right*/
    receive ( v[1,*] ) ;      /* Receive from left; matches send() below*/
} else /* {
/* I must be even */
    receive ( v[1,*] ) ;      /* Receive from left; matches send() above*/
    send( right, v[N-1,*] ) ;/* Send to right*/
};
```

> Use a combined primitive. This is not exactly an unusual thing we're doing here, so several packages that support message-passing provide it as a primitive operation. For example, the *de facto* standard for message-passing, MPI [Wal93, SOH[+]96], contains a sendrecv() procedure. This procedure incorporates both a send and a receive, guarantees a lack of deadlock, and might even be implemented to use some special hardware by the system vendors. That would turn this fragment of our program into something like[8] the following:

```
get_neighbors( &left, &right, &above, &below ) ;

sendrecv( right, v[N-1,*],/* Send to right */
        left, v[1,*] ) ; /* Receive from left */
```

We actually don't run into any deadlock problems here, because we don't have periodic boundary conditions. Therefore, we don't shift data off the

---

8. This is not the exact MPI syntax. There are several other arguments to all the MPI communication primitives, all well motivated, which make things more complicated than appropriate here.

right and into the far left, and thus avoid creating the cycle that's needed for a deadly embrace. For our case, the simplistic version of the code would look like this instead:

```
get_neighbors( &left, &right, &above, &below ) ; /* Set left, right, … node ids*/
if I_am_not_rightmost() then send ( right, v[N-1,*] ) ; /* Send to right*/
if I_am_not_leftmost() then receive ( v[1,*] ) ; /* Receive from left */
```

This is deadlock-free, but at a price: serialization. Everybody does a send() except the rightmost, which does a receive(); that lets the next-to-rightmost's send() complete, so it does a receive(); that lets the next one loose, and so on. The operation ripples from right to left, serially, so if the logical grid of nodes is W wide, it takes W steps. The checkerboard method takes two steps, no matter how big W is. This might not matter much in smallish clusters, where W might not be much bigger than two.

All right, we've now successfully exchanged our edge values; shifting data in the other directions, left, up, and down, is obviously similar to the right-shift case. Next the program does an iteration of averaging, in the course of which each node computes its local max_change. How do we form the global maximum and let everybody know whether it's time to stop?

Since we're still not doing anything very uncommon, the simplest way is to exploit what is now a common facility of many programming packages, called collective communication. These are group communication facilities into which every node is expected to join.[9] A very common one is reduction, as in reduce(in_v, out_v, op, root). Reduction takes an input value, in_v, from each node and a function op, and does op(in_v_1,in_v_2); then reduce() takes that result and combines it with in_v_3: op(prior_result,in_v_3); then combines that with in_v_4, and so on for all the nodes. It deposits the ultimately combined ("reduced") result of this in the variable out_v, but only at the node named root. With an op of max(), which is usually provided as a primitive, this is the basis for exactly what we want:

```
reduce( max_change, global_max_change, MAX, 1) ; /* find global max */
broadcast(global_max_change, 1) ; /* tell everybody what it is */
if global_max_change < good_enough then quit; /* stop if it's good_enough */
```

Putting the above fragment after the averaging loop will compute the maximum, putting it in node 1. Then, use of another common collective commu-

---

9. Well, not necessarily every node. It's common to provide some form of "node group" and have every node in the group participate. This is one of the otherwise-irrelevant things alluded to in a prior footnote, where I said I was leaving out some things in MPI.

nication procedure, broadcast(), tells everyone what that global maximum was. Finally, everybody looks at the maximum and decides whether it's time to quit or time for another iteration.

These are very common primitives. If they're not available, however, a typical technique is to use a binary tree to do the reduction and the same tree to do the broadcast. (This is the source of the term "root" used above.) The use of such a tree for reduction is illustrated in Figure 86. It is one of those things that has terrifically simple implementation that depends in detail on the properties of binary numbers. A hint if you try programming it yourself, since I'm not going to do it here: Multiply a loop index by two every time around the loop.

Figure 86   A Binary Tree for Reduction (and Broadcast)

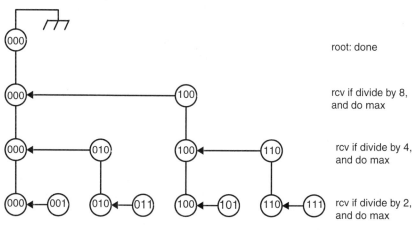

root: done

rcv if divide by 8, and do max

rcv if divide by 4, and do max

rcv if divide by 2, and do max

"if divide by N" means mod(node_number, N) == 0

9.5.2   Implicit Synchronization and Alternation Schemes

When we did the SMP implementation, we were driven to alternation schemes because of a lack of consistency: The program gave a different answer every time it was run on the same input data. That problem doesn't arise here, because a node cannot be given data surreptitiously. Nobody's invisibly messing with somebody else's cache; each receipt of data is an active act, requiring execution of a receive() operation. This implicitly synchronizes all the nodes, so none can go running off doing something without coordination. As a result, our basic, original program will always give the same answer when it is given the same input data.

So, we don't have the same motivation for using alternation schemes that existed in the shared-memory case. However, they might still be desirable because their properties are well known, unlike the properties of the rather *ad hoc* "mixed" iteration used. Better the devil you know, even if it is known to be a devil.

The use of alternation schemes poses no big challenge in the framework of the base program. To do whole-array alternation, for example, the principal thing that must be done is to change the individual node-averaging loops to read from one array and write into another. Then, when edge values are exchanged, the values from neighbors are placed in the array that will be "old" in the next iteration. Nothing otherwise changes.

The red/black methods are handled similarly but the amount of data sent between nodes is halved on each interchange: Only newly computed values need be sent, and on each half-iteration only half the edge values are changed. The checkerboard version is somewhat easier to do, because equal quantities of data are then exchanged on all four sides. The "striped" version may have no new data to send vertically on alternate half-iterations.

Of course, throughout all this we are still not getting the same answers as the original serial program. A way must be found to do true Gauss-Seidel iteration.

9.5.3 *Wavefronts and Multiple Waves*

Once again, we'll approach this by using a wavefront (or hyperplane) method, and will reuse the data distribution pattern already presented. Figure 87 shows the execution pattern. Whenever a node completes its portion, it sends updated edge data to the nodes below and on its right; when a node receives both messages, it starts.

The global max_change calculation can be piggybacked on the main data communication: Each node sends a max_change with each slab of edge data and uses the larger of the two received as its initial value, rather than 0, when computing its own local max_change. Then the max_change of the lower-right node is the global max_change, which can be broadcast to let everyone figure out whether to stop.

This is actually simpler than the original mixed-iteration program. High-level code for it appears in Figure 88 and is explained below.

The only node through both receive() statements at the start is the one in the upper left; it does an iteration, then sends data and max_change to the nodes to its right and left. Then it reaches the barrier(). This is another collective communication routine, possibly the most basic. It's a kind of inverse lock,

Figure 87 First Try at Message-Passing the Wavefront

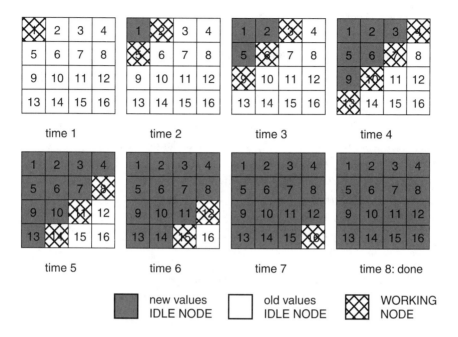

| new values IDLE NODE | old values IDLE NODE | WORKING NODE |

whose function is to synchronize everyone: Nobody exits the barrier() proce-dure until everybody has entered it; then everybody exits it at the same time. When the top left node reaches the barrier(), it just stops for a while.

When the top left node executed its send() statements, it allowed the nodes below and to its right to complete their receive() statements. Both of them do work, send data down and to their right, and wait at the barrier() along with the top left node.

This keeps going on until the last node, with more and more nodes piling up at the barrier, until the one in the bottom right hits it. Now everybody's signed in, so they all continue. The universal max_change value from the lower right is then broadcast. Everybody checks to see if it is good_enough and, if so, quits. Otherwise the whole process starts again.

The message-based commencement of computation used here is reminiscent of the load-balancing technique used in the SMP version. Unfortunately, in this case it results in a truly horrific load-balancing problem. While Figure 87 looks at first glance just like the SMP case, look again at the legend. In SMP execution, there were a total of four processors; each processor was recy-cled—used on multiple diagonals. Here, we have 16 nodes, and no node is ever used more than once. Only the nodes marked as "working" are

Figure 88   First-Try Message-Passing Wavefront Program

```
get_node_ids( &right, &below, &lower_right_node ) ; /* Find out who's who. */
do forever;
    m_c1 = m_c2 = 0;              /* Make sure they are initialized if I'm top left. */
    if I_am_not_top_row() then
        receive ( v[*,1], m_c1 ) ;   /* Get top boundary & max_change from above */
    if I_am_not_left_column() then
        receive ( v[1,*], m_c2 ) ;   /* Get left boundary & max_change from left */
    max_change = max( m_c1, m_c2 ) ; /* Initial value for my max_change */
    /* Run an iteration of the averages, returning new max_change value. */
    max_change = do_useful_work ( max_change ) ;
    send ( below, v[*,N-1], max_change ) ;/* Give new bottom values to node below */
    send ( right, v[N-1,*], max_change ) ;  /* Give new right values to node at right */
    /* Wait for everybody to finish, then get global_max_change
       (or send it, if I happen to be lower_right_node). */
    barrier() ;
    broadcast ( max_change, global_max_change, lower_right_node ) ;
    if global_max_change < good_enough then leave do_forever;
end /* of do forever */;
```

active—the others are idle. At most 4 out of 16 nodes are active simultaneously. This could be called a serialization problem, rather than a load-balancing problem; either way, it's bad.

One way around this is to pursue the suggestion at the very end of the SMP section: Run multiple wavefronts simultaneously. This promised to be a coordination nightmare with shared memory; in this context, it's very natural. As soon as a node finishes an iteration and ships off its edge values, it simply immediately starts on the next one. The global max_change calculation flowing through the processors is completely unchanged.

In fact, the program for multiwave wavefront is exactly the same as the one in Figure 88, with one exception: While data first passes through the array—until the lower-right node has run for the first time—everybody skips the barrier(), broadcast(), and termination check and instead returns to the head of the loop unconditionally. For example, while the second two nodes are running for the first time, the upper left one doesn't wait. It computes its second iteration and is ready to send new values at (approximately) the same time the second two are ready to receive them again.

This has the effect of "priming the pump" of the logical array of nodes. After the lower right node has run the first time, and every time it runs following that, there is a new valid global max_change to be distributed and checked. So from that point on, everybody waits at the barrier() for a much shorter time, gets and checks the global max_change, and continues or not.

So, simultaneously running multiple waves is not such a big deal in message-passing and uses all the processors continuously. It doesn't give exactly the same answer as the original; when everything stops, the values distributed in the array are from a mixture of different iterations, not all from one iteration. But it does practice Gauss-Seidel relaxation and therefore is, in all probability, mathematically acceptable.

9.5.4   Wavefronts in Strips

There is a way, and in fact there are probably many ways, to obtain better load balancing without resorting to multiple simultaneous wavefronts. It involves using a different way to distribute the data among the nodes— which should come as no surprise; that is, as has been emphasized, what message-passing programming is really all about. Instead of dividing the array up into blocks like before, let's divide it up into horizontal strips, with one strip per processor. We're also going to divide each strip into blocks; this is illustrated in Figure 89 for the case of dividing the array among four processors, with eight blocks in each strip.

Processing now proceeds from left to right across each strip, by blocks. Node 1 does the block labelled 1 in the figure. As soon as that block's done, node 1 sends the bottom-edge values from that block to node 2. Then both can start doing the blocks labelled 2. When done, they both send their newly computed block edge data down; this gets node 3 into the act. Once node 4 gets into the act, all four nodes crank away until block 8 is done; then one by one they shut down. When block 11 is finished, max_change (which has been piggybacked on other data transmissions) for the whole array has been computed; it's broadcast, tested, and another iteration starts, or we're done.

Compared to the multiple wavefront version, this is a little disappointing in its load balancing; only some nodes are used at the beginning and end of each iteration. However, this version, without multiple wavefronts, is nearly as good as the SMP solution before we resorted to a global queue; its use of nodes looks as efficient as that version's use of processors.

However, at least for small problems that's an illusion. We haven't yet discussed the overheads involved yet and the resultant size of the blocks needed.

Figure 89 Another Data Distribution

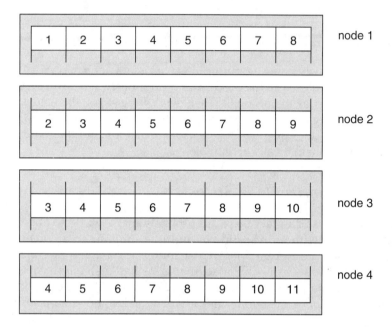

9.5.5   *Communication Overhead in Message-Passing*

In an SMP, all we need be concerned about regarding the size of the blocks is cache utilization. By making the blocks as small as feasible without hurting caching, we can split the array into many small blocks and obtain good load balancing.

In message-passing, cache utilization on each node is still important; doing less than the most efficient job of using a node amounts to parallelizing an inferior algorithm. For that reason, it is wise to use "cache blocking" in the computation used within the nodes. However, the blocks shown in Figure 89 (for example) must be very significantly larger than the blocks required for cache efficiency. The reason is the speed of communication between nodes, compared to communication between processors in an SMP. This has two aspects: bandwidth, the amount of data per second send; and latency, the time before the first bit of data is received.

On widely deployed, standard, nonproprietary media such as Ethernet, peak bandwidth is 10 Mbits/second. The bus or other facilities within an SMP typically operate in the range of high hundreds of Mbytes/second. Taking 500 Mbytes/second as typical (though low), the speed ratio is a factor of 400. That is bad. But as pointed out in Chapter 3, newer communications techniques will raise that bandwidth to the point where it is at least competitive with the interprocessor system bus bandwidth of SMPs between the same number of processors. So, bandwidth is not, or at least will not be, a problem.

Latency and overhead are another matter altogether.

Communication between nodes, especially over standard, nonproprietary media using standard protocols, has fixed overheads that are currently on the order of milliseconds. For PVM, a popular message-passing package using the standard TCP/IP protocol, this has been measured at 1.2 milliseconds between 40–50 MIPS workstations when no data is sent (this was independent of the communication medium, Ethernet or FDDI) [SGDM94]. Similar latencies are reported for intermachine communication within distributed operating systems, such as Amoeba and Sprite [DOKT91], and in systems using special, non-IP protocols over ATM [HM], so this is not a fluke. Those references are several years old now, and the microprocessors are getting faster (I have to say that at least once a chapter), so let's assume it's dropped by a factor of four to 300 microseconds.

An SMP sending a cache line by cross-interrogation between processors can take, on a very bad day, 20 cycles—and at 5 nanoseconds/cycle, a rational current clock rate, this is becomes 100 nanoseconds, a *factor of 3000* different from 300 microseconds. This is Extremely Bad.

What is worse, it is software *overhead*, not hardware latency: The nodes' processors must actively compute for around a millisecond to figure out what must be done and move the data to where it must be for the I/O device to pick it up. This has to be done independently of communication time used to actually send something; bandwidth doesn't help. Since it's processor time expended, that time is intrinsically not available to do the "real" work on the problem.

All this means that to achieve 90% efficiency the nodes have to compute for 9 milliseconds before sending a single message. That's what our second version requires per block. Suppose we're running on systems able to do 50 MFLOPS average on our problem (reasonable, but perhaps a little low). Since each run through a block with N values on a side requires $5N^2$ floating-point operations, we need a block that measures 950 elements on a side to get 90% efficiency. That compares with the range of 30 to 300 for good cache efficiency in an SMP; a factor of 3 to 30 larger.

Unfortunately, you seldom get away with just one message. The first version of our program had two messages (two sends, each matched with two receives), a barrier, and a broadcast for each block of "real" computation done in the node.[10] The latter internally involve multiple messages; the number depends on the number of nodes. Again for PVM [SGDM94], with eight nodes it's 15 milliseconds for a minimal-data broadcast and about 30 milliseconds for a barrier. Now, 90% efficiency requires 400 milliseconds of work, or nearly 6800 elements on a side—over 48 million elements. This is a factor of 20 to 200 worse than an SMP. It obviously is going to be usable only on very big matrices. Furthermore, it doesn't change even if multiple wavefronts are used at the same time; doing that doesn't alter the efficiency. What this means is that our original versions are useless except on problems with enormous amounts of data.

This whole discussion has to do with what is called, in the parallel computing jargon, **grain size**: a computation with a large grain size does a lot between synchronization points, and one with a small grain size does a little. The overhead involved in sending messages forces a large grain size on message-passing systems that use standard communications channels and protocols. This means they're no good for small problems: a block size of 6800, with our 8x8 blocking, means a matrix with 54,000 values on each side!

Combining this with megabit rates of currently deployed LANs, one can readily wonder how anything gets done on LAN-connected clusters. It obviously depends on what's being done, and how. Batch systems, for example, effectively have enormous granularity; the same is true of the multi-job parallel class mentioned in Chapter 8. Grand Challenge problems, under PVM, can attain 80%–90% efficiency [SGDM94]. Grand Challenge problems are *big*, and aptly named. So even this is not insuperable under various circumstances—some occurring in widespread everyday use (batch and multijob parallel), and others when you're taking the afternoon off to do the equivalent of build a Renaissance Cathedral or a Great Pyramid.

Well, now you know why many of the efforts at cluster acceleration discussed in Chapter 5 focused so heavily on inter-node communication efficiency. If inter-node communication drops down to the single-digit microseconds or less, the utility of clusters becomes far greater.

9.5.6   Clusters of SMPs

Before we leave message passing, consider a final possibility: A collection of SMPs connected by message-passing—a cluster of SMPs. This seems like it's just squaring the technical complexity and adding the social difficulty that experts on SMPs and experts in message-passing are seldom on speaking terms with each other (this will be discussed shortly).

---

10. The second version also requires a barrier and a broadcast, but only one for every complete iteration through the array, after computing all blocks.

Consider, however, that from past work one might already have (or be able to get) an already parallelized, SMP version of a program. Now recall that in message-passing versions all had a section labelled, in effect, "do the node's work here." It is not unreasonable to believe that "the node's work" could be done using an SMP within the node. A message-passing "wrapper" surrounding that then allows the use of multiple SMPs together, in a cluster. This is actually the situation with many important commercial subsystems, as will be discussed in the next chapter.

On the other hand, if one is starting from scratch, the effort to make either version work will militate against putting large quantities of work into the other. Then, it is notable that the message-passing code can be made to work within an SMP; a block of shared memory, appropriately carved up into queues, can take the place of intermachine wires. On the other hand, the shared-memory code will be difficult if not impossible—probably a significant rewrite, at least—to run in a message-passing environment. But the message-passing version won't use the shared-memory system at its full potential...

I draw no final conclusion from this. A major point of this chapter, which should be clear by now, is that shared-memory and message-passing programming are just plain different. There are no magic wands that turn one into the other. That is part of what different programming models are all about.

9.6 CC-NUMA

Finally, how do we do this on a CC-NUMA system?

Don't worry, I'm just about as sick of this problem as you are by now, and probably more. This will be the shortest of our three cases—not because it's being shortchanged, but because we've developed so much machinery that the possibilities are rather easy to run through.

The first possibility is to believe some of the press releases and just run the SMP code. Will this work efficiently? It will just plain "work," of course; efficiency is the issue.

After the effort we expended in the SMP case to get better cache locality, worrying about how long it takes to get to an SMP's (UMA) memory, thinking about increasing the memory delay by a factor of three, four, or more is at best distasteful.

However, having done all that chunking and blocking and reducing interprocessor synchronization to a minimum, we may have wound up with a program that runs very well indeed with few accesses outside its cache. So, suppose we simply ignore the node location of the data, and just run the fool thing, without changing it at all from the SMP version. Won't the result be fair efficiency—possibly not as good as on an UMA SMP, but certainly able to effectively use processors in different CC-NUMA nodes?

For examples similar to the one we have been working on here, that might actually be the case, always assuming the inter-node latencies aren't truly abominable. Our example happens to belong to a class of operations called dense matrix operations, which usually have the property that they can be manipulated into a form that has very high cache locality. This is by no means a property of all programs. Practical dense matrix manipulation does, however, often do a lot more sheer arithmetic on each point than we're doing and so should work fairly well.

However, in our particular example we won't have as nice a situation as one would like, because we've reacquired a significant load balancing problem.

Let's assume we're using the most efficient program with the best load-balancer we've got, the one that was developed in Section 9.4.10 on page 276 and used a global queue. Since we don't do much arithmetic per point, the time it takes to process each block is not likely to be gated by processor speed. Instead, it's gated by how fast we can get the data from memory.

We are definitely not alone in that; as was emphasized in the chapter on SMPs, memory subsystems are often the gating factor, even though processors get all the press. We're particularly not alone in technical computing. When the original Cray 1 supercomputer was delivered, many users found performance not really what they expected, primarily because there wasn't adequate memory bandwidth. The follow-on machine was able to load two floating-point numbers and store another every cycle, matching the processor's speed for a standard vector operation $\vec{A} = \vec{B} \cdot \vec{C}$. There's lots of code that still fits that model, and the amount of bandwidth to provide per "FLOPS" remains a hotly debated issue in technical computer design circles.

Given that global queue code, which processor gets which block is basically a random choice. For an UMA SMP, that doesn't matter; it's all in the memory. Using multiple nodes on a CC-NUMA, however, it means that some blocks will, at random, be local to their processors, while others are remote. Let's assume a reasonably good CC-NUMA remote latency, meaning one that is only three or four times worse than the latency to local memory. Given that we're memory limited, doesn't that mean some blocks take three or four times as long to complete as others?

For memory limited code, that appears to be the case. There are techniques that can be used to hide memory latency. For example, many processors allow multiple outstanding load operations to proceed simultaneously. That means our code for the four-point stencil accessing remote memory doesn't go load 1, wait 3X, receive data 1; load 2, wait 3X, and so on. It can instead go load 1, load 2, load 3; wait 3X; receive 1, receive 2, receive 3. The latency of multiple operations can be overlapped by this pipelining. However: Local memory is already far enough away that these tricks are already played to the hilt just for accessing local memory.

So while the code will, indeed, execute without error, it may well lose a significant amount of performance when remote data is accessed, more or less at random. The degradation certainly won't exactly equal the remote access penalty; since other operations are still overlapped, and others can't, exactly how it comes out depends on more detail than can be considered here. However, the difference is clearly enough to worry about. In addition, let's not forget that synchronization for locks that goes across nodes will also be delayed by the additional remote latency.

It certainly sounds like we should be more careful about where data is placed. There's no good place to put a global queue, for example.

No place to put a global queue.

Hmmm. What does that remind you of?

When it comes right down to it, well, perhaps...

Yes. The data layout issues that were the primary issue in message-passing are right at home here. For instance, laying out the data in CC-NUMA nodes in strips like those shown in Figure 89 on page 292, and doing the local processing and inter-node communication just like it was done there, will clearly give excellent results.

There is a significant difference from message-passing, however. The CC-NUMA case looks a lot easier to implement, because it can use shared-memory operations and normal SMP synchronization rather than messages.

For example, when node 1 of Figure 89 finishes with a block, it doesn't have to explicitly send a message with the edge values of that block to node 2. It can just set a synchronization variable that node 2 tests, a variable indicating that the edge is now finished and available for use.[11] Node 2 can then simply start executing, using those edge values in node 1 as the unchanged boundary conditions. When node 2 reaches this line,

---

11. Note: That had better be a synchronization variable, one whose access is hedged with all the issues of sequential consistency ("Sequential and Other Consistencies" on page 174). Otherwise node 2 may start running before all the edge data is available for it in memory.

```
/* replace each value with the average of its neighbors */
v[x,y] = ( v[x-1,y] + v[x+1,y] + v[x,y-1] + v[x, y+1] ) / 4 ;
```

the normal load operation produced to get the v[x-1] value will simply fetch the datum from the other node. Only for those edges will the remote access penalty be paid—assuming that the data layout in memory is compatible with putting whole rows in different pages. If it is not, then some additional node 2 accesses will be remote, and/or so will be some of node 1's accesses.

This example really demonstrates that there is a difference between distributed memory programming and message passing. This is not generally appreciated in the industry, which is why "distributed memory" is used as a synonym for clusters, distributed systems, and the like. It is not. Those are message-passing; this kind of thing is distributed memory.

The processing within each CC-NUMA node, each of which is an UMA SMP, can use the regular SMP techniques, as was described in Section 9.5.6 on page 294, "Clusters of SMPs." Doing so will suggest, for example, "locally global" queues, one per node, to internally keep things well-balanced.

Furthermore, if Simple COMA (discussed on page 210) turns out to win, it's unnecessary to "manually" lay out each node's data in different arrays and make sure those arrays are in the proper nodes; this is particularly a chore when the program is parameterized to allow use on arbitrary-sized arrays. You "simply" write a program that accesses data in the pattern of Figure 89, and the data is automatically moved to the appropriate nodes.

Finally, note that while the data structuring and locality issues may be rather similar to those or message-passing, the communication between nodes is, while worse than between UMA SMP processors, enormously better than between cluster nodes connected using standard communication. That means the grain sizes can be smaller, and in general the system will be more forgiving of serialization.

A different question is how CC-NUMA compares to the specialized structures now appearing to accelerate communication in clusters ("Cluster Acceleration Techniques" on page 108). For really short messages and simple synchronization, CC-NUMA provides a structure that is hard to beat. For larger data transfers, it's not all that clear. In the example used above, for example, should node 2 really use its loop-carried loads to get the data, or is it faster in the long run to do a block transfer—a message—that moves the entire edge into the local memory? I strongly suspect that the answer to this question depends entirely on how well each is implemented and supported, rather than on general architectural issues.

Finally, done. You can now stop thinking about averages. That's certainly what I'm going to do.

9.7 SIMD and All That

Speaking of different programming models, however, the three discussed above are certainly not the only ones. This was pointed out at the start of this chapter, where a summary of some of the others was promised. Here it is. This section provides what is in effect a dictionary of programming models. Since several are best known as elements of an (always limited) taxonomy, where appropriate the taxonomy will also be briefly described.

9.7.1 SIMD, MIMD, and SPMD

Unquestionably the most famous taxonomy of computational or programming models was published all the way back in 1972 by Michael Flynn [Fly72], who picked two characteristics of computers and tried all four of the possible combinations. Two stuck in everybody's mind, and the others didn't. Here are the four.

- ➤ **SISD: Single Instruction, Single Data.** This is a conventional, single-processor Von Neumann-style computer. There is one instruction stream ("single instruction") and one data stream ("single data"). This term is almost never used; it didn't stick.

- ➤ **MIMD: Multiple Instruction, Multiple Data.** This is a broad class of machines that includes all the types that are the subject of this book. There are multiple processors independently executing instruction streams ("multiple instruction") and each has its own, separate stream of data ("multiple data"). SMPs and clusters are members of this class, as are many other types. This is one of the two terms that stuck; it is very frequently used. For example, the MPI message-passing standard is described as a way to program "MIMD distributed memory concurrent computers."

- ➤ **SIMD: Single Instruction, Multiple Data.** This is a class of machines that rises and falls in fashion; most recently it's out, perhaps permanently. In this class, there is a master controller (executing the one, single, instruction stream) that figuratively stands in the middle of a large roomful of slaves and shouts ADD! Everybody adds, each adding a different pair of data values ("multiple data"). If one does matrix arithmetic for a living, this type of organization sounds reasonably appealing. ILLIAC IV was of this type. It was a rectangular array of arithmetic units, each with local storage, presided over by a central controller. Early offerings of the Thinking

Machines Corporation were of this type, although their last offering abandoned it for the flexibility of MIMD. Vector facilities, typified by the traditional Cray offerings, are effectively more flexible but less parallel variants of SIMD; they perform operations between whole columns of numbers with a single instruction. The inflexibility of having every computing element always do the same thing makes this organization harder to bend to general use than MIMD, although special-purpose systems often use it. This is particularly true in areas like image processing and signal processing. It's a great way to put a large amount of arithmetic processing in a small box, but it cannot readily use the power of standard microprocessors. This term also stuck; it's commonly used.

> **MISD: Multiple Instruction, Single Data.** It's a little hard to imagine how to do multiple things simultaneously to a single data item, so even Flynn was hard-pressed to give a convincing example of this category. Pipelined systems through which data flows may qualify. This term, representing a vacuous set, didn't stick and is never used.

More than a decade after Flynn's publication, I coined a related term as a conscious extension of Flynn's taxonomy: **SPMD,** for **Single Program, Multiple Data.** The intent was to concoct a term that described the way in which virtually all multiple-processor operating system code, and virtually all application code, was in practice being written: There is one program, and every processor executes it. The processors may take different paths through the program because they evaluate conditional statements (including locks) differently, but everybody's executing the same program.

Both SMPs and message-passing systems typically use SPMD; every program in this chapter is SPMD, and every subsystem discussed in the next chapter is SPMD. The term is now fairly widely used, usually without attribution. Its first publication was [DGNP88] (hint, hint).

The **SPPS (Serial Program, Parallel (Sub-) System)** term introduced in the first edition of this book is another obvious spinoff from Flynn's taxonomy.

By the way, even after well over two decades the jury is out on how you pronounce these. Should they be acronyms, like mim-dee and sim-dee? Or should they be abbreviations: em eye em dee, and ess eye em dee? Take your pick. In the usual tradition of parallel processing, there's no consensus. I suspect I'm not alone in being inconsistent, using sim-dee and ess eye em dee (for example) interchangeably.

9.7.2 Distributed Virtual Memory and COMA (ALLCACHE)

There are those for whom it is an article of faith that parallel programming using shared memory is inherently simpler than parallel programming using messages. This is nowhere so clear as among the developers of **distributed virtual memory** (otherwise known as shared virtual memory, or distributed shared virtual memory, or shared distributed...), who universally begin every paper by saying, with little or no explicit justification, that they're doing this because shared-memory programming is easier. What they're doing is extending the standard notions of virtual memory—allowing a program to think it's using more memory than really exists by transparently putting currently unused parts on disk—across multiple machines.

In everyday virtual memory, when a program tries to access data that it thinks is in memory but isn't, the operating system is automatically called. It clears some space, brings in the necessary data from disk (in fixed-size units called "pages"), and restarts the program where it left off. Distributed virtual memory is the same, except that the page of data may be obtained from another machine, which may, shared-memory fashion, also be using it.

This is just like moving lines between caches for cache coherence, except that each "line" is the size of a page, typically multiple kilobytes long; and instead of nanoseconds, by the time one goes through the operating system and communications to retrieve the page, the delay is at least multiple milliseconds. These differences—a factor of around 100 in "line size," and a factor of 10^6 in time—mean that to write an efficient parallel program one must be exquisitely aware of that "line size" and where one's data lies within it. False sharing is otherwise going to be rampant, and the attendant "thrashing" of pages between machines will bring efficiency as close to zero as desirable.

This makes a rather substantial difference in how programs must be organized if they are to run efficiently. Programs written to an SMP programming model, where the hardware tries very hard to make even the length of a cache line invisible, will not run efficiently under distributed shared memory except by accident. This doesn't mean that as a programming model it's bad or even hard to use; just that it's different, and not the same as what is in practice "shared memory": the SMP.

It is quite possible to use the techniques of distributed virtual memory to simplify the task of migrating processes from one cluster node to another; this has, in fact, been done [PW85]. However, using distributed memory this way is not the same thing as writing programs using a distributed virtual memory programming model.

A related notion was dubbed **COMA, Cache-Only Memory Architecture,** by a NUMA-inspired group, and is referred to as **ALLCACHE** by its developer, Kendall Square Research [Rot92]. This is rather like distributed shared memory, except for two things: All movement of data is done by hardware, not software, bringing typical "miss times" down into the microseconds and below; and there is no "main memory," only multiple levels of caches with ever-larger line sizes, reaching the point where the cache "lines" are, like distributed virtual memory, page-sized.

Whether the hardware actually helps has been studied [SJG92]; that one study came to the conclusion that it did not—you could, in effect, do just as well with DASH-like CC-NUMA structures and software to migrate pages to where they were used—but the conclusion is controversial. That didn't stop people from continuing to develop this notion into Simple COMA, which was discussed in Chapter 7.

Since the one company that sold a product based on COMA has failed—not necessarily for any reasons having to do with the merit of this technology—the future of the hardware-based technique is at best uncertain. The technology might diffuse to other companies, might be abandoned, or might re-emerge as additional hardware assists for Simple COMA.

9.7.3   *Dataflow and Reduction*

And now for something completely different: **dataflow** and **reduction** programming models. Neither of these has processors in the conventional sense. Neither even has a program counter, and they might not have a conventional memory. Instead, computation is performed as soon as the data required is available (dataflow) or when its results are needed (reduction). Dataflow has therefore also been called data-driven computation, and reduction called demand-driven [TBH82].

Both have the common characteristic that, unlike conventional programming models, one does not and indeed cannot say exactly *how* to do something; one can only *declare what* is to be done, and leave it up to the language and/or hardware to figure out the details of "how." The specifications (declarations) leave plenty of scope for the language processors or hardware to perform operations in parallel, without explicitly parallel programming of any sort. While languages for dataflow look more-or-less conventional, typical functional programming languages often look like nothing you've ever seen unless you have a close acquaintance with abstract algebra. (APL doesn't even come close.)

A discussion of these programming models that is anywhere near adequate is far beyond the scope of this book. Although prototypes of dataflow-based hardware have been constructed [e.g., GKW85], a practical production machine or a pervasive programming language based on these principles has yet to emerge, although it does continue to influence some more conventional architectural work [e.g., A+91]. For further information see [AG94, Hwa93], which contain thorough discussions and references to the rich literature on these subjects, or [Vee86], a dataflow survey.

It is, however, fairly common to use the dataflow notion of scheduling a chunk of work as soon as all the requisite data is available. It was used earlier in this chapter, when a global queue in shared memory was employed to overcome load-balancing problems: blocks of the array were enqueued as soon as they could be processed. It was also used in the message-passing wavefront methods. Strictly speaking, this is **macro dataflow**, the use of dataflow concepts on large chunks of work rather than items the size of single instructions. As indicated in the discussion of global queues, it is effectively used in every operating system and database scheduler; they employ global queues, and put work on them as soon as the work is eligible for processing.

9.7.4   Linda

In a category all by itself is the **Linda** system [CG89]. This is a software system that effectively implements in any system—including message-based ones—a global queue. But not just any global queue. Linda implements a relational-database-like **tuple space**: Any process(or) can drop a "tuple," a linear list of data of varying data types, into the tuple space by using a put() operation; any other processor can, by using straightforward pattern-matching syntax in a get() operation, retrieve tuples and work on them. Simultaneous execution of multiple put() and get() operations by many processors or nodes is taken care of within the put/get software itself.

The simplicity of using just two operations, get() and put(), to do parallelism is appealing. The practicality of doing so, measured in terms of the popularity of Linda compared with shared memory or message-passing, is definitely not clear—although there are circumstances where paired put() and get() operations known to be run on different machines can, at preprocessing or compile time, be automatically turned into a straightforward pass of a message.

9.7.5   General Comments on Other Programming
Models

All the less-common programming models suffer from a chicken-and-egg problem. Substantial applications and subsystems will not be created using them until practical production systems have been deployed that implement them, and there is little point to constructing such systems until there is a sufficient mass of applications and subsystems written to use them.

This is true no matter what their intrinsic merit might be. Distributed virtual memory, for example, may offer a very practical way to program message-based hardware. But programs written to the SMP programming model, with the characteristic global queue, will (except by lucky accident) thrash horribly when run in a distributed virtual memory system. Therefore, rewriting is necessary to use distributed virtual memory. But the current rewriting that's being done to applications and subsystems targets the SMP and message-passing models. Who's writing major applications and sub-systems using distributed virtual memory? Nobody. The same is true of dataflow and all the others.

This situation has been called the "critical mass" problem: Without a mini-mum critical mass of already installed systems, application developers won't be attracted. On the other hand, without the applications, you can't sell that many systems.

The importance of critical mass is often lost in the research and/or univer-sity contexts that engender programming models. With a few exceptions, each generation of graduate students can't figure out the previous genera-tion's code and is inclined to rewrite it anyway. That may be as it should be. Everybody can't be inhibited by short-term practicality; new ideas have to arise somewhere.

In the market, however, the critical mass issue places an immense inertial drag on the use of programming models that are not accepted nearly univer-sally. The only way around this dilemma is application portability, and changing the programming model is the antithesis of portability; this is fur-ther discussed below.

9.8   Importance

Having covered a number of programming models and demonstrated some of the pitfalls and intricacies of parallel programming, it's time to return to the question of why this stuff is important.

Programming models are vitally important for two reasons: First, since some are easier to use than others, they have an effect on how difficult it is to write a program in the first place. Second is the issue of portability; as indi-cated at the start of this chapter, a program written using one model can be extremely difficult to move to a computer system implementing another model.

9.8.1 Ease of Use

The ease-of-use question is very controversial.

Well, so are most of the topics of this book. But this one is *very* controversial, even compared to the rest.

Recall the analogy that a programming model is like the rules of a game, while programs are particular plays or game strategies. Using that analogy, imagine getting a bunch of basketball fans and football fans to agree about which game is the more difficult to play. If you like less violence, try bridge players and chess players. (On second thought, maybe that wouldn't be less violent.)

The resulting melee is mirrored, usually at a more civilized level of discourse, in ease-of-use debates between proponents of various programming models. Agreement has certainly not been attained, and its prospects are at best unlikely. In particular, holy wars have raged over whether shared memory is or is not an easier way to write parallel programs than message-passing—the paradigmatic programming-model distinction. Note that one of the big claims of CC-NUMA advocates is that they maintain the shared-memory programming model. Guess which side they're on?

At present, all that can be said is that any programming model *may* be equally easy to use in the following sense: If one starts with *both* (a) a blank sheet of paper, that is, one is writing an application from scratch; *and* (b) a mind attuned to the particular programming model involved; *then* it is probably as easy to write an application in one programming model as in another.

I do not expect shared-memory proponents, in particular, to agree with that statement; I know, because I used to be one of them. They are likely to say that their way is easier to use because it is closer to the uniprocessor model that everybody knows. But the message-passing bigots will counterclaim that the shared-memory bigots have had their minds hopelessly polluted by programming in FORTRAN, C, BASIC, COBOL, or whatever. If they would only just get used to thinking another way, they would see the light and discover that the discipline of message-passing ends up making the problem easier.

This would seem to fly in the face of some other evidence, however. Distributed computing uses message-passing, and we have all found out just how hard distributed computing is: very. The promises of client-server computing turned out to be rather hard to fulfill.

But the fact that distributed computing uses message passing does not mean that message-passing is distributed computing. In addition to its use of message-passing, distributed computing is characterized by heterogeneous systems; communication that has high overhead, low security, and low reliability; and a consequent need for robust operation in the face of failure and even overt attack. As was mentioned back in Chapter 5, the use of hardware with these characteristics, while enormously convenient, complicates life very considerably for the programmer of cluster or parallel functions.

An example of this added complexity appears in the discussion of parallel processing grain size in this chapter. The most straightforward message-passing solution to our problem simply does not work with normal standard communication overhead because it is too inefficient. This was true even in a version enhanced with techniques beyond what shared memory used—multiple wavefronts, which happen to be easily incorporated into message-passing. Having to find *a very large grain* message-passing solution is significantly harder than just finding *a* message-passing solution; much more ingenuity is required [Bel92b].

In short, distributed computing involves embedding into one's program the ability to tolerate very bad message-passing systems. Message-passing using fast, reliable, secure hardware and low-overhead software should not be damned by association with distributed systems.

Given this distinction between message-passing parallelism and distributed processing, I am at present inclined to agree with the message-passers that their approach *may* be as easy to use as shared memory. Aside from some experience, there is reasoning behind this. There seems to be some connection, albeit probably superficial, between object-oriented programming and message-passing models. These are not the same, any more than procedure calls and remote procedure calls (RPCs)—discussed in the next chapter—are the same, and for much the same reasons. (Among other things, you can't pass pointers in a message, and OO systems just dote on pointers.) However, they are similar enough in overall structure to invite comparisons of the learning process.

It is well documented that successful use of object-oriented methodologies requires a phase of reeducation that involves "unlearning" old ways of thought, following which the practitioners are better off than they were before. It is not unreasonable to believe that a similar situation exists for message-passing. The message-passers were actually saying this for many years before object orientation was picked up by the software community.

Such reeducation is neither simple nor free. At the same time, very significant education and experience is required to pursue any parallel programming at all—definitely including shared-memory parallel programming; recall all the pitfalls we stumbled into when doing the example in shared memory. The "unlearning" phase, however, is certainly an addition to the retraining required.

Is that addition a significant additional burden compared with the total that must be learned?

I consider that last question unanswerable, at least at present, and so conclude that under the two conditions mentioned above, all that can be said is that shared memory and message-passing *may* be equally bad.

But, and this is a very significant "but," SMPs have a very significant market presence; there are many more memory-sharers out there than there are message-passers. So, you're vastly more likely to find shared-memory programs already written and programmers already able to write programs using the shared-memory model.

9.8.2   Portability

The "blank sheet of paper" qualification on ease of use was extremely significant. There is rather less controversy about how hard it is to *move* a program written in one programming model to another, the primary difficulty that motivates this whole chapter.

Let's start by inspection. Was the code for the message-passing version of our example anything like the code for the shared-memory version? No. They were simply nothing alike. We didn't try to translate one into the other; for message-passing we re-thought the problem. Were the thought processes, the mental models of how the system was operating, even similar? No. One concentrated on how threads of control interacted with each other (shared memory), and the other concentrated on how data was distributed and passed around; in fact, message-passing programming or variations on it have been called "data parallel" programming [FHK+90]. How about CC-NUMA? Where we ended up there was using the key thought processes of message-passing, but implementing it using shared-memory tools. The final mental orientation was based on distributed-memory, not SMP-style common memory.

Why does this happen? Consider the game analogy again, recalling that programs are like plays or strategies. This time, consider a play that works well in, for example, (American) football. Imagine trying to apply it to basketball. Doing so may be possible, but it certainly isn't going to happen without a lot of reinterpretation and reorganization at a very abstract level, stripping the play down to its essential philosophical core. The underlying organizations of the two sports are simply too different.

Translation within one game is, by comparison, straightforward: A soccer strategy expressed in Portuguese, for example, can be translated into Italian rather straightforwardly. Some subtlties may be initially lost in translation, but for all practical purposes they can be expressed by using appropriately vigorous gestures.

The implicit translation provided by traditional high-level languages and system standards is like the single-game language translation example above. (Vigorous gestures don't work, however, unless perhaps they're directed at the compiler writer.) This translation works well as long as one is moving from one vendor's implementation of a programming model to another vendor's implementation of that same programming model.

A program written in programming model A, however, may well simply not work at all when run on a computer system that efficiently supports only model B. If it does work, it will most often work so inefficiently that it might as well not work.

System software standards do not help because the different programming models use different standards. For example, standard UNIX SVR4 (System V Release 4) shared segments are often used to create a shared-memory environment, but they do not work at all between processors that are not memory-coupled in a conventional way, like an SMP or a CC-NUMA system. In the other direction, UNIX BSD 4.2 sockets (or SVR4 streams) are standards used for communication between machines that don't share memory. They will work within an SMP, but they impose a stiff overhead penalty that is totally unnecessary in the SMP environment and will significantly decrease performance.

Traditional high-level languages do not help for two reasons. First of all, they are being used to call the standard facilities. A procedure call creating a socket is not going to produce a shared segment just because you compiled it on an SMP—there are sockets on SMPs, too, so a socket is a socket is what you get.

The second reason high-level languages do not help is that the algorithms used and the way they are expressed will in many cases change radically when one moves from one programming model to another. For example, consider the techniques used to find the maximum error in the sample problem used in this chapter. For the straightforward shared-memory SMP case, locking a global location and updating it was appropriate, with a bit of fairly straightforward loop chunking to lower the serialization overhead. In message-passing, equally straightforward, but different, techniques were used: a packaged reduce() or piggybacking a local maximum on another message. Compilation is not going to translate chunked loops into piggybacking; they're different programs.

Can't automatically parallelizing compilers, the AMO systems mentioned in the previous chapter, help? Yes, but at the current state of the art they can't switch programming models in the sense meant here—including appropriate algorithmic change—and it's reasonable to question whether that situation will ever change without having to say "A Miracle Occurs."

What current automatically parallelizing compilers (APCs) can do, and it is extremely valuable, is take a program that has been written in serial form and turn it into the corresponding parallel program: a program that runs in parallel, and has the same overall structure and algorithms as the original serial code. The programmer is freed from debugging parallelism; this is a huge benefit since it eliminates worrying about races and deadlocks and transient, nonrepeatable errors; if they occur, it's a compiler error. Go make some vigorous gestures at its author.

This kind of shortcut could have been used in the examples above, more or less by coding the forall loops as simple for loops; if we had made some error that invalidated parallelizing those loops, the compiler wouldn't have turned the loops parallel, thus avoiding runtime errors. Some of the worst versions presented in this chapter, like the original one with multitudinous race conditions on the v[] array, would never even be produced by any self-respecting (and correct) compiler; it would refuse to parallelize the loop or, if adequately sophisticated would jump directly to the wavefront method—which was originally developed as a general automatic loop-parallelizing technique. We would still have had to write the various programs in different ways to produce the later versions, like the one with a global queue, or one using multiple wavefronts.

In addition, there are versions of languages, such as "data-parallel" High-Performance Fortran [Ste93], in which the compiler can be given declarations of how data is distributed for message-passing, plus serial code; from that, message-passing parallel programs can be automatically generated. But the original serial code must still be written in a manner that executes well on the target architecture—and that means it's different for machines supporting different programming models.

APCs can actually help more than that; they can help manually restructure programs, either for better performance when using one programming model, or for moving between programming models. Since they analyze the program in great detail, they can point out internal dependencies of one datum on another that inhibit parallelism; letting the programmer know about that is an aid to restructuring. Some provide that capability already.

But this is still not automatically moving a program from one programming model to another.

Can that ever be done? Well, the definition given at the start of this chapter effectively precludes it by saying that a programming model is inherently above the level of traditional high-level languages. The qualifier "traditional" was used because some as-yet-undeveloped, even-higher-level language might provide the cross-model portability, perhaps by allowing programs to be expressed in a more general programming model that spans all the others. However, this is not even on the horizon at present. Should it occur, it will probably have a hard time because it will be a new *language*, not just a new compiler of an already deployed language, and the language will have to get past the pervasive, all-but-deadly inertia of the "critical mass" problem discussed earlier.

What can really help, where it is applicable, is the SPPS technique: Don't write applications in parallel at all, period. Let somebody else, a specialist, do it. Let different implementations of a subsystem, for different programming models, worry about all the parallelism. Databases do this, as will be discussed in more detail in the next chapter. Facilities like Fermilab's CPS (see "Fermilab" on page 25) do this, too. These systems only do it, of course, for database applications and for applications fitting the model of CPS. But in the areas where they apply, they are a tremendous help.

Even with SPPS, though, there's a possible pitfall. For databases in particular, the applications written under them can explicitly or implicitly use, for example, shared memory. Commonly used programming techniques closely associated with distributed programming do this (threads). Then, even though the database operations are immune from programming model changes, the applications are not.

So we finally reach the conclusion that there's no way around making a choice, and that choice is not a simple one.

Furthermore, because of the critical mass problem, everybody is going to be screaming in your ears that their programming model, the one on which they bet their business, is clearly superior. That is the real reason for all the varicolored deep-spectrum prose that surrounds these issues. As usual, it's money. Fame, too, but mainly money.

Commercial Programming Models

Never underestimate the inertia of software.

The previous chapter discussed the types of programming models realistically available and the ways in which programs are written using them, using an example from the technical computing realm. The next question is: Where and how is such programming used in commercial computing? This is a crucial question, because the existing multiple millions of lines of commercial software may not be right—in fact, they may be nowhere *near* "right," in any aesthetic or technical sense of the word—but they for sure are not going to get rewritten any time soon. This fact alone has kept (and will keep) many computer hardware vendors in a rather lucrative business for long periods of time.

To answer this question, we must extend the usually processor-centric notion of "programming model" to include input/output facilities, because several of the cases to be discussed differ most prominently in the way they treat input/output. In addition, we will use a somewhat more fine-grained distinction between programming models; there are, for example, at least two different ways in which shared-memory SMP programming is implemented, and here we need to distinguish between them.

This chapter will also justify the raw assertion of the last chapter that the shared-memory (SMP) and message-passing models are the only parallel programming models worthy of practical consideration at the present time; at this writing, CC-NUMA has not yet really crashed the party. The origin of the previously alleged connection between distributed computing and SMPs is explained here, too.

That said, take a look at Table 8. That table summarizes the programming models in use by a number of database vendors, other commercial contexts, and several technical/numerical areas. It also illustrates the inertia of software: except for some additions that should have been there originally, that table has not significantly changed in at least five years. That's practically an eternity in this business. The remainder of this chapter consists entirely of an explanation of that table.

As was the case with caches, an immense body of work will be short-changed here. This time I'm doing transaction-processing systems a disservice. Some topics (like what a transaction actually is) will be covered in Chapter 12, "High Availability." For more background, consult a text such as [GR93, KS86].

Also keep in mind throughout this discussion that moving from one of these programming models to another is an arduous task.

10.1 Small N vs. Large N

The programming models currently in use depend strongly on the size of the parallel system: **Small N** refers to the model implemented and preferred for a small number of active processors or nodes, usually processors; **Large N** refers to the model preferred for a large number of active processors or nodes, usually nodes.

The boundary between Small N and Large N differs depending on the application or subsystem involved, and is somewhat vague. In general, Small N means "SMP size," that is, four to around 16 processors, and Large N means bigger than that.

What, then, about great big SMPs and CC-NUMAs? A reason for this distinction, rather than just saying "SMPs" and "clusters" is that the CC-NUMA case, as implied by the discussion of the previous chapter, will probably gravitate towards Large-N application architectures that use CC-NUMA facilities in their implementations. However, none of those have formally appeared as this book goes to press. Should they begin to do so in numbers, it will be a significant mindshare victory for CC-NUMA systems. For the largest SMPs, on the other hand, the challenge of extending SMP-

Table 8   An Inventory of Programming Models

Type	User	Small N	Large N	
			Processor-Memory	Input / Output
Commercial	Oracle	SMP with shared segments	global lock *SMP	global disk; other I/O local
	Ingres	SMP with threads	global lock *SMP	global file system; other I/O local
	Sybase	SMP with shared segments	RPC *SMP	local
	Informix	SMP with threads	RPC *SMP	local
	IBM DB2/6000 Parallel Edition	SMP with threads	DCE RPC *SMP	local
	IBM DB2/390	SMP with threads	global lock *SMP	global disk and other I/O
	IBM VSAM	SMP with threads	global lock *SMP	global disk and other I/O
	commercial batch	OS interprocess communication; queue software	OS interprocess communication; queue software	global (desirable, not always available)
Technical	Grand Challenge	none; Small N is uninteresting.	message passing	little I/O (except graphics)
	seismic	SMP with threads	message passing	global (desirable)
	engineering analysis	SMP with threads	none (no Large N)	none (no Large N)
	computational chemistry	SMP with threads	message passing	little I/O (except graphics)

based, Small-N solutions to larger numbers of processors has been taken up by several important middleware vendors. It is not easy, and will take a while before performance promises are met and will in the end incorporate

✳ *Commercial Programming Models*   313 many of the techniques that are necessary for the Large-N cases discussed here.

10.2 Small N Programming Models

Each programming model actually has two parts: on the one hand, how it treats processors and memory; and on the other hand, how it treats I/O. Since all the Small-N models treat I/O identically—specifically, they all use the global I/O model—Small-N I/O models were not separately listed in Table 8 and won't be discussed in this section. The global I/O these models use is described later, under "Large-N I/O Programming Models."

10.2.1 Threads

Suppose one were programming a server system to do something for its client machines that involved server I/O. The simplest example of this is the familiar file server, but databases and other more complex operations fit this description also. The course of execution might look like that shown in Figure 90.

Figure 90   Single-Thread I/O Server Operation

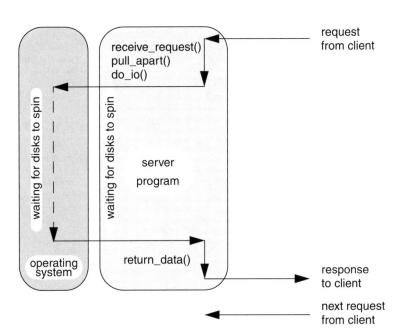

In Search of Clusters ✳

The server receives a client request, does some computation that figures out exactly what I/O to which file, disk, or device is appropriate, and calls on the local server operating system to do that I/O operation. Since external devices are usually rather lethargic, a fairly long delay (milliseconds) ensues; then the I/O operation completes and returns to the server program. Finally, the answer is passed back to the client, and another request can be accepted.

The code to do this would, in outline, look something like this:

```
do forever
    receive_request ( client_data );
    pull_apart ( client_data, client, io_data );
    do_io ( io_data, result );
    return_data ( client, result );
end /* of do forever */;
```

The operation called pull_apart() separates out the pieces embedded in the client_data to find out who the client is (client) and what I/O operation to do (io_data).

The wait for I/O to be completed is the chief element limiting how fast that server can handle requests. This will be true even if multiple disks are attached, with client data spread among them, since only one I/O operation, and therefore only one disk, is used by this server program at a time. The operating system itself need not impose any such limitation and usually does not; it can overlap processing of multiple I/O requests and might even reorder I/O to each disk so disk seek times are optimized, reducing the total time to do all the operations. These commonly available abilities do not matter, though, because the server program never does more than one I/O operation at a time.

Obviously, we'd like to do something about this. The solution of choice in distributed computing is to use **multiple threads of execution** within the server code, along with asynchronous I/O operations. The latter initiate I/O operations, but do not wait for them to finish; instead, they return right away to the user program. Completion is signalled by an interrupt when the operation actually completes.

10.2.2   User-Mode Threads

The notion of multiple threads of execution is actually a programming language construct. Related terms and concepts include *coroutine* (the oldest use of the notion), *procedure activation*, and *generalized label*; there are others. Very closely related concepts appeared in languages for Artificial Intelligence that incorporate backtracking, such as Prolog and the long-ago (early 1970s) Planner and Conniver languages.

The basic idea behind all of this is nothing more complicated than a bookmark. With a bookmark, you can stop reading, put the book down, go do something else, and later pick up the book again and restart where you left off.

In a program, the thread/coroutine/activation/label equivalent of a bookmark is an execution context. It is a complete record of what a processor is currently doing: the next location to execute (program counter), the contents of all relevant registers, and the current language stack of called procedures, temporary data, and so on.

There is always an execution context. Manipulating that context—changing registers, allocating and altering variables, and so on—is what an active program does. The unique thing about multithreaded operation, however, is that there can be more than one execution context.

This is just as if you were reading a book and got bored, so you put in a bookmark and put the book down. Then you picked up another book, read it for a while, and put it down with a *different* bookmark. With multiple bookmarks, you can restart reading any of the books whenever you like. Picking up a new book is like creating a new thread; putting in the bookmark and putting it down is like bundling up the execution context into a data structure and tucking it away somewhere.

This doesn't sound particularly abstruse. But here comes the good part.

The wacky, weird and wonderful thing about multithreaded systems is that by reactivating a context, you can go *back into* a procedure *from which you've already exited.* When you come back, you find everything just like you left it: your old variables have the same values, do-loop indices are the same, and if you return from the procedure (another time!) you return to the place you were called from, which has its old local variables and so on. All this was packed up in the context and put into suspended animation.

This isn't done willy-nilly, of course. You only return to a point that you've previously marked, and you can only have one point marked in a thread.[1]

---

1. The AI languages weren't such party poopers—they let you have lots of places in the same program at which execution could be resumed. This requires using a tree structure to hold the description of the execution contexts. It can get pretty hairy.

Let's see how this is used in practice, by rewriting that server loop as follows:

```
do forever
    receive_request ( client_data );
    create_thread ( do_client_stuff, client_data );
end /* of do forever */;
```

The create_thread() procedure makes a new thread, starting it off executing the procedure do_client_stuff() with the argument client_data. In other words, create_thread() just calls do_client_stuff() like a normal procedure, but it interjects creation of a thread at the start of the procedure invocation. do_client_stuff() is where we put all the work, more or less like before:

```
do_client_stuff ( client_data );
    pull_apart ( client_data, client, io_data );       /* figure out what's to do */
    until_io_done = async_do_io ( io_data, result );    /* start up the I/O */
    suspend_me ( until_io_done );                       /* Stop here, */
    return_data ( client, result );                     /* ...but start again here. */
    suicide();                                          /* Done. Good-bye, all. */
end /* of do_client_stuff procedure */;
```

async_do_io() does the same I/O request as before, but asynchronously. It doesn't wait for completion but instead merely initiates the I/O, and returns something—called until_io_done—that can identify that particular piece of I/O when it's completed.

The thread magic is in suspend_me(). It actually *returns* from do_client_stuff() back into create_thread(). This drops you back into the original main loop! That main loop then continues executing, just as if do_client_stuff() had returned, which it has, and proceeds to call receive_request() to get the next client request.

But suspend_me() is no ordinary return. An ordinary return would "pop the stack" and effectively destroy all the information about where the program was within do_client_stuff(). suspend_me() uses the fact that this is in a multi-threaded environment to save that information; it tucks away the context (where the program is in do_client_stuff()) on a list, together with the information in until_io_done.

As indicated, since we've returned to the main loop, that loop simply continues: It cycles back to receive_request() and will receive another request from another client if one's been sent. When that happens, the loop will call create_thread() to start another thread; that thread will initiate I/O and suspend() itself, returning into the main loop again. The main loop then cycles up to get another request, which starts up and suspend()s yet another thread; then another, and another…

In the meantime, the disks have been churning away. Finally they start rolling in the data and interrupt the main program. This interrupt initiates the other half of the thread magic.

The interrupt handler looks at why the system got whacked upside the head by an interrupt and passes that data to the thread manager, which compares the reason for the interrupt to the values of until_io_done it's got tucked away. When it finds a value that matches, it reinstates that thread's context and restarts it.

Presto, you're back inside do_client_stuff(), right after the suspend() and about to execute the return_data().

The values of local variables are restored, so when return_data(client,result) is done, the right client and the right result are used. There are, of course, lots of different client and result variables existing at any time—specifically, there's one set for each suspended thread. The right ones are always used—they're the ones in a thread's context. (The client and result variables really should have been declared in the do_client_stuff() procedure. If they're declared outside, then, by normal language variable scope rules, there is just one copy of each, shared by all the threads; this is not what we want. I just didn't want to complicate the example, which isn't written in any formal language, anyway.)

After the result has been sent back to the client, the work this thread was created to do is finished. So it commits suicide(), returning the thread data structures to free storage and, in the process, returning to the thread manager. This is the true final exit of a thread. The thread manager then picks something else to do.

The net result of all these shenanigans is shown in Figure 91: Many more clients are serviced in the same interval.

All this amounts to is the use of the classic technique of overlapping I/O with computation. It can increase throughput by a large factor. Exactly how much depends on the amount of computation done by the server program, how fast client requests can be received, and so on, but increasing throughput by a factor of 10 to 100 is certainly in the realm of possibility.

Such large increases in performance are not to be trifled with; client-server support packages really like threads. They are included, for example, in the Tivoli's DCE (Distributed Computing Environment) and are directly built into facilities for doing remote procedure calls, which are the client-server control structure of choice in a majority of contexts.

Figure 91 Multithreaded I/O Server Operation

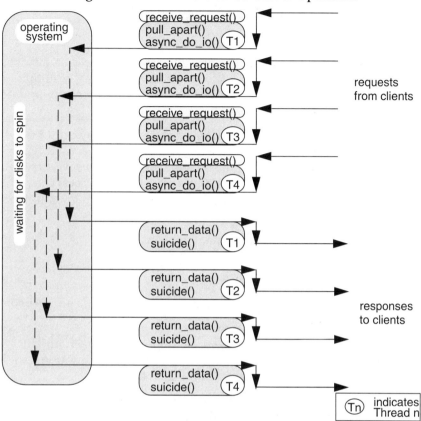

Even such large performance gains, however, are not the only reason for enthusiasm about multithreading. The fact that the local variables are automatically allocated and unique to each thread makes it very useful to have a separate thread for each client request, even if performance is not an issue. It simplifies the code, which otherwise would have to deal with storage allocation and deallocation on a request-by-request basis, explicitly programming the relationship between requests and their allocated data. Instead of doing all that, one simply spins off a thread per request and declares local variables; the system automatically associates the variables' data with the request, because the data is part of the thread's context. Anything that significantly simplifies programming is highly desirable, and threads do that for server programs.

This simplification is particularly notable when remote procedure calls, themselves a simplification, are used. Remote procedure calls will be discussed later.

Not all the data a thread accesses need be, nor should it be, completely local to the thread. As parenthetically mentioned earlier, data that's not locally declared is shared by multiple threads, so common resources and information can readily be shared.

Of course, should one do that, one should be careful, shouldn't one, when updating *shared* data? An interrupt could occur at any time, resulting in a switch to another thread, which might then access some partly updated shared data... Uh-oh.

Remember races? Locks? Unrepeatable results? Deadlocks and deadly embraces? Yes, they're all here when thread-shared data is used. There is only one processor acting at any time, so this is multi*programming*, not multi*processing*, but the same difficulties exist. As was stated back near the start of Chapter 9, multiprogramming and multiprocessing have a lot of things in common.

But hey, as long as we're partly pregnant, why not...

10.2.3   SMP with Threads

...use different processors to execute the different threads and get some computational speedup?

Indeed. There is a natural affinity—some might even say an unholy alliance—between threads, hence client-server distributed computing on the one hand; and shared-memory programming on the other.

They are very close to being the same programming model. While there are differences, those differences can (with care) be encapsulated inside locking, scheduling, and synchronization routines. For example, it is totally useless to spin in a tight loop, waiting for a lock to free up, when you're multiprogramming. No other processor is ever going to reset the lock; only another thread can do so. So you must switch to another thread. Conversely, you don't have to be careful about sequential consistency, since only one processor is involved. But otherwise there's quite a large overlap of techniques.

The way multiple processors get into the act is through the good graces of the operating system. In fact, the term "thread" was most widely popularized by its use in the well-known Mach operating system [BRS⁺85, Ras86], which became the basis of the OSF/1 AD system from the Open Software Foundation. Mach dissected the traditional UNIX notion of "process" into (a) an address space, (b) one or more threads of control executing inside that address space, and (c) a bunch of other stuff that need not concern us here.

The reason the operating system has to get into the act is that it owns the processors. There must be something in there that's recognized by the operating system if the OS is going to assign a processor to it. For multithreading systems, that something is called a **kernel thread**. It is essentially just like the threads we've talked about until now, which in contrast are **user-mode threads**. The big difference is that the "bottom" of the language stack of a kernel thread, and a chunk of its context, resides in and is presided over by the operating system, which can apply a real separate hardware processor to it.

A kernel thread is created by a system call, of course, usually syntactically-sugared through a subroutine package such as an IEEE standard UNIX pthreads package, or Tivoli's DCE threads package (which actually implements an early draft of the IEEE standard). When a kernel thread commits suicide(), it's a system call that deallocates a processor-dispatchable thing from within the operating system kernel.

Kernel threads are what is meant by the notation "SMP with threads" in Table 8 on page 313. The thread techniques described above are used by the commercial subsystems and applications listed in that table. As for the technical applications, well, now you have some idea what goes on inside that innocent-looking forall construct used in Chapter 9.

"SMP with threads" was used in the table only to indicate the use of kernel threads. Virtually all the commercial subsystems use user-mode threads, often with their own unique support code, for the program structure benefits described above. Some use both kernel-mode and user-mode threads. Others just use user-mode threads; for example, Sybase has its own user-mode threads for program structure and uses a different technique (described below) for multiprocessor speedup.

Why use both user-mode and kernel threads? Overhead.

A pure user-mode thread is, or at least can be, a very svelte, fast construct. Not a single system call need be involved in either creating or switching between them; a bare minimum thread switch can involve very little more overhead than a subroutine call (although figuring out which thread to switch to adds to that cost). If one is aiming at supporting thousands of clients, with at least one thread per client, such low-overhead operation is very important.

Kernel threads, on the other hand, require trips to the operating system to create and destroy. Also, there's little point to having many, many more kernel-mode threads than there are processors; all that does is hand over the thread scheduling to the operating system, which will do the best it can but really has no idea what the program is trying to accomplish. However, you'd like to have many, many threads for software structuring.

As a result, in many if not most cases, a user-mode thread package multiplexes a smaller number of kernel threads among a larger number of user-mode threads. This adds to the complexity and hence the overhead of the user-mode threads but is a good tradeoff between program structure and overhead.

Historically, "SMP with threads" is less common in the Open Systems area because it was only very recently standardized in UNIX. "SMP with shared segments" (below) was standardized many years ago with the System V release of UNIX. The equivalent of kernel-mode threads has existed in proprietary operating systems for a long time. In MVS, for example, jobs (like UNIX processes) can have within them multiple tasks; these are like kernel-mode threads.

10.2.4 SMP with Shared Segments

What do you do when you haven't got threads? Try shared segments; they work out just fine.[2]

That's what the "SMP with Shared Segments" category in Table 8 on page 313 is all about. It can be considered a stone-age version of kernel threads for UNIX. Never underestimate the inertia of software, but what the heck, it can be made to work fairly well. The way it operates is described below.

First, you use the standard UNIX fork() and exec() calls to create a whole new UNIX process. The system works a while, and there it is, complete with address space, file pointers, paging space, and the rest of the kitchen sink. Now you use UNIX System V system calls to create another address space, with a name: "Joe." Joe is tacked onto your address space, so the process just created can load and store into that region of (virtual) memory.

Now create some more processes. After a suitable pause, there they are: N address spaces, lots of paging space allocated, and so on. Each of those processes, unlike the first one, does not create yet another address space; instead, they politely ask the system "link me to Joe, please" and lo, it is accomplished. The result is illustrated in Figure 92: several processes, each with some private memory, but all sharing Joe in the normal, shared-memory, SMP fashion.

Since each process is known to the operating system as an active entity, it will (as the Gods of scheduling and dispatching decree) be assigned a processor; so we can get computational speedup. The usual way to use this is to

---

2. And what have you got when you get through a lock? / I'm not certain, but I know it's mine. This time, *Pace* The Beatles. I may have to learn to control myself more.

In Search of Clusters ✳

Figure 92   Shared Memory Using a Shared Segment

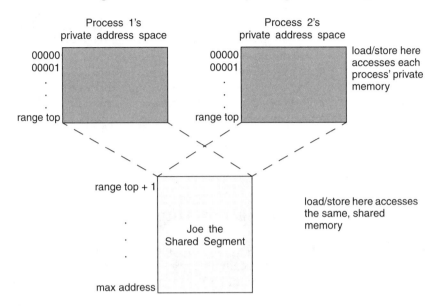

run with absolutely the minimum possible private area, placing everything in the shared segment that can possibly be put there. A database's "cache" of disk-resident data, for example, goes in the shared segment so every processor can get at it. Also, the structures for managing user-mode threads usually go there, too; that way, the processors (one per process) can be used at will to run any user-mode thread for good load balancing. The ubiquitous global queue of work items to do goes there, too. And so on.

There's really very little wrong with this technique, and it was the only portable way of getting computational speedup out of an SMP UNIX system prior to the standardization of kernel threads. Software inertia being what it is, this technique is still commonly used. The process-creation overhead occurs only once, at start-up, unless an application or subsystem dynamically adjusts the number of processors requested during its operation. Since few presently feel the need to do this, little is lost, aside from the kernel data structures and other appurtenances that processes require but threads do not.

Depending on the particular support system used, the shared segment technique may also be found in a number of technical areas despite what appears in Table 8 on page 313.

10.2.5   OS Interprocess

Commercial batch processing typically involves multiple job steps that are programmed as completely separate processes. To the degree that they communicate at all, they use standard OS primitives for communication and synchronization. For UNIX, which is rather typical, that includes pipes, semaphores, sockets, files, and so on. Since the communication facilities come from the OS, this is called the **OS Interprocess** model in Table 8 on page 313. Nowadays System V shared segments are also a standard UNIX interprocess communication facility, but using that facility produces a program structure different enough to warrant calling it a different model.

And with that, the discussion of the Small-N cases is complete.

10.3 Large-N I/O Programming Models _____

Since the I/O Model for Small-N systems was left for the Large-N discussion, it seems only reasonable to begin the Large-N discussion by skipping a column in the table and starting with I/O.

Two general I/O programming models are in use: global and local, and a variation or two on each. They are described in the sections following.

There is, however, a great degree of coupling between the use of Large-N I/O models and Large-N processor/memory models. In addition, cross-dressing of I/O programming models—putting software on one kind of hardware that makes it look like another—is significantly easier and more practical than processor/memory cross-dressing. The reason is that I/O data rates are lower, and techniques for overlapping I/O and processing are well understood and deployed.

The net effect of all of this is to turn the separate discussions of each into a somewhat dry recitation until the combinations are compared. This is done in the section titled "Shared Disk or not Shared Disk?" on page 330, which directly addresses the controversy involved—one that's at least as big as shared memory vs. message-passing. Hang on, we'll get there.

10.3.1   Global I/O

In the **global I/O** model, all devices and files are equally usable and equally visible to any program running anywhere in the system. Furthermore, the same name is used to refer to a device or file no matter where in the system that reference is done. In the jargon: There is a single global name space for devices and similarly a single global name space for files. The kernel or other subsystems accept those global names as the target of I/O operations.

This is, as was mentioned, the I/O model used for all the Small-N programming models. This is not surprising, since the Small-N models are basically variations on the shared-memory SMP programming model, and the "symmetric" in symmetric multiprocessor implies hardware support for global I/O (among other things).

There are variations on global I/O. In particular, some subsystems (primarily Oracle's database system) require global device I/O, specifically UNIX "raw" mode disk I/O; no other devices or capabilities need be global. Others (Ingres' database system) require global file I/O and nothing more. Needless to say, it is possible to provide one without providing the other. Or vice versa.

It's worth noting that the two databases requiring global I/O were originally written to exploit the DEC VAXCluster back when that was what Digital's OpenVMS Cluster was called. This provided global disk I/O via the Star Coupler, as was described in Chapter 2. None of the more recent cluster/parallel database designs has this requirement; it is out of fashion. Running multiple serial jobs, particularly commercial but also technical, is facilitated by global I/O since it makes cross-cluster workload management substantially more feasible and effective. This is particularly the case for global file I/O, rather than global raw disk I/O. Both IBM Parallel Sysplex and DEC's OpenVMS Cluster provide such file systems.

Use of a global I/O model requires the same kinds of programming considerations present in shared-memory operation. Cluster-wide locks are required, for example, so that multiple processors don't attempt to give commands to the same disk at the same time with the usual disastrous results. This is why the deadly embrace discussion in the previous chapter referred to "resources," not just memory. Database use of shared disks is interesting in this connection. Each separate node has a very large—multiple megabytes to Gigabytes—in-memory database cache of disk data. This, naturally, leads to cache coherence issues, which are solved using techniques rather like those used for processor cache coherence. This is further discussed later in "Global Locks" (page page 328) and "Shared Disk or not Shared Disk?" (page 330).

Distributed facilities effectively provide part of the effect of global I/O to application programs. Distributed file systems, for example, provide global file I/O for that part of the file system that is held on a server: As far as the application is concerned, it is doing normal, local I/O, using regular old operating system calls, with a perfectly normal file name. Remote queueing systems for printers perform a similar function, allowing system calls that put a file on a queue to do so as if it were local, but with global effect; with appropriate conventions a large group of machines/nodes can use the same names for a physically distributed collection of printers. This is a one-by-one conversion process, however; other devices—scanners, tape libraries, and so on—are not typically globalized, except under the aegis of a full-system cluster implementation or a kernel-level single system image (to be explained in Chapter 11).

10.3.2   Local I/O

In the **local I/O** model, each node of the system has its own local name space for devices attached to that node. A node cannot do I/O to a device attached to another node—at least, not using normal operating system I/O operations. The same is true of files: There is a local file system, and that's all a node can access.

This, obviously, is not all there is to it; an application or subsystem running across a group of nodes must somehow access devices and data on other nodes. The way this is done is by pulling the necessary function up into the program: A program on node Argus sends a message to a program on node Brutus—and we are here talking explicitly about normal inter-program communication; the only thing the operating system does is send the message. That message requests that the Brutus program do something, for it, such as accessing a disk attached to Brutus or twiddling some other device. If what is requested is a plain I/O operation, such as reading a "raw" disk sector and sending the data back, this process is called **I/O shipping**. If what is requested is a higher-level function, requesting some processing be done on the data and only the results be sent back, the process is instead called **function shipping**. These terms arose in the distributed database community, which has had great fun over the years debating which is better and/or easier to implement and/or more efficient under what workloads.

Note, however, that it was the program that did those operations. The programming model under which that program was written was still local I/O, since the Argus program was explicitly using a name for the operation that was not a normal I/O file or device name.

I/O shipping done within the operating system, however, can give the appearance of the physically-interconnected global I/O model to user programs; this is further discussed later in this chapter.

10.4 Large-N Processor-Memory Models _____

There are three Large-N programming models in use: messages, remote procedure calls, and global locking. In addition, each of these can be present with a variation: the SMP-node variation. This is noted by ***SMP** in the table. The SMP variation will be discussed after the basic models.

10.4.1   Message-Passing

The programming model indicated by **message-passing** in Table 8 on page 313 refers to the pure form of the message-passing model described in the previous chapter. It involves the use of multiple disjoint address spaces, each with a only a single thread of control active at a given time. In other words, multiple, traditional UNIX processes are used, although multiple user-mode threads might be used for program organization. (The *SMP variation is noted in the table only when the nodes can use SMPs for speedup.)

10.4.2   Remote Procedure Calls (RPC and DCE RPC)

The **remote procedure call (RPC)** programming model is a higher-level model usually built on top of the message-passing model. The intent is to simplify message-passing by allowing a program to invoke a function on another node much the same way as a procedure call is done: The program specifies the name of the operation and the arguments, and off it goes; sometime later, execution resumes with the requested operation carried out and the results returned in some of the provided argument slots, just like a procedure call [And91].

There are, however, differences from a normal procedure call.

> ➤ The name of the procedure called cannot be given in the normal syntax for a procedure, resolved by a compiler and linker. Cross-node agreement is required, with names declared specially; usually, a preprocessor is provided to make it easier to use such names, and to make things implied by the other differences more palatable.

> ➤ There is no shared memory between the caller and the callee, so pointers to addresses cannot be used as arguments, nor can the argument data itself contain pointers. This makes passing data structures difficult, to say the least. Structures must be "flattened" into simple concatenations of pure data before they can be either sent out or received back.

> ➤ It takes a lot longer. RPC operation over LANs is measured in milliseconds, whereas a procedure call is done in microseconds or even nanoseconds. Nobody is likely to confuse an RPC with a procedure call when there is a factor of a thousand to a million involved in performance. Part of the reason for the difference is that the arguments must be "marshalled": all packed into a simple string of data, with descriptors, that can be sent to another machine; on the other end,

they must be "unmarshalled," pulled apart again. This is at least a semi-interpretive process, usually involving data copying, and simply takes time. The other reasons are the usual overhead in using I/O-attached communications gear: operating system invocation, the interaction of the operating system with a protocol stack, and so on.

RPC follows the procedural semantics of suspending the caller until the operation is complete. This appears to make attaining speedup, even given the overhead, a mite difficult. However, RPCs are usually used in the context of multithreading or other forms of multiprogramming; suspending the thread that did the RPC does not necessarily stop all local computation, just one thread's. In addition, forms of RPC that are "asynchronous" also exist. The asynchrony involved is the same as that in asynchronous I/O: The RPC is invoked, but the caller does not wait for completion; rather it continues and is later informed when the operation completes. This is occasionally debated as something that destroys the whole concept of a remote *procedure* call and, furthermore, the same effect can be obtained by multithreading; nevertheless it's often offered and used.

The notation **DCE RPC** is used in Table 8 on page 313 for those cases where the specific RPC support being used is that provided by the OSF's Distributed Computing Environment.

10.4.3   Global Locks

In several of the cases—the Oracle, Ingres, IBM DB2/390 and IBM VSAM Large-N programming models—the primary communication between nodes is via global I/O and **global locks.** These are locks guaranteed to be atomic across an entire system. Little other explicitly internode communication takes place, since data is transferred between the nodes implicitly, using global I/O, after it has been appropriately locked. This is the mechanism by which these systems perform database cache management across multiple nodes.

Global locks are not, however, the simple locks we used back in Chapter 9, with a simple acquire() and release() interface. They are complex structures, which separate read locking from write locking; allow multiple simultaneous readers; provide for "promoting" a reader to a writer; allow locking any arbitrary thing, indicated by an arbitrary character string as the lock "name." Perhaps most interesting, they often keep sufficient track of things that in the event of a failure, all the data owned (locked) by a failed node can be identified and released for use by others.

In Search of Clusters ✳

This model, like RPC, is often implemented in software using the message-passing model. A node sends a lock request as a message to a lock manager residing somewhere among the nodes of the system; this message may require the lock manager to send a request to the current holder of a lock, asking that it be "demoted" to read or completely released so that someone else can write. The lock manager can be centralized on one node, which produces a bottleneck, or in Very Large N situations—and in this case, Very Large can be as small as 8—distributed across multiple nodes, each holding a subset of the lock data. Obviously, in the last case, you need some way to find out who has the lock; typically, a hash function applied to the lock name is used.

There is obviously significant overhead involved in this if standard message-passing techniques are used, which is why the IBM Parallel Sysplex provides specialized facilities for this function; they were discussed in Section 5.5, "Cluster Acceleration Techniques" on page 108. The Digital (Encore) Memory Channel, discussed in the same section, can also be quite effective in accelerating locking protocols.

10.4.4   The SMP Variation (*SMP)

All of the database subsystems adapted for Large-N processing can simultaneously use two levels of programming model: The nodes of the Large-N model can be symmetric multiprocessors, so the Small-N model is used on nodes and joined by the Large-N model. This is indicated by the notation ***SMP** in the table.

This characteristic is not shared by any of the technical computing areas, as was discussed back in Chapter 9. The programmers and writers of automatically-parallelizing compilers for technical applications, who usually have many different programs to deal with *en masse*, tend to throw up their hands at the notion of effectively dealing with two levels of programming model simultaneously, which is what the *SMP variation implies: one between the processors of an SMP and another between the nodes that are SMPs. They can, of course, use message-passing between the processors of SMPs as well as between nodes that are SMPs, but that's nearly as bad because the two types of message-passing—inter-SMP and intra-SMP—have vastly different costs.

Database vendors, on the other hand, have only one program to deal with (although it's a *great big* program...). So, they manually do what's required to deal with two levels simultaneously.

10.5 Shared Disk or not Shared Disk?_____

Global I/O vs. local I/O is, within the database community at least, at least as controversial a topic as the shared-memory vs. message-passing imbroglio continues to be within computationally-oriented parallel programming. This is to be expected, since it's the same issue, just at a different level of the storage hierarchy: Should one use physically shared disks, which can be directly accessed by all the nodes, or should only one node "own" each disk?

Note that the issue is whether sharing should be part of normal operation. Multiple physical connections to disks are required to provide the availability that is a major benefit of clustering (a point that will be raised again in Chapter 12, "High Availability") and local I/O systems usually have that; but in local I/O, the "other" connections are used only in the in case of failure, at which time ownership of a disk switches from one node to another.

On the shared side, we have Oracle Parallel Server, Ingres' distributed version, and IBM's DB2 and IMS DB and VSAM; on the local side, we have Sybase (and NCR's) MPP, Informix' XPS, IBM's DB2/6000 Parallel Edition, Tandem Himalaya, and Microsoft's SQL Server. The winner so far in market share among open systems appears to be Oracle, if for no other reason than that they've been selling systems for years longer than the others. Even so, the Tandem, IBM, and Microsoft offerings are not to be trifled with, and the universal choice for new implementations has been local I/O.

Before getting into who can claim what and how, let's describe how the three chief variations work: true physically shared disk, I/O shipping, and function shipping. The discussion will deal with issues other than just database systems, since the same issues arise in cluster file systems.

10.5.1   Physically Shared Disks

The key issue with physically shared disks is that, just as with shared memory, nodes cannot simply whack away at the disks without some control being placed on what they're doing, where they're doing it, and when they do it. Races and other evil things can occur, so some form of control—meaning locking—is required.

In addition, we've got caching to worry about again. Both file systems and databases cache data from disk in primary memory, for the same reason that caches are used in processors: Real workloads exhibit locality of reference to stored data, not just data in main memory, so caching the data in primary memory often eliminates the need for a slow reference to the spinning brown stuff.

Processor cache coherence and the shared-memory programming model use separate techniques to deal with the coherence and logical problems of sharing; coherence is done in hardware, and the logical problems are dealt with primarily in software. Shared disk systems, on the other hand, usually use global locks as a combined solution to both types of problem.[3]

Suppose, for example, node Able wants to write into a block on a shared disk. Node Betty has recently written into that block, so it's in Betty's main-memory database cache. Somehow Betty has to be told to give it up. That's the job of the lock manager. The lock manager could reside in Able or Betty, but to reduce the confusion we'll assume it resides in a third node: Carlos (with IBM's Parallel Sysplex, Carlos would be the Coupling Facility).

The sequence of operations required is shown in Figure 93.

1. Able sends a write lock request for the block to the lock manager, Carlos.

2. Carlos looks up the block in his table of locks, sees that Betty has it, and sends Betty a request to give up the block.

3. Betty gives up the block by first writing it back onto the disk, which she's allowed to do because she currently owns the write lock. Having done that, she deallocates that block from her primary memory, and then sends Carlos an "unlock" message. (If Able had just wanted to read, Betty could have kept the block in her cache with a read lock on it; since Able is writing, that copy would be wrong.)

4. Carlos gets Betty's unlock, notes an ownership change from Betty to Able in the table of locks, and sends Able a "lock granted" message.

5. Able now reads the block from disk and proceeds to scribble all over it to his heart's content.

The similarities between this and processor cache coherence protocols should be blindingly obvious. In fact, the actions of Carlos are very like those of a cache coherence scheme using a centralized directory, carried out in ultraslow motion. One big difference is that transfer of data is through the disk: Betty writes, then Able reads it. This is like writing processor-cache data to main memory, and then reading it back again. Why do that? Why not just send the data direct from Betty to Able?

Well, I keep hearing people threaten to do it, but it hasn't happened in an open systems context. One reason is that, unlike the processor case, there

---

3. The only current exception is disk cache coherence support in IBM's Parallel Sysplex; we'll address that a few sections below.

Figure 93 Writing to a Shared Disk

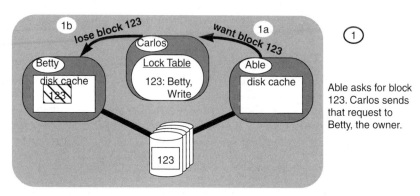

①

Able asks for block 123. Carlos sends that request to Betty, the owner.

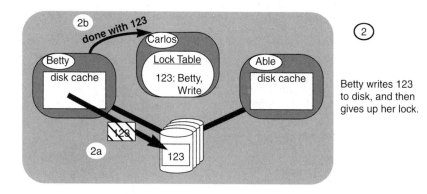

②

Betty writes 123 to disk, and then gives up her lock.

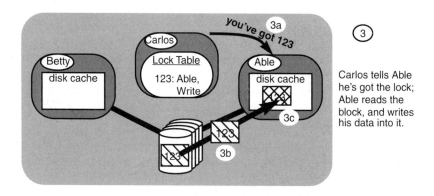

③

Carlos tells Able he's got the lock; Able reads the block, and writes his data into it.

In Search of Clusters ✳

have been few deployed high-speed inter-node buses and switches. In contrast, centralized directories (and snooping caches) for processor cache coherence use high-speed internal switches and buses to flush the data around. Even though it would save waiting for two disk latencies, LAN communication overhead is such that the change would barely be worth it. In one case, where faster communication has been deployed and the system totally reoriented towards shared-data (of all kinds) operation, it has happened: The IBM Parallel Sysplex, discussed in Section 10.5.4 on page 336, just a little further on.

However, there are other issues involved; they are discussed more fully in "Further Comparisons" on page 342.

10.5.2   I/O Shipping

Even if disks are not physically shared, they can be logically shared. That's what I/O shipping is: shared-memory cross-dressing for physically unshared disks.

A typical sequence of events for obtaining a disk block by I/O shipping is shown in Figure 94. Node Able is getting a block from Node Betty this time, and Carlos isn't involved. The sequence is this:

1.   A program on Able issues a request to read a block, number 123 again. This proceeds through Able's operating system to the device driver (although it could be elsewhere), which looks in a table and discovers that block 123 isn't on a disk attached to Able. It's attached to Betty. So the device driver sends a request over to Betty.

2.   On Betty's side, the request again goes into a device driver, Betty's this time, which sees that the block requested is on a local disk, gets it, and sends it back to Able.

3.   Able's device driver picks up the data just as if it had been read from disk and presents it to the requesting program.

Well, that was a whole lot simpler than the first case.

But wait a minute. What about the locks, data integrity, and all that? Who checks to see if somebody else is scribbling away in it like mad in another copy of that block?

The answer is that I/O shipping doesn't handle that. It only ships I/O. The coordination must be done at a higher level—meaning, in the program that requested block 123 in the first place. In effect, I/O shipping treats Betty as if it were a particularly intelligent disk controller, attached using a LAN and a TCP/IP protocol rather than by a conventional disk adapter and SCSI bus.

In other words: I/O shipping is simply an emulation of a multi-tailed disk, using software and interprocessor communication rather than a direct physical attachment. It is more "scalable" than multi-tailed disk, because interprocessor communication allows many, many nodes to be connected no matter what limitations the disk devices themselves may have; the disk drives only need be attached to one computer.

Figure 94 I/O Shipping

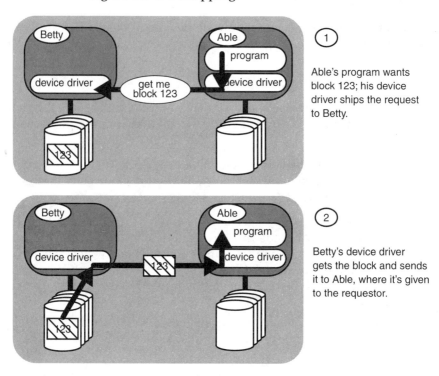

I/O shipping has actually been used by Oracle in place of physically shared disks in an implementation that runs on an NCube highly parallel computer. It is also used in Oracle's implementation on the IBM Scalable Parallel systems [LC94], and will probably be used by Oracle to effectively simulate shared disk on any number of other similar systems. When I/O shipping is used this way, a number of the nodes are designated as I/O controllers, and internode communication is used to send requests to them. In addition, for the NCube implementation a very carefully designed, highly-distributed lock manager was also implemented, and used in its usual fashion to control access to the disk blocks.[4] A locking protocol like that of Figure 93 was used,

In Search of Clusters ❋

but instead of just reading the data from disk, the protocol of Figure 94 was then used to transfer the data.

There is one potentially significant difference between I/O shipping and physically shared disks, however. The "owner" of a disk can maintain its own cache, in its own primary memory, of the data on its disks. That cache is not directly subject to coherence issues, because the owner is the only node that can write to the disk. So, instead of reading the data from disk in step 2, the data might well be sent directly from the in-memory cache; when this happens, it is likely to save enough time to overcome any communications overhead that might arise.

On the other hand, high-performance disk controllers have their own caches; so in the physically shared disk case, the data might well be read from the controller cache. This also saves a mountain of time—rotation latency is 20–30 milliseconds at best—and transfer rates in disk subsystems are 3 or more Mbytes per second, not the 10–16 Mbits per second of current typical LANs.

Yet on the third hand, the intensely faster intermachine communication that is arriving may dwarf the data rate to single disks; the amount of memory in a node is usually significantly larger than that on an adapter; the algorithms used for caching can at least potentially be better tuned to the application; and this cheap general-purpose memory can replace a fancy, expensive disk controller with cache. Now, with the various cluster accelerators we saw in Chapter 5…

Didn't I mention before that this was controversial?

10.5.3   Function Shipping

The final technique draws its name from the database area, but in a more general context can be seen to be common in distributed computing. **Function shipping**, as it is called, is somewhat similar to I/O shipping. But instead of simply requesting I/O, the requestor asks that a significant piece of work be done and only the results be shipped back.

The typical example involves an SQL database select statement: select, applied to a relational database table, returns another table consisting of only the rows of the original table that match some criterion. For example, one might ship to another node, owning a table of employees, a request to

---

4. I have been told by an Oracle representative involved in that lock manager design, tailored to work well with several hundred processing nodes, that creating that highly-tuned, highly-distributed lock manager was the hardest, most painstaking programming he had ever been involved in. Massive parallelism has its drawbacks.

select out of that table all the employees who are in department 77; or out of a list of credit card receipts, the ones for airline tickets.

A common application of function shipping in the database arena involves the parallelization of queries. As in message-passing, the data involved are first distributed among the nodes involved; for example, a big table of credit card receipts might be partitioned into many tables of approximately equal size, uniformly distributed across the disks of all the nodes of the system. Then, when a query comes in asking who bought airline tickets, the select function is shipped out to all the nodes of the system. Each one operates on its own partition and returns the subset of the data requested.

The same kind of thing can be and is done with shared disk systems, but without the logical requirement that the tables be prepartitioned; each node is simply assigned a chunk of the table, much as chunking is used in a forall loop, and goes at it. (However, this requires qualification; see "Further Comparisons" below.)

Function shipping is, as a programming model, very close to RPC, so that's what is typically used to implement it—by IBM's DB2/6000 Parallel Edition, Informix' XPS, and Sybase's MPP. Tandem Himalaya also uses partitioned tables and function shipping.

In a sense, function shipping is also what every distributed file system does (just to pick one common distributed example). A symbolic file name and offset is shipped over, the function of finding that symbolically addressed data is done, and the result shipped back. In that sense, function shipping is extremely common.

10.5.4 Cache Coherence Again, and IBM's Parallel Sysplex

As was mentioned way back in Chapter 5, whole-system vendors who do their own hardware and control most of the system software have the opportunity of optimizing both together. While several vendors have done this to some extent (Tandem, DEC), IBM is unique in doing it wholeheartedly, at a high level, for shared disk. As part of that optimization, obtaining a cluster-wide global lock became a single instruction. (See "The S/390 Parallel Sysplex Coupling Facility" on page 121.) It is a pretty long-running instruction, and does usually require several prior instructions to set up the data structures it uses, but it executes quickly enough that switching to another task is (by design) not worthwhile.

Another part of that optimization is support for coherence among database caches on different nodes. The issue and that solution are described here, both because it's interesting and because it usefully highlights the difference between locking (synchronization) and disk cache coherence, the latter being a much more widespread issue.

Suppose node Able, some time in the past, read block 123 into its disk cache. Able got a read lock for 123, looked around in it for a while, then was finished with it and let go of the read lock like a good citizen. See Figure 95, part 1.

After finishing with that block, what did it do with it? Zero it out, or randomly scribble on it? There's no point to that; why waste the time? Instead, Able just let block 123 lay there, in its disk cache. Maybe Able wiped out its copy of block 123 by reusing that storage are, reading another block on top of it. Then again, maybe not. It depends on the replacement algorithm used, and that can vary both by database implementation and by the type of operation being performed.

As a result, there's a decent chance that block 123 will still be hanging around in Able's own disk cache when Able wants to read it again. (Figure 95, part 3.) That chance will obviously be better if the workload has some locality of reference, which is typical of transaction processing (but not large queries).

So, Able wants to read block 123 and gets a read lock on it. Able is now free to look at block 123. But what does Able do with that copy of block 123 in its memory?

Sure would be nice to just use it again, without having to re-read it from disk. Single-node (non-clustered) systems do that all the time, and gain a significant performance improvement as a result. People spend significant effort tuning replacement algorithms to maximize the possibility that this will happen. The same replacement algorithms are re-used in cluster systems, so the possibility is quite real that block 123 is perfectly OK to use a significant fraction of the time. Furthermore, all the discussion in "I/O Shipping" about caching in disk controllers vs. inter-system speed of transfer is moot for this case: Not having to transfer the data at all is nearly always better than having to move it.

Unfortunately, this isn't a single node system. *Able doesn't know whether another node has scribbled on block 123,* as happened in Figure 95, part 2, making the copy in Able's disk cache out of date. Having given up its original read lock, Able simply lost track of any use of block 123 elsewhere in the system. Getting the second read lock tells Able nothing about whether his copy is clean or tainted. That's the difference between serialization issues and cache coherence issues.

This problem isn't unique to shared-disk databases. Shared-nothing I/O-shipping organizations have this problem, too, if they attempt the optimiza-

Figure 95 The Disk Cache Coherence Problem

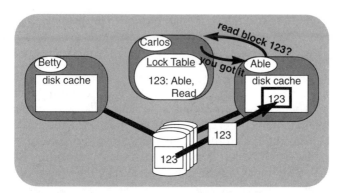

Able gets a read lock on block 123, reads it into his cache, looks at it, and releases the lock. Keeps the copy in cache. Why not?

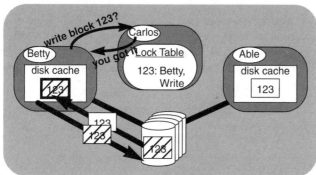

Betty gets a write lock on block 123, reads it, scribbles in it, writes it back to disk, and releases the lock. Able still has his old copy.

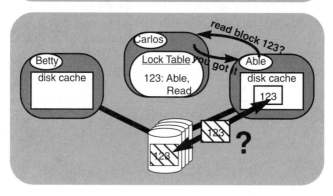

Able gets a read lock on block 123 again.

How does Able know not to use the copy left in his disk cache?

tion of keeping a local cache of data they're obtained from another node. Cluster-wide file systems have the problem if they do local data caching. Distributed file systems like AFS or DFS, which cache data locally, also have this problem. The real issue isn't shared-disk or shared-nothing, it's the fact

In Search of Clusters ✳

that maintaining local caches—usually a very good thing for system efficiency—requires that something be done about cache coherence.

The usual distributed solution is that somebody maintains a directory that tracks who has copies of which disk blocks at all times. Then whenever a write is attempted on a block, the "somebody" with the directory is told first. It uses the directory to inform everybody with a copy that their copy is no longer any good—multicasts an invalidate signal for a block; after that, the write is allowed to proceed.

The steps involved in maintaining the directory and using it were left out of Figure 95, part 2 to illustrate the problem when this isn't done. (This was also left out of Figure 93 on page 332.) Those steps eliminate the question in part 3 of Figure 95, because Able would have been told back in part 2 that its copy is no longer any good.

This whole approach is extremely close to the omniscient central directory approach to SMP processor cache coherence that was discussed all the way back in Section 6.4.2 on page 162.

It's possible to speed up the process considerably by judicious use of some hardware. The way IBM did so in their Coupling Facility entwines this operation with the use of the Coupling Facility as a "second-level" global shared cache for disk data. It essentially provides a hardware assist which multicasts the invalidate signal with low node overhead. The important most interesting hardware components used for this are shown Figure 96.

Figure 96   Coupling Facility Coherence Components

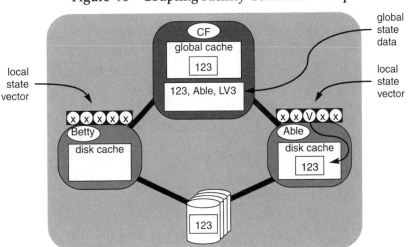

Each system node has an added structure called its local state vector (LV). The CF itself has a global state data and the global disk cache. It also has the lock table information, but for clarity that's left out. These will be explained, as usual, through example.

When Able (for example) read-locks and then reads a block from disk, it *registers* that block under a global name at the coupling facility; the block is (optionally) stored in the global cache, using the high-speed CF links. At registration, Able also assigns a bit in the LV to correspond to that block, sets it to indicate "valid," and tells the CF which bit that was. The CF records that correspondence, along with the node name (Able) in the global state data. In Figure 96, the block named 123 has been assigned the third LV position and copied into the global cache.

Recall that the CF is just another node, although running a special code load; it does not run the normal OS. The global cache and the global state data are normal program data structures in that node's normal memory.

The LV, on the other hand, is in the S/390 more-or-less equivalent of memory-mapped I/O. A section of memory that the processor can diddle with normal memory operations, but which external devices can read and write, too. It is, for example, where I/O channels deposit their status. So, things are arranged so that the CF can change the bits in the nodes' LVs. See where this is going?

Suppose, now, node Betty wants to write into block 123. It first checks its own local disk cache; not there. So it tries the CF, finds it, and reads in the block (fast), registering it and picking its own LV bit. We're now in the state shown in Figure 97.

Figure 97 Coupling Facility Coherence, Write (part 1)

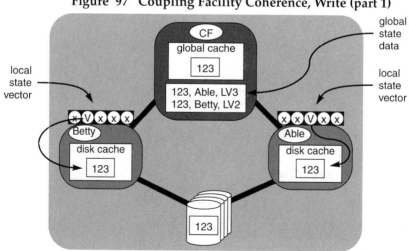

In Search of Clusters ✳

Next, Betty acquires a write lock on block 123 (not illustrated). Until it lets go, nobody can mess with block 123 in any way, so Betty is free to scribble in its local copy of that block, which it does with merry abandon. When done, it sends the data back to the CF with a subcommand that causes the CF to go through the global state data, find all the nodes where 123 is hiding, and set the LV bit in each node to "invalid!" for block 123 (see Figure 98). Sooner or later it also writes it onto disk, to ensure stable storage, and releases the write lock. (It appears logical that some future version will make the CF caches themselves a stable storage site.[5]) Now we're in the state shown in Figure 98, which also illustrates the invalidation operation.

Figure 98   Coupling Facility Coherence, Write (part 2)

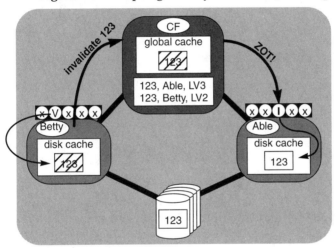

The CF's ZOTting of Able's local state bit 3, however, did not cause an interrupt or otherwise disturb Able. That means that Able, if it wants to look at block 123 sometime later, must first check whether it already has a copy *and* the local state vector says that copy is valid. If the copy is valid, use it— answering the question originally posed in part 3 of Figure 95 on page 338. If it's not, it sees if there's a copy in the global cache; if none is there, oh well, guess we've got to get it off the disk.

While this description has been long, it illustrates not just how IBM's particular implementation on Parallel Sysplex works; other than the fast invalida-

---

5. The original CF proposal used memory that was hardware fault-tolerant, never-die, good as duplexed disk. When this was passed by some customers, the reaction was "That's nice, but if my system is going to fail if I lose that thing I want two of them, and by the way, why does it cost so much?" So much for that idea. Plain old memory was used instead, along with the ability to reconstruct CF data in another CF.

tion, the same kinds of functions must be performed whenever cached data is used on any system.

It's also simplified. For example, the discussion above assumes that the unit of storage moved to and from disk and memory is the same unit locked, and the same unit that has to be tracked for coherence. For many databases in particular, this would lead to thrashing due to "false sharing" behavior, just like CPU caches can exhibit. (See "Cache Coherence" on page 158.) Betty might have changed just 16 bytes in a page-size unit (for example, 4K bytes), and Able might never need to have anything to do with those bytes. So the locking unit, the coherence unit, and the unit of transfer need not be the same. Parallel Sysplex also supports this, using multiple local state vector entries to dissect a block into the pieces the program actually wants to play with; for more detail, see the references (e.g., [NMCB97, Str97]).

10.5.5   Further Comparisons

A number of other points can be raised about the shared vs. non-shared disk issue.

An issue often cited in the shared vs. non-shared debate is the requirement, when disks are physically shared, to provide direct access from all nodes through their I/O systems to all the disks of interest (there may be private disks local to each node, but that won't concern us here).

This means the disks themselves must be "multi-tailed," meaning they can accept commands and data from more than one source. Conventional mass market SCSI, SCSI-2 and SCSI Fast/Wide disk interfaces don't do this very well, even though they can be physically connected to multiple nodes. The problem is in switching from one master to another when multiple nodes are actively using the disks, not in "failing over" in the event of a failure. In addition, these multi-tailing facilities are usually limited to two- or four-way sharing, limiting the size of the systems that can be constructed. So, this looks like a dual score for local I/O: You need proprietary disk technology to make shared disks work well and support even middling-sized clusters.

While this argument used to be quite strong, it is rapidly evaporating for several reasons:

> Within the SCSI paradigm, some vendors, like DEC, have provided "SCSI hubs" which allow many nonproprietary disks to be attached to good-sized clusters.

> "Loop" technologies, like SSA and FC-AL, have appeared, soon to merge into FC-L, and intended to replace SCSI. These allow many disks to be attached to many nodes at costs that are as low as SCSI.

In Search of Clusters   ✳

This was not instigated by clustering; it came from the need to attach more disks to a single adapter, which was inhibited by the physical size of the SCSI connector and the electrical characteristics of the bus. Fibre Channel Standard (FCS) also provides this capability very well, but at a large scale, longer distances, and for more money.

➤ It turns out that even shared-nothing systems need the I/O disk connectivity that has been assumed to only be a requirement of shared-disk systems. The reason lies in load balancing after a node failure, and is discussed in Chapter 10.

So, physical connectivity issues are not necessarily a way to differentiate the two paradigms.

From a marketing viewpoint, shared disk is easy to explain. Instead of one computer processing the workload, N computers do. See those cables right there? That's how they all access all the data! Local I/O systems require further explanation just to reach the point where customers understand how all the machines can get to everything.

Shared disk advocates typically point to issues like load balancing and convenience as being in their favor: You just put all the data out on the disks, and whoever needs to get at it, gets it. For a recent summary of those arguments, see [KDY97], which emphasizes system performance under varying workloads. In comparison, the local I/O folks have to partition the data ahead of time, spreading it out among disks according to the anticipated query workload. Some have elaborate front-end tools to help this process. Sybase's MPP, for example, has a tool that take the anticipated types of queries as input, determines a good partition for that on the basis of analytical models or simulation, and outputs a pile of shell scripts that will perform the partitioning for you.

However, simply dropping data in any old way on the disks of a shared disk system does not necessarily lead to good performance. It's seldom useful to parallelize a query, for example, if all the tables being used are on the same disk; that disk's bandwidth will be the bottleneck. At least some partitioning is necessary, just as it was necessary to have multiple memory banks with interleaving when putting together an SMP.

Another difficulty with sharing arises from the database equivalent of cache cross-interrogation. This can lead to trouble if some of the database records are "hot"—frequently accessed by many different nodes. In that particular case, intelligent local caching of I/O data can help, and function shipping can be a significant gain: If everybody's function on the "hot" item is queued up, it's entirely possible that significant performance gains from processor cache locality of reference can result. A major reason for IBM's use of a global disk cache in the Parallel Sysplex Coupling Facility is to deal with that problem.

There's another issue here, too, that brings in an issue completely different from the discussion that's been going on so far. It concerns the key ability of a database or transaction system to actually perform **transactions**—internally consistent alterations to data that either completely, consistently happen, or do not happen at all—no matter what hardware, and most software, failures occur. This will be discussed in some detail in Chapter 12, "High Availability."

With shared disks or I/O shipping, the special processing necessary to ensure transactional semantics can be done on a single node: All the data and all the control over the disks is implicitly gathered into a single place. With function shipping, however, even a simple transaction cannot usually be done on a single node; several nodes, all doing part of the work, must cooperate. Performing operations as true transactions, even though the operations are spread across multiple nodes, is by no means impossible. The technique called **two-phase commit** is probably the most common way to accomplish that feat. This is described further inChapter 12; in the meantime here's a horribly simplified description: A controlling node first makes sure everybody is "prepared" to commit the transaction (phase 1), and if everybody agrees then all are told to move from the "prepared" state to the fully "committed" state (phase 2). This method works. It also requires significantly more processing at each node and, perhaps more importantly, significantly more internode communication to accomplish it. Function-shipping systems must incur this additional overhead on many transactions; the gathering process used in the shared systems avoids it, but of course imposes its own overhead.

Of course, if the sharing systems are used to do parallelism inside a single large operation, they, too, do things simultaneously on multiple nodes and must use two-phase commit or an equivalent protocol. And the tradeoff of shipping function may reduce the total communication enough that even with two-phase commit, there's little if any additional overhead. Overall, the function-shippers appear as this book is written (mid-1997) to have a definite disadvantage in attaining high throughput on many small transactions, particularly if internode communication is subject to large overheads.

10.5.6   *The Ultimate Direction*

So, what is the ultimate direction? It's going to at least depend in part on the particular environment and circumstances.

If one starts with a blank sheet of paper—a new installation, for a new application—and does so soon (the short run), the relative simplicity of the shared-disk systems and the heavy overhead involved in current standards-based internode communication make physically shared disk systems hard to beat when data updates must be done. Decision support and other large-query, read-mostly applications are favoring the simplicity, in that context, of shared-nothing.

In the longer term, blank-sheet-of-paper case, as cluster acceleration facilities become more widespread, internode communication rates will rise and overhead will be reduced, hopefully dramatically. It used to be the case that one could use this to argue for the eventual domination of I/O shipping and function shipping, since they effectively exploit less expensive, non-proprietary hardware that doesn't share large numbers of disks effectively. That is no longer the case, since non-proprietary disk interconnects are now showing up that eliminate that disadvantage (FCS, SSA, FL-L). It might turn out that shared-nothing advocates have been unknowingly seduced by a temporary hardware situation and, primarily, a false analogy with more commonly understood distributed systems (lack of the concept of "cluster" again).

On the other hand, there's seldom any such thing as a blank sheet of paper.

One axis of non-blankness is illustrated by a major reason IBM decided on shared disks for Parallel Sysplex. This reason is not even touched on in the usual contentious, workload-dependent arguments about which is bigger/better/faster/efficient/whatever. They wanted to upgrade existing customers to a cluster-based solution with as little pain as possible. In particular, they wanted the customers' existing data—which is rather massive—to stay put on disks, without changing the layout of the data. Since that data was organized under the assumption that sharing in memory would be available—prior systems were SMPs—that meant that sharing data between nodes was utterly necessary to maintain performance, and it had better be done efficiently, too. Hence the Coupling Facility, global caches, support for disk cache coherence, and so on. To the degree that clustering is used as an upgrade for a large SMP system, this can be a compelling argument.

However, there are other axes of non-blankness. Some important ones have to do with integration into existing facilities and market position. How well a cluster "slides in" without changing the way a system is viewed for administration and other functions makes a huge difference. Over all of this is the fact that technical merit is by no means the key determinant of the ultimate winner. Market position, pricing, and other factors will play a huge role.

As will ease of use. I've spoken with at least one ex-administrator of a system using partitioned data who has done everything but swear on a stack of Bibles to never again have anything to do with data partitioning as long as he lives. Whether this is a personal idiosyncrasy, a comment on the tools available, or an indication of the intrinsic difficulty involved—I do not know. But it does give one pause.

Single System Image

If there is a single unifying element to the concept of "cluster," it is the notion of a **single system image (SSI)**. A single system image is the illusion, created by software or hardware, that a collection of computing elements is a single computing resource.

Despite my initial denials when defining a cluster, this definition of SSI definitely is part of the definition of a cluster. A collection of connected machines is not a cluster unless it is used as a single computing resource, so single system image is what makes a cluster a cluster.

Many discussions of single system image focus on something not mentioned in the SSI definition given above, namely system administration. System administration is actually just one aspect—although a critical one for practical cluster use—of the more general issue. It is not the only aspect of a cluster that should exhibit a single system image, and it is certainly not the sole defining characteristic of single system image.

Some examples: The cluster batch job submission facilities described in Chapter 2 effectively provide a single system image *from the point of view of the user* submitting a job. Front-end dispatcher described in that same chapter provides a single system image *from the point of view of the network*. The database systems running across clusters, described in Chapter 2 and Chapter 10, effectively provide a single system image *for their applications* and often for their own administration. The cache coherence schemes used in SMPs and CC-NUMA systems (Chapter 6 and Chapter 7) effectively provide in hardware a single system image *of memory, for all programs.*

The availability of the batch submission, network, and database single system images, which are obviously independent of each other, is the basis of much of the current utility of clusters. Flaws in currently available single system images for administration—unity of the system *from the point of view of an administrator*—constitute one of the greatest difficulties that currently inhibit the use of clusters.

Once the above has been pointed out, the fact that there are multiple single system images floating around appears obvious. The next question is: Are all those images completely independent, randomly generated things, or is there some order limiting, and suggesting, what is possible?

A key that provides structure to the universe of single system images lies in noting the following two points:

1. every single system image has a **boundary**; and
2. single system support can exist at different **levels** within a system, one able to be built on another.

Why this happens and what it means is the subject of the rest of this chapter.

11.1 Single System Image Boundaries_____

Consider a reasonably designed batch submission system for a cluster, such as any of the ones mentioned back in Chapter 2. A user submits a job to the batch system, and so to the cluster as a whole, not to any specific element of the cluster. The batch system runs it on one of the machines of the cluster—the user does not necessarily know which one, just that it's in the cluster somewhere—and returns the results. During execution, the user can submit queries about the job or cancel it by asking the batch system—not by referring to a machine on which it may be queued. As far as that user is concerned, the cluster as a whole is one thing, a single, job-queueing system. That is a single system image.

But suppose the user issues some command not in the batch facilities—for example, the UNIX ping command that "bounces" a message off another machine to see if it's alive and talking to the communication network. That command (at least in exposed clusters) will distinguish the various cluster machines; each has its own name, and each individually may be functional or not. In general, if the user performs any operations that aren't part of the batch system's suite, the illusion of a single system is undone: The user is outside of the SSI boundary. The many machines again appear as many machines, not as a single facility.

A way to visualize an SSI boundary is illustrated in Figure 99: When you're inside the SSI boundary, the cluster as a whole looks like—exhibits the image of—one big machine; in this case, the machine illustrated is a classic supercomputer. But if you do anything outside that boundary, the cluster again appears to be just a bunch of connected computers.

Figure 99 An Application's Single System Image Boundary

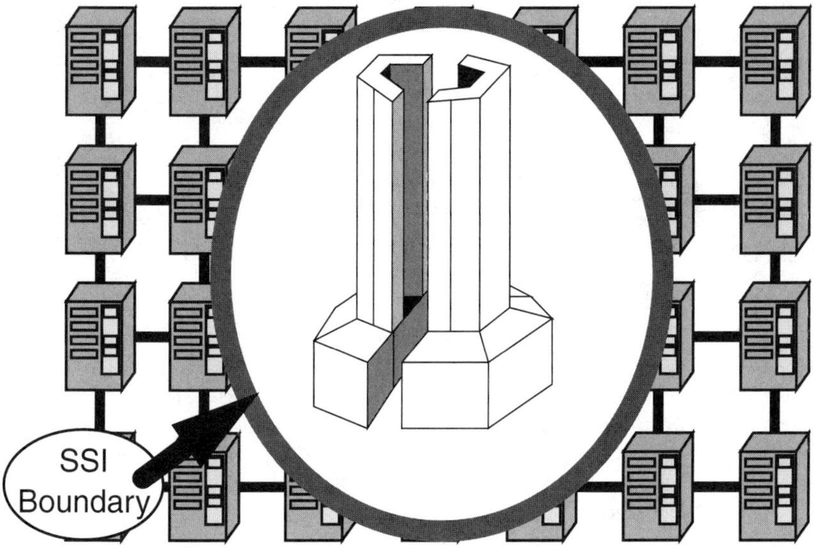

Different SSI-creating applications can provide different images of the same cluster. Consider using two, for example a database system and a batch submission system (Figure 100). As you move from one to the other, you're moving from inside one SSI boundary to inside another. In both cases, by definition, you see a single system image. However, their (single system) images—plural—are different, as illustrated.

This difference in appearance is inevitable and obviously desirable. Batch and database systems (for example) are different things; they have different functions, and different commands. If they looked the same, why have them both? Their single system images are just plain different.

However, there are common elements that SSI applications can, and should, share. For example, it is in many cases a wholly unnecessary irritant to require users to have different user identifiers and passwords for different

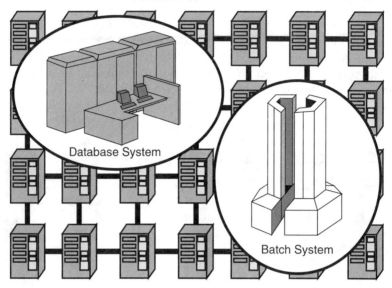

Figure 100 Two Applications' Single-System-Image Boundaries

applications and to go through different, separate, authentication rituals when moving from one application or subsystem to another. In other cases, the issue isn't merely a question of irritation, but of function. For example, the batch and database applications may require access to the same data. Their function can't be provided if they use different, incompatible ways to obtain a single system image of that data.

So, the supporting structures and facilities must themselves exhibit a single system image if they're to be useful to SSI applications; but that support is not, in itself, a usable application. The implication is that there are multiple levels of single-system-image support.

11.2 Single System Image Levels _____

The notion of "levels" of single system image is the computer science notion of levels of abstraction. A house, for example, is at a higher level of abstraction than walls, ceilings, and floors; those in turn are at a higher level than lumber and plasterboard. It is certainly not impossible to build a house directly from lumber and plasterboard (and nails, and so on); in fact, this is common practice. But construction is vastly simplified if prefabricated walls, ceiling, and floors are used—in other words, if a level is built using the level of abstraction below.

Types of single system images can similarly be recognized as belonging to different levels in a hierarchy of levels of abstraction. Table 9 shows the three groups of levels that will be used in the discussion here: the application/subsystem levels; the operating system kernel levels; and the hardware levels. (The table headings will be used later.)

Table 9   Outline of the Levels of Single System Image

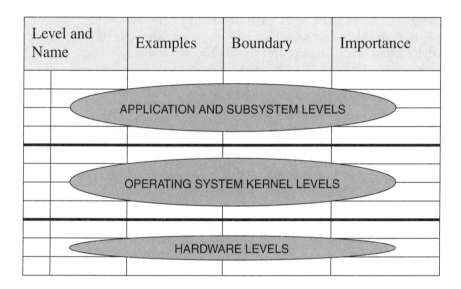

Level and Name	Examples	Boundary	Importance
APPLICATION AND SUBSYSTEM LEVELS			
OPERATING SYSTEM KERNEL LEVELS			
HARDWARE LEVELS			

By basing applications on common support structures (lower levels of SSI support), it is possible both to save effort and to avoid the kinds of gratuitous incompatibilities mentioned in the previous section. What this means is that the lower levels of support provide common SSI semantics to applications. In general, the lower the level, the more pervasive and deep the common SSI semantics becomes. Different applications can still choose to present those semantics to users in different ways, but that is an issue outside the bounds of this discussion.

While is easier to obtain an SSI by using the levels below it, two points must be emphasized: First, "easier" does not mean "free"; in general, work must still be done to obtain the single system image desired for a program that exploits the multi-node nature of a cluster. A purely serial program may indeed get a kind of SSI for "free." Second, skipping levels in our construction technique is certainly possible and, under some circumstances, preferable or necessary. We'll see examples of all of this as our discussion covers each of the three major levels in turn, illustrating how each can be further subdivided.

There are undoubtedly other choices of levels into which single system images can be divided and different ways to subdivide the levels used. The one presented here appears to be a useful one, but it's probably not unique.

11.3 The Application and Subsystem Levels ___

The application and subsystem levels are the highest levels at which a single system image can exist. They include the ultimate level—the application level, the one that a user sees. However, there are other levels. The collection of these levels, in order, appears in Table 10; each is described below.

11.3.1 The Application Level

The application level is the highest and in a sense the most important level because it is what the user sees. One common example, a batch job submission system, has already been covered. Another example is the electronic forms applications that form part of the office applications of several companies, including Digital and IBM.

These systems typically run across multiple machines, so that a form filled out on one machine is routed to the appropriate personages whose approval is implicitly sought by the original filer—whether or not the filer knows who they are (or why they've got to approve a request). A user can typically submit a query for a form that's entered the system, finding out who's seen and approved it, and who has to be nudged to get the thing out of his or her electronic in-basket. During the query, the user need have no idea on which of a collection of machines the form, or the data about it, actually resides; the application has created a single system image potentially spanning a large enterprise.

This level is, in a real sense, the most important because it is the only level an end-user ever sees. It is therefore the only thing for which any anybody will ever hear a "market requirement." The only purpose of all the other levels is to make it easier for developers to create top-level applications exhibiting a single system image to the user.

The term "end-user" is perhaps misleading, since by it I simply mean anyone who uses an application. In particular, if the application involved happens to be system management, the "end-user" is the system administrator. And this, by the way, is where system management comes into the picture; it's the one application suite that every computer necessarily has. There will be more discussion of this subject later.

Table 10 The Application and Subsystem Levels of SSI

Level and Name		Examples	Boundary	Importance
A 4	application	cluster batch systems, system management, electronic forms	an application	what a user wants and needs
A 3	subsystem	distributed DB, Lotus Notes, MPI, PVM	a subsystem	SSI for all applications of the subsystem
A 2	file system	Sun NFS, DFS, NetWare, IBM VSAM on Sysplex, DEC OpenVMS Cluster file system, and so on	shared portion of the file system	implicitly supports many applications, subsystems
A 1	toolkit	Tivoli TME, Sun ONC+, Apollo Domain, Microsoft "Wolfpack" API, and so on	each toolkit facility: users, service names, time, membership, ...	best level of support for heterogeneous systems
		KERNEL (OPERATING SYSTEM) LEVELS		
		HARDWARE LEVELS		

11.3.2 The Subsystem Level

The next important level of SSI support is that of subsystems. (The term "middleware" has become popular in referring to what is meant here by "subsystems.") These are programs not an integral part of the operating system that provide desirable or necessary services to other, application, programs. Database and On-line Transaction Processing systems are the typical examples of subsystems, but communication and other subsystems are common. Tivoli's TME, a subsystem for administrative applications, is another example.

**Figure 101 Applications Using a Subsystem's Single
System Image**

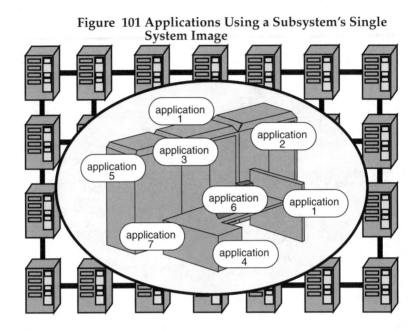

One of the more valuable services a subsystem can provide to an application is a single system image. If it is provided, application programs written to use that subsystem will automatically see a single system image, without any effort on their own part. As illustrated in Figure 101, the applications ride within the single system image created by the subsystem.

The single system image boundary in this case is the API (Application Program Interface) of the subsystem: As long as an application uses only facilities provided though the subsystem's API, that application will see a single system image—assuming, of course, that the subsystem has provided a complete SSI over its entire API interface. Step outside the boundary—for example, by bypassing the subsystem's facilities and directly using an operating system call because it's faster or more convenient—and again the illusion is undone.

Several examples of databases providing an SSI over a cluster have been given in Chapter 2; virtually every vendor of an "open systems" database provides this as a feature (or will provide it soon), as do several vendors of proprietary database systems. The kinds of clusters on which these SSI databases can run varies, but all provide the ability to span multiple machines.

Application programs neither know nor care about that as long as they operate through the database API.

Another example of this type of subsystem is Lotus Notes [OHE94], a groupware subsystem that facilitates mail, conferencing, electronic form submission systems, and similar applications. Applications written under this system are distributed across multiple workstations in a client-server fashion, and multiple servers communicate to form a web of connections in which any change to Lotus Notes' databases is visible to any user of the system at that user's workstation. As far as users of the many client machines are concerned, there is just one copy of each collection of data. The important thing at this level is that the applications did not have to work to bring that about—it was inherited by virtue of being an application using the Notes subsystem. Were the application to access data outside the Lotus Notes framework, this inheritance would no longer work: The many machines in the web, including the ones Notes runs on, would again appear as multiple machines and not a unified resource.

As mentioned previously, probably to the point that the reader is bored with the emphasis, this is an important layer; it provides crucial enablement for commercial use of clusters by supporting the SPPS model of application execution. It could be implemented without significant lower-level SSI support, but no examples the author is aware of do that.

While subsystems are important and are often the primary workload run on a system, it is must be realized that they still have a single-system-image boundary, and there are important things outside that boundary that must be done.

If one needs to do anything outside a database—such as, for example, add a new disk to one of the machines, check system error logs, and so on—one is outside the boundary and does not see a single system image. (That example was used because workers in the database area seem particularly prone to forgetting that anything exists outside the bounds of the database.) That the examples here come from system management is significant; that's the application, as will be mentioned, that must be run on every system.

11.3.3   The File System Layer

The file system layer is familiar to many because of its ubiquity. Distributed file systems such as Sun's NFS [S+85], CMU's AFS [San90], OSF's DFS [Ope93], and Novell's NetWare are well known. Full-system clusters such as IBM's Parallel Sysplex and DEC's OpenVMS Cluster also have cluster-specific SSI file systems. Many users of clusters believe they have a perfectly adequate single system image just because they have a distributed file system. This belief provokes arguments with others who believe single system image is single system image system management. The position taken here is that the file-system side is correct—if you restrict your vision, looking only within the SSI boundary of the distributed file system. Of course, the administration side is correct, too, if you look only within the SSI boundary of administration.

The SSI boundary induced by a distributed file system is the portion of the file system (usually a subtree or subtrees) that is shared with others. File operations performed within that boundary exhibit a single system image in the following sense: They are visible to anyone who has access to those files, without any further action than normal open/close/read/write calls to the operating system. This implicit support for many unchanged applications makes this level of the SSI support hierarchy also valuable.

Once again, of course, it is possible for an application to step outside that SSI boundary. If one accesses files *not* in the shared portion of the file system, the fact that the files reside on different machines becomes excruciatingly visible. In the full-system clusters, that is often impossible, or at least highly unlikely for user data; that is all in one name space.

The position of the file-system layer in this support hierarchy is somewhat problematical. The file system API is part of the kernel API, a lower layer that is discussed later, and distributed file systems are generally installed as part of the kernel or a kernel extension. I've placed the file-system layer where it is, however, since every known instance of a distributed file system is supported by the toolkit layer that certainly comes next, and subsumption into the kernel is actually a later occurrence, an optimization of earlier implementations outside the kernel, an organization that is still going strong in the PC world.

11.3.4   The Toolkit Layer

The name for this layer is problematical.

On the one hand, I've called it the "Toolkit Layer" because it consists of a variety of tools and toolkits designed to support higher layers: naming services, communication services such as remote procedure calls, lock and other synchronization services, grouping services such as group membership and group multicast, and so on *ad bizarrum*. Examples include Sun's ONC+ [Ram93], OSF's DCE [Ope93], various high-availability subsystems' programming support, such as IBM's for HACMP/6000 and Microsoft's Windows NT Cluster Services ("Wolfpack"), IDS ISIS [Bir95, BJ87], the elderly and innovative Apollo Domain system [Pek92], and others. As with the subsystem layer, as long as an application or subsystem uses the API of such a system, there is the image of a single system; go outside that API and the illusion is undone.

On the other hand, it could easily have been called something like the "Over-Kernel" layer to reflect a very important characteristic: This is the level at which the greatest breadth and depth of SSI support is possible without significant modification to an operating system kernel itself. This is an important implementation distinction because it's necessary to provide intersystem portability. In addition, distinctively, that in turn implies that this level is the best that can be achieved for heterogeneous clustered systems containing different operating systems (and possibly different hardware).

Achieving breadth of SSI support is important, for a reason first mentioned under "Single System Image Levels" above. The broader the common semantic base on which applications are built, the more feasible it is for them to avoid a confusing proliferation of different types of single system images. That is why integrated, comprehensive toolkits that provide a consistent broad framework, such as Tivoli's DCE, are important.

At this stage it is worthwhile to pause and consider the kind of "overall" single system image that can be provided at this, the best possible heterogeneous level. That situation is illustrated in Figure 102.[1] Each SSI-enabled application has its own single system image, as semantically common with the other applications as feasible. However, each also has its own SSI boundary, and there are definitely cracks between the applications into which users fall if they fail to use, or do not have, the SSI version of an application.

Unless literally every application and command is (re)implemented to use the toolkit SSI facilities, and those facilities are broadened to include all possible things every application needs to use, the SSI illusion cannot be complete. Is it possible to achieve completeness? This is a debatable question.

Building an SSI directly into important subsystems, with semantics provided by a general tool layer, provides that SSI in great measure without burdening the programmer. Examples where this works well are distributed file systems and SSI-enabled database systems; neither simple commands like dir or ls nor a debit transaction need change in their programming to inherit an appropriate SSI. These capabilities could, perhaps, be extended to all facilities and to all applications.

However, the author knows of nobody actually proposing literally distributing *every* element of a system in an over-kernel manner. This would be a never-ending job. Instead, what is proposed and implemented are the facili-

---

1. Figure also called "Author goes nuts with limited set of clip art."

Figure 102 Achievable Over-Kernel "Overall" Single

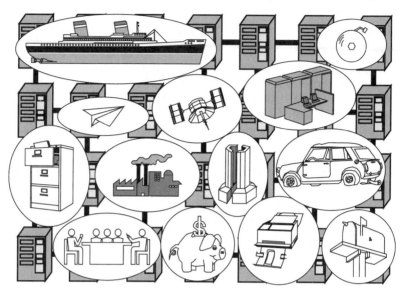

ties required to support specific important applications and subsystems, not wall-to-wall total coverage. Halfway measures, leaving cracks in the overall SSI, are both common and inevitable.

For example, consider X Windows. Use of this facility gives all graphics applications a distributed structure, but this is not the same as a single system image. Actually making an application run somewhere else while displaying on one's home display requires arcane (to a user) creation of strange files with odd names and contents. This is not just another user-hostile UNIX interface; from the viewpoint used here, it is revealed as a crack in the single system image because the names of each source of graphics must be explicitly listed.

Similarly, under UNIX it is impossible at the over-kernel level to attain a complete SSI in the file system. The reason is that the file system contains more than files; the /dev directory provides access to the devices attached to a machine. Conventions can produce a near-equivalent to complete file-system SSI, but near-equivalents are continually subject to errors and mistakes.

11.4 The Operating System Kernel Levels _____

The next levels of single system support lie at the edge of the operating system or within the operating system kernel itself. They deal with providing the unifying illusion at the boundary of the operating system and with how that illusion can be implemented within the operating system. The levels involved here are shown in Table 11 and discussed below.

Table 11 The Operating System Kernel Levels of SSI

Level and Name		Examples	Boundary	Importance
	APPLICATION AND SUBSYSTEM LEVELS			
K 4	kernel (operating system)	Locus, TCF, QNX, Sprite, Amoeba, IBM OS/390 Parallel Sysplex, Tandem NonStop	each name space: files, processes, pipes, devices, and so on	kernel support for applications, administration, subsystems
K 3	kernel interfaces	UNIX vnode, Locus (IBM) vproc	types of kernel objects: files, processes, and so on	modularizes SSI code within kernel
K 2	virtual memory	none supporting operating system kernels	each distributed virtual memory space	may simplify implementation of kernel objects
K 1	microkernel	Mach, Chorus, Amoeba, (Windows NT)	each service outside the microkernel	implicit SSI for all system services
	HARDWARE LEVELS			

11.4.1   The Kernel API Layer

Dissatisfaction with cracks in the single system illusion, the inability to ever completely finish the entire job, to support everything and do it right—these are significant motivations for moving to the next lower layer, that of the operating system kernel itself. The operating systems Sprite, QNX, Locus,

AIX TCF, OS390 for Parallel Sysplex, and Tandem's NonStop Kernel are examples of systems providing this level of SSI support.

As rather feebly illustrated in Figure 103, supporting SSI at this level means that a consistent, coherent single system image is seen on every system call made by every program running on the system: application, subsystem, and tool.

Figure 103 Kernel-Level Single System Image

Furthermore, this SSI is enforced by hardware facilities, not convention: No program can access anything outside its address space without using through a system call, a requirement that forces it through the system code maintaining the SSI. The primary way this is manifest is that all the names used for every facility throughout the system—files, processes, devices, pipes—are guaranteed to be unique system-wide identifiers that allow users to gain access to all the types of "thing" the system defines, without specifying where any of it is.

In addition, the implied subsumption of several kernel capabilities into the single system image produces a requirement that the kernel do some things that over-kernel support seldom does. High availability support (failover), and the migration of jobs from one node to another are two examples of this.

11.4.1.1 Effects

From the point of view of a user or administrator, there is a dramatic difference between the best that over-kernel systems can do, on the one hand, and a true kernel-level SSI, on the other. Perhaps an analogy is the best way to get at this difference.

Think of trying to actually get something completed on a multiple computer system as being like crossing a river. You *really* don't want to fall in; getting swept away will at least cost you time that may ultimately prove calamitous.

All the various individually distributed tools of the over-kernel layer are like a collection of stepping stones that can be used to walk across. They may be flat, dry, with good traction, and even linked in some underlying basalt. But there are still cracks between them. When crossing, you're never quite secure; you always have to be careful where you place your feet.

A kernel-level single system image, on the other hand, is a bridge across those troubled waters, one with solid guardrails (they're hardware-enforced).

"Objectively," meaning using a reductionist one-on-one feature comparison, that bridge might not provide one tiny shred of additional function. It might even provide less—for example, its maximum allowable load might be less than that allowed by the stepping stones.

Nevertheless, like a bridge over troubled waters, it eases your mind.[2] You don't have to think about where you put your feet (which commands you use) because there are no cracks, and if you lose your balance, you'll just bump against the guardrail and not fall in. People who are naturally highly coordinated, with an excellent sense of balance, and physically quick probably won't notice the difference. The rest of us poor slobs will prefer to take the bridge.

There happens to be a reflecting pond in the center of the IBM Austin campus that has, across it, a delightful-looking set of broad, flat, regular stepping stones that provide a quite usable and direct path across the pond from one of the buildings to another. I've walked across them many times. Between the stones, there are cracks where the water is visible. They're small cracks, narrower than typical men's shoes, and help form an overall effect that is visually and architecturally pleasing. But I have to say that I am always watching where I put my feet when I use that route. It's not a huge burden. But it's another thing to worry about, and that is something we can all do without.

---

2. Tell me you didn't see that one coming. *Pace* Paul Simon again.

11.4.1.2 Sources

What, technically, is the source of this mind-easing benefit?

A primary factor, which directly follows from having a kernel-level SSI, is that SPPS processing is by default enabled for everything run on a cluster—just as it is enabled for traditional SMP-supporting operating systems, as well as the initial wave of CC-NUMA system.

> ➤ Separate jobs (or processes) are "automatically" placed on separate nodes as appropriate, just as they are "automatically" placed on separate processors in an SMP—and this happens for standard, unaltered, serial uniprocessor programs; it is built into the (serial) system primitives they use to create and manipulate jobs.

> ➤ Operations that are split into multiple processes using standard, uniprocessor, serial communications facilities (in UNIX: pipes, sockets, signals, and so on) can, as they do on an SMP, exhibit speedup by being run on multiple nodes simultaneously.

> ➤ Individual jobs may run with increased efficiency because system-provided parallelism can off-load system operations—for example, I/O—onto nodes other than the one on which the user program is running. (This again is equivalent to common SMP operating system function.)

These factors make a cluster of machines remarkably more useful. Programs do not have to be written in a new form, do not have to use a "distributed" version of operations that is different from the operating system's version, do not have to wait until the standards for the new, distributed form have been negotiated. The existing, standard operating system interfaces are *preserved*, reinterpreted for a cluster environment; new ones are not necessary.

Of course this reinterpretation is precisely what SMP operating systems do, and it is why SMPs are as widely used, and as usable, as they are. The same advantages, for the same reasons, accrue to the initial wave of CC-NUMA systems. The system-level, SPPS parallelism that is broadly enabled by this level of single system image is often the primary, and in many cases only, way that parallelism is exploited by SMP installations.

If individual programs are to internally run in parallel, the way databases and other economically important, high-use subsystems do, they must of course be rewritten under a kernel-level SSI—just as they must be rewritten for an SMP. To target an SMP, they must be rewritten for an SMP shared-memory programming model—threads, shared segments, or syntactic sugarings of those constructs such as forall; to target a cluster, they must be rewritten to a message-passing programming model.

In Search of Clusters ✳

For a cluster supported at this level of single system image, that does not mean programs must be rewritten to be what is commonly called "distributed" environments today; it may be significantly easier. Current distributed programs must in general deal with a complete lack of single system image among the machines they use, as well as high-overhead, low-bandwidth communication (as discussed near the end of Chapter 9); current parallel programs on highly parallel message-passing machines must deal with a paucity of operating system services. The writing of message-passing programs in an environment that has both high performance communication and broad SSI system services should be significantly easier, as has been discussed previously. Also, there's the issue of stepping stones vs. bridges again, which can be very significant. The mere use of a message-passing programming model, without the other extraneous complications, definitely does not guarantee excessive difficulty in comparison to the difficulties of shared-memory parallel programming; demonstrating that was why I dragged you through Chapter 9.

11.4.1.3 Cost

All of this function is not achieved for free. Substantial, skilled, expensive software effort must be put into creating this grand illusion of a single system. Furthermore, much, if not a majority, of the work is actually outside the kernel; and that work doesn't deal with intellectually amusing computer-science topics like unifying name spaces. Instead, it deals with the grubby details of getting the commands and libraries of an operating system to work.

In many cases commands and libraries just work without modification. Debuggers, for example, (mostly) port without change because kernel-level SSI maintains, across nodes, the same process tree and interfaces to processes—even remote ones—that is provided on uniprocessors. In other cases, however, utilities must be modified to do their job correctly on an SSI cluster. As many of these modifications are in the system management arena, examples are given later in that discussion.

Command, library, and utility modification constitutes the real bulk of the work required to implement kernel-level SSI support, because that's the location of the bulk of the code by an overwhelmingly large margin. This is not bad; it means the "tools" philosophy that began with UNIX works. It's also true that a many of the tools "just work" without modification. But even the remainder is large; so there's much work to do, and it all must be done before the kernel-level SSI support hits the street. Systems lacking a full range of command and library support at introduction are crippled.

The command and library modifications required, by the way, are by and large the same elements that must be rewritten—although in some cases less completely—to deal with multiple processors of an SMP.

The prior discussion dealt primarily with implementation cost. There is another type of cost that a kernel-level SSI potentially incurs, a cost in performance. If the intent is to exactly duplicate the semantics of system calls within a single machine, then there are a number of things that must be done which can induce overhead or serialization that isn't present if separate operating systems are used on each node.

The simplest example is undoubtedly the UNIX file pointer. UNIX requires that child processes inherit the standard input and output files of their parents. When characters are read or written into those or any other files, the location of the "next" thing is updated in the system-internal file descriptor. It is part of UNIX semantics that if any process reads or writes a file, all processes accessing that file see that change: when they next read, for example, they see data after that read by the last process. This allows some abysmally cute tricks between parent and child processes, but was probably defined that way simply because it was convenient and easy to implement: Everybody updates the (one) file data structure, and everybody sees the results.

Well, it's not convenient any more when the parent is on one computer and the child is on another, placed there by a cross-machine load balancing facility. A child process might, through a global file system exploiting multiple physical paths to disks, be able to read its inherited standard input just fine by itself, without disturbing the machine the parent inhabits. It *can* do that, but, to quote the standard pedantry, it *may* not. The file pointer semantics imply that somehow the parent must be told of every change as it happens (and vice versa, if the parent keeps running). This might imply routing all I/O through the parent's machine, or doing some fancy cross-machine locking while maintaining a local copy of the relevant data structure; however one does it, there is software development cost, overhead and additional serialization that wasn't there if the nodes ran separate operating systems.

There are many such examples in UNIX—inter-process signals for halting and continuing are a slightly less obvious one—and undoubtedly many examples in most other operating systems.

On the other hand, complaining about this is somewhat like hardware designers complaining about the SMP hardware requirement that memory be coherent. You can complain all you want, but if you don't strictly adhere to the standard there will be too many non-obvious cases where innocently written, debugged, customer code simply stops working.

11.4.1.4 Evaluation

Is it worth it?

At present, the vote of the general computing community appears to be much more in favor of over-kernel facilities than kernel-level SSI. Many more people are engaged in creating over-kernel facilities than in creating kernel-level SSI systems.

One reason for this choice is the proliferation and influence of distributed systems, which, as opposed to clusters, must handle heterogeneity among the operating systems of the nodes. It's just a bit hard for a kernel-level SSI operating system to handle heterogeneous operating systems—in fact, it's a contradiction in terms. The effect of this on systems with a kernel-API single system image is discussed later, in Chapter 14, "Why We Need the Concept of Cluster"; in the author's opinion, the effect has been profoundly negative.

There is, however, another reason why kernel-level SSI has not caught on, a reason that has nothing to do with the ultimate desirability of kernel-level vs. over-kernel SSI; it has to do with incremental funding and reward.

Over-kernel SSI facilities can be implemented one at a time, with visible gain from each piece implemented. When an application works, it can be shipped; the revenue from that can be used to fund the next application, and so on. Kernel-level SSI, on the other hand, is a kind of "big bang theory" of SSI: You do it all, you do it completely, you do it once; and you don't have one single blasted thing you can sell until everything's done. This is a heavy economic decision to undertake, and most of the industry has so far voted with its feet for the venture that was less economically risky.

In addition to the above, a factor that has strongly impressed several of the brave souls who have attempted kernel-level SSI is the performance loss and complexity of actually implementing all kernel-level semantics across machines. (For instance, the UNIX file pointer discussed in the prior section.) There is a technically informed opinion that says maintaining such semantics puts a significant limit on the ultimate scalability of kernel-level SSI systems because of serialization that was inadvertently designed into most operating systems' definitions. It is hard to assess how true this is, and whether it would seriously affect clusters as opposed to MPPs. Since the latter have virtually no agreed-upon limit to scalability, it obviously affects them. It is the case that most of the kernel-level SSI systems used as examples in the table came into existence before most of the Posix standards were defined, and many of those standards are things that, when examined in detail, are troublesome.

If "standard" system definitions are in fact unsuitable as a base for a kernel-level SSI, well, clearly there are niches—some quite substantial, like high availability— where the advantages of clusters are so great that they out-weigh the problems of having to write code that follows some rules other than the "standard." That is in fact what has happened so far in the industry. Are those niches large enough to effectively define their own de facto standard? Even though that standard is more painful to deal with in some areas that are known problems today—system administration, in particular?

I don't know. I do know that many, but not all, discussions of kernel-level SSI are terminally infected with a massive parallelism virus that vigorously attacks anything looking like it might cause scalability problems, no matter what the possible benefit. So I am not at all sure that this issue is bad a problem as it may appear in some quarters.

11.4.2   The Level of the Kernel Interfaces

Just as various underlayers in the Application and Subsystem layers supported SSI applications, an SSI at the Kernel API layer can be supported by several layers of constructs that reside inside the operating system kernel. Here we are in the realm of operating system structuring, tools used by kernel-level system programmers. A variety of techniques, not all necessarily mutually compatible, are possible.

The level of the kernel interfaces is one at which particular collections of objects used by the kernel independently acquire what amounts to a single system image: All of them, no matter where they are, are manipulated through the same programming interface. Of necessity, these are each specific to a particular operating system kernel.

One example of such an SSI construct is the UNIX vnode interface. With this in place, the existence of a distributed file system (or indeed any number of different file systems) is modularized away from the remainder of the kernel. By use of the vnode API, a single system image of the file system is essentially maintained. Outside that API the illusion is, of course, shattered.

Another example, modelled after vnode, is the vproc interface. As vnode does for files, vproc allows internal kernel code to manipulate a process no matter where it is without getting involved in the details of how the distribution is accomplished.

The purpose of such constructs is modularity. Without them, implementation of a kernel-level SSI can pervade a kernel, involving a very large number of very small changes to a very great fraction of the modules comprising the operating system. Such modifications are ugly and miserable to debug and maintain compared to a a few changes to a few modules, and the addition of one large-ish, separate module.

In Search of Clusters   ✳

The vproc interface was developed by Locus Computing Corp. and IBM as part of a proposal made to OSF for an SSI kernel. (OSF decided they were buying tools, not kernels, at the time; they did DCE instead.) Prior implementations of the Locus-derived kernel-level SSI, embodied in the UCLA Locus operating system and the IBM TCF product, were of the pervasive, ugly persuasion. vproc modularizes another piece of the puzzle quite well; too bad name-space resolution in the kernel isn't the only thing that a kernel-level SSI requires.

11.4.3   The Distributed Virtual Memory Level

There are levels within the level of the kernel interfaces, as there are for other levels. At one of the lower ones resides distributed virtual memory. This sublevel produces the effect of a single system image for the memory of the system under circumstances where the hardware does not support it directly. While distributed virtual memory can be surfaced all the way to application programs as a means of parallel (or distributed) programming, one of the hopes of some of its adherents is that it could be used to simplify the implementation of a single system image at the kernel level.

As indicated previously, however (page 301), distributed virtual memory is a distinct, different programming model that requires the programs using it to be significantly modified for efficient operation. In this case, that requirement applies to programs within the kernel itself. Using distributed virtual memory techniques selectively on user processes, however, as opposed to its own separate programming model, is certainly a feasible way to simplify the task of migrating processes between nodes for various purposes, including load balancing.

11.4.4   The Microkernel Level

Operating systems based on the microkernel concept have a structure that is particularly well suited to supporting kernel-level single system image across message-passing clusters. This is inherent in the structure that a microkernel imparts to an operating system, plus one additional "feature."

The notion of a microkernel is to provide, in the operating system kernel, only the absolute minimum set of facilities required in any operating system: process creation, the bases of virtual memory management, primitive I/O, and, very importantly, interprocess communication. That set of facilities is chosen to be just minimally sufficient, in the sense that the facilities can't be made from each other and all other required operating system function can be created using them.

The rest of the required operating system functions are provided by service programs that are written, and run, outside the kernel. These provide the services of file systems, trees of process structures, particular algorithms and techniques for virtual memory management, and so on. The true application processes communicate with those service providers, and the service providers with each other, using microkernel-provided communication; that communication comes in the form of message passing.

Thus, if an application process wants to create or open a file, it sends a message to the file system service; if it wants to create another process with the UNIX-like semantics of a hierarchy of processes, it sends a message to the UNIX-process service; and so on. This is a client-server paradigm within an operating system.

Obviously, when you're sending messages there must be a way to identify the service to which you're sending a message. This is another of the required minimum facilities the microkernel provides.

Well, All You Have To Do Is Just make the message-passing work between machines—implying that the identifiers form a cross-machine single system image—and presto change-o, you've got a kernel-level single system image. Every application automatically talks to the (one) file system server on all the machines, the (one) UNIX-process server, the (one) external communications server, and so on, automatically unifying every one of the traditional operating system facilities implemented under the microkernel.

Microkernel systems such as Chorus [A+92], Amoeba [Tan92], QNX [Hil93], Mach [Tan92, BRS+85, Ras86] and OSF/1 AD [WLH93] provide such cross-machine message-passing. The identifiers are unified in Chorus through Universal Identifiers (UIs), and in Mach through what's called NORMA IPC (IPC = Inter-Process Communication; for NORMA, see page 186), and QNX through what's called FLEET.

Once you've enabled cross-machine message passing, you've instantly got a very workable single system image. Unfortunately, you very probably also have a massive serial bottleneck. Or rather, a collection of them. Every application reading from a file, for example, has to go through the file server even if the files are on different machines; every application creating a process has to get a process identifier from the process-id server; even more ludicrous, every application using virtual memory would have to go through a single server on every page fault. As a result, it's still necessary to parallelize the servers, distributing them through the machine.

I did say "*may*" have a bottleneck, right? The above is utterly true, no "may" involved, for massively parallel systems. What if you've just got a li'l 'ol cluster of four or so machines? Some things still have to be done as part of release 1.0; a centralized bottleneck in a virtual memory system, for example, will cripple anything. Nevertheless, you no longer have to do everything all at once. The work of parallelizing different servers can be prioritized—and shipped incrementally, just as over-kernel applications can be shipped and might just begin returning incremental revenue. Or, machines in a cluster that are specialized for file serving might be the only ones running the (parallelized) file server. While there's still no such thing as a free lunch, the incremental shipping of function may at least break the logjam of funding a kernel-level SSI as a "big bang."

All of the above discussion of microkernel benefits is relevant only if microkernel-structured systems are good for server systems, with their high system and I/O demands. While prior experience seems to have been negative, at least one microkernel-structured system, Microsoft's Windows NT, is certainly making a run at that one.

11.5 Hardware Levels

To round out this discussion, it should be noted that there is no reason for single-system-image support to come to a halt even with the lowest levels of software. Levels of hardware-supported single system image are shown in Table 12.

Memory-coupled clusters using non-coherent (NC-) NUMA, such as Digital's TruCluster when Memory Channel is used, can be viewed as creating a single system image for the address space. The boundaries of this SSI are the addressing regions that have been mapped between the systems. This is a way to achieve low overhead communication and synchronization between nodes of a cluster. (We have seen back in Chapter 5, however, that it is not the only way.)

NC-NUMA, with its programmatically odd semantics, does not give an SSI for the memory, though. That step is the one cache-coherent (CC-) NUMA takes, and it is the feature on which the first wave's single copy of the operating system rests.

At the very bottom level we of course have the SMP, which provides hardware-level SSI support not only for memory, but also for I/O within a system. Perhaps such lowest-layer hardware support is one of the reasons why SMP software exhibiting an SSI is common, whereas more general cluster-based kernel-level SSI is not. On the other hand, perhaps that support is common because an SMP is totally useless without it, whereas clusters can limp along.

Table 12 The Hardware Levels of SSI

Level and Name	Examples	Boundary	Importance
APPLICATION AND SUBSYSTEM LEVELS			
OPERATING SYSTEM KERNEL LEVELS			
H 3 address space	NC-NUMA; DEC Memory Channel	mapped portions of the memory space	low overhead communication, synchronization
H 2 memory	CC-NUMA	memory space (restrictions possible)	single copy of the operating system
H 1 memory and I/O	SMP techniques	memory and I/O device space	lower overhead cluster I/O

11.6 SSI and System Management

Having divorced system management from the notion of single system image, it is necessary to indicate where it fits in. The functions involved in system management are many; the general areas involved and some examples are listed in Table 13. Notice that these functions do not include load balancing or other issues more directly related to performance; here we are discussing management only.

System management is, in the SSI formulation used here, a suite of applications. Furthermore, it is the one application suite that every system must provide. No matter what else is done with a computer system—OLTP, number-crunching, multimedia gropeware, whatever—system management must always be done. It is the one universal application.

Table 13 Aspects of System Management (Not Exhaustive!)

Resource Management	Subsystem Management	Network Management	Security Admin.	Problem Management
Installation	Subsystem	Alerts	C2 func-	Alerts
Install	Configur-	SNMP	tions	Diagnostics
Update	ation	NetView	Authentica-	Error Report
Merge	Control	...	tion	Logging
Uninstall	Start		Users	...
Device	Stop		...	
Configura-	Status			
tion	Subsystems			
Users	Spooler			
Accounting	TCP/IP			
...	SNA			
	NFS			
	...			
	...			

It is also a large, messy, tedious, and generally ugly task whose minimization is earnestly desired by everybody. On top of that, it is pure overhead: It does not directly contribute one iota to the functions for which the system was purchased.

All the above implies that of all applications that could be SSI-enabled for clusters, system management is the most desirable. Nobody wants to multiply a large, already-messy task by the number of nodes in a system. Some would go so far as to say that without SSI-enabled system management, there is no single system image at all. I do not, because there are useful applications and subsystems (for example, batch systems, databases, OLTP) that provide major SSI function in the absence of SSI system management.

There are significant differences in system management depending on whether it is done in the context of a non-SSI kernel (the toolkit layer) or in the context of an SSI kernel API. Those two cases will be discussed separately.

11.6.1   Over-Kernel SSI System Management

SSI constructed by using over-kernel facilities, such as is supposed to be supported by Tivoli TME, HP OpenView, IBM NetView, and Sun NIS+, is a kind of meta-application suite. It provides a framework that glues together individual machines' independent system management functions, collecting data from them and controlling them. The individual machines' system management facilities must still be present and, in general, must be modified to communicate with the framework and be consistent with it.

This organization is wholly consistent with the origins of this type of support in distributed computing, where heterogeneity is a fact of life. It would be impossible to create one system management program suite that directly managed all manufacturers' systems; many system management functions are there to deal with specifics of the operating system and the hardware that differ from vendor to vendor.

The distributed origin of over-kernel facilities causes the functions provided to be overkill for clusters (they are also insufficient in some ways, which will be noted later). The task these facilities set for themselves is much harder than the management of clusters, because clusters are single, not multiple, computing resources and so their nodes should be managed uniformly.

As an example, consider software distribution. Elaborate mechanisms are typically defined that allow an installer to take into account which systems have licences for the software to be installed and which do not, as well as the update level of each system. All of this is specified in a way that handles problems of very large scale; in particular, data and storage structures are used that are capable of handling thousands of distributed system nodes. The resultant subsystem allows the construction of sophisticated software distribution applications; it is not a solution in and of itself.

Virtually none of this complexity is necessary with clusters. Problems of scale for around ten or so machines, kept as similar as feasible, do not require such sophistication. The software environment on each node can, for most clusters, be identical, since it is a single computing resource and any job could be run on any node; in fact, the issue with clusters is often how one manages to make and keep that environment identical.

TME or similar facilities could certainly be used to construct a distribution system, and other management systems, very appropriate for clusters. Object-oriented frameworks (like TME's) could certainly have subclasses added that dealt with a cluster of nodes as a unit at higher levels, applying commands and collecting data as uniformly as feasible with each cluster.

However, to the best of my knowledge, that has not been done; furthermore, the chances that it will be done are minuscule. The primary issue appears not to be technical, but rather a question of the business model being used.

Systems such as TME earn their keep by selling thousands of copies for installation in client systems. Cluster installs, to run on servers, will never be more than, say, twenty times smaller than that. Each cluster installation would, of course, cost more and bring in more profit. However, producing and selling widgets of any kind for sales in the thousands or millions is a

In Search of Clusters ✳

different business than doing so for sales that are a twentieth of that: The sales channels are different, the individual customers are different, the service and support issues are different, the process of defining products is different—in fact, just about everything from a business standpoint is different. Companies that do one just don't do the other, or if they do it's in divisions separate enough that they might as well be different companies.

So I wouldn't expect that any time soon there will be cluster administration tools from the folks who bring us distributed system administration tools.

Instead, the cluster developers—server hardware and server software vendors—will do and are doing their own separate thing. This will of course hook into the grand scheme of distributed system administration through alerts, traps, and the like. However, the cluster administration tools will be a completely different implementation, extending single system administration tools rather than specializing distributed system administration tools.

11.6.2   Kernel-Level SSI System Management

System management for systems providing an SSI at the kernel level is a very different proposition from the over-kernel case. Rather than being a meta-application suite, it must be the *same* as the system management functions of a traditional single system.

The reason is that many of the functions of system management involve changes to data used by the operating system: descriptions of devices, tables of users, and so on. There is exactly one "logical" operating system in a kernel SSI system; it is a single, large, distributed/parallel program.

So, from the point of view of an administrator, there is exactly one copy of all this information, and exactly one application to manipulate it. That application is (invisibly, more or less) distributed among all the nodes of the cluster; and it will (really invisibly) maintain multiple copies or otherwise bulletproof that information, using transaction semantics (discussed in Chapter 12), to enable high availability. Nevertheless, managing a kernel-level SSI system is precisely like managing a single machine using that single machine's normal management facilities.

This is precisely the most desirable solution for clusters: Manage them as if they were single, giant computers. Within a wider distributed management context, it still is the desired solution. The (single) system management functions of a kernel-level SSI system can interact with the distributed management framework, when it exists, exactly the way any other individual system would. It is "one" system and acts like that in the framework.

The development cost of this solution is essentially the cost of taking the existing administration applications and, to use a parlance now being adopted, making the "cluster aware," meaning highly available—since administration is certainly one thing that wants to survive the failure of a node.

A key issue in this is making sure that all applications adhere to transaction semantics (see Chapter 12 again) when storing data. This is of course much facilitated if those applications now use a uniform means of storing data— essentially, a database—which can be modified once and then used by all the applications. Unfortunately, it is seldom the case that administration tools are that uniform in their treatment of the data they maintain. Some newer systems have that property, but, for example, traditional UNIX has a huge number of different files for administrative data, whose formats range from the trivial to the totally bizarre.

If simple function, and not high availability, is deemed adequate for an initial release, however, many of the required functions will just port without change, taking advantage of the kernel-level SSI provided by the system. For example, a printer management subsystem will work fine and automatically take advantage of multiple nodes in a kernel-level SSI cluster. This follows from kernel-level SSI's maintenance of the uniprocessor image of process structures and I/O devices, and from an assumption of at least primitive automatic load balancing. This inheritance factor greatly simplifies the job of making the applications function under the cluster.

There will be functions that require modification. For example, consider a function that reports on the state of the various jobs running on the cluster, like the ps command does in UNIX. It will still get data from the kernel in the same form it did previously, except that it will undoubtedly have to be enhanced to accept, and report to the user on which node of the cluster the jobs are running.

More serious than modifications to ps-like functions are the implications of having multiple physical I/O subsystems, one for each node in the cluster. This implies each I/O device description must have something added that indicates which node it's plugged into. Devising such an identifier is easy; it's sure to be directly derived from whatever is used to name a cluster node. However, the use of that identifier must now permeate all device manipulation programs, at least to some degree, and right up to the user level interface. In a specifically UNIX context, one might be able to avoid some of the complexity, kludgeing something together by using some strange encoding within the major and minor device number fields. However, systems using an interactive, iconized, graphical user interface to ease system management will have to grow some graphical representation that allows visual grouping of devices according to the node they're plugged into. (Making that representation work with multi-tailed disks is an interesting problem.)

All this work would, of course, be unnecessary if good distributed system management were universal. So would any and all enhancements to the management of single machines. I don't see that work stopping yet.

On the other hand, while the computer-science-theoretical issues of name spaces and parallelizing ("distributing") operating system functions are getting some play in the research community, I don't see anybody lining up to do the same for system management. It's viewed as boring.

Part 4:

Systems

High Availability

Having slogged our way through both hardware topics and software topics, it's time to consider the whole system. That makes this chapter's topic both appropriate and inappropriate as a starting point.

It's very appropriate because "availability" is always system availability. If a computer can't be used, it's broken, period, whether the cause was hardware or software. At the same time, this topic is inappropriate because it involves far more than merely hardware and software. Welcome to the realm of the professionally paranoid, dedicated warriors who doggedly fight the entire universe, known and unknown, in what they all know, or soon learn, is an ultimately futile battle against Murphy's Law: "Whatever can go wrong, will go wrong." With singularly appropriate self-reference, that often-quoted law is an example of itself. What Edward A. Murphy actually said in 1946 was "If there are two or more ways of doing something, and one of them can lead to catastrophe, then someone will do it." The most commonly used form of the law is a misquotation [Mat97].

This topic is about as far as one can get from the intellectual endorphin rush of designing and building the biggest, fastest computers. One imagines a nasal, monotone drone: "This very computer system right here has been running continuously, without error, for four hundred and seventy-two

days, seven hours, fourteen minutes and twenty-two seconds. Exactly."
"Really?" "Yes. And now [checks clock], it's been running for …"

That just doesn't get the juices flowing for most people. It's more exciting to say "This machine does a gazillion whizzaflops!" "Really? Let's see it." "Sure, as soon as it's fixed." That's like loving a sexy sports car that spends half its life in the shop. Can't deny the attraction. Can't deliver the goods with it, either. Reliability "like a rock" is a theme of some truck commercials, and we're talking practical trucks here.

That's not to say that high availability doesn't have its share of really interesting, clever notions and solutions, some certainly in the heroic class.

For example: There's a major investment firm famed for its consistent delivery of high investment yields. The risk that entails is enough; they don't want more in their data center. That caused them a problem, because zoning restrictions prohibited installing a water tower. Huh? This is a problem? Well, they had some older mainframes that used water cooling, and didn't want to get caught (ahem) high and dry if there were a break in the water mains.

Their solution: Build a swimming pool. It's a fine, good-looking, well-landscaped pool, perfectly within the legal zoning requirements, and employees make good use of it for exercise and recreation, but it's "Everybody out of the water!" if there's a break in the mains. (Why do I feel like Louis Ruykheuser?)

That's heroic and ingenious to be sure, and underlines the point made above: To achieve really good levels of availability, you have to consider much more than just the computer-internal hardware and software issues that will be discussed here. Disciplined system management is utterly indispensable. So is consideration of environmental factors—power, water, air conditioning, physical security, and so on—that are outside the usual topics of computing.

There's no denying the large and growing importance of this issue. That was discussed in Chapter 3, so reasons why high availability is important won't be repeated here. Instead, this chapter's primary focus is on what "high availability" means, and how it's accomplished.

It's necessary to note before beginning that the importance of high availability has predictably resulted in an enormous amount of money, and therefore effort, being spent on issues of reliability and availability. Just as was the case with SMPs, there are an enormous range of techniques that have been developed and applied, and more are being invented every day by very ingenious, dedicated people. They range from innumerable *ad hoc* patches of difficulties with busses (at the moment, PCI is prone to being patched) all the way to formal theories of error correcting codes, trimodular redundancy, reliable voters, electronics burn-in, and multi-version programming, to name just a few.

This chapter cannot, therefore, claim to even attempt to cover the entire range of availability techniques. It will not even attempt to raise all the high availability *issues*, although it will raise many of the more common ones. Instead we'll discuss only techniques and issues directly related to clusters, with some passing reference to the purely hardware reliability techniques that are clusters' chief competition in this area. What this chapter will do is explain how clusters cover more common errors than the older techniques, and do so far more affordably, but do not cover all types of software; and how they perform this feat, making clear the sources of clusters' capabilities and restrictions.

First, however, we need some idea what it is we are aiming for.[1]

12.1 What Does "High Availability" Mean?____

Is "high availability" just another public relations buzzword? Well, at least partly. "High availability" is actually relatively recent terminology. The term that used to be heard, and often still is, is "fault tolerant."

In the past, "fault tolerant" had a specific meaning. It referred to systems that used various hardware techniques to make a single, stand-alone piece of computer hardware more or less bulletproof (sometimes, in military contexts, literally). Many vendors still provide systems like that in 1997. There's NetFrame and Marathon (who also use cluster techniques); Tandem, with a traditional hardware fault-tolerant offering in addition to their main-line cluster facilities; IBM, who used to have a hardware fault-tolerant offering;[2] Sun Microsystems, who added one to their product line in 1996; and so on. There are some ways in which pure hardware fault tolerance has advantages over clusters, as we will see, but many other ways in which it does not.

1. I am indebted to several IBM colleagues for some of the information presented in this chapter, especially Section 12.1. The members of the 1997 Server Availability study group of the IBM Academy of Technology are particularly to be thanked, and especially to Lisa Spainhower, a chief IBM availability guru in Poughkeepsie, and IBM Fellow Jim Rymarczyk. What appears here, unless otherwise noted, are entirely my own (not so) humble opinions, of course.

2. Among about a zillion other offerings. At one time there were even helicopters flying around Broome County, NY, with IBM part and serial numbers on them. The electronics were a far bigger part of the contract than the airframe, so IBM was the prime contractor, subcontracting the self-propelled cabinetry.

Ah, for the Olde Days when that kind of fault tolerant system was the only "highly available" one. They were much simpler. Everybody could count the size of the "fault tolerant" market easily, just by looking at the sales of the few vendors who supplied systems using such techniques to customers willing to pay for them. With the advent of clusters, it's harder to get a handle on both the market and the terminology. "Fault tolerant" and "highly available" are used with merry abandon, chosen more often than not according to what the customer happens to want to hear. If a customer's been lead to believe that "fault tolerant" has its traditional hardware-oriented meaning, cluster-like systems get called "software fault tolerant."

This can be a crucial marketing issue. There are customers who will quite literally stop listening and throw you out if you can't at the outset say your system is "fault tolerant," using those exact words. Among other groups, the finance industry—stock exchanges, commodity exchanges, and the like—is particularly famous for this attitude,[3] with some obvious justification. You can imagine the heart attacks on the trading floor and elsewhere if it were announced that the last 10 minutes of trading wasn't recorded. Saying a system is "fault tolerant" and then, two hours later, saying "well, it's *implemented* as *software* fault tolerance" can buy two hours with the customer, which just might get a sale on other valid grounds to people who don't demand deep discounts. Usually.

There is also a converse problem on the customer side. Not infrequently the ears have walls, and the customer hears what he or she wants. One respondent on a recent high-availability survey was absolutely irate because his expensive "fault tolerant"—hardware fault tolerant—system crashed nearly every day. The details of the survey revealed that the hardware was operating just fine; it had, in fact, ridden out several hardware problems without a glitch. However, the customer was modifying and updating the application on a daily, or even more frequent, basis, and its buggy state caused repeated crashes. The customer was still irate, and about to replace the system, because it said "fault tolerant," and it wasn't tolerating his faults.

As a result of this sometimes innocent but often deliberately-generated confusion, some more technically scrupulous types have simply given up and

---

3. Outside of brokers, there's another group that apparently must hear "fault tolerant." Apparently a very large number of people in the People's Republic of China have been convinced that they must have "fault tolerant" computer systems. This is despite the fact that in many cases electrical power is only available a few hours a day. Apparently, the argument is that the system absolutely must work during those few hours. In too many cases, HA/FT marketers have much in common with unscrupulous insurance salesmen: both prey on the fears and insecurities of their customers.

started calling the whole area "HA/FT," the ultra-scrupulous not even being willing to expand the abbreviation.

Marketing aside, there is an extremely significant techno-economic difference involved here. The traditional hardware fault tolerant systems rely on specialized hardware (and software) with features unique to those systems. For completeness, some of these techniques are discussed in a later section (Section 12.11.3 on page 440). Here are some of the buzzwords: tri- or bi-modular redundancy, inter-module comparators, reliable voting logic, intensive internal error checking/correction, automatic hardware-based checkpoint/restart, robust electrical design, and so on. That's why they were easy to count: You count shipments of that specially designed, low volume, and thus rather expensive, hardware.

The newer crop, more likely to be labelled "high availability" (except to customers who want to hear "fault tolerant") is harder to count precisely because it does not use specialized, and therefore expensive, hardware.

Instead, "high availability" clusters use high volume, low cost, common off-the-shelf system hardware elements to deliver high availability—*potential* high availability, anyway, depending on whether they are configured and managed well, with attention to detail. Cluster-based high availability thus represents a significant step towards the reliable and commoditized large-scale computing. The use of commoditized elements is not the only cost issue, however; there is a significant link between cluster performance scaling and the cost of high availability, as will be discussed in Section 12.11.1.

That said, it would still be nice to be able to know what "high availability" means in some slightly more technical sense.

12.1.1   How High is "High"?

One approach to attempting rational discussion of these issues is to focus on the question "how high is High?" In other words: If a system is available for use X% of the time, how big does X have to be for its availability to be "High"?

The result of this reasoning is, of course, that there's a continuum. It's commonly expressed with reference to a table like Table 14 below, which shows how much total non-operation (outage) time per year is implied by various availability percentages. Systems are then characterized has having a certain number of 9s ("this is a five 9's system") or being a certain availability class ("class 5") according to the band of availability it achieves. A class 1 system, for example, has 90%-99% availability (class 1 = one to two 9s).

Table 14 Classes of Availability

Availability	Total Accumulated Outage per Year	Class ("# of 9s")
90%	more than a month	1
99%	just under 4 days	2
99.9%	just under 9 hours	3
99.99%	about an hour	4
99.999%	a little over 5 minutes	5
99.9999%	about half a minute	6
99.99999%	about 3 seconds	

Where do various types of systems fit on this scale? Campus-wide LANs, according to two surveys [Conn92, Data90] are "in a permanent state of disrepair," falling into class 1 at about 95% availability. Class 1 is bad. Stand-alone, non-clustered open/commodity systems with average system management are typically in class 2, while typical open system-based cluster systems achieve class 3; class 4 is possible, but a challenge. Telephone switches are specified as class 5, and in-flight aircraft computers similarly should be class 6. Traditional mainframes have ranged from class 3 or 4 on up in the past, depending on the configuration and whether some form of clustering was used. However, like other systems, their position on this scale is rising: IBM states that its 1997 crop of S/390 Parallel Sysplex (cluster) systems can achieve class 5 relative to hardware failures, in a well-managed environment.

As a final step in creating tables like Table 14, names are usually given to the classes. Class 1, for example, has been called "unmanaged." (So much for LANs.) One of the levels—3, 4, or 5—is usually chosen to bear the label "high availability." So there's our definition.

Unfortunately, I consider this naming a useless exercise because, as mentioned above, the term a customer likes is the one that customer is going to hear. Also, it doesn't help that there appears to be little agreement about the labels. For example, while "fault tolerant" usually labels a higher class than "highly available," I've seen versions of that table with the opposite ordering, undoubtedly originating from vendors who chose to call their systems "highly available." Additional terms like "Fault Resilient," "Very Highly Available," and "Ultra High Availability" get thrown in, too, in fairly arbitrary places. I, for one, certainly can't tell from the names whether "Fault Resilient" is better or worse than "Very Highly Available."

Other attempts have been made to define an availability spectrum, implicitly giving meaning to "High Availability" or some other substitute phrase. Several analyst companies have done so in particular. For instance, IDC has a four-level availability spectrum [IDC96] labelled AL4 (best, Availability Level 4) to AL1, based on how a failure appears or doesn't appear to a user—which must be the ultimate criterion, of course. In AL4, failure of any component is transparent to a priority user. There's no interruption of work, no degradation of performance, and so on. In AL1, work stops and there's an uncontrolled shutdown, although data integrity is ensured.

Nearly all these spectra and hierarchies seem fairly reasonable. The problem is that few, if any, other organizations or users understand them, much less agree that they abstract the most relevant properties.

The classes alone, or the number of 9s, are at least unambiguous and fairly widely accepted.

12.1.2   Facets of Availability

This nails down "High" about as well as possible, which is to say not very firmly. How about "Availability"? Table 14 presupposes two states of a computer system: available, and not available. How do we know when we're counting time spent in one state versus the other? Unfortunately, that's even less simple than defining "high."

First of all, a system may be partly functional. One third of the disks might be inaccessible, or only two of 2,500 attached terminals. This issue can be patched by making availability a fraction: the fraction of its intended workload that the system can perform acceptably. This isn't completely reasonable in all cases; for example, I'd rather not be on the airplane whose class 6 navigation computer decided to get the wrong answer 25% of the time for several minutes of a year that happened to occur during a runway approach. However, in most data processing applications this is a reasonable approach.

The door starts opening to larger problems when we take into account the fact that a system need not operate all the time. In-flight computers, for example, don't have to operate when the airplane isn't flying, and the systems used to track stock transactions needn't run when the stock exchange is closed.

It seems unreasonable to count that time as "outage," since apparently nobody cares if the system's functional during those periods. Indeed, that unused time usually isn't counted. Also, there's the mathematical problem that our availability fraction isn't defined in those "unused" periods since the denominator, the workload to be done, is zero. Or is it?

Those non-operational hours are almost never 100% time spent with the power off. They're the time when system maintenance is done. That means housekeeping chores like adding memory, replacing disks that show signs of failing, applying upgrades to application or operating system software, taking backups, and so on. If those chores can't be done, the system is non-functional; it must be "available" during the time that's not counted. So, let's call those tasks part of the workload, and count the time when they're done against normal availability requirements.

Now that we've talked ourselves into considering upgrades part of the workload, we can take down the system in the middle of the day to do them, right? There's obviously a problem here.

It arises because we've implicitly been considering only one kind of service outage, the kind that most people initially consider when worrying about availability: Outages caused by something breaking or operating incorrectly when it wasn't expected—**unplanned** outages. There's another type of outage, an outage that's **planned** in advance. You know what it's for and you know ahead of time when it's going to occur. So maybe you can plan a picnic or something while it's happening, because you can't use the system.

Planned outages are a very significant source of system down time. For mainframe systems running mature applications in the mid-1990s, planned outages are actually a much larger cause of down time than unplanned outages. See Figure 104, which shows what resulted when some dedicated people put on some green eyeshades and, in excruciating detail, pored over the system logs of 16 very well managed S/390 systems, searching out the sources of system outage over a six month period. The vast majority—92%—of the outages were planned, not unplanned. This speaks well for S/390 hardware and software maturity; or perhaps, looking at the breakdown of reasons for the outages, speaks badly of the database backup and reorganization facilities available at that time (that was back in 1990; it's since been fixed).

I'm certain many people reading this who run PC-based systems are thinking they wish they could say that planned outages were their primary problem, but even for those systems planned outages can be a real issue. The reason, as was discussed in detail in Chapter 3, is that for a rapidly increasing number of uses of computers, there is no time when the system isn't supposed to be delivering service. Bank ATMs, grocery stores, the Internet (of course) and many other services operate 24 hours a day, 365 days a year (24x365). There are literally no empty slots for maintenance.

Figure 104 Sources of Outage in IBM S/390 Systems (1990)

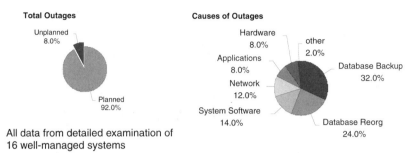

Total Outages

Unplanned 8.0%

Planned 92.0%

Causes of Outages

Hardware 8.0%

Applications 8.0%

Network 12.0%

System Software 14.0%

other 2.0%

Database Backup 32.0%

Database Reorg 24.0%

All data from detailed examination of 16 well-managed systems

Clearly, systems which aspire to 24x365 operation must find ways to eliminate planned outages as well as unplanned ones. There are three interesting implications that can be drawn from this.

First, clusters rule. The traditional bulletproof hardware fault tolerance techniques do not address this issue.[4] Clusters at least provide the hardware basis on which one can erect systems which avoid planned outages. Exactly how will be covered in the next section. As usual, of course, the "challenge" is in the software.

Second, a new set of design criteria is involved. The techniques for avoiding planned outages are very different from the ones used to avoid unplanned outages. Error checking, hardware redundancy at the detail level of adapters and processors, and the other paraphernalia of normal high availability design don't help. That prompts construction of the "design space" illustrated in Figure 105. To accentuate the difference, "high availability" is used in that figure to refer only to avoiding unplanned outages; "continuous operation," in contrast, is the avoidance of planned outages. Putting them both together simultaneously results in "continuous availability."

Not all applications require continuous availability, and Figure 105 gives examples of applications for each quadrant. The cases to the right and top are straightforward; obviously emergency communications require continuous availability, and the Internet never sleeps. Nobody likes to see their application on the bottom left, however; keep in mind that "basic availability" isn't necessarily "high unavailability" unless you have a catastrophically inept system administrator. Finding a case for the upper left quadrant is problematical; e-mail seems the least inappropriate.

---

4. Some may claim to address planned outages because they have "hot plug" disks or other hardware that can be added or removed without bringing the system down. However: First, does the software support this? (It might, for some devices.) Second, this doesn't address software maintenance at all.

Figure 105 An Availability Design Space

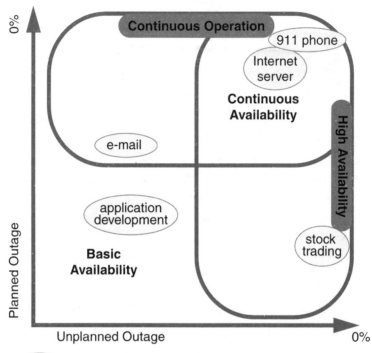

indicates an example application requiring a particular
combination of immunity from planned and unplanned outage

The third implication to be drawn from considering 24x365 availability is
that we might suspect that if there is one new class of outages and associated
avoidance techniques, there may well be others. We would be correct about
that. And therein lies a problem: How do you usefully discuss the entire
world's slings and arrows of outrageous fortune? All attempts to break it
into usable parts are somewhat arbitrary. Gray and Reuter, for example,
divide sources of outages into six categories: Environment, Operation,
Maintenance, Hardware, Software, and Process (the latter meaning "other").
A 1996 work group on server availability in IBM divided it differently, as
shown in Table 15.

The purpose of dividing outages along the lines of Table 15 is to better high-
light the fact that different kinds of actions are required to avoid them. No
matter what, however, many of the distinctions are relatively arbitrary and
leave room for interpretation. For example, suppose a bearing wears out in a
disk drive. Was that a physical error, or did it occur because of poor design?
All such lists really do, and it is a valuable exercise, is to raise our conscious-

In Search of Clusters ✳

Table 15   Causes of Outages

Type	Name	Description
unplanned	physical	something physically wore out or broke
	design	design errors in software and hardware
	environmental	loss of power or cooling
	operator	operator or user action: accidents, inexperience, or malice
planned	upgrades	software or hardware upgrades
	maintenance	preventative or deferred maintenance
	regulations	government/policy regulations
disaster	natural	natural disasters like hurricanes, earthquakes, or floods; or more localized "disasters" like accidentally setting off a file sprinkler system
	forced	"unnatural," human-caused disasters such as terrorist activity

ness about all the things that can cause outages. The real issue is: Which ones matter? What are the most prevalent causes of errors?

I wish there were a good, firm answer to that, but there isn't. Few studies are published by computer system vendors, simply because publicly admitting that your systems fail is corporate masochism that no sales team will willingly allow the company to undergo. As for giving the reasons, well. Consider the designers of whatever's worst (there has to be something that's worst). After they get finished denying that the study is correct, and pointing out why it doesn't matter, they'll say the next release fixes the problem, so why publish ancient history?

Here and there some data is available, but when it is, no two studies separate the slings from the arrows in the same way. For example, a study published in 1985 of 1,383 Japanese banking systems [GR93, Wat86] showed that 42% of the outages were due to "the vendor." It doesn't say what portion of that was vendor-supplied hardware, or software, or unplanned outages, or planned maintenance. It does an interesting job of placing blame, however.

Without formal studies, folklore is what's left. All right, what's the folklore? Here is what I hear floating about the corridors as a rough ordering of the expected causes of failures of open and commodity systems running competent vendor-supplied system software.

1. The most common cause of outage is loss of power, unless you happen to live in Japan or Germany; their power systems are excellent. This doesn't mean you should immediately rush out and buy a UPS (Uninterruptable Power Supply). If power's off, will it matter if the server is down? A large U.S. retailer I visited didn't think so for the inventory systems in his warehouses. If the lights are off, nothing can move in the warehouse; so why run inventory? Better boot up fast when power returns, though.

2. The second most common source of outages is application software. Interestingly, this agrees with the Japanese study mentioned above; that attributed 25% of the failures to application software.

3. At this point, the folklore says there is a huge gap in frequency. Then several other things show up. The order within this set isn't clear. They are, in no particular order: operating system software, subsystem software (like databases), hardware with moving parts (fans, disks, tapes, printers), and I/O adapters.

4. Memory is next.

5. Finally, with another huge gap from the prior items, there is the complicated central electronics of the computer: central processing unit, caches, and so on. Furthermore, many of the failures here come not from things wearing out but from design errors, bugs in the manufacturing process, particular odd lots that are bad, and so on.

Take this with a large grain of salt for two reasons. First, it is folklore. It's fairly informed folklore, more or less agreed to by what few fragmentary studies exist, but still folklore. Second, individual circumstances can totally overwhelm any average behavior. If you live in the lightning capitol of the world,[5] some form of power supply protection is rather likely to be a good investment to ride out momentary outages and avoid power surges. If you run a multi-Terabyte disk megafarm, it doesn't take too many smarts to see that you will have more disk failures than the average Joe, simply because you have more disks than the average Joe. Same comment for memory if you have a gigantic main memory installed. You also could be unlucky and happen to be the recipient of a batch of cache chips that just barely squeaked by quality assurance, moving your processor complex way up the list of likely outage causes.

---

5. Central Florida, USA.

All of this also depends on what's being counted and which users are counting it. Very recently, a large but so far unpublished survey of 200 users of highly available servers was conducted by Harvard Research for International Data Corporation (IDC). In terms of number of outages, it basically agreed with the ordering above, but the gaps between the various levels weren't as large as intimated above, and software beat out everything, even power failures.

However, their analysis of that data revealed that the outage distribution was highly skewed. The typical respondent had many rather short outages, and a few real whoppers, so the mean and the median outage duration were very different. It turned out that when you filtered the data to consider only the whoppers, the ranking of causes changed significantly. Power outage was #1. However, #2 was now disks, and the rest of the hardware was tied with software for third place. Unfortunately, this survey didn't separate electronics from things that move, so it's not clear whether this was fan failures or CPU chip failures. However, there's nevertheless a lesson to be drawn: Hardware doesn't break very often, but when it does you're in really big trouble, probably because it takes much longer to find the parts and repair the hardware than to reboot a software-catatonic system.

Whatever the source, formal study or informal discussion, one thing stands out: Once power, cooling, and the rest of the non-computer-internal elements are discounted, *a major source of system outages is software.*

This poses a dilemma. Software doesn't wear out or physically break. The only causes of software failures are design flaws. How do you fix or avoid that? Various design disciplines can be used, successful in rough proportion to increasingly traumatic expense, but if you're running purchased software, no such option is available.

Furthermore, it turns out that a large number of the software errors encountered are the kind that are extremely difficult to track down and fix. These are unrepeatable, transient errors that occur due to a particular combination of inputs arriving in a particular sequence, nevermore to recur. **Heisenbugs**, named after Heisenburg's uncertainty principle. Ugly things. (The repeatable ones have been called Bohrbugs, after Bohr's simpler, more deterministic model of the atom, but the term hasn't caught on like "Heisenbugs.")

Heisenbugs are nearly impossible to stamp out because, of course, they don't recur when you run through the problem again.

Wait a minute. *They don't happen when you run it again.*

Running it again is exactly what happens when a cluster fails over to another node. These particularly nasty, latent errors don't show their ugly heads if the system does reexecute the exact same functions but, deliberately or inadvertently, does so in a slightly different sequence. This is a kind of hopeful, probabilistic approach to fixing errors, which turns the very nature of the problem—nonrepeatability—into its own solution. Does it work in practice?

The answer appears to be a resounding "yes." It works much better than we have any right to hope it will. So clusters still rule.

12.1.3   Outage Duration

Even after all the discussion above, there remains a dimension of failure that hasn't been touched: the duration of each individual outage. Take, for example, a class 4 system that experiences an hour of total outage a year. If that outage happens as a single, one-hour period—naturally, by Murphy's law, at the busiest time of the year—it will be much more disruptive than if it happens as $60 \times 60 = 3600$ one-second outages spread throughout the year. No matter when they happen, nobody will notice.

This is one area where the traditional hardware fault tolerance techniques rule over clusters. They can, and in most cases do, reduce outages to durations that are so short that they're indiscernible by people and by most physical mechanisms. Clusters, in contrast, usually (but not always, as we'll discuss in Section 12.6) require at least 30 seconds to resume service, and often longer. It may take several minutes to be fully back on the air, or even hours depending on how it's counted (see Section 12.6). With that amount of time involved, the system's users will usually notice that something has happened. In many cases, however, systems come back fast enough if they are back on-line quickly enough that the users aren't tempted to take a coffee break.

Another deficit of clusters compared with pure hardware fault tolerance, which in many ways is much more serious, is that clusters cannot perform their magic on every kind of software. As will be discussed later, only applications or subsystems with very specific characteristics—transactional semantics—are able to fail over reliably; furthermore, avoidance of planned outages for software changes requires additional, different, software characteristics. Hardware fault tolerance, in contrast, works to keep the hardware running no matter what the software. On the other hand, don't forget that irate customer who was mad at his fault tolerant hardware because his system kept crashing due to bugs in his application. As the introduction said up front, availability is a system issue; down is down.

12.1.4 So, OK, What Really is High Availability?

After all that, have we really defined high availability? We've talked all around the subject, poked at it from different angles, and seen its complexity, but not really nailed it down.

There's yet another way of coming at it that's not been covered, involving the notion of a **single point of failure**. This is a single element of hardware or software which, if it fails, brings down the entire computer system. When dealing with high availability, single points of failure are obviously highly undesirable. With one addition, their avoidance is the basis of the working definition I personally prefer.

A computer system is highly available if it has two properties:

1. No replaceable piece is no single point of failure.

2. Overall, it is sufficiently reliable that you are overwhelmingly likely to be able to repair or replace a broken part before something else breaks.

This doesn't speak to many of the causes of failure, give a mathematical percentage of outage, or even give a popular N-hours x M-days statement, and ignores many of the issues. However, if a system has the two properties above, it is potentially immortal. When something breaks, it keeps running, and does so long enough that you can fix what broke. The basic reliability of most system components today is high enough that condition (2) is satisfied in most cases, so we just need to configure out systems as clusters to satisfy the first.

Immortality is an adequate definition of high availability for me.

This has been a long discussion of a collection of things that really has no beginning, no end, nor to my taste any satisfactory structure (another bloody survey). So let's quickly summarize the really relevant points:

➢   For 24x365 operation, you must do a good job on many things that are not the usual computer-technology-related stuff. Power, cooling, physical environment, and so on are important. Careful and disciplined system management is extremely important.

➢   24x365 operation also implies dealing with planned outages and disasters, not just breakage and errors.

➢   Software causes the largest number of outages, after power failure.

➢   However, the worst, meaning longest, unplanned outages are caused as much by hardware as software (again, after power failure).

> Configure systems to avoid single points of failure.

> Clusters can help with planned outages and unplanned errors in both hardware and software, but don't do so for all software.

> Pure hardware-based fault tolerance "fails over" instantaneously, but doesn't help with software errors or planned outages.

> As a customer you'll hear, and as a vendor you'll hear from competitors, whatever words you want. There is no industry consensus on what "high availability" and "fault tolerance" mean. Think of them as yet more synonyms for "good," and ask about single points of failure and levels of availability.

Now let's get on with how one achieves all these noble ends.

12.2 The Basic Idea: Failover

The basic technique used in clusters to achieve high availability is **failover**. The concept is simple enough: One computer (Alice) watches another computer (Bozo); if Bozo dies, Alice takes over Bozo's work, as shown in Figure 106.

Figure 106 Basic Failover

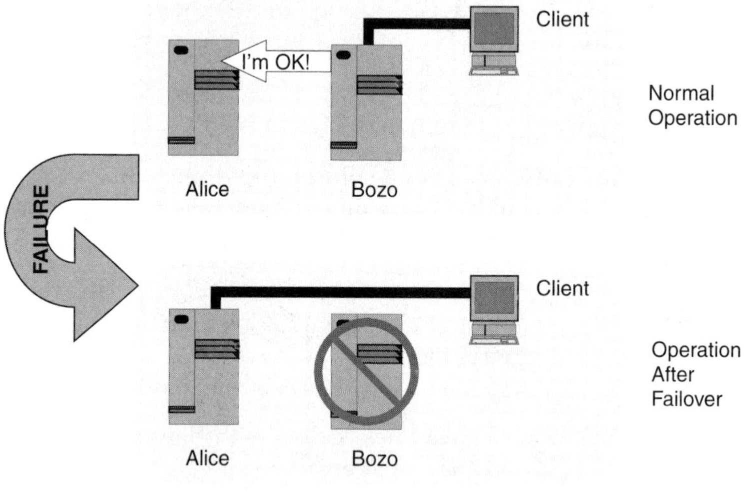

In effect, Alice is a back-seat driver who must be continually assured that Bozo is awake. Unless Alice continually hears "I'm awake, Dear. I'm awake, Dear. I'm awake, Dear," it's going to reach over and grab the steering wheel. That is exactly what failover does.

12.2.1   First, Do No Harm

That mental image suggests a real danger: If Alice jumps the gun, both of them end up struggling for the steering wheel, with disastrous consequences. Of course, Bozo is most likely to slow down the recitation of his mantra at the most dangerous possible moments, since that's when it needs to focus most intently on the "real" work, relegating Alice's pacification to second place. So you're more likely to get both pairs of hands on the steering wheel in the middle of heavy traffic at a intersection (or during the heaviest workload of the day).

This analogy is absolutely spot on. Out-of-control high availability cluster software can indirectly do damage much worse than it tries to prevent by persuading different computers to believe they both "own" the same data, communications lines, or other resources. Two pairs of hands on the steering wheel does not work. Totally scrambled data can easily result if the takeover process is not programmed with an experienced, sharp eye to being conservative—"first, do no harm"—and has not been wrung out with extreme thoroughness on the configurations it is to protect.

So really, really try to avoid putting Release 1.0 of any high availability system into production use. For this case (and others), there is terribly significant value to software maturity, meaning that the code has been used in many installations and gone through an extensive sorting-out process over a significant amount of time. In other words: Use other people to debug it.

If you've an interest in seeing that a system currently at Release 1.0 becomes mature, lean on it as hard as you can in a pre-production environment. Beat it up. And report the bugs. Loudly. Often. In detail.

Also, be very circumspect about installing any high availability software on a system whose configuration doesn't *precisely* match one that's already certified as working. Salesfolks will push, saying a configuration isn't "significantly" different and so will work, but their motives are always suspect; they want to move the hardware.[6]

12.2.2   Avoiding Planned Outages

When all is working correctly, the basic failover scenario also becomes the basis of an important availability issue: avoiding planned outages.

---

6. I was walking in Manhattan one day with a sales rep when she paused, looked into a shoe store window, and then turned to me, saying "Do you want to know how sales reps think? I just said to myself 'I really like those shoes. If I sell five more workstations, I can afford to buy them.'" From the look on her face, I concluded that it would be downright dangerous to get between her and those shoes.

This scenario is like a planned swap of drivers: Bozo gracefully yields the wheel, Alice takes over, and Bozo takes a nap or has a bite to eat. Gracefully shutting down a system can be a special command to the cluster software, or, in more sophisticated systems, a use of cross-machine workload balancing software.

Once Bozo is not in use, anything required can be done to it. In effect, everything on Bozo becomes "hot plug" because the heat has been transferred to Alice. Once the upgrades are finished, the reverse of failover is performed—**failback**—and normal operation is resumed on Bozo. Then Alice can be upgraded in a similar fashion.

This is a very significant use of clusters. Confirming the data of Figure 104 on page 387, a 1995 survey of 15 UNIX accounts using clusters, done by D.H. Brown [Brow95] found that failover to avoid *un*planned outages accounted for only one-third of the failovers performed. The other two thirds were deliberately instigated in order to apply upgrades and maintenance. So failover is used twice as often to avoid unplanned outages as to avoid planned outages.

Hardware upgrades and modifications are fairly straightforward in this scenario, with the exception of hardware that's shared by cluster members. Alice hasn't stopped using them, so failover doesn't help. They are upgradable only if the hardware is "hot plug" and the software can deal with that. The hardware this most often applies to is disks, which often have the desired properties if they're configured as freestanding RAID subsystems.

Software is a more difficult story. It's certainly the case that anything at all can be done to Bozo while it's disconnected; the issue is whether it will work when reconnected to Alice. There are two cases where that is potentially a problem:

1. the software change requires a change to data formats held on disk
2. the software runs in parallel across the nodes of the cluster.

Databases and file systems, along with many other subsystems and applications, quite often come under class 1; parallel databases can be in both classes simultaneously. The cluster availability and control software itself is always in case 2 and, depending on its design, may be in case 1 also.

In both cases, an outage-free change requires compatibility between the version currently running and the version being installed. This is not a commonly accepted, much less satisfied, requirement on many software upgrades. When it is available, it usually goes by the name **N and N+1 version compatibility**, occasionally abbreviated as **N/N+1 compatibility**. As the name implies, it means you can get from where you are to any later version by going through intermediate steps, without any outages.

The first software systems I knew of that programmed to that requirement were the cluster subsystems used to control failover themselves. Naturally, they were the first to realize there was an issue involved. Several major subsystems of full cluster systems (IBM Parallel Sysplex, DEC VMScluster, Tandem Himalaya) have also adhered to this discipline when, for example, updates to the core operating system is required.

Future NUMA systems have a potential difficulty here. Imagine attempting to attain N/N+1 version compatibility in a NUMA-organized system. On a conventional cluster, each node can be taken off-line and have version N+1 of the OS installed; when it is brought back, there are functional compatibility issues with version N on the other nodes, but at least it can communicate. If an enhanced NUMA system is in place—either NC-NUMA or CC-NUMA, one with firewalls and other safeguards required for high availability—then presumably a node can be taken off-line; it's also not unreasonable for that node to be initialized with a new version of the OS. But if inter-node communication directly uses addresses in other nodes and data structure formats in its inter-node communication, integrating version N+1 into a functioning cluster running version N is a rather difficult prospect. It can be alleviated by restricting communication to particular areas, in particular formats, but when this is done sufficiently to cover most functional changes, one begins to wonder whether it is actually equivalent to just using the memory access facilities for passing messages.

12.2.3   Some Questions

If all of this is beginning to sound rather less simple than it looks at first glance, you're getting the idea. There are several things glossed over so far that need further explanation.

> ➢ How did Alice get at Bozo's data in the first place? What about communication, since Figure 106 shows a client's communication switching over to Alice. How did that happen?

> ➢ How do you accomplish reliable monitoring and takeover that doesn't end up with two pairs of hands on the wheel?

Those are the next major topics. As we'll see, they have significant areas within them that involve many possible design alternatives.

As we go through them, for convenience we'll use the term **target** to indicate the system that's taking over the work (when we don't call it Alice, as in Figure 106 on page 394) and **source** to indicate the system that failed (when we don't call it Bozo). The term "backup" might be a little more mnemonic than "target," but it has the undesirable implication that Alice is just sitting there, doing nothing but acting as, well, a backup for Bozo. While this can be done, and should be done in some circumstances, it is unnecessarily expensive in many cases. This will be covered in section 12.11.1.

12.3 Resources

Failover involves moving "things" from one node to another. Many different kinds of things are potentially involved: physical disk ownership, logical disk volumes, IP addresses, application processes, subsystems, print queues, collections of cluster-wide locks in a shared-data system, and so on. The less-informal name for "things" like those is **resources**, a term borrowed from operating systems.

Resources depend on one another. This relationship matters because, for example, it will not help to move an application to one node when the data it uses is moved to another. Actually, it will not even help to move them both to the same node if the application is started before the necessary disk volumes are mounted.

Early high-availability support systems, as well as current primitive ones, left to the user the problem of keeping such relationships intact. When a node failed, the high-availability support code on the other cluster nodes would simply start execution of a user exit, telling it what node went down. It was up to the user code, typically a shell script or visual basic program, to do what was necessary to attach and/or start up appropriate tasks in the right order.

Keeping this straight and consistent across the cluster is a nontrivial administrative task, and when this technique is used it is a very significant part of what makes clusters more difficult to manage than single systems. Of course, if mistakes are made, the rule of "first, do no harm" can be egregiously violated. However, more usually the failover simply does not work, which is probably bad enough.

A way to help avoid these problems is to maintain a cluster-wide data file that records all the resources that are of interest, and then use that to restart things. The file would typically contain, implicitly or explicitly, some identification of each resource and an indication of what to do to start it. It is typically kept within, or in a similar format to, operating system files that similarly list the resources within a single system—for example, the Microsoft Windows NT Registry, or the IBM AIX/6000 Object Data Manager (ODM). Then, adding the further ability to define groups of resources that are moved together (like a database manager and its disk volumes) allows the user to specify what's to be done in a much less error-prone manner: Move this group to there, and that one to here.

Unfortunately, mistakes are still very easy to make in specifying the groups, since the relationships between resources can quickly become difficult to keep straight. Furthermore, the system administrator must be careful to update the relationships when seemingly unrelated things are altered.

For example, if a logical disk volume is extended to a different physical disk, it may suddenly be the case that otherwise unrelated applications must now belong to the same "group" in the sense that they can only be relocated as a unit. The reason is that you can't move the same physical disk to two different places, and the logical disk volumes involved may now share the same physical disk. (This specific example doesn't, of course, happen if a physical disk can't be split into different logical volumes; but other things like that can happen.)

A way to help eliminate that source of error is to record the dependencies between the resources in that data file. This is typically a hierarchy that shares subtrees. This is illustrated in Figure 107, which shows a database that needs an IP address and disk volumes in order to run, and a separate application needing a print queue and a file system, which also needs logical and physical disk volumes.

Figure 107 A Resource Hierarchy

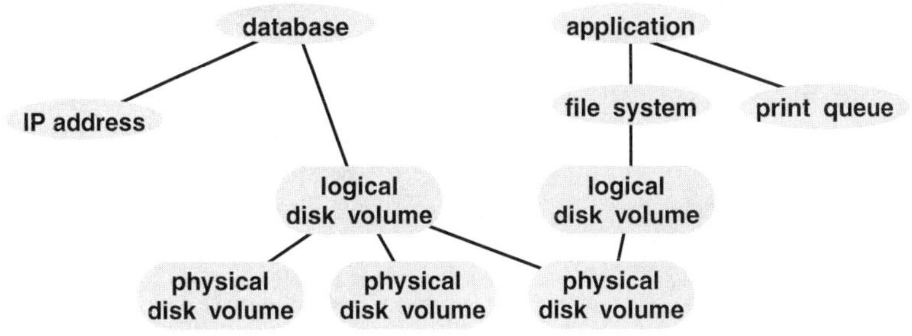

database   application

IP address   file system   print queue

logical disk volume   logical disk volume

physical disk volume   physical disk volume   physical disk volume

Once the relationships have been defined by the system administrator, the failover support can know that the database and the application in Figure 107 must be moved as a unit, because they share a physical disk volume. Furthermore, it can know the order in which resources must be brought into service to make the entire operation succeed. The user need only say what top-level resources move where, and the rest is deduced automatically.

Ideally, this specification of the inter-resource dependencies is integrated with the normal system administration tools that define and manipulate resources. Otherwise errors can still easily be made, as in the case mentioned earlier of extending a logical volume. Doing so effectively involves creating a single system image for system administration across the cluster; this is desirable in any event, but is a significant amount of work.

There are a few more issues related to resources in general and their relationships:

➤ Resources can potentially depend on individual cluster nodes. Only certain nodes might have a program installed, for example, or by administrative fiat certain applications might be allowed only in certain places; or only particular nodes may have a connection to a given physical disk.

➤ What is done to bring a resource on line can depend on the node to which it is moved. For example, a print queue may already be defined on all the nodes of the cluster; an attempt to initialize it when it's already running could lead to further errors. A similar situation exists with shared data systems; usually they do not need, and it would be an error to try, to mount a disk volume they are already accessing.

➤ The dependence and resource information must itself be reliably available to all nodes at all times, even when it is being modified. Chaos can easily result if the node being used to change that information happens to crash while the change is being made. This implies that all changes must be self-consistent, indivisible, and have other properties—a collection of traits called "transactional semantics," which is discussed in Section 12.4.2.

That more or less takes care of general issues with resources. There are significant questions about how one actually fails over (moves) particular kinds of resources which can have large implications on system structure and cluster characteristics such as failover time. These are covered in the sections immediately following.

One general issue not discussed, however, is: Where do resources fail over to? When there are only two nodes, and one of them just died, this isn't much of a question. It becomes much more exciting in clusters of several nodes, and is discussed in section 12.7.

12.4 Failing Over Data

In order for a target system to take over data from the source, several issues must be confronted: How does the data get there? Is it good data—consistent and correct? A system was just lost; how do you rebalance the workload? Finally, how much time does this all take, and how can it be made faster?

The sections following describe how different styles and structures of clusters answer those questions in very different ways.

12.4.1 Replication and Switchover

Getting the data to the backup can be done in two ways: First, the backup can keep its own independent copy, a method called **replication**; or, second, the backup can get physical access to the storage devices that were being used by the failed system, a method called **switchover**. Each has advantages and disadvantages, and their use is independent of whether the system as a whole uses data sharing or a shared-nothing philosophy (as was discussed in Chapter 10).

Replication is illustrated in Figure 108. In order for the data to be kept up to date, Bozo must ship every change over to Alice, who must apply the change to its copy. If the data is in a file system, each write must be sent; if the data is in a database, a convenient method is to ship Bozo's database log over to Alice, who applies the log to its own copy of the database. An alternative to the update-driven version described above is to scan for changes at some regular interval, copying them in bulk over to the second system.

Figure 108 Accessing Data by Replication

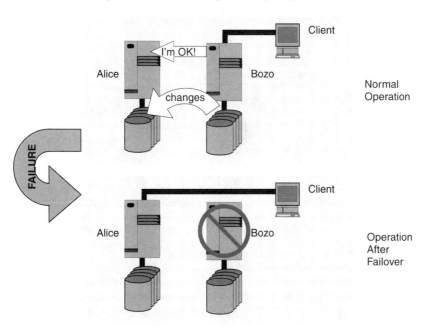

Switchover, in contrast, is shown in Figure 109.

With switchover, some form of external storage interconnect provides a path to the storage units from both systems. When the source (Bozo) dies, the target (Alice) activates a path through the interconnect directly to the devices

Figure 109 Accessing Data by Switchover

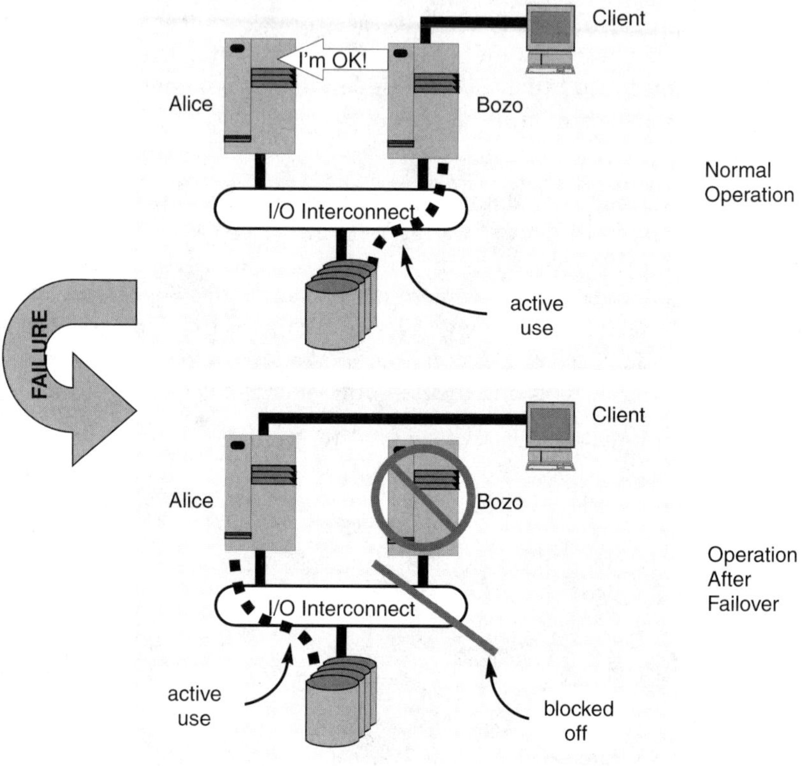

that Bozo was using, and also does its best to keep Bozo from accessing the data. Remember, first, do no harm. Bozo failed, so it's state is unknown; keep it quarantined.

The I/O interconnect itself can be an industry standard bus or ring, such as SCSI, SSA, Fibre Channel Switch (FCS), Fibre Channel Arbitrated Loop (FC-AL) or the negotiated merger of SSA and FC-AL, which at least initially had the rather ungraceful abbreviation FC-EL; apparently it will now be called FCL. Alternatively, the interconnect can be a proprietary arrangement, such as Digital's broadcast-based Star Coupler, IBM's S/390 switch-based ESCON director, or Tandem's ServerNet system area network.

All these interconnects are, for the most part, designed not just for failover but for active sharing of data. For high availability purposes, however, no two systems need be actively banging on the same device at the same time.

(Both Figure 108 and Figure 109 are slightly simplified in that both Alice and Bozo also usually have private disks to hold their own copies of system data; those aren't explicitly shown.)

As a way to implement high availability, replication is often deprecated. I've heard a leading light of clusters refer to replication-based systems as "not real clusters." What constitutes a "real cluster," however, is very much in the eye of the beholder. I've heard others complain that marketing must be the reason people use "cluster" to describe systems that don't "even" have a lock manager, while the leading light mentioned above is a staunch zealot if not a high priest of the shared-nothing sect, which of course don't need no steenkin' lock managers (as recounted in Chapter 10).

Since I tend to be a multicultural pluralist about these issues (maybe a cluster anthropologist), damn the buffalo and here's Table 16, comparing the two.

Adding insult to injury, here's a discussion of the issues listed in Table 16, which will bring out important points about switchover (for those of you who may be replication-intolerant):

> **adding a second node**: For replication, you usually add another communications adapter to carry the updates to the replica. While it's painful to add even a two-port network, doing so is nowhere near as bad as messing with the disk cabling already in place on a system, possibly having to add additional disk adapter if the external interconnect would otherwise be overloaded, and possibly having to rearrange volume information. The latter is obviously much worse.

> **synchronizing configurations**: A replicating target system is independent of the source in most ways. With switchover you had better be sure the two systems agree on disk partitions, volume organizations, volume names, and other details of administration concerning the switched-over disks. If you don't, you will likely get severely scrambled data on switchover. This is one area where single system image administration tools help a lot; a big advantage of a kernel-level single system image is that it isn't possible for the systems to disagree on such stuff.

> **distance**: Switchover requires that the disk interconnect span the distance between the nodes. In the case of FCS, this isn't much of a restriction, since it can cover kilometers; the other standard (and proprietary) methods cover tens of meters at best. Raw distance aside, however, each disk being switched must be in one place, unless that hardware is truly sainted and achieved bilocation; that

Table 16 Replication vs. Switchover

Replication	Switchover
✔ easier to add to an existing single machine	harder to add; must alter existing system cabling
✔ easier to configure; systems are fairly independent	harder to configure; disk configurations must be synchronized
✔ nodes can be a distance apart, which gives some disaster-like tolerance	nodes must be physically close, and disks are in one place; everything drowns if a fire sprinkler goes off
✔ can use any old I/O adapters and controllers	requires adapters and controllers that actually implement their specifications
✔ can use simple storage units	must use hardened storage, such as RAID
one-to-many backup is feasible up to the point where the backup saturates; limits ability of backup to do useful work	✔ 1-to-many backup is feasible up to the limit of the disk interconnect
requires another copy of storage	✔ shares a single copy of storage
uses CPU and I/O capacity in normal operation	✔ no overhead in normal operation
tight synchronization causes performance loss; loose synchronization can lose data at failure	✔ natural complete synchronization without performance loss
failback can present new problems of re-synchronization	✔ failback issues are no different from failover

place can be flooded, lose power, etc. Replication allows the use of standard communications between the machines, which can span continents—or, cheaply, go to another floor and/or power grid. For this reason it is a key technique in disaster tolerance, as will be discussed in section 12.11.2.

➢ **adapter/controller issues**: Replication works with any disk adapters able to operate on a collection of disks attached to one computer, which really should be all of them. Switchover requires that the adapters be able to switch "master" designations on the I/O interconnect. That is a part of the specification of every I/O interconnect, including the ability to "unlock" an adapter that was set to keep others out during an uninterruptable sequence of operations. However, not every disk adapter sold for PC systems has been adequately tested for the switchover (or shared data) case; you will have a hard time finding one that works at Joe's Cheap Computer Parts Shack. Most adapters sold for workstation and midrange systems are well-behaved in this regard, but they naturally come with higher price tags.

➤ **storage units**: If the disks themselves are not part of a unit that internally has redundancy and no single point of failure—such as external RAID storage subsystems—then switchover has a single point of failure in the disks. Thus more expensive and slower disk units must be used. Replication can use anything able to remember bits.

➤ **one-to-many backup**: Both schemes can be used to allow one otherwise idle server to back up several others. Replication's limit on this is how busy the backup unit becomes; beyond a certain number of primaries, it will run out of ability to keep up with all the changes. This also limits how well replication can be used if the backup is to do useful work, not just sit around waiting for something to fail. Switchover, in contrast, is limited only by how many systems can be attached to the same interconnect and, unlike replication, has no inherent performance-related limitations.

➤ **duplicate storage**: Replication is, well, replication. You have to keep a complete separate copy of the data on the second system, so you have to purchase twice as many disks; in effect, replication mirrors the data. Since disks can easily be the single most expensive unit in a commercial installation, this cost penalty can be quite large, as we'll discuss in Chapter 13. This is the biggest single failing of replication in 1997. The economics of disk storage in the future are not necessarily those of 1997, though.

➤ **overhead**: Replication is an active process. The source must send copies of changes to the target, and the target must write them on disk. This uses both system CPU power and I/O bandwidth on both the source and the target. In one case, the overhead on an active transaction processing system was estimated at 10% of the CPU capacity on the source, and 15% on the target, assuming the remaining capacity of the source was fully occupied doing transactions. If two systems are mutually replicating to each other, so both are in active use, that means 25% of the CPU capacity is lost on both. While those numbers will be significantly lower in systems with less update activity, such as most file servers, it nevertheless is a noticeable advantage of switchover that there is no overhead at all during normal operation.

➤ **synchronization**: Replication takes time. If the source waits for the target to signal a completed write for every update, significant performance can be lost, particularly on write-intensive transaction workloads. If the source does not wait, on the other hand, there is a chance that data will be lost if it wasn't written when a failure occurs. Switchover simply doesn't have this problem.

➤ **failback**: For switchover, reinstating the failed node incurs no problems not present when the target took over for the source in the first place. With replication, you have a copy of the data on the target that has been getting out of date for as long as the source was out; a significant collection of changes must be sent over to re-synchronize the two before the normal lower update traffic can resume. In mild cases, higher than usual overhead will be incurred while re-synchronization takes place; in severe cases, a planned outage may be needed to accomplish the re-synchronization.

12.4.2   Avoiding Toxic Data: Transactions

Alice (the target) now has physical access to the data. Data that was last written by Bozo. Dead Bozo. Bozo who may well have been deranged before kicking the bucket. How do we know it didn't scramble the data in its death throes?

This problem is illustrated for its worst case in Figure 110. There, Bozo's mess isn't just wrong, it's positively toxic: Alice, encountering it, crashes. This toxic data syndrome is a real bummer. We can take heart in that it's not the usual case (but I've had it happen, as have many other people). Most often, the software on Alice won't crash; it will, instead, do sufficient consistency checks that it'll just refuse to run. Either way, this is not exactly the effect failover is supposed to have.

This problem actually isn't any worse with clusters than with stand-alone systems. If a singleton computer drops dead, it may well have been behaving in a deranged fashion just before rigor mortis set in, and so may have damaged the data. However, people purchasing clusters usually do so with some expectation of high availability, and this problem keeps the customer from getting what was paid for. So, how do we fix it?

Figure 110 Toxic Data Syndrome

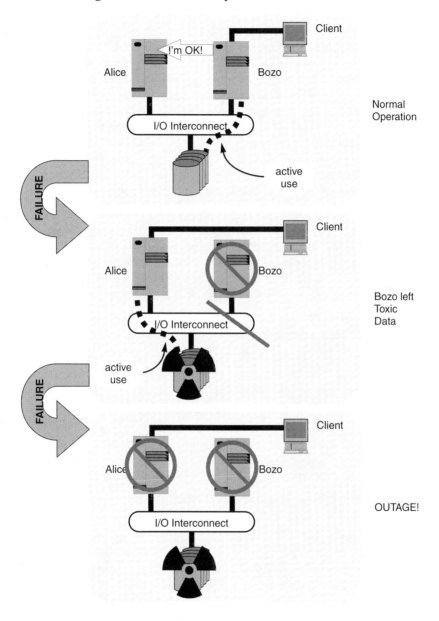

As with any toxic waste, there are two ways to avoid this problem: Clean it up, or avoid creating it in the first place.

Cleaning it up involves running some sort of "check" or "fixup" program; the most familiar of these are the UNIX fsck command, DOS CHKDSK command, and the many useful DOS/Windows disk utilities. Programs like these have the unenviable task of rooting through nastily twisted tangles of incorrect data, trying to make some sense out of what used to be a file system, database, or other collection of usually crucial data. On large collections of data, they can take quite a while; UNIX fsck, applied to a large disk volume, was famous for running for hours. Programs like this are utterly invaluable when they work. Nevertheless, injecting them into normal failover processing to be sure the data won't bring down the target system is unlikely to meet anybody's requirements for speedy resumption of service.

Avoiding the problem seems like a far better idea, and in fact the techniques for doing so form a a very well-developed body of theory and practice in the commercial data processing community. This is the notion of making all changes to data as **transactions**. Transactions are defined to be operations on data that have a collection of properties called, in a superb acronym, the ACID properties; taken together, they define transactional semantics:

➤ **Atomic**: Changes are made as indivisible units, even if they affect multiple separate data items

➤ **Consistent**: The relationships between data items are what they're supposed to be. For example, if two indices are supposed to indicate the same data item, they in fact do that.

➤ **Isolated**: Each change is independent of the others. If two are done to the same data item, it's as if they happen in sequence. If something is changed to red by one transaction, and changed to blue by another, it will end up red. Or blue. You don't necessarily know which. But you do know it will never, ever, end up purple.

➤ **Durable**: Transactions that have completed ("committed") will survive failures.

This sounds great, particularly the last item, since that item implies that transactions will resist anything Bozo might do in its dementia. However, this definition says nothing about how such magic is actually accomplished. There are a a wide variety of techniques (for example, see [GR93, KS86]), and an enormous technology has been developed for transaction processing.

In brief, transactional semantics are usually implemented by using a separate file on stable storage (such as mirrored disks) that's called the log file. The log is a sequentially written record of everything done to the data: The values before it was changed, with a unique identifier of this change; then the values after it is changed, with the same identifier; and then, crucially, as a single atomic write, a short item with the identifier and the notation "did it." The application doing the changes has to note when it's starting the change; let the system know (or go through interfaces that automatically let the system know) what's being changed; and let the system know when it's completed a consistent change so the crucial "did it" record can be written. (Locks are also obviously necessary on the data being changed, to ensure the isolation and consistency properties. They were discussed in Chapter 9.)

Having atomically written that "did it" record, the transaction is **committed**. Assuming the application was correct, and really did a consistent change to the data, you're safe. No matter what happens—assuming the stable storage stays stable—a consistent state of the data can be recreated by scanning through the log. If a "did it" record is present, you plug in the new values, and the change has happened, completely; if it's not present, plug back in the old values, and it never happened. This isn't too difficult, so making sure things are in a consistent state can usually be done rather quickly as part of the takeover process when failover is performed. The actual writing of the data onto disk files in its proper format can occur after the log is written. The log file sees all, knows all, and gets mighty big mighty quickly if it's not pruned of unnecessary old committed transactions on a regular basis.

This indicates how transactions are done on a single system, or in a parallel system that uses data sharing (as discussed in Chapter 12), but shared-nothing systems seem to have a problem in doing transactions where changes must be done to data "owned" by different computers in the cluster. That's performed, as briefly mentioned in Chapter 12, by a technique called two-phase commit.

Two-phase commit is equivalent, to use a wonderful analogy mentioned in [GR93], to a marriage. A third party coordinates the operation, the minister, who in effect follows this sequence:

Minister:	Alice, do you take this to be your lawfully committed data, to have and to hold, through normal operation and failure, at least until the next database reorganization?
Alice:	I do. I am ready to commit.
Minister:	Bozo, do you take that to be your (etc.)
Bozo:	I do. I am ready to commit.
Minister:	I now pronounce you transactional. You may write your logs.

If Bozo had backed out, for example, the Minister would tell Alice "Tough luck, you were left at the altar. Don't write that commit record to your log." Then the transaction is said to have aborted: without those records written, the whole operation, in effect, never happened.

Of course, this minister has no objection to sanctifying a *ménage à trois*, or even *a quatre, a cinq*, or any number. All it cares about is commitment. First it gathers commitment from everyone (phase one); and then he tells them all to complete (phase two). The minister could actually be Alice or Bozo, in disguise or being schizophrenic (as a separate process). Multi-phase operations like this are not just for transactions processing in clusters, as we shall see.

That's all well and good, but what does it mean in terms of the software that can reliably be used to fail over in a cluster? Does anybody really do all this stuff? Transaction processing systems do. (No surprise.) There are many of those, such as Digital's Reliable Transaction Router (RTR), IBM's CICS (nobody cares what the acronym stands for any more (it's resolutely non-meaningful), but more programmers know how to write for it than for any other commercial system), Transarc's Encina, BEA Tuxedo, and many others.

Transactional semantics are also a *sine qua non* of database systems; all of them provide it, and it's tested for in all popular commercial benchmarks.

Furthermore, everybody finally got sick and tired of running fsck in UNIX, so now virtually every modern UNIX has a transactional file system, although they're usually referred to as "log-based," Windows NT's file system has followed suit.

So databases, transaction systems, and file servers are OK for failover. That covers a lot of useful ground. It's at least the majority, if not the overwhelming majority, of uses of server systems, but it's by no means everything.

Technical computing in particular seldom has anything to do with transactions, except indirectly through the file system. Without it, you are not in good shape availability-wise. If your application doesn't have transactional semantics, cluster failover simply can't be depended on to work reliably. There is an alternative: Do a great, big transaction every once in a while by taking a checkpoint. By keeping successive checkpoints in alternating files, a system can always "back up" to the last consistent state and start over, which in some cases is quite adequate, and can serve to help technical computing quite a bit.

Also, just because you are using a database does not mean you always have useful transactional semantics in every case. In particular, when running a large query for decision support, it is quite possible that nothing will be committed until the query is complete. While you can start everything over again in the event of a failure, this isn't much consolation if the query is really large—and some have been known to run for multiple days. This is really very analogous to a long-running technical job, and the solution is the same: checkpoints. In this case, however, the database helps. "Simply" (it may not be all *that* simple) splitting the query into separate parts that commit intermediate results will allow restarting from those intermediate points, with transactional semantics assured at the checkpoints.

That completes the discussion of avoiding toxicity in your data.

As an aside, it leaves a niggling little question: Why on earth is that crucial file called a "log" file? Perhaps surprisingly, the answer involves logs. Wooden logs. The kind with bark on them. A little etymology:

In olden tymes, sailors needed to know how fast their ship was going, so they could figure out where they were when they couldn't see landmarks.[7] To do this, they would attach a rope to a log and toss the log overboard. The rope had knots in it at specific, regular intervals, and someone holding the rope would count how many knots passed through his hands in a specified time, giving a measure of speed. (That probably answers an unrelated niggling little question.) The number of knots, with related information like the time and compass heading, was entered by the navigator into what was called, with admirable directness, the log book. Obviously the log book was important and had to be kept safe, so it became the natural place to record any crucial information that had to be kept safe. Eventually the important data itself was referred to as the ship's log after its container. From there it's a natural progression, through other merchant-related professions, to the general notion of "logging" information sequentially in permanent form.

Pity the poor bloke who had to haul the log back on board a fast ship. Or, for that matter, has to write the log file on a big, fast transaction-processing system. The speed with which the log can be written can easily become a performance bottleneck.

12.5 Failing Over Communications _____

It took a bit or work, but Alice (the target) now not only has access to data, it has some assurance the data is valid. All that's needed is some clients, and it can start processing.

Clients get attached by telling a lie. Alice resets one (or more) of its communications adapters to respond to the IP address(es) that Bozo was using. Since communication is assumed not to work in the first place, it contains

---

7. Yes, that's also why they're called landmarks.

code that expects failures and lost messages; so it just tries again if nobody answers. So if **IP takeover**, as it is known, happens quickly enough, the clients never know the difference; they're still connected.

Unfortunately, connected does not necessarily mean totally functional. The client *people* using the computers may very well know the difference. When they began using the server, those people sat down and logged on, setting up sessions and doing things: navigating to various places in the data, entering information in advance of a query or update, and so on. We've just been through an exercise that ensures that the final results of the people's actions—data in the database, file system, or whatever—is not lost. But what about the sessions?

In many cases, they will be lost. It is common for the state of the session—for example, where someone is in their navigation—to be held on the server, but not kept in the database itself; that is deemed to be too slow for the response time required, or require too many database accesses, or something.

Thus the clients fail over their connections, all right, and then when the database or whatever has started on the target (Alice), they are all immediately presented with the log-on screen they saw when they originally connected.

After emitting mass groan, everybody logs on at once, which of course immediately brings the server to its knees. In large cases, for example with several thousand terminals attached to a server, the simultaneous re-log-on of all those clients can take hours. Once again, this is not exactly a prescription for speedy recovery from failure.

There are two basic techniques for fixing this one: persistent sessions on the server and using the intelligence of client workstations.

Persistent sessions are essentially what they sound like: The session state data is kept on stable storage and updated with transactional semantics. It's not necessarily part of the database, but if it's not it is kept in files that do fail over to the target system. Thus when things restart, the target system picks up that session data, too, and keeps going from where it left off. On IP-based systems, this must be done at some level of the application code, since IP has no notion of a "session"; that was one of the levels in the standard ISO communication model that was deliberately left out of IP on the grounds that it was too application-specific and complex. IBM SNA systems, on the other hand, have a session layer; in fact, it was SNA's session layer that was the starting point for the ISO session layer. That SNA layer can optionally be persistent, and fail over so clients maintain the state of their sessions. This is particularly useful when the clients are dumb, inexpensive terminals, of which there still are rather a lot out there.

Intelligent clients offer other options. On the Internet, for example, state is maintained between requests for Web pages by several means. In the first place, general navigational position is kept locally, as a stack of past-seen URLs. More detailed state data is kept locally too, in a unit called a "cookie." By passing the cookie back over the network to the server, the server can know from whom this request came. State data—for example, whether this person has an account, is logged on, has seen data posted since date so-and-so—can be kept in the cookie or stored in the server; if in the server, the cookie is used as an index to stored user data.

As a result of the cookie convention, Internet clients have no problem whatsoever failing over between servers in a cluster. The cookie contains or has a pointer to the entire state of the session, and the failover target system receives it on every communication after the first. (Cookies are also the source of a potential security hazard, since it is possible for them to pass arbitrary information back to the server without the user's knowledge. This hole has been patched in recent releases of browsers, however.)

Lotus Notes uses a slightly different but similar technique. A user logs on at a client workstation, which locally verifies that this person is allowed access by comparing with a locally-stored identification file. From then on, the client includes the logged-on user's encrypted identification with all accesses to servers, keeps session data on the client, and passes the needed information to the servers which trust the client. Some distributed file systems, such as Windows NT's, use a similar technique. Each of its remote procedure calls to the file server includes a userid validated locally; the security service fails over itself, and it's used to ensure that the userid is allowed to do whatever is requested in the remote procedure call.

All of this was prefigured, and to some degree has been surpassed, by transaction monitors. For many years their client code has understood failover explicitly. Their clients hold not just the IP address of the server but, optionally, the communications addresses of multiple servers: a primary one, and one or more backups in case the primary fails to respond. This is a much more reliable means of obtaining failover than blindly retrying the same IP address, while, on the server, the failover code frantically tries to move that IP address before time-outs expire and the client decides it's lost communication.

In some cases communication events themselves have been given transaction semantics: Either the entire data was sent, completely, and guaranteed to have arrived; or nothing has happened. This is the case with DEC's RTR, and may be the case with others (IBM's CICS, BEA Tuxedo, Transarc Encina, NCR's Top End, and so on); most support at least primary/secondary server specifications.

So, as was the case when considering the problem of toxic data, not all applications and subsystems will adequately cause clients to fail their communications over to the target in a cluster. However, the most important cases—Internet servers, file servers, transaction monitors—are covered.

12.6 Towards Instant Failover

The discussion above, with its discussion of users re-logging in and taking large amounts of time to get up to speed, brings up the issue of failover time. If hardware fault tolerance is used, failover is, for all practical purposes, instantaneous. The redundant hardware takes over in midstream with time delays that are either literally zero or measured in microseconds. However, hardware fault tolerance doesn't handle software failures. Where is the time spent in cluster-based failover?

Parts of it are spent in housekeeping: Mounting the volumes of disks that are taken over, reorganizing communications to take over IP address, etc. In addition, as we shall see later, response to heartbeat signal loss is usually deliberately delayed to avoid false error reactions; but that amounts to seconds at most, and usually less. The time to perform that housekeeping is usually what is quoted in high-availability cluster products as a minimum failover time, with a variation to cover the time to mount large numbers of disk volumes or very large disk volumes.

However, when those chores are finished, the target system isn't yet doing useful work. The programs and subsystems that the source was running have to be loaded and restarted. That can take quite a while. Some database subsystems do have a feature that allows them to be loaded and ready to go, on a trip wire, waiting for something to happen. That can speed things up quite a bit, but even after the load there are other tasks. First, the starting database has to run through the log file, making the updates that happened but aren't yet in the main data files, and potentially backing out partial updates that weren't committed; this is its part in maintaining transactional semantics. Second, it's necessary to warm up the database cache. Until the most repeatedly used information—particularly indices—are loaded from disk, the database won't be performing at full speed. Paradoxically, if the workload is a bad one with little reuse of data, this part doesn't take long at all since the contents of the cache aren't all that crucial to performance. Some measurements of startup on the TPC-C benchmark, which has some locality built into its references, indicate that on that benchmark the warm-up period on recent machines is only on the order of ten seconds.

In addition to the above, the user sessions that were in place at the time of failure have to be recreated, either automatically (durable sessions, cookies) or manually (everybody logs on again).

Adding this of all together it can easily take a long time to fully restart a large subsystem after a failure. Many cases do not; client-side session information, for example, is instantly available again after failover, and warming the cache doesn't always take forever. Nevertheless, the minimum times specified by vendors—typically a few tens of seconds—are usually lower bounds. However long it is, though, everyone would like it to be less than that, and in some cases even ten seconds is simply deemed inadequate.

There is, however, a technique that can produce nearly instantaneous failover in clusters. This is the notion of process pairs, originally developed by Tandem and always referred to in their literature as "Tandem's patented process pair technique."

The idea here is that for each source process of interest on one node, there is another strongly coupled target process on another node. Every time the source process changes its state, that change is reflected in the state of the target. This coupling can be performed by repeated node-to-node checkpoints of the contents of memory. Alternatively, it can be performed by structuring both processes to be "stateless" in the sense that they maintain none of their internal state in the normal manner. Instead, all changes to internal main memory data are treated like transactions, with a the second copy in the target used much like stable (disk) storage in a transaction system. When work comes in, the source process does it, makes a transactional change to its main memory as a result, and uses two-phase commit to ensure that it is recorded on the target side of the process pair. When another work item comes in, the state is queried to find out everything that normally would hang in main memory in the process. Since only memory-to-memory operations are involved, very fast inter-node communication will keep the overhead of all of this far below the overhead normally associated with transactional semantics.

Given a heartbeat from the source to the target—which can be piggy-backed on the state change messages—the target process is now completely primed to take over if the heartbeat stops. This effectively provides near-instantaneous failover, since none of the session-resumption, database cache warming, process starting, or other delays are required. The target has been kept current in all ways—including all those things—fully mirroring the state of the source.

Tandem has claimed that by using this technique, sub-second failover is achievable in the version of their NonStop SQL/MX database that they have ported to Windows NT.

This technique does have limitations. In particular, using it places limitations on the workload rebalancing that one must do when a node fails in a cluster. All the work done by the source process must be moved over to that target, because that's where the other half of the pair lies; it cannot be divided up and split among nodes. This may not be as bad as it sounds, however, as discussed in the next section.

12.7 Failover to Where?

We've not solved the whole problem when we've successfully attached correct data to the target, reattached the clients with their session state intact, and started up the services required. Those are the final steps, but we've left something out back at the start: Which system is the target?

When there are only two nodes in the cluster, and one of them just died, this is a reasonably straightforward question to answer. It becomes interestingly nontrivial when there are more than two nodes. Which work gets moved to which system? There are three sets of sub-cases to consider here: High-availability cluster add-on packages vs. full cluster systems; cross-cluster applications or subsystems; and shared data vs. shared-nothing.

There is a huge difference between whole systems designed as clusters and high-availability "add-ons" that concentrate on simply adding failover function. The difference is that the system clusters—such as DEC VMScluster, IBM Parallel Sysplex, and Tandem NonStop—have cluster-wide workload management functions to begin with. Work can be deployed across them automatically or semiautomatically to meet the combination of the load and user-selected work priorities. The add-ons don't have that function, unless it is itself another add-on, and in that case the functions provided are usually a straightforward load-based batch subsystem.

For the most part, the add-on packages provide a user exit allowing the customer to write a shell script or visual basic program with which anything can, in theory, be done. However, few users are going to use that to create their own full-scale workload management. A few static cases are all that is really feasible, for example:

> ➤ If Bozo dies, put jobs A & B on node Alice, the rest on node Clara;

> ➤ if Clara dies, put job D on Alice and E on Bozo;

> ➤ if Alice dies, (and so on).

"Groups" of jobs (resources) can be used to simplify the problem somewhat. If a resource dependency system is used, (as described in Section 12.3 on page 398) the system can ensuring that, for example, everything a resource depends on is in a group with that resource. Even with that aid, however, administrator-written scripts are unlikely to take into account daytime vs. overnight system loads, or the fact that one of the applications is currently under higher load than usual, and so on.

Of course, the exact same problem exists when a node rejoins the cluster (failback), or joins it for the first time. This can all be taken into account, but nobody is likely to write code for their own cluster that handles all cases; more general workload management solutions are far preferable.

If the cluster as a whole is primarily dedicated to one function, however, and that function is itself a cluster-parallel operation—such as a parallel database, or a cluster-parallel file system, or a cluster-parallel Internet server—then that subsystem can do a lot more if it has its own workload management built in, as many do. The user exits are then all that's needed, since all they will do is a passive translation; they merely turn a system failure notification into a subsystem call saying the same thing, telling the subsystem it can take action.

It would appear that those subsystems (as well as whole systems with cluster-wide workload management) have a decided advantage in this if they are organized as shared data, as opposed to shared nothing. With shared data, the work that came off the failed node can be uniformly distributed among the survivors in accordance with whatever priority rules are normally in force. With shared nothing, switching the disks from the failed node to another moves all the work over in a big lump. This would give one node double its normal load, unless a spare node was purchased that sat around doing nothing but waiting for this hopefully infrequent situation.

However, while this shared-disk advantage is not nonexistent, it is not quite as huge as the description above would make it appear. The reason is that shared-nothing systems can, and at least some do, divide the work on each single node into multiple parts; then those parts can independently failover to different nodes. Informix' parallel data base, for example, divides the data on each node into separate logical units that can independently be moved to other nodes. As another example, IBM's DB2 Parallel Edition for AIX operates in terms of "logical nodes," each of which is a work unit containing both processing and associated disk storage; several logical nodes are normally assigned to each physical node, and each logical node can independently fail over to other physical nodes.

Techniques like these don't directly give as fine-grained control over work reallocation as shared-disk appears to, but shared nothing never has that degree of control even under nonfailure situations; its proponents trade that off for other advantages, as was discussed in Chapter 10.

There is an interesting hardware implication of this discussion. In order to allow this flexibility—failing over one node's disks to many other nodes—*shared-nothing needs physical connectivity to disks that is the same as shared-disk.* Simple disk connectivity schemes, such as using only two-way connections in a chain, imply significant difficulties in load balancing after a failure. This assumes, of course, that every other node is not a spare; that is overkill.

12.8 Lock Data Reconstruction

For their part, shared-disk systems have to deal with a problem that shared nothing simply does not have: Reconstructing the state of system-wide locks after a failure. This is a obviously a problem whether the lock data is distributed among nodes (as with most shared-disk parallel databases, and DEC VMScluster), since some of the lock information will be held in memory on a node that just died. It is also a problem with a centralized locking implementation, such as IBM's Coupling Facility, since failure of the CF (which holds all locks) has to be managed too.

There are two distinct reasons why system-wide locks have to be recovered. First, the node that failed was without doubt holding locks of its own when it kicked the bucket. Unless those are unlocked and purged, they'll be held forever since nobody's ever going to "unlock" (release) them; the owner's dead. This will quickly cause system lockup as others run into those forever-held locks. The second reason is that whatever node failed was probably holding information for locks that other nodes were using; they won't be able to proceed far until that information is reconstituted.

The only way lock recovery can be accomplished is for redundant locking information to be held elsewhere in the system. In some cases this is simply a requirement placed on every subsystem or application using it by the global lock manager: You must keep track of all locks I give you, and be prepared to give me a list of them on notice. While ugly from a structuring point of view, the global-lock-using subsystems probably keep track of those locks already (for example, they have to check for deadlocks). So it's not as bad as it sounds, and it is potentially more efficient that the other alternative, which of course is for the global lock manager to itself keep a duplicate copy of the data.

That said, I will here deliberately refrain from even attempting to describe global lock state reconstruction, aside from saying that its implementations may well be the most complex programs ever put into production use on this planet. (Hint: What happens if, in the middle of the process, one of the other nodes dies?) That means they are also some of the hardest programs to get right.

While I won't say who, since the problem has since been fixed, it's been documented that in years past more than 80% of the whole-cluster outages of a certain well-known and widely-deployed cluster system (or maybe subsystem?) were caused when the system tied itself up into teeny tiny knots attempting to reconstruct the state of the global locks after a node failure.

12.9 Heartbeats, Events, and Failover Processing

We have now covered various issues involved in moving resources of many types from node to node in response to a failing node. What's left is to define the trigger: figure out when a node has died. Then we have to bring everybody together to actually run the detailed failover process.

As discussed back in Section 12.2 on page 394, failure information is extracted from a negative event: The node stops sending what are called **heartbeat** signals to other nodes. These are simple no-data or little-data messages sent around the system. The receivers set a time-out, and if it expires without receiving a heartbeat, the node whose heartbeat didn't arrive is declared dead.

Oh, if it were only that simple.

Heartbeat processing is actually a real-time task with hard, externally imposed deadlines. If a node misses its deadline, it will be presumed dead; other nodes will take over its IP address(es), fence it from interacting with its disks, and otherwise dismember it, with concomitant delays to the users of the system. We would really like to avoid that happening to a live node. However, virtually none of the operating systems to which clustering is applied has nearly adequate facilities for dealing with such tasks, meaning getting them done, on time, guaranteed. Such highly-constrained tasks are traditionally the domain of specialized real-time control systems, which do not provide all the other capabilities and features of a normal full-function operating system.

In a conventional operating system, the heartbeat send and receive processes can be "pinned" into dedicated memory that's never swapped out; and they can be given very high priority, so when it's time to run, they do tend to run immediately. However, it is much more difficult to give equivalently high priority to the complete stream of processing that must be done to actually send a message from node to node. What guarantees that even a promptly-initiated message doesn't get stuck behind a huge stream of application traffic in the communications stack?

This is like having a bunch of guys ready to confiscate your bank account, your house, your wife, your dog, and your pickup truck if one of them doesn't get a letter from you on time. And you sent it by normal mail. And it might be Christmas. (Sounds like a country song.)

These problems can be drastically alleviated by use of a bonded courier—in other words, use of the various low-overhead, virtualized, user mode cluster communication accelerators discussed in Chapter 5. Traffic problems never go away completely, since the communications media are shared. However, for example, it will be rather reliable, fast, and independent of other workload elements to slip a single NC-NUMA "store" into a traffic stream and cause a location on another node to be changed—which is all that's needed for a heartbeat.

One must, however, ask what is being verified by receiving messages over such a channel. It does little good to be getting reliable, fast, precise heartbeats from a system that might otherwise be completely waxed. The messages coming through a TCP/IP stack may be relatively unreliable, slow, and sloppy, but receiving them means more. It of course means that the communications stack and adapters are operating; it also implies that much of the scheduling and dispatching machinery of the transmitting system are functional, as is probably a great deal more.

Well-designed heartbeat subsystems, following this line of reasoning, attempt to get maximum information about a cluster's health by running multiple heartbeats that couple the cluster's nodes through every possible orifice. That includes using:

> ➤ normal communications, such as LAN and other communications adapters;

> ➤ all the cluster acceleration gear available;

> ➤ slightly less normal paths, such as RS232 links added between cluster nodes just to have a non-traffic-bearing, inexpensive link; and

> ➤ even signals sent across the I/O interconnect from node to node, using, for example, the "target mode" of SCSI busses. The latter is actually particularly valuable, since its operation gives evidence that much of the I/O and disk subsystem is functional.

This strategy has two implications.

In the first place, it means that somebody, somewhere, knows what all those orifices are, to say nothing of how they're connected and what all the nodes are. This is often an additional part of the system file that holds all the resource information, discussed in Section 12.3 on page 398, but it could be a separate file. Using that information, plus the current state of each node (up, down, quiescent), a heartbeat chain can be constructed that threads through every adapter or other portal once, connecting all the nodes of the system with minimal added overhead for heartbeating. Consistently communicated to all the heartbeat monitors (transaction semantics again), this forms the basis of heartbeat operation.

The second implication is that the immediate response of the system to loss of a heartbeat is: Wait.

The reason for waiting isn't to see if the heartbeat finally does arrive. The time-out values used should by themselves be adequate for that. Rather, the reason is that the first heartbeat loss doesn't provide enough information to conclude that a node is down.

If node Alice reports a lost heartbeat from node Bozo across a LAN adapter, it could mean that Bozo kicked the bucket. However, it could also mean that Bozo's LAN adapter croaked, or Alice's LAN adapter did likewise, or the network those adapters use is hosed by a broadcast storm originating elsewhere. If you wait a while—a kind of inverse time-out—more events will usually come rattling in that clarify the situation.

For example, if in short order node Clara also loses heartbeat from Bozo across RS232, and node Fred loses heartbeat across SCSI, and together all those things mean that none of Bozo's ports is responding, then it's a pretty good bet that you should "roll up" all those events into a single one, namely: Bozo has gone South (or West, if you live in the UK); it has become retrosand; it is in casters-up mode; it is an ex-computer.

That final rolled-together event, reliably broadcast to the remaining nodes of the cluster, begins Bozo's funeral rites.

Those rites are a sequence of cluster-wide events that must vary depending on the needs of the applications and subsystems running on the cluster. However, a typical sequence might include the following events, done by every member of the cluster, with each completed by all members before the next starts:

> establish a new heartbeat chain that excludes Bozo;

> inform parallel subsystems that were running on Bozo, such as databases, of what has occurred and is about to happen;

> fence Bozo off from its resources—disks and other storage devices in particular;

> form a cluster-wide, consistent plan defining how Bozo's resources and workload should be redistributed among the remaining nodes;

> execute the plan;

- This means actually move the resources, with each node acquiring them in the order defined by inter-resource dependencies. For this part in particular, individual subsystems may require their own unique sequences of cluster-wide coordinated steps; for example, shared-data databases or file systems will have to undergo global lock data reconstruction.

➤ inform subsystems that the resource reallocation process has been completed;

➤ resume normal operation.

The order of some of the steps above is somewhat arbitrary. For example, work could begin on the plan for moving Bozo's resources at any time prior to the fifth step where the resources are moved. For the most part, however, it is important that each step in a sequence like this be reliably complete throughout the cluster before the next step begins. For example, it would not be good at all to start moving resources without a plan that every node consistently follows, or to do so before Bozo has been fenced off; either case can result in "two sets of hands on the steering wheel" and chaos.

When Bozo comes back to life and wishes to rejoin the cluster, a similar sequence of events is followed, initiated by a message from Bozo to an advertised port listening for such messages. Obviously the step fencing Bozo off is not performed, but much the same collection things have to happen. When a brand new node arrives that has never before been part of the cluster, the sequence is again fairly similar but it has an added step: The new node must let the cluster know what resources it has to offer, how it is attached, and so on; and the cluster-defining resource files have to be updated.

Also note that what this process does, as is particularly evident in the planning phase, amounts to workload reallocation—load balancing—among the cluster nodes. Failure of a cluster node is a particularly drastic reason to perform such reallocation, but it need not be the only one. The whole process could instead be triggered by a substantial change in the workload, arising either from external causes (one of the home pages on your Internet server just got selected as the "cool site of the day") or from internal causes (a seismic program stopped reading Gigabytes of data and started analyzing it).

The implication is that if true cluster-wide workload management is performed, events like this are part of normal, not abnormal, operation. They are also much less traumatic if the subsystems and applications are cluster-aware and already running on multiple nodes, since less resource redistribution is required; they're already distributed.

It should be fairly clear from all the above that the cluster-wide parallel subsystem managing all this could make rather good use of a general facility for carrying out cluster-wide operations that have multiple global phases. These are rather like the two-phase commit process discussed back in Section 12.4.2 on page 406; that is still required as a basis for doing basic data updates, but additionally there's a need to extend such operations to many phases, such as the sequence described above. That is indeed the case, and a structure for doing so will be discussed in the next section.

Before doing that, however, a couple more points to complete the discussion of heartbeats and failure detection.

The discussion of heartbeating through every orifice was correct, but left something out. All it does is tell us that several hardware and system software pieces are functional. What we would really like to know is that the subsystems and applications are functioning. The cluster nodes could be communicating to beat the band, up and down every hole they have, while the database (for example) running across them sits there sucking its thumb and staring at its navel, catatonic.

Unfortunately, it is hard enough to get even marginally reliable real-time monitoring signals out of a process specifically designed to just do that function. Extending a general, large application to meet the requirements of avoiding page faults and obtaining short, regular, high-priority execution, is difficult to the point of near impossibility, particularly with the support provided by general-purpose operating systems.

Even embedding heartbeats in special-purpose processes hasn't been easy to tame in practice. For example, a typical error in cluster installation is to set the heartbeat rate too fast; because there's not enough time to get the heartbeats off under load, spurious failures are detected and failover processing started against fully functional nodes.

This problem can be attacked by doing the opposite of a heartbeat: a liveness check. Active system resources are sent messages whose only purpose is to elicit a response, thus giving an indication that the resource is still functional. Going back to our original analogy for failover, this is like node Alice (the back-seat driver) repeatedly asking Bozo, "Are you awake? Are you awake? Are you awake?" Putting aside its highly annoying aspects, obviously Bozo need only grunt in reply. Occasionally that isn't enough. People can grunt in their sleep, and programs can potentially respond adequately to such a test without being otherwise functional. So some systems go further, including less-frequent requests for a thorough investigation of how well the resource is functioning. Alice would make spurious conversation requiring a non-grunt reply: "Is it windy?" "How are we doing on gas?" "Have you changed the oil recently?" "Shouldn't you clean the windshield?"

Even liveness checks aren't foolproof. For the same reasons that heartbeats are hard to maintain in applications, the response time to a liveness check can vary radically. So, to more carefully follow the principle of "first, do no harm," a further addition is made to many heartbeat generators and cluster managers: a deadman switch.

The generator checks itself to see if it's managed to get its heartbeat sent, and the cluster manager watches to see if it's gotten a message that's its own obituary. If a node doesn't get its heartbeat sent in time, or has reason to believe that the rest of the cluster thinks it is dead, the best thing to do is to immediately commit suicide: force a system shutdown. That ensures that its hands, at least, are off the steering wheel. If the programmers of the system have some class, this will of course produce a console message starting "It is a far, far better thing that I do..."

12.10 System Structure _____

Up to now, we've examined the piece parts of high availability: failing over disks, communication, etc. We'll complete the discussion by looking at how the those pieces can be glued together to form complete high availability subsystems. While few examples of this have been published at any level of detail, two have: Microsoft's Windows NT Cluster Services, code-named "Wolfpack" after the cover on the first edition of this book[8]; and IBM's RS/6000 Cluster Technology, code-named "Phoenix." These target very different levels of support, as is described below.

12.10.1 IBM's RS/6000 Cluster Technology ("Phoenix")

"Phoenix" proper is not intended to be a complete high availability cluster implementation. Instead, it is a collection of services generally needed in any cluster. The services themselves are described later, since there is an question that must be answered first: What's the purpose of this product?

The point of Phoenix is that the services it provides are actually always present in any high availability cluster product, but have been, up to now, implemented under the covers of the cluster manager, usually in an idiosyncratic manner intended only to support the cluster manager itself. Phoenix' intention is to "clean up" and generalize those services, since they are in fact needed not just by the cluster manager but also by any cluster-parallel subsystem or application that wishes to achieve high availability.

Today, all such high availability, parallel programs must re-implement these services themselves. Not only is this extraordinarily difficult (*expensive*) pro-

---

8. They thought "dogpack" didn't sound cool enough. That may be right. But Savage Multiheaded Wolf doesn't cut it, either.

gramming to get right in the first place, it also has to work around cluster managers' user exits that often provide insufficient flexibility. The "Wolf-pack" product described in the next section, for example, has many situations where its own components "talk among themselves" to decide what to do, so it must internally do the kinds of operations Phoenix supports; but it externalizes nothing corresponding to Phoenix to simplify the creation of high-availability parallel applications.

It is, perhaps, not too far-fetched to suggest that the lack of Phoenix-like support is a major reason for the relative lack of sophistication of open system clusters compared with proprietary implementations. The proprietary versions, more tightly coupled to their privately implemented subsystems, have included those private subsystems as elements whose idiosyncrasies must be supported (see, for example, the comments about the IBM Parallel Sysplex lock manager on page 128). So whatever else may be true of that support—it could be very odd in structure—it is adequate for the subsystems. Open systems, on the other hand, have generally exported only the most primitive facilities—a user exit to which a shell script can be attached, for example. This means that the kind of system-wide, multiple phase operation necessary to actually perform failover in a parallel program—like that discussed on page 421 in the last section—must be reimplemented within the subsystem in response to that shell script. Phoenix provides an infrastructure that makes such coordinated actions simpler to implement.

Since Phoenix originally arose out of a desire to extend IBM's HACMP cluster product to the large number of nodes available on IBM's RS/6000 Scalable Parallel system, its implementation is also highly scalable. Designed to work on at least 512 nodes, it has achieved operation on over 400 nodes in the lab and is the basis of a high-availability cluster manager—HACMP Enhanced Scalability (HACMP ES)—that operates on 16-node clusters.

The core services of Phoenix are called Topology Services, Group Services, and the Event Manager. They interrelate as shown in Figure 111. All three are parallel/distributed programs: The entire set of core services runs on every cluster node, and each node's instance communicates with its counterparts on other nodes. Each also is highly available; failure of any node doesn't compromise its operation, including in particular failures that occur while that operation is under way (not a trivial thing to do). Figure 111 also shows a recovery driver. This is not one of a core components, but is necessary in any high-availability failover implementation. Other applications that wish to use Phoenix' services—which was the whole point of cleaning up and externalizing them—plug into those services in exactly the same place as the recovery driver, as shown in the figure.

Figure 111 IBM "Phoenix" Organization

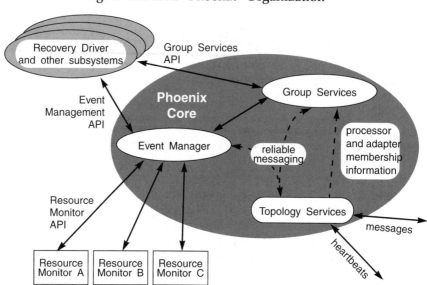

Topology services is a layer underlying the other two components; it has no externally visible interface. Topology services performs heartbeating across all nodes and through all adapters, using the information gathered to dynamically maintain a map of the cluster that shows the state of all nodes and inter-node adapters; that map is maintained on every node. In addition to membership information, the map is used to provide a reliable messaging service to the other components: If any path exists between cluster nodes, Topology Services knows about it and can use it. This ensures that network failures can't be misinterpreted as node failures unless all the adapters into a node fail.

The **event manager** provides a way to inform a program running anywhere in the cluster when something of interest happens anywhere else; the intention is to allow programs to monitor the health of resources on which they depend, so appropriate action can be taken when those resources fail. It is, in effect, a reliable way to transfer information either (a) from outside the collection of Phoenix-supported applications into that collection; or (b) between different process groups using Phoenix' services (inter-group). In contrast, as we shall see, group services provides, a way for the processes of a group to communicate among themselves (intra-group).

An event can be literally anything: a file system running out of space, processor utilization going too high, or anything else measurable. A general application program interface (API) allows the creation of custom resource

In Search of Clusters ✳

monitors (as shown in Figure 111) which supply information to the event manager about the state of resources in the form of resource variables; for example, one resource variable might be the amount of paging space left on node Bozo. Resource monitors change the state of those variables whenever they wish, calling the event manager's API. Events actually "happen" not when a resource variable changes, but rather when a predicate associated with it becomes true. For example "paging space < 500KB on node Bozo."

While the currently deployed implementation does not do so, it is planned that at some point the event manager will guarantee that client processes monitoring multiple events on different nodes see all events in the same sequential order, even if they occur nearly simultaneously on different nodes. Because of unpredictable communication delays, that order may not be the "real" order as seen by some omniscient observer—which, as in general relativity, cannot exist inside the system—but it will be a consistent order. This is an extremely important property that avoids the nasty problem of having one part of a cluster-parallel program go off and react to event A (like moving work from node A to node B) while another part is reacting to a different event in a possibly conflicting way (like the paging space on node B is dangerously low, so work should be shifted from B to A). The parenthetical example is tough enough to deal with without having conflicting notions of what is happening. This consistent-order property was not part of the initial implementation, however, since that targeted at supporting HACMP ES, which does not directly use it.

While the event manager provides a way to inform parallel/distributed programs that events of interest have happened, it does not give those programs any help in actually responding to those events. That is the province of group services.

Group Services is Phoenix' key externalized interface help programs to deal with issues of high availability. As the name implies, it deals with groups: groups of processes spread across the nodes of the cluster.[9] What group services does—and all it does—is communicate changes of group membership and group state in a consistent way among all members of each group. "Group state" can of course include any information at all, such as the

While any process can apply for membership to any group, the usual situation is that all the instances of each parallel application or subsystem, one or more per node, will form a group, separate from other parallel applications.

9. These are completely different from the resource groups discussed in Section 12.3 on page 398. Those were collections of resources that were to be moved from one node to another together. These groups are the collections of processes that, running on different nodes, form a parallel program.

The event manager processes, for example, form a group; so would processes of a parallel database system. In fact, most database systems have enough different kinds of processes that they may form several groups: one for the back-end database engine proper, one for printing, one for communications front ends, and so on. This makes it easier for those different functions to do their own, modularized, recovery from the failure of a node. The printer queue recovery code, for example, need know nothing of the horrors of lock data reconstruction.

Changes to the group state can be proposed by any member of a group. It is performed by a general N-phase protocol which can implement several useful operations:

> **One-phase** operation simply transmits information to all members, guaranteeing that everybody sees it in the same order. It is, in effect, a reliable, ordered broadcast. For greater efficiency, a "window" of three to five of these transmissions can be in operation at once. It is nevertheless guaranteed that every client process sees them all in the same order, even under a variety of nasty failure conditions (nodes, communications, etc.). This is decidedly nontrivial to implement.

> **Two-phase** operation is a way to provide the two-phase commit processing necessary to achieve transactional semantics, which has numerous applications in allowing an application to maintain consistently nontoxic data.

> **Multi-phase** operation provides a series of steps in which everybody in the group completes the tasks of each step before anybody begins doing the next. The failover sequence described in the previous section (page 421) is a case where this is useful. In general, it is a form of control referred to as "barrier synchronization": Everybody must wait at a "barrier" that is lowered only after all the participants have reached it.

Except for one-phase operations, which are labelled as such when proposed, the number of phases is in effect controlled by a "while" loop rather than a fixed-iteration "for" or "do" loop. This is done by having the client processes' return messages be votes. They vote on whether to stop successfully, abort the whole process, or continue with another phase. A concluding message brodcast at the end of each operation informs the clients of the difference between success and failure. Any client returning "abort" causes failure, as required by two-phase commit; all must agree to "accept" for a successful termination.

One-phase operation is actually different in kind from the others, for two reasons: First, it's really not "proposed;" it is unconditionally sent out, and

            In Search of Clusters ✳

nobody votes to accept or reject it. (They can ignore it, however.) Second, multiple one-phase broadcasts can be in operation at the same time, allowing higher efficiency. Multi-phase operations (including two-phase) are, in contrast, atomic throughout the cluster in the sense that each phase is completed across the entire group before another one begins. The effect of an atomic, rather than just ordered, broadcast may be required anyway, despite the increase in serialization it entails; this can be achieved by proposing a a change using the multi-phase protocol, with everybody accepting the change on the first returned vote.

The voting protocol is also followed when a client tries to join a group. A prospective member can be "blackballed" by a single rejection—for example, it might not know the secret password needed for security purposes. In addition, leaving a group can be voluntary (orderly shutdown, for avoiding planned outages), the result of failure (crash!), and *involuntary*: a client can be *evicted* if one group member proposes it and the rest of the group agrees.

This is potentially useful. One can imagine a scenario where one member says "I've been getting garbled, trashy data from Joe, which makes me think he should be rebooted. The rest of you guys agree?" "Yeah." "Sure, why not." (Joe: "No, no, I'm all rigRhfd&%@!") "OK, let's give him the wedgie of death." However, it also makes joining a group a little like joining a fraternal organization. One imagines group names like "The Benevolent Protectorate of Volume Groups." It appears that someone in Phoenix development with a subtle sense of humor is be aware of this, since what I've called a "client" they call a "supplicant." (At least they did in development. Lawyers nixed it for the product, being afraid it would offend someone.)

While group services guarantees that only one multi-phase operation is in progress for a given group at a time, it will simultaneously run different groups' operations. Thus, for example, several different applications can be recovering from node failure simultaneously. This is desirable for efficiency, but causes a problem with resource dependencies. The group controlling disk volume access, for example, had better finish its work before the group controlling a parallel file system starts recovering. To avoid this, a group can designate itself as the target of another group, called the source. When this is done, all operations of the same type—like membership changes—are performed on a source before any target groups' operations are begun.

Throughout the Phoenix core services there is an underlying current of cluster-wide consistency and ordering: topology services presents a consistent map of the cluster, event services spreads gossip to everyone, group services makes cluster-wide groups act in parade ground formation.

A single technique is used throughout the current implementation to achieve this: A leader process is chosen on one of the nodes, and all operations flow through the leader. Thus, for example, a group services peon daemon (non-leader) on one node doesn't just broadcast a state change request it receives; instead, the peon sends that request to the leader, who queues it with other received requests and broadcasts the queued elements back out, one change per group at a time (except for one-phase requests).

Use of a leader in this way makes the implementation of Phoenix' ordering and consistency functions dramatically easier than otherwise would be the case. Several hard distributed problems must still be solved, in particular electing the leader in the first place, and arranging for an orderly, consistent transfer of the mantle of leadership when nodes go down and up (particularly when they go down and up while transferring the mantle). However, those exact algorithms can be reused in every component, letting the leader code alone contain the code that provides the subservice's function.

As a final comment on Phoenix, note that as stated at the start of this section it doesn't actually do anything itself. Using Phoenix, one can much more easily create parallel applications that gracefully recover from failure, and provide for resources like disks, and so on. But it is not intended to do those things itself.

12.10.2   Microsoft's Cluster Services ("Wolfpack")

Microsoft's "Wolfpack," on the other hand, is a self-contained high-availability cluster product[10]—one of many available, from many vendors, as was shown in Chapter 2, "Examples." Phase I of Wolfpack, while designed and written to handle more than two nodes, is more restricted than most such products since it has been tested only for the two-node case.[11] Phase II will support more nodes.

The primary components of Phase I and their relationships are shown in Figure 112 [MS97]. To understand what all the parts do and how they interact, let's walk through the process of starting up a node in a cluster and failing something over.

When a cluster node is booted, the cluster services are automatically started under the control of the event processor. In addition to its normal role of dispatching events to other components, the event processor performs initial-

---

10. As this is written, "Wolfpack" is actually not a finished product, but rather in its second Beta phase. Presumably it will have reached general availability by the time this book is published.

11. Given the characteristics of this area, that means that it is guaranteed to exhibit instant catatonia if presented with three nodes. Two is always a special case, even if you try not to make it so.

Figure 112 Microsoft "Wolfpack" Organization

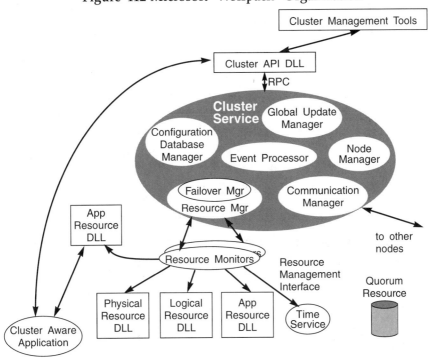

ization and then tells the node manager, also called the membership manager, to join or create the cluster.

The node manager's normal job is to create a consistent view of the state of cluster membership, using heartbeat exchange with the other node mangers. It knows who they are from information kept in its copy of the cluster configuration database, which is actually part of the Windows NT registry (but updated differently, as we'll see). The node manager initially attempts to contact the other nodes; if it succeeds, it tries to join the cluster, providing authentication (password, cluster name, its own identification, and so on). If there's an existing cluster and for some reason our new node's attempt to join is rebuffed, it immediately dies of a broken heart: system shutdown. Have to go fix the password or provide a better pick-up line or something.

However, if nobody responds to a node's requests to join up, the node manager tries to start up a new cluster. To do that, it uses a special resource, specified like all resources in the configuration database, called the quorum resource. There is exactly one quorum resource in every cluster. It's usually a disk; if it is, it's very preferable to have it mirrored or otherwise fault tolerant, as well as multi-ported with redundant adapter attachments, since otherwise it will be a single point of failure for the cluster. The device used as a quorum resource can be anything with three properties: it can store data durably (across failures); all cluster nodes can get at it; and it can be seized by one node to the exclusion of all others. (SCSI and other disk protocols like SSA and FC-AL allow for exactly this operation.)

The quorum resource is effectively a global control lock for the cluster. The node that successfully seizes it *uniquely defines* the cluster. Other nodes must join with that one to become part of the cluster. The very important thing this prohibits is the nasty problem of a partitioned cluster.

It's possible (but you should configure things so that it's highly unlikely) for internal cluster communication to fail in a way that breaks the cluster into two or more parts that can't communicate with each other. What do you do in such a split brain cluster? Keep both running? Then how do you reconcile the inevitable differences that will arise between them?

The solution used here is: He who controls the quorum resource *is* the cluster, and there is no other cluster. Any node that can't talk to *the* cluster, or get control of the quorum resource to be the cluster, should please drop dead. Which is what a node partitioned from the cluster does: an immediate system shutdown.

So the owner of the quorum has a "quorum" in the parliamentary sense that it alone is the nucleus of the group that can perform the cluster's business. This is true even in the—cosmically unlikely—event that it's a partition of just one node in a 32-node cluster, and all the other nodes are operational but can't talk to that one. At least this serves to keep the state of the system consistent, correctly following the "first, do no harm" rule.

The quorum owner's job isn't permanently secure, however; if it fails, someone else must pick up its position. In addition to the normal heartbeat monitoring, Wolfpack also employs a challenge/defense protocol that keeps trying to take ownership of the quorum device away from the cluster leader. Should a challenge succeed, the leader is replaced.

Once a node joins or forms a cluster, the next thing it does is update its configuration database to reflect any changes that were made while it was away. The configuration database manager can do this because, of course, changes to that database must follow transactional semantics consistently across all the nodes and, in this case, that involves keeping a log of all changes stored on the quorum device. (Transactional semantics, mediated by the configuration database manager and the global update manager, are the key difference previously mentioned between updating the configuration database and a normal Registry update.) This arrangement has the good property that node Bozo can fail; then the rest of the cluster can fail; then Bozo can come up again, with nobody else around, and start from where they left off, including the stuff done while he was asleep.

After catching up on the latest gossip using the quorum resource's log, our new node should now start doing something useful. This means acquiring resources. These can be disks, IP names, network names, applications, or anything else that can be either off-line or on-line. They're all listed (where else?) in the configuration database, along with the nodes they would prefer to run on, the nodes they can run on (some might not connect to the right disks or networks), their relationships to each other, and everything else about them. Resources are typically formed into and managed as groups. For example, an IP address, a file share (sharable unit of a file system), and a logical volume might be the key elements of a group that provides a network file system to clients. Dependencies are tracked, and no resource can be part of more than one group, so sharing of resources by two applications is prohibited (and, as a result, Figure 107 on page 399, which I used to illustrate dependency, would be illegal).

Our new node's failover manager is called upon to figure out what resources should move (fail over) to the new node. It does this by negotiating with other nodes' failover managers, using information like the resources' preferred nodes. When they have come to a collective decision, any resource groups that should move to this one from other nodes are taken off-line on those nodes; when that is finished, the Resource Manager begins bringing them on-line on the new node.

The actual calls to the resource-specific code that bring things off- and on-line are performed in a resource monitor. This is in a separate address space from the cluster services for safety, since resource monitors potentially invoke third-party or user code that actually brings up the resources, and there's no guarantee that code won't Do Harm, and Grievous Bodily Harm at that, to the whole cluster by hosing the cluster services. The interface is through a standard resource API, which calls dynamic linked libraries (DLLs) that translate from that API into something the resources understand. Any application can, like Tommy, become aware by having a set of those DLLs written. If some of those pinball wizards are known to be particularly flaky (read: being debugged) (even if they're at release 7), separate resource monitor processes can be created to isolate them from the more well-behaved resources. There's a "generic" DLL to handle unaware applications, just bringing them up and down with parameters.

The new node is now up and being useful. Its resource monitors regularly call on its resources for liveness checks ("Tommy, can you hear me?"), and the node manager keeps heartbeating, and all's right with the world until something goes wrong.

If it's a resource gone bad—no reply to a liveness check—it can be restarted in the same node, or, perhaps after trying that a few times, moved elsewhere; maybe it'll be happier on another node. (Dratted Heisenbugs. Who knows?) If any resource group member is caught failing, the whole group is recycled or moved as a unit.

However, if the node manager stops getting heartbeats on some channel, a few additional things happen. First, it immediately starts talking among the other node managers to construct a cluster-wide consistent state (maybe it's just him). While that's happening, any nodes detecting something funny cease all writes to all shared devices—kind of a reverse, hopeful fence operation—until the event roll-up is complete and everybody knows whether it's just a dead adapter, or a dead network, or a dead node, or whatever. The agreed-upon change in state is written to the configuration database, and the failover managers start renegotiating who gets what resources. This whole operation is called "regroup," and is a five-phase protocol (of the kind discussed in the prior section on Phoenix).

A few further items, and then we're done.

Another resource, other than the quorum, that's always in a Wolfpack cluster is the time service. This is implemented as a normal resource; esthetics kept me from trying to make it connect to a resource monitor through a DLL in Figure 112, but it does. It is used to establish a consistent notion of time across the cluster. Doesn't have to be correct, of course, just consistent.

There is also, naturally, an API into the cluster services itself that can be used to create a nice GUI for cluster system management and allow mediated access to cluster information (like the resource database) from applications.

Wolfpack, and before it Digital Clusters for Windows NT, speaks of presenting a kind of cluster single system image to clients by providing *virtual servers* (or exporting virtual resources). What this really means is associating a service with an IP name (or other network name) and making the IP name and the rest of the stuff needed to do the service into a resource group. The group can then fail over from one node to another in a cluster, moving the server to another node while retaining the same external identity.

12.11 Related Issues

The preceding parts of this chapter covered issues directly related to high availability in clusters. There are, however, some related issues that bear further discussion: the link between high availability and scaling; disaster recovery; a summary of hardware fault-tolerance techniques; and finally, a discussion of why the cluster competition—SMPs and CC-NUMA systems—are not highly available, and why their problems in this regard not simple to deal with.

That is what follows.

12.11.1   The Link To Scaling: Cost

Back in Section 12.1 it was mentioned that clusters' use of standard (and in some cases "commodity") systems intrinsically lowered the cost of clusters' high availability compared with traditional hardware fault tolerance. It was also mentioned that there was another element.

That is the relationship between high availability and scaling. This relationship is some combination of trivial, arcane, or very significant, depending on your point of view. It does, however, place a rather different light on scaling.

Take a look at Table 17, which makes this relatively obvious, but seldom made, point: The more nodes there are in a cluster, the less you pay for high availability.

Table 17   Scaling Makes Availability Affordable

Number of Nodes	Primary	Performance Loss on 1 Node Failure	Backup for 100% Capacity	Cost of Backup
1		100% (outage)		100% minus disks
2		50%		50% minus disks
4		25%		25% minus disks

The assumption in that table is that the same amount of computational work is done in each case, but there's a choice: It could be done on just one node; or it could be done on two nodes by using cluster parallel operations with performance scale up; or it could be done on even more nodes, with more scaling of performance. As the number of nodes increases, the performance loss on node failure becomes less and less severe, and the cost of backup facilities to maintain 100% capacity becomes less and less.

Furthermore, the cost is actually substantially less than shown. The reason is that a large proportion of the cost of most commercial systems lies in the disks, and, assuming a switchover organization with a highly available disk subsystem, it is unnecessary to duplicate the disks.

Obviously if the scaling is less than perfect this exact ratio won't hold, and in any event there will be "breakage": No number of smaller systems will add up to exactly equal the power of one, even counting inefficiencies. This, however, is nitpicking.

The main point is that it is *desirable* to use computers that *individually cannot fulfill the job requirements*. This result stands in sharp contrast to the directions of those who target ever larger single systems, usually SMPs. It is also in contrast to the usual motivation for scaling, which is to perform a task that is too big for the largest available single system.

It also implies a different target for scaling efforts. There is a problem with design for scaling, namely: Where do you stop? What number of nodes is sufficient? Working with the usual motivation—"Power. Must get more power."—there is, as with the human hunger for power, no defensible maximum. This ends up leading to wholly qualitative arguments, and a final choice that may be based on felicity of advertising or individual developers' strengths of personality, since there is no good reason, ever, to put a lid on it.

In contrast, the motivation shown here, arising from cost of availability, has a built-in limiting factor. The utility of this use of scaling drops in inverse proportion to the system size. For example, when the number of nodes is 16, the availability costs are at worst on the order of 6%. Even without taking the "disk factor" into account, this is negligible. Systems with thousands of nodes are clearly not a necessary response to the extremely important system requirement of high availability.

12.11.2   Disaster Recovery

Disasters differ from other failures in that they are distributed over an area. While "normal" failures (interesting concept) or maintenance may render a single device or piece of software inoperable for a while, disasters take out *everything* in a room, building, city, or other geographical area. While one thinks of earthquakes, terrorism, floods, and so on as disaster causes, it's far more common to have a disaster-class outage from power loss or storm damage. The key to riding out events like these is the ability to resume operations—in some sense, fail over—on a system that is outside the scope of the disaster, and so necessarily in a different geographical area.

In businesses that use computers heavily, disasters can really hurt. In fact, the corporate mortality rate they can produce is astonishing. The University of Minnesota conducted a study in the Minneapolis regional area, looking at insurance, banking, and other heavily computer-dependent industries. With disaster-caused outages of less than six days, 25% of the companies studied immediately went bankrupt, 40% were bankrupt within two years, and less than 7% were still in business after five years. That should enough to scare anybody into putting together a disaster recovery plan. Less than 7% of companies ultimately survive a loss of their computing facilities that lasts 6 days. That's a mortality rate worse than the Ebola virus. However, take it with a grain of salt. I do, since I have to say that I'm reporting this only from a summary of the study; I've no way to know, for example, whether it is corrected to include the effects of "normal" business failures from other causes during that same period. Even discounting that, a 93% death rate is cause for alarm.

Just as the second sure thing after death is taxes, another reason for doing disaster recovery is that government regulations sometimes require it. For example, U.S. Federal Reserve regulations require that banks connected to the federal banking network limit any service interruption to under six hours.

How is disaster recovery accomplished? Obviously, some form of data replication is required; disk switchover in the sense discussed in section 12.4.1 can't be used, because the disks that are switched are all in one place. However, the replication isn't necessarily what was implied by the figures in that section. Quite often, seemingly crude methods are used quite effectively. This is illustrated in the seven "tiers" of disaster recovery that were defined at the 1992 SHARE conference (IBM user's group) by the Automated Remote Site Recovery Task Force.

> **Tier 0** obviously contains nothing worth discussing, even though it's rather common.

> In **tier 1**, you occasionally take a backup of all data, load it on a truck, and take it somewhere else—preferably fairly far away. In the event of a disaster, you get out the truck again, retrieve the data, and go look for a computer to put it on. There are companies that can be contracted with to provide systems equivalent to yours to use in cases like this.

> **Tier 2** is like tier 1, except that you drive the truck to your own duplicate system site. There you store the data and load it on when there's a disaster. Again, there are companies that provide such duplicate sites, hoping that not all their clients will want to use them at the same time (just like insurance companies).

Table 18 Tiers of Disaster Recovery

Tier	Description
0	no disaster recovery
1	PTAM (Pickup Truck Access Method[a])
2	PTAM to a hot site
3	electronic vaulting
4	active secondary
5	two-site, two-phase commit (of key data)
6	zero data loss

a. "Access Method" is mainframe-ese for "file system." Approximately. So this could be a PTFS, but that's unpronounceable. "Pee-tam" rolls off the tongue.

➤ In **tier 3,** electronic vaulting, you replace Tier 2's pickup truck with wires, making it more convenient to send backups more regularly.

➤ **Tier 4,** active secondary, also sends data electronically to a duplicate site. In addition, however, this tier keeps the data loaded and ready to go on the secondary site, not just sitting in a room on tape. At this point, you need to own (or rent) that duplicate site for your own permanent use.

➤ **Tier 5** makes sure the secondary is continuously up to date by doing a two-phase commit between the primary and the secondary for key data. Other data is handled less rigorously by occasionally sending backups. Note that any data with transactional semantics can be handled this way, including not just databases but file systems; with such semantics, "geographical mirroring" products exist which mirror disks over distances and make this and higher levels relatively easy to implement.

> ➤ The ultimate zero data loss situation is the highest tier, **tier 6**. There, all data, not just some, is continuously updated at a secondary site that's ready to go.

It's worth emphasizing that a key difference between the higher-tier techniques and "normal" clusters is the distance between the nodes. That causes delays that can strongly affect performance in the cross-system commit tiers. Grey and Reuter [GR93] point out that a full two-phase commit isn't always necessary, and in fact is seldom used. They divide the possibilities for Tiers 5 and 6 into three cases:

1-safe: The primary site commits all transactions. After committing each, it asynchronously writes the log to the backup site. This has only a minor impact on performance. It can lose transactions, but won't lose many if the delay to the other site is low.

2-safe: If the backup site is operational, each transaction's log records are written to the backup before committing the transaction. The primary commits only after getting a response that the log was received. This arrangement cannot lose transactions. On the other hand, it does impact performance because commitment is delayed. The size of the impact obviously depends on the delay to the backup site.

Very safe: This is the only case that literally performs two-phase commit between the sites. Each transaction is committed only when both primary and secondary commit. It loses performance and, while more reliable, is actually less available than the others, since it cannot function if either site is out of order. Grey and Reuter [GR93] commented that they knew of no places where it's used in practice.

Several database vendors provide facilities for 1-safe and 2-safe systems, and all transaction monitors can do the very safe case. Support for file systems and other non-database applications is spottier, but as of mid-1997 at least one disk subsystem vendor (EMC) and at least cluster vendor (IBM's HACMP) provided a "geographical mirroring" facility that at least supports 1-safe processing for transactional file systems and other transactional applications.

Are systems like these, sometimes spread across a whole continent, really clusters?

My personal mental image of a cluster is of something physically compact. There is an argument that continent-spanning systems like these are clusters, too, since they share many of the same characteristics. Customers want the same kind of single system administration across disaster recovery boundaries that they want for clusters (and only get in a few cases). In addition, there are disaster recovery scenarios with more than two sites. For example, at least one rather large communications service provider splits its U.S. tracking and billing operations among three centers distributed across the continental U.S. Disaster recovery is also done between those sites. This results in the same kinds of workload redistribution issues that clusters have when there are more than two nodes. It also brings in the cost advantages of using scaling with high availability in clusters. Furthermore, two of the full-system cluster products on the market, Tandem's Himalaya and DEC's OpenVMS Cluster, provide support within their cluster image for systems far enough apart to encompass true disaster tolerance. DEC's OpenVMS Cluster, for example, can operate with FDDI links up to 40 km long.

So I'm doing stretching exercises on my mental image. It's not quite there yet, but it is getting closer.

12.11.3 *Hardware Fault Tolerance & Repair Techniques*

The techniques by which hardware can be made to tolerate failures are not directly the subject of this book. However, the nodes of clusters, and data stores, must make adequate use of these techniques or the second half of the requirements for immortality—the definition of "high availability" proposed in Section 12.1.4 on page 393—cannot be fulfilled: Each node must be sufficiently unlikely to fail in the first place that it's highly likely that repairs can be done before a second point of failure brings down the entire system. So a short summary is included here for completeness, and the issue of repair ("hot plug") is discussed at the end of this section.

Hardware fault tolerance techniques can be divided into four categories, as illustrated in Figure 113

As indicated in the figure, different techniques are used depending on whether the purpose is to find out that faults have occurred (fault detection) or keep on operating in the presence of faults (fault tolerance). Actually, what everybody really wants to do is the latter. Detection techniques are used to "kick the problem upstairs" to a higher level—software, cluster control code—which then fixes the problem or arranges to tolerate it. Similarly, different techniques are used depending on whether the thing being

Figure 113 Hardware Fault Tolerance Techniques

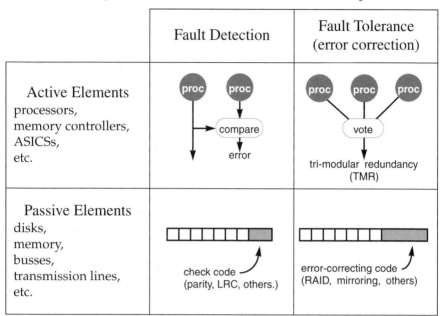

	Fault Detection	Fault Tolerance (error correction)
Active Elements processors, memory controllers, ASICSs, etc.	proc proc compare error	proc proc proc vote tri-modular redundancy (TMR)
Passive Elements disks, memory, busses, transmission lines, etc.	check code (parity, LRC, others.)	error-correcting code (RAID, mirroring, others)

checked is active—a processor, or logic in general—or passive, a container of some sort for data.

Fault detection on active elements is done by having two of them and comparing their outputs. If they differ, something's wrong. You don't know which one is wrong, but you do know something is wrong. This is useful because the system can stop immediately—a technique called *fail-fast*—rather than waiting for the error to propagate into somewhere noticeable. This is extremely useful. It was (and is) used by Tandem in their systems for that reason, and is also used by others. Fault tolerance is attained by having at least three copies of a unit, and a voter: the majority is considered the correct output. If there's an error, an additional output is turned on to indicate that, but the system does not have to stop. There are intellectually interesting logical puzzles involved in these arrangements: How do you know that it's not the comparator or voter that's wrong? When you add those compare or vote elements, you add more things to the system that can fail; how do you keep them from decreasing the system availability as a result? *Quis custodiat custodies?* There are techniques that solve these conundra, (for computers, anyway) but they're well beyond the scope of this book.

A long time ago, as this industry goes, both of those techniques were typically used on small logic elements, even individual logic gates. The innards of processors, registers, internal busses, and so on were individually checked. This is seldom done to the extent it used to be; there may be parity checking the data in some register files and caches (see below for what that means), but nobody builds, for example, self-checking adders that make sure the addition logic hasn't fouled up. They used to.

Instead, it's now more common to apply comparison or voting to whole microprocessors—hence the "proc" in Figure 113—or even to whole computers. Occasionally variants on standard microprocessors are provided that optionally turn every output into an input, and compare that input with the internally generated signal that would have been output; this makes it a lot easier to compare two microprocessors, since otherwise the compare logic would require an inordinate number of pins (and not much logic). Whole-computer comparisons (or voting) are done by comparing the data they emit through their I/O streams. In both the whole-computer and whole-processor cases, what's effectively being argued—fairly reasonably—is that you don't care what's gone on inside as long as the effect on the external world is correct. This is a behaviorist psychology school of computers, as it were.

The TMR organization is not infrequently supplanted by a slightly different one, called "pair and a spare." This uses two sets of units, each set a pair that does self-checking like the upper left quadrant of Figure 113. All are run in lock step, with identical inputs and (barring errors) identical outputs; no performance is gained by having four processors instead, for example of one. Instead, the idea is that if one self-checking pair goes casters up, the other can keep running—and, even before repair takes place, the system is still fail-fast.

All these techniques are generically called NMR, for N-way Modular Redundancy. TMR is the most frequently used of the possible *MR acronyms, but others do occasionally appear.

Techniques for protecting data are completely different. They all consist of appending additional redundant data that provides an internal consistency check on the entire ensemble. There is a well-developed theory associated with this that can be used to provide a continuum of checking from the minimal to the incredibly paranoid. So it is strictly incorrect to divide it as I have done in the figure, between error detection and error correction; but in practice that division is appropriate.

The familiar parity bit is an example of pure checking. It exists only to enforce the condition that there always is an odd number of "1" bits in a section of data, typically a single byte. If there's an even number, you know something's wrong, but not what. The Longitudinal Redundancy Code (LRC) often added to transmitted data are another example. This is effectively a collection of parity bits (or more complex functions) applied verti-

In Search of Clusters ✳

cally to a column of numbers in binary notation. The value the code should have is recomputed at the receiver, and once again if it doesn't match what's transmitted something is known to be wrong.

What's wrong can be deduced by using more bits, forming what's called an error-correcting code (ECC). For example, there is a rather clever scheme called a Hamming Code in which the last $\log_2 N$ bits of a N-bit ensemble (data plus check code) is used to pick out the bit in that number that is incorrect. This includes pinpointing errors in the added check code. Obviously, if you know which bit is incorrect, flipping its value fixes the error. This kind of thing can be taken to extremes, allowing codes that can correct N errors or detect M (M>N) errors. The usual practical stopping point is abbreviated as SECDED, for Single Error Correction, Double Error Detection.

However, losing a single bit or a collection of bits is often less likely than what's called a *burst* error: A bunch of mistakes all at once. When a disk drive stops spinning, you sure do get that. Similarly, it happens when a whole memory chip goes dead, or there's a lightening strike near a transmission line that turns all transmitted bits to 0 for a few milliseconds. Yet more techniques have been developed to counter these slings and arrows of outrageous fortune. They often consist of arranging the error correction in an appropriate distribution that takes into account the physical units likely to fail. That's done for memories, for example, by making sure the codes span chips appropriately.

Applied across disks, this is the well-known RAID-5 technique: For every N disk drives, there's an extra one added. This allows a parity block to be written on a different drive for every N blocks on different drives. Parity normally would not provide error correction; in this case it does, because you know which unit failed, so, conversely, you know which ones are correct. Since the number of 1s must be odd, you can look at all the others and figure out what the missing one must be.

It's worth noting that all of these techniques of course have a price, either in additional logic, or performance loss, or both. RAID-5 in particular turns every write into a read and two writes: you have to read the parity block, compute the new parity values given the new data to be written, then write both the parity block and the data. Furthermore, the read operation has to sequentially precede the writes; it cannot overlap them. This contrasts with the other popular disk data protection technique, mirroring (also RAID-1): just keep a full copy of all the data on another disk. Read performance can improve under mirroring, since data can be read from one disk while a completely separate block of data is read from the other. Write performance is slightly worse, but since the two writes can be scheduled independently and done in parallel, the overhead involved is minimal. Of course, you do have to buy twice as many disks. Which is better depends on whether the number of disks you need is determined by disk capacity (number of bytes stored) or by disk performance (number of reads or writes per second). If performance is the determining factor, you may actually end up with fewer disks by using mirroring.

All these techniques of fault tolerance will keep systems running in the presence of hardware that has failed. However, it is still necessary to repair that failed hardware, or a additional failure may bring the system down. RAID-5, for example, will keep operating in the presence of a single failed disk in a RAID array, but if a second disk bites the dust, the data stored on the disks is toast. It's highly desirable to replace that failed component as soon as possible. This means, however, that while these techniques have avoided an unplanned outage—the system will keep running until the replacement part is found and the repair dude arrives on the scene with the part in hand— you still have a planned outage to deal with while the repairs are made.

This planned outage can in many cases be avoided by a technique called "hot plug." To make it work, both a hardware and a software component must be in place. The hardware component consists of electrical and mechanical design of enclosures, connectors and electronics that allow a unit—very often a disk, or an I/O device, but "hot plug" processor cards do exist—to be physically removed from the system, and another plugged back in, while the system stays "hot": power is on. The software component similarly allows this action while the system is not only powered-on, but also still actively running. Unfortunately, the software component is often ignored; it is a key element, even though it sometimes exists anyway; often the simple ability to emphatically ignore devices—take them off line—is built in normally, and so no added software support is necessary. This is not guaranteed, however.

It's worth emphasizing that "hot plug" is a technique for avoiding planned outages, not unplanned outages. Pre-existing fault tolerance of some kind must exist if it is to help—although it can, of course, definitely help for fault-less planned outages, such as the upgrading of a system by adding hardware. The planned/unplanned distinction is particularly confusing in situations where the fault tolerance required doesn't exist, or only partly exists, as is the case with several "hot plug" processor cards. In most cases, the system cannot survive hard failure of any significant components on those cards, as discussed in detail in the next section. Hot plug doesn't change that situation. It can help upgrades, or preventive maintenance.

12.11.4 Lowly Available Systems: SMP, CC-NUMA

If the other end of the spectrum from "highly parallel" is "lowly parallel," the other end from "highly available" must be "lowly available," right? Besides, I couldn't figure out how to hyphenate "Non Highly Available."

It's not that SMP and CC-NUMA systems break every time you look at them cross-eyed. On the contrary, as the technology has matured over time (or will mature, in the case of CC-NUMA) they have become rather robust, reliable server workhorses.

Nevertheless, they are not highly available in this sense: Their architecture provides no way to configure them to have no single points of failure.

We have to be careful, though, about exactly what that statement means. It does not mean that it is not possible to build a hardware fault-tolerant SMP or CC-NUMA system. It is clearly possible to build a hardware fault-tolerant *anything*, with no single points of failure, even if the system is a uniprocessor. In fact, hardware fault-tolerant SMPs have certainly been built and sold. However, those systems' lack of single points of failure had nothing to do with their SMP or CC-NUMA architecture; that was not the source of the higher availability. Unlike the situation with clusters, the SMP and CC-NUMA architecture in itself is not a source of high availability.

Where do these availability problems come from? For SMPs, there are obvious single points of failure in the memory and the I/O. There's only one of each, so if they fail the entire system goes down. This is a partial simplification, since if just part of the memory dies, at least not a bad part holding key system data, it is certainly not impossible for the system to recover at least partial operation (given sufficient software). However, the hardware controlling the memory—decoding addresses and turning them into row and column strobes that pick the actual bits read or written—is a single point of failure.

Perhaps more surprising is that virtually no SMPs or CC-NUMA systems can survive the loss of a single processor/cache subsystem anywhere in the complex. If one processor fails, the entire system goes down.

Why this happens isn't as obvious. There are other processors; how come they can't just take over the work, the way a cluster fails over?

CC-NUMA systems, in particular, certainly look rather like cluster hardware. Each CC-NUMA node has its own memory, and its own I/O; why shouldn't it be able to fail over?

This is a natural assumption, and equally naturally the purveyors of CC-NUMA systems don't deliberately drag skeletons out of the closet on sales calls. Many customers are therefore left believing that these systems naturally can fail over. In fact, this assumption is so natural that I have encountered customers who simply will not believe otherwise, despite being given the explanation presented below; technical gobbledegook couldn't sway the natural presumptions. On asking the NUMA vendor point-blank, however, reality prevailed (along with an apology from the customer).

Perhaps more surprisingly, a somewhat similar situation also occurred with a major computer industry analyst. I'd been invited to give a talk about clusters at a conference they held, and in the course of the introduction mentioned that CC-NUMA systems weren't highly available. This caused many surprised looks, multiple questions, and a rather large extension of the time I was scheduled to talk. They'd just the day before had a briefing from a CC-NUMA vendor—replete with technical details about interconnect speeds, bits, bytes, nanoseconds and such; good technical gorp, they loved it—in which this little-bitty fact about availability happened never to have been mentioned. Well, why deliberately hang your dirty laundry out? (The analysts did believe my technical gobbledegook.)

It is of course true that a cluster whose nodes are separate CC-NUMA systems can fail over between those separate CC-NUMA systems, just like any cluster. That's not the issue. The issue is whether a single, non-clustered CC-NUMA system is highly available. In the "pure" form taken by at least the first wave of CC-NUMA systems in 1997, they are not.

(Later variations on the CC-NUMA theme may fix this, as was discussed back in Section 7.5.2 on page 203, but the result of those variations is to turn the CC-NUMA system into what's effectively a cluster of CC-NUMA systems.)

It does turn out that there is a cache-coherent shared memory multiprocessor implementation that can survive processor failure, but nearly all cannot. After explaining the common case, we'll cover the exception; a look at what it takes to fix the problem will definitely make that the exception that probes the rule.

12.11.4.1   Hardware Issues

There are two classes of reasons behind SMP/CC-NUMA's inability to survive loss of a processor. The first primarily involves hardware, and derives from issues of cache coherence. Recall from Chapter 6 that in virtually all cases, a cache coherent system in operation looks like Figure 114 (copied from Chapter 6): The memory is randomly measled with wrong data, because data updated in the caches hasn't, at random, made its way back to main memory.

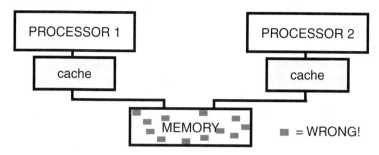

Figure 114 SMP Cache Coherence and Measled Memory

The correct data is of course held in one or another cache. It is up to the cache coherence algorithm to find it, no matter where it is, and present it to a requesting processor on demand.

Therein lies the difficulty. Those cache coherence algorithms assume that the processors and caches holding the data are working. If they don't work— give the wrong answer or give no answer at all—the correct data is inaccessible. As a result, one of two things will happen: Either the requesting processor will halt because a memory reference isn't satisfied; or, particularly when snoopy busses are used, the lack of a response from a processor's cache results in wrong data being retrieved from memory. See Figure 45 on page 168, for example, and consider what happens when the cache holding the correct data doesn't intervene by saying "WRONG" to the transfer of data from memory. What happens is that the wrong data simply gets returned to the processor that requested it.

In either case, whether there's a hang or bad data, the system won't last long.

It is worth emphasizing that this also definitely affects CC-NUMA systems, and therefore virtually all the systems today called "NUMA." They also rely on the active participation of processors and caches to maintain memory correctness. So if a single processor-cache element of a large CC-NUMA system fails, the entire system will fail even though there may be hundreds of processors involved. Also, for similar reasons each directory unit connecting the memory subsystems of NUMA nodes (see Figure 49 on page 188) is another single point of failure.

There is another problem with cache-coherent systems that may or may not be directly hardware-related. It's been observed [CRD⁺95, SC91] that "wild writes"—basically, processors writing the wrong data and/or to the wrong place—occur regularly when systems fail. Repeatedly encountering processor failure modes that actively causes writes to be issued to the wrong place is unlikely. It's more likely that one of the still correctly operating processors obtained wrong data because cache coherence failed elsewhere, and then that good processor did a wild write because it performed a correct operation on invalid data. However, since software errors cause more outages than hardware failures, the most likely usual culprit is a software bug. Whatever the cause, the fact that all of memory is an open target for any processor in an SMP or the first round of CC-NUMA systems means that wild writes can corrupt memory. One could provide memory protection techniques that could help alleviate this problem, but they haven't appeared yet.

12.11.4.2 Single-Copy Operating System Data

There is a completely different set of availability issues with SMPs and CC-NUMA systems that arises from a totally different source. These systems have a single copy of the operating system, and hence a single copy, in memory, of operating system data: memory allocation information, process or task descriptions, I/O control blocks, and so on. This data amounts to one great, big, single point of failure, particularly in the face of processor failure. (Again, as discussed in Section 7.5.2, this assumes the characteristics of the first wave of CC-NUMA systems as shipped in 1997.)

For example, suppose some processor (Able) is doing something inside the operating system on behalf of an application. It could be allocating memory, or setting up I/O, or something else. Whatever it does, it's operating on data structures that must also be used by the other processors. So Able sets locks that keep other processors from changing things out from under it until it finishes its work. Deep in the bowels of this manipulation, Able breathes his last.

That means nobody ever unlocks the locks that Able set.

Sooner or later, other processors will come along, see the lock set, and wait forever. Only Able can reset them, and Able can't; it's dead. The failure of the whole system will follow. It may take a little while, since on finding locked data operating systems often put the task needing the lock on a queue and go off to do something else. Sooner or later, though, every task in the system—or enough of them that it really doesn't matter—ends up on queues waiting for a lock or locks that are never reset.

For this reason, as well as the hardware-related reasons discussed in the previous section, SMPs (and now CC-NUMA systems) have often been said to exhibit "sympathy sickness": A single processor's failure spreads to others, bringing down the entire system.

Before proceeding on to describe the exception that does survive processor failure, a couple of other items must be mentioned.

In Search of Clusters ✳

First, at least one vendor has stated by mid-1997 that it is working on fixing the availability problems with CC-NUMA. The "Cellular IRIX" operating system of Silicon Graphics, apparently based on the Hive system of Stanford [CRD+95], will replicate operating system structures in separate "cells" within a CC-NUMA system, allowing one cell to fail over to others. Once they do that, it becomes in effect a cluster using NUMA (non-CC, or controlled CC) for communication. Unlike other styles of cluster, it can run single jobs that share memory on different cluster nodes. For the reasons given above, however, while the system will survive failure, an application sharing memory with a failing node will not survive. If you are running multiple application, this is better than the previous situation. If you run an application with transactional failover semantics, it can survive, but those to date have been written only for message-passing (cluster) semantics.

The second item: This whole discussion may seem to have directly contradicted the statements of some system vendors that they have "hot plug" processors that can be removed and replaced while the system is running. If it seems that way, it's because too much has been read into the term "hot plug." (Or, like the case of CC-NUMA availability, customers were (naturally) allowed to read too much into it.)

The implementations of "hot plug processors" on the open system market in 1997 do not survive *unplanned* failures. If the operating system is informed ahead of time that a processor is to be removed, it can remove work from the processor and execute special instructions that eliminate all data from its cache; then it can be unplugged. Plugging back in, or possibly adding an additional processor, also requires no magic beyond a goodly, but feasible, amount of operating system function. So outages for planned processor maintains can be avoided, but not unplanned processor failures.

CC-NUMA systems will also have to evolve "hot plug" NUMA nodes for them to be as available as an everyday cluster.

Finally, all of the issues mentioned above can be avoided if memory is not treated as the usual form of memory that prevails in SMPs. That's the case, for example, in NC-NUMA (Non-Coherent) cluster systems. It is treating memory as normal memory, holding normal data structures, that is the source of the difficulty. "NUMA," meaning NC-NUMA, systems can in that sense "share memory" (sort of, not in the normal way), and be highly available.

12.11.4.3   The Case of the Tightly-Coupled Multiprocessor

At this point anyone familiar with traditional IBM S/390 mainframes, and many S/390 plug-compatible competitors, is probably wondering what's going on.

Those systems can, and do, survive failure of a processor and keep operating. They're also SMPs, and very definitely treat memory as normal, everyday, main memory, with a single copy of operating system data. Recall that anything can be made more highly available, including SMPs, with appropriate effort; it's just that being an SMP doesn't help, even though it looks like it should since there are multiple processors involved. However, IBM didn't use the seemingly straightforward route of plain old fault tolerant, redundant, bulletproof hardware. When the techniques mentioned here were devised, the hardware of mainframes was expensive enough without resorting to that. Nevertheless, non-"standard" fault tolerance techniques can still be applied.

IBM's S/390 flavor of SMP, which they specifically refer to as a Tightly-Coupled Multiprocessor (TCMP), has features not found in the run-of-the-mill *de facto* standard SMP. I'll briefly describe how S/390 TCMPs can survive processor failure, just to give some idea of what must be done if the inherent processor availability problems of cache-coherent shared-memory multiprocessors are to be fixed while retaining the characteristics of normal memory. If something like them, or plain heavy-duty hardware redundancy, doesn't appear in an allegedly highly-available shared memory system, you should react with skepticism and surprise.

First, there are two levels of caching (see Figure 115), with the level 2 cache shared between processors. Moreover, the level 1 cache uses a policy called *store through*: Every time data is written to the level 1 cache, it is also written "through" it into the level 2 cache. This technique is normally only used on rather low-end processors, but here it's deliberately used for higher availability because it ensures that there is always good data in that level 2 cache.

Figure 115 TCMP Two-Level Caching

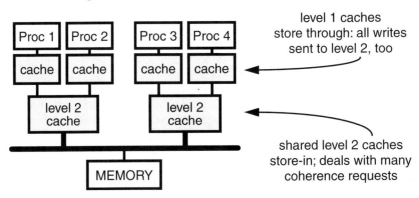

The level 2 cache does not store through to memory, but because that cache is used in the coherence protocols with other processors, the others can get correct information even if the level 1 cache and processor are inoperable. (This also decreases the coherence traffic load on the level 1 caches, so it's not totally a performance-degrading exercise.) Since a working level 2 cache is crucial to processor recovery, heavy-duty hardware fault tolerance techniques are used to make it as bulletproof as feasible: lots of redundancy, very heavy error-correction codes, and so on.

More than that is involved, however.

Should a processor fail, a section of processor hardware is invoked that is deliberately kept primitive, robust, and as tolerant of all sorts of faults as possible. This reptilian hindbrain takes over from the higher functions in a reversion to a primitive survival mode. It dumps the state of the processor into a predefined area of memory (meaning into level 2 cache, of course).

That stored processor state can be loaded onto another processor and continue execution there, like a ghost haunting the system, unable to rest after the untimely death of its body. Running the ghost on the other processor uses a kind virtual machine facility (based on logical partitions), so it proceeds along with the regular work of the processor that accepts this burden.

Once it begins haunting another processor, the failed processor state is lead through a trap into functional recovery code. This is additional software whose purpose in life is to clean up the mess. As quickly as feasible, that code moves the ghostly process into a state where one of two things can be done: The ghost can be taken up as regular work on another non-ghostly processor; or the ghost can be cleanly terminated. That recovery code backs out system locks, repairs damage to data structures, and tries to enqueue the cleaned-up task somewhere where the rest of the system will find it, and so on, as appropriate.[12]

Note that this means that every time any function is added to the operating system, an associated functional recovery routine had to be written to back it out if the processor failed at any time during its execution. No such thing is done in any open system I'm aware of.

Once the functional recovery code safely restores sanity to whatever was running, or cleanly terminates it if nothing better can be done, the continued

---

12. This describes a bad case where unconstrained damage occurred in the processor. There's also a good case. Processors check to see if an error left it in a state known to be legal and well-defined. If that happened, the "Processor Availability Feature" (PAF) dumps the known good state to storage, where it is queued for execution on another processor. Everything then continues from that point with no special software invoked. This is effectively "instruction retry" on a different processor. It also relies on a store-through L1 cache keeping cached data up to date in shared L2 cache.

ghostly state of the failed processor stops rattling its chains and is put to its final rest.

This is complicated, large, and expensive stuff to implement. It is, in fact, sufficiently expensive that IBM no longer focuses on it, preferring to invest its effort in the cluster-based availability of Parallel Sysplex, particularly since that also provides a good measure of protection from many possible errors not covered by this scenario, such as software failures.

Symmetric Multiprocessors, "NUMA," and Clusters

Which car is better, a Lexus LS400 or a Corvette?

We all know the kind of never-ending argument that type of question can start. We all should also recognize that it's obviously a trick question, because "better" isn't defined. Better at what? Carrying four people? Lexus wins. Impressing adolescents of any age? Corvette wins. Different types of cars fulfill different needs for different people. That's why there are hundreds of types of motorized transport, from single-seat race cars to 18-wheel tractor-trailer rigs.

The direction this chapter is going to take should be clear. None of the three types of computer server systems discussed in this book is unequivocally the "wave of the future" to the exclusion of the others. That is because there are differences between them, and those differences are not minor. For the most part, they are not even particularly subtle, once you know where to look. They cause different types of systems to be meet different needs. This is important from two points of view:

> ➤ Purchasers of server systems need to understand both the differences in the systems and the characteristics of the tasks they need to do so the two can be matched. That a certain type of system is

new, or being talked about a lot, does not make it right for your needs.

➢ Vendors of server systems need to understand the differences between the systems and the needs of the market they are targeting so they can design systems that satisfy those needs. The implication is that they do have to choose a market. Just because there's a lot of money to be made in a particular area does not mean that a company's systems, or even the systems a company could realistically design, deliver, and support, can meet those needs.

What are these differences? Just as differences between cars can be divided into incommensurate areas—seating capacity, price, power, luxury, and so on—the differences between the systems discussed in this book can be divided similarly. This is yet another one of those taxonomy-like things that can validly be done in any number of ways. The areas that fall most readily to my hand are: performance, cost, and high availability. Each is discussed separately in this chapter, followed by some miscellaneous other comparisons and a seemingly unrelated issue, partitioning.

But first, we have some preliminaries to attend to.

13.1 Preliminaries

"What?!" I can hear you saying, "More? We've already had 454 bloody pages of *$%&@#@ preliminaries!"

That's true. And to those of you who have actually slogged all the way through this book to here, congratulations—and thank you for the implied compliment.

However, I know from experience that there are people who will go directly to this chapter without reading anything that came before. In fact, one of the reviewers of this edition did exactly that. To be fair, he was looking for something specific; but then again, so probably is everybody who dives in this late in the game. So, sorry, I have to be a little redundant, and also include an unconscionable number of references to prior discussion. Otherwise what's said here may be taken by those who pick it up here as blatant assertions worth no more than uninformed prejudice, and ignored beyond the trivial level of "He agrees/disagrees with what I already know is true."

Also, I think you would want to be sure exactly what is being compared here—like, why there are sometimes four, sometimes two, and seldom three cases; and why there is a real sense in which the entire comparison is bogus.

13.1.1   What's Being Compared?

It was pointed out in Chapter 5 that cluster hardware organizations can vary all over the map. How can we compare SMPs and CC-NUMA systems with something so nebulous? The comparisons, as it happens, are based on just a few characteristics, shared by nearly all forms of cluster. Specifically:

> ➤ **Local Memory.** Each machine in the cluster has its own local memory. Communication with the other machines is less efficient than access to a machine's own memory. There may be memory that's shared in the sense that multiple machines can reference it by addresses. If the memory is not all shared, the local memory referred to here is the unshared, private part. If, on the other hand, all the memory is accessible by all processors, it's assumed that there is a local-remote distinction wherein remote access is less efficient.

> ➤ **Local I/O.** Each machine has its own attached I/O. Access to another machine's I/O is less efficient than access to a machine's own I/O. There may be shared disk, access to which is less efficient than access to private disk; this inefficiency may be due, for example, to the protocols involved.

In contrast, an SMP can be crisply defined as was done in Chapter 6. It's a computer with multiple processors and only multiple processors, no multiple memories or multiple I/O systems, and every processor has equal (therefore complete) capabilities. "One memory" implies cache coherence and uniform access time to all of memory.

A cache-coherent, CC-NUMA system—NC-NUMA, not cache-coherent, is a different case, as explained in Chapters 5 and 6—is a computer composed of SMPs linked at the memory level to provide a single, cache-coherent, view of memory as seen from all processors, but whose memory is divided into parts, one part for each SMP used. Accessing a remote part takes at least two or three times longer than accessing a local part. We will have more to say about how long it takes to access a remote cache, not memory.

In the comparisons, CC-NUMA will often be divided into two categories, thereby forming the four cases referred to above: Current CC-NUMA, and Potential CC-NUMA.

By Current CC-NUMA is meant "NUMA" systems as they first appeared on the market in mid-1997, with a single operating system and a single memory space covering all the nodes of the systems, treated as much as possible as if they were SMPs in their programming model. This is what the proponents of CC-NUMA want it to be—another way to build an SMP—because the programing costs are otherwise too large.

Potential CC-NUMA refers to CC-NUMA modifications that fix the bottle-necks and single points of failure implied by those characteristics, with pro-gramming (including system programming) that actually admits that these machines have a distributed memory programming model. While individual applications, and some subsystems, have been partially programmed this way (none fixes high availability yet), no complete system has those characteristics at the time this book is written.

Even though most comparisons are covered within the above characteristics, the many possible variations on cluster hardware organizations may still cause variations in the details of the discussion below. While not every nub-bin can be examined in detail, most of the larger effects will be noted.

13.1.2   Good Twin, Evil Twin

That explains why comparisons will sometimes compare four cases. How-ever, it sometimes comes down to just two when Potential CC-NUMA is considered.

SMP systems, on the one hand, and both clusters and CC-NUMA systems on the other, use globally different approaches to increasing a system's size. In a metaphor that's well-known in the parallel processing community, SMPs are "dancehall" machines while the other two are "boudoir" machines. See Figure 116.

Figure 116 The Dancehall and the Boudoir

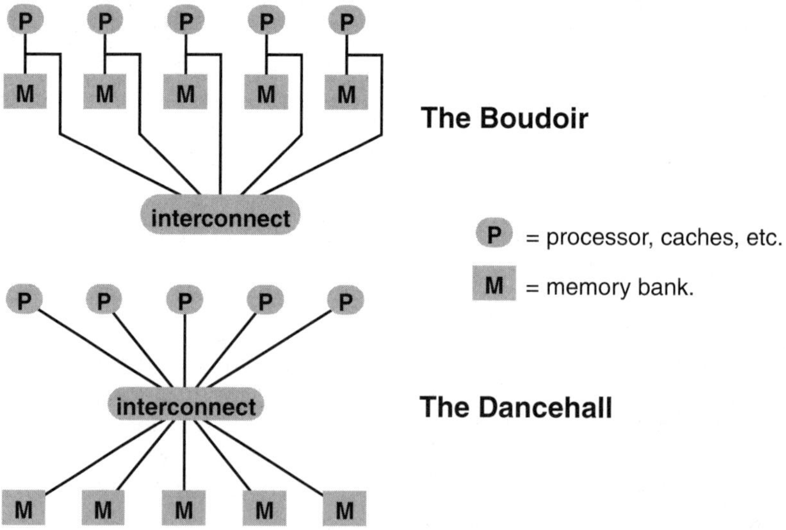

The Boudoir

P = processor, caches, etc.

M = memory bank.

The Dancehall

UMA SMPs get the memory bandwidth needed by adding memory banks on the other side of the ballroom floor (so to speak) from the processors. As a result, each memory back is equidistant from every processor. To maintain the performance of the system, the interconnect and associated things listed in must increase in bandwidth as the number of processors goes up, while maintaining latency, or the result will be UBMA: Uniformly *Bad* Memory Access.

Clusters and CC-NUMA systems, on the other hand, snuggle a memory up to each processor or to a few processors; that the nodes can be modest SMPs was left out of Figure 116 for clarity. Bringing processors and memories together ensures that at least one processor has an easy time getting to each memory, and so, for that node, heroic measures are not needed in the memory subsystem. But there is a price to be paid: Memory as a whole gets "lumpy" (CC-NUMA) or chasms appear between the memories (cluster). As a result, the techniques for programming it have to change.

The use of SMPs as boudoir nodes alleviates a problem that has existed in boudoir organizations, specifically that one memory bank usually does not meet the exact requirements of one processor except by happy accident. The use of SMP nodes allows other ratios to be used.

Of course, the use of different types of inter-node coupling in the boudoir (you know, this could get risqué) causes differences between clusters and CC-NUMA systems that are so major that the relationship between the two is more like an imaginary good twin/evil twin pair than even like siblings. The programming models are related, but different (distributed memory, vs. message passing, as discussed in Chapter 9); high availability is a natural characteristic in one case, but not the other (Chapter 12); and running the whole complex under a single operating system is more natural in one case than in the other (Chapters 7 and 13).

Nevertheless, one would expect that in some respects these two are similar. Indeed they are, as we shall see.

There's another factor complicating this crisp dichotomy. Do you notice something odd about Figure 116? Unlike nearly all the similar diagrams in this book, it leaves out caches. If caches are added to the dancehall, in particular, it begins to assume some of the characteristics of the boudoir because there is memory snuggled up to the processor. Rather fast memory, at that.

In fact, if the cache has large enough capacity, a dancehall SMP system effectively becomes a boudoir system. Certainly it does if "large enough" means "holds an entire application's data." In some cases this is in fact possible; in others it is not. The strong hardware tendency is to increase the size of caches to compensate for memory that's ever-slower relative to processors, but there's also a strong tendency for applications to use more data as their function increases.

So, which wins? Probably the applications—unless the SMP applications are specifically programmed to maintain sufficient locality, which effectively means they must, like CC-NUMA systems, be programmed as if they were a distributed-memory system. It seems a somewhat different kind of distributed memory, however, because it can be discontiguous, using data blocks only in cache-line-size units rather than pages or other larger units. But at the same time, the size of cache lines is increasing, so some convergence appears likely even there.

These factors have to be taken into account, particularly in performance comparisons.

13.1.3   Architecture vs. Implementation

All of the characteristics described in this chapter are tendencies, not iron-clad truths true in every instance. That is the sense in which any comparison must be bogus.

The reason for this situation is that this book is about parallel computer architecture, meaning the overall organization of a parallel computer, not its implementation details. Architecture, however, is not destiny.

Implementation, the execution of the architecture in creation of an actual system, can override general architectural tendencies. A good implementation of a less-desirable architecture can be better than a poor implementation of a more-desirable architecture. Consider, for example, Intel's X86 architecture Pentium Pro implementation. Despite general agreement that the X86 CISC instruction set architecture is far less desirable than any RISC, the Pentium Pro kicked butt. Its performance was a major wake-up call to all RISC vendors.

More: With sufficient effort, almost any characteristic of any architecture can be provided in almost any other architecture. For example, Section 12.11.4 on page 445 explained in gruesome detail why SMPs and CC-NUMA systems do not have high availability. Then in Section 12.11.4.3 on page 449, I turned around and explained, in equivalent detail, how a particular, special implementation—IBM's S/390 TCMP—overcame the problems described, and did provide it.

So, what good is architecture?

The key is in the phrase "with sufficient effort" above. Saying "computer architecture X has characteristic Y" is really saying "it will be *easier* to implement a computer with characteristic Y if you the implementation follows architecture X." Each of the two counter-architectural examples above extracted a price in development resources, chip area, power, and other areas that is not present when more appropriate architectures are used.

"Easier" does not mean "free." However, since nobody has unlimited resources, it can mean "possible." Intel is moving to a new 64-bit architecture to get higher performance. IBM S/390 has moved to clusters (Parallel Sysplex) to get higher availability. With the resources they had available, it was not possible to get enough of what they wanted using the old architecture.

So, there may well be product implementations that appear to violate the architectural characteristics described here, but they're swimming upstream. They may have found some particular rocks or eddies to hide behind to make it feasible for a while, but reasonable people find it easier to swim with the current.

Progress does depend on unreasonable people, however. Most are just stubborn, and get nowhere. Occasionally, however, there can be a breakthrough implementation that proves the architectural verities wrong. Those are, actually, no more than averages over many implementations.

That does it for the final preliminaries. Let's start the match.

13.2 Performance

Which car goes faster, a Formula 1 race car, or a U-haul truck?

That's right, when considering performance alone, we immediately run into the same kind of trick question that a general "who's better than who" comparison raises: It depends on what you use it for. A truck is faster if you're moving refrigerators, for example.

In this case, there's a temptation to try to answer the question in a seemingly absolute sense, since only a Martian would answer that initial question by saying "it depends." Most people would say "the Formula 1 car." (That is, except for the ones who didn't immediately realize that such an absurd comparison could only be a trick question.) The "absolute sense" usually corresponds to picking an application that itself maximizes speed, and seeing which is best in that particularly agreeable case.

That's a temptation best resisted. Even within the analogy used here, it's the case that the race car's "application" is very strictly defined to *not* be merely "fastest speed." The "formula" of "Formula 1" specifies a maximum engine displacement, implicitly defines the kinds of courses on which it runs, and so on. Without rules, Formula 1 cars would probably end up looking like the strange contraptions used to set land speed records, and would have much less popularity than Formula 1's spectator following. The rules were picked to make the contest interesting to reasonable range of people.

The exact same thing is true of computers. Comparisons that aren't interesting to a good-size range of people aren't useful. And just as some people prefer Formula 1, while others prefer NASCAR, drag, or truck racing, there are different areas of computing that different people find interesting and relevant. Unfortunately, this is far less obvious in the abstract, invisible arena of computer server performance than it is in the world of racing.

Also unfortunately, things are even more complicated than the above analogy suggests. The reason is that parallel computer performance is really the same thing as what's called "scaling": Making a computer faster when you make it bigger by adding more computing units of some kind.

This complicates matters. Even within a particular application area, no hardware, alone, scales up in performance as more of it is added. Performance refers to how fast a system does something, and getting it on a parallel system is a process of elimination. All your ducks have to be lined up in a row:

1. Yes, hardware that avoids serialization is necessary.

2. That hardware, however, does no good unless the operating system also scales up, avoiding serial bottlenecks.

3. Even if you have the hardware and the OS in good shape, it still does you no good if middleware layers exhibit serialization.

4. And even if the hardware, the OS, and the middleware are all fine, you still lose if the application *tells* the whole confabulation to do something that's heavily serialized. This is a question of algorithm, not application area, and can vary all over the map.

13.2.1   Workload Characteristics

A way to look at the above list of is to mash the last three items together and call them "the workload": The combination of operating system, middleware, and application characteristics with which the hardware must deal, all at once. Now, can anything be said about workload characteristics that is relevant to the characteristics of the types of hardware we are comparing?

One relevant spectrum of characteristics is illustrated below in Figure 117.

This classifies workloads by two characteristics: amount of bulk data traffic, and amount of synchronization traffic. The reason those characteristics were chosen is that they stress different characteristics of communication:

Figure 117 A Two Dimensional Workload Spectrum

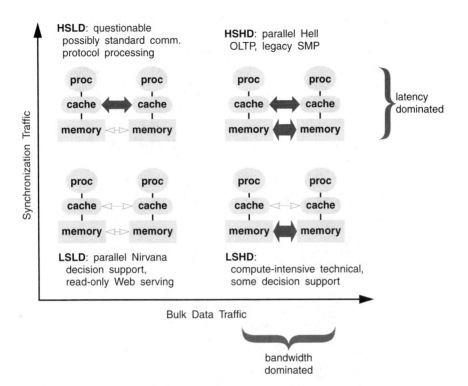

- ➢ Bulk data traffic primarily stresses inter-node bandwidth. Since in high traffic cases there is a lot of data, it will tend to stress bandwidth to main memory since the data doesn't fit in cache.

- ➢ Synchronization traffic primarily stresses inter-node latency. Since in high traffic cases there are many communication events on small amounts of highly reused data (synchronization variables), it will tend to stress latency between the caches of each node—assuming, for the case of clusters, memory-based communication or some rather sophisticated, virtualized acceleration (see Chapter 5).

These differences are what the graphics in Figure 117 attempt to suggest: memory traffic vs. cache traffic. The graphics aren't literally accurate, since the transfer is ultimately to the processors, not between the storage units; but direct memory-to-memory transfer certainly is done, and besides, the figure would get ugly were more complexity shown.

While in reality there is continuous variation along those characteristics for different workloads, the four possible extremes are, as Figure 117 indicates, useful and interesting to characterize. They are covered below. See the discussion at the end of the list regarding the examples chosen.

> **High synchronization, high data traffic (HSHD)**: This upper right corner is Parallel Hell. Communication is so frequent that there is little opportunity to overlap it with processing. So latency is the key issue, and high efficiency is attained only with substantial effort.

  - Unfortunately, some commercially important application areas tend to live there, particularly on-line transaction processing with short transactions (checking an account or credit balance) and "legacy" programs that were constructed and optimized with a little too much faith in the uniform data accessibility of the SMP programming model.

> **Low synchronization, low data traffic (LSLD)**: This lower left corner is, in contrast, Parallel Nirvana. This is the corner at which parallel performance tuning aims. The processing nodes run in splendid isolation, barely communicating or interrupting each other at all, and are therefore left in peace to be one with their assigned task, computing at high efficiency.

  - Decision support—large read-only query processing, on-line analytical processing, and so on—tends to live here when it's not in the LSHD quadrant. So does the job of serving read-only information to the Web, as do a workloads consisting of many separate jobs. In the latter case, the only communication may be incidental, forced by operating system semantics such as the implicit locking of data structures when files are opened. HSHD workloads that can be "partitioned" into separate units can thereby become LSLD. Unfortunately, that happens to be the case with the most popular transaction processing benchmark; see Chapter 14.

> **Low synchronization, high data traffic (LSHD)**: The lower right corner is neither Hell nor Nirvana. There is a lot of data transfer, but ways can sometimes be found to overlap it with computation. Particularly when it cannot be overlapped (and often even when it can), the inter-node bandwidth is what limits the time a node can spend doing useful work rather than communication.

  - A significant number of compute-intensive technical problems fit this characterization. Some of the more nasty decision support cases might fit this case also, but so far the evidence appears to indicate that in practice, decision support is currently LSLD; this may change.

> **High synchronization, low data traffic (HSLD)**: The upper left corner is problematical. The author is unsure whether there are many real examples with these properties.

  • A possible example may be the use of multiple processors to feed many data streams into a single very high speed adapter, using standard, high-overhead communications protocols. At the higher levels of the protocols, there would be little interference between the streams, but as lower levels are reached there is a funnel effect, finally ending up with intense synchronization feeding the adapter with small packets.

The slippery part of dealing with categories like the above does not lie in defining them. It is ascertaining where, in the spectrum they sample, typical applications or application areas are to be placed.

In particular, it can be argued that high-performance transaction processing systems belong in seemingly vacuous HSLD (low data traffic) case, not in HSHD (high data traffic). Certainly they do not have the bandwidth requirements characteristic of many technical codes. On the other hand, my experience is that referring to those workloads as "low" data traffic seriously underestimates them; so perhaps they truly are HSMD (medium data traffic): Parallel Purgatory. If your experience points to lower data rates, feel free to interpret HSHD in the next section as HSLD or HSMD.

Beyond that issue, there are two reasons to consider any such collections of examples as only approximations:

First, workload behavior is data dependent. While a given program may generally inhabit one area in the twofold spectrum, it may change its characteristics significantly depending on the data it is supplied. Nowhere is that more clear that with database managers, which change their characteristics dramatically depending on whether heavily read/write transaction processing or mostly read-only decision support is performed.

The second reason this can only be an approximation is that all programs are moving targets whose characteristics are changed over time. The function of any live program, application, or subsystem is continually being enhanced or generalized; this can have a significant effect on the amount of data transferred and the rate of synchronization. In addition, significant effort is spent moving performance-critical software down and to the left on the diagram in an attempt to make it more efficient. This is what happened for the two-year period in the mid-1990s during which best-of-breed transaction performance "flattened out," as noted about the historical graph presented in Section 3.4 on page 60. There are indications that this may occur in a different direction for decision support; as database vendors respond to this burgeoning application area, developers are working making their serial portions substantially more efficient, which will in effect increase the rate of communication, primarily of data but also of synchronization.

13.2.2 Workload-Relative Performance

Applying the four architectural cases to the workload types, leaving out high synch/low data traffic (HSLD) as a likely vacuous case, we arrive at Table 19 on page 464.

Table 19   Relative Performance Matrix

	High Synchronization, High Data Traffic (HSHD)	Low Synchronization, Low Data Traffic (LSLD)	Low Synchronization, High Data Traffic (LSHD)
SMP (UMA)	best	good, but memory design limits number of processors	good, but memory design limits number of processors
Current CC-NUMA	synchronization latency disadvantage	OS synchronization traffic limits system size	OS synchronization traffic limits system size, but overlap with data traffic may allow larger systems
Potential CC-NUMA	synchronization latency disadvantage	excellent; can use many processors on large problems	excellent; can use many processors on large problems
Cluster	large synchronization latency disadvantage without special acceleration	excellent; can use many processors on large problems	excellent; can use many processors on large problems

That table requires both explanation and qualification, since the answers in that table can vary depending on implementation. We'll approach it column by column.

The UMA SMP is the undisputed ruler of Parallel Hell (HSHD). The reason lies in its ability to do fast inter-cache transfers of data, particularly for synchronization. CC-NUMA systems have the disadvantage that their remote references must at least traverse two memory subsystems (plus communication), versus one for an UMA SMP. This can be hidden behind large and increasing main memory latencies when the transfers are to memory, but the inter-cache transfers of this workload leave nowhere to hide. Clusters are even worse, but examples exist in rather elaborate acceleration facilities have made them adequate. There is no particular reason why such techniques could not also be applied to CC-NUMA systems, but to date they have not.

The above discussion of CC-NUMA vs. SMP in HSHD assumes that the SMP's memory subsystem has latency roughly comparable to the memory subsystem within a single CC-NUMA node. This may be hard to achieve for large SMPs; on the other hand, a latency less than half that of an SMP is a stiff challenge for even a small CC-NUMA node.

Moving on to the middle column of Table 19:

Both clusters and Potential CC-NUMA systems serenely attain Parallel Nirvana (LSLD). Both can be extended in size as far as the problem requires and the customer's pocketbook allows. This assumes that each almost autistic part of the problem fits within a single node; if it does not, the result is effectively a nested collection of workloads, and the inner one may be HSHD; that would be bad news for the CC-NUMA and cluster systems.

SMPs can do well on this workload also, but must support in their one memory subsystem all the memory requirements of all the workload's nearly-incommunicado pieces; their otherwise independent memory access streams are mixed together in the SMP's single interconnect. Clusters and CC-NUMA systems (Potential or Current) have an advantage because of their boudoir structure; they can incrementally add more memory subsystems as needed, and the streams don't mix. So, the dancehall structure of an SMP ultimately limits its ability to support an arbitrarily large workload, even of this particularly congenial type. Where the limit appears is heavily dependent on implementation; in mid-1997, it ranged from four to possibly as many as 64 processors—assuming that all 64 can in fact be used at once on a meaningful workload, which hasn't been demonstrated.

All of the above paragraph's comparisons are actually only true if the independent problem sections do not fit wholly, or nearly wholly, inside the caches of the SMP. If they do, we have the situation, discussed in Section 13.1.2 on page 456, in which the SMP's ballroom is effectively turned into a boudoir. There is little traffic across the SMP's interconnect and therefore there is no problem with scaling it to infinity and beyond. It is unwise to bet that one's applications will do this "naturally," without programmer effort; but as discussed, it is possible to program this in by organizing the SMP code as if it were CC-NUMA or cluster code, providing the basic cache capacity is large enough. So implementation—both of the software and the hardware—can turn this comparison around.

Aside form these factors, Current CC-NUMA systems have a limit imposed from another source: the inherent internal synchronization required within a single image of a single operating system. In effect, that means there can be no true extremely LSLD workload for a Current CC-NUMA system, because the operating system always injects additional synchronization traffic. This does depend heavily on the characteristics of both the workload and the operating system. If the workload, in addition to being LSLD in its internal communication, makes very little use of operating system facilities, Current CC-NUMA can scale up readily. It is also possible to (laboriously) modify the operating system to exhibit very little internal stray synchronization or serialization, but CC-NUMA's synchronization overhead makes that harder than it is for an SMP with an equal number of processors.

Finally, the last column of Table 19 on page 464:

The low synchronization, high data traffic case is a lesser Nirvana for Potential CC-NUMA and clusters. Providing their inter-node communication has adequate bandwidth, both can provide customers with a great opportunity to part with large amounts of cash for large systems that run large problems. For the clusters to meet the capabilities of most CC-NUMA systems, however, this will require use of non-standard communication such as the accelerators discussed in Chapter 5 or the fast communication hardware often listed as special hardware support in Table 5 on page 47. CC-NUMA's potential for faster synchronization than clusters doesn't help in this case; however, the ability to do distributed memory programming rather than message-passing undoubtedly may strongly appeal to many.

Notice that in this case, the issue of SMP cache size doesn't arise because the assumption is that there is, like it or not, a lot of inter-node memory-level traffic—in other words, by definition this case does not fit into the caches of an SMP, no matter how much effort is put into the programming; there's just a whole lot of memory data.

Current CC-NUMA is limited by single-system operating system synchronization as in the pure Nirvana case. However, the key example in this area, compute-bound technical work, is notorious for using very little by way of operating system facilities; so that is less of a problem. In addition, it is far from impossible that the required synchronization can be overlapped with the large data transfers assumed to exist in this workload.

That completes the discussion of workload-dependent performance, but a final comment must be made. The above discussion was in terms of absolute types. There is no such thing. Those types are interesting extremes in a two dimensional spectrum, and a real workload will lie somewhere among them. Furthermore, a single workload might be a mixture of those types—for example, a HSHD transaction processing workload that is sharply partitioned into LSLD segments. And, of course, there are those customers who persist in having more than one kind of work they want to perform on a single computer.

13.2.3   Projecting to a Single Dimension

There is another point from which to view the prior discussion that emphasizes different things. It is seemingly simpler, corresponding to the "obvious" answer a non-Martian would give to the speed question posed at the start of this performance discussion. For that reason, it is usually found in marketing literature, while the prior discussion is not. But it also obscures the effects of different workloads, which is why that issue was covered first.

This viewpoint is illustrated in Figure 118, which is actually rather more complex than most such graphs. They typically have only two humps.

Figure 118 SMP, Cluster, CC-NUMA: A Marketing Graph

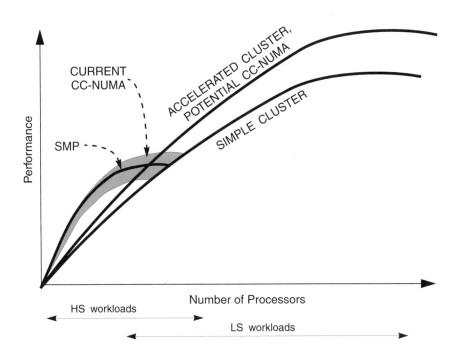

Notice that the graph in that figure contains no numbers whatsoever. (That, and the fact that its content goes up and to the right, would make it a perfect marketing chart if it were simpler.) It is, in fact, exceedingly difficult to get any two individuals to agree on any of the key numbers on the horizontal axis, particularly the intersection points. I have even had people nitpick the detailed shapes of the curves, despite the fact that the graph is only claimed to be qualitative. That nitpicking is why, for example, the curves exhibit only the faintest actual drop from their peaks as the number of processors is increased. God forbid it should look like the performance can decline noticeably when you *add* processors. For any of the architectures being considered. (P.S.: It most definitely can. Analogy: Committees.)

What this graph does make clearer than the detailed discussion is that in the region to the left, where all the systems have the same number of processors, the more tightly-coupled systems—SMPs, Current CC-NUMA—tend to win. The Current CC-NUMA case is shown here as a range above and below SMPs because it is workload-dependent; the top of the range corresponds to LSLD, and the bottom to HSHD, as explained in the prior section. In reality all the curves should be ranges, but they would overlap in too complex a fashion to be useful. That one range is included because it stuck out in my mind, for some reason.

The other thing Figure 118 makes clear is that Potential CC-NUMA and accelerated clusters can be extended in size far beyond any reasonable limits for SMP systems—or, given single operating system constraints, Current CC-NUMA systems.

Those are useful things to make clear. Unfortunately, graphs like those of Figure 118 profoundly obscure the workload issues. The only way I've found to really interpret them is to assume that they implicitly change the workload when moving form left to right (as shown at the bottom of Figure 118):

> ➤ On the left, with few processors, they probably mean HS workloads, where low-latency synchronization is needed. That workload is needed to argue that the tightly-coupled systems are faster than the more loosely-coupled ones.

> ➤ And on the right, with many processors, they probably mean LS workloads, where little synchronization is needed, so that the problem itself allows the use of many processors.

Of course, these complications are never mentioned when such graphs are shown. Only a Martian could be so dense as to think that graph is unclear. Formula 1 cars are obviously faster than U-Haul trucks. Where do you want me to put this refrigerator?

13.3 Cost

Meanwhile, back on Earth, somebody's got to be willing to pay for these things at a price high enough that the people selling them can make a buck or two. The discussion here will focus on the *cost* to design and manufacture these systems, rather than on the price for which they are sold. The price has only a fleeting acquaintance with the cost, since competition, psychology, market dynamics, the other things the sales rep hopes the customer will buy, the time of year, and for all I know the phase of seventeen-year locust cycle all play a strong role in setting prices.

13.3.1 Does Processor Complex Cost Matter?

Back in Chapter 6, rather a large amount of discussion was focussed on how (UMA) SMP semantics required various heroic measures on the part of designers, implicitly leading up to an argument that SMPs cost a lot.

We'll still bring that up, but another issue has to be considered first, namely: Does it matter? Does the cost of the CPU, cache, memory subsystem, and I/O subsystem—the processor complex—matter at all?

The source of that probably surprising question lies in the bar graphs shown in Figure 119 below.

Figure 119 Cost Content of Large Transaction Systems

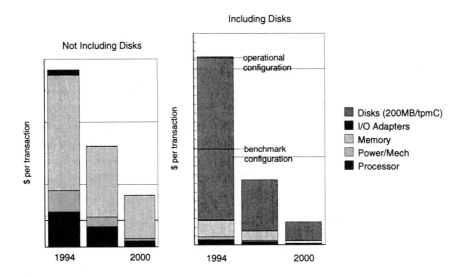

These charts have no numbers because cost data is one of the more confidential items any company has. However, the absolute values aren't relevant to our discussion; we're interested in the relative sizes of the components. The dates on the charts are also not really relevant, except to note that the relative contribution of the various elements isn't expected to change much, except to get worse from our point of view. (It's additionally not relevant, but highly interesting, that the total cost per transaction is expected to decline precipitously between now and the end of the century. It probably won't stop then.)

First, look at the bar graph on the right, which shows the relative cost of all the components making up a typical large, mature, commercial transaction processing system. If that graph represents reality, and I assure you it does, who in his or her right mind would care what the processor complex costs? You could platinum plate the fool thing and charge well over ten times its cost and nobody would even notice, because virtually all the money is being spent on disks. The processor complex is down in the noise level.

That this is saying that real, heavy-duty, large commercial customers buy a lot of disks is a terrific understatement. Notice the marks labelled "benchmark configuration" and "operational configuration." The benchmark case, well down the chart, corresponds to the amount of disk storage used when running the TPC-C transaction processing benchmark. One of the criticisms of that benchmark is that it has become far too expensive to run because of the huge disk farm needed. Figure 119 says that when genuine large-scale production gets going its disk farms leave those allegedly-overstuffed benchmark configurations in the dust.

Well, OK, maybe other workloads, like technical computing, are different. They don't use anywhere near as much disk storage. Usually. At least in universities and some national laboratories. (Seismic processing, anybody?) Ignore the fact that there's much less money in that much smaller, poorer, market. This is all to no avail; the hope that the technical case is different is dashed by the bar graph on the left. What that shows is that even when the disks are subtracted, the system cost is still dominated by another commodity item: memory. Furthermore, the domination apparently increases as time passes. What these figures refer to is not, in fact, a technical system; but technical systems do, for real production systems, incorporate a lot of memory; so the graph at least indicates the general trend.

The conclusion to be drawn from this is that processor complex cost does not matter, right? Not exactly. Certainly one can draw the conclusion that any system had bloody better well allow the customer to buy disks and memories at the least expensive, wholly commodity cost level; any other solution will price you out of the market. So special, fancy, costly memories and high-priced proprietary disk systems are Right Out.

Against Figure 119 must be placed the fact that engineers designing processor complexes really do care about cost a whole lot. They also know, or the company employing them had better know, about the ratios implicit in Figure 119. So, are all those engineers deluded? Are they wearing blinders of some kind? Hardly.

First, recall what I said earlier about the non-relationship of cost and price. The bar chart shows production (or vendor purchase) cost. The processor complex, unless it is a near-commodity item, will have a price that reflects its development cost, not its production cost, since the development cost is the largest fraction of the total cost that the price must recoup. So, again unless commodity production volumes enter the argument (we'll bring those up in a later section), the price of the processor complex is significantly larger than those bar graphs would indicate. That fixes at least the case on the left, without disks. But the case on the right is still an issue; the processor complex could be a very large multiple of its cost and still not be noticeable there.

There is a second factor, however. The ratios shown above, particularly those for disks, are for mature systems that have been successfully deployed and in full operation for a significant period of time. It took years, in most cases, to reach that point. Consider instead systems that are just being purchased for a new application area. It may indeed be true that the customer wants a system that can be expanded to the state shown in the bar charts. The processor complex may in fact be an insignificant fraction of the total price—as the system exists in, say, five years' time. That does not mean it is an insignificant fraction of the price today, when it is initially purchased for system development, and must be paid for out of this year's budget.

Putting this another way: The cost of the processor complex makes a difference for *new* business. It may, in fact, make little direct difference in *replacement* business, where the customer is upgrading an already mature system to a new level of performance. So any company that wants to capture new business, and not just keep re-selling things to the same customer installations it already has—not just the same customers; even old customers put in new systems—had better be concerned with the cost of the processor complex.

And there's the other little fact that for most business models it's difficult to get into a replacement business unless you manage to capture, at some point, some new business.

13.3.2   The Cost of Scaling Up SMPs

Now that we know that the cost of the processor complex matters, the next issue is whether there is a systematic cost difference among the architectures we are comparing that's not just a matter of a particular version's implementation. This is where we haul out all the things prepared for back in Chapter 6. There is a systematically larger cost associated with scaling up—adding more processors to—an SMP that comes from its nature as a ballroom organization. The boudoir organizations, cluster and CC-NUMA, do not share these problems.

Before starting, however, I should note that many people will undoubtedly disagree with this section. So, what else is new? Lots of people have disagreed with lots of the statements in this book. But this is about *cost*. Cost is different.

Several times, over several years, I have been involved in attempts to compare product costs across different organizations, or attempted such comparisons myself. Without qualification, I have found that this issue is the most highly charged and politicized issue I have ever come across. When the subject of cost comes up, organizations that are rife with internal backstabbing and bloody internecine feuds will instantly lock arms, circle the wagons, and join as a seamless unit with a single focussed objective: repel that invader who is attempting to unfairly compare their product costs with anybody else's. The definition of "unfair," is, of course, "unfavorable." Or, more precisely: Done by anybody but them. In the room with the competition. Where they can stare each other down in a game of bluff poker, mutually deciding through eloquently minimal body language how much lying, um, I mean emphasis on appropriate aspects of the situation, can be achieved without the whole thing blowing up in their faces. The end result, if any agreement is reached at all, is usually a collection of people who are quite happy mutually swearing that the moon is made of green cheese. Unless, of course, the original point of the exercise was to discover if there was any Roquefort to be found. Then the location of the lunar Roquefort mines will be mapped out to within centimeters.

The reason for all of this is, of course, that old survival instinct coming to the fore. Performance and other elements be damned, it's cost that most directly affects net profits, and those profits are what pay for that organization staying intact. Nothing matters more. If something did, the organization wouldn't stay intact for long.

Anyway, the net of this is that I no longer can believe a word any development organization says about its own costs or any other competing development organization's. Neither should you. The only way to find out the truth is to use an outside auditor. Preferably an outside auditor flanked with a battalion of the corporate equivalent of internal police armed with bales of the equivalent of subpoenas, and riding in M1A1 Abrams tanks.

Now that that's off my chest:

The problem is that the base cost of a few-processor SMP system, and the incremental cost of adding a processor, gets larger as the maximum usable number of processors goes up. Figure 120 illustrates what this means. It plots the cost of five hypothetical SMP systems against the number of processors installed in them. The five systems are assumed to be identical, including the efficiency with which their processors can be used, except for the maximum usable number of processors each supports: 1, 2, 4, 8, and 16. (The 1-processor system isn't an SMP, of course; it's a uniprocessor.)

Figure 120 The Cost of SMP Scaling

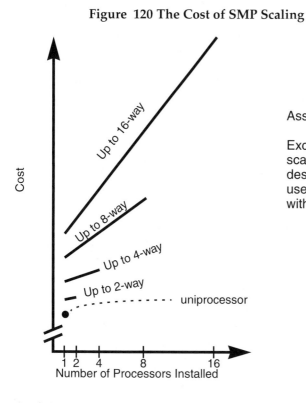

Assumption:

Except for their maximum scaling, all five system designs are identical and use all of their processors with equal efficiency.

Supporting a larger maximum number of processors injects more fixed cost into the system, so the 1-processor version of the 16-way costs more than a 1-processor version of the 8-way, and so on. That fact sets the differing heights of the leftmost point of each line. The support structure that must be included with each processor becomes more costly when a larger maximum number of processors is to be supported. This makes the slope of the 16-way's cost line larger than that of the 8-way, and so on.

In addition, the problem gets worse as processor speed goes up. With reference to Figure 120, the leftmost points of the lines spread further apart and the slopes diverge even faster.

It would be nice to be able to inject some hard data into that qualitative graph, since the quantitative issues are crucial. Who cares if the base cost goes up if it goes up only 1% when moving from a 2-way to a 32-way maximum system? As explained earlier, however, accurate cost data is virtually impossible to find outside of an auditor's office.

Nevertheless, and under these circumstances justifiably not naming names: There was at least one open-systems-based, UNIX-oriented SMP on the market, the product of a successful vendor, designed to scale to at least 16 processors, whose base list price was nearly 100 times the base list price of several uniprocessors that are very comparable in uniprocessor performance, technology, general market, and so on. Prices are still fuzzy, and high end prices are certainly inflated relative to low end ones, where broader competition forces a closer relationship between price and cost. Nevertheless, a factor of 100 is sufficient to pierce the fuzz surrounding this comparison and indicate that there are differences.

Why is scaling SMPs up expensive? If doubling the maximum number of processors more than doubles the price, and it does, perhaps we should be looking at other ways of getting a bit more lowly parallelism—like clusters or CC-NUMA systems.

Some of the reasons for a larger base cost are blindingly obvious. If you're going to fit more processors into a box, you need a bigger box. You also need larger basic circuit boards (motherboards or backplanes), a larger power supply, more fans to carry away more waste heat, and significant engineering to keep those hot chips thermally stable (barely). You also have increased shipping costs because all of those things make it heavier, and you quite possibly have to invest more of your field force's time in setup because the whole thing is physically more unwieldy. Did I mention increased insurance premiums because it does more damage when dropped on someone's foot?

Such things add up to a significant difference in cost; see the size of the "power/mech" (mechanical) segment of the left bar chart in Figure 119 on page 469. This, however, is hardly of the magnitude suggested by the price difference mentioned. They also don't readily explain why the incremental cost of adding a processor should be larger. This is where the memory contention, memory coherence, and sequential consistency discussed in Chapter 6 start coming in.

That chapter did not demonstrate, nor could it, that SMPs don't scale in a usable, marketable, customer-oriented sense. It couldn't because it's not true. You can build big machines in which many processors can be effectively used. What it did attempt to demonstrate is that there are intrinsic costs to building large SMPs that are disproportionate to the size of the system. Compared with much smaller SMPs, large ones must have:

> larger caches

> longer cache lines (but not too long, or false sharing does you in)

> more memory banks

> more expensive switches

> bigger, faster buses

> more complex coherence protocols

> shared caches

> more expensive serial consistency facilities

Moreover, these are not artifacts. They are necessary responses to the required SMP programming model and the resulting Von Neumann bottleneck.

The costs do not, of course, increase in a continuous linear fashion; adding one bit to a 128-bit cache line doesn't increase the cost by one-128th. There are thresholds, under which additions are "free" but beyond which costs suddenly rise. These are primarily related to size, packaging, and power. It is really expensive to need one more pin that a particular package provides, since it means going to a larger package which is probably much more expensive because it is made in lower volumes. It is really expensive to need more than some number of watts of heat dissipation, because after that point you can't use such-and-such a standard heat sink, and must resort to more exotic (expensive) measures.

In effect, there are "knees" in the cost curves of many elements that reflect discontinuous increases in the prices of the components as size, power, and so on are scaled up. At times it appears that they all line up to form a single, giant, overall "knee," so that SMPs with Z processors are cost-efficient, while SMPs of with Z+1 or more processors are grossly costly. However, in a world where SMPs are for sale with everywhere from four to 64 processors, it's hard to believe that any such overall knee exists. The discrete cost-increase events are apparently dense enough to form a continuum.

Nevertheless, the net result of all these increases, in addition to the "blindingly obvious" cost increases mentioned above, is that scaled-up SMPs are intrinsically less cost-effective than small ones.

13.3.3　The Production Volume Issue

The cost of any item is directly related to the number of them that are manu-factured because what are called fixed costs—the non-recurring costs needed to produce any at all—must be allocated across all the units built. The larger the denominator (number of units), the smaller the fraction of that fixed cost appears in each unit. Typically, fixed costs include things like development cost and the cost of setting up the manufacturing line.

There is another factor at work here, too. Competition forces any develop-ment organization to pay far more attention to cost issues for higher volume products. If high-volume units are not heavily cost-optimized, someone is bound to weigh in with a lower cost unit and price it lower, hoping to make up the profit differential in number of units sold. That doesn't happen if the market size is too small to make up the difference by selling larger numbers.

Large SMPs are intrinsically a low-volume business. Due to their ballroom organization, their memory subsystems must be built to accommodate the large number of processors and so must be a different design point from higher volume units, which must be cost-optimized for their size.

CC-NUMA systems, on the other hand, can potentially use high-volume units—*if*, and only if, those high-volume units are designed to accept on their system bus the additional directory unit that connects the nodes (see Chapter 7). This is not just a matter of having a socket on a system board. The chips interfacing to that bus—memory controller, I/O controller, proces-sor cache controller—must also be able to drive the additional electrical load and address the additional unit. That happens to be true for the 1997 genera-tion of the most important high-volume board around, Intel's Standard High Volume (SHF) 4-way Pentium Pro SMP. Whether it will continue to be true for the indefinite future is anybody's guess.

Clusters can also be built of cost-optimized high volume units. Here there is no qualification, unless cluster acceleration techniques are used that extrava-gantly require modification of the base unit the way CC-NUMA systems do.

However, the story is not quite that simple and clean, for two reasons.

To begin with, the architectures discussed here differ primarily in their memory and related subsystems; the same processors could be used throughout. This is an issue because the primary contributor to system cost is not those subsystems; it is, rather, the processor. So while there is an advantage to using a higher-volume processor "nest," that advantage can be small compared to the advantage of using a high-volume processor.

The other complicating factor is that while many more small servers than large ones are sold, the numbers involved are all rather small compared to the numbers of client systems sold. This does not eliminate hardware volume cost advantages, but it does mute them, and it places the largest hardware cost advantage squarely on those systems that use the same processors that client systems use.

As a result, while clusters and to a lesser extent CC-NUMA systems do have an architecture-based hardware cost advantage from production volumes, it is not clear that this advantage is always overwhelming. In this area in particular, execution may override architecture. A good, low-cost but low-volume implementation can be better than a slightly less competent high-volume implementation. You do, however, need to have that less-competent high-volume implementation sitting there to be picked off. It is not wise to bet on that.

13.4 High Availability_____

It is truly unclear whether anybody is really interested in a large server system that does not incorporate a significant degree of high availability. In fact, it appears that the desire for an increasing level of high availability grows in proportion to the size of the system.

This makes sense. The bigger the system, the larger the number of people who depend on it, or the more important the job that system performs. This can be true in reality: the number of people and the job importance was why the customer paid that much for a large system. Alternatively, it can be true by attribution, reversing the argument: It must be important, and a lot of people must depend on it, because the customer paid a lot for it.

Furthermore, the more components a system has, the higher the likelihood that one of them will fail. So, in an absolute sense, larger systems need more attention paid to availability issues. This produces a double whammy: Not only are more people more unhappy when a large system fails, it is more likely to fail.

This means high availability is doubly important as server size grows, and the trends favoring increased server sizes are many; this was discussed in Section 3.5 on page 64.

Here, at last, we have an area with a clear-cut, definitive answer.

> Among the alternatives considered in this chapter, only clusters have high availability now.

> Compared with other high availability alternatives not considered in this chapter, clusters achieve this goal at much lower cost by using high volume components. Here, the high volume issues are

clear cut because the alternative, hardware fault tolerance, is but a sliver of an elite market.

The reasons why SMPs and Current CC-NUMA systems lack high availability are the maintenance of cache coherence itself, and the use of a single operating system. This was explained in Section 12.11.4 on page 445, "Lowly Available Systems: SMP, CC-NUMA," which also describes how bloody awful it is for implementation to overrule architecture in this particular case.

Potential CC-NUMA systems may provide recovery from unplanned outages in the future. However, continuous availability—avoiding both unplanned and *planned* outages, including outages for system upgrades—will remain a problem for the foreseeable future as far as I can tell; some breakthrough might be made, but it's unclear that the problem is even well-recognized at this point. So, this is a fairly permanent problem—if these systems remain CC-NUMA systems in their programming. If CC-NUMA proponents give up on "SMP programming model" claims and become, in effect, clusters, that problem can be overcome. This appears at present to be a remote possibility.

13.5 Other Issues

While important, performance, cost, and high availability are not everything. In many cases, none are not even the first bar over which a product must pass when being considered. How SMPs, clusters, and CC-NUMA systems compare in other areas is summarized in Table 20, and discussed in this section. In these cases, the distinction between Current and Potential CC-NUMA doesn't matter, so for this section it will be dropped

13.5.1 Memory Utilization

Given how much of a system's cost is memory, it is important that clusters and CC-NUMA systems are slightly poorer at utilizing a given aggregate quantity of memory than are SMPs, even though this disadvantage is probably insignificant in useful server cases. This disadvantage arises from two directions.

For clusters, each node must contain an independent copy of at least the kernel of an operating system, whereas a single copy is shared by all the nodes of an SMP. It's not clear which is normally chosen in the first wave of CC-NUMA systems, but in any event this really doesn't make as much difference as one might suppose.

The actual space used by an operating system kernel is in large part determined by data structures whose size is proportional to the system resources

Table 20 Other Comparisons

Feature	Symmetric Multiprocessor	Cluster	CC-NUMA
memory utilization	optimal due to existence of single memory pool	suboptimal because of boundaries between nodes' memories, but usually not a large effect	suboptimal because of boundaries between nodes' memories, but usually not a large effect
load balancing	increasingly expensive, but routine use of global queues provides good results if grain size large	degradation due to the need to have separate queues per node	degradation due to the need to have separate queues per node, overhead of inter-node job migration
application & subsystem support	common using industry-standard techniques, e.g., threads	not as common as SMPs, but all most important subsystems covered	not common
administration	simplest; natural single system image because one OS	most difficult unless single system image support provided; then as good as SMP	first wave (non-highly available) simple, because it has one OS; later will inherit cluster difficulties
programming model	SMP shared memory; will not work on clusters, performance often will not scale well on CC-NUMA	message passing; works with greatly reduced efficiency on SMP	distributed memory; will not work on clusters, works on SMPs

and load. For example, tables for memory management are in many cases proportional to the total real memory available and to the amount of memory allocated for all active jobs. For comparison purposes, one should assume that the aggregate, job-required memory size and job load is the same on an SMP and a cluster. Then, the aggregate table size added up across all cluster nodes will be in the same range as the total allocated in an SMP's memory.

Nevertheless, there are unique items, such as the code itself, base table structures, standard per-machine daemon processes, and so on, that must be replicated. So clusters, and possibly CC-NUMA systems, are at a disadvantage in this regard, but it is seldom a significant disadvantage. In particular, if one is running a large commercial database system, Internet server, or file server, the amount of "real" data overwhelms the system-derived items to such an extent that this difference is completely insignificant.

The second memory utilization issue arises because the aggregate memory of a cluster or CC-NUMA system is divided into chunks, one at each node. CC-NUMA systems provide access to remote nodes, but the system should try to avoid this because it's less efficient. This means that there are job mixes that can run on SMPs that cannot run as efficiently on a cluster or CC-NUMA system. Assume, for example, that the aggregate memory in both a two-node cluster or CC-NUMA and a two-node SMP is 100 Mbytes: 100 Mbytes in the SMP, and two 50 Mbyte memories in each of the nodes in the other cases. The SMP can simultaneously run two jobs with memory requirements of 30 Mbytes and 70 Mbytes respectively. The cluster cannot run the 70 Mbyte job without degradation anywhere, since no one node's memory is larger than 50 Mbytes. The CC-NUMA system can't either, without degradation.

13.5.2   *Load Balancing*

Load balancing, or workload management, is a performance issue; but it did not fit well with the earlier performance discussion, so is covered here. This subject refers to distributing work across the nodes of any system in an attempt to keep all nodes equally busy, or, more precisely, to meet the performance goals of the customer (which may have nothing to do with whether all the nodes are always busy). As was discussed in Chapter 9, load balancing is not a trivial operation on SMP systems. Nevertheless, it is routinely performed in what is usually judged to be an adequate manner; examples were given in Chapter 9 and Chapter 10. The existence of a common global pool of memory and I/O resources is a significant, if not crucial aid in accomplishing load balancing.

Clusters have a harder time of this. Unless something like the Parallel Sysplex Coupling Facility is used, there is no good place to keep a global queue of tasks; other, less satisfactory techniques must be used. If a global pool is maintained, the additional overhead of communication between cluster nodes comes into play. It is much easier on a cluster than on an SMP for a global queue to become a serial bottleneck, and even on an SMP it is common to have trouble with it.

In Search of Clusters   ✳

Even if there is no problem finding out what jobs are to be done, the additional internode communication overhead of clusters is a negative factor. Compared to an SMP, a cluster requires the use of more processing power and time to migrate a job from one node to another. This overhead limits a cluster more than an SMP in how well it can balance the load. This may change, however, as the faster communications facilities become more widely deployed.

CC-NUMA systems share many of the characteristics of clusters in this area. Once again, it's hard to find a place to put a global queue. On the other hand, it may be easier to get to it than in clusters. Similarly, the need to migrate jobs between nodes is there in CC-NUMA and not present in SMPs.

13.5.3 Application and Subsystem Support

Another point that must be reckoned with is how well subsystems and applications can make use of the system.

SMP hardware is effectively an industry standard. Threads and other techniques, covered in Chapter 10, are common, and, by whatever means, support is nearly ubiquitous.

Clusters are now well-represented in major subsystems and middleware: databases, transaction monitors, and some groupware (for example, Lotus Notes) have versions that are appropriate for cluster use. However, one must almost always purchase, at added cost, the "distributed" version of that middleware; the SMP support, in contrast, is built into the base product. In general, the facilities available for support of general use of clusters have nowhere near the universal availability of such facilities for SMP systems.

If clusters are weak here, CC-NUMA systems are pusillanimous. A few middleware vendors have announced support for individual hardware vendors' CC-NUMA systems, but in general it lacks the breadth of support available for clusters. Yes, CC-NUMA advocates say that doesn't matter because they run SMP code. We've discussed that in Chapter 5.

13.5.4 Administration

System administration is another area where many current cluster offerings have a disadvantage, but not all.

Since an SMP is running a single operating system, of course it is administered as a single unit. CC-NUMA systems as they appeared in mid-1997 have the same characteristic.

Clusters, on the other hand, are usually multiple operating systems administratively glued together, if at all, by a collection of multisystem administration tools. Those tools make it much easier to administer than would be the case if they did not exist, and administrators had to deal with each node separately. Nevertheless, it is not as easy as administering a single system.

However, there are cluster systems that exhibit a genuine single system image for administration. This is particularly true for the full-system clusters (IBM Parallel Sysplex, Tandem Himalaya, DEC OpenVMS Cluster). It will also be true for any generally-available kernel-level SSI systems that make it into general production availability. These systems have no significant disadvantage in administration compared with SMPs and CC-NUMA systems.

13.5.5 Programming Model

The largest nonperformance difference between SMPs, clusters, and CC-NUMA systems is that they naturally support different programming models. This difference is the one that underlies many differences: system availability, workload balancing, the number of applications and subsystems that run on one or the other, and so on. Two chapters were devoted to this issue, so little will be repeated here.

13.6 Partitioning

The real need for high availability brings up an issue with respect to large SMPs: Who would want a huge system that isn't highly available? Not many at all.

This fact has been long known in the mainframe arena. The response there has been complex hardware (Section 12.11.4 on page 445), clustering, and a third element: partitioning.

Partitioning consists of taking a large single system and separating it into smaller pieces that are, as far as the software running on it is concerned, separate computers. A 12-way SMP, for example, might be partitioned into two 6-way systems, or a 2-way and a 10-way, and so on. In addition to processors, each has its own separate area of memory, its own collection of I/O devices, and so on; each partition is a separate, fully-functional computer, running an independent copy of the operating system.

This at first appears illogical. After going to all the effort of creating a huge single machine, why break it up? There are several reasons:

- ➤ Avoiding software failures. Hardware FT doesn't help here; partitions keep error situations isolated from other processing.

- ➤ Tuning to very different workloads. It is often far easier to parameterize two systems in different ways than to attempt to mix them both together on one system.

- ➤ As a combination of the previous two, isolating a development or test system from a production system. The development system is more likely to fall over, and this way it doesn't take the production system along.

Those are good reasons for wanting separate systems, and large open systems SMPs are now offering partitioning that attains those ends, but why not use a cluster instead? Well, initially few people were thinking about clusters, had only one big mainframe box, and couldn't afford a second for development and testing. So this was a useful tool. But now?

The answer lies in the ability to make the partitioning dynamic, variable over time. This allows, for example, a development partition to use few resources when they're needed for production, and a production partition to give up resources to development when the load is light. This is having your cake—cluster-like availability—and eating it too, with a kind of system wide load balancing.

This dynamism has been implemented on mainframes since the late 80s by facilities like IBM's LPAR (Logical **Par**tition) and Amdahl's MDF (**M**ultiple **D**omain Feature). There, it is implemented as a kind of hardware-assisted time sharing. Partitions are effectively a kind of virtual machine, presided over by a hypervisor (above the supervisor, what else?) that alone has control over various permission and routing registers that keep the virtual machines separate from one another, even when running operating systems in supervisor mode.

Using this technique, a physical 10-way SMP can be turned into two 10-way partitions overlaying one another, time-shared on the same hardware, neither aware of the other's existence. The fraction of the use of the system that each gets can be varied by hypervisor-controlled event-driven scheduling according to the load applied to each partition; or by operator command, turning one on and the other off; or by weighting attached to each by the hypervisor, set by the customer. The current implementations only allow creating a new partition when the system is booted, but this time-sharing allows the needed dynamics.

However, all this only works within the bounds of a single SMP. Cluster-like MPP systems, such as the IBM RS/6000 SP systems, also provide partitioning in the more obvious way: This set of nodes does one thing, that set does another, and the two are isolated from one another by virtue being on physically separate machines and having settings in the interconnect hardware and/or software that keep them from inadvertently bugging each other. This allows multiple workloads to coexist under the roof of a single administration system, which is quite useful. Dynamism here is achieved by retiring nodes from one partition, and recruiting them into another.

Open systems providers of large SMPs are also providing partitioning within their SMPs, but as this book is written, they do not have the dynamic qualities of traditional mainframe partitioning.

Now, recall the comments made in the chapter on "NUMA" systems, Section 7.5.2 on page 203, about the architectural additions that would be necessary if CC-NUMA systems were to attain high availability. This sounds familiar, because what was required actually was partitioning of exactly this sort.

Putting all this together could result in a system that looks like the one shown in Figure 121.

This is a system that, overall, is a single cluster; it is managed as a single unit. The whole computers of which it is formed, however, are partitions of two sorts: A separation of a sea of CC-NUMA nodes into individual systems; and a logical separation of a single large SMP node into separate elements. The whole is joined by an single interconnect, but what flows over that interconnect is either CC-NUMA load/store traffic, on the one hand; or on the other hand some form of message or NC-NUMA access. Which flows depends on the relationship between the nodes communicating: members of the same cache-coherence domain, or not. That hardware and software would not involve any particular difficulty or unknowns at this point. Going further and providing the dynamic membership that customers need from partitioning would be harder, but certainly not impossible. The intent there would be to allow nodes to retire from one cache coherence domain, and be recruited into another; or, as shown in the blown-up segment of Figure 121, individual processors, segments of memory, and I/O facilities could be treated similarly, by building the ability to partition into a single large SMP.

I know of no vendor that is actually building such a system today. There are clusters of SMPs, and clusters of separate CC-NUMA systems, and vendors providing partitioning of large SMP systems allow making clusters out of those partitions, too (just Sun and IBM as this book goes to press). However, nobody, so far, uses the interconnect that makes the tighter bond to do the cluster communication. So everybody is poking around the edge of a synthesis system like that of Figure 121, but nobody's yet jumped in. Perhaps there is some reason why not, when one considers it in more detail. I suspect, however, that most have just not done all the work yet.

In Search of Clusters ✳

Figure 121 A Synthesis Using Partitioning

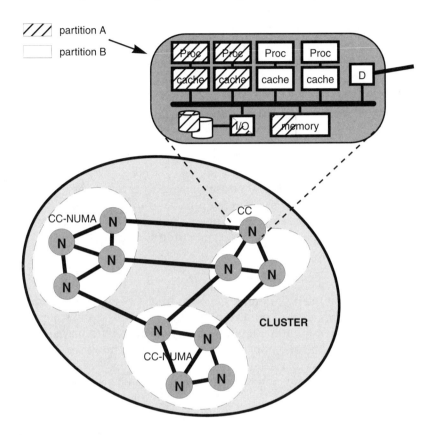

An interesting question is whether the resultant system is, or should be, considered a "massively" parallel system. Certainly there can be a huge number of processors if the individual nodes are large SMPs or CC-NUMA aggregations with many processors. However, there is no particular reason why the number of cluster nodes should be enormous. A cluster node count of 32 or less is probably sufficient to satisfy the two requirements that exist: Sufficient partitions for logical purposes, separating independent workloads and keeping development out of the way of production; and providing enough granularity for scaling to make high availability inexpensive, as discussed in Section 12.11.1 on page 435.

So who knows, perhaps this reunites clusters with the MPP crowd once again. Unfortunately, spectacle will probably win the name game, and the lowly cluster will once again be forgotten, particularly among those who smoke too many of their own press releases.

13.7 Conclusion

SMP, CC-NUMA, and cluster systems are, indeed, different. Optimally, each would be used for the particular area that suits them best. This is particularly true with regard to performance; while there is significant overlap in capabilities, there are pockets in which each is a better solution. Cost of SMPs, particularly for new business, is an issue; but that issue is counterbalanced by their greater familiarity and general pervasiveness. I therefore expect that each will persist in the market for the foreseeable future. Particularly because of the overlap in their capabilities, this should make for particularly entertaining marketing wars.

Furthermore, as cache-based performance effects drive SMP programming towards a boudoir model, even the programming of all these systems may ultimately converge. The inertia of software being what it is, I would not anticipate this to have a huge effect any time soon, however.

However.

Remember that the programming model differences between these competing architectures create a critical mass issue, as discussed in Chapter 9. That makes the situation ultimately unstable; once even random perturbation—or perception—makes it appear that one of these architectures has the upper hand, the industry zeroes in on it: more software breeds more hardware which breeds software, and so on to convergence on a single architecture.

It is tempting to say, therefore, that the battle is over and clusters have won, because clusters, while at least showing no major disadvantages on the cost and performance fronts—and arguable advantages in both those ways—are unique in their ability to satisfy the requirement for high availability, and so already have the upper hand. Certainly this guarantees that, no matter what is used for the nodes, clusters will survive and be a significant piece of the server market indefinitely.

However, the server purchases that drive the actual market convergence are based to a very significant degree on factors that have nothing to do with such technical issues. Business relationships, service, ability to run required software, service, and a host of other factors enter into the decision to purchase, as does a necessary conservatism wrought by cost: costs of migrating to a new model, a new architecture, a new operating system, and so on.

Architecture isn't even technical destiny. How can it possibly define the destiny of the market?

Why We Need the Concept of *Cluster*

The preceding chapters have been concerned with defining and elaborating on the concept of a cluster of computers, along with the comparisons and issues raised by that concept. All this has hopefully been interesting and useful.

But before those discussions, the introduction indicated that even more was involved—that we *needed* the concept of a cluster, distinct from general parallel or distributed systems. Lacking that concept as a normal part of our thinking, a number of bad things are happening without our intention or notice.

1. Benchmarks are not giving us the information that we expect.

2. Research and product development directions are misguided.

3. Conceptual issues are confused, to the detriment of a variety of areas.

4. Products are being pursued that are maladapted to the market.

This is the chapter that backs up those assertions, explaining exactly how, and in what sense each of them is meant.

14.1 Benchmarks

Ideally, standardized benchmarks should provide purchasers and developers of computer systems with many different types of information. They should let you:

> ➤ compare systems of similar architecture—for example, a collection of SMPs;

> ➤ compare systems of differing architectures—for example, SMPs vs. uniprocessors vs. "NUMA" vs. clusters;

> ➤ identify the parts of systems whose enhancement will yield the biggest benefit—for example, a developer might analyze benchmark execution to determine whether total performance is enhanced more by increasing the cache size or by increasing the CPU speed;

> ➤ choose an initial list of candidate systems for implementing a particular application, in two senses: first, by narrowing the performance range to the approximate level required; and second, by determining the interest of a vendor in that type of application, as indicated by the vendor's willingness to go through the often expensive process of running a related benchmark. The cut on performance can only be approximate, of course, because no benchmark's characteristics exactly match the real application that is to be run.

No benchmark is perfect. Otherwise, there wouldn't be so many of them, each emphasizing different aspects of system performance. That's the reason for the qualification mentioned at the end of the above list: All a benchmark measures is how fast the benchmark runs, not how fast your application will run—even though that's what everybody wants to use it for.

Unfortunately, some of the most common benchmarks in use for commercial processing do not recognize the difference between distributed systems and clusters: They lack the concept of a cluster. As a result, their ability to provide every one of the benefits listed above is, for clusters, significantly compromised.

14.1.1 The TPC Benchmarks

The most widely used and quoted benchmarks in commercial data processing are those of the Transaction Processing Performance Council (TPC). The TPC is a consortium of 44 leading hardware and software companies worldwide; it was founded in 1988 to define transaction processing and database tests. The council's TPC Benchmarks A, B, and C (TPC-A, TPC-B, and TPC-C) have been far and away the most popular standard benchmark for determining performance and price/performance in a commercial context [Tra93a, Tra93b, Tra93c].

For all practical purposes, these are *the* industry benchmarks for on-line transaction processing; there is no other game in town. Since on-line transaction processing is a very large market, these benchmarks are widely used even though they are large, expensive, and require a very significant investment in equipment and time to run. Publication of the benchmarked system's price every time the performance is mentioned is one of TPC requirements.

These benchmarks are also quite carefully defined and controlled. Compliance with the definitions is independently audited for each system whose results are published.

The various TPC benchmarks are based on different commercial scenarios. TPC-A and -B were modeled on a branch banking debit/credit scenario and used to be widely quoted; TPC-A was interactive, whereas TPC-B was a batch version of the same thing. The current TPC-C benchmark is modeled after a warehouse order entry and fulfillment facility. The TPC-A and -B benchmarks have been withdrawn; now, only TPC-C is current, and there is work under way to define what is being called TPC-98 during development; it is intended to replace TPC-C. Another benchmark, TPC-D [Tra94], also exists to provide performance information in a decision-support scenario.

14.1.2   Parallel Execution

When any of the TPC's transaction benchmarks are (or were) run on a symmetric multiprocessor, the benchmark's workload is distributed among processors the way one might intuitively expect, as illustrated in Figure 122.

No distinction is made between a uniprocessor and an SMP. A single input stream of transactions to be performed is simply presented to the machine. Exactly how that stream is presented, whether through front-end machines or via terminals, or whether a client-server variation is used, is the subject of very detailed specifications that have nothing to do with this discussion.

The issue we're concerned with is this: It is up to the operating system, database system, and possibly transaction monitor (if used) to divide the work among the processors to obtain the best possible throughput. This is, at least, what I'd expect—that the effectiveness of a parallel system's distribution of work is one of the things implicitly measured by the benchmark.

The request stream may happen to be internally partitioned into groups of transactions that affect each other very little. That's provided for by the TPC rules, which model distributed processing as a defined way to increase the

Figure 122 TPC Workload Distribution in an SMP

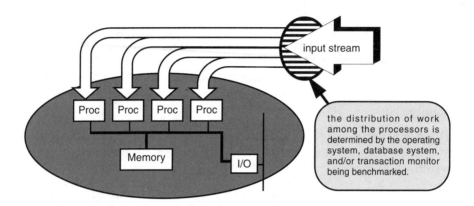

input stream

Proc Proc Proc Proc

Memory

I/O

the distribution of work among the processors is determined by the operating system, database system, and/or transaction monitor being benchmarked.

size of the workload. TPC-A and -B did this by coarsely modeling branch banking, while TPC-C similarly models multiple warehouses. The rules specify that the branches do most of their processing locally, as do warehouses, so each branch or warehouse is represented by a sub-stream of transactions that are mostly independent of others.

This is illustrated in Figure 123, which also shows the particular percentages used in the most common case: 85% is local, and 15% is uniformly distributed across all sites. Since half of the uniformly distributed workload comes back home, it ends up 92.5% local and 7.5% remote.

Figure 123 TPC Benchmark Workload for Distributed Processing

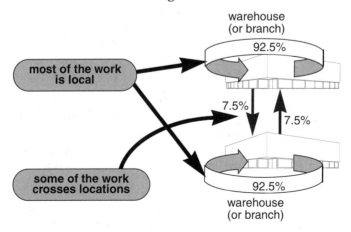

warehouse (or branch)

92.5%

most of the work is local

7.5%

7.5%

some of the work crosses locations

92.5%

warehouse (or branch)

In Search of Clusters ✳

As far as I know, no SMP systems attempt to take advantage of the internal partitioning that the distributed case provides. The situation with clusters is different, but not because the rules specifically call out clusters. It's indirect. All that happens is that the TPC rules specifically and deliberately do not state how many warehouses or branches there are to be, or how the system under test is configured in detail—that's all up to the vendor—and when there are multiple systems involved, multiple input streams can be used.

So, everybody does the obvious optimization, very clearly allowed under the rules: They all use one warehouse per node, with the stream from that branch going into a single node. Or, if they have big SMPs at the nodes, they put several warehouses at each node. However, nobody with any understanding of the benchmark—and believe me, you don't get into this game unless you understand the benchmark very well indeed—is so stupid as to split a warehouse between two nodes.

The effect of this, for a two-node system, is illustrated in Figure 124. 92.5% of the workload on each node is known when it arrives at the node to be completely local, requiring no communication between the nodes; only 7.5% requires any communication.

Figure 124 TPC Workload Distribution in a Two-Machine Cluster

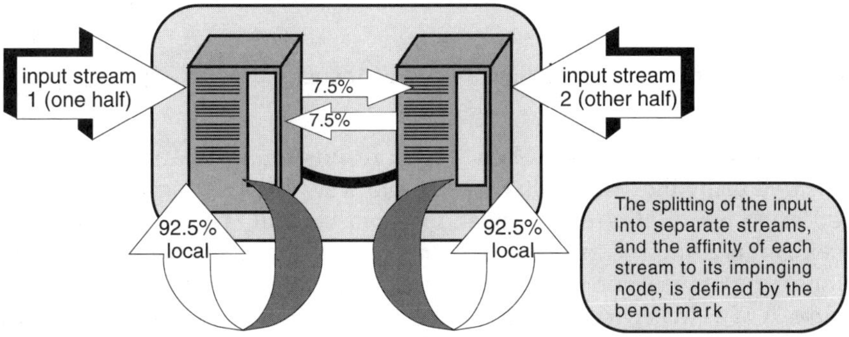

input stream 1 (one half)

7.5%

7.5%

input stream 2 (other half)

92.5% local

92.5% local

The splitting of the input into separate streams, and the affinity of each stream to its impinging node, is defined by the benchmark

Unlike the SMP case, *the benchmark definition itself* is doing much of the load balancing for a clustered or scalable parallel system. The benchmark furthermore ensures that very little communication must pass between nodes; the vast majority of the processing is local to a node.

This is the way every published TPC benchmark result for a cluster should be interpreted. It is the accepted, audited interpretation of the benchmarks and is performed in this manner by every vendor of clustered systems.[1] Distributed systems are defined to be evaluated in the way described, and clusters, as is usual, are lumped in with distributed systems while SMPs are not. The concept of a cluster, as distinct from a distributed system, is missing.

Actually, the situation is a little more complex—and worse—than that. TPC-A and -B had only one type of transaction. TPC-C has several different types, and each is distributed according to different rules. In TPC-C, the transaction type, which is defined to be (at least one of the) the most voluminous, the Payment transaction, is governed by an 85/15 rule. The other transaction types also have locality rules: 99/1, or even 100/0. So the total benchmark-derived locality is actually stronger than indicated above.

This situation is why the discussion of Tandem's record TPC-C result on page 36 emphasized that it was benchmarked as a 7-node cluster, even though each of those nodes, a 16-cell loosely-coupled multiprocessor in Tandem's terminology, could technically have been considered a 16-way cluster of itself.

14.1.3   Difficulties

If someone intends to use a cluster for on-line transaction processing with multiple input streams that have significant locality, this benchmark definition, and its cluster interpretation, is very reasonable. If that is not the intended use, this benchmark is not suitable. This is just like any other benchmark: If it matches the intended use, the benchmark is appropriate; if it doesn't, it's not.

Nevertheless, the characteristics of the TPC benchmarks as applied to clusters cause difficulties.

The first problem is that TPC benchmark results for SMPs and clusters are measured using the same unit. For example, a system's performance is specified as so many "tps-A" (transactions per second, TPC Benchmark A) whether it is a uniprocessor, an SMP, or a cluster. The use of the same unit, to say nothing of the same benchmark name, encourages everyone to compare the tps-A of a cluster with the tps-A of an SMP, as if they measured the same thing. Even if the TPC were to shout the difference from the housetops (it doesn't), people would still compare them just because they've got the same name. For a uniprocessor and an SMP, they are the same. For a cluster, clearly they are not.

This name confusion alone limits the ability of these benchmarks to perform one of the four functions mentioned at the start of this section, namely perform meaningful comparisons between different architectures. Such comparisons breaks down particularly in the area of scaling: how performance increases (or doesn't) as one adds additional, parallel, processing capability.

The predefined locality present in the benchmark causes clusters to demonstrate rather good scaling characteristics: Their tpm-C ratings usually increase quite nicely as more cluster nodes are added, even if internal cluster communication facilities are relatively meager. SMPs, which do not enjoy this predefined locality, have a much harder time scaling their performance on these benchmarks.

Unlike clusters, whose internal communication is bounded by the 15% limit, SMPs must contend with interprocessor communication that keeps increasing as the number of processors rises. As a result, the measurements published for SMP systems are more robust than they are for clusters, meaning: The SMP results tend less than the cluster results to predict lower performance than one will achieve in practice. In practice, you can encounter a worse workload distribution than is used for a cluster; but you cannot encounter one worse than the SMP benchmark uses. Note that the clusters may indeed be more robust than the SMPs. However, the benchmark results cannot be used to measure how much more robust they are.

This disparity between SMPs and clusters affects another item in the list of things benchmarks should be good for: choosing a candidate list of systems appropriate to a particular application. Often neither sales personnel nor customers understand the difference between the SMP and cluster benchmarks. Actually, my experience is that this is an understatement. In the last few years, I've met with over a hundred customers and potential customers for server systems, and a good fraction of that many sales representatives. I have yet to find *one* of them who understood this difference before it was explained.

The results of this confusion? Customers include clusters in their initial list of choices on the basis of the published standard benchmarks. Then, when they run their own benchmarks, everybody is dumbfounded over why the system isn't performing as well as anticipated. (This is the point at which I receive an often frantic phone call from the field.) Time and money has been wasted. Even more of both is wasted if the cluster is installed solely on the basis of the standard benchmark, without benchmarking the customer's application—absolutely never recommended, but it happens often enough—and shortly thereafter the machine is thrown out, accompanied by suitable invectives, because it doesn't perform adequately. These situations are far from universal; more cluster installations are successful than not. However, customers do encounter these problems on a regular basis, and as a result end up convinced that clusters simply don't work or require inhumanly complex data and input partitioning efforts to work adequately. Sales

---

1. Specifically, the rules stated in sections 2.4.1.5, 2.5.1.2, 2.6.1.2, 2.7.1, and 2.8.1 of the *TPC Benchmark C Standard Specification Revision 2.0* [Tra93c].

representatives wind up with similar opinions, reducing the number of customers to whom clusters are even suggested.

So far, the discussion has deliberately avoided a key question: Is the benchmark as defined appropriate for clusters? Another way of stating that is: Does the benchmark adequately predict the performance of clustered systems as they will typically be used? My experience has been indicated above. None of the *cluster* situations I've personally observed had multiple input streams with the kind of locality exhibited by the benchmark. Distributed situations are, of course, another issue; locality is usually quite apparent there. Several years ago I heard of, but did not personally investigate, one cluster installation that did exhibit such locality; it involved a cluster of mainframes.

It's therefore my personal opinion that for clusters, as opposed to distributed systems, the vast majority of customers (to say nothing of the hapless sales and other field personnel) would be better served by a benchmark that can be compared to the uniprocessor/SMP case without being misleading. This could be accomplished in at least two ways: If locality is considered normal, one could incorporate it into the SMP as well as the cluster benchmark. If locality is not considered normal, eliminate it from the cluster benchmark. Or, if it's impossible to decide whether locality is normal, have two benchmark variations—one with and one without locality—and publish separately labelled results.

All this presumes, of course, that one recognizes that a cluster is not the same thing as a distributed system.

Let's assume that a "0/100 rule" (no locality) is closer to "typical" customer use—a hard thing to define; everyone thinks they're typical—than the "85/15 rule" used in the benchmark. Under that assumption, the current benchmark's ability to provide the other benefits one can expect from standardized benchmarks is also compromised.

If 0/100 is more typical, then, with the current benchmark, comparison between machines of the same architecture—between clusters—is compromised because of the small amount of internal, intermachine communication engendered by the 85/15 rule. This low level of communication means that after one has installed minimal communication, additional communication facilities will not improve benchmark performance. Machine A, with minimal communication and faster processor complexes, might well benchmark faster than Machine B, with much better communication but slightly slower processors. This result would certainly not be bad if the 85/15 rule corresponded to "typical" use; in fact, it would then be the answer one would want the benchmark to give. But if 0/100 is closer to actual use, one will never find out that Machine B might well be better.

Improving the breed, pinpointing areas that yield the most cost-effective performance improvements, is the final area where these benchmarks are compromised if the 85/15 rule is not representative of most situations. In parallel systems of all stripes, including clusters, the important issues are always communication, synchronization, and load balancing, with administration hanging in there as the very important but grubby practical issue that nobody ever wants to work on. The TPC benchmarks are not intended to deal with administration (as I said, nobody wants to work on it). But the 85/15 rule does most of the load balancing for the system; and the internal communication and synchronization required under the 85/15 rule are sufficiently minor that clusters could probably be connected by wet string and still benefit from faster processors, not better communication.

In fact, this rule leads to the silly result illustrated in Figure 125. Suppose you take three collections of identical processors, with eight processors in each collection. One collection you make into a cluster of uniprocessors connected to each other using shared disks and Ethernet (even if it's not wet). Another collection you make into a single large SMP, internally connected by a great, big, fast bus. The third you make into a cluster of moderate, say four-way, SMPs. Assume everything else is as similar as possible: everyone has at least enough memory, large caches, the same aggregate I/O bandwidth and I/O initiation rate (harder for the SMP, but assume it anyway), the same number of disk drives, and so on. Benchmark them using the TPC benchmark rules. Ignore cost (but the clusters are probably cheaper). Because of the 85/15 rule, the cluster of uniprocessors will win by a large margin, and the cluster of SMPs will come in second. Every time.

Figure 125 Handicapping a TPC Race

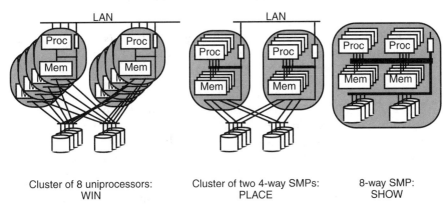

Cluster of 8 uniprocessors:
WIN

Cluster of two 4-way SMPs:
PLACE

8-way SMP:
SHOW

✳ *Why We Need the Concept of Cluster*   **495**

The reason this result is so silly is that it says Ethernet (10 Mbits/second) plus disk bandwidth (a few Mbytes/second, with milliseconds of rotational latency) is a *better* communication medium than multi-hundred-mega-byte/second or even gigabyte/second internal busses connecting the same number of identical processors.

14.1.4   Why Am I Doing This?

This section, by far the longest of this chapter, has been devoted to showing in some detail why clusters might not give as good performance on commercial workloads as we have been lead to believe. This probably seems like an odd thing for a proponent of clusters to do. It may quite possibly lead to fewer of the current crop of clusters being sold.

Even if the standard benchmark results for clusters aren't directly compara-ble to those of uniprocessors and SMPs, pretending they are can still get you in the door, and anybody with any exposure to marketing knows how valu-able that is. Once you're in, even if performance isn't, well, quite as good as was anticipated, it will still be possible to emphasize some of the many other factors present in any purchasing decision: high availability, lower cost, sup-port, scalability (with appropriate tap-dancing around performance), financ-ing, customer relationship, delivery schedule, warranty, and so on. These things make a large difference, and a customer might very well be happier with the whole package that can be offered with a cluster than with, for example, an SMP system lacking the other goodies. But an initial perfor-mance cut is like single-issue politics: No matter what else you have to offer, you don't get in the door and don't even get a chance to bring up the other issues.

But truth will out, in the long run truth in advertising is best, and the good guys always win in the end. Right?

OK, I had long hair and a beard (actually, a goatee) in the 60s too, but along with everybody else I've grown a 90s reality bump and it's uncomfortable with that.

The real problem is not that clusters might not be as good as the current crop of numbers indicates. The problem is that word "might." To design systems you have to have a workload against which to evaluate them. For commer-cial systems, the TPC benchmarks are it. Nobody I know of looks seriously at much else when designing systems for commercial data processing.

This is not entirely bad. They could do much worse, especially for unipro-cessors and SMPs; the TPC benchmarks definitely have cache, memory, and I/O characteristics that appear to be at least roughly appropriate for com-mercial data processing. Besides, you have to publish the benchmark numbers eventually anyway; might as well know what they are likely to be, so the planners can do pricing, compare with competition, and so on. As a result, TPC-C gets used, and since there are always limited resources very little else gets looked at. Result: Nobody knows the degree to which artifacts like the 85/15 rule are affecting system designs. We can't understand clusters without breaking this mold. While it holds, we don't know what we're doing.

A short story:

Once upon a time there were two system designs, call them A and B, and only enough money to pursue one. Happens all the time. Design B—not mine, by the way; I was an onlooker, and for a number of reasons irrelevant to the current discussion I didn't like it—I've called "B" because it was a very Bad Boy. Not only was it politically unpopular, it also egregiously violated several of the more religiously held technical dogmata concerning how parallel systems should be built. But wow, did it have a whale of a lot of internal communication and fast synchronization. Its internal communication was exceeded only by the stubbornness of its advocates, without which it never would have lasted as long as it did. (Also happens all the time.)

Design A, on the other hand, followed the path of righteousness. Politically and techno-aesthetically correct, it boasted moderately good internal communication with the usual overhead entailed by righteous communication that eschewed any of the cluster acceleration gadgets previously mentioned; they didn't exist then. This would merely be a typical story of product development politics, since Design A did of course win (for a number of complicated reasons having little if anything to do with the point of this story), except for one thing.

In the course of the struggle, some performance modeling was carried out, based on benchmarks very much like those of the TPC. Unlike other such modeling, this version had the ability to vary the local/global ratio. At the TPC-standard 85/15 value, assuming the same processors and support gear all 'round, you couldn't tell the difference in performance between A and B; the difference was infinitesimal, certainly below the error bounds of the modeling. At 0/100, under the same assumptions, the Bad Boy won Big. In fact, it won big enough to represent almost an entire generation of microprocessor development, worth millions of dollars.

Is that what we're throwing away?

Does anybody really know?

By the way, that modeling was officially judged irrelevant to the decision between the designs. Why?

It was declared that the modeling showed the designs to have identical performance in customer situations officially sanctioned as "typical."

14.2 Development Directions _____

There really is more than one reason why we need the concept of clusters. I will now stop droning on about benchmarks and discuss more of those reasons.

The next reason on the list is the issue of development direction. Without the notion of a cluster as a target for development, a home for various products and projects, there are hardware and software efforts that are expending unnecessary effort trying to be something they are not; they are also not getting the recognition and success they deserve for doing things that are natural to them. This section will concern itself with just one example of this, the development of kernel-level, single-system-image (kernel-level SSI) operating systems.

Kernel-level SSI systems such as Locus TNC [Thi91], Amoeba [Tan92], Sprite [O+88], and QNX [Hil93] have been developed in the distributed computing milieu.[2] They had to be developed there; traditionally there is no other place for them. Usually they are positioned as alternatives to over-kernel toolkits like DCE [Ope93, CP93]; again, there is no other place for them. But such systems are not the best fit to the requirements of distributed computing for at least three reasons.

The first reason is that distributed computing places a very high value on the coupling of heterogeneous systems, specifically including machines running different operating systems and having different hardware data formats. This is a very important issue in distributed computing; much of the distributed computing market lies in creating order out of an existing chaos of previously purchased workstations.

Pursuing this goal is abundantly right and proper for distributed systems, but kernel-level SSI systems have a hard time of it. Portability across operating systems is a contradiction in terms, since they are the operating system; how can they not replace what's there? Denigration city. (Locus TNC is an extension of an operating system personality under a microkernel, which is not quite the same thing but is close enough.) Dealing with different hardware data formats is certainly possible, but the degree of coupling such systems entail causes this to be a much larger performance burden than afflicts

---

2. Amoeba actually targets what amounts to a cluster; good for them. QNX targets embedded control situations, which is a different milieu altogether. They are all, however, published and evaluated against the standards of distributed computing.

the looser coupling of over-kernel toolkits. Despite such problems, heterogeneity has been pursued by kernel-level SSI developers because it is of great value in distributed computing—and, lacking clusters, there is no other place for these systems.

The second reason kernel-level SSI systems are disadvantaged derives from the need to accommodate local autonomy. This is highly desired within distributed computing: This is my workstation, with the software tools and hardware widgets I paid for, but please update all the standard stuff for me, but I didn't mean *that* stuff—I don't use it and I need the space for something else; oh, and this whole department all wants it like this except for Joe, and the dummies in Accounts Receivable across the hall want something totally different. Like hardware heterogeneity, local autonomy probably can be done within kernel-level SSI systems; Turing machines are indeed universal. But it is against the grain; it's not what they naturally do, which is make everybody exactly the same; so it is awkward and expensive. That they find it harder counts against these systems. It's irrelevant that this is most often precisely what's desired in clusters.

The third reason concerns a less well advertised characteristic of the distributed computing environment: high-speed variation. In any sufficiently large collection of workstations, somebody's always turning their machines on or off (to say nothing of spilling coffee on them), messing with the communications links, and so on. Therefore, machines are always popping in and out of visibility and whole collections may be isolated for some periods. With respect to kernel-level SSI systems, Turing was still right, doggone him; techniques have been developed that allow those systems to cope with this variation (see [Thi91]), and their developers are probably, justifiably, quite proud of them. It's an enormous mental and probably physical effort to make that work.

From the standpoint of clusters, that effort could have been saved. How often is communication within a single room (or rack) going to be interrupted, much less split into autonomous survivable groups, or one machine go down while the others stay up? It's not that such events will never happen, but an order of magnitude or two difference in how often they happen can make an enormous difference in the complexity of the programming needed to respond to them. Even after accomplishing coping with this temporal irregularity, the developers get little recognition for their efforts, because the techniques devised depend heavily on a kernel-level SSI context. Therefore it's dismissed as not being terribly relevant. It's indeed not relevant—to distributed computing.

As a result of difficulties like those mentioned above, kernel-level SSI systems have not attained any great degree of popularity. Unlike over-kernel toolkits, they are mismatched to the market they are trying to serve. They do continue to be pursued; good researchers are nothing if not persistent.

Yet in their pervasive, well-defined, and cleanly delineated single system image, kernel-level SSI systems have significant advantages that over-kernel toolkits lack—when considered in the context of clusters. It is difficult to conceive of dynamic load balancing with process migration, for example, outside of the context of such systems; in the canonical fully heterogeneous, widely distributed system with provision for local autonomy such load balancing goes against the grain—a task so difficult it is not worth doing outside of special cases. Kernel-level SSI systems' all-encompassing, single-system administration for clusters has been mentioned earlier as an area where these systems provide a tremendous advantage; yet because it results in OS-specific administration of multiple machines, it is anathema to traditional heterogeneous distributed computing, which must supply a common denominator. It's regarded as a problem rather than the major benefit it can be—for a cluster. Without the concept of a cluster, these benefits are hard to appreciate.

Kernel-level SSI systems may yet flourish, as they have not so far. But they will not flourish as *distributed* operating systems, as they are more commonly known. Rather, they may flourish as excellent *cluster* operating systems.

This is starting to happen today, now that clusters are part of the vocabulary of nearly every computer-industry-oriented magazine and analyst's report. However, as far as I can tell it is just beginning to penetrate the Computer Science research establishment.

14.3 Confusion of Issues

Another reason why we need the concept of a cluster is to enhance diversity. By adding any new system concept to our repertoire, comparing and contrasting it with existing ones can clarify issues that otherwise remain confused.

For example, consider Chapter 11 on the subject of single system image. This has been an area of significant confusion, replete with meaningless adjectives like "seamless," and thoroughly confused with the separate issue of system management. The discussion in that chapter arguably brings to this subject some order and structure that was not previously present. It certainly applies not just to clusters but also to other forms of computing.

Could this clarification have taken place without consideration of clusters? Possibly. But it did not. Consideration of clusters brought it into the high relief necessary to resolve some of the muddle.

Are there other areas that consideration of clusters might clarify? Perhaps, but it is hard to tell until the job has been done. One I hope might become more clear is communication. It's certainly confusing to me that it takes more effort and overhead to communicate between "intelligent" devices— programmable computers—than between one "intelligent" device and a dumb one, like a disk drive. But I fear that this may be too much to hope for. Communication has been a subject crossing the distributed and parallel boundaries for a long time, and little has come of that cross-fertilization. On the other hand, so has the notion of single system image.

14.4 The Lure of Large Numbers _____

If you hang around marketing people long enough, some of their thought processes inevitably rub off whether you like it or not. A flake that's rubbed off on me, a rather elementary aspect of the area, is represented by what's called a generic market volume pyramid, shown in Figure 126.[3]

Figure 126 The Generic Market Volume Pyramid

- really, really big ones
- big ones
- medium-sized ones
- little bitty ones

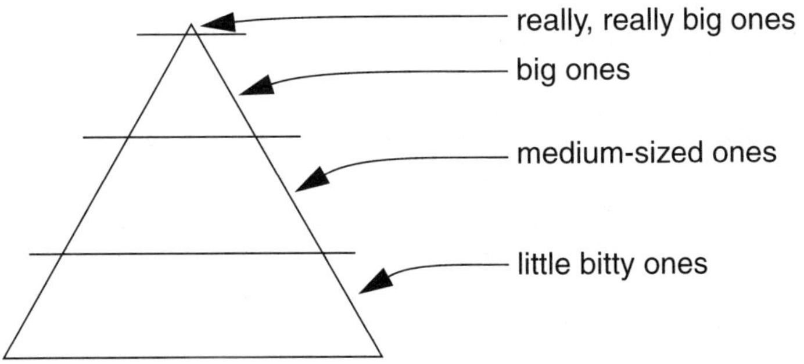

That figure illustrates how many of any kind of widget will be sold, based solely on its size and/or price. Whether one is selling cars, potato chips, or computers, you sell a whole lot of little ones, fewer medium-sized ones, and rather few really, really big ones. The differences in market volume can be dramatic. The sides of the pyramid really should be nonlinear—bowing in, to make the base wider and the top narrower—but no marketing diagram I've seen has curved lines, either.

_____

3. This is the only marketing diagram I have ever seen that does not go up and to the right.

Here is one way to segment the computer market in that manner. The bottom segment is the "client" personal computer market: machines used by individuals, one person to a machine. That is a market of millions of units per year; enormous revenue, but thin profit margins. Next up are the PC servers. These have, to use a very rough number, less than one-tenth the sales volume of PCs; but each server is a larger machine, with larger revenue, that is not quite as price-sensitive because users buy fewer of them and need not be as penny-wise about each. Above that lie larger, more complex system servers and multiuser systems capable of handling large, active databases, Internet servers, and heavier computational loads.

Other slices can be made, and rather intense discussions occur over how many slices there are and where they reside (and in which industry, geographic area, and for all I know what ranges of customer hair length), but for this discussion we're interested in the peak: That's where the massively parallel machines have their target. The point of the pyramid diagram is to make it blindingly obvious that few of those big machines are going to get sold.

This is well known and understood by the people who build and market massively parallel machines. They expect to sell only a few, if any, of their machines fully populated with the largest possible number of processing nodes. They also expect to sell many more that are less fully packed. That's what happens. But that's not the issue. The issue is the fact that their design target is the biggest feasible machine.

When you have targeted a design to highly massive proportions, scaling it down does not produce the best fit to the requirements of the market for smaller machines: systems that scale *up* to very large numbers of parallel nodes do not scale *down* to few nodes in an appropriate way. This has already been exhaustively discussed for the case of SMPs. It is equally true for massively parallel systems, for reasons that are entirely analogous to the heroic SMP case, but different in some technical details.

For example, the blindingly obvious issues apply directly. Massively parallel machines can participate in industry economies of scale by using processor and support chips in common with lower regions of the pyramid. But of necessity, since they target large numbers, they have to use bigger boxes. And bigger frames, power supplies, shipping costs, and so on, just as was mentioned for heroic SMPs back in "The Cost of Scaling Up SMPs" in Chapter 13. Paradoxically, they require smaller-than-standard packages, too; since the point is to pack many processors into a small floor space, the repackaging performed on workstations (or PCs) results in units that are nonstandard because they contain less memory, less disk capacity, and fewer I/O slots than are considered adequate for stand-alone systems. Just as was the case with large SMPs, all of those things cannot participate in the much larger volumes available lower in the volume pyramid.

The less-populated versions of massively parallel machines, therefore, can't match in cost what's possible by simply sticking together a few of the higher-market-volume units without changing their packaging at all—quite feasible when the number of units stuck together is in the range of eight or so. The high-end designs have been warped to the needs of the lure of large numbers.

The large SMP situation had an additional technical problem with caches and memories, as was dissected in gruesome detail earlier. There's an analog in the massively parallel world: communication networks. There are problems in the design of very large communication networks, problems that are sufficiently technically interesting to have occupied many researchers for decades and generated an immense technical literature which demonstrates that some quite non-obvious effects can occur (for example, there's what is referred to as the "'hot spot' controversy" in [AG94], initiated by the myself and Alan Norton [PN85]: unbalance communication by 0.1% with 1,000 nodes and everything goes to pot). Also, the sheer design problems of wire routing for large machines pose quite interesting problems for packaging.

None of this says that large machines cannot be built. They can. Also, the issues involved are technically challenging and interesting to deal with. If the small (but exorbitantly publicized) population of customers for those machines can afford them, so be it; there's no reason not to satisfy those customers and make some money in the bargain. However, the depopulated versions, the versions one would hope to sell in larger numbers, are, like big SMPs, vulnerable in their market position compared with systems *designed* to the more modest, higher market volume, segments.

There is a similar story to tell for software. The issues and problems of large numbers exert a strong lure there, too. They're interesting, challenging, and justifiably cause practitioners to feel that they're working on something of immense significance. They may well be.

But those large number problems lure effort away from the mundane, boring, grubby, practical issues—like, making the machine as easily administered as an SMP. The people who really want enormous systems expect that they'll be cantankerous, "bleeding edge," messes to deal with, so the issue of simple administration is usually made secondary. Targeting the high end also injects synchronization and control overhead that is unnecessary for smaller numbers, a practice that unnecessarily reduces efficiency when used in more modest ranges. This lure appears to be affecting the kernel-level SSI developers, too.

But the market volume pyramid says something about this. It says that the effort is being expended for a market segment that is small. And the processor speed increases that continue to occur indicate that market segment will become ever smaller over time.

The lure of large numbers is, therefore, deluding many vendors, and an unconscionable number of researchers and teachers, into ignoring the real mass of customers who need smaller systems and more ease of use—the old system administration story again, from which one is easily distracted by intrinsically interesting large number effects. The middle layers of the pyramid need clusters, but the lure of large numbers keeps people working on systems that cannot scale down to produce good cluster products.

Without even the notion that there is a respectable conceptual target—the cluster—there is no antidote to this lure.

That has been the point of this chapter. We need the concept of cluster.

CHAPTER

15

Conclusion

Attempts to use overtly parallel processing have previously been crippled by wimpy microprocessors, slothful communication, and the need to rebuild painfully complex parallel software from scratch on each attempt.

The result of this situation has been the completely justifiable conviction that this form of computing simply was not worth the trouble unless it provided enormous gains in performance or function. With a performance focus came a fixation on massive parallelism; with a functional focus came a fixation on massively distributed processing.

The sole exception to this has been the symmetric multiprocessor (SMP), which has nearly always used the most powerful possible processors and the fastest possible communication. As a result, its practical use requires the parallel programming of only a handful of key system and subsystem programs. All other software, the broad and deep mainstream, can remain serial; it need not cope with the Byzantine intricacies of parallelism on top of the already back-breaking complexity that is its primary limitation. Fixations on massiveness have been unnecessary for symmetric multiprocessors.

Nevertheless there is a demonstrable need for server computing facilities with greater performance, cheaper entry configurations, and, especially, higher availability than modestly scaled SMPs. SMPs can, technically, achieve those goals, but in doing so, they become disproportionately expensive.

Three things have happened to alter this situation. Microprocessors are now fast enough, are becoming ever faster at a tremendous rate, and tremendously fast ones are on the threshold of becoming tremendously inexpensive. Communication rates over standardized media have increased dramatically. The foundations of reusable message-based software support have been laid on an initial framework derived from distributed processing—a usable framework, though actually more difficult to use than this case requires.

Furthermore, the proliferation of low-end servers and the ever-advancing microprocessor speeds that make them hardly "low-end" have created a new market—a mass market for high availability that is unwilling to pay the elite prices associated with traditional fault-tolerant systems.

These factors make *clusters* of computers—groups of whole, standard computers each used as a single, unified resource—an adequate way to meet the needs of server systems now and in the future.

The future holds even greater promise because the technology trends producing the cluster conquest and the market forces requiring high availability are not abating. They will continue for good and sufficient reasons having nothing to do with clustering. The dramatic differences in price that once differentiated "open systems" from proprietary mainframes and minicomputers are playing out again in the midrange field of clusters and heroically large SMPs and CC-NUMA systems—which are becoming, where they aren't already, partitionable into clusters.

This trend has in recent years become apparent throughout the computer industry. There are no major hardware nor software vendors who do not now have at least one cluster product. Practically no industry analyst nor industry magazine has not issued at least one report, if not several, on the subject. Clusters are now a substantial part of the midrange market, and are poised to become a major factor in the "low-end" market; they've always been a significant part of the high-end market, but nobody ever bothered to count them before.

Clusters have arrived. That is not to say, however, that they have reached anything like their full potential. With very few exceptions, the possibilities they offer to fulfill the needs of customers are not being completely realized. The remaining few sections of this book reemphasize where the problem areas lie, and say a little about fixing them.

But let there be no doubt: The problems will be fixed. The only question is who will be the first, among computer hardware vendors, software vendors, and customers, to profit from the result.

15.1 Cluster Operating Systems

The one most crucial element most clusters lack is a highly-available, complete illusion of a single machine—a single system image—as serviceable as that presented by uniprocessors or SMPs, particularly with respect to the one universal application suite, system administration and management.

This single system image already exists adequately in several full system proprietary cluster solutions. However, people doing open system clusters are, with a few exceptions, either in a state of denial about the need for this capability, or woefully ignorant of both its benefits and its costs, or oscillating between those two states.

So-called "distributed" operating systems, just a little to the side of the main distributed programming bandwagon, provide an excellent solution framework. However, none are as yet fully industrial-strength products, particularly in the areas of system administration and high availability. This is in contrast to several high-end proprietary solutions, which have addressed those areas adequately.

This is the primary problem that must be fixed. There are no theoretical roadblocks to doing so, although an elegant and modular way to structure all the requisite function in an operating system remains to be found. The use of microkernel structuring appears to help greatly, but does not encompass the whole problem. Pragmatically, however, this can be accomplished now, with sufficient effort. Someone simply needs to make the investment and provide the function on cost-effective hardware platforms. It is not impossible that some vendors are already doing this.

15.2 Exploitation

Having discussed removing a reason *not* to use clusters, the next element must be providing positive reasons to use them.

Operating systems in general, and administration in particular, are pure overhead. They are not interesting for what they do, but for what they let users do: run applications. There is where the value of computers lies. Unless applications explicitly or implicitly exploit clusters, clusters are not useful.

Implicit exploitation is far easier than explicit, so while direct application use of clusters is by no means foolish—and may be the primary mode of use in the technical area—middleware that exploits clusters for all its dependent applications is a higher-leverage area of focus.

The situation in this area is promising, but incomplete. Several important pieces of middleware—databases and transaction monitors in particular, with some Internet server action—already exploit clusters quite well. If they didn't, there would be no market today. However, those subsystems certainly do not exhaust the field. File systems generally do not do a good job of exploiting cluster scalability, although most of them can now exploit clusters' high availability. Mail servers remain blissfully cluster-ignorant, as does nearly all groupware. The Java language, as of mid-1997, includes "Enterprise Beans" for OS-independent transaction support, which is a necessary high-availability function, but otherwise deals only in threads and traditional distributed processing.

The concept of cluster must become a valid, normal part of the armamentarium of large server applications. If they are not exploited by applications, clusters are useless.

15.3 Standards

Adequate exploitation and single system image are the primary areas where progress must be made. Exploitation will obviously be easier, though, if adequate standards are in place, allowing a single implementation to suffice on multiple platforms. There are three areas where standards could make it easier for clusters to be used by applications: common functions, communications, and transactions; these are discussed below.

The standards discussed here are all software. There is a group attempting to define hardware and very low level (device driver) software standards for clusters, namely the I_2O SIG (Intelligent Input/Output Special Interest Group). This is a collection of about 40 companies, initiated by Intel. It is primarily focussed on general I/O issues, but one of their target areas is cluster communication. This may be an interesting thing to standardize, if done at a level high enough that future advances in communication aren't locked out, but as mentioned back in Chapter 3, "Why Clusters?", the real issues aren't hardware; they're all software. So software is where the standardization efforts will have the greatest effects.

15.3.1   Common Functions

At present, every vendor of a cluster-oriented batch system, availability system, parallel programming package, database system, or OLTP system reimplements their own versions of a collection of functions which virtually every cluster-exploiting application or subsystem must have. These include cluster membership, event multicast, occasionally cross-system locking, and other basic facilities. Few of these implementations are particularly large, but they are, to put it mildly, very tricky to implement. In addition, few have complete functionality—not all functions are needed for every product—and few are fully robust, able to take advantage of clusters' intrinsic availability characteristics. They are also unnecessarily inefficient, because to be portable they have to use only standard, least common denominator capabilities.

Without standards, this situation cannot change. Independent database vendors, for example, do not want to use a system vendor's package; they don't want to be locked into that vendor's systems. The system vendors, contrariwise, can't afford to do a special implementation of every database vendors' support layers; they don't want to lock their system into one database vendor.

15.3.2   Intra-Cluster Communication

The problem of communication overhead using currently standard protocols has been stressed enough in the rest of this book; further discussion is either superfluous or useless.

Commercial parallel efforts, such as those for parallel databases, must now constrain themselves to write in terms of standard facilities such as sockets or streams, because they cannot afford to invest in a nonportable implementation. However, that locks them into very specific system structures and protocols designed for another era. The technical computing community, on the other hand, is now well into the process of bypassing that hurdle by defining a standard higher-level Message-Passing Interface (MPI) [Wal93, Mes94, SOH$^+$96] that is independent of any specific system interface and has been adopted by a large number of parallel computer vendors. The efficiencies potentially, and in some cases demonstrably, attainable by vendor-specific implementations at that level are spectacular relative to the normal modes of communication: microseconds of overhead, compared with milliseconds.

The MPI interface does not address all the needs of commercial users; that wasn't its intent. Availability issues, in particular, were deliberately not addressed, and neither were remote procedure calls. MPI does, however, suggest itself as a very solid start towards a more universally usable communication standard, one that system vendors could strongly optimize to allow highly efficient use of ever more macho interconnects, setting the hardware jocks free again to invent even more wondrous switches. How fast can you build something to multicast to a specific set of processes spread across a group of computers? (First, you had better ask the system programmers what to do when those processes are swapped out.)

The beginning of a mostly appropriate standard are visible in the VIA effort initiated by Intel (Chapter 5). This author thinks parts of the initial proposal are mistaken, particularly the part making reliability an option. He'd promote it as it stands in a nanosecond, however, if it were accepted by a wide enough segment of the industry. A standard like this is desperately needed.

15.3.3   Transactions

It should be apparent to anyone who has made it through the chapter on high availability that a means of simply providing transactional semantics for data, without necessarily having to buy an entire relational database in the bargain, would make it significantly easier for applications to be highly available in a cluster. Without it, they cannot, except by accident.

This might be built directly into a file system; such file systems have been constructed in the past. Better, though, would be a standard portable interface providing basic transactional begin, rollback, and commit work facilities that could be portable across implementations.

Nothing of this nature appears to yet be on the horizon as this is written.

15.3.4   Comments on Standards

The standards involved here certainly do not have to be formal, *de jure*, efforts. *De facto* standards can work just as well, and when they are successful usually require a lot less time.

Vendors of proprietary systems, of course, have an advantage in this. Since they are not worried about inter-system portability, they can set and use their own internally-defined standards. If their market position is strong enough, those can become the industry *de facto* standards. This process may well be in operation now for the application program interfaces defined by Microsoft's Windows NT "Wolfpack" Cluster Services.

Whether this is good, bad, inevitable, or avoidable—and if so, how?—is a topic of enormous importance to many people that is, thankfully, well outside the scope of this book.

15.4 Software Pricing

Suppose you've purchased a cluster. You have four cluster nodes, each node a four-processor SMP. You did so because it provides more performance than a sixteen processor SMP and higher availability, all for a lower price.

How many copies of the operating system did you purchase?

Oops.

How about the compiler? The communication subsystem? The database, the application, ...?

What was that about "a lower price" than a sixteen processor SMP?

Software licenses for a sixteen processor SMP cost more than licenses for the corresponding uniprocessor, but the price rise is much less than proportional to the number of processors. For example, a license for a sixteen processor SMP costs substantially less than four times the cost of a license for a four-way SMP. As long as the cluster is considered a group of separate machines, however, each machine must bear the burden of its own software license. So, as a cluster owner, you are paying four times the cost of a four-way SMP license—substantially more than the SMP software cost. Software costs commonly exceed hardware costs, so the total cluster cost can easily exceed that of a roughly equivalent (but usually inferior) SMP.

The price break for SMPs is partly based on the fact that SMP performance is far from proportional to the number of processors. That's been discussed at length, and it's not surprising; it's true, as a general rule, of every parallel system. However, it's also true of clusters. Why don't they get the same price break?

Well, for one thing the concept of a cluster doesn't exist. It's rather hard to price something that most people don't believe exists.

Another reason clusters don't get the same price break is the potential for abuse. Are those four workstations part of a cluster, therefore eligible for a cluster pricing, or are they separate computers? How do you tell? Are they in the same room? (Does that matter? Recall campus-wide clusters.)

By the way, there's room here for some hardware paranoia, too. If cluster hardware is priced by aggregate performance, then a cluster of N nodes will cost less than N times the cost of a single system, just because perfect speedup doesn't ever happen. That opens an undesirable door. Third-party resellers could buy large clusters, cut them up, and make money selling the parts at a price that undercuts the normal individual node price. This is not far-fetched; it has actually happened, not with clusters, but with old mainframe SMPs that were built as separable halves.

Getting back to software: As was mentioned in Chapter 2, preassembled vendor-constructed clusters can get around the software pricing issue by assigning a single serial number to the cluster as a whole. Then software licenses can simply follow serial numbers, and cluster software licensing can scale up with nodes as slowly as SMP licensing scales with processors. This arrangement is by no means automatic. It exists only because of negotiation with each software vendor by each hardware vendor—negotiation that starts right at home with the hardware vendor's own software shop, trying to get a reasonable price for the operating system. Talking to a software vendor who hasn't yet been "softened up" to clusters will almost always elicit the knee-jerk reaction of requiring a fully-priced, separate license per machine.

The serial number dodge doesn't help user-assembled clusters. Their nodes were bought as separate computers, and that's that.

This problem has an analog in distributed systems that share a single centrally-administered copy of a program. It's not yet fully solved there and, as usual, clusters add their own bit of complication not addressed by the distributed case.

Until this software pricing problem is solved, the real cost advantages of cluster hardware may be moot, and will constitute a real disadvantage compared with CC-NUMA systems, which undoubtedly will follow the SMP model. It will be solved, however, because the current situation is unstable. Once one software vendor moves its pricing policy, others will be forced to follow suit or endure being noncompetitively priced on the most cost-effective hardware platforms in the computer industry.

15.5 What About 2010?

A central theme of this book has been that clusters and similar systems owe their existence to the ever-increasing power of microprocessors. It is worth examining, then, whether that trend is nearing a close.

There is a hue and cry being raised about how the era of Moore's Law—the factor of two increase in chip density every 18 months that's fuelled the computer industry—is coming to an end sometime around 2010. The reasons cited are several:

> ➢ The cost of chip factories, "fabs," will increase enormously. A new state-of-the-art fab is a one to two billion dollar investment in 1997. A fab producing chips at the tremendously smaller feature sizes anticipated past the turn of the century might be $15 billion or $20 billion. This may be beyond private investment's ability to handle.

In Search of Clusters ✳

> The small number of electrons moved at these new small feature sizes may not be enough for reliable computing. It's hard to reliably tell the movement of ten or so electrons from noise.

> The feature sizes will be so small that quantum effects raise their nasty heads. Phenomena like tunnelling (going where it's impossible to go), and state superposition (being two places at once) will limit the ability of these devices to do what they classically have done for computing, namely, be reliable digital switches.[1]

It's easy to jump from these predicted difficulties to the conclusion that massively parallel computing will, in 2010, finally arrive. With no further advances in raw clock rate, this reasoning goes, ever increasing parallelism will be indispensable to future increases in computer performance.

As a result, clusters will finally and permanently give way to massively parallel systems. Most of what's been discussed in this book will still be valid, since it is applicable to massive systems as well as clusters, but the unending drumbeat I've tried to maintain about "cluster" vs. "massive" must inevitably go the way of the Dodo.

This might happen. The problems certainly must be addressed, and the lead time for constructing semiconductor fabrication facilities is long enough that now is not too soon to worry about it. However, assuming immediately that radical changes must be in store is a bit premature, for three reasons.

First, only unwarranted feature-size myopia has caused us to believe that circuit speed continues to be the primary driving force behind the bulk of computer speed increases. Of the 154% CGR of commercial speed increases documented in Chapter 3, only about 60% can be attributed to circuit speed alone. The other 94%, the majority, already comes from other factors: non-massive parallelism and algorithms in compilers, databases, operating systems, and so on. These elements are already a major force. Whether they can continue to be so can be questioned, but they face no known physical barrier in 2010.

Second: Once bitten, twice shy.

Back in about 1982 I attended a talk by Bob Dennard, the IBM Fellow who invented the single-transistor DRAM cell that is now the most replicated artifact in all of human history. In that talk he forecast a somewhat similar

---

1. Some people have proposed that these phenomena be used to do a new type of computing that follows multiple paths at once, finally collapsing the wave function down to the (or "a") right answer. I suggest that those people learn a bit about the limitations that speculative execution and SIMD exhibit when attempted on practical computing problems.

end to increases in circuit speed. Below a certain feature size—I believe the magic number then was around 7 microns—the Boltzmann statistics that underlay the behavior of electrons and holes in semiconductors no longer held.

This sure as heck sounded like a fundamental problem to me. It wasn't. In 1997 we were at 0.5 microns or less and counting down. What happened? It turned out that the real issue was the density of dopants, the selected necessary impurities diffused into silicon to give it necessary semiconducting characteristics. The people involved couldn't see how to get them dense enough in small features. A year or so after that talk, the technologists involved figured out new techniques of doping, got the densities up where they had to be, collectively said "oh, well," and kept on shrinking the feature sizes.

The point is that what appears from the outside to be a smooth continuous process—the shrinking of device size—is and always will be the successive solution of a long series of discrete problems of widely varying difficulty. Most yield straightforwardly to normally-skilled practitioners. Some require breakthroughs. The people most deeply engaged in the technology always see the problems. They have to; it's their job. They never know how to get from here to there. If they did, there wouldn't be any problems, and they wouldn't have jobs. So they may be collectively stumped for a while. It happens. They may get over it.

The third and final reason why it's wise to take such apocalyptic visions with a grain of salt is that 2010 is an awfully long way off. Granted, many of the issues involved are long lead time items, and preparations must begin for many rather soon; but there's still a huge amount of time to cover in an industry and technology that has reinvented itself on a regular basis in far shorter time spans than is available until 2010. If this book is still sold in other than garage sales in 2010, I will be astounded. Virtually every page had to be revised for the second edition, just to account for the two years since its original publication. A *lot* will happen by the time 2010 rolls around.

Of course, no exponential process can continue forever. At some point circuit speeds will saturate, and it might just be that 2010 is the magic date. However, it is premature to assume that massive parallelism will finally be triumphant then, or ever.

15.6 Coda: The End of Parallel Computer Architecture

Finally, a thought that arises from an entirely different direction.

Discussing the political and economic ramifications of the events surrounding and following the end the Cold War, Francis Fukuyama writes in *The End of History and the Last Man*:

> The apparent number of choices that countries face in determining how they will organize themselves politically and economically has been *diminishing* over time. Of the different types of regimes that have emerged in the course of human history, from monarchies and aristocracies, to religious theocracies, to the fascist and communist dictatorships of this century, the only form of government that has survived intact to the end of the twentieth century has been [...] democracy. [Fuk92, p. 45; italics in the original]

The issues Fukuyama is discussing obviously overreach this book's technical topics so broadly that no connection between their causes, even extremely indirect, is defensible in the slightest degree. Nevertheless, there are striking similarities in computer architecture to the situation he describes.

Specifically, deliberately constructing a direct paraphrase:

> Is it not the case that the apparent number of choices that people face in determining how they will organize overt parallelism has been *diminishing* over time? Of the different types of overtly parallel computer organizations that have emerged, from SIMD to vector supercomputers, from associative arrays to dataflow, from reduction machines to MIMD-SIMD combinations, from hierarchies to webs to pyramids, the only forms of overtly parallel computer organization that have survived intact to the mid-90s have been symmetric multiprocessors, clusters, and clusters' flamboyant sisters, the massively parallel multicomputers.

There may yet be scope for new, wild, weird and wonderful covert parallelism. Internal processor organizations can still incorporate any number of possible schemes for covert parallelism, from the sublime to the unusually bizarre. Nor is there a barrier to flamboyant intermachine communication systems. There is also nothing inhibiting thought experiments in parallel architecture that are at least interesting, if not able to shed dramatic light on other aspects of computer science.

But the external, software-visible architecture of practical, marketable, overtly parallel computer systems is another matter. On the one hand, there is the mass-market economics of integrated circuit manufacture, driven by stupendous and ever-increasing requirements for investment in production facilities; it is also driven by the smaller, but not negligible and also increasing individual chip development costs. On the other hand, there are the license-counting economics, perpetual development crisis, and awesome inertia of software. Those two hands have a death grip on overt parallelism because they combine to create a critical mass problem—if it doesn't exist already, you can't sell it—so ever-increasingly severe that it is impossible to conceive of a situation where the basic unit of overt computer parallelism is not a standard, Von Neumann architecture machine, communicating with other such machines via messages.

This is the problem that "NUMA" advocates have. It doesn't matter if you're better in some well-defined way. Just being different is enough to prefigure your doom, which is why they are determined to say they're just like SMPs.

This conclusion is not one that can be reached lightly, and it is, perhaps, rather sad to contemplate. It may be the price of increasing maturity. Fukuyama also says of democracy that we've reached this point after utter exhaustion, exhaustion caused by experimenting with all the other possibilities, using two world wars in our experimental procedure. The same could again be directly paraphrased—with market shake-outs substituting for world wars—for the case of overt parallelism.

It's not impossible that this may also be true of *covert* parallelism, as manifested in different processor instruction-set architectures. As was noted several times, processors are getting faster more quickly than are memories. Once a processor is fast enough to continuously saturate a memory system, what difference does its internal architecture make? For computer performance in a wide and increasingly broad class of applications, "It's the memory, stupid!" The ability to saturate the memory system does depend on the processor architecture, but not on many, if any, of the characteristics currently hyped in the RISC/CISC/VLIW/EPIC wars that continue.

The general loss of freedom being discussed here may not be inevitable. I'd like it not to be. But I do not at present see any practical way around it. The computer industry naturally gravitates to standards, wherever they come from, and once in place they are almost impossible to dislodge.

Whether it is true or not, and whatever changes the future rings into the computer industry, I am certain of one thing.

We will not have to search for clusters any more.

They will be commonplace.

Annotated Bibliography

Parallel and distributed processing has accumulated a technical and popularized bibliography of cosmic proportions. As a result, there are lots of references here. Furthermore, the entries in this bibliography span a very wide range of types. They range from press releases that appeared during the final phases of writing to heavily mathematico-logical treatises, graduate and undergraduate textbooks. Those who might want to pursue some of these topics more deeply might end up sorely disappointed without some indication of what they're in for.

Therefore, I've annotated each of the entries that appears here. The annotations are by no means a complete capsule reviews of every entry, although my opinions will not be found to be in short supply; nor is there an interwoven collection of cross-references that disentangles a cross-coupled web of literature. I've simply tried to provide some idea of what you can expect if you dig into these reference materials.

As far as possible, I've augmented traditional reference information with World-Wide Web URLs, since that is the most easily-used form for many readers. However, the lifetime of the average URL has been estimated at 18 months, so some may disappear during this book's lifetime. Hopefully the URLs referenced here will last longer than most of the faddish ones.

[AB86]   James Archibald and Jean-Loup Baer. Cache coherence
              protocols: Evaluation using a multiprocessor simula-
              tion model. *ACM Transactions on Computer Systems*,
              4(4):273–296, November 1986. Describes in a consistent
              way the bus-based protocols most popular at the time
              it was written (Dragon, Firefly, Illinois, and so on) and
              compares their performance against a consistent set of
              workloads. Unsurprisingly comes to the conclusion
              that the most complicated wins.

[AE+97]   J. Aman, C.K. Eilert, D. Emmes, P. Yocom, and D. Dil-
              lenberger. Adaptive algorithms for managing a distrib-
              uted data processing workload. *IBM Systems Journal*,
              Vol. 36, No. 2, 1997, pages 242-283. Also available at ht-
              tp://www.almaden.ibm.com/journal. One of eight pa-
              pers in that issue about Parallel Sysplex. How S/390's
              intensely feature-full workload management facilities
              were extended, with additions, to work across a Paral-
              lel Sysplex cluster.

[AG94]   George S. Almasi and Allan Gottlieb. *Highly Parallel
              Computing, 2d edition*. The Benjamin Cummings Pub-
              lishing Company, Inc., 390 Bridge Parkway, Redwood
              City, CA , 1994. Good, broad, highly readable coverage
              of many of the aspects of traditional areas of highly
              parallel computing, both hardware and software. Lots
              of sidebars and a number of interesting anecdotes and
              asides in addition to good coverage of the technical
              bases.

[AGZ94]   R. C. Agarwal, F. G. Gustavson, and M. Zubair. Im-
              proving performance of linear algebra algorithms for
              dense matrices, using algorithmic prefetch. *IBM Journal
              of Research and Development*, 38(3):265–275, May 1994. A
              demonstration of how to improve the performance of
              an RS/6000 Model 590 on dense-matrix linear algebra.
              The authors went from about 36 to about 44 MFLOPS
              by doing loads of data prior to when they were needed,
              just to overlap the cache fill time.

[AH90]   Sarita V. Adve and Mark D. Hill. Weak ordering-a new
              definition. In *Proceedings of the 17th Annual International
              Symposium on Computer Architecture*, pp 2–11. IEEE,
              June 1990. This description of weak ordering of inter-
              processor instruction execution is the one most refer-

enced in later years. I think that's because hardware guys think software guys understand and/or accept this definition—at least, that was the point of the presentation as made in this paper—creating a definition that was comprehensible in software terms.

[Amd67]   G. Amdahl. Validity of the single-processor approach to achieving large-scale computer capabilities. In *Proceedings of the AFIPS Conference*, pages 483–485, 1967. The original appearance of the famous Amdahl's Law, which states that a parallel machine can only speed things up to a limit governed by how much serial execution must still be done.

[And91]   Gregory R. Andrews. *Concurrent Programming: Principles and Practice*. Benjamin/Cummings Publishing Company, Inc., Redwood City, CA, 1991. Excellent reference on all the issues involved in writing parallel programs: Shared variables, RPCs, message-passing, monitors, heartbeats, and so on. Very significant emphasis on proving that such programs work, which is extremely appropriate but makes for nontrivial reading.

[AR94]   Thomas B. Alexander, Kenneth G. Robertson, Deal T. Lindsay, Donald L. Rogers, John R. Obermeyer, John R. Keller, Keith Y. Oka, and Marlin M. Jones II. Corporate business servers: an alternative to mainframes for business computing. *Hewlett-Packard Journal*, pp. 8-33, June 1994. A description of the Hewlett-Packard T500 series of SMPs.

[A$^+$91]   Anant Agarawal et al. The mit alewife machine. In *Proceedings of Workshop on Scalable Shared Memory Multiprocessors*, Boston, MA, 1991. Kluwer Academic Publishers. Dataflow concepts live on in the new proposal for a highly parallel machine. (The Alewife Brook parkway is in one of the towns making up the Boston metroplex.) (An Alewife is also a kind of herring with a big belly.)

[A$^+$92]   L. Albinson et al. UNIX on a loosely coupled architecture: The chorus/mix approach. *Future Generations Computer Systems*, 8(1-3):67–81, July 1992. Description of the Chorus microkernel system, and how it can be used to distribute Unix semantics across multiple machines.

[BARM97]   N.S. Bowen, J. Antognini, R.D. Regan, and N.C. Matsakis. Availability in parallel systems: automatic process restart. . *IBM Systems Journal*, Vol. 36, No. 2, 1997, pages 284-300. Also available at http://www.almaden.ibm.com/journal. One of eight papers in that issue about Parallel Sysplex. The surprising complexities involved in "just" restarting something that died elsewhere in the cluster.

[BBDS94]   David H. Bailey, Eric Barszcz, Leomardo Dagum, and Horst D. Simon. NAS parallel benchmark results 3-94. Technical report, NASA Ames Research Center, Moffett Field, CA, March 1994. Evaluation of various machines on parallel jobs. Includes redefinition of some of the benchmarks to avoid unintended implementation methods. Shows workstations very competitive with current Crays.

[BBK$^+$68]   George H. Barnes, Richard M. Brown, Maso Kato, David J. Kuck, Daniel L. Slotnick, and Richard A. Stokes. The ILLIAC IV computer. *IEEE Transactions on Computers*, C-17(8):746–757, 1968. The original paper on the ILLIAC IV computer, one of the first efforts, if not the first effort, in multipurpose massively parallel computing.

[BDG$^+$91]   A. Beguilin, J. Dongarra, G. A. Geist, R. Manchek, and V. S. Sunderam. A users' guide to PVM: parallel virtual machine. Technical Report # ORNL/TM-11826, Oak Ridge National Laboratory, July 1991. Detailed users' guide to PVM, the most popular system for parallel programming of clusters. A required document if you want to use PVM.

[BDM97]   T. Banks, K.E. Davies, and C. Moxey. The evolution of CICS/ESA in a sysplex environment. . *IBM Systems Journal*, Vol. 36, No. 2, 1997, pages 352-360. Also available at http://www.almaden.ibm.com/journal. One of eight papers in that issue about Parallel Sysplex.

How the most-used transaction processing system in the world has evolved over time to use the cluster acceleration facilities of S/390 Parallel Sysplex.

[BEIW97]   N.S. Bowen, D.A. Elko, J.F. Isenberg, and G.W. Wang. A locking facility for parallel systems. *IBM Systems Journal*, Vol. 36, No. 2, 1997, pages 202-220. Also available at http://www.almaden.ibm.com/journal. One of eight papers in that issue about Parallel Sysplex. Discussion of the cross-machine locking facility in Parallel Sysplex. I wish this could have been better written; it's unnecessarily dense.

[Bel92a]   Gordon Bell. An insider's views on the technology and evolution of parallel computing. In *Software for Parallel Computers*, R. H. Perrott, ed, pp 11–26. Chapman & Hall, 2-6 Boundary Row, London, 1992. Quite interesting reading. Atypically readable, typically curmudgeonish look by Gordon Bell at how parallel machines have evolved over time, what's proven practical, and what's really not.

[Bel92b]   Gordon Bell. Ultracomputers: A teraFLOP before its time. *Communications of the ACM*, 35(8):26–47, 1992. Trying to reach a teraFLOP too soon has produced machines that scale in only one sense—the amount of money you can pay for them. Better to wait, since it will only be a few years for the technology to naturally reach the point where these performance levels are achievable with reasonable ecomony. Many useful insights in a paper that is unfortunately not as well organized as it might be.

[Ber94]   Josh Berstin. Sybase for HACMP/6000: An architected approach to clustered systems. *AIXpert*, pp 46–52, May 1994. One of a series of articles on cluster database systems in that issue of AIXpert. Describes how Sybase is approaching the problem for clusters, as opposed to NCR's approach (which is sold as Sybase Data Navigator).

[BGvN62]   A. W. Burke, H. H. Goldstine, and J. von Neumann. Preliminary discussions of the logical design of an electronic computing instrument, part ii. *Datamation*, 8:36–

41, October 1962. A later reprint of some of the design notes written during the birth of what is now known as the Von Neumann architecture computer.

[Bir95]   K. P. Birman. Replication and fault-tolerance in the ISIS system. *Operating Systems Review*, 19(5), December 1995. Discussion of the reliable multicast protocol technology used as the basis for the ISIS system at Cornell, later commercialized by ISIS Distributed Systems (IDS). Also appears in the Proceedings of the Tenth ACM Symposium on Operating System Principles.

[BJ87]   K. P. Birman and T. A. Joseph. Reliable communication in the presence of failures. *ACM Transactions on Computer Systems*, 6(1):47–76, February 1987. Detailed discussion of how one can have a reliable multicast by using a special protocol, when media and nodes are unreliable. This is the core technology of the ISIS distributed system support, developed at Cornell and later commercialized by ISIS Distributed Systems (IDS).

[BJS88]   F. Baskett, T. Jermoluk, and D. Solomon. The 4D-MP graphics superworkstation. In *Proceedings of Spring Compcon '88*, pages 468–471, 1988. Description of the Silicon Graphics SMP workstations used as nodes (they call them clusters) in the Stanford DASH system.

[BL92]   R. Butler and E. Lusk. Users' guide to the p4 programming system. Technical Report ANL-92/17, Argonne National Laboratory, 1992. Detailed users' guide to a popular portable system for parallel programming, used for clusters as well as other machines. Developed at Argonne Lab.

[BMR91]   Sandra Johnson Baylor, Kevin P. McAuliffe, and Bharat Deepu Rathi. An evaluation of cache coherence protocols for micprocessor-based multiprocessors. In *Proceedings of the International Symposium on Shared Memory Multiprocessing*, pages 230–241, April 1991. Looks at data-sharing aspects of several scientific programs by simulation, comparing several hardware-based and a software-based coherence protocol. Less than 3% of references turn out to be shared, which is a very interesting and extremely useful result. But watch out if the cache line size gets too big; you get false sharing galore.

[Boo83]   Daniel J. Boorstein. *The Discoverers*. Random House, New York, 1983. A really extraordinary book. Extremely interesting, nontechnical(!) history of many important basic technologies, such as printing, geography, music, and so on.

[Bou92]   J.-Y Le Boudec. The asynchronous transfer mode: A tutorial. *Computer Network and ISDN System*, 24:279–309, February 1992. An introduction to ATM. Fairly readable.

[Brow95]   High Availability Trends: A Poll of Leading Edge Users. D. H. Brown Associates Inc., 222 Grace Church St., Port Chester, NY.

[BRS$^+$85]   R. Baron, R. Rashid, E. Seigel, A. Tevanian, and M. Young. Mach-1: An operating environment for large-scale multiprocessor applications. *IEEE Software*, 2:65–67, July 1985. Description of the Mach microkernel operating system, developed at Carnegie-Mellon University. Clearly the most influential microkernel system ever developed, and the origin of the term "microkernel.

[Bry90]   Bill Bryson. The Mother Tongue: English and How It Got That Way. Avon Books, 1990. A good read for anyone interested in words and language. Tends to be a little long on trivia and short on discussion and background, but the trivia is very entertaining.

[BW89]   J. L. Baer and W. H. Wang. Multilevel cache hierarchies: Organizations, protocols and performance. *Journal of Parallel and Distributed Computing*, (6):451–476, 1989. Technical description of several multilevel caching schemes, with their performance analysis.

[CKA91]   David Chaiken, John Kubiatowicz, Anant Agarwal. LimitLESS Directories: A Scalable Cache Coherence Scheme. *Proceedings of the Fourth International Conference on Architectural Support for Programming Languages and Operating Systems (ASPLOS IV)*, pages 224-234, April 1991. Also available at http://cag-www. lcs. mit. edu:80 /Alewife.

[CRD+95]   John Chapin, Mendel Rosenblum, Scott Devine, Tirthankar Lahiri, Dan Teodosiu, and Anoop Gupta. Hive: Fault Containment for Shared-Memory Multiprocessors. *15th ACM Symposium on Operating Systems Principles*, ACM, December, 1995.

[CF93]   Alan L. Cox and Robert J. Fowler. Adaptive cache coherency for detecting migratory shared data. In *Proceedings of the 20th Annual International Symposium on Computer Architecture*, pages 98–108. IEEE, May 1993. Description of a snoopy, bus-based cache coherence protocol that dynamically switches between updating and expunging lines in other caches on write. Also, a good root for a tree of cache coherence references.

[CG89]   N. Carriero and David Gelernter. Linda in context. *Communications of the ACM*, 32(4):444–458, April 1989. A description of Linda, a system for parallel programming of clusters that takes a unique approach to communication and program organization that some people like a lot. Linda began life as a project by Gelernter at AT&T Bell Laboratories, an attempt to make use of a typically nonstandard, clusterish parallel machine dreamed up by engineers who had no idea how hard it might be to program. Later expanded as a major Yale research project (Gelernter and Carriero are Yale faculty), then became the primary product of a spinoff company, Scientific Computing Associates.

[CGST94]   H. Jonathan Chao, Dipak Ghosal, Debanjan Saha, and Satish K. Tripathi. Ip on atm local area networks. *IEEE Communications Magazine*, pages 52–59, August 1994. The various techniques a number of people are using, including the ATM Forum, to provide standard LAN (IP) communications protocols over ATM's nonbroadcast medium. Includes a description of the standard LAN techniques of bridging and routing.

[Chr94]   Gregg A. Christman. Informix-online's dynamic scalable architecture. *AIXpert*, pages 32–36, May 1994. One of a series of articles on cluster database systems in that issue of AIXpert. Describes how Informix is approaching the problem. This is written and published before this product was shipped or even officially announced.

Indicates that they're attempting to conquer SMP, NU-MA, and NORMA parallelism all with one program structure. It'll be great if it works.

[Col92]   William W. Collier. *Reasoning About Parallel Architectures*. Prentice Hall, Inc., Englewood Cliffs, NJ 07632, 1992. An intense, detailed, mathematical treatise dissecting issues such as sequential consistency, organized around ways of telling whether computer architecture A exactly equals computer architecture B—which is another way of saying that a program running on machine A will do exactly the same thing when run on machine B, a rather useful thing to know. Extremely useful if you really want to get interprocessor consistency right. Not for those lacking a mathematical bent.

[Conn92]   Keeping Systems Running, Connexion 2, September 1992.

[Cos94]   Terry Costlow. Sci gaining acceptance as scalable link. *Electronic Engineering Times*, (787), March 7, 1994. Overview of progress to the publication date on implementations of SCI.

[CP93]   Daniel Cerutti and Donna Pierson. *Distributed Computing Environments*. McGraw-Hill, Inc., New York, 1993. A collection of generally rather good and readable papers that discuss many of the issues involved in distributed computing. The papers are tied together by introductions written by the editors. Very complete coverage of issues and trends, and all papers maintain a high standard of readability.

[CY93]   Christopher Cheng and Leo Yuan. Electrical design of the xdbus using low voltage swing cmos (gtl) in the sparccenter 2000 server. In *Symposium Record of Hot Interconnects '93*, pages 1.3.1–1.3.4. Stanford University, August 1993. Sun Microsystems paper on how they built a bus to support 20 SuperSPARC processors. Unlike other papers at this workshop, this one is a complete written paper rather than a collection of presentation transparencies.

[Data90]   Lan Downtime: Clear and Present Danger. Data Communications, March 21, 1990. Reference to a survey by Infonetics on how truly bad campus LAN reliability actually is.

[DG97]   Data General, Westboro MA. Data General's NUMALi-iNE Technology: The Foundation for the AV2000 Server. Also available at http://www.dg.com/about/html/numaliine_technology_av2000_foundation.html

[DGNP88]   Frederica Darema, David A. George, V. Alan Norton, and Gregory F. Pfister. A single-program-multiple-data computational model for epex fortran. *Parallel Computing*, 7:11–24, 1988. Original definition and first use of the term SPMD to describe the programming model that is effectively used everywhere on both shared-memory and message-passing machines.

[Dig93]   Digital Equipment Corporation, Maynard, MA. *Open-VMS Clusters Handbook*, 1993. Document # EC-H2207-93 Rel. #79/93 06 43 60.0. Introduction to the various forms and capabilities of Open VMS Clusters. Really quite readable; other vendors should copy the style and format of this series of small books.

[Dig94]   Digital Equipment Corporation, Maynard, MA. *Digital's Unix Clusters Lead Industry in High Availability Commercial Solutions*, October 4, 1994. Announcement at 1994 UNIX Expo, mentioning both 18-second failover time for DECSafe high-availability and the Memory Channel work with Encore.

[Dij65]   Edsgar W. Dijkstra. Solution of a problem in concurrent programming control. *Communications of the ACM*, 8(9):569, 1965. The original, and most famous, mutual exclusion algorithm. Like most classics, short: a one-page paper. Expect to spend several hours figuring out why it works.

[DOKT91]   Fred Douglis, John K. Ousterhout, M. Frans Kaashoek, and Andrew S. Tannenbaum. A comparison of two distributed systems: Amoeba and sprite. *Computing Systems*, 4(4):353–383, Fall 1991. Very interesting comparison along a number of different axes: Assumed system structure (glass-house vs. campus-wide cluster), microkernel vs. macrokernel, UNIX base vs. written from scratch, and so on.

[Dol95]   Dolphin Interconnect Solutions, 5301 Great America Parkway, Suite 320, Santa Clara, CA. *SBus-1 Product Overview*, 1995. Product flyer for Dolphin's SBus card that provides an SCI-based link between machines for clustering.

[DKMT96]   Danial M. Dias, William Kish, Rajat Mukherjee, and Renu Tewari. A scalable and highly available web server. *Proceedings of Compson '97: Technologies for the Information Superhighway.* IEEE Computer Society Press, Los Alamitos, CA. February 1996. Analysis of how much better it is to do load balancing on an IP address rather than let a standard round-robin domain name server balance your web-request load across a cluster. Not difficult reading, rather worthwhile.

[Edd94]   Guy Eddon. *RPC For NT: Building Remote Procedure Calls for Windows NT Networks.* Prentice Hall, Englewood Cliffs, NJ, 1994. An entire book about all the ways to create and use RPCs, sparing no detail, to simplify life when doing client/server computing using Microsofts Windows NT system.

[Edi91]   Edinburgh Parallel Computing Centre, University of Edinburgh. *Chimp Concepts*, June 1991. Overview of Edinburgh's parallel message-passing system, one of the systems whose concepts had a significant influence on the MPI emerging standard.

[EGKS90]   Suzanne Englert, Jim Gray, Terrye Kocher, and Praful Shah. A benchmark of nonstop sql release 2 demonstrating near-linear speedup and scaleup on large databases. In *Proceedings of the 1990 ACM SIGMETRICS Conference*, pages 245–246, New York, 1990. ACM. Demonstration of increased speed and increased scaling as you add nodes to a Tandem system.

[Exe87]   Executive Office of the President, Office of Science and Technology Policy. *A Research and Development Strategy for High Performance Computing*, November 1987. The official, government-approved definition and list of Grand Challenge problems.

[EY92]   David John Evans and Nadia Y. Yousif. Asynchronous parallel algorithms for linear equations. In *Parallel Processing in Computational Mechanics*, Hojjat Adeli, editor, pp 69–130. Marcel Dekker, Inc., 270 Madison Ave., New

York, 1992. Discussion and comparison of a wide variety of ways of solving linear and differential equations in parallel, with emphasis on shared memory techniques. Shows chaotic relaxation (called "pure asynchronous" here) is best in many cases.

[FBH+92]   D. Frye, Ray Bryant, H. Ho, R. Lawrence, and M. Snir. *An external user interface for scalable parallel systems.* Technical report, International Business Machines Corp., Armonk, NY, May 1992. Description of the EUI message-passing subroutine library developed for the IBM Scalable Parallel series of machines. EUI stands for End User Interface, a name thought up by folks in the IBM Research Division, giving you some idea who they thought the "End" users were.

[Fec94]   Giles Fecteau. Db2 parallel edition. *AIXpert*, pages 24–30, May 1994. One of a series of articles on cluster database systems in that issue of AIXpert. Describes how IBM DB2/6000 is approaching the problem of parallel/cluster database processing, using function shipping.

[FHK+90]   G. Fox, S. Hiranandani, K. Kennedy, C. Koebel, U. Kremer, C. Tseng, and M. Wu. Fortran d language specification. Technical Report # TR90-41, Department of Computer Science, Rice University, December 1990. A complete specification of FORTRAN D, which was the predecessor to High Performance FORTRAN. The D stands for Data-parallel, as opposed to Control-parallel.

[FJL+88]   Geoffrey C. Fox, Mark A. Johnson, Gregory A Lyzenga, Steve W. Otto, John K. Aalmon, and David W. Walker. *Solving Problems on Concurrent Processors, Volume I: General Techniques and Regular Problems*. Prentice Hall, Englewood Cliffs, NJ, 1988. An excellent introduction to techniques for message-based parallelism on regular scientific and technical problems. Many of the methods described arose from the Concurrent Computation Program at California Institute of Technology, originator of the original hypercube machines.

[Fly72]   Michael J. Flynn. Some computer organizations and their effectiveness. *IEEE Transactions on Computers*, pages 948–960, September 1972. The original paper defining the programming models MIMD, SIMD, SISD, MISD.

[Fuk92]   Francis Fukuyama. *The End of History and the Last Man*. The Free Press, A Division of Macmillan, Inc., New York, 1992. With the collapse of authoritarian regimes, is there an endpoint to history-directed change in human affairs—with liberal democracies and capitalism the final, ultimate socio-political system? What kind of people inhabit such an end-result world? Is it stable?

[Gal93]   Mike Galles. The challenge interconnect: Design of a 1.2 gb/s coherent multiprocessor bus. In *Symposium Record of Hot Interconnects '93*, pages 1.1.1–1.1.7. Stanford University, August 1993. Silicon Graphics' paper on how they built a system bus to support 36 MIPS R4400 processors. Unfortunately, the proceedings contains only the presentation transparencies, not a complete paper. Much information is nevertheless contained here.

[Gil96]   R. Gillett. Memory channel network for PCI: An Optimized Cluster Interconnect. *IEEE Micro*, Vol. 16, No. 1, pp. 12–18. Also available at http://computer.org/micro/. While there are a zillion papers from DEC authors on programming Memory Channel, this is the only paper I found that actually describes the hardware and admits that it really does broadcast.

[GK97]   Richard Gillett and Richard Kaufmann. Using the Memory Channel Network. IEEE Micro, Vol. 17, No. 1, January/February 1997. Also available at http://computer.org/micro/. This is one of a set of articles in that issue about "hot" interconnects. It is quite adequately readable.

[GKW85]   J. R. Gurd, C. C. Kirkham, and I. Watson. The manchester prototype dataflow computer. *Communications of the ACM*, 28(1):34–52, January 1985. Description of one of the few live, working dataflow machine ever constructed; done at the University of Manchester. This work was quite influential and often cited in dataflow literature.

[GLL^{+}90]   Kourosh Gharachorloo, Daniel Lenoski, James Laudon, Phillip Gibbons, Anoop Gupta, and John Hennessy. Memory consistency and event ordering in scalable shared-memory multiprocessors. In *Proceedings of the 17th Annual International Symposium on Computer Architecture*, pages 15–25. IEEE, June 1990. Description of release consistency, the inter-processor memory access ordering used in the Stanford DASH project.

[GR89]   Jim Gray and Andreas Reuter. Transaction Processing: Concepts and Techniques. Morgan Kauffman Publishers, Inc. 1989. More than you ever thought it was possible to understand about transaction processing. A well-written, highly readable treasure trove.

[GS89]   G. A. Geist and V. S. Sunderam. The evolution of the pvm concurrent computing system. In *Proceedings of the 26th IEEE Compcon Symposium*, pages 471–478, San Francisco, February 1989. A description of the most popular system for parallel programming of clusters. PVM is a highly portable system making message-passing programming easier. Supports heterogeneous, as well as homogeneous, collections of machines. Highly portable freeware.

[Gus92]   David Gustavson. The scalable coherent interface and related standards projects. *IEEE Micro*, 12(1):10–12, February 1992. Very readable description of the SCI interconnect and the issues it addresses, written by one of the primary proponents and principal parents of this technology.

[Hal94]   Tom R. Halfhill. 80x86 wars. *Byte*, 19(6):74–88, June 1994. How all the "other" 80x86-architecture vendors— Cyrix, AMD, IBM—are now going to start doing their own designs, not waiting for Intel do something new and then copying it.

[HC85]   Robert W. Horst and Timothy C. K. Chou. An architecture for high volume transaction processing. In *Proceedings of the 12th International Symposium on Computer Architecture*, pages 240–245, Boston, MA, 1985. IEEE. Description of Tandem's cluster and/or parallel database system architecture, used in the Tandem Cyclone and later products.

[Hem91]   R. Hempel. The anl/gmd macros (parmacs) in fortran for portable parallel programming using the message passing model - user's guide and reference manual. Technical report, GMD, Postfach 1316, D-5205 Sankt Augustin 1, Germany, November 1991. Detailed users' guide to the the PARMACS system for portable message-passing parallel programming of clusters.

[Hil93]   Dan Hildebrand. An architectural overview of qnx. In *Proceedings of the Usenix Workshop on Micro-Kernels and Other Kernel Architectures*, April 1993. QNX is a microkernel designed for real-time and embedded applications that has been successfully used in many cluster-like products, as well as extended downward to PDAs. This paper outlines its architecture and compares its performance to a traditional macrokernel (SVR5). Paper available by ftp from quics.qnx.com /pub/papers and ftp.cse.ucsc.edu /pub/qux. The proceedings where it appeared are ISBN 1-880446-42-1.

[HKM94]   Chengchang Hwang, Eric P. Kasten, and Philip K. McKinley. Design and implementation of multicast operations for atm-based high performance computing. In *Proceedings of Supercomputing '94*, November 1994. How to do collective communication operations for parallel processing over an ATM-based LAN.

[HM]   Chengchang Hwang and Philip K. McKinley. Communication issues in parallel computing across atm networks. *IEEE Parallel and Distributed Technology*, to appear. Overview of ATM and parallelism, then results of doing experiments in broadcast, reduction,and so on, over an ATM-based LAN. It still takes a minimum of a millisecond to get anything out of a computer.

[HM89]   A. Hac and H. B. Mutlu. Synchronous optical network and broadband isdn protocols. *IEEE Computer*, 11:26–34, November 1989. Introduction to ATM at a mildly technical level. Broadband ISDN is ATM, for all practical purposes.

[Hor95]   Robert W. Horst. TNet: a reliable system area network. *IEEE Micro*, February 1995.

[HP90]   John L. Hennessy and David A. Patterson. *Computer Architecture A Quantitative Approach*. Morgan Kaufmann Publishers, Inc., San Mateo, CA, 1990. Excellent

※   **531** textbook on computer architecture, with special emphasis on quantitative measurements, RISC vs. CISC, and caches. Currently clearly the best textbook on the subject. Too bad it stops short of SMPs, but it's pretty big already.

[Hwa93]   Kai Hwang. *Advanced Computer Architecture: Parallelism, Scalability, Programmability.* McGraw-Hill, Inc., New York, 1993. Broad coverage of many of the aspects of parallel processing. Includes descriptions of SMPs and cache coherence issues, which is rare. Aggressively technical and formal.

[IBMa]   IBM Corporation, Armonk, NY. *High Availability Cluster Multi-Processing/6000 System Overview.* Document # SC23-2408-02. Description of the IBM HACMP/6000 system for clustering RISC System/6000 workstations and servers.

[IBMb]   IBM Corporation, Armonk, NY. *Introduction to JES3.* Document # GC28-0607-2. Not-too-basic introduction to IBM's JES3, a system for distributing work across a cluster of mainframes.

[IBMc]   IBM Corporation, Armonk NY. *LoadLeveller General Information Manual.* Document # GH26-7227. General description of IBM's LoadLeveller product, a technical computing batch facility originally developed for the IBM Scalable Parallel (SP) series but also running on a variety of vendors' workstations.

[IBMd]   IBM Corporation, Armonk, NY. *Sysplex Hardware and Software Migration.* Document # GC28-1210-00. All the things to worry about, hardware and software, if you are considering clustering IBM mainframes together in an IBM Sysplex.

[IBMe]   IBM Corporation, Armonk, NY. *Sysplex Overview.* Document # GC28-1208-00. Well written. Basic introduction to parallel processing (and data sharing) targetting readers familiar with large-scale commercial computing. Good description of the basic IBM Sysplex (mainframe cluster) hardware facilities, but insufficient depth for real technical satisfaction.

[IBM94]   IBM Corporation, Armonk, NY. *IBM Delivers New Versions of its PowerPC RISC Microprocessors*, October 10, 1994. Press release announcing availability and pricing for 100 MHz PowerPC 601 and 604, and 66/80 MHz PowerPC 603 microprocessors.

[IBM97]   IBM Corporation, Armonk, NY. *IBM's Parallel Sysplex Overhead: A Reality Check*. April 14, 1997. Also available at http://www.s390.com/marketing/gf225009.html. Someone in IBM attempts in a two-page memo to get out of the corner the company wrote itself into in the way it portrayed Parallel Sysplex efficiency. As the word "overhead" in the title shows, however, they still don't get it.

[IDC96]   International Data Corporation. *Commercial Systems and Servers: Highly Available Systems*. ICD #11503, September 1996.

[Ins93]   Institute of Electrical & Electronic Engineers, New York. *IEEE Standard for Scalable Coherent Interface (SCI)*, August 1993. IEEE Std 1596-1992.The official definition of SCI. Required reading for anyone attempting to implement or really understand it. Hideously detailed, as one would expect from a standards document.

[Int94]   International Data Corporation (IDC). *Cost of Unix Midrange Systems*, 1994. A study of all the costs of ownership of a midrange commercial UNIX system; not just the hardware, but software, maintenance, staffing, and so on. Uniquely, it was done by studying not artificial configurations but actual, "live" sites—hundreds in both the US and Europe.

[Joh91]   Mike Johnson. *Superscalar Microprocessor Design*. Prentice Hall, Englewood Cliffs, NJ, 1991. Excellent, quantitative, detailed technical discussion of the issues involved in superscalar processor design, done with a consistently maintained "everything in moderation or it will cost too much" viewpoint. Very good appendix on why RISC is intrinsically better than CISC, and how hard it is to use RISC-y techniques on a CISC machine. However, the author has apparently changed his position on how bad CISC is, given recent comments on the HP/Intel alliance. He's entitled; time passes and more thought ensues.

✳

[Joh97]   P. Johnson. The importance of systems management for a parallel sysplex. . *IBM Systems Journal*, Vol. 36, No. 2, 1997, pages 301-326. Also available at http://www.almaden.ibm.com/journal. One of eight papers in that issue about Parallel Sysplex. Customers install S/390 Parallel Sysplex just to get the cross-systems management facilities that are included, which substantially simplify the complex task of running multiple large mainframes with enormous applications.

[JMNT97]   J.W. Josten, C. Mohan, I. Narang, and J.Z. Teng. DB2's use of the coupling facility for data sharing. . *IBM Systems Journal*, Vol. 36, No. 2, 1997, pages 327-351. Also available at http://www.almaden.ibm.com/journal. One of eight papers in that issue about Parallel Sysplex. Specifically how IBM's DB2 database internally makes use of the shared-data cluster acceleration provided in Parallel Sysplex.

[KAP96]   K. Keeton, T.E. Anderson, and D.A. Patterson. LogP Quantified: The Case for Low-Overhead Local Area Networks. *Hot Interconnects III*. According to this paper, OLTP used four message pairs per transaction and never had more than 200 bytes per transaction. ("The Case for X" papers have been very popular at Berkeley ever since Stonebraker wrote "The Case for Shared -Nothing Architectures," which became the battle-cry of the shared-nothing zealots.)

[KDY97]   G.M. King, D.M. Dias, and P.S. Yu. Cluster architectures and S/390 parallel sysplex scalability. *IBM Systems Journal*, Vol. 36, No. 2, 1997, pages 221-241. Also available at http://www.almaden.ibm.com/journal. One of eight papers in that issue about Parallel Sysplex. An excellent description of cluster system architectures, particularly aimed at indicating why shared data was chosen for Parallel Sysplex. (Obviously written by shared data zealots; there are no middle positions in this religious debate.)

[KEW+85]   R. H. Katz, S. J. Eggers, D. A. Wood, C. L. Perkins, and R. G. Sheldon. Implementing a cache consistency protocol. In *Proceedings of the 12th Annual International Sym-*

posium on Computer Architecture, pages 2–11. IEEE, June 1985. The Berkeley cache coherence protocol, one of several popular bus-based snoopy protocols.

[KLS86]   Nancy P. Kronenberg, Henry M. Levy, and William D. Strecker. Vaxclusters: A closely-coupled distributed system. *ACM Transactions on Computer Systems*, 4(3):130–146, May 1986. Description of the highly successful Digital VAXCluster hardware and software architecture. One of the more successful and popular clustered systems. Now called Open VMS Cluster.

[KLSM87]   Nancy P. Kronenberg, Henry M. Levy, William D. Strecker, and Richard J. Merewood. The vaxcluster concept: An overview of a distributed system. *Digital Technical Journal*, 4:7–21, September 1987. Keynote paper in an issue of the Digital Technical Journal that has several papers devoted to the VAXCluster (now called the Open VMS Cluster).

[Knu97a]   Donald E. Knuth. *The Art of Computer Programming: Fundamental Algorithms (Vol 1, 3rd Ed)*. Addison-Wesley Publishing Co., 1997.

[Knu97b]   Donald E. Knuth. *The Art of Computer Programming: Sorting and Searching (Vol 3, 2nd Ed)*. Addison-Wesley Publishing Co., 1997.

[KOH$^+$94] Jeffrey Kuskin, David Ofelt, Mark Heinrich, John Heinlein, Richard Simoni, Kourosh Gharachorloo, John Chapin, David Nakahira, Joel Baxter, Mark Horowitz, Anoop Gupta, Mendel Rosenblum, and John Hennessy. The Stanford FLASH Multiprocessor. *Proceedings of the 21st International Symposium on Computer Architecture*, April 1994. A very readable description of their CC-NUMA implementation, also available at http://www-flash.stanford.edu/architecture/papers/ISCA94.

[Kol91]   Adam Kolawa. The express programming environment. *Workshop on Heterogeneous Network-Based Concurrent Computing*, October 1991. A description of Parasoft's Express product for message-passing on clusters and massively parallel machines. It began life as a very successful programming system for the CalTech cosmic cube, then migrated to a spinoff company, Parasoft.

[KP97]   J. Kay and J. Pasquale. The Importance of Non-Data Touching Processing Overheads in TCP/IP. Technical Report, Department of Computer Science and Engineering, University of California, San Diego. Another documented measurement showing that most (80%) messages are short (<200 bytes).

[KS86]   Henry F. Korth and Abraham Silberschatz. *Database Systems Concepts*. McGraw-Hill, Inc., New York, 1986. A standard textbook on database systems, covering many of the topics of interest in general but not (in this version, anyway) adequately dealing with newer parallel models of database execution.

[KSS$^+$91] H. T. Kung, R. Sansom, P. Steenkiste, M. Arnould, F. J. Bitz, F. Christianson, E. C. Cooper, O. Menzilciogly, D. Ombres, and B. Zill. Network-based multicomputers: An emerging parallel architecture. In *Proceedings of Supercomputing '91*, pages 664–673. IEEE CS Press, 1991. Clusters can do grand challenge problems, particularly when connected by ATM and highly intelligent adapters.

[Lam]   Leslie Lamport. The parallel execution of do loops. *Communications of the ACM*, 17(2):83–93. Derivation of the notion of a hyperplane of array computations that can be done in parallel when ordinary indexed loops are parallelized. Referred to in this book as the wavefront method.

[Lam79]   Leslie Lamport. How to make a multiprocessor computer that correctly executes multiprocess programs. *IEEE Transactions on Computers*, C-28(9):690–691, September 1979. The original definition of sequential consistency. This two page paper—actually, a short note—is rigorously referenced by everybody who ever says anything about interprocessor instruction ordering, all the way up to 1997.

[LBD$^+$96] James V. Lawton, John J. Brosnan, Morgan P. Doyle, Seosamh D. Ó Riordáin, Timothy G. Reddin. Building a high-performance message-passing system for memory channel clusters. Digital Technical Journal, Vol. 8, No. 2, 1996. Also available at http://www.digital.com /info/DTJ000/. Possibly the best I found of many papers available on DEC's Memory Channel.

[LC94]   Sandra Lee and Annie Chen. Oracle parallel technology empowers aix systems. *AIXpert*, pages 37–42, May 1994. One of a series of articles on cluster database systems in that issue of AIXpert. Describes how Oracle is approaching the problem, with description of Oracle Parallel Server implementation for the IBM SP2 highly parallel system.

[LD95]   Daniel E. Lenoski and Wolf-dietrich Weber. *Scalable shared-memory multiprocessing*. Morgan Kaufmann Publichers. 1995. Excellent description of the various ways to do CC-NUMA systems and the measured results of running code on them, as well as a well-researched descriptive comparison of many other parallel architectures.

[LLG$^+$92] Daniel Lenoski, James Laudon, Kourosh Gharachorloo, Wolf-Dietrich Weber, Anoop Gupta, John Hennessy, Mark Horowitz, and Monica S. Lam. The Stanford DASH multiprocessor. *Computer*, pages 63–79, March 1992. Introduction to DASH, a Stanford University CS project in coupling multiple conventional SMPs into one great big coherent-memory NUMA SMP.

[LLJ$^+$92] Daniel Lenoski, James Laudon, Truman Joe, Luis Stevens, Anoop Gupta, and John Hennessy. The dash prototype: Implementation and performance. In *Proceedings of the Annual Symposium on Computer Architecture*, pages 92–103, April 1992. How the Stanford University DASH (in this case, capitalized) project is implemented, how much hardware it takes and how long memory accesses take. Pictures of circuit boards as well as technical data.

[LLJ$^+$93] Daniel Lenoski, James Laudon, Truman Joe, David Nahahira, Luis Stevens, Anoop Gupta, and John Hennessy. The dash prototype: Logic overhead and performance. *IEEE Transactions on Parallel and Distributed Systems*, 4(1):41–61, January 1993. Stanford University DASH implementation in detail with lots of measurements of various shared-memory applications rewritten to run on the completed prototype.

[Llo92]   I. Lloyd. Oracle parallel server architecture. In *Proceedings of Super-Computing Europe 92*, pages 5–7, 1992. Description of Oracle's parallel database, the Oracle Parallel Server product. Unlike everybody else's approach, it uses the much-maligned, old-fashioned shared disk technique, which everybody else's paper feels obliged to trash. But Oracle Parallel Server was out there in many installations, working, while they were still in beta at the time this paper was written.

[LO87]   Ewing Lusk and Ross Overbeek. *Portable Programs for Parallel Computers*. Holt, Rinehart and Winston, Inc., 1987. Many examples of portable parallel programming, focused on programming using the P4 system developed at Argonne National Laboratory, home location of the authors.

[Man93]   M. Morris Mano. *Computer System Architecture Third Edition*. Prentice Hall, Englewood Cliffs, NJ, 1993. Revered and heavily used textbook on computer architecture. Getting a bit dated in its emphases. I would prefer Hennessey and Patterson now.

[Mar94]   John Markoff. Bigger, faster hardly matters. *Austin American-Statesman (also NY Times)*, C1, C5, August 8, 1994. Newspaper article about the death of supercomputers, pointing out how they are dying with shrinking defense spending. Confuses Thinking Machines with a traditional supercomputer vendor, but otherwise makes good points.

[Mes94]   *MPI: A Message-Passing Interface Standard (Version 1)*, May 1994. Message-Passing Interface Forum, available from the University of Tennessee, Knoxville, Tennessee. Multihundred-page, highly detailed, standard definition for the newly proposed standard for message-passing, created by an international *ad hoc* group called the Message Passing Interface Forum. This is the first version (not a draft) of the specification from which vendors will build their implementations of MPI.

[Mat97]   Robert A. J. Matthews. The science of Murphy's Law. *Scientific American*, April 1997, pages 88-91. It actually is provably built into the fundamental nature of the physical universe that toast will fall butter side down.

[MS97]   Microsoft Corporation, Redmond, Washington. *Microsoft "Wolfpack" Technical Architecture. March, 1997.* Also available at http://www.microsoft.com/ntserver /info/wolfpack.htm. My description in this book is more readable, but this isn't bad and it's the genuine horse's mouth. Lots of papers available at Microsoft's web site if you search for "cluster."

[NMCB97] J.M. Nick, B.B. Moore, J.-Y. Chung, and N.S. Bowen. S/390 cluster technology: Parallel Sysplex. *IBM Systems Journal*, Vol. 36, No. 2, 1997, pages 172-202. Also available at http://www.almaden.ibm.com/journal. One of eight papers in that issue about Parallel Sysplex. A rather detailed introduction to S/390 Parallel Sysplex, overviewing all its facilities. Not the world's easiest reading.

[OHE94]   Robert Orfali, Dan Harkey, and Jeri Edwards. *Essential Client/Server Survival Guide*. Van Nostrand Reinhold, 115 Fifth Ave., New York, 1994. Join Zog the Martian on a fun-filled trip through the jungles and swamps of client-server computing. Stacks, NOSs, SQL, transactions, groupware, Lotus Notes, distributed system management and other assorted topics treated in a usefully light-hearted way. A very large amount of useful information is contained herein, and a spoonful of sugar helps the tech content go down.

[Ope93]   The Open Software Foundation. *Introduction to OSF DCE*, 1993. Prentice Hall, Englewood Cliffs, NJ. General high-level but technical introduction covering all of DCE's features and capabilities, with a glossary and a listing of all other DCE documentation.

[O$^+$88]   John K. Ousterhout et al. The sprite network operating system. *Computer*, 21(2):23–26, February 1988. Description of the Sprite operating system developed at Stanford. This is a macrokernel system that distributes UNIX semantics across multiple workstations. Interesting file system caching at the workstation enhances response time significantly.

[PBG$^+$85]   G.F. Pfister, W.C. Brantley, D.A. George, S.L. Harvey, W.J. Kleinfelder, K.P. McAuliffe, E.A. Melton, V.A. Norton, and J. Weiss. The research parallel processor prototype (rp3): Introduction and architecture. In *Proceedings of the 1985 International Conference on Parallel Processing*, pages 764–771, August 1985. Description of one of the typical highly parallel processing projects that sprang up in reaction to the Japanese Fifth Generation projects. Up to 512 processors, with a particularly interesting memory organization. (Well, I thought so anyway.)

[Pek92]   M. Fernin Pekergin. Parallel computing optimization in the apollo domain network. *IEEE Transactions on Software Engineering*, 18(5):296–303, April 1992. Description of the Apollo Domain distributed computing support system, one of the most influential, original distributed computing environments. Influenced Hewlett-Packard's work in this area.

[Pfi86]   Gregory F. Pfister. The ibm yorktown simulation engine. *Proceedings of the IEEE*, 74(6):11–24, June 1986. Description of a special-purpose, highly parallel computer for the simulation of computers. The machine architecture of that system is yet another brainchild of John Cocke, who invented the concept of RISC computer architecture.

[PN85]   Gregory F. Pfister and V. Alan Norton. "hot spot" contention and combining in multistage interconnection networks. *IEEE Transactions on Computers*, C-34(10):943–948, 1985. How to get in a huge pile of trouble if your internode communication is even 1% away from uniformly distributed. Spawned a whole research sub-industry of network simulators trying to prove the results were wrong or get around them. Didn't happen.

[PP84]   Mark S. Papamaroos and Janak H. Patel. A low-overhead coherence solution for multiprocessors with private cache memories. In *Proceedings of the 11th Annual International Symposium on Computer Architecture*, pages 348–354. IEEE, June 1984. Original paper on the MESI cache coherence protocol (although it's not called that in this paper). This is the bus based cache coherence protocol that is one of the most commonly used.

[PW85]   Gerald Popek and B. J. Walker. *The LOCUS Distributed System Architecture*. MIT Press, Cambridge, MA, 1985. A description of the original, non-microkernel Locus system developed at UCLA. Provides a detailed description of how UNIX operating system semantics can be distributed across multiple machines.

[QD94]   Gregory Quick and Kelley Damore. Workstation arena feels growing heat of pentium. *Computer Reseller News*, page 1 & 317, July 25, 1994. Article about how Intel is specifically targeting the technical workstation market. Now that Pentium has caught up sufficiently in floating-point performance, system designers are embedding 3-D graphics capabilities as the other thing needed to crack this arena.

[Ram]   Rambus Inc., 2465 Latham Street, Mountain View, CA USA. *Rambus Architectural Overview*. Rambus is a new kind of memory channel and DRAM memory chip interface that allows higher-performance memory access in general. This report and related information are available by ftp from rambus.com, in the /pub/doc/rambus directory.

[Ram93]   Rick Ramsey. *All About Administering NIS+*. Prentice Hall, Englewood Cliffs, NJ, 1993. NIS+ is Sun Microsystems' facility for easing the administration of distributed workstations. This book's title describes its contents well—a readable, administrator-oriented description of everything you ever wanted to know about how to use NIS+ to administer systems.

[Ras86]   R. F. Rashid. Threads of a new system. *Unix Review*, 4:37–49, August 1986. Description of the Mach microkernel operating system, developed at Carnegie-Mellon University, written by one of its primary architects. Mach is very possibly the most influential microkernel system ever developed, and the origin of the popularization of the term "microkernel."

[Ray86]   M. Raynal. *Algorithms for Mutual Exclusion*. MIT Press, Cambridge, MA, 1986. More ways to keep processors out of each other's shorts than you ever imagined could possibly exist.

[RBG95]   John G. Robinson, David C. Baxter, and Jim Gray. Advantages of COMA. Kendell Square Research, April 1995. Also available at http://www.research.microsoft.com/research/barc/Gray/COMA.ps

[Rot92]   James Rothnie. Overview of the ksr1 computer system. Technical Research Report TR92020001, Kendall Square Research Corporation, Cambridge, MA, March 1992. Description of the KSR1 "ALLCACHE" machine architecture, a highly-parallel system with a unique approach to organizing memory: everything's a cache; there are no absolute memory locations; the cache lines just get bigger and bigger. Company now defunct, primarily due to financial finagling by its chief officer(s), so this may be hard to get hold of directly.

[RS96]   Eric S. Raymond and Guy L. Steele Jr. The on-line hacker jargon file, version 4.0.0, July 24 1996. Available at http://www.ccil.org/jargon, or contact Eric Raymond at esr@snark.thyrsus.com. Also published as *The New Hacker's Dictionary*, compiled by Eric S. Raymond. MIT Press, Cambridge, MA. This is the definitive hacker jargon and culture reference. No, a hacker is not somebody who breaks computer security, the stupid and ignorant newspapers be damned for misappropriating the word. A blast from the past for me; I hung around MIT's Project MAC (not LCS) and AI Lab getting my Ph.D. just before or when many of the people mentioned in the file arrived, and was embedded in that culture. It's a trip into a strange small world for most other people.

[San90]   Mahadev Santayaraman. Scalable, secure, and highly available distributed file access. *Computer*, 23(5):9–21, May 1990. Description of the Andrew File System (AFS), a distributed file system developed at CMU to serve thousandss of users simultaneously. The Distributed File System (DFS) of the Open Software Foundation (OSF) Distributed Computing Environment (DCE) is based on AFS.

[SC91]   M. Sullivan and R. Chillarege. Software Defects and Their Impact on System Availability—A Study of Field Failures in Operating Systems. *Proceedings of the 21st International Symposium on Fault-Tolerant Computing*, pp. 2-9, June 1991.

[Seq97]   Sequent Computer Systems, Inc., Beaverton Oregon.
              Sequent's NUMA-Q SMP Architecture. Also available
              at http://www.sequent.com/news/papers/qnu-
              masmp/numa.html. NUMA-touting purple prose at its
              deepest ultraviolet level, exceeded only by what HP is
              writing these days about the IA64 processor
              architecture.

[SGDM94]   V. S. Sunderam, G. A. Geist, J. Dongarra, and
              R. Manchek. The pvm concurrent computing system:
              Evolution, experiences, and trends. Technical report,
              Oak Ridge National Laboratory, to appear. Good over-
              view, performance data, and examples of use for PVM,
              the very popular portable parallel programming
              system.

[SGI97]   Silicon Graphics Inc., Mountain View, CA. Technology
              overview of the origin family. Also available from
              http://www.sgi.com/Products/hardware/servers
              /technology/ overview.html. A readable technical de-
              scription of their NUMA system, which they call SSMP.
              Nowhere near as purple prose as most NUMA promul-
              gators, but still at that end of the spectrum.

[Sha91]   Jay Shah. *VAXclusters*. McGraw-Hill, Inc., New York,
              NY, 1991. A detailed description of how to work with,
              and on, Digital Equipment Corp.'s VAXClusters. Pre-
              dates the change to Open VMS Clusters. Describes in
              minute detail how to configure and use the system.

[SJG92]   Per Stenstron, Truman Joe, and Anoop Gupta. Compar-
              ative performance evaluation of cache-coherent numa
              and coma architectures. In *Proceedings of the 19th Inter-
              national Symposium on Computer Architecture*, 1992.
              Compares NUMA, with page migration in software, to
              the KSR system (COMA), which moves all data around
              by using hardware. Comes to the conclusion that all
              that hardware doesn't help much, if at all. In my opin-
              ion, it's unclear that a fair comparison has been made;
              judge for yourself.

[SOH+96]   Mark Snir, Steve Otto, Steven Huss-Lederman, David
              Walker, and Jack Dongarra. *MPI: The Complete Refer-
              ence*. The MIT Press, 1996. Also available free, in Post-
              Script format, from ftp.netlib.org; or see
              http://www.netlib.org/utk/papers/mpi-book/mpi-

✳

book.html. The official complete reference for the "Message-Passing Interface," now the most standard way to deal with message-passing programming for technical and scientific applications.

[SSCK93]   M. Swanson, L. Stoller, T. Critchlow, and R. Kessler. The design of the schizophrenic workstation system. In *Proceedings of the USENIX Mach Symposium*, April 1993. In terms of this book, these folks are building a campus-wide cluster system and have noticed in great detail that it must have multiple personalities.

[Ste93]   Guy L. Steele Jr. High performance fortran: Status report. *ACM SIGPLAN Notices*, 28(1):1–4, 1993. Current (11/89) status and readable, short description of High Performance Fortran, extensions to FORTRAN making it not intrinsically impossible to automatically compile it to run in parallel on message-passing systems.

[Str97]   J.P. Strickland. VSAM record-level data sharing. *IBM Systems Journal*, Vol. 36, No. 2, 1997, pages 361-370. Also available at http://www.almaden.ibm.com/journal. One of eight papers in that issue about Parallel Sysplex. How the most important "file system" (sort of) on S/390 runs in parallel across S/390 Parallel Sysplex, using its shared-data cluster acceleration features.

[S⁺85]   Ralph Sandberg et al. Design and implementation of the sun network file system. In *Proceedings of the Summer Usenix Conference*, pages 119–130, 1985. The original description of the original, *de facto* standard for UNIX, NFS distributed file system.

[Sun94a]   Sun Microsystems, Inc., Mountain View, CA. *New Sun Parallel Database Servers Deliver Leading Performance and Availability for Mission-Critical Applications*, October 1994. Announcement of the availability of the new SPARCcluster 1000 PDB and 2000 PDB systems, two- to (eventually) eight-way high-availability clusters. Initially these systems will run Oracle Parallel Server; eventually, they will run Sybase and Informix' parallel offerings.

[Sun94b]   Sun Microsystems, Inc., Mountain View, CA. *SPARCcluster 1 Product Overview*, October 1994. General description, features, and specifications of Sun's cluster dedicated to providing NFS performance and higher availability. Little detail on how things like load balancing are actually accomplished.

[SWCL95]   Ashley Saulsbury, Tim Wilkinson, John Carger, and Anders Landin. An argument for simple COMA. *Proceedings of High Performance Computer Architectures - 1*, 1995, pp. 276-285. Also available at http:// playground.Sun.COM:80/ pub/ S3.mp/ simple-coma/ hpca95/ paper.html. I'm sorry, but I have to say that I found this almost unreadable. Apparently somebody else told the author that, since some extremely general, vague, marketing-like charts were ungraciously grafted on at the start. It didn't help.

[Tana]   Tandem Computers Incorporated. *NonStop Himalaya Range*. Document # CD0194-0993, order number 102603. Overview of Tandem's Himalaya series of computers, their top of the line at this time.

[Tanb]   Tandem Computers Incorporated. *TorusNet Interprocessor Connections*. Document # CD0194-0194. Overview of Tandem's Himalaya series of computers, with emphasis on the TorusNet interconnection topology.

[Tan92]   Andrew S. Tannenbaum. *Modern Operating Systems*. Prentice Hall, Englewood Cliffs, NJ, 1992. Really good book on operating systems. Reads like a novel. Basic issues, plus descriptions of classical UNIX, DOS, Mach, others, and a primary reference for Amoeba distributed OS.

[TBH82]   Philip C. Treleaven, David R. Brownbridge, and Richard P. Hopkins. Data-driven and demand-driven computer architecture. *Computing Surveys*, 14(1):93–143, March 1982. Description and comparison of the dataflow and reduction programming (computational) models, two highly nonstandard ways to do computing that have been intensely popular in academic computer science programming theory circles.

[Thi91]   Greg Thiel. Locus operating system, a transparent system. *Computer Communications*, 14(6):336–346, July-August 1991. Description of Locus, a system developed at UCLA that distributes single-system UNIX semantics across multiple machines. The version described here did not localize the changes required, but rather made a huge number of small changes to a huge number of code modules. Brrr.

[Tra93a]   Transaction Processing Performance Council (TPC). *TPC Benchmark A Standard Specification, Revision 1.2,* March 1993. The Transaction Processing Performance Council, 777 North First St., Suite 600, San Jose, CA 95112, e-mail: shanley@cup.portal.com. The official definition of the TPC-A interactive-use benchmark. The TPC benchmarks are probably the most important commercial transaction processing benchmarks there are. This benchmark has been phased out in favor of TPC-C.

[Tra93b]   Transaction Processing Performance Council (TPC). *TPC Benchmark B Standard Specification, Revision 1.2,* March 1993. The Transaction Processing Performance Council, 777 North First St., Suite 600, San Jose, CA 95112, e-mail: shanley@cup.portal.com. The official definition of the TPC-B batch-mode benchmark. The TPC benchmarks are probably the most important commercial transaction processing benchmarks there are. This benchmark has been phased out in favor of TPC-C.

[Tra93c]   Transaction Processing Performance Council (TPC), *TPC Benchmark C Standard Specification, Revision 2.0,* October 1993. The Transaction Processing Performance Council, 777 N. First St., Suite 600, San Jose, CA 95112, e-mail: shanley@cup.portal.com. The official definition of the TPC-C benchmark, which contains a mixture of transaction types. The TPC benchmarks are probably the most important commercial transaction processing benchmarks there are.

[Tra94]   Transaction Processing Performance Council (TPC), François Raab, editor. *TPC Benchmark D Standard Specification, Working Draft 7.0 for Company & Public Review,* May 1994. The Transaction Processing Performance Council, 777 N. First St., Suite 600, San Jose, CA 95112, e-mail: shanley@cup.portal.com. Preliminary version of the definition of the TPC D benchmark, which is not yet final. It is intended to be a benchmark for decision-support, as opposed to transaction-processing operation. The TPC benchmarks are probably the most important commercial transaction processing benchmarks there are.

[TS87]   Charles P. Thacker and Lawrence C. Stewart. Firefly: A multiprocessor workstation. In *Proceedings of the Second International Conference on Architectural Support for Programming Languages and Operating Systems*, pages 164–172. ACM, June 1987. The Firefly cache coherence protocol, another popular, bus-based, snoopy cache coherence protocol developed at the now-defunct DEC Western Research Laboratory.

[vDR94]   Ronald van Driel and Daan Reuhman. The x station: A high-end workstation in disguise. *HP.Omni*, pages 22–25, August 1994. Description of the cluster used at Philips National Laboratory; users connect from X stations to the cluster nodes via ethernet switches. Locally developed software is used for login (xldb) and batch load balancing (SQS), as well as for cluster system administration (SOS).

[Vee86]   Arthur H. Veen. Dataflow machine architecture. *Computing Surveys*, 18(4):365–396, December 1986. One of the more recent surveys of all the various types of dataflow machines that have been proposed and built, including some chip-level parts available for purchase.

[Wal93]   David W. Walker. The design of a standard message passing interface for distributed memory concurrent computers. Technical Report ORNL/TM-12512. Oak Ridge National Laboratory, Oak Ridge, TN, 37831, October 1993. Compact, readable, general description of the currently-emerging standard interface for message-passing systems.

[Wat86]   E. Watanabe. Survey on computer security. Tokyo: Japan Information Development Corp. March 1986. I admit it, this is a second-level reference; I found it in [GR89], so I repeat it here. I never actually read it myself.

[WH88]   D.H.D. Warren and S. Haridi. Data Diffusion Machine—a scalable shared virtual memory multiprocessor. *International Conference on Fifth Generation Computer Systems 1988*. ICOT, 1988.

✳

[WLH93]   Bruce J. Walker, Joel Lilienkamp, and Joe Hopfield. *Open Single System Image Software for the Multicomputer or MPP (Massively Parallel Processor)*. Locus Computing Corporation, 9800 La Cienega Blvd., Ingelwood CA 90301-4400, 1993. Description of how Locus was applied to a UNIX personality server under the OSF/1 AD microkernel to achieve application transparency for the Intel Scientific Computing Corp.'s Paragon massively parallel machine.

[WP89]   B. Walker and J. Popek. Distributed unix transparency: Goals, benefits, and the tcf example. In *Winter 1989 Uniforum Conference Proceedings*, 1989. Description of the Locus distributed operating system, with the example of how it was embedded in UNIX-equivalents for the IBM S/370 and PS/2 as the Transparent Computing Facility (TCF). A potentially useful idea that did not sell well for a variety of reasons, like apparently there are a total of 12 customers worldwide interested in buying a native UNIX system that runs on S/390.

[ZR93]   Syrus Zial and Cheryl Ranson. Summit: A 1 giga-byte per second multiprocessor system bus. In *Symposium Record of Hot Interconnects '93*, pages 1.2.1–1.2.9. Stanford University, August 1993. Hewlett-Packard paper on how they built a system bus supporting 16 HP PA processors, type unspecified. Remarkable for its electrical engineering: inputs switch on the leading edge of the wavefront of the electrical signal. Unfortunately, the proceedings contains only the presentation transparencies, not a complete paper; much information is nevertheless contained here.

Index

K

About the Author

Dr. Gregory Pfister has been attempting to make parallel computer systems useful since 1969, when he noticed that nobody made decent use of some computer graphics hardware he had designed. This bothered him sufficiently to send him from computer hardware to software, and he has been oscillating between the two ever since. He is currently an IBM Senior Technical Staff Member in IBM's cross-divisional System Architecture and Performance group in Austin, Texas, working in the areas of clusters, competitive analysis, and system architecture. Born in Detroit, MI through a fluke of his father's World War II posting, he was soon moved to Long Island, NY, where he grew up. He received his S.B., S.M., and Ph.D. from MIT in 1967, 1969, and 1974, respectively. He has taught Computer Science as an Instructor at MIT and an Assistant Professor at the University of California at Berkeley; and he has worked in IBM development, research and corporate headquarters on computer graphics, parallel programming, highly parallel computer architectures, and clustered systems. In IBM Research he was Principal Scientist of the RP3 project, a research effort in highly parallel computing. He has been elected to the IBM Academy of Technology, Eta Kappa Nu, Tau Beta Pi, Sigma Xi, and Senior Membership in the Institute of Electrical and Electronic Engineers (IEEE), and has been a Distinguished Visitor of the IEEE Computer Society. He has earned six patents and an IBM Corporate Technical Recognition Award. His numerous published papers include two that received "best paper" awards at major technical conferences. He lives in Austin, Texas, with his wife, Cyndee, children Danielle and Jonathan, and a Bichon Frise (that's a dog, folks) named Dallas Belle who knows she runs the house. When he's not doing this stuff he's travelling for pleasure, skiing, playing computer role-playing games, and reading science fiction.